PRACTICE AND RESEARCH

Contemporary Social Work Studies

Contemporary Social Work Studies is a series disseminating high quality new research and scholarship in the discipline and profession of social work. The series promotes critical engagement with contemporary issues relevant across the social work community and captures the diversity of interests currently evident at national, international and local levels.

CSWS is located in the School of Social Sciences (Social Work Studies Division) at the University of Southampton, UK and is a development from the successful series of books published by Ashgate in association with CEDR (the Centre for Evaluative and Developmental Research) from 1991.

Other titles in this series:

Sexual Identities and Sexuality in Social Work
Research and Reflections from Women in the Field
Edited by Priscilla Dunk-West and Trish Hafford-Letchfield
978-0-7546-7882-3

Spirituality and Social Work
Beth R. Crisp
978-0-7546-7734-5

For information about other titles in this series, visit www.ashgate.com

UNIVERSITY OF Southampton
School of Social Sciences

Practice and Research

IAN F. SHAW
University of York, UK

ASHGATE

Published by
Ashgate Publishing Limited
Wey Court East
Union Road
Farnham
Surrey, GU9 7PT
England

Ashgate Publishing Company
Suite 420
101 Cherry Street
Burlington
VT 05401–4405
USA

www.ashgate.com

British Library Cataloguing in Publication Data
Shaw, Ian, 1945-
Practice and research. -- (Contemporary social work studies)
1. Social service--Research. 2. Qualitative research.
I. Title II. Series
361.3'072-dc23

Library of Congress Cataloging-in-Publication Data
Shaw, Ian, 1945-
Practice and research / by Ian F. Shaw.
p. cm. -- (Contemporary social work studies)
Includes bibliographical references and index.
ISBN 978-1-4094-3917-2 (hbk) 1. Social service--Research.
2. Social service--Evaluation. 3. Social work education. 4. Social case work. I. Title.
HV11.S4825 2011
361.3--dc23

2011052187

ISBN 9781409439172 (hbk)

MIX
Paper from responsible sources
FSC www.fsc.org
FSC® C018575

Printed and bound in Great Britain by the MPG Books Group, UK

Contents

List of Figures and Tables

Figures

Tables

Acknowledgments

I would like to place on record my appreciation of my co-writers in a number of articles republished in this book.

I am also grateful to the following for permission to republish my work.

SAGE Publications Ltd. for the following articles and chapters:

Bull, R. and Shaw, I. (1992) 'Constructing Causal Accounts in Social Work', *Sociology* 26 (4): 635-649.

Shaw, I. (1999) 'Evidence from qualitative evaluation' in I. Shaw (ed.) *Qualitative Evaluation*, London: Sage.

Shaw, I. (2003) 'Qualitative research and outcomes in health, social work and education', *Qualitative Research* 3 (1): 57-77.

Shaw, I. (2004) 'William J. Reid: an appreciation', *Qualitative Social Work* 3 (2): 109-115.

Shaw, I. (2006) 'Human Services' in I. Shaw, J. Greene, and M. Mark (eds) *Sage Handbook of Evaluation*, London: Sage Publications.

Shaw, I. (2008) 'Ethics and the Practice of Qualitative Research', *Qualitative Social Work* 7 (4): 400-414.

Shaw, I. (2009) 'Rereading *The Jack-Roller*: hidden histories in sociology and social work', *Qualitative Inquiry* 15 (7): 1241-1264.

Shaw, I. (2009) 'Ways of Knowing in Social Work' in M. Gray and S. Webb (eds) *Social Work Theory and Methods*, London: Sage.

Shaw, I. and Faulkner, A. (2006) 'Practitioner Evaluation at Work', *American Journal of Evaluation* 27 (1): 44-63.

Shaw, I. and Gould, N. (2001) 'The consequences of qualitative social work research' in Shaw, I. and Gould, N. *Qualitative Research in Social Work*, London: Sage.

Shaw, I. and Ruckdeschel, R. (2002) 'Qualitative social work: a room with a view', *Qualitative Social Work: Research and Practice* 1 (1): 5-23.

Cambridge University Press for the following article that first appeared in the *Journal of Social Policy*:

Shaw, I. (1976) 'Consumer Opinion and Social Policy', *Journal of Social Policy* 5 (1): 19-32.

The British Association of Social Workers for:

Shaw, I. (1997) 'Participation, Empowerment and the Rhetoric of Quality' in A. Pithouse and H. Williamson (eds) *Engaging the User in Welfare*, Birmingham: Venture Press.

Shaw, I. (1999) 'Seeing the Trees for the Wood: the Politics of Practice Evaluation' in B. Broad (ed) *The Politics of Research and Evaluation in Social Work*, Birmingham: Venture Press.

Oxford Journals for:

Shaw, I. (1984) 'Consumer Evaluations of the Personal Social Services', *British Journal of Social Work* 14 (3): 277-284

Shaw I. (2003) 'Cutting Edge Issues in Social Work Research', *British Journal of Social Work* 33 (1): 107-116.

Taylor and Francis for:

Shaw, I. (1995) 'The Quality of Mercy: the Management of Quality in the Personal Social Services' in I. Kirkpatrick, and M. Lucio (eds) *The Politics of Quality in the Public Sector*, London: Routledge.

Shaw, I. (2007) 'Is social work research distinctive?', *Social Work Education* 26 (7): 659-669.

Professor Rodreck Mupedziswa and the *Journal of Social Development in Africa* for:

Shaw, I. and Al-Awwad, K. (1994) 'Culture and the Indigenization of Quality in Third World Social Research', *Journal of Social Development in Africa* 9 (1): 59-71.

Jessica Kingsley Publishers for:

Shaw, I (2000) 'Just Inquiry? Research and Evaluation for Service Users' in H. Kemshall and R. Littlechild (eds) (2000) *Participation in Social Care: Researching for Practice*, London and Philadelphia: Jessica Kingsley Publishers.

National Association of Social Workers, and Rights Link for:

Shaw, I. and Shaw, A. (1997) 'Game Plans, Buzzes and Sheer Luck: Doing Well in Social Work', *Social Work Research* 21 (2): 69-79.

Polity Press for:

Shaw, I. (2010) 'Evaluating in Practice' in T. Evans and M. Hardy with I. Shaw *Evidence and Knowledge for Social Work*, Cambridge: Polity Press.

The following first appeared in books from the present publisher:

Shaw, I. (1996) 'Unbroken Voices: Children, Young People and Qualitative Methods' in I. Butler and I. Shaw (eds) *A Case of Neglect?* Aldershot: Avebury.

Shaw, I. (2004) 'Evaluation for a Learning Organization' in N. Gould and M. Baldwin *Social Work, Critical Reflection and the Learning Organization*, Aldershot: Ashgate.

The closing chapter, 'Users' and Practitioners' Research', is a previously unpublished essay first presented in 2009 to the Annual Meeting of the Inter-Centre Network for the Evaluation of Social Work Practice', Kristiansand, Norway.

To those social work and social science colleagues in all countries who have enriched my vision of social work practice and research

Introduction

Serendipity, Misfires and Occasional Patterns: A Career in Social Work Research

Ian Shaw

Donald Campbell once remarked on the value of being able to 'reduce the need to put up a brave front of continual competence, and enable one to talk about intelligent hypotheses that proved wrong, stupid investments of research energy that were never worth undertaking even in anticipation, and promising lines of research that were dropped before fruition due to faintheartedness or doing too many things at once', and how such a story illustrates 'the chancy indirectness of discovery, and the further chanciness of recognition' (Campbell, 1981: 455). Fragilities of memory and the danger of hubris put at risk any effort to trace a career. I am answerable for too many periods of dull inactivity and ill-thought through investments of energy, and the recipient of too many unplanned good fortunes, to justify claims to more than occasional patterns in the following account. While I reflect in the first part of this essay on the influences that seem to have shaped my work, I then play a more conventional note by considering the inter-relation of practice and research, and how I think the pieces included in this collection fit.

Incidents and accidents[1]

I am not sure I know what brought me into social work – actually into being a Probation Officer working with offenders. Being a tolerably bright working class boy in the English Midlands[2] heading for a semi-profession; close acquaintance with a probation officer; a Christian faith – all no doubt played some part. Following an unremarkable grammar school education (how I envied the added yellow bar in the prefects' ties!), I took a Sociology degree at Sheffield University in the north of England in the 1960s. British sociology was in its vigorous post-war expansion phase. The year I commenced sociology the following books made their appearance:

1 The reference is to Paul Simon's 'You Can Call me Al': 'All along, along there were incidents and accidents, there were hints and allegations.'

2 I have included personal history only insofar as it seems relevant to the course and content of my career.

- Howard Becker's *Outsiders*
- Michel Foucault's *The Birth of the Clinic*
- Erving Goffman's *Stigma*
- Thomas Marshall's *Class, Citizenship and Social Development*
- C. Wright Mills' *Power, Politics and People* (the year after his death)
- Karl Popper's *Conjectures and Refutations*
- Lloyd Warner's *Yankee City* series

I do not recall any mention of Foucault, Becker or Popper, but the other names figure in my dusty undergraduate notes. Sociological theory, research methods, social administration, social structure of modern Britain, social anthropology, an option in urban sociology, and statistics[3] are the courses that linger – 'glimpses of notes like the catch of a song.'[4]

I was deeply shaped by my experiences of undergraduate sociology. I recall the struggles with weighty library tomes by Talcott Parsons, Max Weber, Robert Merton and, although I cannot be sure, Emile Durkheim, and the (almost too) late discovery of Levi Strauss as I spent long hours revising for finals. I recognise the political scepticism that inured me to the counterpoint of functionalism *versus* Marxism. It was Peter Mann's methodology course and to some extent his urban sociology that had the most lasting impact. His teaching, as I recall, was not popular, but for me it was the highlight of the week, brought to life when the class undertook an audience survey at a Sheffield theatre, and also when I undertook a crude observation study of a Sheffield Juvenile Court.[5]

I fell immediately into a professional social work training course at Swansea. As with sociology, UK social work courses were springing up from the early sixties. The course was psychodynamically infused. To the doubtless disbelief of the present generation of social work students and faculty, we were required by Elizabeth Clarkson, the programme director, to read Florence Hollis' *Casework: A Psychosocial Therapy* cover to cover before we arrived on the course.[6] Margaret Stacey's uncomfortable and early feminist sociology course, and still more David Fowler's practice teaching, provided counterweights. But in all it was an oddly disjointed experience. It may not have dulled my early interest in research, but it scarcely reinforced it.

I spent the first five years of my career as a Probation Officer back in Sheffield. The Sheffield Probation Service at the end of the sixties was one of the best places to be for someone with an interest in research. The Home Office Research Unit in

---

3 I was later to teach basic statistics, but made little sense of the Sheffield course.

4 Perhaps the best known phrase from 'Forty Years On', the main school song at Harrow School, but adopted by many other schools including mine.

5 Mann moved out of university life into research on libraries. His methodology teaching was captured in a now little known book (Mann, 1985). His urban sociology was reflected in Mann (1965).

6 The seriousness of my failure to do so was made clear in an early tutorial!

London and Manchester was commissioning excellent research by Martin Davies, Ian Sinclair and several others. Influenced by North American work, especially in Canada, a major experimental study was commissioned in Sheffield and elsewhere to assess a model of intensive intervention (e.g. Smith, 1977). Hugh Sanders, then Principal Probation Officer,[7] set the tone of the learning culture when he remarked in words that linger in the memory that some probation officers have 20 years' experience – others have one year's experience 20 times over.

I had been working for about two years when I registered for a research degree. This was the second period in my life when I had cause to be grateful for the stimulus of scholars at Sheffield University's Department of Sociological Studies. Sociologists and social work faculty were in the same department – a combination I was to hugely appreciate when I encountered it in my subsequent career. On this occasion I was supervised by Eric Sainsbury in the period when he was doing fieldwork for his remarkable research on client and practitioner experiences and interpretations of social work (Sainsbury, 1975, 1982).[8] My own work was relatively mundane. I was working in a newly decentralised team in a tough area of Sheffield and gathered what data I could to ascertain the consequences in terms of agency networking and proactive engagement with the agency by local residents. It became my first publication (Shaw, 1973). It would be some years before I began to question the careful but naïve realism of this kind of data. In the closing months of my time in Sheffield I had started a lunch time seminar for colleagues interested in doing research. There are those who recall me running that group in my early 20s and sending out required reading to fellow officers![9] Nothing came of that group though I recall being attracted by the potential of Robert Bales' interaction process analytic categories for exploring court practice.

So it came to be that the big ideas for me have come as much through methodology as through theory. It was years later that I gratefully picked John Madge's *The Origins of Scientific Sociology* off the shelf of a second hand bookshop in Hay on Wye.[10] I was probably the only student of my year who read the now long-forgotten heavyweight Madge cover to cover. Methodology has always been for me what theory is for others – a source of frameworks. A distinction needs making. I do not treat methodology as an *alternative* to theorising,

7 Or was it the remarkable Jack Porter – a wonderful and influential model for several of that generation of able young Sheffield probation officers.

8 I was not the only person to appreciate Eric's work. He supervised an excellent doctoral thesis by Michael Bayley (Bayley, 1973) who convened an occasional discussion group of young researchers. Joan Orme's tribute is a worthy record of Sainsbury's contribution (Orme, 2009).

9 Including, so Joan Orme remembers, an early article by Joel Fischer on the effectiveness of social casework.

10 If you do not know about Hay – its famous bookshops and festival – then follow this link. http://www.hay-on-wye.co.uk/

but as an implicit way of theorising, an act of interpretation. Over the years it has been the doing of, and the reflection on, inquiry that has given me whatever purchase I may have on social work practice, sociology, social policy, and so on.

I had seen myself as applying for promotion in the Probation Service, and, courtesy of a continued contact with David Fowler, I applied for a position heading up a student training unit in Cardiff's probation service in South Wales. I was turned down. Having spent my energies doing a research degree, my lack of experience of supervising students counted against me. As Plan B I applied for a lectureship at Cardiff University. UK social work was still in expansionist phase. Generic Social Services Departments had been set up in 1970 following the Seebohm Committee's report in 1968, the British Association of Social Workers was formed, universities were growing apace and people like me fell into academic posts with minimal qualifications. So I ended up at the university that became my home for 31 years.

The Department of Social Administration and Social Work, as it then was, was headed up by Howard Jones, an able criminologist. Not long before I arrived, personal and academic issues had triggered a split between sociologists on the one hand and social policy, criminology and social work academics on the other. These ran so deep that it was not until all the original protagonists had retired in the late 1980s that the two departments came back together as the Cardiff School of Social Sciences. In the early 1970s national assessments of research performance, with their associated funding settlements, were not even a gleam in the government's eye. Social work in the universities was expanding rapidly, and delivering professional programmes figured more largely than developing excellent research. Some of the best research was being done outside of universities, e.g through the Home Office Research Unit.

In the 1960s and 1970s in the UK experiments and quasi experiments (the distinction was not too often made until the classic Cook and Campbell book of 1979), and the responses that bounced off them, provided the real excitement as well as the reference point for social work research. Some of the most stimulating writing was by those who engaged with this work (eg Briar and Miller, 1971; Fischer, 1976). I spent many hours writing detailed abstracts of these studies for my students (Meyer, Borgatta and Jones' *Girls at Vocational High*, Matilda Goldberg's *Helping the Aged*, Clarke and Cornish' Kingswood study in Bristol, the IMPACT studies in the UK's Probation Service, Reid and Shyne's *Brief and Extended Casework* and so on). The edginess of this field can still be encountered in reading Mary MacDonald's response to the *Girls at Vocational High* study (MacDonald, 1966), and even around the experimenters' camp fires there were sharp elbows (e.g. Fischer, 1976).

The 1960s onwards witnessed substantial social work research in Britain that was based on quantitative expertise or a combination of quantitative and qualitative excellence. The early work of people such as Sinclair, Davies, Clarke, Cornish and others linked to the Home Office Research Unit, the influence of epidemiological models on the work of Matilda Goldberg and others, the cross-fertilising work of Tizard,

Sinclair and colleagues on small institutions, the solitary cluster of British research on task centred models of intervention, and the research on childcare issues that led to the establishment of the Dartington Social Research Unit in 1963,[11] were often marked by a methodological enthusiasm and innovativeness.[12]

I am not sure whether scientific controversies take place in social work in the same sense they occur in the more established sciences, but this field was perhaps as near as it gets, and is perhaps one reason why all this quickens the pulse. It appeared to offer tough-mindedness combined with an empirical rigour marked by a mindset that was ready to listen to the evidence. For example, the original task centred casework experiment *Brief and Extended Casework* (Reid and Shyne, 1969) was carried out with the assumption that open-ended casework would prove more effective than brief interventions, given ideal circumstances. When the contrary was supported by the evidence it led to a sustained programme of research led by Bill Reid to develop and test the effectiveness of the model. It was this resistance to ideological interests that gave me something to challenge the psycho-dynamic hegemony of social work.[13]

My early work had two strands. While I was enticed by the general rigour of experimental designs, I applied it to a series of survey-style projects that culminated in a large dataset doctoral study of the social characteristics of those who sought to gain entry to social work, and the predictors of success or failure in doing so (Shaw, 1985). Second, I was drawn to several research and writing projects that aimed to give voice to those who were on the receiving end of social work and related interventions (Shaw, 1976, 1978, 1979).

And yet the experimental work of the period had left me (and others) with a sense of a dead-end – 90 miles an hour down a dead end street to borrow a song title. One by one I stumbled on things. I read the first edition of Denzin's *Research Act* (1970). I found John Mayer and Noel Timms' *The Client Speaks* (1970) – a book that was a revelation to me – a world that made perfect sense yet which required assumptions about research and practice that challenged equally the psychodynamic culture of professionalism and the version of research rigour that had led to the dead end just mentioned. This was deepened by Eric Sainsbury's work mentioned above – a form of research that was debunked by early emancipatory researchers for 'consumerism' in ways that I still think missed the point. I was teaching a year-long research course every academic year to postgraduate social

11 http://www.dartington.org.uk/about-us.

12 The decline and partial loss of this creative stream of research in the UK can be understood in the light of the withering and eventual demise of the Probation Service link to social work, the crisis of confidence in the face of 'nothing works' arguments, and the decline of quantitative skills associated with the flowering of qualitative methodology from the early 1970s. At the time of writing there is a determined revival of quantitative skills in the UK through Forrester, Shemmings, Macdonald, Carpenter and others.

13 This was not the exclusive property of quantitative researchers. It was one reason why Mayer and Timms' *The Client Speaks,* was so influential.

work students. I read Aaron Cicourel's *Method and Measurement in Sociology* (1967) and Giddens' essay on forms of explanatory accounts (1976), and a bit later John Hughes' *The Philosophy of Social Research* (1980). More generally, my sociological identity pushed persistently in new directions. My early work on matters such as client and patient accounts of their experience of service delivery led me into a series of qualitative case study evaluations (Shaw, 1979, Shaw et al, 1992; Shaw and Walton, 1979) and further efforts to make general sense of the voice of the client[14] (Shaw, 1984a and 1984b).

The culmination of my efforts to conduct rigorous survey research coincided with my growing convictions as to the descriptive and explanatory limitations of data of that nature, and I only published one paper from my thesis (Shaw, 1985). Most of the work included in this collection falls into this later period. In the 1980s I published relatively little. Social work academic expectations about publishing were still ambiguous. I wrote and edited Christian books and articles, and was published outside the academic world. It helped hone my writing and editing skills (e.g. Shaw, 1988), but it served to remind that '(t)hings always take longer than anticipated. Fluencies in writing and thinking are highly variable' (Campbell, 1981: 479).

Transitions

I think I went through two overlapping but distinct transitions in the period from the end of the eighties through to the early years of the century. I already have picked out the shift that – slightly over-simply – can be read as one of methodological commitments. There were various strands to this, which are represented in the section divisions of this book. Qualitative methodology, an awareness of the challenge of feminist research methodology, a concentrated decade-long interest in the agenda posed by the evaluation movement, especially in the USA, a modest attempt to engage with user-led research, and an engagement with the puzzles posed by the seemingly mundane activity of practitioner research. These have all led to relatively extensive writing, which, in ways I am still not sure I can explain, I find to be mutually reinforcing. Some of this was empirical (although not much is represented in this book) and other was more reflective and position-taking. This latter multi-stranded output *is* well represented in the following pieces, possibly because they date less easily. Neither of these kinds of work – empirical and position-taking (indeed, position-making) – feels at all finished.

The efforts to express a standpoint on this and that gradually pushed me towards more strategic writing. I must knowledge a major debt at this point. Around 2002 or 2003 I took over as chair of the Research Sub-Committee of the UK's Joint Universities Social Work Education Committee. It occurred at a point when, if my judgement is right, one of the most creative and visionary periods of UK social

14 'Client' because that was the term universally in use at that time.

work research was about to start. The committee came to be the main voice for social work research in the UK; social work became recognised as a distinct field by the Economic and Social Research Council; and the deeply invested national strategy for social work research was drafted.[15] A generation of academics who came into social work in the 1960s and 1970s joined forces and voices to bring these and other developments to a sort of fruition. Among those who played a central role in this were Paul Bywaters, Audrey Mullender, Jackie Powell, Joan Orme, Mike Fisher and Peter Marsh.[16]

My own work was shaped by a further shift and development, best labeled as a growing membership of and participation in international networks. My core interests have given me access to and membership of invaluable networks in the USA, Canada, Germany, each of the Nordic countries, Australia, New Zealand, Japan, Spain, Hong Kong, Cyprus and Morocco. Aspects of my work – mainly around evaluation and qualitative methods – have appeared in Japanese, Chinese, Finnish and Spanish. Working for 30 years or so in Wales also pressed on me the challenges of a bilingual nation, and has been just one of the influences that has kept me preoccupied with language, despite my inability to gain competence in any other language than English. From the turn of the century I have been part of INTSOCEVAL – the Inter-Centre Network for the Evaluation of Social Work Practice. Mainly but by no means exclusively European in membership, the annual meetings of this small group have been a valuable discipline. My links with colleagues internationally have been a pleasure, such that my academic identity has been only loosely linked to the Fabian research traditions of my home university in more recent years. This intellectual widening was probably facilitated by a resurfacing of my ever present but previously less explicit sociological identity.

It was in this context that I undertook a number of initiatives and research projects that were partly methodological and partly strategic. I co-drafted the statement characterising the field of social work research that became the ESRC statement for the discipline. I worked with American evaluation scholars to produce the *Sage Handbook of Evaluation* (Shaw, Greene and Mark, 2006). I led two projects aimed at 'placing' social work research (Shaw, Arksey and Mullender, 2004, 2006; Shaw and Norton, 2007, 2008). The latter yielded one of the outputs that I think said something about the nature and quality of social work research that had not been expressed hitherto, though its influence is not yet apparent. Perhaps the high water mark for this kind of work is embodied in the *Sage Handbook of Social Work Research* (Shaw, et al, 2010) – a project with Katherine Briar-Lawson, Joan Orme and Roy Ruckdeschel, plus writers and peer reviewers from

15 See the special issue of the *British Journal of Social Work* Volume 38 (5) for the key papers behind this strategy, and http://curlew.cch.kcl.ac.uk/ipi_scwru/redist/pdf/Strategy_Final_2.pdf for the Strategy document.

16 The weighty significance of network links with able social work scholars elsewhere in Europe, especially in the Nordic countries, should not be overlooked.

over 60 countries – that was deeply satisfying, both as a colleaguely venture and for the originality of its final form and content.

I hold a position about social work that may seem paradoxical – even to me. I have written quite a lot that tries to exemplify how social work as a coherent field with its own purposes, domains, and contexts, lays down a range of challenges to cognate fields and disciplines. Yet at the same time I refuse to go along with the tendency too often found in social work, to take a position of professional virtue stemming from a presumed distinctiveness of values and aims. But the contradiction is only apparent – it is a paradox not an antinomy. The latter failing leads to intellectual isolationism, which abates and atrophies any effort to develop a strong social work voice. This conviction supports my current work on the history of social work as a field of research (Shaw, 2008a, 2009b, 2010c, 2011b), that has taken me to archival work at Chicago, the location of one of the first university-based social work schools in the USA and the first university Sociology Department, and to one or two nascent research projects. As an aside, most (not all) of my work that I have found most rewarding has been the result of small research grants, or even personal unfunded inquiry. We should never be sucked into the deceptive assumption that grant size and importance are positively related.

As will be apparent, much of my writing in the last 20 years has had a broadly methodological agenda running through it. The article on causal accounts, included in this collection probably triggered this unfinished series. Conversations with my then colleague Rodney Bull prompted the article, which, despite the courtesy of the name sequence, was written by me (Bull and Shaw, 1992). Even when I have been drawn into writing about methods, there has usually been an agenda-setting purpose (e.g. Shaw, 2003a; 2003b; Shaw and Ruckdeschel, 2002), and that remains true in my more recent work (Shaw, 2011a). Perhaps the high point of this commitment, intellectually and emotionally, was the founding, with Roy Ruckdeschel, of the journal *Qualitative Social Work* and its launch in 2002.

Over against the frequent tea-room grumble, I stress what I see as the crucial significance of the emergence of email in the early 1990s. I doubt that most of my international network links would have happened without the facility of email. Two examples must suffice. First, I applied, jointly with a writing colleague, to edit the *British Journal of Social Work* around 1999. We were turned down. I decided that it was the moment to promote a dream I had nursed for a few years – the need for a social work journal that would counterbalance the dominant emphasis on quantitative, accountability, and evidence-based practice agenda in most social work research internationally. I embarked on an international personal consultation that was the foundation of the afore-mentioned *Qualitative Social Work* but which would have been impossible without the still infant internet. Some of my most valued international colleagues are part of that journal network. It is also down to email that I have been able to nurture the privilege of encouraging and possibly mentoring emerging scholars around the world. Second, I had for a while wanted to undertake a major rewrite of my *Evaluating in Practice* book. I opened an email conversation with Bill Reid, as a result of which we agreed to co-write a book that would bring together his and my perspectives on this theme. Sadly Bill died in late 2003 and it took several years before I navigated the project through my mind and the publishers (Shaw, 2011a). I have sometimes chided American colleagues for their intellectual insularity evidenced in the 99 per cent 'in-house' citation lists at the close of most USA social work journal articles. Had the project happened as originally hoped, it would have represented one way of bringing together voices from each side of the Atlantic.[17]

I have never taken an unequivocal position for or against this or that methodology (cf Shaw, 1975 with Shaw, 2010b). I have been a career-long admirer of the late Bill Reid (cf Shaw, 2004a) and, like the iconic qualitative scholar Howard Becker, have found Donald Campbell's arguments richly repay engagement and perhaps still more those of Lee Cronbach (e.g. Shaw, 1999a; Shaw, 2012a). I have attacked sentimental attachments to favoured positions, perhaps especially in the quarters where I am most at home (Shaw, 1999b, 2011a). My vision behind the inaugural European Conference for Social Work Research in 2011 was for a Europe-wide forum for the development of the best possible social work research of whatever variety.

I agree with Greene when she dissents from the methodological pragmatism that avers epistemological purity does not get research done. Rather, 'epistemological integrity does get meaningful research done right' (Greene, 1990: 229). But I do not believe that qualitative and quantitative methods are undergirded by incommensurable philosophical standpoints (Shaw, 1999a, Shaw and Norton, 2007; Shaw, 2009a) and have continued to engage with the challenges of quantitative methods (e.g. Shaw et al, 1996; Shaw, 2012a). I describe my position as epistemologically constructivist and ontologically realist. Skagestad expresses each element well when he describes the former as 'the view that our knowledge *of* the world is itself a fact *in* the world and that the theory of knowledge may therefore be regarded as a part of empirical science' (Skagestad, 1981: 77). He characterises ontological realism as the view that 'There is a real, theory-independent world, which exists independently of what we know about it and even independently of our existence as knowers' (p. 84).

These several positions are, needless to say, very difficult to jointly affirm. If we know the world only through the theories of science, how can we conclude there is a real world? Also, can we deduce that there are any grounds for believing that science gives an incrementally closer approximation to the real world? I have been influenced in holding this position by Lakatos, Campbell, Phillips and MacKay (c.f. Shaw, 1999a, Ch 3). I do not follow Campbell, Popper or Lakatos' social evolutionary grounds for its defence, but find a Christian position adequate (c.f. Harrison, 2007; McKay, 1988) – that the tree continues to be when there's no one about in the quad. Yet in reality '*all* hypotheses are … underdetermined by the evidence available for them' (Skagestad, 1981: 82).

---

17 I have briefly voiced this misgiving about American myopia (Shaw, 2012b).

To repeat the gist of something I said above, I have for many years been skeptical when encountering claims for the distinctiveness of social work – whether in terms of values or substantive field. I discuss some aspects of the question in an essay included in this compilation (Shaw, 2007). It is no accident that a third of the items included in this collection were first published in non-social work journals or books. I have increasingly felt that I practice on various borderlands – between social work and sociology, research and practice, Britain and the wider world. My current research on the history of sociology and social work takes me further in that direction.

Practice and research

One of the umbrellas for this work is perhaps a constant effort to problematise and develop a multifaceted argument about the relationship between practice – diversely understood – and research. I will develop a more conventional review of this question in the remaining pages of this essay.[18] I take the term 'research' very broadly to include all forms of disciplined inquiry, by whomever they are undertaken. 'Practice' is not limited to social work intervention. The final essay in the collection has the most to say about ideas of practice.

I am at least as much interested in what practice has to say to research as *vice versa*. 'Knowing' and 'doing', research and practice, are not two wholly distinct areas that need mechanisms to connect them, but are to a significant degree part and parcel of one another. Two of the most stubborn and difficult to avoid options for presenting the relation of research and practice are to give research priority over practice (rationalism) or to give practice priority over research (romantic conservatism). These distinctions are not intended to carry any evaluative judgements – for example, I do not believe that social work research will necessarily be better the closer it is to practice (Shaw and Norton, 2007; Shaw, 2010a).

Social workers often face the dominance of social science and research 'experts' over practice 'beneficiaries'. This tends to lead to a deeply unhelpful situation in which practitioners are routinely blamed for their perceived failure to act on the 'findings' of research. Kirk and Reid elegantly criticised 'practitioner-blame' responses that take the form of discussions of science as progress, of science as having to struggle against 'organizational banality', and practitioners as subverting research and easily being threatened. They responded:

> Omitted from these portraits of research is any suggestion that researchers' motives may extend beyond the good and worthy; that scientists are not strangers to aggrandizement or status seeking; that the research process itself can be subjective and biased, sometimes fatally so; or that researchers may have a personal, as well as a professional, stake in persuading practitioners to value their work. There is

18 I first developed the core of this argument in Shaw, 2011a, Chapter 2.

> little recognition that scientific technology has limits or that what researchers have labored to produce may not be particularly usable. (Kirk and Reid, 2002: 190)

A particularly helpful way in to understanding these issues was provided by the systems theorist, Norma Romm. Her basic premise is that 'the process of attempting to "know" about the social world already is an intervention in that world which may come to shape its constitution' (Romm, 1995: 137). Romm says that 'The view that theory is applied in practice and may be tested in that practice, can amount to an unreflected/unreflexive endorsement of a theoretical position' (Romm, 1996: 25). 'One is not just applying "findings", but intervening in the social discussion in a specific way, that is, in a way which authorises particular conceptions' (1995: 145). She is not only doubtful about the wisdom of traditional research application perspectives, but raises questions about other positions.

For example, most but not all participatory approaches advocate reflective deliberation as a means of reaching agreement. Romm chides by saying that such approaches 'fail to consider that their "understanding" *already gears practical activity* in a certain direction, and excludes other options for action' (1995: 151-52). What she means is that participatory models direct research processes towards dialogue, debate and accommodation of interests. Viewing the world 'in a way which suggests that debate can be initiated between participants engaged in purposeful activity, already directs participants towards activities in which they communicate with the hope to achieve an accommodation of interests' (1996: 30) and does not press us to consider the fairness of the accommodation reached, and whether contention or confrontation are ever appropriate. Borrowing a phrase from the sociologist Alvin Gouldner that echoes the criticism of sentimentality I mentioned above, she argues that critical self reflection must include 'acceptance of the need to open oneself to "bad news"' (1995: 158) which she defines as 'news springing from opposing positions'.

Approaches that fall within advocacy research recognise this problem, and are cautious about pseudo-compromises. Yet even here there is a risk that 'knowing' predisposes certain action. 'By "knowing" that there "is" an inevitable and unnegotiable conflict of interests, one may contribute to rendering this so – through the political action that one adopts' (p. 163). This may seem a collection of pessimistic recipes, but I do not think so. Indeed, the abrasive tendencies in the research/practice context are, for me, simply as they should be, and nor or they at all special to social work.

There are several options on offer for squaring the circle of understanding and action, including evaluation, applied research, action research, advocacy research, action science, participatory inquiry, and practitioner research. The issues can helpfully be unlocked through the recognition that research and practice need linking in ways that release the potential for practice to challenge social work science, and in so doing contest conventional hierarchical ways of seeing expert/beneficiary relationships. I have found for me that these linkages are best approached through considering five questions.

- What do we mean when we talk about social work practice?
- How does thinking qualitatively help?
- What is involved when we make use of research?
- How does the social context in which research and practice takes place influence the practice/research relationship?
- Does qualitative research offer a pattern for practice?

Most of the chapter in this book can be linked to one or more of these questions.

Practice

A useful way of thinking about the issues has been offered by Trevillion. He helpfully – if discomfortingly – raises five issues he believes we need to think about when we talk about the idea of social work practice (Trevillion, 2010: 166):

1. Practice is to some extent shaped by changes in government policy and a considerable amount of research is paid for by national governments so as to help them to achieve policy objectives. In this situation, can we distinguish between policy and practice, and if so how?
2. Practice is increasingly inter-professional and multi-disciplinary. What does it mean to talk about a specifically social work practice domain in an increasingly inter-professional and multidisciplinary context?
3. The practice context may look very different to practitioners, service users, carers and managers. Is there a way of describing the influence of practice on research that does justice to all these different perspectives?
4. In order to examine the influence of the practice context on research there is a need to model the relationship between the two. How do we go about building a model based on the idea that research is an emergent property of practice?
5. Practice means different things at different levels of social reality. How do we incorporate the concept of 'different levels of practice' in our emergent model?

His arguments are well worth pursuing on each of the five challenges he poses. He is being particularly helpful when he asks us to consider whether social work research can be seen as an emergent property of practice. He says,

> To suggest that practice can have a significant formative influence on research is to suggest that we think about research as a particular kind of practice outcome. This is a startling proposition. It runs counter to the rather romantic idea that research is the outcome of an independent community of scholars exploring issues in a process driven exclusively by intellectual curiosity. It also challenges the assumption that the world of research is essentially rational and linear and that the researcher is in control of the research agenda by suggesting that

> research is a product of the same messy world that social workers and service users inhabit. (p. 168)

Trevillion is not claiming that practice determines or causes research, but that it is 'rather a way of pointing out that the process of searching for knowledge is itself rooted in the conditions being examined' (p. 168). I find this kind of head-over-heels argument refreshing and pointed, in that it challenges the usual top-down assumption that research is autonomous and drives social work practice, while being untouched by that same practice. Extending how we should think about practice, I like the way Sheila Spong seeks to resolve the theory/practice dualism in her helpful reflections on counselling (Spong, 2007). She argues that effective relationship-based practice requires what she calls pragmatic belief, which obliges the practitioner 'to hold in tension the belief needed for therapy to be effective and the scepticism required to maintain openness to alternative interpretations' (p. 55). This entails an ability to retain 'an "as-if" position: ... immersed but not absorbed; ...utterly present and to have a meta-view, understanding that there are other possibilities and perspectives' (p. 62).

Thinking and practising qualitatively

Bornat and Walmsley, writing about 'biography as empowerment research', remind us that this is an area where there has been considerable interest in research applications in care settings. They develop a 'more questioning appraisal of claims for empowerment through biographical work' (Bornat and Walmsley, 2004: 221). Claims that self-worth or reclaimed identity have been achieved are hard to measure, and there is tendency to partisanship eg that they 'give voice' or are authentic. We may show commitment but must remain sceptical about our own commitment, in the way that Spong urges.

A somewhat different basis for making a plea to think and practise qualitatively rests on a determination to respect the 'rough ground' of practice. Schwandt and Dahler-Larsen engage in an illuminating conversation regarding their encounters with resistance to evaluation programmes (Schwandt and Dahler-Larsen, 2006). Dahler-Larsen reflects on an attempted evaluation of a free school with a Christian tradition in Denmark. He suggests that some communities may be characterised by 'a substantive value ... which cannot be made the object of reform'.

> My proposition is...that there are some basic ingredients in communities that define themselves in a particular way which make these communities incompatible with the idea of evaluation, at least at some level or for some issues some of the time.. I think that perhaps the reason why some communities resist evaluation is that they have sensed that evaluation is the capacity of asking exactly those questions that may threaten the very existence of the community (p. 499)

The possible lines of connection to social work are easily read. But in response Schwandt suggests a different interpretation, when drawing on a study of rehabilitation in a cardiology hospital. He poses what he views as 'the basic question of the justification for the evaluator's role to challenge and engage in critique' and says 'I am continually perplexed by this problem' (p. 502). He reflects on the metaphor of 'rough ground' as 'signifying that evaluation cannot always smooth out the creases in the intricate, uneven fabric of social practices or iron out difficulties in the appraisal of the value of those undertakings' (p. 503). Practice is rough ground because 'different ideas of what constitutes good practice and a good practitioner always compete for attention and because the moral, the political and the instrumental are always intertwined', and the very idea of critically engaging tradition is 'placing oneself in a place of being vulnerable to changing one's own ways of thinking' (p. 504). Schwandt concludes in constructive terms (in both the moral and intellectual sense),

> Perhaps evaluators should listen more carefully and respond more prudently to voices in communities that are hesitant or sceptical about evaluation...Perhaps beneath their apparent 'resistance' to evaluation, communities...are saying that they do not regard evaluation as smoothing and fixing things but rather as an activity that touches the rough ground of their lives, values and practices that constitute the world as they know it, and live in it, in other words, their *community* (2006: 504).

Utilising research

We have already heard the gist of Norma Romm's argument that 'practice cannot become the tool to substantiate theory, because *criteria for judging the relevance of practice are already written into the* theory' (Romm, 1996: 27 italics in original). The relationship between research and action cannot be seen simply as 'scientists understand' and then 'social workers do'. Reid described this view of utilisation whereby findings are applied to the solution of a problem as 'instrumental utilisation', and argued that it does not occur very often (Reid, 1988). Probably a more common form of utilisation is 'conceptual utilisation', in which findings are added to a storehouse of information, and emerge at some future point. Finally, there is what Reid terms 'persuasive utilisation', in which evidence, ideas and understandings are used to advance a point of view. This portrayal of utilisation processes suggests that implementation is always likely to be 'murky and convoluted' (Reid, 1988: 55).

Romm proposes the formula 'comprehension=application'. This says more than application is *based on* comprehension but rather comprehension is 'inextricably tied to' application (1996: 26). She believes that this formulation 'provides a way of challenging the (excessive) partiality which ensues, ironically, in the quest to ground knowledge in an impartial "inquiry" moment' (p. 28). She helpfully insists on 'not suppressing alternative ways of conceiving and seeing the world' and 'the need to be critical or suspicious of our intellectual assumptions' (p. 26). So our social work practice decisions 'can be defended only on the grounds that one has *thought-and-acted having taken one's encounter with other arguments and possibilities seriously*' (p. 27).

Hence we need a form of discursive accountability in which we 'defend our choices of vision and of action in the light of serious confrontation with alternatives' (p. 34) This brings us to the fourth question, in that reflection on what is entailed in research utilisation is sufficient for us to realise that research to practice perhaps never occurs through formulated rules uniformly implemented across research projects. Practice and research relations develop over time and variously according to the social context (Shaw, 2010a).

Does qualitative research offer a pattern for practice?

There are signs that some qualitative sociologists have an interest in the relevance of such work for practitioner audiences. Bloor, for example, has returned to this theme. He concludes that 'ethnographies of everyday professional practice may have such rich descriptions of everyday practice that practitioner audiences are able imaginatively to juxtapose their own everyday practices with the research description'. 'More radically, street ethnographers have sometimes opted for a dual role of both researcher and service provider, both street ethnographer and outreach worker' (Bloor, 2001: 184). He cites examples from ethnographies of prostitution and drugs outreach.

More recently Ellen Bogolub started from the stance that social work researchers have an ethical responsibility to bring about good for research respondents, and illustrates this from how she responded to an emerging awareness from a pilot study that there may have been significant service gaps for children receiving foster care services. She suggests that 'qualitative research seems particularly likely to raise such unanticipated questions'. She reflects on the costs and benefits – both ethically and methodologically – of her options for action and her decision to raise the service issues with the host agency (Bogolub, 2010). Michael Bloor responds to this. He relates tales from his own experience as a sociologist, observing as he does so that methods texts rarely provide embarrassing examples for others to cite. His main development of Bogolub's position is to suggest that 'The hallowed first rule of research, "Do no harm", is surely inadequate'. While well aware of the likely reactive consequences of his position, he claims 'one should always try actively to perform those small courtesies for one's research participants that will ensure that … one's research presence is not a burden, a threat, or an onerous additional task for others who are co-present in the setting' (Bloor, 2010: 19).

This is not quite to suggest that ethnography offers a template for practice, but does helpfully remind that the borders between disciplines are rarely as watertight as discipline insiders may believe or even wish.

Sociological social work

Given the title of this chapter it would be implausible to suggest in concluding that there is coherence to the academic work outlined above – and these do not exhaust the themes that have taken up my energies at one time or another. But the social work/sociology interface is one theme that I would like to mention, because it connects areas of work that otherwise may seem distant from one another. The sociology connection is perhaps most obvious in the steady stream of methodology books (Shaw, 1999a; Shaw et al, 2010; Shaw and Gould, 2001; Shaw and Lishman, 1999), facets of which are represented in this collection. Conceptually and substantively my empirical work has been infused by aspects of sociology. For example, my more recent work on technology and professional practice has been influenced by the sociology of scientific and practical knowledge (e.g. Shaw and Clayden, 2009; Shaw, Morris and Edwards, 2009), and my research with Neil Lunt and others has been driven by related areas of thinking (e.g. Shaw and Lunt, 2011; Shaw and Lunt, forthcoming). The latter is represented in this volume by a paper written with Alex Faulkner from a previous project in this field.

But neither of these could be described as crafting a sociological social work. Two areas of unfinished business best represent this strand. First, my book writing has been bracketed by two very different versions of my book *Evaluating in Practice* (Shaw, 1996a, 2011a). This is incompletely represented in this collection in a summary paper from this work, and in passing in the 'Just Inquiry' essay. I have tried through this writing to respond to four connected problems.

1. A narrowness of conception of intervention possibilities. For most practitioners it assumes practice as delivered through interviewing – and more than that, a certain kind of interviewing that easily becomes routinised and formulaic.
2. An unhelpful – because again narrowly conceived – conception of the relationship between research and practice. The 'application of research knowledge' approach has a number of problems but the central one for our purposes is that it renders the 'method' of social work invisible.
3. An unduly deferential conception of the relationship between social science and social work.
4. A constrained view of what is entailed in social work evaluation. Typically a *post hoc*, evaluation-as-accountability model.

In responding to these problems I have endeavoured to refashion the relationship of research and practice by demanding a methodology-led at least as often as a findings-led relationship. I draw on a process of 'translating' and 'reinhabiting' qualitative sociological methods. In doing so I want to decolonise the subordinate relationship of social work to social science, and hence liberate social work by placing it in an egalitarian and reciprocal relationship with sociology and cognate social science disciplines. I see this as entailing a radical reinvention of the role of evaluation as a methodological practice that permeates all of social work rather than functioning as a retrospective inspection and appraisal, and as serving a wider range of purposes than accountability. Kuhn speaks of a switch of gestalt as 'a useful elementary prototype for what occurs in a full-scale paradigm shift' (cited in Richards, 1981: 46) such that 'until the scientist has learned to see nature in a different way the new fact is not quite a scientific fact at all.' Without wanting to claim far too much, I suspect there may be elements of a prototype gestalt switch within these arguments, which relates to how people may not immediately 'get' the argument.

My endeavours to develop a sociological social work are undergirded more generally by a long term project that explores the historical emergence of social work and sociology. Following some initial articles on Clifford Shaw, Ernest Burgess and Frederick Thrasher (Shaw, 2008a, 2009b, 2010c, 2011b), I am working on archival material from the University of Chicago that previously has not been examined by social work researchers. Influenced once more by work in the sociology of knowledge (e.g. Collins and Pinch, 1998a, 1998b), I anticipate that this archival research may further challenge any remaining comfort about essentialist delineations of social work and sociology, and of the relationship between what sometimes are contrasted – perhaps invidiously – as more research-based and more application-based social sciences.

There is a common thread running through the previous paragraphs – a moderate skepticism of the kind that is represented in the essay on 'Ways of Knowing' in this volume. This cautious skepticism follows from the critical realism set out in the first part of this introduction. It also necessitates an awareness of the flawed and incomplete nature of any one person's efforts to describe and explain the world, in particular one's own.

References

Bayley, M. (1973) *Mental Handicap and Community Care*. London: Routledge and Kegan Paul.

Bloor, M. (2001) 'The Ethnography of Health and Medicine' in P. Atkinson, A. Coffey, S. Delamont, J. Lofland and L. Lofland, (eds) *Sage Handbook of Ethnography*. London: Sage Publications.

Bloor, M. (2010) 'The Researcher's Obligation to Bring about Good' *Qualitative Social Work*, 9 (1): 17-20.

Bogolub, E. (2010) 'The Obligation to Bring About Good in Social Work Research: A New Perspective' *Qualitative Social Work*, 9 (1): 9-15.

Bornat, J. and Walmsley, J. (2004) 'Biography as Empowering Practice: Lessons from Research' in Chamberlayne, P., Bornat, J. and Apitzsch, U. (eds) *Biographical Methods and Professional Practice*. Bristol: Policy Press.

Briar, S. and Miller H. (1971) *Problems and Issues in Social Casework*. New York: Columbia University Press.

Fischer, J. (1976) *The Effectiveness of Social Casework.* Springfield: Charles Thomas.
Campbell, D.T. (1981) 'Comment: Another Perspective on a Scholarly Career' in M. Brewer and B. Collins (eds) *Scientific Inquiry and the Social Sciences*. San Francisco: Jossey Bass, pp. 454-486.
Cicourel, A. (1967) *Method and Measurement in Sociology*. New York: Free Press.
Clarke, R. and Cornish, D. (1972) *The Controlled Trial in Institutional Research.* London: HMSO.
Collins, H. and Pinch, T. (1998a) *The Golem: What You Should Know about Science*. Cambridge: Cambridge University Press.
Collins, H. and Pinch, T. (1998b) *The Golem at Large*. Cambridge: Cambridge University Press.
Cook, T. and Campbell, D. (1979) *Quasi Experimentation: Design and Analysis Issues for Field Settings.* Chicago: Rand McNally.
Cornish, D. and Clarke, R. (1975) *Residential Treatment and its Effects on Delinquency*. London: HMSO.
Denzin, N. (1970) *The Research Act in Sociology*. Chicago: Aldine.
Giddens, A. (1993) *New Rules of Sociological Method.* Stanford: Stanford University Press.
Goldberg, E.M. (1970) *Helping the Aged.* London: Allen and Unwin.
Greene, J. (1990) 'Three Views on the Bature and Role of Knowledge in Social Science', in Guba, E. (ed) *The Paradigm Dialog*. Newbury Park: Sage.
Harrison, P. (2007) *The Fall of Man and the Foundations of Science*. Cambridge: Cambridge University Press.
Hollis, F. (1964) *Casework: a Psychosocial Therapy.* New York: Random House.
Hughes, J. (1980) *The Philosophy of Social Research*. London: Longman.
Kirk, S. and Reid, W.J. (2002) *Science and Social Work*. New York: Columbia University Press.
MacDonald, M.E. (1966) 'Reunion at Vocational High' *Social Service Review*, 40: 175-189.
Madge, J. (1963) *The Origins of Scientific Sociology*. London: Tavistock Publications.
Mann, P. (1965) *An Approach to Urban Sociology*. London: Routledge and Kegan Paul.
Mann, P. (1985) *Methods of Social Investigation*. Oxford: Blackwell.
Mayer, J. and Timms, N. (1970) *The Client Speaks*. London: Routledge and Kegan Paul.
McKay, D. (1988) 'Value Free knowledge: myth or norm?' in D. McKay *The Open Mind and Other Essays*. Leicester: Inter-Varsity Press.
Meyer, H., Borgatta, E. and Jones, W. (1965) *Girls at Vocational High*. New York: Russell Sage Foundation.
Orme, J. (2009) 'Eric Sainsbury' *Qualitative Social Work*, 8 (3): 409-414.

Reid, W. (1988) 'Service Effectiveness and the Social Agency' in R. Patti, J. Poertner, and C. Rapp (eds) *Managing for Effectiveness in Social Welfare Organisations*. New York: Haworth.

Richards, R.J. (1981) 'Natural Selection and Other Models in the Historiography of Science' in M. Brewer and B. Collins (eds) *Scientific Inquiry and the Social Sciences.* San Francisco: Jossey Bass.

Romm, N (1995) 'Knowing as an Intervention' *Systems Practice*, 8 (2): 137-167.

Romm, N. (1996) 'Inquiry-and-Intervention in Systems Planning: Probing Methodological Rationalities' *World Futures*, 47: 25-36.

Sainsbury, E. (1975) *Social Work With Families*. London: Routledge.

Sainsbury, E., Nixon, S. and Phillips, D. (1982) *Social Work in Focus*. London: Routledge.

Schwandt, T.A. and Dahler-Larsen, P. (2006) 'When Evaluation Meets the 'Rough Ground' in Communities' *Evaluation*, 12 (4): 474-495.

Shaw, I. (1973) Agency Decentralization: Planning and Assessment' *British Journal of Social Work*, 3 (3): 229-241.

Shaw, I. (1975) 'Making Use of Research', in H. Jones (ed.) *Towards a New Social Work.* London: Routledge, pp 151-166.

Shaw, I. (1976) 'Consumer Opinion and Social Policy' *Journal of Social Policy*, 5 (1): 19-32.

Shaw, I. (1978) *Patient Participation in General Practice*, Welsh Consumer Council, Cardiff.

Shaw, I. (1979) 'Patient Participation in General Practice' *Journal of Consumer Studies and Home Economics*, 3: 255-263.

Shaw, I. (1980) *Community Service: Attitudes and Practice*. Cardiff: South Glamorgan Probation Service.

Shaw, I. (1984a) 'Consumer Evaluations of the Personal Social Services' *British Journal of Social Work*, 14 (3): 277-284.

Shaw, I. (1984b) 'Keeping the Customer Satisfied?' in H. Jones (ed.) *Issues in Social Welfare*. Cardiff: University College, pp. 11-28.

Shaw, I. (1985) 'A Closed Profession? – Recruitment to Social Work' *British Journal of Social Work*, 15: 261-280.

Shaw, I. (1988) (ed.) *Social Issues and the Local Church*. Bridgend: Bryntirion Press.

Shaw, I. (1996a) *Evaluating in Practice*. Aldershot: Ashgate.

Shaw, I. (1999a) *Qualitative Evaluation*. London: Sage Publications.

Shaw, I. (1999b) 'Seeing the Trees for the Wood: the Politics of Practice Evaluation' in B. Broad (ed) *The Politics of Research and Evaluation in Social Work*. Birmingham: Venture Press.

Shaw, I. (2003a) 'Cutting Edge Issues in Social Work Research' *British Journal of Social Work*, 33 (1): 107-116.

Shaw, I. (2003b) 'Qualitative Research and Outcomes in Health, Social Work and Education' *Qualitative Research*, 3 (1): 57-77.

Shaw, I. (2004a) 'William J. Reid: an appreciation' *Qualitative Social Work*, 3 (2): 109-115.

Shaw, I. (2008a) 'Merely Experts? Reflections on the History of Social Work, Science and Research' *Research, Policy and Planning*, 26 (1): 57-65.

Shaw, I. (2009a) 'Ways of Knowing in Social Work' in M. Gray and S. Webb (ed) *Social Work Theory and Methods*. London: Sage Publications.

Shaw, I. (2009b) 'Rereading *The Jack-Roller*: Hidden Histories in Sociology and Social Work' *Qualitative Inquiry*, 15 (7): 1241-1264.

Shaw, I. (2010a) 'Places in Time: Contextualizing Social Work Research' in I. Shaw, K. Briar-Lawson, J. Orme, and R. Ruckdeschel (eds) *Sage Handbook of Social Work Research*. London: Sage Publications.

Shaw, I. (2010b) 'Logics, Qualities and Quality of Social Work Research' in I. Shaw, K. Briar-Lawson, J. Orme and R. Ruckdeschel (eds) *Sage Handbook of Social Work Research*. London: Sage Publications.

Shaw, I. (2010c) 'An Unresolved Legacy of the Chicago School' in C. Hart (ed) *The Legacy of the Chicago School*. Poynton, Cheshire: Midrash Publications.

Shaw, I. (2011a) *Evaluating in Practice*. Farnham: Ashgate.

Shaw, I. (2011b) 'Social Work Research: An Urban Desert?' *European Journal of Social Work*, 14 (1): 11-26.

Shaw, I. (2012a) 'The Positive contributions of quantitative methodology to social work research: a view from the sidelines' *Research on Social Work Practice* 22 (2): 129-134.

Shaw I. (2012b) 'Professional Voices from the Field: A Story' in Maschi, T., and Youdin, R. *Social Worker as Researcher: Integrating Research with Advocacy*. Boston: Pearson Publishing. Online at. http://www.pearsonhighered.com/product?ISBN=0205594948#tabbed.

Shaw, I., Arksey H. and Mullender, A. (2004) *ESRC Research and Social Work and Social Care*. London: Social Care Institute for Excellence.

Shaw I., Arksey H. and Mullender A. (2006) 'Recognizing Social Work' *British Journal of Social Work*, 36 (2): 227-246.

Shaw, I. and Clayden J. (2009) 'Technology, Evidence and Professional Practice: Reflections on the Integrated Children's System' *Journal of Children's Services*, 4 (4): 15-27.

Shaw I. Greene, J. and Mark M. (2006) *Sage Handbook of Evaluation*. London: Sage Publications.

Shaw, I. and Gould, N. (2001) *Qualitative Research in Social Work*. London: Sage Publications.

Shaw, I. and Lishman, J. (1999) (eds) *Evaluation and Social Work Practice*. London: Sage Publications.

Shaw, I. and Lunt, N. (forthcoming) 'Constructing practitioner research' *Social Work Research*.

Shaw, I. and Lunt, N. (2011) 'Navigating Practitioner Research' *British Journal of Social Work* 2011; doi: 10.1093/bjsw/bcr025.

Shaw, I. and Norton, M. (2007) *Kinds and Quality of Social Work Research in Higher Education*. London: Social Care Institute for Excellence. http://www.scie.org.uk/publications/reports/report17.asp.

Shaw, I. and Ruckdeschel, R (2002) 'Qualitative Social Work: a Room With a View' *Qualitative Social Work: Research and Practice*, 1 (1): 5-23.

Shaw, I. and Walton, R. (1979) 'Transition to Residence in Homes for the Elderly' in D. Harris and J. Hyland (editors), *Rights in Residence*. London: Residential Care Association, 19-31.

Shaw, I. Bloor, M., Cormack, R. and Williamson, H. (1996) 'Estimating the Prevalence of Hard to Reach Populations: Illustration of Mark-Recapture Methods in the Study of Homelessness' *Social Policy and Administration*, 30 (1): 69-85.

Shaw, I., Morris, K. and Edwards, A. (2009) 'Technology, Social Services and Organizational Innovation *or* How Great Expectations in London and Cardiff are Dashed in Lowestoft and Cymtyrch' *Journal of Social Work Practice*, 23 (4): 383-400.

Shaw, I., Williamson, H. and Parry-Langdon, N. (1992) 'Developing Models for Day Care Services' *Social Policy and Administration*, 26 (1): 73-86.

Skagestad, P. (1981) 'Hypothetical Realism' in M. Brewer and B. Collins (eds) *Scientific Inquiry and the Social Sciences*. San Francisco: Jossey Bass.

Smith, D. (1977) *IMPACT (Intensive Matched Probation and After-Care Treatment) – the Major Findings* http://www.ncjrs.gov/App/Publications/abstract.aspx?ID=55996.

Spong, S. (2007) 'Scepticism and belief: unravelling the relationship between theory and practice in counselling and psychotherapy' in S.R. Smith (ed) *Applying Theory to Policy and Practice: Issues for Critical Reflection*. Aldershot: Ashgate.

Trevillion, S. (2010) 'From Social Work Practice to Social Work Research: An Emergent Approach to a Basic Problem' in I. Shaw, K. Briar-Lawson, J. Orme and R. Ruckdeschel *Sage Handbook of Social Work Research*. London: Sage Publications.

PART I
Perspectives on Social Work Research

This opening section acts as a reference point for the following four sections of the book. The 'cutting edge' chapter started from the main British institution for assessing the quality of research in universities – then known as the Research Assessment Exercise – and offered a critical overview of where social work research stands in relation to research methodology; social work's relationship to science; the relationship between social work practice and research; governance and research ethics; building research capacity; and establishing research quality. I offered a basis for arguing that good social work research will:

1. contribute to the development and evaluation of social work practice and services;
2. enhance social work's moral purpose;
3. strengthen social work's disciplinary character and location;
4. promote social work inquiry marked by rigour, range, variety, depth and progression.

The following chapter, on whether social work research is distinctive, picks up and develops these questions. Taken together, these chapters set out the general position I have taken when warning against an unduly introspective standpoint on social work research, that claims too much by way of special character, and in doing so loses too much by way of understanding social work research as part of a loose affiliation of cognate social science disciplines.

Part of the empirical work undergirding this argument was undertaken as part of a study assessing the presence of social work research in the many bids and funded projects within the UK's Economic and Social Research Council (Shaw, Arksey and Mullender, 2004 and 2006). A more substantial research project was undertaken immediately following this, to get to grips with the general questions of what kinds of research may be characterized as social work research, and how may and should we assess the quality of such research. This yielded what I believe may be the first fully elaborated scheme to categorize the kinds of social work research, and also a set of detailed conclusions, principles and recommendations regarding how research quality should be understood and assessed (Shaw and

Norton, 2007 and 2008). This is an area that opens up opportunity for further work, but is one that so far has not had the influence I had hoped.

The cross-cutting assumptions of this line of reasoning are also reflected, if rather differently, in the final chapter in this section, on the career of William J. Reid (Shaw, 2004a). Reid died in late 2003, still at the height of his powers. I had already made an effort to place his work in the context of the evaluation movement in the USA (Shaw, 1999a, Ch 2) – a place that may seem incongruous given the absence of any engagement either way. The appreciation offered here takes a less than conventional view of his contribution to social work research.

As with the critical tribute to Bill Reid, the chapter on 'Re-reading *The Jack-Roller*' is not an immediately obvious choice for inclusion in a section on the general perspectival issues raised by social work research. However, it is one of the first fruits of the historical work outlined in the opening chapter of the book. Intended as an act of historical deconstruction, I explore a range of material that is barely known to sociologists and in some cases not known at all within the social work field. I understand the Chicago School of sociology as an intellectual melting pot that sheds as much light on the emerging field of social work as it does on sociology. This is the least finished area of work represented in this collection – but one that holds promise for especially challenging conclusions about the social work project.

Sandwiched by the general pieces on social work distinctive and the specific articles on Reid and the Chicago School is one of the pieces of writing where I have tried most explicitly to work through the implications of holding to epistemological constructivism and ontological realism, and expands on earlier work (Shaw, 2009a). I have continued to work on these wide issues as part of work subsequent to that included here, especially in terms of the general logic of social work research (Shaw et al, 2010a, 2010b, Shaw et al, 2010), and on aspects of the history of research and the Chicago School (Shaw, 2010c, 2011b).

References

Shaw I., Arksey H. and Mullender A. (2006) 'Recognizing Social Work', *British Journal of Social Work* 36 (2): 227-246.

Shaw, I. (1999a) *Qualitative Evaluation*. London: Sage Publications.

Shaw, I. (2004a) 'William J. Reid: an appreciation', *Qualitative Social Work* 3 (2): 109-115.

Shaw, I. (2009a) 'Ways of Knowing in Social Work' in M. Gray and S. Webb (ed) *Social Work Theory and Methods*. London: Sage Publications.

Shaw, I. (2010a) 'Places in Time: Contextualizing Social Work Research' in I. Shaw, K. Briar-Lawson, J. Orme, and R. Ruckdeschel (eds) *Sage Handbook of Social Work Research*. London: Sage Publications.

Shaw, I. (2010b) 'Logics, Qualities and Quality of Social Work Research' in I. Shaw, K. Briar-Lawson, J. Orme and R. Ruckdeschel (eds) *Sage Handbook of Social Work Research*. London: Sage Publications.

Shaw, I. (2010c) 'An unresolved legacy of the Chicago School' in C. Hart (ed) *The Legacy of the Chicago School*. Poynton, Cheshire: Midrash Publications.

Shaw, I. (2011b) 'Social Work Research: An Urban Desert?' *European Journal of Social Work* 14 (1): 11-26.

Shaw, I. and Norton, M. (2007) *Kinds and Quality of Social Work Research in Higher Education* London: Social Care Institute for Excellence. http://www.scie.org.uk/publications/reports/report17.asp.

Shaw, I. and Norton, M. (2008) 'Kinds and Quality of Social Work Research' *Br Journal of Social Work* 38 (5): 953-970.

Shaw, I., Arksey H. and Mullender, A. (2004) *ESRC Research and Social Work and Social Care*. London: Social Care Institute for Excellence.

Shaw, I., Briar-Lawson, K., Orme, J., and Ruckdeschel, R. (2010) 'Mapping social work research: pasts, presents and futures' in I. Shaw, K. Briar-Lawson, J. Orme, and R. Ruckdeschel (eds) *Sage Handbook of Social Work Research*. London: Sage Publications.

Chapter 1

Cutting Edge Issues in Social Work Research*

The aim of this critical commentary is to set out what I think are some important issues regarding social work research, and to imply what I think should be the contributory factors towards a general strategy. I prepared the initial version of this chapter for a workshop of social work doctoral students in Nottingham in the spring of 2002, and the tone and pitch of the chapter reflect its origins. I was not speaking to government officers, social work students, practitioners or fellow academics. I assume some knowledge of the field, and have an action agenda, but have not attempted the detailed 'so what' work.[1] I have tried to avoid being too parochial. I owe much to international links, but my main focus is on Britain, and suspect that readers can make the 'translation' to their own circumstances.

I have been involved with social work research for most of my life, and I am inevitably shaped by my biography. I got hooked on social science research while doing an undergraduate degree in sociology in the 1960s. I was recently asked to write a comment on an article by a former colleague on the sociology of trust, for a housing journal. The exercise evoked memories of how much I have been shaped by those early experiences. I recalled the struggles with weighty library volumes by Parsons, Merton, Weber and so on. I called to mind the political scepticism that inured me to the counterpoint of functionalism *versus* Marxism. The big ideas for me came not through theory but through methodology. It was years later that I enthusiastically picked up an old copy of John Madge's *The Origins of Scientific Sociology* off the shelf of a bookshop in the British Mecca of second hand bookshops, Hay on Wye. For better or worse, I was possibly the only student of my year who had read the now long-forgotten Madge cover to cover. Methodology has always been for me what theory is for others – a source of big ideas. Of course, the theory/methodology distinction should not be overdrawn. Was it William James who said you need a theory to pick up a stone in a field?

It is not easy to obtain barometric readings of the strength of social work research. One of the more rounded assessments, based on a relatively wide

---

* Originally published as Shaw, I. (2003) 'Cutting Edge Issues in Social Work Research', *British Journal of Social Work* 33(1): 107-116. Reprinted with permission of Oxford University Press.

1 This is not a research strategy for social work, albeit some elements of a strategy are suggested. For a draft social work research strategy see Fisher, 2001.

database, is in the overview report on social work submissions to the 2001 Research Assessment Exercise in British universities.[2] The panel concluded that,

> Research in Social Work has matured intellectually and includes both theoretical and empirical work. More attention is being paid to user involvement. Qualitative research is a growing strength and includes, for example, use of case studies, ethnological work, document analysis and participant observation as well as thematic analysis of free-flowing interviews. These methods are used in a number of new and emerging bodies of work – especially with regard to issues of sexuality, abuse and violence. (RAE 2001: Overview Report on UOA41 Social Work)

The panel concluded that 'there is some evidence of strength in those institutions which have specialized and have grown over time. Particularly marked improvements have taken place in some institutions which have specialized in sub-areas of the discipline or particular methodological approaches'. This may have been part of what the panel had in mind when commenting that social work research 'is changing its shape and looking less like traditional social work. There appears to be less research being carried out on what used to be seen as core topics'.

We can get some clue to panel members' thinking by noting what they believed to be the weaknesses of social work research.

> There was less attention paid to social work in the field of mental health than might have been expected. There was a paucity of quantitative analysis, particularly that combined with qualitative approaches. Quantitative work, while sometimes of a high quality, is rare and not always good when found. Exciting practice developments are not always well described and are often written up with too little regard for method.[3]

Taking the Research Assessment Exercise (RAE) report as a starting point, what are the key questions against which to assess social work research? I want to organize them under six themes.

---

2 For an initial general assessment of the 2001 RAE in the UK see Fisher and Marsh (2003).

3 Interesting as it is, the RAE panel report should not be taken as a gold standard for future research. It represents an academic panel view on the thirty submissions received, covering just over 400 staff. Universities that rolled up social work staff as part of submissions to other panels are not represented, and the report has a bitty feel to it, and reflects a panel probably wishing to present social work research in a generally positive light, given its relatively low volume. The Sociology panel, by comparison, received forty-eight submissions representing over a thousand staff – more than twice the staff return of social work. Sociology submissions averaged over 20 staff compared with an average of about 13 staff for social work.

1. Social work research methodology.
2. Social work's relationship to science.
3. The relationship between social work practice and research.
4. Governance and research ethics.
5. Building research capacity.
6. Research quality.

Research methodology

The RAE report is probably a safe guide on methodology. It covers what social work academics and their academic managers believe to be their best research undertaken in the years from 1996 to 2001, and for that reason is likely, if anything, to overstate the strengths of the generality of social work research.

Social work is not alone in the weakness of its quantitative research. The Economic and Social Research Council is responsible for accrediting training outlets for doctoral research in British universities. The most recent recognition exercise conducted in 2001 started from the general premise that the quality of quantitative methods across a number of social science disciplines was at risk, and developed generic guidelines for training outlets that gave additional emphasis to quantitative skills as a core requirement (http://www.esrc.ac.uk).[4]

Social work clearly has considerable ground to gain. In some cases it is ground to *re*gain. The 1960s onwards witnessed substantial social work research in Britain that was based on quantitative expertise or a combination of quantitative and qualitative excellence. The early work of people such as Sinclair, Davies, Clarke and Cornish and others linked to the Home Office Research Unit, the influence of epidemiological models on the work of Matilda Goldberg and others, the cross-fertilizing work of Tizard, Sinclair and colleagues on small institutions, the solitary cluster of British research on task-centered models of intervention, and the research on child care issues that led to the establishment of the Dartington Research Unit, were often marked by a methodological enthusiasm and innovativeness.

The partial loss of this creative stream of research can be understood in the light of the withering and eventual demise of the Probation Service link to social work, the crisis of confidence in the face of 'nothing works' arguments, and the decline of quantitative skills associated with the flowering of qualitative methodology. The parlous state of quantitative skills among the rank and file of social work academics remains a cause of serious concern.

Qualitative methodology may not be as soundly based as first impressions suggest. There are twin risks of routinization and dilution. There is a 'follow-my-leader' tendency whereby fruitful ideas such as focus groups and narrative analysis become the uncritical method of choice. Qualitative social work research

4 I have reviewed this recognition process in Shaw, 2003 (b).

is also at risk of dilution (Shaw and Gould, 2001). A high proportion of master's dissertations[5] draw on qualitative methods, but few such dissertations include anything other than semi-structured interviews and focus groups. The RAE panel's complaint about poorly described and methodologically indifferent accounts of practice suggests one end result of this dilution. The core problem is an absence of a methodological imagination, without which the much-extolled 'research-mindedness' is rudderless pragmatism.

There are welcome straws in the wind suggesting a reaction against these trends (eg Edgar and Russell, 1998; Jokinen et al, 1999, Shaw and Gould, 2001, and the recently launched journal *Qualitative Social Work*). There are also efforts to develop principled mediating positions that bring qualitative and quantitative methods into conversation with one another. For example, Reid in the USA and Sinclair in Britain have developed mediating positions (Reid, 1994, Sinclair, 2000). Researchers have also addressed the relationship between different methodologies in ways that fruitfully extend the debate (eg Bryman, 1988, Greene and Caracelli, 1997), and have explored the relative contributions different methodologies make to evaluation studies of the processes and outcomes of social work service interventions (Shaw, 2003 [a]).

It would be highly premature, however, if we assumed that using multiple methods will lead to sounder consensual conclusions in an additive fashion. Naïve versions of triangulation arguments are sometimes resorted to in support of this argument. One of the most insightful illustrations of the problems raised by this assumption is Trend's early classic account of an evaluation of a USA programme designed to test the effectiveness of direct payment of housing allowances to low income families (Trend, 1979). His conclusion still stands as a warning against such easy solutions:

> The complementarity is not always apparent. Simply using different perspectives, with the expectation that they will validate each other, does not tell us what to do if the pieces do not fit. (1979: 83)

He quoted approvingly Paul Feyerabend as saying 'It seems that it is not the puzzle solving activity that is responsible for the growth of knowledge, but the active interplay of various tenaciously held views' (p. 84).

There are other core methodological issues for social work research. Technological developments that enable meta-analysis, text manipulation, and the emerging uses of visual data are in themselves value-neutral, but will increasingly shape the field. More broadly, I think we have yet to appreciate the significance of the internationalization of the research community that has come with the Internet and electronic mail. Internationalization need not mean lowest common

5 A 15-20,000 word research requirement for completion of a master's degree in the UK and elsewhere.

denominator globalization. Indeed, it opens up new scope for addressing issues of methodology and culture.

Social work and science

Preoccupation with methodology poses the wider question of social work's relationship to science. The question is not new (cf Timms, 1968, England, 1986, Kirk and Reid, 2002). I suggest below that research should be judged in part according to its contribution to strengthening social work's disciplinary character and location, but this does not require that we argue for social work as a distinct discipline. Leaving aside logical reasons for this, there are pragmatic disadvantages to claiming disciplinary autonomy for social work. For example, small university departments and research groupings do less well in the RAE, and a strong disciplinary emphasis can promote a 'you in your small corner and I in mine' mentality when it comes to research training.

Despite the British government's allergic reaction to theorizing in social work training, there is a welcome emergence of theoretical literacy in social work, including European social theory, feminism, the sociology of knowledge, and concepts such as risk, time, practice, and expertise. Some of this work is obfuscating, but at its best a theoretical awareness delivers from naïve pragmatism, facilitates innovation, fashions connections, challenges practice, and undermines sentimentalism.

Practice and research

Social work practice and services have gained in three broad ways from research. Research may shed light on the processes and outcomes of practice, thus assisting in building knowledge and skills for practice. Social work has also gained from the wider range of knowledge-questioning research that seeks to describe or explain social problems encountered by human services practitioners.[6] Practice and research may mutually benefit from considering how far the perspectives and methods of one provide a template for the other.

There is a risk of short-termism in some practice-related research, particularly when instrumental, social engineering concepts of research predominate. Short-termism can be countered through doctoral research, including emerging professional doctorate schemes, and also through the slowly increasing opportunities in Britain for employer-university partnerships through collaborative studentships funded by the ESRC (Shaw, 2003 [b]). Mutual openness to developments in fields such

6 The phrase 'knowledge-questioning' serves partly to ensure we keep open the question whether social work research is progressive and beneficial.

as health and education research, and the evaluation community in the USA and elsewhere would increase the attractiveness and potential value of collaborative research, and help cure social work of a tendency to parochialism sometimes evident in otherwise excellent journals (cf the exchange between Gilgun, 2002 and Heurtin-Roberts, 2002).

An associated shortcoming arises from a naïve view of what evidence-based practice entails – an assumption that unambiguous 'evidence' can be readily elicited through routine research designs with a strong control element, and that this evidence can be unproblematically 'applied' to practice, if only practitioners are willing to face the facts and act on them. Uncritical partisanship about the virtues of evidence-based practice tends to discourage assiduous development of understanding of what works.

The RAE social work panel's comment that 'practice developments are not always well described and are often written up with too little regard for method' is worrying and receives at least anecdotal support from the conference circuit. One rarely mentioned failing of British social work research lies in the absence of a research and development model in the development of social work intervention. A comparison with the American research scene is illuminating. Take task-centred intervention models for example. A cumulative programme of intervention research on task centred intervention can be traced in the USA from the 1960s through to the 1990s. By contrast, the typical advocacy of task centred intervention in Britain is innocent of any empirical work, apart from a single publication bringing together linked projects in the 1970s (Goldberg et al, 1976).

There is an emerging insider argument to the effect that standards of quality in advocacy research should not be different from those in mainstream social research, but that such research should and can be defended on the grounds that it yields good research. For example, Sally Oliver's extensive work on involving health care consumers in identifying research topics, and prioritizing, commissioning and reporting research, has led her to conclude that consumers tend to highlight issues about patients' views, social contexts, information and support needs, long term outcomes, and dissemination of research findings to consumers. Her work suggests that these issues are less usually addressed by academic research reviewers, who tend to focus more on technical and economic aspects of research (Oliver, 1999). It is unclear for the moment where this unifying argument will lead, although it may attract a badge of orthodoxy in Britain if, as seems possible, it is adopted by bodies such as the Social Care Institute for Excellence.[7] Advocates of justice-based research approaches and promoters of recent scholarly reactions against partisanship in social research triggered by research on racism in schools (eg Hammersley, 2000 and 2003), will need to take dispassionate account of the serious arguments advanced by the other.

7 http://www.scie.org.uk.

Governance and research ethics

'Governance' has a sober, measured ring to it, and helpfully emphasizes the need to take issues of standards and ethics seriously in social work. For example, in the United Kingdom, the spate of concerns over consent for storage of body organs, developments in genetics, and linked innovations in technology, and new problems in privacy issues have destabilized confidence in the ethical regulation of medical research and led to the development of wide-ranging standards of research governance (Department of Health, 2000). Codes of research ethics have an established tradition in countries such as the USA, and there are recent tentative moves to seeking support for a code of social work research ethics in Britain (Butler, 2002).

A preoccupation with governance and standards is, of course, not an unmixed blessing. The basic thrust of the BBC Reith Lectures for 2002 was to raise and develop the thought that the revolution in accountability, of which research governance frameworks are a part, paradoxically *undermines* rather than enhances public trust (O'Neill, 2002). O'Neill's analysis is overly conservative, but should not be ducked altogether. There are two related risks from governance developments that are germinal to the development of social work research. First, a concern with governance readily transmutes into over-regulation. Institutionalization of decisions about ethics can become a medicalization of decisions about ethics, which in turn can render research *less* sensitive to the particular ethical challenges of social work research. Similarly, concern with ethics can lead to a solution of codification, with risks on the one had that ethics decision-making becomes the sole criterion for research access, and ironically on the other hand that ethics decisions are confined to access, research design and research management (Shaw, 2003 [c]).

Research capacity

Research capacity-building is in fashion. Community based health programmes are one example in the health services field (eg Shediac-Rizkallah and Bone, 1998). In Britain, the Economic and Social Research Council has invested heavily in a Research Capacity Building Network for teachers. In social work the recent pleas for social work agencies to be learning organizations is one manifestation of a similar concern (eg Baldwin and Gould, 2004).

In the mid 1990s it was possible to count the number of British social work research units on the fingers of one hand, with fingers to spare. One form of growing capacity can be seen in the fact that such units have more than doubled in the last five years, and a growing international network of social work research centres is beginning to solidify. The opportunities mentioned earlier for individuals to engage in research that avoids short-term activity could lead to further welcome evidence of research capacity. But unfortunately there are more negatives than positives.

First, there is little funding support for explicit mechanisms that encourage alliances between disciplines, pump-priming multi-disciplinary discussion, work and systematic review, and investment in the methodology for such work, in areas of need such as complex intervention studies. Second, the rhetoric of 'joined-up research' is honoured in the breach as much as the observance. There is an increasing amount of health and social care research, but how much collaborative research takes place in the fields of planning, housing, education, criminal justice and public health? Still more, has there been a single good concept paper on social care and transport research, or on civil engineering and social work? Too little of the healthy theorizing that takes place among social scientists about the environment, practice, time and risk percolates through to social work. The structures and discipline boundaries of universities and relationships between government departments are partly responsible for this. Third, the career opportunities for social work researchers are poor. The difficulties facing short-term contract staff are considerable, and it needs a joint response by universities and government research funding agencies to tackle the problem. A serious problem in Wales, to mention the country with which I am most familiar, is the lack of longer/permanent contracts for more experienced researchers. This aspect of research capacity has not been adequately addressed. It stems from the fact that the main funding sources are discontinuous and linked to projects rather than people.

The RAE social work panel report concluded that particularly marked improvements had taken place in some institutions which had specialized in sub-areas of the discipline or particular methodological approaches. A continued and strategic development of research specialisms is necessary. There will need to be a mixture of principle and pragmatism on this matter. It will not be feasible for national research budgets to cover the full range of research specialisms in any one country or region. This leads to a linked need for the establishment of priority-setting mechanisms in which practitioners, policy makers, researchers and service users all have an input.

These issues will not easily be resolved. There will continue to be a tension between, for example, encouraging participation in research and development and multi-disciplinary working, versus the need to allow focus and specialization to promote academic excellence. But the time has come for social work agencies and academics to join forces in lobbying governments for national audits of the social care research workforce similar to the audit of the public health R and D workforce promised in the Department of Health document *Research and Development Strategy for Public Health* (Department of Health, 2001).

Research quality

The pleas for the development of a cutting edge social work research need locating in the context of a larger picture. Such research should

1. Contribute to the development and evaluation of social work practice and services.
2. Enhance social work's moral purpose.
3. Strengthen social work's disciplinary character and location.
4. Promote social work inquiry marked by rigour, range, variety, depth and progression.

These four broad criteria have been implicit in the foregoing. For example, the expectation that social work research should be assessed by the extent to which it enhances the strength with which the moral purpose of social work is promoted, is both substantial and complex. The infusion of practice, methodology and research utilization with criteria of justice is one of the most contested and central issues facing social work.

If social work research is also to be judged according to its contribution to strengthening social work's disciplinary character and location, then social work researchers and academics need not be too preoccupied with the more arcane reaches of debates as to whether social work is a distinct discipline. But I do believe that disciplinary issues such as theorizing, conceptualization, doctoral level work, the practice/higher education interface, and research ethics are ignored at our peril.

Finally, social work research, and writing about it, should be judged by the extent to which they promote social work inquiry marked by rigour, range, variety, depth and progression. This is more likely to be achieved if we

1. Avoid ethnocentrism. Social work and its research enterprise are not hermetically sealed from cognate enterprises in the fields of education, health, criminal justice, and evaluation. We have no reason to be precious regarding our professional enterprise.
2. Remember – but are not stifled by the realization – that regimes of truth are regimes of power.
3. Eschew sentimentalism of the kind that refuses to question dearly held positions, or launches attacks on straw figures.

Universities can lead through, for example, setting up expert workshops on topics such as meta-analysis, visual data, research ethics, ethnography, cohort studies, theorizing, research and justice issues. Agencies can earmark modest proportions of training budgets to the promotion of longer term research excellence by social work practitioners. The devolved governments in Britain can audit research social work capacity. Social work centres of research excellence could establish a fixed term, small international 'think-tank' with colleagues in the USA, the Nordic countries, Australia, Canada, New Zealand, Germany, Israel, Spain and so on, to develop a radical research-mindedness. We do not have time to sit on our hands and do nothing.

References

Baldwin, M. and Gould, N. (2004) (eds) *Social Work, Critical Reflection and the Learning Organisation*. Aldershot: Ashgate.

Bryman, A. (1988) *Quantity and Quality in Social Research*. London: Unwin Hyman.

Butler, I. (2002) 'A Code of Ethics for Social Work and Social Care Research' in *British Journal of Social Work* 32 (2): 239-248.

Department of Health (2000) 'Research Governance Framework for Health and Social Care'. London: Department of Health.

Department of Health (2001) *Research and Development Strategy for Public Health*. London: Department of Health.

Edgar, I.R. and Russell, A. (eds) (1998) *The Anthropology of Welfare*. London: Routledge.

England, H. (1986) *Social Work as Art*. London: Allen and Unwin.

Fisher, M. (2000) 'A Strategic Framework for Social Work Research' in Mullender, A. (ed.) Theorising Social Work Research: Report to ESRC, University of Warwick, available at www.nisw.org.uk/tswr.

Fisher, M. and Marsh, P. (2003) 'Social work research and the 2001 Research Assessment Exercise: an initial overview' in *Social Work Education* 1 (22): 71-80.

Gilgun, J. (2002) 'Conjectures and Refutations: Governmental Funding and Qualitative Research' in *Qualitative Social Work* 1 (3): 359-375.

Greene, J. and Caracelli, V. (1997) *Advances in Mixed Method Evaluation: the Challenge and benefits of Integrating Diverse Paradigms*. New Directions For Evaluation, No 74, San Francisco: Jossey-Bass.

Hammersley, M. (2000) *Taking Sides in Social Research: Essays on Partisanship and Bias*. London: Routledge.

Hammersley, M. (2003) 'Social Research Today: Some Dilemmas and Distinctions' in *Qualitative Social Work* 2 (1).

Heurtin-Roberts, S. (2002) 'Thought on qualitative research methods at NIH' in *Qualitative Social Work* 1 (3): 376-379.

Jokinen, A., Juhila, K. and Pösö, T. (1999) *Constructing Social Work Practices*. Aldershot: Ashgate.

Kirk, S. and Reid, W.J. (2002) *Science and Social Work*. New York: Columbia University Press.

Madge, J. (1963) *The Origins of Scientific Sociology*. London: Tavistock Publications.

Oliver, S. (1999) 'Users of Health Services: Following their Agenda' in Hood, S., Mayall, B. and Oliver, S. (eds) *Critical Issues in Social Research: Power and Prejudice*. Buckingham: Open University Press.

O'Neill, O. (2002) *A Question of Trust*. Cambridge: Cambridge University Press.

Reid, W.J. (1994) 'Reframing the Epistemological Debate', in Sherman, E. and Reid, W. (eds), *Qualitative Research in Social Work*. New York: Columbia University Press.

Reid, W.J. (1995) 'Research Overview' in Edwards, R.L. and Hopps, J.G. (eds) *Encyclopedia of Social Work* 19th Edition Volume III Washington DC: NASW Press.

Research Assessment Exercise, 2001 (2002) 'Overview Report on UOA41 Social Work'. http://www.rae.ac.uk/2001/.

Shaw, I. (2003 [a]) 'Qualitative Research and Outcomes in Health, Social Work and Education' in *Qualitative Research* 3 (1): 57-77.

Shaw, I. (2003 [b]) 'Process and Outcomes: The 2001 ESRC Recognition Exercise' in *Social Work Education* 22 (6): 613-617.

Shaw, I. (2003 [c]) 'Ethics in Qualitative Research and Evaluation' in *The Journal of Social Work* 3 (1): 9-29.

Shaw, I. and Gould, N. (2001) *Qualitative Research in Social Work*. London: Sage Publications.

Shediac-Pizkallah, M.C. and Bone, L.R. (1998) 'Planning for the Sustainability of Community Based Health Programs: Conceptual Frameworks and Future Directions for Research, Practice and Policy' in *Health Education and Research Theory and Practice* 13 (1): 87-108.

Sinclair, I. (2000) 'Methods and Measurement in Evaluative Social Work' in Mullender, A. (ed.) Theorising Social Work Research: Report to ESRC, University of Warwick, available at www.nisw.org.uk/tswr/sinclair.html.

Timms, N. (1968) *The Language of Social Casework*. London: Routledge and Kegan Paul.

Trend, M.G. (1979) 'On the Reconciliation of Qualitative and Quantitative Analyses', in Cook, T. and Reichardt, C. (eds) *Qualitative and Quantitative Methods in Evaluation Research*. Beverly Hills: Sage Publications.

Chapter 2
Is Social Work Research Distinctive?*

The UK's Economic and Social Research Council (ESRC)[1] gave recognition to social work as a subject for which doctoral students could register and train for the first time in 2005. This implies a question which, although embedded in the context of doctoral research, is more general. Are efforts by the social work community across different countries to achieve greater research recognition of social work only a device to build the capacity of social work? This is not to demean such a motive, but are such efforts *only* about this? If we were to think that social work research differs only in place and people from politics, sociology, psychology or geography, then the question whether social work research is distinctive would be merely rhetorical.

What does make social work research distinctive? And how is our answer linked to how we do social work research? In this chapter I will take ESRC statements about social work research as a starting point. I will argue that it makes some degree of sense to ask what is distinctive about social work research. But I will go on to claim that the more significant question is what might make social work research distinctively good? I will suggest six criterial benchmarks.

Social work research

One way to understand how different social science communities see their identities is to compare several of the subject/discipline statements in the ESRC Guidelines (ESRC, 2005). This is not the only way to open up this question. Its limitation is that it tends to be aspirational. A different way would be to do empirical work on the methods and methodology actually used by different social science communities. Yet aspirational claims-making sheds no less illumination on how communities see their identities. There is a lot of similarity, but differences of emphasis. One of the main differences is how far the nature of the area is described in terms of understanding/theorizing and how far it also includes some notion of 'application'.

---

* Originally published as Shaw, I. (2007) 'Is social work research distinctive?' in *Social Work Education* 26(7): 659-669. Reprinted with permission of Taylor and Francis.

1 The ESRC is the leading funder of academic social science research in the UK. The nearest funding parallel in the USA is the federal system of national research institutes. Social work doctoral students were able to compete for ESRC funding previous to 2005, but under the 'flag' of existing recognized disciplines such as social policy, sociology or psychology. They could also gain funding from other sources.

Some disciplines are weighted quite differently from others in that respect. There are differences also in how each subject sees the balance between generic research skills and subject specific ones. Some of the subject specific statements (social work included) are quite a lot longer than others, thus appearing to imply that they regard their distinctives as relatively more important than those subjects where briefer subject accounts are given. This is what is said about social work:

> 4.1 In addition to the generic research methods training, students undertaking research training in social work will be expected to demonstrate:
>
> - Awareness of and sensitivity to the ethical and governance aspects of their research.
> - Reflexivity about their own and others' roles in the research process.
> - Knowledge of the social and political contexts and uses of research.
> - Knowledge of and sensitivity to conducting research in emancipatory ways.

Much of the content of the first three points could be found in any social science 'benchmark' description of research. But we are being told here that these issues may take special 'shape' in social work. The fourth point is, beyond reasonable contradiction, an area that is stressed more heavily in social work than in any other discipline[2] and in most not at all. The Guidelines go on to say that:

> 4.2 Students undertaking research in social work study and interact with people as individuals and as members of families, networks, communities and societies. Research training must therefore give students:
>
> - A clear understanding of the ways in which inequality and diversity shape research questions, and the skills, understanding and sensitivity to understand, reflect and, where appropriate, challenge these issues at all stages of the research process.
> - An understanding of the need to incorporate the perspectives of all research users in an appropriate manner, and an appreciation of the tensions this may produce within the research process, especially where it is developed within a participatory framework.
> - A critical awareness of the potential and limitations of multidisciplinary and interdisciplinary approaches to social work research, and how these may usefully be integrated to further research in social work and social care.

This emphasizes value issues and also the relevance of work in a range of other disciplines. When the Guidelines deal with the details of the research process they emphasize particular designs and data collection methods. For example, on design

2 The social work research community in the UK includes a range of positions on whether good research will always be emancipatory.

> knowledge and skills in experimental and quasi-experimental designs, n=1 designs (i.e. single case designs), longitudinal studies, case studies, applied ethnographies, action research, intervention research and development, and evaluation designs.

Also, on data collection

> Knowledge of the scope, value and utility as sources for social work research of archival, documentary, institutional and agency records, official statistics, and policy reports.

A particular social work research agenda can plausibly be detected. The quoted example of a research design requirement reflects the centrality of broadly evaluative questions, and the data collection example derives from the significance of institutional settings in social work.

The implications of these requirements seem not to require a claim for any distinctive methods *per se*, but suggest how the choice of methods will (and ought to be) connectable to the characteristic disciplinary (social work) purposes of the research. (Similar inference could be drawn from the way data analysis is discussed in the Guidelines.)

If taken as a reference point or benchmark, the text helps illuminate where there are gaps in current efforts. It also helpfully suggests that the social work research community ought to avoid thinking of research in simply 'technical' ways. Social work rightly foregrounds wider issues. The sort of wider questions to consider include:

1. What is the role and purpose of social work research?
2. What contexts shape the practice and purpose of social work research?
3. How can we maximize the quality of the practice and method of social work research?
4. How can the aims of social work be met through social work research?

Good social work research will include this wider agenda. There are some interesting comments on how to achieve parts of this programmed in another part of the ESRC Guidelines. Annex Two deals with professional doctorates – doctoral qualifications typically pursued part-time and based on a roughly 50/50 balance of taught course work on themes relevant to research in their occupation, and a thesis or dissertation. It raises some questions about how professional knowledge might be infused in research. While not specifically about social work, much will easily transfer. The document writers say at one point (Ann. 2.3):

> ESRC sees the focus of a professional doctorate as a dual one – to make a contribution to both theory and practice, and to develop a contribution to professional practice through making a contribution to (professional) knowledge.

This duel direction is helpful. A later paragraph says that a key issue for such a doctorate is, 'Does the professional doctorate provide a bridge between theory and practice and vice versa?' (App. 2.3.i), and regards the approach taken to this complex link to be a key issue.

The point is meant to apply across a wide variety of professional fields. But in a social work connection the point should be made still more strongly. One distinctive characteristic of social work research ought to include the development of strategies through which research (or more broadly, social science) might be challenged by practice. This perspective can be worked through in several directions, for example, by rethinking what it means to do 'practical' research, and also by trying to give more bite to what is usually called 'practitioner research'. Endeavours have been made to liberate practitioner research from a personalized model that takes academic research and disciplines as given, and limits practitioner inquiry to applying research to practice (e.g. Fahl and Markand, 1999; Shaw, 2005; Shaw and Faulkner, 2006). Fahl and Markand's project sought to create an identity for practitioner research as critique rather than individualized application – critique of social science as well as of practice. Their point about psychology will stand for social science in general when they conclude that 'if existing academic psychology and existing professional psychological practice can only be brought together with difficulty, then this "only" says that this type of psychology needs to be criticized and developed' (p. 75). An emphasis of this kind prevents social work from falling into the temptation to be intellectually defensive.

A caution

Should we conclude from the foregoing that social work research is and ought to be different from research in social science disciplines, and even from other areas of 'applied' research, such as education or housing? An illustration may clarify. It has sometimes been suggested that social work research has a distinctively radical critique of positivism. The references to positivism in social work are almost always negative, as when the broadside is fired that 'positivists not only see their work as uncontaminated: they see themselves as pure and safe in their objectivity, an elite who have managed to transcend the constraints of subjectivity' (Everitt et al., 1992, p. 6).

I have at least two problems with this and similar arguments. First, the key terms – positivist, objectivity, and subjectivity – tend to be treated as self-explanatory, and in need of no unpacking. It becomes a form of sloganizing – 'a swearword by which no-one is swearing' (Williams, 1983) – and leaves proponents vulnerable to being regarded as ill-informed, and as a consequence risk being ignored. Second, it undermines a culture of reciprocal exchange and argument that should mark social work activity at all levels. Lying behind claims to social work's special character is, I suspect, an old heresy that for many years was prevalent – the belief that social work has a basic value position that has greater merit/greater human authenticity/is more whole-person oriented, etc. than other professions.[3]

Even when the term 'paradigm' is not used, these sorts of arguments have the marks of a naïve paradigm position. Hammersley is right to warn that paradigm talk on this level 'obscures both potential and actual diversity in orientation, and can lead us into making simplistic methodological decisions' (Hammersley, 1995, p. 3). To pick up his second point, it is primitiveness when one hears the occasional argument that quantitative analysis is inherently 'positivist', and that qualitative methodology is somehow more reflective of social work values than quantitative. There are, of course, positivist hangovers in some quite roomy corners of social work, for example in parts of the evidence-based practice movement and in the American plea for scientific practice. The journal *Research on Social Work Practice* offers a congenial domicile for this general position. Criticisms of foundationalist science, naïve realism, and a correspondence theory of truth – all characteristic of most forms of positivism – do need making [cf. Sommerfeld (2005) for a recent review that is sharply critical without being hectoring].

But social work and social work research will be the poorer if we over-emphasize the distinctives. It will make us disinclined to listen to the voices of colleagues in other disciplines and professions. If we espouse joined-up services, why not disciplinarily joined-up research? On most occasions the right question to ask is not what makes social work research distinctive, but what might make it distinctively good? The first three points in the second part of this paper take research as their starting position. The final three start from social work and practice.

What makes social work research distinctively good?

Social work research will be distinctively good when it:

- Aims for methodological excellence in whatever it does.
- Promotes social work inquiry marked by rigour, range, variety, depth and progression.
- Sustains an active conversation with the social science community.
- Achieves a thoroughgoing consistency with broader social work purposes.
- Gives serious attention to aspects of the research enterprise that are close to social work.
- Aims to unsettle its preconceptions by taking seriously aspects of the research enterprise that seem on the face of it far from social work.

3 I have tried to develop this criticism in a preliminary way in an earlier book (Shaw, 1996, pp. 106-109).

Methodological excellence

There is too much methodologically thin social work research. This was hinted at in the panel report on the 2001 UK Social Work Research Assessment Exercise, which concluded, alongside several positive remarks, that in social work submissions from UK universities:

> There was a paucity of quantitative analysis particularly that combined with qualitative approaches. Quantitative work, while sometimes of a high quality, is rare and not always good when found. Exciting practice developments are not always well described and are often written up with too little regard for method. (RAE, 2001: Overview Report on UOA41 Social Work)

The reservations expressed in the report should not be disregarded as if they over-emphasize negative points about social work research in the UK during 1996-2001. The Research Assessment Exercise considers what social work academics and their academic managers believe to be their best research, and for that reason is likely, if anything, to over-state the strengths of the generality of social work research.

The core problem may be an absence of a methodological imagination, without which the much-extolled 'research-mindedness' is rudderless pragmatism. We need better ethnography, better attention to the best ways of tackling outcomes research, a disavowal of narrative research that is simply given a narrative 'tag' without accompanying substance, and so on.[4]

Social work inquiry marked by rigour, range, variety, depth and progression

This is more likely to be achieved if the social work community avoids a polarized attachment to this or that method or methodology. This is emphatically not a plea for either diversity of methods at all costs, or for a position that has no place for careful argument about the merits of one particular method over another. Once the argument for mixed methods becomes a pragmatic choice, it will reduce research to the lowest common methodological denominator.

The case for mixed methods entails tough thinking and practice around several questions. It is first of all an epistemological question. Are there philosophical reasons for concluding that quantitative and qualitative methods are fundamentally different in their assumptions and hence in their methodological outworkings? Second, it is a question about data relationships – whether we should expect that qualitative and quantitative data will most of the time yield a harmony of explanations and conclusions. Third, it is a question about methods and knowledge

---

4 On ethnography and narrative see the special issue of the journal *Qualitative Social Work*, vol. 4, no. 4, 2005, edited by Christopher Hall and Susan White.

claims. In this regard it is important to think through in advance of fieldwork decisions, what sorts of knowledge claims derive from different methods. Fourth, it is a logic question. One of the more fruitful ways of rethinking the logic of the boundaries of methods is when we consider using the logic of one in association with the fieldwork methods of the other. The examples I can most easily think of are when we use qualitative methods to tackle the logic issues of quantitative studies (Shaw, 2003). Finally, there is a different area of thinking that pushes us to be clear about the basic assumptions of our methods, whether qualitative or quantitative. This is the question of whether we can agree criteria for good research. This is tricky, but may be achievable if we can get beyond the language and practice barriers of validity–reliability–objectivity on the one hand and plausibility–trustworthiness–authenticity on the other.

Practitioners of social work research should also actively remember – but not be stifled by the realization – that regimes of truth are regimes of power. And they should eschew sentimentalism of the kind that refuses to question dearly held positions, or launches attacks on straw figures

Active conversation with the social science community

The motto to stick on the kitchen fridge in this regard is 'avoid ethnocentrism'. Social work and its research enterprise are not hermetically sealed from cognate enterprises in the fields of education, health, criminal justice, or evaluation. We have no reason to be precious regarding our professional or disciplinary enterprises. There will not always be reciprocity as we venture this, and sometimes the conversations will need to be sharp. But we can adapt G.K. Chesterton's aphorism about Christianity in this context. 'It is not that Christianity has been tried and found difficult', he remarked, 'But that it has been found difficult and not tried'. So it is with cross-border conversations.

Social work purposes

It will achieve consistency with broader social work purposes when it severally aims to:

- generate or enhance theory and knowledge about social work and social care;
- provide impartial evidence about and for decision-making;
- instrumentally improve practice and organizational learning;
- highlight the quality of lived experience and advance practical wisdom; and
- promote justice, social change and social inclusion.

To take the final point, the social work academic community still has much to learn from service users about good research. The dimensions of this lesson-learning are beginning to take shape. The reflections emerging from the UK-based Toronto Group, for example, make useful distinctions between involving service users in mainstream research, involving service users in peer review, involving people from black and minority ethnic communities in research, and emancipatory research (Hanley, 2005). These distinctions are helpful both in avoiding generalities about the merits or otherwise of these forms of research, and also in setting clear agenda for a much longer list of questions and challenges than is sometimes assumed. More generally, we should not forget Bob Holman's exhortation about 'Research from the Underside' (Holman, 1987). We should attend much more to 'voices' within social work research. Sociologists, especially those influenced by what is often called the crisis of representation, have led on this issue. Social work ought to be in the front line on this (cf. Gilgun and Abrams, 2002; Gray, 2002; Terrell and Staller, 2003). I do think this is an area where qualitative researchers have been far more active than those of a quantitative ilk.

Included within this 'benchmark' is the implicit assertion that social work research will be distinctively good when it contributes to professional knowledge and practice. The discussion of the ESRC Guidelines at the opening of this chapter dwelt on aspects of this point in some detail already. But the five bullet points above give emphasis to the necessary breadth of this enterprise. 'Theory', 'knowledge', 'evidence', 'instrumentally improving', 'practical wisdom', 'justice' and 'social change' are 'big' words and phrases in every sense. 'Practice research', for example, is often associated with strongly voiced discussions about ways of evidencing and knowing. This is as it should be, but it ought not make us exclusive in our view of the scope of the project. Practice research, as a working definition, may be accepted as comprising

Any disciplined empirical inquiry (research, evaluation, analysis), conducted by researchers, practitioners, service users/carers, that is intended, wholly or to some significant degree, to shed light on or explain social work intervention/practice with the purpose of achieving the goals of social work within and across national cultures.

Aspects of the research enterprise that are close to social work

Such aspects include, for instance, the nature of the interview, applied research, usefulness in research, the social work context, and so on. Take the last – social work context – as an illustration of where this can lead.[5] Much of the best qualitative research in social work can often be described as 'constructivist' in orientation. There is far less research that carries the imprint of ethnography and traditional aspects of social anthropology. This is not an 'anorak' preoccupation with

5 See Shaw and Gould (2001, pp. 17-23) for a fuller discussion.

intellectual bypaths of methodology. On the contrary, thoroughgoing ethnography sets in the foreground the liberating or constraining features of everyday life, the particularities of culture, and above all an emphasis on context – and these are all central to understanding and good practice in social work.

'Context' should not be treated as a taken for granted feature of social work. What are our assumptions of the meaning of 'social work context'? Possibly roughly the same as 'setting' or 'agency' and as something that is a 'given' of social work practice. Something we can 'touch, taste and handle' – that is relatively fixed and durable – social work's material culture. Maybe we distinguish in our minds the local from the extended setting. This extended setting may be spatial, or defined by membership. Service users may well appear in our image of the social work context. Possibly we envisage the extended context as including policy and managerial contexts. But what about the time dimension? Contexts are retrospective as well as prospective, and context cannot be restricted to spatial models. Professional and organizational discourses, and the almost endless deposit of written texts, also form core elements of social work contexts.

It will be clear from this that the frameworks of meaning within which social workers practise are not fixed and given. They are the result of mutual 'labour' on the part of actors. Such labour encompasses the methods that members engage in, for making their activities 'accountable' – visible, rational, and reportable.

But contexts are more – much more – than the collaborative endeavour of peers. One weakness of some interpretive sociology has been 'a failure to examine social norms in relation to the asymmetries of power and divisions of interest in society' (Giddens, 1993, p. 164). Giddens argues

> that the creation of frames of meaning occurs … in terms of the differentials of power which actors are able to bring to bear … *The reflexive elaboration of frames of meaning is characteristically imbalanced in relation to the possession of power* … What passes for social reality stands in immediate relation to the distribution of power. (Giddens, 1993, p. 120, emphasis in original)

This underlines the central importance of both language and structure in grasping the significance of social work contexts. There is a risk that a too exclusive emphasis on 'constructivist' orientations neglects issues of power, space, place and time – context. This is particularly true when we slip into speaking of constructions as if they were merely mental constructs, as when Guba, for example, says that 'realities exist in the form of multiple mental constructions … It is the mind that is to be transformed, not the real world' (1990, p. 27). But reality is not simply and solely a mental product. It comprises social, collective acts, and these collective acts are material transactions with the world (Atkinson, 1995).

Aspects of the research enterprise that seem distant from social work

This final claim may appear to contradict the previous point, but the questions are quite different. The thrust behind the previous line of reasoning is a conviction that close inspection of what we 'know' is needed if we are to discover what we know. This point looks away from conventional social work identities and boundaries to the unfamiliar, while the previous one proceeds by defamiliarizing the known.

Take, for example, theorizing about and for social work. Ideas of knowledge, theory and practice open up linked themes of evidence, learning, reflection and expertise. Welfare and wellbeing – on which much work is being done across the social sciences – turn our attention in new ways to professional practice, risk, attachment, resilience, and power. New thinking about technology, as not solely about machines and hardware, but as a social manifestation, takes social work to developments in health, the biosciences, sociology, social policy, management and business. Social work has made rich contributions to thinking about social justice. This could be taken further through engaging with work done in disciplines such as philosophy, law and jurisprudence, political science, international development, social policy, criminology, and socio-legal studies. Language, culture and communication open up allied themes of globalization, expertise, and practical knowledge. Finally, concepts of time, place and community suggest the potential fruitfulness of collaboration with colleagues in social geography, area studies, transport studies, sociology, environmental planning, and social anthropology.

Conclusions

This chapter is relatively brief and sketched intentionally as a cartoon outline. But it is a cartoon on a wide canvas. I have argued that it does make sense to ask what is distinctive about social work research, but the more significant question is what might make social work research distinctively good? I suggest six benchmarks. These address the case for methodological excellence; inquiry marked by rigour, range, variety, depth and progression; active conversation with the social science community; consistency with broader social work purposes; attention to aspects of the research enterprise that are close to social work; and taking seriously aspects of the research mission that seem on the face of it far from social work. However, social work and social work research will be the poorer if we over-emphasize the distinctives at the expense of commonalities in fostering and assessing best practice and best purpose.

It was suggested by an anonymous reviewer that the paper was mistitled and should be 'Distinctiveness and quality in social work research'. While I appreciate the probable thinking, I have resisted for fear of dramatically over-claiming. The argument about quality is subordinate to that about distinctiveness.[6]

The argument has implications for social work education, in terms of two kinds of continuity. First, there are important continuities between teaching and learning practice and research. This kind of connection is not special to social work, but the character of the continuities will be distinct. For example, being a reflective practitioner and committed to enhancing social inclusion have analogies, although not replicas, in both research and practice. Second, there are important continuities between qualifying, post-qualifying and doctoral learning. In the UK this is only weakly appreciated, due in significant part to a chronic failure over many years for the regulatory bodies – or at least key stakeholder interests within them – to recognize the continuity or commit to it. The academic and practice social work communities have been weaker both severally and jointly as a consequence.

Acknowledgements

Thanks are extended to the network of UK social work doctoral students who responded valuably to an earlier version of this paper.

References

Atkinson, P. (1995) *Medical Talk and Medical Work*, Sage Publications, London.

Economic and Social Research Council (2005) Postgraduate Training Guidelines, ESRC, Swindon, Section F15 and Appendix 2.

Everitt, A., Hardiker, P., Littlewood, J. and Mullender, A. (1992) *Applied Research for Better Practice*, Macmillan, London.

Fahl, R. and Markand, M. (1999) 'The project "Analysis of Psychological Practice" or: an attempt at connecting psychology critique and practice research', *Outlines*, vol. 1, pp. 73-98.

Giddens, A. (1993) *New Rules of Sociological Method*, Stanford University Press, Stanford.

Gilgun, J. and Abrams, L. (2002) 'The nature and usefulness of qualitative social work research: some thoughts and an invitation to dialogue', *Qualitative Social Work*, vol. 1, no. 1, pp. 39-55.

Gray, M. (2002) 'Art, irony and ambiguity: Howard Goldstein and his contribution to social work', *Qualitative Social Work*, vol. 1, no. 4, pp. 413-433.

Guba, E. (ed.) (1990) *The Paradigm Dialog*, Sage, Newbury Park, CA.

Hammersley, M. (1995) *The Politics of Social Research*, Sage, London.

6 Shaw and Norton have explored judgements of the nature and quality of social work research (Shaw and Norton, 2007).

Hanley, B. (2005) *Research as Empowerment? Report of a Series of Seminars Organized by the Toronto Group*, Joseph Rowntree Foundation, York.

Holman, B. (1987) 'Research from the underside', *British Journal of Social Work*, vol. 17, no. 6, pp. 669-683.

Qualitative Social Work (2005) Special Issue on Narrative and Ethnography, vol. 4, no. 4, edited by C. Hall and S. White.

Research Assessment Exercise, 2001 (2002) Overview Report on UOA41 Social Work. Available at: http://www.hero.ac.uk/rae/.

Shaw, I. (1996) *Evaluating in Practice*, Ashgate, Aldershot.

Shaw, I. (2003) 'Qualitative research and outcomes in health, social work and education', *Qualitative Research*, vol. 3, no. 1, pp. 57-77.

Shaw, I. (2005) 'Practitioner research: evidence or critique?', *British Journal of Social Work*, vol. 35, no. 8, pp. 1231-1248.

Shaw, I. and Faulkner, A. (2006) 'Practitioner evaluation at work', *American Journal of Evaluation*, vol. 27, no. 1, pp. 44-63.

Shaw, I. and Gould, N. (2001) *Qualitative Research in Social Work*, Sage Publications, London.

Shaw, I. and Norton, M. (2007) *Kinds and Quality of Social Work Research*, Social Care Institute for Excellence, London.

Sommerfeld, P. with Herzog, P. (Eds) (2005) *Evidence-Based Social Work – Towards a New Professionalism?* Peter Lang, Bern.

Terrell, J. and Staller, K. (2003) 'Buckshot's case: social work and death penalty mitigation in Alabama', Qualitative *Social Work*, vol. 2, no. 1, pp. 7-23.

Williams, R. (1983) *Keywords: a Vocabulary of Culture and Society*, Fontana, London.

Chapter 3
Ways of Knowing in Social Work*

> … and if you stay barren, (of conceptions of knowledge) you'll be less burdensome to those who associate with you, and gentler, because you'll have the sense not to think you know things which in fact you don't know. That much my art can do, but no more (Socrates, in Plato, 'Theaetetus')

My aim in the chapter is to facilitate the reader in gaining competence – and confidence – in asking tricky questions about knowledge for social work practice and research. Knowing how and when to ask the right questions – of oneself and others – and to gain an appropriate disposition towards social work knowledge, are hard won and more easily lost. Once lost, there is a danger of wrenching doing apart from knowing, so that no-one recognizes the importance of the question, 'How do I know when I have got it right?' Much of this book will be more readily understood and assessed if we undertake some preliminary ground clearing.

I am not a philosopher, and would have little plausibility were I to claim expertise in philosophical work on knowledge and reality. Perhaps I have should have shown minimal modesty and declined the invitation to write. I don't know. And as philosophers might remind us, 'I don't know' may be either an acknowledgement of ignorance or a philosophical position.

Thinking about ways of knowing in social work takes us immediately to epistemology – that branch of philosophy concerned with the theory of knowledge, its origin, and nature (compared, for example, with 'belief' or 'opinion'):

> Epistemology, or the theory of knowledge, is driven by two main questions: 'What is knowledge?' and 'What can we know?' If we think we can know something, as nearly everyone does, then a third main question arises: 'How do we know what we do know?' (Greco, 1998, 2007, unpaginated)

The three questions are closely related, and it is unlikely that someone will address one of them without addressing the others, or at least assuming something about the others. The first part of the chapter picks up the questions of what is knowledge, and how we know. The chapter moves on to consider how the social work community has responded to questions of how we can know what we know and, in particular, asks if it makes helpful sense to think of social work

---

* Originally published as I. Shaw, 2009. 'Ways of Knowing in Social Work,' in Gray, M. and Webb, S. (ed.) *Social Work Theory and Methods.* London: Sage. Reprinted with permission of Sage Publications Ltd.

knowledge as socially constructed. I conclude the chapter with a brief reflection on scepticism and advocate a moderate Socratic scepticism as essential for social work knowledge based on evidence, understanding, and justice. I will refer quite frequently to arguments about evidence-based practice in social work (see Chapter 16). However, the chapter is not meant to smuggle in either a critique or defence of evidence-based practice (see Shaw, 2006), but simply this – exploring a strong version of evidence-based practice (or scientific practice, empirical practice, and similar terms) is a helpful way of making some of the issues stand out.

Forms of knowledge in social work

Requirements for the accreditation of social work training programmes have much to say regarding knowledge. Skills for Care for social work programmes in England, for example, include the requirement that:

> In your specific area of practice you must understand, critically analyse, evaluate and apply the following knowledge:
>
> 1. The legal, social, economic and ecological context of social work practice.
> 2. The context of social work practice for this area.
> 3. Values and ethics.
> 4. Social work theories, models and methods for working with individuals, families, carers, groups and communities (http://www.topssengland.net/).

Each element is spelt out in detail. The relevant point for our purposes is that there are different kinds of knowledge and understanding in this list. To understand and apply social work theories or the legal context of work in a given area of practice is not the same as to understand and apply values or methods of working. To express this differently, knowing *that* something is the case is not the same as knowing *how* to do something.

Furthermore, knowledge clearly entails more than being right. Take a simple hypothetical example from social work practice: You are convinced that task centred intervention will prove effective in applying cognitive behavioural intervention approaches with a young person who has serious school refusal problems. Let us suppose that there is research evidence somewhere – but unbeknown to you – that yields plausible evidence that your belief is correct. Does your correct belief count as knowledge? While hypothetical, it seems likely that this scenario may be quite common on social work programmes.

The classic answer from Socrates is that 'someone who can't give and receive an account of something isn't knowledgeable about that thing' (Plato, Theaetetus).[1] I have knowledge about something if I believe it, my belief is justified, and it is true – knowledge on this reading is justified true belief. What is entailed in

1 Socrates did not, in fact, find this argument convincing.

justifying, or giving a good enough account of something, is not straightforward. Perhaps we should say that the person with knowledge believes something in a good way – perhaps as an act of intellectual virtue – whereas the person with mere opinion assents to the merits of task centred intervention in a way that lacks some intellectual merit. But what exactly counts as a good way of believing is not easy to agree upon.

Take a different example to illustrate this difficulty. There has been much (welcome) attention to diverse arguments for reflective learning and practice in social work (e.g. Fook, 1996; Gould and Taylor, 1996; Martyn, 2000; Schön, 1991). While Schön (1991) has little to say explicitly about social work, his distinction between reflecting *on* action and reflecting *in* action has entered the vocabulary of many social work students. We can call this a strong version of 'internalist' approaches to giving an account of a belief. We assume that we can find out what we are justified in believing primarily by a process of learned reflection; that this process is internal to our mind (at least to a significant degree); and that it is a process we can consciously access.

Tacit knowledge

None of these three assumptions is without controversy. Take the third assumption. Can we always access our reflective processes? Commonsense knowledge, for example, will often be tacit knowledge. When we think of tacit knowledge in professional work, it can be defined as knowledge or abilities that can be passed between experts by personal contact but cannot be, or has not been, set out or passed on in formal statements, diagrams, verbal descriptions, or instructions for action (Collins, 2000). There are actions, judgements, and recognitions which we accomplish spontaneously. We do not have to think about them prior to performance. We are often unaware of having learned to do them. While we may remember once being aware of the understanding necessary for action, we typically are now unable to describe the knowing that our actions reveal. It has become 'thinking as usual' knowledge: 'Tacit knowledge exists in that time when action is taken that is not understood, when understanding is offered without articulation, and when conclusions are apprehended without an argument' (Altheide and Johnson, 1994, p. 492).

There is nothing intrinsically wrong about an implicit, unarticulated theory: 'Reality is what we choose not to question at the moment … [and] … the better shape science is in, the more the positions are implicit' (Becker, 1993, p. 220); 'When we watch new scientific consensus emerging we are watching the growth of new bodies of tacit knowledge' (Collins, 2001, p. 111). Tacit knowledge is not limited to what goes on in an individual's mind. For example, sociologists of knowledge in practice have explored ways that practice is a social form: 'People in different social groups take different things to be certain knowledge but they are not aware of the social basis of their certainties' (Collins, 2001, p. 110).[2]

A consequence of prioritizing reflective practice in social work ought to be that different kinds of tacit knowledge will be recognized. The significance of personal contact and practical knowledge sharing between social work practitioners will be brought out, and sources of trust and mistrust between social workers made clear. This is a big agenda, and one that social work has only begun to tackle.

Is tacitness inherent in our knowledge? Is it a part of how we are or is it a 'God of the gaps' kind of explanation, where we might conceivably be able to render our knowledge explicit? The question 'matters' when we are engaged in identifying the different forms of knowledge that are part of professional work. For example, in a recent helpful example of such an attempt in the case of social care knowledge, Pawson, Boaz, Grayson, Long, and Barnes (2003) devote effort to suggesting how tacit practitioner knowledge can be rendered explicit. The aspiration may be wise, if only to avoid the alchemy of intuitionism and appeals to 'personal style' that beset some professional practice – so long as we do not deceive ourselves that the goal is fully achievable.

The question arises whether tacit, implicit understanding is in tension with more explicit, planned research-based practice. The evaluation writers, Stake and Trumbull (1982), may seem to suggest as much when they argue that 'For practitioners ... formal knowledge is not necessarily a stepping stone to improved practice ... We maintain that practice is guided far more by personal knowings' (p. 5).

There is a frequent tension in social work between 'internalist' and 'externalist' ways of justifying what we believe. Reflective practice is clearly a different approach from evidence-based practice (EBP) as we have seen in Chapter 16. EBP is strongly externalist, and rests on the view that we can only find a sufficient basis for knowledge-for-practice from empirical evidence external to ourselves.

Practical knowledge

We discover the same tension within the social work research community, when social work researchers talk about what they believe are appropriate criteria for judging the quality of research (Shaw and Norton, 2007). Needless to say, knowledge from reasoning or from experience does not exhaust kinds of knowledge. Schwandt (1997) distinguishes theoretical knowledge ('knowing that'), craft or skill knowledge ('knowing how'), and practical-moral knowledge ('knowing from'). For Schwandt, when we talk about 'application', something more is intended than the instrumental sense of practicality (as though a social work model of intervention, or a finding about effectiveness could be applied like a 'tool'), but the more fundamental sense of making something relevant to

2 For an engaging review of major controversies in the history of science and an exemplification of how scientific certainties do not come from experimental method, but from the way ambiguous evidence is interpreted, see Collins and Pinch (1998).

oneself. This involves a particular kind of knowledge – 'knowing from within or practical-moral knowledge' which 'requires not cleverness in application but understanding' (Schwandt, 1997, p. 76). 'Practical-moral knowledge aims to actually move people, not simply give them good ideas' (p. 81). If being practical means having an impact, then 'practical' *per se* is neutral rather than a good thing. We can have bad as well as good practical research. We cannot predefine whether social work will be practical. Its practicality is created.

How do we acquire knowledge that is not observed?[3]

To begin with, we do so empirically. There is a major field of study in the sociology of science that has extensively explored these issues. As part of acquiring an empirical understanding of epistemology within social work, we should not ignore the common sense ways in which practitioners endeavour to make evaluative sense of their practical activities (Shaw and Shaw, 1997a, 1997b). In a similar way, recognizing the role of informal logic means that we also need to discover how researchers draw conclusions about evidence. For example, Kirk and Reid (2002) argued that we know little of the everyday epistemologies of practitioners.

But there is a problem with this kind of research. While empirically we may learn what social workers believe, do these beliefs constitute knowledge? We face a logical problem – the relationship between 'evidence' and 'conclusion': 'These empirical investigations may enable us to describe the ways in which people arrive at *beliefs* about unobserved facts, but they leave open the question of whether beliefs arrived at in this way actually constitute *knowledge*' (Salmon, 1967, 2007 p. 252).

Philosophically this is the problem of inductive evidence. 'Evidence-based-practice' has been criticized partly because it appears to some that the relationship between evidence and conclusion is treated too straightforwardly, as if the evidence spoke unambiguously and the inferences for practice were indisputable and obvious. There are two sorts of inference. A *demonstrative* inference is one where, logically speaking, the conclusion says no more than was in the premises. A *non-demonstrative* conclusion is one where the premises do not necessitate the conclusion – where the premises could be true while the conclusion false. The critique of 'evidence-based-practice'[4] I have in mind at the moment can be expressed as saying that some advocates present the argument for evidence-based practice as if the inference were demonstrative, whereas it is indubitably non-demonstrative. The social work version of this problem can be observed in other fields, for example, evaluation: 'Everyone agrees that information somehow informs decisions, but the relationship is not direct, not simple. Often the more

3 This problem is associated with the work of the Scottish philosopher, David Hume.

4 I have hyphenated the phrase in this passage as an indication of the assumption that inference and conclusion are demonstrative and inseparable. I have placed it in inverted commas because I do not accept the assumption.

important the decision, the more obscure the relationship seems to be' (House, 1980, p. 68).

House (1980) goes as far as to say that, 'subjected to serious scrutiny, evaluations always appear equivocal' (p. 72) and hence concludes that evaluations can be no more than acts of persuasion: 'Evaluation persuades rather than convinces, argues rather than demonstrates, is credible rather than certain, is variably accepted rather than compelling' (p. 73). When, as social workers or evaluators, we underplay the role of judgement and hence of argumentation, this results in an unduly technical, methods-oriented analysis, an over-confidence in quantification, and a tendency to represent knowledge in an impersonal, objectified form. Those who fail to accept the 'compelling' conclusions drawn from the evaluation are dismissed as irrational. If results were unequivocal then those who failed to accept them would be 'wrong'.

The pervasiveness of non-demonstrative inferences in identifying and making use of knowledge in social work makes practice more demanding. There have been several attempts to take a different approach to thinking through the reasoning process involved in constructing justified evaluative arguments (Fournier, 1995; Fournier and Smith, 1993; Scriven, 1997). These typically emphasize the complex connection between evidence and conclusions, and commence from the differences between formal and informal reasoning. Whereas formal reasoning assumes a tight fit between the premises and conclusions within an argument, informal logic 'deals with ordinary, everyday language, where rules of inference are less precise and more contextual' (Fournier and Smith, 1993, p. 317). Toulmin's *The Uses of Argument* (1958) has been perhaps the most influential text. In explicating the connection between claims and evidence, he gives a central role to 'warrants'. A warrant provides the grounds explaining how we get from evidence to claim, and hence, he argues, a warrant legitimizes the inference we make.

So far we have seen that social work knowledge calls for more than simply having an opinion or even being correct, but needs some kind of justifying account. We have seen that some accounts are 'externalist' (e.g. evidence-based practice) and some are 'internalist' (e.g. reflective practice), and that there are perhaps unavoidable tensions between the two – albeit we should remember that the tensions are logical and philosophical and may not always be pragmatic. We return to this point in the next section of the chapter. We have also seen that the relationship between evidence and practice inferences is rarely self-evident, or demonstrative. Finally, we have reminded ourselves of Schwandt's point that knowledge includes 'knowing from' – practical-moral knowledge – as well as 'knowing that' and 'knowing how'.

Experience and knowledge

Two final distinctions are in order. First, knowledge by acquaintance – what we derive from our senses – is distinct from knowledge by description. But the distinction is shaky. When we express knowledge by acquaintance in language it becomes knowledge by description. The face to face interview between service user and social worker entails knowledge by acquaintance on both sides, but as soon as the social worker refers to that interview verbally or in writing (in a record, email or report), it becomes knowledge by description. Likewise with a research article or report. 'It is a deep question how we learn to name objects of common experience ... from our private knowledge by acquaintance' (Gregory, 1987, p. 412).

While the distinction is not absolute, I am not sure that it is well enough observed. Take a recent influential and interesting account of kinds of knowledge in social work and social care that I mentioned earlier. Pawson et al. (2003) helpfully invite us to distinguish between knowledge held by practitioners, the policy community, service users and carers, researchers and organizations, and set out to develop provisional criteria for assessing knowledge through a common framework of quality criteria. One of the difficulties of this scheme is that there may be as much diversity of knowledge by acquaintance and description *within* each of these as there is *between* them. However, the acquaintance/description distinction has limited purchase in practical terms, in that it is now very widely accepted that there is description within perception and experience, evident for example, in understandings of the world as being (socially) constructed.

Stake and Schwandt (2006) have recently explored a different though related distinction – that between experience-far and experience-near knowledge. This is the second of our final distinctions. In their discussion of discerning quality in evaluation they distinguish between 'quality-as-measured' and 'quality-as-experienced' (we might say 'knowledge' rather than 'quality'). In the first case quality is regarded as measurable and judging quality takes on the characteristic of 'thinking criterially', through explicit comparison of the research in question to a set of standards for it (is it reliable, valid, free from bias, etc). Judging quality criterially is more or less an 'experience-distant' undertaking. 'Quality-as-experienced' starts from the view that quality is a phenomenon that we personally experience and only later make technical, if need be:

> This view emphasizes grasping quality in experience-near understandings, that is, in the language and embodied action of those who actually are undergoing the experience of a program or policy. Criterial thinking is important but it is rooted in interpretation of personal experience (Stake and Schwandt, 2006, p. 408).

The importance of experience is closely related to another question addressed in several places in this book – the relation between knowledge and power. Class, gender, race, and education are all factors that indelibly shape who is accepted as having knowledge. Feminist work illustrates this powerfully. Although there are important variations on questions of epistemology within feminism, all feminist positions start from the proposition that the social workers must ask questions that make sense within women's experience and for women (Hawkesworth, 1989). While most feminists would now reject the idea that there is one single woman's experience, they would also reject a relativist position (see Chapter 6). Perhaps the strongest form anti-relativism takes is through feminist 'standpoint' theory which has its origins in Marxist and Hegelian arguments that reality is obscured to people from certain backgrounds because of the effects of ideology:

> Standpoint theory builds on the assertion that the less powerful members of society experience a different reality as a consequence of their oppression ... To survive they must have knowledge, awareness and sensitivity of both the dominant group's view of society and their own – the potential for 'double vision' or consciousness and thus the potential for a more complete view of social reality (Swigonski, 1993, p. 173).

This theory makes two linked assertions – the double vision of the oppressed and the partial vision of the more powerful – 'privilege and its invisibility to those who hold it' (Swigonski, 1993, p. 174). My own position is that a strong standpoint position is hard to sustain, but a moderate standpoint position is persuasive (Shaw, 1996; Shaw and Gould, 2001). Ideas about knowledge by acquaintance, experience-near research, power, and social construction take us to the remaining discussion in this chapter regarding social constructivism and scepticism.

Realism and constructivism

Can we know the world as it really is, or are we restricted to knowing it as shaped by our thoughts and experience? Can our knowledge be objective or is it 'only' subjective perspectives? Discussions in social work about this issue are often presented through a question as to whether social work is 'positivist' or 'postmodern'. I do not intend to address this issue, primarily because I believe it is often ill-conceived, presented in an unduly polarized form (cf Shaw, 1999a, Ch 3; 1999b), and rarely illuminating.

There are different understandings of what may be meant by 'objective' (e.g., Greco, 1998, 2007). I find myself psychologically drawn to a moderate realism, taking the view that what is represented by at least some of our beliefs is objective, that is, logically and causally independent of how we conceive of that thing. Such a position is not easy to defend, or to show that it does not beg relevant questions in an arbitrary way. It follows that an appropriate humility about human reasoning is warranted.

An important driver of such diffidence about human reasoning is the realization that critical, emancipatory approaches to social work and research conceptualize problems as part of the social, political, and cultural contexts in which social work is formed. Hence, the basic logic is not preoccupied solely with the formal organization of argument, 'but also particular forms of reasoning that give focus to scepticism towards social institutions' (Popkewitz, 1990, p. 49). Hence, critical knowledge from social work is never neutral: 'It is always for some particular subject' (Comstock, 1982, p. 374). For many this involves an obligation to pursue political commitments through active participation in political movements. But before we say anything more about realism, it is worth pausing in parenthesis to recognize that for many practitioners and researchers the pathway of pragmatism is more attractive: 'What should count is not the favoured method of a particular group, but rather how well we answer the question or achieve the purpose ... it matters little which perspective or purpose has been adopted' (Chelimsky, 1997, p. 109).

Becker (1993), writing of epistemological issues, says, 'I think it is fruitless to try to settle them ... These are simply the commonplaces, in the rhetorical sense, of scientific talk in the social sciences, the framework in which the debate goes on. So be it ... There's nothing tragic about it' (p. 219). Rather, like Bill Reid, Becker believes we should take an empirical perspective on such matters, treating them as 'a topic rather than an aggravation' (p. 222). But we should beware the paralysing effect of too much methodological discussion. 'We still have to do theoretical work, but we needn't think we are being especially virtuous when we do' (p. 221). Rather than regard such theoretical work as the responsibility of all, he is content to view it as a specialism – the profession of 'philosophical and methodological worry' (p. 226)!

We should distinguish between *methodological* and *philosophical* pragmatism. Methodological pragmatism rests on impatience with philosophy and an emphasis on real world evaluation and practice, and it is claimed that methods can be separated from the epistemology out of which they have emerged. The emphasis is thus on practical utility and the credibility of the methods used. Most of the pleas for pragmatism referred to above are of this kind. Thus, in complaining about the 'philosophically besotted' (Scriven, 1997, p. 478), Scriven (1997) says 'it is better to build on what might conceivably be sand … than not to build at all … It is a waste of time to try to solve the problems of epistemology without getting on with the job' (p. 479). Reid (1994) argues to similar effect, if more temperately, for social work: 'Irreconcilable conflicts may indeed exist in the discourse of philosophers, but their perspectives are not essential to the task of resolving differences and building consensus in the practical worlds of social work' (p. 478). Despite its disclaimer, this is, of course, a philosophical position, and one that seems to assume a fairly strong acceptance of a realist position. Holding to a realist position does not necessarily entail either positivism or even strong confidence in objective knowledge. The sociologist, Herbert Blumer (1969), argued that a view of knowledge as socially constructed:

> … does not shift "reality", as so many conclude, from the empirical world to the realm of imagery and conception … [The] empirical world can "talk back" to our picture of it or assertions about it – talk back in the sense of challenging and resisting, or not bending to, our images or conceptions of it. This resistance gives the empirical world an obdurate character that is the mark of reality (p. 22).

Constructivism of this kind is thus not incompatible with realism. On this view of things we can maintain belief in the existence of phenomena independent of our claims about them, and in their knowability, 'without assuming that we can know with certainty whether our knowledge of them is valid or invalid' (Hammersley, 1992, p. 50): 'The essence of this position is that, although a real world, driven by real natural causes, exists, it is impossible for humans truly to perceive it with their imperfect sensory and intellective mechanism' (Cook and Campbell, 1979, p. 29).

There is a wide range of positions within this broad approach. I take the position that, while some version of objectivity remains as a 'regulatory ideal' (Phillips, 1990, p. 43), social work processes and results are always significantly jeopardized by interests, the social location of the practitioner and agency, powerful stakeholders, and, in Guba's (1990) surprisingly realist phrase, 'nature's propensity to confound' (p. 19).

Such epistemological modesty does not necessarily lead to modest aspirations for social change. For example, from within social work Reid (1988) has asked, 'Is it better to make limited but well documented progress or to work toward more important goals with less certainty of what we have attained?' (p. 45). Yet fallible realist social work practitioners and researchers are less likely to pronounce confidently that they have got it right. They are likely to concur with Phillips (1990) when he admits that 'the objectivity of an inquiry does not guarantee its truth … *nothing* can guarantee that we have reached the truth' (p. 43).

We have taken constructivism too much for granted. Suppose a given intervention X is found to be effective in working with young people with challenging behaviour problems. Assume that for someone this can be stated as 'It is a fact that X is effective in working with young people with challenging behaviour problems'. Is this a fact for everyone? Not in the sense that all social workers believe it to be a fact (a trivial case of 'not a fact for everyone'). Is it possible, then, to say 'It holds true for you but not for me'? Is it true independently of what I believe, or of how society is organized? A social constructionist would respond by saying that:

1. Facts are socially constructions rather than being objects.
2. It is constitutive of a given fact that it is so constructed.
3. The construction is contingent and not universal.

The interest lies in exposing constructions where none is thought to exist – 'where something constitutively social had come to masquerade as natural' (Boghossian, 2006, p. 18). To 'de-construct' is then thought to be potentially liberating.[5]

This is a strong version of social constructionism. The classical philosophical view is that it is sometimes possible for the evidence alone to explain why we

5 There is a philosophical problem in the deconstruction project, in that it seems to require an assumption that the 'deconstructor' is able to see through the construct. This risks the accusation of 'ontological gerrymandering' (Woolgar and Pawluch, 1985).

come to believe something. Task centred social work may be considered a case in point. The original experiment, *Brief and Extended Casework*, (Reid and Shyne, 1969) was carried out with the assumption that open-ended casework would prove more effective, given ideal circumstances. When the contrary was supported by the evidence it led to a prolonged programme of research to develop and test the effectiveness of the model. A strong version of constructionism would respond by asserting the *descriptive dependence of the facts* in this experiment. A moderate constructionist would respond by asserting the weaker position of the *social relativity of descriptions*. However, even if we go for the weaker position, judgement about evidence still remains a demanding task. If we accept that there are some mind-independent facts, 'This argument ... does not tell us all by itself which facts obtain and which ones don't; nor does it tell us, of the facts that do obtain, which ones are mind-independent and which ones aren't' (Boghossian, 2006, p. 57).

Judicious scepticism

'I don't know' might, I suggested at the chapter's opening, be a philosophical position. Is evidence-based practice the right way to improve quality of services? I do not know. The philosopher most associated with scepticism is perhaps Descartes. To provide a firm ground for knowledge he began by 'doubting all that could be doubted' (Grau, 2005/2007, p. 195), for example by asking what if he was only dreaming. Contemporary films explore this idea via speculations about technology (e.g. *The Matrix*). Hume saw no way out of Descartes' problem, and thought we have to live with it, on the grounds that we can be philosophical sceptics yet sustain a practical belief in reason.

Does (moderate) scepticism lead to paralysed inaction? Not necessarily. It is possible to be philosophically sceptical yet practically committed to action.[6] This tension between philosophy and practice is perhaps inescapable. Greene (1996) talks of qualitative evaluators, but her remarks will stand for social work practitioners and probably researchers:

Many qualitative practitioners struggle with the dissonance invoked by the assumed mind-dependence of all social knowledge claims in the face of the contextual (as well as personal, ego-related) demands to '*get it right*', to '*find out what's really going on in this setting*' (p. 280).

---

6 Off-stage, as it were, I would also argue that such skepticism is not incompatible with a strong faith-based position.

Selective bibliography

Collins, H. and Pinch, T. (1998). *The Golem: What you should know about science.* Cambridge: Cambridge University Press.

Kirk, S. and Reid, W.J. (2002). *Science and social work.* New York: Columbia University Press. Chapters 1 and 2.

Pawson, R., Boaz, A., Grayson, L., Long, A., and Barnes, C. (2003). *Types and quality of knowledge in social care.* London: Social Care Institute for Excellence.

Shaw, I. (1999). *Qualitative evaluation.* London: Sage Publications. Chapter 3 and 4.

Stake, R.E. and Schwandt, T.A. (2006). On discerning quality in evaluation. In I. Shaw, Greene, J., and Mark, M. (Eds). *Sage handbook of evaluation.* London: Sage Publications. Chapter 18.

References

Altheide, D. and Johnson, J. (1994). Criteria for assessing interpretive validity in qualitative research. In N. Denzin and Lincoln, Y. (Eds). *Handbook of qualitative methods*. Thousand Oaks: Sage.

Becker, H. (1993). Theory: The necessary evil. In D. Flinders and Mills, G. (Eds). *Theory and concepts in qualitative research: Perspectives from the field.* New York: Teachers College, Columbia University Press.

Blumer, H. (1969). *Symbolic interactionism: Perspective and method.* Englewood Cliffs, NJ: Prentice-Hall.

Boghossian, P. (2006). *Fear of knowledge.* New York: Oxford University Press.

Chelimsky, E. (1997). Thoughts for a new evaluation society. *Evaluation*, 3(1), 97-118.

Collins, H. (2000). *Tacit knowledge, trust and the Q of Sapphire.* Cardiff University School of Social Sciences. Working Paper. http://www.cf.ac.uk/socsi/ (subsequently published in *Social Studies of Science*).

Collins, H. (2001). What is tacit knowledge? In T. Schatzki, Cetina, K., and von Savigny, E. (Eds). *The practice turn in contemporary theory.* London: Routledge.

Collins, H. and Pinch, T. (1998). *The Golem: What you should know about science.* Cambridge: Cambridge University Press.

Comstock, D. (1982). A method for critical research. In F. Bredo and Feinburg, W. (Eds). *Knowledge and values in educational research.* Philadelphia: Temple University Press.

Cook, T. and Campbell, D. (1979). *Quasi-experimentation.* Chicago: Rand McNally.

Fook, J. (1996). *The reflective researcher: Social work theories of practice and research.* St Leonards: Allen and Unwin.

Fournier, D. (Ed.). (1995). *Reasoning in evaluation: Inferential links and leaps.* San Francisco: American Evaluation Association/Jossey-Bass.

Fournier, D. and Smith, N. (1993). Clarifying the merits of argument in evaluation practice. *Evaluation and Program Planning*, 16(4), 315-323.

Gould, N. and Taylor, I. (1996). *Reflective learning for social work.* Aldershot: Ashgate.

Grau, C. (2005/2007). Bad dreams, evil demons and the experience machine: Philosophy and *The Matrix.* In J. Perry, Bratman, M., and Fischer, J.M. (Eds). *Introduction to philosophy: Classical and contemporary readings.* New York: Oxford University Press.

Greco, J. (1998). Introduction: What is epistemology? In J. Greco and Sosa, E. (Eds). *The Blackwell guide to epistemology.* Oxford: Blackwell Publishing. Blackwell Reference Online. 15 February 2007. http://www.blackwellreference.com/subscriber/tocnode? id=g9780631202912_chunk_g97806312029123.

Greene, J. (1996). Qualitative evaluation and scientific citizenship. *Evaluation*, 2(3), 277-289.

Gregory, R.L. (Ed.). (1987). *The Oxford companion to the mind.* Oxford: Oxford University Press.

Guba, E. (1990). The Alternative paradigm dialog. In E. Guba (Ed). *The Paradigm Dialog*. Newbury Park: Sage.

Hammersley, M. (1992). *What's wrong with ethnography?* London: Routledge.

Hawkesworth, M. (1989). Knowers, knowing, known: Feminist theory and claims of truth. *Signs: Journal of Women in Culture and Society*, 14(3), 533-557.

House, E. (1980). *Evaluating with validity*. Beverly Hills: Sage.

Kirk, S. and Reid, W.J. (2002). *Science and social work.* New York: Columbia University Press.

Martyn, H. (2000). *Developing reflective practice.* Bristol: Policy Press.

Pawson, R., Boaz, A., Grayson, L., Long, A., and Barnes, C. (2003). *Types and quality of knowledge in social care.* London: Social Care Institute for Excellence.

Phillips, D. (1990). Postpositivistic science: Myths and realities. In E. Guba (Ed.). *The paradigm dialog.* Newbury Park: Sage.

Plato, *Theaetetus.* In Perry, J., Bratman, M., and Fischer, J.M. (Eds). (2007). *Introduction to philosophy: Classical and contemporary readings.* New York: Oxford University Press.

Popkewitz, T. (1990). Whose future? Whose past? In E. Guba (Ed.). *The paradigm dialog*. Newbury Park: Sage.

Reid, W. (1988). Service effectiveness and the social agency. In R. Patti, Poertner, J., and Rapp, C. (Eds). *Managing for effectiveness in social welfare organisations.* New York: Haworth.

Reid, W. (1994). Reframing the epistemological debate. In E. Sherman and Reid, W. (Eds). *Qualitative research in social work.* New York: Columbia University Press.

Reid, W. and Shyne, A. (1969). *Brief and extended casework.* New York: Columbia University Press.

Salmon, W.C. (1967/2007). The problem of induction. In J. Perry, Bratman, M., and Fischer, J.M. (Eds). (2007). *Introduction to philosophy: Classical and contemporary readings.* New York: Oxford University Press.

Schön, D. (1991). *The reflective practitioner.* Aldershot: Ashgate.

Schwandt, T. (1997). Evaluation as practical hermeneutics. *Evaluation*, 3(1), 69-83.

Scriven, M. (1997). Truth and objectivity in evaluation. In E. Chelimsky and Shadish, W. (Eds). *Evaluation for the 21st century.* Thousand Oaks: Sage.

Shaw, I. (1996). *Evaluating in practice.* Aldershot: Ashgate.

Shaw, I. (1999a). *Qualitative evaluation.* London: Sage Publications.

Shaw, I. (1999b). Seeing the trees for the wood: The politics of evaluating in practice. In B. Broad (Ed.). *The politics of research and evaluation.* Birmingham: Venture Press.

Shaw, I (2006). The human services. In I. Shaw, Greene, J., and Mark, M. (Eds). *Sage handbook of evaluation.* London: Sage Publications.

Shaw, I. and Gould, N. (2001). *Qualitative research in social work.* London: Sage Publications.

Shaw, I. and Norton, M. (2007). *Kinds and quality of social work research.* London: Social Care Institute for Excellence.

Shaw, I. and Shaw, A. (1997a). Keeping social work honest: Evaluating as profession and practice. *British Journal of Social Work*, 27(6), 847-869.

Shaw, I. and Shaw, A. (1997b). Game plans, buzzes and sheer luck: Doing well in social work. *Social Work Research*, 21(2), 69-79.

Stake, R. and Trumbull, D. (1982). Naturalistic generalizations. *Review Journal of Philosophy and Social Science*, 7, 1-12.

Stake, R.E. and Schwandt, T.A. (2006). On discerning quality in evaluation. In I. Shaw, Greene, J., and Mark, M. (Eds). *Sage handbook of evaluation.* London: Sage Publications. Chapter 18.

Swigonski, M. (1993). Feminist standpoint theory and questions of social work research. *Affilia,* 8(2), 171-183.

Toulmin, S. (1958). *The uses of argument.* Cambridge: Cambridge University Press.

Woolgar, S. and Pawluch, D. (1985). Ontological gerrymandering: The anatomy of social problems explanations. *Social Problems*, 32(3), 214-227.

Chapter 4
Re-reading *The Jack-Roller*: Hidden Histories in Sociology and Social Work*

The early tales of sociology and social work at Chicago are ones of rich and complex inter-relationships. But the departmental and eventually disciplinary parting of the ways after 1920, with their associated shift of (women) sociology faculty into a new social work school, while welcomed to some extent on both sides, led to an eventual closure of conversation that worked against the interests of both fields of study. In universities across the world, this continues to hobble both sociology and social work. It may not need to be so. I revisit these moments in the history of sociology and social work with the intention, echoing Geertz, to enhance 'the precision with which we vex ourselves' (Geertz, 1973: 29).

I start by revisiting one of the iconic Chicago School studies, Clifford Shaw's *The Jack-Roller*. A comparatively naïve reading of Shaw's book leaves the reader, almost eight decades later, with a sense of having been inducted into a blend of what we now know as sociology and social work, but which to Shaw is no *melange*, but a coherent stance. A historical sidelight on the period will suggest that this is close to the heart of how things were, and not a temporary distortion in the separate flows of history in sociology and social work. The longest part of this article develops and illustrates this argument through a hidden history of an intellectual case for reciprocity between the two disciplines as seen in some barely noticed work of Ernest Burgess. I conclude with a suggested re-reading of *The Jack-Roller* that offers support for a relationship between sociology and social work based on egalitarian respect and a commitment to practising history in the sense of positioning ourselves in a historical context.

Reading *The Jack-Roller*

Stanley – the *Jack-Roller* of the title of Clifford Shaw's compact book – is a Chicago 'delinquent'. His story is prefaced by several chapters in which Shaw reflects on the value of a delinquent boy's 'own story', a sketch history of Stanley's 'behaviour difficulties' and of his cultural and social background. Shaw gives the reader a detailed schedule of Stanley's school and work history,

---

* Originally published as I. Shaw, 2009. 'Rereading *The Jack Roller*: hidden histories in sociology and social work', *Qualitative Inquiry* 15(7): 1241-64. Reprinted with permission of Sage Publications Ltd.

and in introducing Stanley's social and cultural background produces two 'base maps' of parts of Chicago where Stanley lived, typical of the maps produced by the Chicago School, detailing the numbers of 'alleged male delinquents' and the residences of adult male offenders. From chapter four onwards we have Stanley's own story, seen, as Shaw expresses it, through six years of 'rather intensive study' and a 'somewhat intensive program of social treatment' (Shaw, 1966: 1). Stanley apparently organized the material and the chapter divisions, and Shaw interpolates comments on Stanley's story. For example, when Stanley remarks that even if he exaggerated the faults of his stepmother, 'I certainly did not exaggerate my feelings towards her' (55), Shaw remarks that this illustrates,

> one of the primary assumptions of this volume, namely, that in the study and treatment of the delinquent child it is essential to deal with his personal attitudes, his definition of the situation... Even if it were true that Stanley's interpretations of the family situation were somewhat exaggerated, it cannot be doubted that he acted 'as if' these interpretations were true. (55)

Most of the material for 'our study of Stanley's career in delinquency' (164) was secured at the time he was released from the House of Correction at age seventeen. Stanley takes us through his time at the Detention Home and the Parental School, on which Shaw observes that 'Case histories of this type suggest the desirability of developing a more informal and diversified institutional program adaptable to the different types of personality' (65). On his discharge at seventeen, 'Upon the basis of the materials available at that time, certain interpretations of the case were made and a plan of treatment was devised' (164).

What later readers would regard as elements of reflexivity are generally absent from the account. It seems very clear that interventions were agreed largely on the basis of Shaw's analysis and interpretations. 'In the light of the foregoing interpretation of the case, it was decided to place Stanley in an entirely new social situation' (165), consisting of a 'sympathetic and informal' (166) foster home in a non-delinquent community, with monitored vocational guidance, and the development of 'conventional' peer relationships in the area of his new home. Stanley writes how, on his discharge from the House of Correction where no aftercare was provided, 'In my desperation I decided to drop in and see Mr Shaw. He had talked to me a few weeks before and promised to help me if I would come to see him at the time of my release' (168). Shaw remarks,

> During the first two years of the period of treatment, we had personal contact with Stanley at least once a week. Through these contracts it was possible to give him insight into his own mental processes, and to assist him in solving many problems which necessarily arose during the course of his adjustment to the new cultural world in which he was placed. (166-7)

Shaw ascribes the 'modifications in his interests and conduct' as 'due, in large part, to changes in group relationships' (183). The account by Stanley – albeit always cast in more informal terms – appears to indicate a less professionalized support and intervention.

> He always encouraged me and treated me as one of his own friends. We would go out to dinner together, and through him I met a lot of other people. He talked friendly to me about all of my troubles but never upbraided me or told me that I was in the wrong. (171)

Shaw talks of weekly meetings and Stanley's account draws to a close with the mention that 'Mr Shaw talked to me many times about getting more education' (177).

Shaw discusses the value of a delinquent boy's own story 'recorded in the first person, in the boy's own words, and not translated into the language of the person investigating the case' (1). He enters a plea that the 'own story' should be seen alongside the other documents of a 'total case history' (2), and cites Thomas as including 'psychoanalytic confession' alongside case study and life records as part of such documentation. Without such material 'any interpretation of the life history is somewhat questionable' (2), though he does not see this as a realist arbiter of the truth of the story, and quotes the famous W.I. Thomas statement of 1928. 'His immediate behaviour is closely related to his definition of the situation...If men define situations as real, they are real in their consequences' (3).

Shaw's language is often cast in the terms of welfare intervention. Life stories reveal 'the essentially human aspects of the problem of delinquency' (17). He says of the 'therapeutic value' (19) of the life history that 'the child's "own story" is of particular importance in the diagnosis and treatment of cases of delinquency' (17).

> The attitudes and intimate situations revealed in the life-story not only throw light upon the fundamental nature of the behaviour difficulty, but, along with the other case material, afford a basis for devising a plan of treatment adapted to the attitudes, interests, and personality of the child. (17)

He develops this further as a critique of probation work, that 'the large amount of failure in probation and parole work' (18) is due to workload pressures that oblige the worker to focus on 'the more formal and external aspects of his cases' when the focus ought to be on 'the delinquent's personal attitudes and intimate situations' based on 'painstaking study and prolonged contact' (18). He complains that 'the treatment consists chiefly of attempts to gain control and effect adjustment through threats of arrest and punishment' (18). He concludes with a discussion of the theoretical value of life-history data as a basis for causal 'hypotheses' (19), and an account of his methodology as consisting of 'various techniques' designed to facilitate spontaneity and to 'follow the natural sequence of events in the life history of the delinquent' (21), usually through a series of interviews 'which in some cases extend over a relatively long period of time' of some months apart (21). They were recorded mostly by a 'stenographic record' to preserve the 'exact language of the interviewee' (22).

Shaw's life history work, as with most of his Chicago colleagues, builds on 'the position that lives have natural histories that unfold over time and that these lives are marked by objective events and experiences' (Denzin, 1989: 50). 'While Burgess (and Shaw) disclaim the pursuit of absolute truth, they seek to uncover...a center to Stanley's personality that will explain his "reactions to the events of his experience"' (52). In their commitment to an objective natural history approach 'the empirical subject merges with the social scientist'. 'Stanley and Clifford Shaw become one in *The Jack-Roller*' (Denzin, 1992: 40, 41). It certainly is the case that in appealing to the value of documents from psychiatrists, parole officers, and social workers to evidence Stanley's life, Shaw and Burgess may seem to fail to see that these are also social constructions. Yet I am not sure Denzin is entirely just when he concludes engagingly of such natural histories that 'an interactionist complicity structured these texts... (T)hey created the sympathetic illusion that a solution to the delinquency problem had been found' (1992: 43) and perpetuated a 'romantic overidentification with society's undesirables' (44). There was an unfinished work-in-progress feel in particular to Burgess' developing stance, that included in a series of almost unnoticed papers a sharp critique of social work records that typically assumes a professional interpretive carapace.

'Sociology' and 'Social Work' at Chicago

In inverted commas, for neither term carried its present meaning, nor was either recognisable as itself. 'Sociology' and 'social science' were often interchangeable expressions, hence part of Albion Small's efforts were devoted to establishing sociology as a definable field of study within the social sciences (e.g. Small, 1903).

Chicago University was founded in 1890 as a Baptist institution by William Harper, its first president. He wanted the university to be marked by fundamental research/training and the improvement of society.[1] Hence he set out to appoint outstanding people rather than to build disciplines as such. The city of Chicago was central for much of this development. 'All of social life was here and being investigated by sociologists' (Plummer, 1997: 8). Plummer expresses it nicely as a place where 'a world of strangers and danger merges with a world of diversity and innovation. Here was the pathos of modernity' (Plummer, 1997: 7).

In sociology's early development '...those methods and indeed topics, which were characteristic of the "Chicago School", were equally characteristic of social workers and voluntary activists who were in the field somewhat sooner' (Platt, 1996: 263). The point is not original (cf Plummer, 1997: 8), but Deegan has developed the argument with force, commitment and in great detail (e.g. Deegan,

1 I am indebted here to Stephen Diner's work.

1991; 1997a; 1997b). Informed by the work of Charles Booth, Addams and her colleagues at Hull-House mapped the structure of the whole city in ways that were subsequently adopted by Chicago sociologists. Published in 1893, the 'Hull-House Maps and Papers' are seen by Deegan as methodologically and substantively central to, yet subsequently 'erased from the annals of sociology' (Deegan, 1997b: 5).

Social work education and research were proceeding in rough parallel to sociology. In 1908, following a series of initiatives in Chicago and in New York, the Chicago School of Civics and Philanthropy was established. The first Bulletin of the School, in 1910 concluded optimistically that relief had become scientific, and that social work had 'attained recognized professional status and those who lead it are rightly regarded as scientific specialists' (Lubove, 1965: 143). The School of Social Service Administration (SSSA) was established as a professional graduate school in 1920, replacing the School of Civics and Philanthropy and independent of the sociology department. The reasons are difficult to disentangle. They were partly financial, and there was an important mutuality in the separation of the two fields. Secularising tendencies were associated with growing confidence among faculty in both fields. With an over-simplification of hindsight, Ruth Cavan, a student in the sociology department from 1922 to 1926, remarked that 'the department also separated itself from courses in social work and thus strengthened its objective approach'[2] (Cavan, 1997: 46). She remembered that for Small, 'the purpose of sociology was not humanitarian or social reform, but an understanding of human behaviour' (47). This is better seen as a vision for sociology that crystallized during the later 1920s primarily through the work of Park and possibly Burgess. Yet at the time the parting of the ways was probably not seen in such binary terms. The changes were more complex and Coghlan may be correct when she concludes that

> (I)t is not likely that permanent, full-time positions in a university affiliated program were seen by Abbott and Breckinridge as banishment from sociology. Rather, it was the culmination of their efforts to that point to define and professionalize the discipline of social work. (Coghlan, nd)

Sociology and social work

The 1920 establishment of the SSSA was a gendered division. The women were defined as social workers and the men as sociologists. 'Women's place in sociology was first established through special qualities of mind and action and later removed from the field to another profession' (Deegan, 1997a: 203). Yet Deegan recognizes that the events of 1920 were not imposed or allocated in the way this complaint suggests. The women who ended up in social work saw their distinctiveness as based on strengths. Small's position as Head of Department was crucial. He held

2 In the context, 'objective' appears to roughly approximate 'empirical' and is set against 'philosophical'.

to the doctrine of 'separate natures but equal ability', but it led him to see women's work as being in social settlements and women's institutions. He wanted equal pay but an absence of competition between men and women.[3]

Jane Addams and most of her colleagues did not resist the change. She worked in other fields and did not cultivate her sociological base. 'Addams' sociology moreover, was buried in these professional realignments' (Deegan, 1997a: 225).[4] Edith Abbott held a different and more interesting position. A Hull-House resident, Abbott was appointed in 1913 as lecturer in social statistics, and by 1924 she was dean of the SSSA. She 'mastered the most advanced statistical and survey methods of the day' (Diner, 1997: 36). She had previously visited London (the London School of Economics) in 1906, and on her return reproduced Beatrice Webb's course in 'Methods of Social Investigation' in Chicago. She became Director of Social Research at the School of Civics and Philanthropy in 1908. Following the separation of the Department of Sociology and the School of Social Service Administration in 1920, Edith Abbott and Sophonisba Breckinridge founded the *Social Service Review* in 1927 with the aspiration of undertaking important work that would combine intellectual challenge with social usefulness. These remarkably able and influential women were exceptional in their commitment to research (cf Deegan, 1991). Abbott and Breckinridge had clear views about the kind of research that was needed.

1. It should solve welfare problems and not simply advance the frontiers of human knowledge. They 'established a tradition of sound research and political advocacy on behalf of the powerless' (Deegan and Hill, 1991: 31).
2. It had to be good research. Abbott complained that 'some of our social science friends are afraid that we cannot be scientific because we really care about what we are doing...' (Diner, 1977: 11). She retorted that 'the social worker may care very genuinely about what happens to the unfortunate child or the broken family for whom she is temporarily responsible without being less scientific' (11).
3. They believed that practitioners must have the skills to contribute to research. Research could not be carried out solely by social scientists. 'Social workers must be so trained scientifically that they belong in the social science group' (Abbott, quoted by Diner, 1977: 11).

Unlike some typical sociology courses for social workers today, Abbott was opposed to sociology being taught in a 'tamed' or instrumental way. She

3 For an interesting account of the response of the men sociologists to the segregation issue, see Deegan, 1997a.

4 Deegan is probably too set upon making her case about the role of women in early sociology. This leads her on occasion to perpetuate an anachronistic sociology/social work divide. Thus, when she is defending the sociological contribution of the *Hull-House Maps and Papers*, she objects on one occasion that they were not about social work.

distinguished the idea that courses like research, law and government should be construed as 'background' for social workers. She saw them as 'foundation' (Lubove, 1965: 149). Abbott and Breckinridge held the interesting view that 'such training is needed for the sake of social research itself, which so often demands a competent understanding of the field of social treatment...and should be carried out by social workers, who are also trained in social research' (Diner, 1977: 12).

Viewing her arguments as a whole, they have enduring interest. They face both ways, in that they challenge both social work and sociology – a stance I find compelling. Hence, asking whether she was a sociologist *or* social work scholar illustrates the intellectual anachronisms of our own time,[5] as well as the tendency to see social work as standing in a client relationship to sociology, psychology and so on. Not surprisingly, Abbott and Breckinridge came under fire in return from both 'sides'. In addition to the doubts of their 'social science friends' they famously refer to 'our eastern colleagues' (the social work programmes at Boston and New York) who 'told us we could not have casework and fieldwork in a university' (Diner, 1977: 7; c.f. Lubove, 1965: 265).

Methodology developments at Chicago illuminate the creatively shadowy interplay of intellectual and welfare elements that were part and parcel of early sociology and social work. Take Diner's remark that Abbott was at ease with the most advanced survey methods of the day. Platt has pointed out that the term 'survey' was used very early, but not to refer in the current sense to a method of data collection or research design. Rather, the term laid 'emphasis on the purpose (which was social reform and local community improvement), and on the coverage of a limited geographical area' (Platt, 1996: 45). In the USA the social survey movement was a reform-minded one.[6]

It is possible that social workers were first in the field in this regard. Cavan (1997) remembers Burgess using psychiatric case histories in class, side by side with statistics. Despite Small's joking aside that 'a great many people have the notion that sociology is merely a pretentious name for slumming' (Small, 1903: 471), Diner remarks that American university teachers – 'generally a sedate class of men' – 'stayed away from low life, from the poor, and from noisy, drunken, brawling conduct'. They 'did the next best thing: they associated with social workers who knew them first hand, and they encouraged their students to study

5 To refer to this network of women as 'The Chicago Women's School of Sociology' is an instance of such anachronistic rhetoric. I am indebted to Javier Treviño for this reference.

6 The reader is often struck in the sociology and social work sources of the period how similar they read to left-leaning social policy research in the UK. Abbott, for example, seemed closer to social policy research as it was understood in post 2nd World War UK than to either later sociology or social work. As Deegan and Hill express it, she 'typically explored institutional inequities that could be documented statistically' and had a vision of social work as 'an aggressive, policy-making and controversial profession' (Deegan and Hill, 1991: 33).

them' (Diner, 1997: 54). Thus, sociology had 'become closely connected to welfare work (obliquely through Hull-House, specifically through the Chicago Area Project)' (Plummer, 1997: 32).

The interpretive problem lies in part in the subsequent construction of a sociological meta-narrative that downplays any counter-claims. There are hints of this even in Platt's work in the apparent normative assumptions behind her remark that 'sociology and social work took a long time to become disentangled' (Platt, 1996: 46).

How Chicago Sociologists Saw Social Work: The case of Ernest Burgess

It is doubtless indicative of buried discipline histories that I stumbled with surprise upon a citation of a paper by Burgess in an early issue of a social work journal when reading for another paper. I had never previously encountered any serious discussion of his research and writing in relation to social work. Apart from brief accounts of sociology's methodological indebtedness to social work there are no hints in the literature of any significant intellectual interaction after the 1920 divide. Yet a preliminary analysis of Burgess' writing and work in the decade following the establishment of the SSSA will help open up a different history and an alternative view of the possible promise of reciprocal work between sociology and social work.

My argument can be encapsulated roughly as follows. Throughout the 1920s Burgess pursued a creative preoccupation with the identity and historical development of sociology and social work in relation to one another. This led him to an early position (1923) that there is an essential interdependence between the two, and that their separate disciplinary developments had converged on a mutual while still distinguishable set of linked research interests. This essentially egalitarian view of their relationship prompted him to a view that there are reciprocal gains to be had, the one from the other. It also enabled him to voice positive criticisms of his own discipline and of social work. In the earlier part of this period he expounded the primary contribution of sociology to social work in terms of emerging conceptualizations of the city and community from leading sociologists across North America. In the later years of the decade he gave closer attention to spelling out the benefits for social work of empirical work carried out in Chicago. His primary application of the contribution social work could make to sociology was in seeing agency records as a radical resource for sociology, and, to a less developed degree, reflecting on the implications of seeing social work as a 'concrete experiment' that gradually focused his mind on the potential for what today we would call 'outcomes research' and on the possibility of predictive judgements. However, by the later years of his career, for reasons that are not altogether clear, he appears to have lost this cluster of interests, and to be speaking to social work, if at all, only from a distance.[7] I will try to tease out and give substance to these threads. In doing so, it is not my intention wholly to own or assess the details of Burgess' position,[8] but rather to engage with his intention to place the interdependence of the two fields at the centre of their respective discipline-health. It is disquieting that the majority in both sociology and social work no longer believe this.

Distinct and interdependent

It was common in the early years of the last century to view social work as a branch of sociology – as applied sociology. Burgess expressed his response to this view without equivocation.

> It is a fallacy, widely current, that social work has been, and is, applied sociology. As things are, nothing could be farther from the truth. The origins of sociology and social work go back to different motives, they have pursued independent paths, each has upon occasion been indifferent, hostile, or even contemptuous of the other. (Burgess, 1923: 366)

As to their respective aims he expands as follows:

> The aim of social work is and will continue to be the maintenance and the raising of the standards of economic, social and civic life. The aim of sociology, in the future as in the past, will be the increase of knowledge of the behaviour of the person and of society. (Burgess, 1923: 370)

He traces the beginnings of sociology to the philosophy of history in the work of Comte, Spencer and Ward, and detects a transition from philosophy to science moving from Comte and Spencer's 'sociology, conceived in the grand style' (367), through a period of various sociological 'schools' to what he describes – as 'the period of investigation and research into which sociology is just now entering' (367).

---

7 I am aware of the various arguments in the sociology literature regarding gender; secularized abandonment of the social gospel inspired ameliorative mission in favour of objective science; the scholarly dynamics of the intellectual hostility that developed between the two disciplines and departments; and the significance of external world events such as the First World War. Yet none of these seems to provide sufficient texture and anchor points. For example, in the earliest paper discussed here, Burgess is categorical that sociology is not about amelioration, yet he is forceful in his case for its 'necessary interdependence' with social work (Burgess, 1923: 370).

8 For example, there are difficulties with his starkly different creation stories for the two fields.

In contrast, social work 'had its origin in attempts to organize and systematize the giving of relief to individuals and families in distress' (1923: 367). He is more tentative about periods in social service history, but suggests an initial period of philanthropy, followed by a period of social reform, social politics and the launching of social movements, and leading to

> The period of social work as a profession, applied social science, with a technique of personal and social adjustment, the period social service is now entering. (367)[9]

Yet he still believes by 1927 that 'the central current of the development of social work has remained in the channels of social economics and social politics' (191) through the influence of books by Richmond (1917) and Breckinridge (part of what he describes as a 'small but promising' social work literature, 1923: 367).

While Burgess' periodizing schemes have limited present value, their interest lies in his wish to see an historical convergence and congruence of interest. He suggests that both fields of enterprise had been too immersed in immediate preoccupations of development and survival to engage in actual field research in the case of sociology or 'have much energy left to deal with the relation of human nature and social forces to problems of case work with individuals and families' (1927: 191) in the case of social work. But

> The inexorable logic of a common social situation, however, is now forcing sociology and social work to recognize and act upon their necessary interdependence. (Burgess, 1923: 366)

The interdependence circles around their respective research interests. As sociology, at Chicago at least, entered a period of investigation, so 'there can be no doubt that social work is moving with increasing momentum toward research' (1923: 367). He detects within this a shift of emphasis, yet in its infancy, to seeing case work 'as a pragmatic art based upon the experimental study of behaviour' (1923: 368).

Contributions of sociology to social work

In the earlier part of this period he expounded the primary contribution of sociology to social work in terms of emerging conceptualizations of the city and community from leading sociologists across North America. He refers to the way

---

9 His later schematizing varies in language. He suggests in 1927 a period 'based upon experience and common sense', succeeded by a stage in which the influence of social economics and its application to social work became dominant. 'The third stage has been marked by the invasion or introduction into social work of the psychiatric point of view and the technique of the psychiatric social worker'. (Burgess, 1927: 191)

that the notion of social forces 'arose independently both in social work and in sociology' (1923: 368), and in both 'the motive...has been to secure an explanation of human behaviour' (p. 368). He illustrates this from Thomas and Znaniecki's 'Polish Peasant' research on social attitudes and human wishes. He suggests also the relevance of Sumner's work on folkways.

> One can hardly overestimate the extent to which the lack of knowledge of European customs and cultural backgrounds has been responsible for the failure of social workers to secure cooperation of immigrant families. (1923: 368)

In addition to Thomas and Sumner, he draws on the work of Charles Cooley regarding human nature as a product of social life, such that the person is an individual with status. 'Insights such as these terms suggest are helpful alike to the social theorist and the social worker' (1923: 369). By 1928 he expresses the connection more forcefully and optimistically. 'The perception that "the relation of the individual to the group" is the basic problem both of research in sociology and of treatment in social work is at last becoming clearly recognized' (Burgess, 1928: 525). He proceeds in this subsequent paper to evidence, in a fascinating way, his wide reading and reflection on the social work literature, and his extending convictions regarding the interdependence of the two disciplines. For example, he cites Mary Richmond in her *Social Diagnosis* who in turn is drawing on Octavia Hill, the major English 19C housing reformer. He borrows from Richmond a quotation from Hill in a paper in 1869 to the Social Science Association, as 'the first description we have been able to find of inquiry with social reinstatement as its motive and aim' (Burgess, 1928: 525). Hill is quoted as saying that

> By character is meant...knowledge of the passions, hopes and history of people; where the temptation will touch them, what is the little scheme they have made of their lives, or would make, if they had encouragement; that training long past phases of their lives may have afforded; how to move, touch and teach them. (Hill in Burgess, 1928: 525)

While he sees neither sociology nor social work as having adequately based their work on the implications of Cooley and Hill's insights, he remains optimistic that 'both sociology and social work have taken long strides in this common (*sic*) direction' (525).[10]

As the Chicago programme of research became embodied in the major research studies of the 1920s, Burgess took a more research-led stance as he developed his

10 He goes on to extol in similar terms and at some length the social work writing of Ada Sheffield in her book on *Case Study Possibilities,* for presenting a social view of the individual over against the 'atomic view of the individual' adopted by 'most medical men' (Burgess, 1928: 526), saying that 'with her theoretic statement I find myself in complete agreement' (525).

interest in the application of sociology to social work. He states this most fully in two papers published at the end of the 1920s and at the opening of the next decade (Burgess, 1929, 1930). His 1929 paper is a detailed report and application of an early study of the potential of parole records to provide a predictive framework in social work. He picks up on early social work intervention studies by Healy and Karpf, and reports a straight quantitative study, (without any obvious statistical calculation), of the records of 3,000 parolees in three Chicago institutions. He prepares expectancy tables, and suggests the application of the basic approach to social work with various child and family risks, and as a stimulus to intervention development.

> In my judgment this same method and variations of it may with profit be widely used wherever a social agency or other organization keeps relatively full records of significant traits of personality and of behaviour. (Burgess, 1929: 545)

Consistent with his assumptions regarding the reciprocity of relationships between sociology and social work, he concludes that the study of prediction in human behaviour 'opens up a new avenue of cooperation between sociology and social work' (545).

His 1930 paper is rather different and offers, in a crystallized form, his sense of the relevance of Chicago sociology to social work. His optimism and efforts over the decade seem to have yielded limited reward. He wishes to

> Throw the question open for general discussion why at present these materials on the basic facts of community life have had but little effect upon the policies and practices of social agencies. (Burgess, 1930: 481)

Drawing on the work of Anderson, Thrasher, Shaw, Wirth, Zorbaugh and others, he discusses the relevance of research in three groups, *viz* the growth and structure of the city, basic social data, and the description and analysis of the groups and institutions of the local community. On the growth of the city, he sketches the main strands of Chicago research, from his own work and that of Clifford Shaw, and argues,

> ...both for purposes of research and for the practical work of social agencies, it is only possible to get a grasp of the form and trends of city life by setting up such an ideal construction. (Burgess, 1930: 482)

He suggests the kind of theoretically and empirically informed application he has in mind when he asks

> ...if the city has, like an organism, a structure that is closely correlated with its functioning, why should this not be taken into account in any plan of districting by social agencies? What is the justification of treating the city not as a living

> organism, but as if it were a corpse which can be cut up arbitrarily into unrelated parts? (486)[11]

His reflections on the importance of basic social data stem largely from the Chicago study of local communities, funded in part by the Chicago Council of Social Agencies. In accord with Chicago theorizing, he advocates gaining community level material on the social forces and trends of local community life, and draws on Vivien Palmer's work, in which she placed special reliance on interviewing older community residents and real estate men, in addition to more conventional small-area data from the Census. Once again he pleads the relevance for social work, and the value of such data to enable social agencies to 'check the effectiveness of their case work processes' (Burgess, 1930: 488).

> It should be feasible to note the effect of the modification of one factor as for example the introduction of a new method of treatment of poverty or of juvenile delinquency. (488)

As with other of his proposals he is not fully confident they will be adopted. He recognizes that 'many social agencies may not wish to subject their work to so impersonal and external a test, but no doubt some agency will have the courage required for experimentation' (488-89). He does not pull his punches and sets out implications as he sees them for social work training.

> These local community studies point unmistakably to the systematic inclusion in training for social work and in the practice of social work of the cultural, or the community or the group treatment of problems of personality, of the family or of the neighbourhood. (490)

Burgess advocates the formation of conference groups of social workers organized around the details of Clifford Shaw's work on juvenile delinquency as offering methods of intervention that, while developed for research, are in his view fully susceptible to transfer to social intervention,[12] and discussion of community factors for each of the districts of the city, as promoting an alternative to what he sees as the existing 'haphazard and unsystematic' approach where 'even the most successful demonstrations of group treatment are ascribed to the "personality" of the worker' (490).

Contributions of social work to sociology

His work is marked by depth, range and specificity in engaging with social work. This is equally evident when he considers the obverse case of social work's contribution

11 Mainstream social work, at least in the UK, still largely ignores this perspective.

12 For a more recent text that adopts a similar logic, see Shaw, 1996.

to sociology. The main argument he develops over three papers (Burgess, 1923, 1927, 1928) is the value of agency case records, especially regarding families, as sources of 'data of distinct value for sociological investigation' (1923: 369). He quotes as the 'proverbial grain of truth' writers saying that 'The student of social work...is himself recording facts that will go to make up new sociological text-books of the future' (370). His interest is far from instrumental or naïve, and reflects the facing-both-ways stance that was prominent in Edith Abbott's position. In pressing his argument he consistently sets his hearers/readers readers back on their heels. Here are two examples of opening sentences from his papers.

> What I am about to say will be astounding and probably disquieting to you all and especially to my fellow sociologists. For I propose to explode the current and soothing convention that because sociology is a required subject for social work...therefore sociology has made a contribution to family social case work... Sociology as I see it has made little or no direct contribution to family social case work. (Burgess, 1927: 191)[13]

> What should social case records contain to be useful for sociological interpretation? They should contain what will render them valuable for social case work, that and no more. This answer will, I know, perplex and astonish many social workers and sociologists. (Burgess, 1928: 524).

Having set expectations on their heads, he goes on to reframe 'the question of the joint interest of social workers and sociologists in the content and form of social case records' (1928: 524). He clears the ground by saying of current literature that 'there is not a single volume – good, bad or indifferent – on the application of sociology to social work' (1927: 191).

His perspective rests, we now realize, on the assumption of a convergence of interest. It is in this light that we need to read his elaborations of the gains sociology brings to social work. Reflecting on the fact that such research had 'not as yet been integrated into the general scheme of training and practice in family social work', he concludes that

> The full value of sociological research for social workers will only come through experimental procedure involving the co-operation of sociologists and social workers. (Burgess, 1927: 192)

---

13 His paper was given to the National Conference of Social Work, Division on the Family, earlier in 1927. In the light of his opening sentences we note that sociologists are assumed to be present in a social work conference audience; that the majority of schools of social work were integrally linked to sociology departments; that social workers of the time got more sociology teaching than from any other social science discipline; and that he places himself as challenging sociological (and presumably social work) convention.

His specific proposal is enticing, even at this distance.

> My proposal is actually quite simple and I think, entirely feasible and reasonable, in spite of the fact that I do not anticipate its immediate and general adoption. It is to enter into the case record statements made by all persons visited in nearly as humanly possible the language which they used. (192)

He immediately glosses this with the complaint that he is

> strongly opposed to having the language of the father and the mother in the home, of the landlord, or the teacher, or of the employer, translated into the language of the social worker on the case. The translation invariably and inevitably distorts the point of view and the attitude of the person interviewed. Each informant has a right[14] to have himself appear in the record in his own language. (192-93)

He foresees this plan as giving 'a human document in place of a routine report' and candidly acknowledges 'How invaluable for case work and, I am frank to admit, for sociological research, would be the case records entirely in the first person' (193).

Having made the case in brief in 1927, he devoted the majority of his 1928 paper to developing his argument. We noted some moments ago his reference to Octavia Hill. He draws the chastened conclusion that

> Existing case records seldom, or never, picture people in the language of Octavia Hill, with their "passions, hopes, and history" or their "temptations", or "the little scheme they have made of their lives, or would make if they had encouragement". The characters in case records do not move, and act, and have their being as persons. They are depersonalized, they become Robots, or mere cases undifferentiated except by the recurring problems they present. (1928: 526-27)

He explains this by reiterating the point of his 1927 paper, that the 'characters...do not speak for themselves. They obtain a hearing only in the translation provided by the language of the social worker' (p. 527). He reflects his nascent interactionist sociology and social psychology[15] by setting the choice as one between a legalistic conception of the interview and a personal one.

---

14 This remark about human rights is not accidental. It is repeated in his 1928 paper, page 527.

15 Herbert Blumer invented the term symbolic interactionism. His doctoral dissertation was published in 1928. Not everyone would regard Burgess as an interactionist. Robert Prus remarks that Burgess 'was really more interested, I think, in family relations from any perspective, rather than being an interactionist, per se' (Kleinknecht, 2007: 233).

> To enter the interview in the words of the person signifies a revolutionary change. It is a change from the interview conceived in legal terms to the interview as an opportunity to participate in the life history of the person, in his memories, in his hopes, in his attitudes, in his own plans, in his philosophy of life. (527) [16]

He continues to be alert to points of common ground with social work writing and cites a then recent paper by a leading social work scholar, Gordon Hamilton. She had suggested a distinction between the natural and the social sciences, where the latter 'are inevitably concerned with preferences and values' (527).

Re-reading *The Jack-Roller*

We should not imagine that Burgess saw his work as sociologically eccentric, or that what may be described as sociological welfare intervention was special to him or to the delinquency research of the former parole officer, Clifford Shaw. 'Personality' was a common category in Chicago thinking, and the life history was on occasion 'seen as something of a confessional exercise. Indeed, there seems to have been an assumption that the life history had a cathartic function' (Lee, 2004: 872).[17]

Burgess often reiterated his appreciation of the work of Clifford Shaw at the Institute for Juvenile Research who had 'as far as I know more consciously developed the method of first person reporting and carried it further than anyone else in the country' (Burgess, 1927: 529). He wrote a careful discussion paper as part of Shaw's book and in this, as in Shaw's work, we find Chicago 'sociologists' crossing theoretical and therapeutic 'boundaries' without any apparent sense that they see themselves as wearing alternating disciplinary hats as they do so. Yet in doing so, there is a challenge to social work methods that fail to take into account sociologically informed analysis and interpretation. Shaw's focus on peer relationships, community and group relationships ran counter to the growing hegemony of individualist social work intervention.

---

16 He addresses and counters likely objections to his plea, *viz*: that such verbatim remarks are trivial; that they are not objective; that it would render records unduly lengthy; and that it would require new social work skills. He also suggests other ways that case records could be improved. The controversial character of proposals is implicitly acknowledged in that his paper is immediately followed in the same issue by a response from Bruno on the limitations of verbatim recording.

17 The social work/sociology connection, whereby sociology drew on the practice methods of social work and counselling, continued at least until the 1950s. Lee remarks of Carol Rogers, the non-directive therapist, 'that the work of Rogers had a significant influence on sociological practice with regard to interviewing…Merton et al. (1956) explicitly drew on Rogers' concept of non-direction in formulating their concept of the focused interview, which in turn underpinned the development of focus groups as a qualitative research method' (Lee, 2004: 876).

Thus Burgess in his 1930 essay in *The Jack-Roller* says of the benefits of Shaw's intervention that Stanley's 'reformation is quite as much or more a matter of changing his social groups as of effecting a change of attitudes or purposes' (Shaw, 1966: 187) and that the second follows from the first. He goes on to press the value of 'materials in the first person'. He repeats his 1927 argument by contrasting this approach with the materials of case records held by agencies as 'subjective records, that is, translations by the visitor of the language, emotional expressions, and attitudes of the person interviewed' (187). While such accounts are likely to be true as to 'objective facts' they yield 'quite often widely different interpretations of these facts' – and it his 'personality reactions and his own interpretations of his experiences' that are of primary significance. He argues that it is the attitude of scientific research that is most likely to elicit truth. It is narrative qualities, rather than answers to 'cut and dried questions', that will yield internal coherence (188). It is not categories such as 'broken home', 'poverty', 'bad housing' etc that explain, but 'His career is a series of acts in response to changing social situations' (189).

Burgess develops what today we would see as a classification of kinds of narrative:

- The Chronicler;
- The Self-defender;[18]
- The Confessant;
- The Self-analyst

He concludes with a 'social work' argument for 'a new technique of treatment' (194) consisting of:

1. Empathy not sympathy, which he defines as 'entering into the experience of another person by the human and democratic method of sharing experiences' (194-5).
2. Telling one's life story. This 'is itself part of the treatment' (195), not simply to be understood as therapeutic catharsis but as giving the subject 'perspective upon his life'. Hence 'Mr Shaw does not use the methods of the psychoanalyst, he is not dealing with the materials of the unconscious, but with the memories, wishes and ambitions of the conscious mind' (195).
3. 'Pay attention to the powerful factors of group and neighbourhood influence' (195).

Burgess also draws on other Chicago work such as Thrasher's *The Gang* and Shaw's large dataset *Delinquency Areas* as foundation for interventions. Social work had been largely centred on case work with the individual, whereas 'the

18 Burgess places Stanley in this category, and also calls him an 'egocentric personality'.

development of techniques of group and community treatment' (196) were needed, along with 'research into the processes of social treatment' (197).

I have been unable to locate any further engagement on the part of Burgess with the relationship of the two fields. Deegan observes, for example, that Burgess in the earlier period was supportive of 'practical sociology' (a quote from 1916) and in 1924 was speaking approvingly of women's 'neighbourhood work', but in his later career writing was downplaying it as 'isolated', and not scientific or objective, and referring to its 'social work' orientation (Deegan, 1997b: 13). Speculatively, this may have been due to an expanding preoccupation of each field with its own development. There is little evidence of critical engagement on the part of social work with the creative challenge posed by Burgess, Shaw and others. For sociology, Burgess was playing a central role with Park, eg in the publication of their benchmark text on sociology in the later twenties. The diminished conversation may – though I am but guessing – have been connected with wider intellectual hostilities between the two disciplines that marked the decade. Burgess himself developed a strand of interest in the relationship between sociology and Freudian psychoanalysis – psychoanalysis and socioanalysis as he somewhere expresses it (Burgess, 1939: 263).

In papers where his earlier interests seemed opportune for further development (e.g. Burgess, 1939, 1947) he makes no mention at all of social work. His 1939 paper is a very interesting discussion of Freud's influence on sociology in which, within his characteristic periodizing of sociology's development, he argues the point that the central methodological problem of the two disciplines is the same. Exploring the reasons as he sees them for divergences between the fields, he moves to discussing the potential for a combination of methods between sociology and psychoanalysis. The underling logic has obvious but unspoken points of connection with his approach to the relationship between sociology and social work, thus tacitly implying how he might have further developed his earlier thinking.

The issues lie fairly close to the surface.

- The nature of the unresolved legacy, and my sense that it might have been otherwise.
- The relationship between the applied, the ameliorative, and what Mills et al (2006) have recently, in a somewhat invidious comparison, contrasted as 'practice oriented' and 'research-based' social science disciplines.
- The social contingencies of discipline recognition (c.f. Shaw, Arksey and Mullender, 2006).
- The institutional shaping of fields of study.
- The hard won gains and easy losses of inter-disciplinary collaboration.
- The continued prevalence of 'friendly fire' actions among the social sciences.

Several disclaimers are in order. I do not, for a moment, want to claim that sociology and social work are part of one and the same enterprise. Small, of course, was correct, at least in principle, when he remarked on the existence of 'practical social workers who have but a vague notion of society in general, and who consequently cannot properly be called sociologists' (Small, 1903: 472). Nor do I believe we should even aspire to a circumstance in which sociology and social work coexist in perfect amity. Neither should we wish to draw a line from 80 or 90 years ago and teleport Edith Abbott, Clifford Shaw or Ernest Burgess to the present.

What I would plead for, however, is a relationship between social work and sociology of intellectual reciprocity based on egalitarian respect. Yet this is all too rare. Sociological history tends still to take the modernist view that wider work in the city was simply the precursor to sophisticated social science.

> Accounts written from within sociology, as history of sociology, generally treat both other disciplines and groups outside the academy as parts of the background. They are seen as instrumental to the main aims of sociologists, or as introducing distortions into the...course of pure sociological development. (Platt, 1996: 264)

In exploring such mutually respectful *rapprochements*, the sense of unfinished labour that emerges from reading Burgess is a helpful benchmark, with its consequences for professional and scholarly work.[19] The realization that Burgess put himself about to place himself before and in social work audiences also has implications for contemporary cross-boundary activity, though perhaps made more demanding in the USA where most universities have long ago followed the Chicago departure into separate schools.

In a rare contemporary example, on the uses of ethnography, Bloor argues from reviews of a street ethnography of HIV-related risk behaviour among Glasgow male prostitutes, and comparative ethnographies of eight therapeutic communities, that there are two ways in which ethnography might speak to the practitioner. In ways that carry over naturalist and realist assumptions not dissimilar to those of Shaw and Burgess, he suggests that *first*, it may 'model' a service delivery that can be transferred to service providers. For example, 'ethnographic fieldwork, in its protracted and regular contacts with research subjects, has much in common with services outreach work' (Bloor, 1997: 227). From his therapeutic community studies, Bloor suggests the very act of comparative judgement can model helpful service practice. 'Rich description of particular kinds of therapeutic practice can assist practitioners in making evaluative judgements about their own practices' (229). *Second*, ethnographers may, where appropriate, draw practitioners' attention to practices they think worth dissemination and further consideration. Bloor and McKeganey list seven practices which seemed to them to promote therapy in their original settings (Bloor and McKeganey, 1989), and which they discussed with the practitioners in the therapeutic communities. Incidentally, they point out the corresponding implications for ethnographers, in that

19 I have tried to 'place' social work with this rubric in mind (Shaw, 2007).

> any attempts to further exploit the evaluative potential of ethnography for a practitioner audience must be paralleled by a growth in ethnographic studies which focus on practitioners' work, not practitioners' conduct. (Bloor and McKeganey, 1989: 210)

Until that time, when 'citizens themselves commend the work of practitioners, then it is not the place of sociologists to murmur of false consciousness and demand resistance to pastoral care' (Bloor, 1997: 235).

For the moment, it is as if we are 'too embarrassed to look seriously at our history, afraid of the disorder we might find, too eager to distance ourselves from the pre-professional beginnings' and are, in consequence, homeless and 'disembedded' (Lorenz, 2007: 599). Lorenz' conclusion has equal point for sociology and social work. 'All social work practices are deeply embedded in historical and cultural habits from which we cannot detach ourselves at will'. He aptly infers from this that we should be practising history 'in the dual sense of positioning ourselves in a historical context and of giving our interventions a historical dimension' (601).

Whatever we may conclude from these *leitmotifs*, Diner is surely correct when he says that above all university departments (sociology or social work) need 'teachers and investigators who are learned, imaginative, curious, scrupulous, patient and tireless in their exertion' (Diner, 1997: 56).

Acknowledgements

I am grateful for the comments of sociology colleagues at a conference on the legacy of the Chicago School at Manchester, England, 2007, and to observations made by social work colleagues at the 2007 Bielefeld meeting of INTSOCEVAL (an international network of social work evaluation centres).

References

Bloor, Michael, 1997, 'Addressing social problems through qualitative research' in Silverman, D. (ed) *Qualitative Research: Theory, Method and Practice*. London: Sage.

Bloor, Michael and McKeganey, Neil, 1989, 'Ethnography addressing the practitioner' in Gubrium, J. and Silverman, D. (eds) *The Politics of Field Research: Sociology Beyond Enlightenment*. Newbury Park: Sage.

Burgess, Ernest W., 1923, 'The interdependency of sociology and social work' in *Journal of Social Forces* 1 (4): 366-370.

Burgess, Ernest W., 1927, 'The contribution of sociology to family social work' in *The Family* October 1927: 191-193.

Burgess, Ernest W., 1928, 'What social case records should contain to be useful for sociological interpretation' in *Social Forces* 6 (4): 524-532.

Burgess, Ernest W., 1929, 'Is prediction feasible in social work? An inquiry based upon a sociological study of parole records' in *Social Forces* 7 (4): 533-545.

Burgess, Ernest W., 1930, 'The value of sociological community studies for the work of social agencies' in *Social Forces* 8 (4): 481-491.

Burgess, Ernest W., 1939, 'The influence of Sigmund Freud upon sociology in the United States' in *The American Journal of Sociology* 45 (3): 356-374.

Burgess, Ernest W., 1947, 'The family and sociological research' in *Social Forces* 26 (1): 1-6.

Cavan, Ruth, 1997, 'The Chicago School of Sociology, 1918-1933' in Plummer, K (ed) *The Chicago School: Critical Assessments Vol I A Chicago Canon?* London: Routledge.

Coghlan, Catherine, L., nd, 'The Graduate School of Social Service Administration: Beginning or End of the Differentiation Process between Chicago Sociology and Social Work?' Unpublished Paper.

Deegan, Mary Jo, 1991, *Women in Sociology: a Bio-bibliographical Sourcebook*. New York: Greenwood Press.

Deegan, Mary Jo, 1997a, 'The Chicago men and the sociology of women' in Plummer, K (ed) *The Chicago School: Critical Assessments Vol I, A Chicago Canon?* London: Routledge.

Deegan, Mary Jo, 1997b, '*Hull-House Maps and Papers*: the birth of Chicago sociology' in Plummer, K. (ed) *The Chicago School: Critical Assessments Vol II, Theory, History and Foundations*. London: Routledge.

Deegan, Mary Jo and Hill, Michael R., 1991, 'Edith Abbott (1876-1957)' in Deegan, Mary Jo, (ed) *Women in Sociology: a Bio-bibliographical Sourcebook*. New York: Greenwood Press.

Denzin, Norman K., 1989, *Interpretive Biography*. Newbury Park: Sage Publications.

Denzin, Norman K., 1992, *Symbolic Interactionism and Cultural Studies: the Politics of Interpretation*. Cambridge MA: Blackwell.

Diner, Stephen J., 1977, 'Scholarship in the quest for social welfare: a fifty-year history of the *Social Service Review*' in *Social Service Review* 51 (1): 1-66.

Diner, Stephen J., 1997, 'Department and discipline: the development of sociology at the University of Chicago, 1892-1920' in Plummer, K., (ed) *The Chicago School: Critical Assessments*. London: Routledge.

Geertz, Clifford, 1973, *The Interpretation of Cultures*. New York: Basic Books.

Kleinknacht, Steven, 2007, 'An interview with Robert Prus: his career, contributions, and legacy as an interactionist ethnographer and social theorist' in *Qualitative Sociology Review* 3 (2): 221-288.

Lee, Raymond, 2004, 'Recording Technologies and the Interview in Sociology, 1920-2000' in *Sociology* 38 (5): 869-889.

Lorenz, Walter, 2007, 'Practising history: memory and contemporary professional practice' in *International Social Work* 50 (5): 597-612.

Lubove, Roy, 1965, *The Professional Altruist*. Cambridge: Harvard University Press.

Mills, D., Jepson, A., Coxon, T., Easterby-Smith, M., Hawkins, P. and Spencer, J., 2006, *Demographic Review of the UK Social Sciences* Swindon: ESRC. Available at http://www.esrc.ac.uk/ESRCInfoCentre.

Platt, Jennifer, 1996, *A History of Sociological Research Methods in America*. Cambridge: CUP.

Plummer, Ken, 1997, 'Introducing Chicago sociology' in Plummer, K. (ed) *The Chicago School: Critical Assessments Vol I, A Chicago Canon?* London: Routledge.

Richmond, Mary, 1917, *Social Diagnosis*. New York: Russell Sage.

Shaw, Clifford, 1966, *The Jack-Roller*. Chicago: Chicago University Press.

Shaw, Ian, 1996, *Evaluating in Practice*. Aldershot: Ashgate.

Shaw, Ian, 2007, 'Is social work research distinctive?' in *Social Work Education,* 26 (7): 659-669.

Shaw, Ian, 2008, 'Merely experts? Reflections on the history of social work, science and research' in *Research, Policy and Planning*, 26 (1)

Shaw, Ian, Arksey, Hilary and Mullender, Audrey, 2006, 'Recognizing social work' in *British Journal of Social Work*, 36 (2): 227-246.

Shaw, Ian and Gould, Nick, 2001, *Qualitative Research in Social* Work. London: Sage Publications.

Small, Albion W., 1903, 'What is a sociologist?' in *American Journal of Sociology*, 8: 468-477.

Chapter 5

William J. Reid: An Appreciation*

The death of Bill Reid in November 2003 brought to an end his work which, over a period spanning five decades, shaped the agenda for research on social work services. He was, at the time of his unexpected death,[1] Distinguished Professor at the State University of New York. Reid spent his career in social work education. His early work grew from mainstream experimental outcome evaluation. His later work harnessed continued development and evaluation of goal-oriented models to a growing engagement with qualitative, process-oriented research.

He first became widely known through Anne Shyne's and his book, *Brief and Extended Casework*, which reported an experimental study comparing short and long-term social work intervention (Reid and Shyne, 1969). Planned short-term service provision yielded results at least as good as and possibly better than open-ended intervention. In the context of the time, when long-term casework was regarded as the ideal, 'in this particular race (Planned Short Term Intervention) needed only a tie to win' (p. 175).

Reid took the lead in developing and testing Task-Centred Practice – a short-term, problem-solving approach to social work where the focus is on the problems that clients acknowledge as being of concern. The model has been research-informed throughout, and has a strong empirical orientation (e.g. Reid, 1997). This connecting strand running though Reid's career provides the context for a range of concerns.

First, his own outcome research and review work on other studies has been one plank in the gradual renewal of confidence in evaluative research (Reid, 1988, 1997; Reid and Hanrahan, 1982). His work notes the increasing 'dominance of structured forms of practice', in particular those influenced by 'the behaviour modification movement' (Reid and Hanrahan, 1982: 329). While he is convinced the helping professions can demonstrate that they are effective, he warns that the practical significance of identified effects is often slight, and their durability ambiguous. He sometimes appears doubtful about the methodological criteria of such studies. In his chastening and memorable metaphor, 'It is like trying to

---

* Originally published as I. Shaw, 2004. 'William J. Reid: an appreciation', *Qualitative Social Work* 3(2): 109-15. Reprinted with permission of Sage Publications Ltd

1 In 2004 there continues to be a steady output of work completed right through 2003. See for example, his essays on computer technology and social work (Petrucci, Kirk and Reid, 2004) and task-centred practice (Reid and Fortune, 2004) in Roberts and Yeager, (2004).

decide which horse won a race viewed at a bad angle from the grandstand during a cloudburst' (Reid, 1988: 48)!

In his observations on the direction of outcome research, he commented favourably that 'the researcher as evaluator is giving way to the researcher as developer of models' (Reid and Hanrahan, 1982: 338). This reflects his *second* cluster of concerns. He regards his task-centred practice research as a step- by-step process of development, testing and further development. He has sought to develop unobtrusive and practitioner-friendly methods for field testing the early trial versions of specific practice interventions (Reid, 1994b).

Reid's modest confidence in the benefits of outcome and developmental research contrasts with more bullish pronouncements regarding evidenced-based practice. Reid responded to these with measured, benchmark reviews of the empirical practice movement (Reid, 1994c; Reid and Zettergren, 1999):

> The empirical practice movement has advanced social work's long and laborious pursuit of the goal of creating a scientifically based profession. However, the gains achieved have been partial, uneven, and not always clear. (Reid, 1994c: 180)

This indicates his *third* contribution – suggesting ways in which considerations of epistemology and methodology should be applied to social work. For example, he explored the potential of 'change process research' (Reid, 1990). Practical and ethical constraints on experiments necessitate, in his view, the naturalistic study of process–outcome relations. A key notion about the process of change is that of understanding intermediate 'micro-outcomes' depicted through intensive study of smaller elements of practice. This gives central importance to the immediate context of practice. This avenue of research has the potential to be pulled towards either a stronger naturalistic, interpretive methodology, or towards more traditional notions of rigour. Reid (1990: 144) opposed the latter and probably the former, and preferred to see the knowledge gained as 'one kind of provisionally valid knowledge'. Behind this careful steering was Reid's concern to reframe debate, away from arguments about epistemological worldviews, and devote our energies instead to clarifying and resolving the specific issues embedded in these arguments (Reid, 1994a: 465). His concerns were good practice, empirical work, a shared vocabulary and rationality, and a lack of enthusiasm about philosophical authority. He falls 'within the tradition of American pragmatism especially as it has been set forth in the writings of Pierce, James, Dewey and Rorty' (Reid, 1994a: 472). He was a methodologist in the widest sense. He increasingly refracted social work and research through its historical, intellectual, philosophical and organizational contexts. His overview essay on research in the 1995 *Encyclopedia of Social Work* (Reid, 1995) is a masterly synopsis of research broadly conceived. This safe-guarded him from rash claims on behalf of social work and research. To him 'research-based knowledge can be only a part, albeit an important one, of a vast network of information that informs practice' (Reid, 1995: 2041). If anything, he grew more cautious as his career progressed. It is only a few years ago that Joel Fischer was predicting that 'by the year 2000, empirically based practice – the new social work – may be the norm, or well on the way to becoming so' (Fischer, 1993). No such bland optimism marked Bill Reid's work. He certainly believed that 'social work research has come a long way' (1995: 2043) 'but it has a much longer way to go'. In one of his final books, with Stuart Kirk, he remarked that, 'within the profession, science remains on the cultural margins, struggling for a voice and a following' (Kirk and Reid, 2002: x). They regarded the social work research community as 'scattered across many academic hamlets' (Kirk and Reid, 2002: 218) and saw their obligation as 'to keep the profession liberated from its own provincialism' (Kirk and Reid, 2002: 219).

His philosophical commitments were not peripheral. He was keen to remind Nick Gould and me, in a pre-publication review of our recent book, that in our discussion of common sense, we 'might consider some reference to the long-held notion that science is, indeed, as Dewey once put it, "common sense, writ large"' (unpublished review, cf. Reid, 2002). Despite his misgivings about positivist bashing and epistemological grandstanding, he was ready to acknowledge that theoretical assumptions *are* implicit in scientific practice.[2] He developed this in one of his invaluable reviews of the empirical practice movement (Reid and Zettergren, 1999), and returned to it in his and Kirk's argument that 'it may make sense to construe scientific practice as a "perspective" on intervention', and his willingness 'to accredit client ideas about measurement, data collection and the like that might not fit conventional research notions'. They went as far as to say that this understanding of a scientific practice perspective 'could be used with advocacy research, even though the practitioner-researcher might need to forgo his or her "neutrality"' (Kirk and Reid, 2002: 89).[3]

Having said this, his epistemology and ontology were perhaps as much a given as they were a focus of preoccupied attention. He would very likely have allied himself with the implicit distancing in Howard Becker's aside about the profession of 'philosophical and methodological worry' (Becker, 1993: 226). It is my view that he did not reach a nuanced development of his position in this area. There is a critical strand submerged just below the surface in some of what proved to be his last work, and yet he retained the allegiance of 'post-positivism' (Kirk and Reid, 2002: 15), of the variety that accepts it is normally possible to gain a substantially true picture through research, and in one of his last essays he happily embraced Michael Patton's pragmatism as a 'sensible strategy' that 'puts epistemological controversies and clashes of paradigms where they belong – on the sidelines' (Reid, 2002: 292).

2 I was impressed by his instant readiness to develop this idea during the development of his and Pam Zettergren's chapter in Shaw and Lishman (1999).

3 This quote and the following point are from his prepublication review of Shaw and Gould (2001).

When it came to methodological choices it was his wish, in one of his many memorable phrases, to 'redefine the nature of the mainstream so that qualitative methodology is a part of it not apart from it' (Reid, 1994a: 477). The Sherman and Reid (1994) handbook stands, in this regard, as the most comprehensive survey of the achievements and possibilities of qualitative research. He was to be the lead editor of the successor volume.

He was neither unconditional nor comprehensive in his backing for qualitative methods. He seemed to take a position that, for me, has much going for it – to regard the relationship between paradigms and methods as an *empirical* question. Thus, with Kirk, he lamented that 'we know comparatively little about notions of bias, error, mistakes and truth – the actual epistemologies used – in the ordinary practice of social work' (Kirk and Reid, 2002: 17). He took a similarly inductive stance when remarking that 'the bottom line for research utilization is what happens in the field among practitioners' (Kirk and Reid, 2002: 194). Take this on board, and the more extreme rhetoric of evidence-based policy and practice would be purged of several excesses. There was an ethnographic streak in his awareness, for example, that 'contextual phenomena often lurk at the blind side of quantitative methods'. Yet he thought the notion of context had its limits. For example, he regarded Lee Cronbach's position on generalization as 'cavalier'[4] and emphasized that generalization across diverse contexts is certainly possible and has been attained to some degree. He was very doubtful about constructivist research, and said little or nothing about critical research, participatory inquiry or reflective practice. Much of this we can take as we find. Yet I wonder if there is just a touch of the social work community's tendency to set up straw figures for the sake of making a point in some social work writing. For example, we do not have to accept the view that research methods are or should be moulded in a deterministic way by the paradigm position of the researcher to recognize that inquiry questions are nonetheless shaped by our paradigm-like starting points. Hence it is not grandstanding to assert that there is a real but imperfect relationship between paradigm and method, and that 'epistemological integrity does get meaningful research done right' (Greene, 1990: 229).

There are inevitable unresolved tensions in his work. There is a gradualist presumption in his welcome for incremental experimentation, and in his comment that 'these small successes of the present are better than the grand failures of the past' (Reid and Hanrahan, 1982: 338). Reid tended to ignore wider issues such as the politics implicit in evaluation research. He was aware that if social workers focus their energy on the achievement of effective but modest results, this can 'discourage more radical, but possibly less testable innovations' (Reid, 1988: 45).

Reid's disavowal of provincialism is worth a second look. 'Provincialism' is not the best term here – its connotations of 'unsophisticated', 'simple' and

4 Cronbach and his colleagues said that 'a program evaluation is so dependent on its context that replication is only a figure of speech' (Cronbach et al., 1980: 222).

'outmoded' are invidious. The more incisive term – to borrow Becker once more – is 'sentimentality'. We are guilty of sentimentality, says Howard Becker,

> when we refuse, for whatever reason, to investigate some matter that should properly be regarded as problematic. We are sentimental especially, when our reason is that we would prefer not to know what is going on, if to know would be to violate some sympathy whose existence we may not even be aware of. (Becker, 1970: 132-3)

Sentimentality is often associated with parochialism. In Britain, for example, there has been little if any effort to develop the design and development approach that Bill Reid, along with a handful of others, actively promoted. In the USA there is insularity in much of our colleagues' writing. Reid was sensitive to this, though his writing still tended to be heavily American oriented.

His personal impact on colleagues, practitioners, and doctoral students has to be assessed by those closer to him year by year. His generosity with his time and support, and his readiness to share his mind and time with others were outstanding. He authored over 20 books and 160 scientific journal articles and book chapters. It was apparently said of him, in one of the nomination letters for his Distinguished Professorship, that 'there would be few social workers in the world who would not know of and respect Reid's work'. Conversations with students following his death suggest that sadly this may not be quite so universal. It ought to be. He was the single most significant figure in social work research, and he will continue to enhance 'the precision with which we vex ourselves' (Geertz, 1973: 29).

References

Becker, H. (1970) *Sociological Work*. Chicago, IL: Aldine Publishing Company.

Becker, Howard (1993) 'Theory: The Necessary Evil', in D. Flinders and G. Mills (Eds) *Theory and Concepts in Qualitative Research: Perspectives from the Field*. New York: Teachers College, Columbia University Press.

Cronbach, L., Ambron, S., Dornbusch, S., Hess, R., Hornik, R., Phillips, D., Walker, D. and Weiner, S. (1980) *Toward Reform of Program Evaluation*. San Francisco, CA: Jossey-Bass.

Fischer, J. (1993) 'Empirically Based Practice: The End of Ideology?' in M. Bloom (ed.) *Single-System Designs in the Social Services: Issues and Options for the 1990s*. London: Haworth Press.

Geertz, C. (1973) *The Interpretation of Cultures*. New York: Basic Books.

Greene, J. (1990) 'Three Views on the Nature and Role of Knowledge in Social Science', in E. Guba (ed.) *The Paradigm Dialog*. Newbury Park, CA: Sage.

Kirk, Stuart A. and Reid, William J. (2002) *Social Science Work: A Critical Appraisal*. New York: Columbia University Press.

Petrucci, Carrie J., Kirk, Stuart A. and Reid, William J. (2004) 'Computer Technology and Social Work', in A.R. Roberts and K.R. Yeager (Eds) *Evidence Based Practice Manual*, pp. 85-94. New York: Oxford University Press.

Reid, William J. (1988) 'Service Effectiveness and the Social Agency', in R. Patti, J. Poertner and C. Rapp (Eds) *Managing for Effectiveness in Social Welfare Organizations*. New York: Haworth.

Reid, William J. (1990) 'Change-process Research: A New Paradigm?' in L. Videka-Sherman and W. Reid (Eds) *Advances in Clinical Social Work Research*. Silver Spring, MD: NASW Press.

Reid, William J. (1994a) 'Reframing the Epistemological Debate', in E. Sherman and W. Reid (Eds) *Qualitative Research in Social Work*. New York: Columbia University Press.

Reid, William J. (1994b) 'Field Testing and Data Gathering on Innovative Practice Interventions in Early Development', in J. Rothman and E. Thomas (Eds) *Intervention Research: Design and Development of Human Service*. New York: Haworth Press.

Reid, William J. (1994c) 'The Empirical Practice Movement', *Social Service Review* 68(2): 165-84.

Reid, William J. (1995) 'Research Overview', in R.L. Edwards and J.G. Hopps (eds) *Encyclopedia of Social Work 19th Edition Volume III*. Washington, DC: NASW Press.

Reid, William J. (1997) 'Research on Task-centred Practice', *Social Work Research* 21(3): 132-7.

Reid, William, J. (2002) 'In the Land of Paradigms, Method Rules', *Qualitative Social Work* 1(3): 291-5.

Reid, William, J. and Fortune, Anne (2004) 'Task-centered Practice: An Exemplar of Evidence-based Practice', in A.R. Roberts and K.R. Yeager (Eds) *Evidence-Based Practice Manual*, pp. 226-32. New York: Oxford University Press.

Reid, William J. and Hanrahan, P. (1982) 'Recent Evaluations of Social Work: Grounds for Optimism', *Social Work* 27: 328-40.

Reid, William J. and Shyne, Anne (1969) *Brief and Extended Casework*. New York: Columbia University Press.

Reid, William J. and Zettergren, Pam (1999) 'A Perspective on Empirical Practice', in I. Shaw and J. Lishman (eds) *Evaluation and Social Work Practice*, pp. 41-62. London: Sage.

Roberts, Albert R. and Yeager, Kenneth R. (2004) (Eds) *Evidence Based Practice Manual*. New York: Oxford University Press.

Shaw, Ian and Gould, Nick (2001) *Qualitative Research in Social Work*. London: Sage.

Shaw, Ian and Lishman, Joyce (1999) (Eds) *Evaluation and Social Work Practice*. London: Sage.

Sherman, Ed. and Reid, William J. (1994) (Eds) *Qualitative Research and Social Work*. New York: Columbia University Press.

PART II
Evaluation

A majority of my books have the word 'evaluation' somewhere in the title. Despite this I regard myself as having relatively circumscribed plausible evaluation knowledge and experience. The evaluation field, understood by Scriven (1997) and others as a meta-discipline that draws a number of social science disciplines into one field, offers a valuable gateway into thinking creatively about the span of issues touched on in this collection.

The section opens with the most recent piece – placed first because it is an overview of human services evaluation (Shaw, 2006). In tune with the approach in the first section, I aim to set out where I believe social work evaluation shares an agenda with the wider evaluation field and where it has some field-specific elements.

I include something about my work on evaluating in practice in the fourth section of the collection. But having written the original book (Shaw, 1996) I was aware that two issues needed addressing, and set about tackling them. First, how does an evaluation agenda shape social work practice (Shaw and Lishman, 1999), and, second, how might we constitute a qualitative framework for evaluation (Shaw, 1999a). The second project is represented in this collection by one of the chapters in *Qualitative Evaluation* – probably the most referenced piece of work I have written, albeit largely by those outside social work. One way of viewing this inclusion is to see it as an application of the issues discussed in the 'Ways of Knowing' essay in the previous section, but spoken about within the evaluation literature.

'Seeing the Trees for the Wood' is another inclusion that crosses different sections of the book, but in this case the links are more to the fourth and fifth sections. I have included it because it is representative of the various efforts I have made to jolt the social work community out of what I fear may be an unduly complacent alignment to this or that set of standpoints (Shaw, 1999b). Hence the title, suggesting that a fondness for big pictures may obscure the appropriate differentiation of the social work field.

Finally, I have been drawn at several different points in my career into aspects of organization research. The piece on evaluation and learning organizations is not fully typical of my work in this area, but does illustrate ways in which connections may be made between developments in different fields. Its treatment of the two literature domains is fairly straightforward, but it does point up a recurring tendency in my writing to engage in rough thought experiments, considering what happens if we bring together two or more themes, or if we turn conventional social work wisdom on its head and ask, 'but what if…?' The Chicago-focused work mentioned previously is one such example, as is some current organization work I am doing with Mark Hardy and Rachael Finn by asking what if social workers are sometimes 'unsafe' in 'safe' environments?

References

Scriven, M. (1997) 'Truth and objectivity in evaluation' in E. Chelimsky and W.R. Shadish (Eds.), *Evaluation for the 21st Century: A Handbook* (pp. 477-500). Thousand Oaks, CA: Sage Publications.

Shaw, I. (1996) *Evaluating in Practice.* Aldershot: Ashgate.

Shaw, I. (1999a) *Qualitative Evaluation.* London: Sage Publications.

Shaw, I. (1999b) 'Seeing the Trees for the Wood: the Politics of Practice Evaluation' in B. Broad (ed) *The Politics of Research and Evaluation in Social Work.* Birmingham: Venture Press.

Shaw, I. and Lishman, J. (1999) (eds) *Evaluation and Social Work Practice.* London: Sage Publications.

Shaw, I. (2004b) 'Evaluation for a learning organization' in N. Gould and M. Baldwin (ed.) *Social Work, Critical Reflection and the Learning Organization.* Aldershot: Ashgate.

Shaw, I. (2006) 'Human services' in I. Shaw, J. Greene, and M. Mark (eds) *Sage Handbook of Evaluation.* London: Sage Publications.

Chapter 6
Social Work and the Human Services*

Evaluative inquiry in social work and the human services[1] goes back at least as far as the parallel debates about whether social work is a profession, and if so, how should social workers be educated and trained for their task (Kirk and Reid, 2002). Evaluative inquiry in social work and the human services should contribute to the development and evaluation of practice and services; enhance professional moral purpose; strengthen social work's disciplinary character and location; and promote human services evaluation marked by rigour, range, variety, depth and progression.

Human services evaluation can be divided for heuristic purposes into:

1. Programme, policy and practice evaluation designed to establish plausible *evidence* regarding best practice and the outcomes of policies, services and intervention.
2. Evaluation that aims to *understand* and learn about social problems, organizational responses, and direct practice.
3. Evaluation seeking to promote *just* forms and outcomes of human services.

I will review the field in terms of these three large purposes.

As with all evaluation domains in this part of the Handbook,[2] there is a very extensive 'body' of evaluation, and I would risk superficiality if I tried to assess evaluation of practice across the fields of e.g. children and families, learning disabilities, older people, mental health and so on. My approach[3] will be to review

---

* Originally published as I. Shaw, 2006. 'Human services', in I. Shaw, J. Greene and M. Mark (eds) *Sage Handbook of Evaluation*. London: Sage. Reprinted with permission of Sage Publications Ltd.

1 'Human services' is an American category, although it is increasingly adopted outside the USA. 'Social care' (eg in Britain) and 'community development' (eg in Africa and some Arab world countries) are other categories that condense a broad scope of formal and informal, state-regulated and independent, secular and faith-based, personal social services. The expression 'human services' is used throughout this chapter as shorthand to refer to these coalescences of agencies, occupations and professions. Within these broad groupings are occupations that are typically a minority within the whole, although more or less professional, linked to higher education, subject to state or national regulatory frameworks, and research-based. Social work is an example of such an occupation.

2 [i.e. in original source].

3 The main thread of this chapter is the work of Shaw. Mowbray and Qureshi's work is contained within the exemplars. The use of the first person singular occurs in places where I do not want to commit all three authors to the view expressed.

key themes, and illustrating them through occasional exemplars of evaluative programmes and projects. However, evaluation in these substantive areas puts flesh on the skeleton of evaluative work. Carol Mowbray (Example 6.1) illustrates this.

Example 6.1 Supported education for adults with serious, long-term mental illnesses

Carol Mowbray

Background

Higher education is now considered a necessity for obtaining decent jobs with adequate salaries, career ladders, and benefits. Despite the importance of higher education, people with psychiatric disabilities are frequently unable to gain access to educational resources or maintain their involvement with educational institutions (Cheney, Martin and Rodriguez, 2000; Unger, 1998). Main-line mental health treatments do not typically address a rehabilitation need like access to post-secondary education. Supported education (SEd) programs arose in response to requests from consumers and family members for services that could help individuals with serious mental illness begin or continue pursuit of higher education goals. Published reports on these SEd programs have been mainly descriptive, with only pre-post changes reported.

Aims and objectives

The Michigan Supported Education Research Program developed and implemented SEd services in the public mental health system, testing effectiveness through an experimental design. We recruited eligible participants from an urban area and randomly assigned them to one of two active conditions versus a control condition. The SEd program provided preparation, assistance and support, in a group format, to address higher education goals. The key features of the evaluation were measurement of service participation levels (not just assignment condition); use of program theory to specify underlying causal mechanisms through which outcomes would be achieved; utilization of quantitative and qualitative measures tapping proximal outcomes reflecting the program theory, in addition to distal outcomes; a longitudinal design with five data collection points over 20 months; and multilevel modeling to optimize use of all available data.

Results, key issues, and likely future directions

The overall intervention effects were that 57 per cent of those enrolled participated at least to a moderate extent, and 41 per cent were engaged in some productive activity (higher education, vocational training, or work) at 12 months follow-up, compared to 27 per cent at baseline. For the intervention conditions, the number of participants enrolled in college or vocational training increased significantly, from 6 per cent to

28 per cent; whereas in the control condition, enrolment over time did not change. Further, participants in the active intervention conditions had significantly higher levels of satisfaction and enjoyment than those in the control condition. In focus group sessions, the benefits frequently mentioned by participants were group support and encouragement, improved self-concept, gaining skills, and a renewed sense of hope (Bellamy and Mowbray, 1998; Collins, Bybee and Mowbray, 1998; Mowbray, Collins and Bybee, 1999).

In multilevel modeling analyses, significant intervention effects were found for three distal outcomes: more school or work activity, decreased social adjustment difficulties, and increased quality of life. The intervention also had significant effects on two proximal outcomes – increased SEd participation and more social support for educational/vocational goals. There were three specific mediation paths: (1) amount of SEd participation completely mediated condition effects on school or work activity; (2) social support for educational or vocational goals partially mediated the effect of the intervention on social adjustment difficulties; and (3) social support and its effect on social adjustment problems completely mediated the intervention effect quality of life.

In summary, the evaluation design not only demonstrated the effectiveness of supported education in multiple domains, but also suggested the mechanisms through which SEd achieves its positive results: more participation in the program directly affects school and work activities; SEd decreases social adjustment difficulties by enhancing social support for educational and vocational goals. Attention to program theory can enhance successful implementations in other sites, as well as resultant long-term outcomes associated with a program.

Supported education is now being disseminated and replicated throughout North America, as well as in Europe and Asia. More effectiveness studies are needed to demonstrate the settings, contexts, and participant characteristics which may optimize SEd success.

References

Bellamy, C. and Mowbray, C.T. (1998) 'Supported Education as an Empowerment Intervention for People with Mental Illness', *Journal of Community Psychology*, 26 (5): 401-414.

Cheney, D., Marlin, J., and Rodriguez, E. (2000) 'Secondary and Postsecondary Education: New Strategies for Achieving Positive Outcomes' in H.B. Clark and M. Davis (eds.) *Transition to Adulthood* (pp. 55-74). Baltimore: Paul H. Brookes.

Collins, M.E. Bybee, D. and Mowbray. C.T. (1998) 'Effectiveness of Supported Education for Individuals with Psychiatric Disabilities: Results From an Experimental Study', *Community Mental Health Journal*, 34(6): 595-613.

Mowbray, C.T., Bybee D., and Collins M.E. (2002) Effectiveness of Supported Education: Regression *vs.* Multilevel Modeling Results. Washington, DC. NIMH Conference on Evidence-Based Practice.

Mowbray, C.T., Collins. M.E., and Bybee, D. (1999) 'Supported Education for Individuals with Psychiatric Disabilities: Long-term Outcomes From an Experimental Study', *Social Work Research*, 23(2): 89-100.

Unger, K.V. (1998) *Handbook on Supported Education.* Baltimore: Brookes.

Evidence, Intervention and Outcomes

The most pervasive – but by no means only – manifestation of evaluation concerns within the human services is with providing objective, impartial evidence for decision-making, providing public accountability, and generating or enhancing knowledge about social policy, social problems and how best to solve them. This particular set of commitments has been present in human services evaluation in three overlapping but distinguishable ways. First, an argument for evidence-based practice that, while shaped in parallel with developments in medicine and the health sciences, has developed some distinctive hallmarks. Second, a range of service and programme evaluations that have been concerned with assembling evidence regarding human services outcomes, and also with fashioning ways of conceiving outcomes such that they are congruent with the special features of human services delivery. Third, there has been a dedication to a research and development model – sometimes referred to as intervention research – that seeks to develop empirically grounded practice strategies through an iterative process of inquiry and practice. I will review each of these three strands in this part of the chapter.

Evidence-Based Practice

Attention to the knowledge and evidence base within the human services has focused on both practice and policy. It is not agreed how far these linked concerns raise similar or different issues. It is also important to note that in social work and human services, the boundaries between evaluation and research (e.g. 'intervention research') and also between evaluation/research and practice are somewhat blurred. This blurring is an interesting distinctive characteristic of the human services field, and marks it off from application of (for example) evidence-based practice in health-related fields, criminal justice, and (to some extent) education.

For the sake of manageability, I will focus mainly on evidence-based *practice* in a USA context, where there has been limited attention to the boundaries of policy and practice. After briefly reviewing ways in which evidence-based practice (EBP) has been defined and characterized, we will observe how its advocates have thought through the implications for social work intervention, management and training. We will observe recent and still emerging claims for modifications of EBP from within and some probable future directions, before considering still-remaining criticisms that might be levelled against evidence-based practice.

Characterizing Evidence-Based Practice

Sackett's definition of evidence-based practice as 'the conscientious, explicit and judicious use of current best evidence in making decisions about the care of individual patients' (Sackett, et al., 1996: 71) is cited often enough in human services and social work literature to give the impression that discussion about definitional issues is redundant.[4] This would be unhelpful. Mullen, for example, distinguishes between

1. A model of intervention that has been demonstrated effective.
2. A way of practising, using critical thinking.

The first of these sometimes has been disaggregated to include basing practice decisions on empirically based evidence as to the interventions of intervention strategies that are likely to produce the desired outcomes, and evaluating the implementation of these interventions to ensure they are being implemented as intended (eg Roberts and Yeager, 2004: 5). The second characteristic, critical thinking focuses more on professional judgement. It 'denotes an approach to evidence, argument and decision-making which is closely related to scientific reasoning' (Macdonald, 2000a: 80) and has been said to include:

1. Assessing accurately the quality of evidence.
2. Recognizing and countering common fallacies of reasoning.
3. Recognizing how affective and cognitive biases can adversely influence professional judgement.
4. Establishing 'a *modus operandi* which promotes accuracy or truth over winning the argument' (Macdonald, 2000a: 80).

Macdonald brings these various aspects together when she says that evidence based practice represents 'an approach to decision-making which is transparent, accountable, and based on a consideration of current best evidence about the effects of particular interventions on the welfare of individuals, groups and communities' (Macdonald, 2000b: 123).

EBP entails underlying claims regarding good practice that seem to go beyond a plea for reason-based professional judgement and practice. For example, when Sackett writes of evidence-use as being 'conscientious, judicious and explicit' this appears to entail three kinds of claim:

- A *moral* claim.'Conscientious' suggests done according to conscience; as a moral duty.
- A *wisdom* claim. 'Judicious' suggests sound judgement, and is a mark of practical wisdom and discretion.
- A claim to transparency and *openness*. 'Explicit' appears to have the sense of leaving nothing merely implied.

Evidence-based practice advocates often appear to distinguish hierarchies of evidence. Yeager and Roberts, for example, refer to evidence levels from meta-

4 Sheldon gives a straightforward adaptation of this definition to social work www.ex.ac.uk/cebss@introduction.html.

analysis through single randomized control trials (RCTs) to 'uncontrolled trials' and finally 'anecdotal designs' (2004: 6). In assessing evidence-based practice it is important to acknowledge that other factors, such as practice wisdom and values, *are* recognized by evidence-based practice protagonists. But there is still a general conviction that these should be subordinated to 'rigorous consideration of current best evidence…of the *effects* of particular interventions'. Again, the more thoughtful advocates of evidence-based practice do not claim that only randomized control trials provide evidence about effects, but rather that RCTs give the most secure evidence about internal validity, and that internal validity is crucial. The net effect of this is that RCTs are often believed to be the 'gold standard, the Rolls Royce of evaluation approaches' in the human services (Chelimsky, 1997: 101).

Commitments to certain ways of knowing typically bring with them, by their epistemological assumptions, constraints on the range of action and interventions that may follow (cf Romm, 1995). This has been particularly clear in countries where supervision of criminal justice orders and youth justice orders is done by social workers or specialist trained professionals. The conclusions drawn by many from 1970s research that 'Nothing Works' led to some demoralization of policy makers and practitioners. There has been a shift since then especially through confidence in cognitive and behavioural interventions. This has been given a major stimulus from work in Canada by Robert Ross and colleagues (Vanstone, 1999). Lipsey concludes that, assuming integrity of implementation, '(T)he more behaviourally oriented, skills-oriented, and multi-service programs tend to have larger effects' (Lipsey, 2002: 204). The general consensus on practice implications is that practitioners should:

- Target factors that have contributed to offending.
- Adopt methods that have structure and require active involvement in problem solving.
- Match degree of intervention to risk of offending.
- Have program integrity, i.e. avoid drift, objective reversals or non-compliance (Davies, 2000).

Promoters of evidence-based practice within the human services are not unanimous on whether professional practice shows up positively as a result. Fischer was predicting that 'by the year 2000, empirically based practice – the new social work – may be the norm, or well on the way to becoming so' (Fischer, 1993). That year has come and gone and Mullen laments that 'for the most part social work practitioners are not engaged in evidence based practice' (Mullen, 2004: 208), and Kirk and Reid remark of social work that, 'within the profession, science remains on the cultural margins, struggling for a voice and a following' (Kirk and Reid, 2002: x).

Practitioners may, of course, suspect they cannot win if they back an evidence-based approach. That would appear to be the case if Macdonald is correct when she claims that 'we frequently overestimate social work's beneficial effects and underestimate social work's capacity for adverse effects. In general, the more rigorous the research design, the less dramatic the former and the more transparent the latter' (Macdonald, 2000b: 124).

EBP Modifications, Directions and Reservations

The evaluative orientation of most evidence-based work in the human services owes most to accountability models of evaluation, and draws largely on quantitative and usually local, medium-scale inquiry projects. Typically, it makes little reference to the mainstream evaluation traditions or writers.

The original, fairly bullish versions of evidence-based practice in the human services have gradually been re-presented in terms that suggest a need to involve service users, and to take account of the local contexts in which services are delivered. General assertions that service users are – or at least ought to be – involved in EBP decision-making at the case level can be found in the recent literature. In the USA, writers who have not been strongly associated with stakeholder or justice based models of evaluation have added their voices to this claim (eg Corcoran and Vandiver, 2004; Gibbs, and Gambrill, 2002; Howard, McMillen and Pollio, 2003; Mullen, 2004). Similarly, the need to take account of local contexts has gradually been acknowledged. In one of the most fully developed examples of this modification, Proctor and Rosen (2003) say that 'Having a solid foundation of empirical support does not guarantee that a given intervention will meet the needs of a particular client' and, 'although sometimes given short shrift, local knowledge is an important complement to research-based knowledge' (Proctor and Rosen, 2003: 196, 197). They warn against the risk of over-committing to standardized interventions. This leads them to the issue of when and how an intervention should be modified to meet local contingencies. They support doing so, albeit in a careful and well-reasoned stepwise process. Practitioners should:

1. Locate evidence-based interventions relevant to the outcomes for pursuit.
2. Select the best-fitting intervention in view of the particular client problems, situation and outcomes.
3. Supplement and modify the most appropriate and best supported treatments, drawing on practitioner experience and knowledge.
4. Monitor and evaluate the effectiveness of the intervention.

Lying just beneath the surface is an acknowledgement that evidence-based practice has to hold on to a tension between routinization of practice and professional judgement. While this is occasionally recognized, it is but fleetingly so (cf Howard, McMillen and Pollio, 2003).

These modifications are unlikely to persuade committed constructivist human services evaluators or those committed to alternative visions for human services evaluation reviewed later in this chapter, but it is a significant shift of position, and one that hopefully will be more extensively developed. There *is* a softening of strong versions of EBP. Munson, for example, pleads for a version of evidence-based practice that is 'balanced with a relationship model' (Munson, 2004: 259). He argues that treatment 'must have a developmental focus using a scientific perspective that relies on evidence that is grounded in a therapeutic relationship' (p. 252). Evidence alone and relationship alone do not produce change, but both – and practice thus based has ethical implications. While advocates of a strong version of EBP appear to believe that the main risks of being unethical lie in being non-rational, Munson suggests that 'There must be monitoring for the subtle belief that only evidence-based tasks or outcomes have value' (254). Evidence-based practice must, he believes, address power issues and ethical aspects of, for example, lack of expressive capacity in traumatized children.

It would be misleading, however, if we assumed that the only direction of evidence-based practice is towards a softening and accommodation with those who have hitherto been its critics. Considerable effort is being made to develop evidence-based practice standards (Proctor and Rosen, 2003; Rosen, Proctor and Staudt, 2003), routinized guidelines (Mullen and Bacon, 2004; Okamato and LeCroy, 2004; Springer, Abell and Hudson, 2002a, 2002b), and strategies for learning and teaching evidence-based practice (Howard, McMillen and Pollio, 2003). Howard and colleagues tacitly acknowledge that evidence-based practice does not in practice provide a deliverable platform and are ready to allow that instructors 'can teach interventions without compelling empirical support as long as…there is sufficient justification for the intervention' and the available 'scientific support' for the intervention is also taught. They include 'strong theoretical justification' and 'practice wisdom' as grounds for teaching non-empirical practice (p. 248).

It is beyond the scope of this chapter to review the achievements and limitations of evidence-based practice, except to say I am not convinced the problems it raises have been adequately resolved by the present generation of evidence-based evaluators. Rationalist ideas of efficiency do not sit comfortably with, for instance, ideas of democratic participation. Cronbach goes as far as to say that, 'Rationalism is dangerously close to totalitarianism' (Cronbach et al., 1980: 95). In response to arguments that quasi-experimental designs are convincing and plausible, he and his colleagues say tartly that

> The demand that an argument be "convincing" is nothing more than a rationalist attempt to define a category of conclusions that in no way rest on belief and values; in evaluation it is an attempt to place decisions outside politics by establishing an inescapable conclusion. (p. 292)

Too often proponents of evidence-based human services suggest they hold undue confidence in the power of science to solve human problems. Evidence-based practice is presented as a continuation of the scientific revolution (Corcoran and Vandiver, 2004: 15), and 'a paradigmatic (*sic*) break with the authority based and idiosyncratic practice methods that have historically characterized social services… interventions' (Howard, McMillen and Pollio, 2003: 239). EBP too often seems to place faith in a discredited naïve falsificationism – a view that fallible theories can be tested with non-fallible facts (cf Howard, McMillen and Pollio, 2003: 247), and to be premised on a simple foundationalist assumption regarding the relationship between evaluation data and the real world. This on occasion tends to dogmatism, as when Howard and colleagues allude, in the context of teaching EBP, to the rise in malpractice actions against social workers, and the dangers of practising from alternative perspectives.

There is a further problem too little appreciated. The question, 'Does it work?' is a sceptical question and 'functions as an exclusionary gatekeeper' (Bogdan and Taylor, 1994: 296). Even assuming that design problems could be solved the question still would not be helpful to practitioners. 'Conscientious practitioners do not approach their work as sceptics; they believe in what they do' (p. 297). Bogdan and Taylor have worked to develop what they call 'optimistic research'. 'We have evolved an approach to research that has helped us bridge the gap between the activists, on the one hand, and empirically grounded sceptical researchers, on the other' (p. 295). The main focus of their research has been on questions of how people with severe disabilities can be integrated into the community. Rather than ask whether services are effective, they ask, 'What does integration mean?' and 'How can integration be accomplished?'

Outcomes and Interventions

If deliberations regarding evidence-based human services in the USA have concentrated on practice, parallel research and debate within the United Kingdom have more often crossed back and forth the borders of policy and practice. It is, of course, possible to find tough-minded proponents of evidence-based practice represented for example in the work of Macdonald, Sheldon, Kazi, McGuire and others. But beside this there can be observed two rather different groupings. First, an intellectual alliance of feminist, post-modern, critical, and learning-oriented social work researchers who are only partly preoccupied with an evaluative agenda, and second, a coalition of service-focused evaluation researchers convinced of the need to develop a broader evidence-based. This mix of stances towards human services evaluation can also be found in countries such as Sweden, Holland, Denmark, Switzerland, Finland, Norway, Spain, Australia, New Zealand, Canada and possibly in an emergent form in several eastern European countries.

Service evaluation in social care

It is the service-focused evaluation researchers that have made the most direct challenge – from within and without – to the case for strong evidence-based practice. The orientation of those identified with this approach has been helpfully captured in a recent review by Qureshi, who premises much of what she says on the belief that

> both policy and practice can be seen as occurring within multiple self-adjusting and interacting systems, characterized by non-linear relationships, uncertainty and fuzzy boundaries, giving rise to inherent unpredictability (Qureshi, 2004: 19)

In situations of complexity 'where uncertainty is high and agreement about action is low...professionals and policy-makers have more in common than might be supposed in terms of their best use of evidence' (p. 20).

Qureshi and her colleagues have developed this stance over some years through a programme of development-oriented research on outcomes with older people. Taking the example of domiciliary care she argues that the purpose of such care is not to *improve* health or quality of life, but to *maintain* quality of life. Put slightly differently she says that while health typically (not always) has 'cure' as its aim, social work with older people has 'care' as its aim. The outcome indicators will be different in each case. It leads to a focus on 'success' in *maintenance*.

Example 6.2 Outcomes into practice in adult social care

Hazel Qureshi

Background

Social workers play key roles in relation to the care of older and disabled people. Their assessments are critical in controlling access to publicly funded residential services, and in designing and implementing packages of care which will keep disabled people (of all ages) in their own homes with an acceptable quality of life. However there is criticism that the focus is too much on services actually available rather than desired objectives. At the same time, available statistical information from routine sources reveals little about outcomes for service users apart from whether or not they remain living at home.

Our initial scoping studies revealed that people at the front line in general did not practice in an outcome focused way, and indeed that people were confused by the prevailing health outcomes model, based on expectations of change and cure, which often did not seem to fit their work (Qureshi, 1999).

Aims and objectives.

The program of research, evaluation and development was designed to find ways to re-focus both practice and information collection on broader outcomes for service users, thus enhancing the scope for a more explicitly evaluative on-going approach in both of these areas.

What strategy was used in the evaluation/research/development described?

The program was conducted in two phases: first, widespread and inclusive consultation; second, collaborative research and development. The consultation was designed to investigate stakeholder concepts of outcome, and to identify realistic opportunities to incorporate a greater outcome focus in routine practice and agency information collection. In the research and development phase researchers worked with local agencies (staff at all levels and service users) to attempt to implement a number of the ideas generated during the first stage. The development process was researched to identify barriers and facilitators.

Results, key issues, and likely future directions.

The consultations generated a new framework for understanding social care outcomes which recognised that although change is sometimes an objective of interventions, maintaining a situation or state unchanged may, equally, be a considerable achievement. In addition, objectives may relate to the way in which services are delivered (Qureshi, 2003). Staff seminars and the joint development of new documentation successfully underpinned the introduction of a focus on appropriate outcomes in assessment and care management, as well as in the collection of evaluative feedback from service users (Qureshi and Nicholas, 2001, Nicholas, 2003).

The work demonstrates that the change issues involved in focussing on outcomes have to be actively addressed (Nicholas and Qureshi, 2004). One stream of work in a subsequent program has been to collaboratively produce materials to assist managers and trainers in adult services to bring about the necessary changes (Nicholas, Qureshi and Bamford, 2003). If these innovations are to spread, the ideas must be implemented without researcher input. There are already examples where people in services have imaginatively integrated the ideas into their own independent developments (Ball et al., 2004).

References

Nicholas, E. (2003) 'An Outcomes Focus in Carer Assessment and Review: Value and Challenge', *British Journal of Social Work*, 33 (1): 31-47.

Nicholas, E., Qureshi, H. and Bamford, C. (2003) *Outcomes Into Practice: Focusing Practice and Information on the Outcomes People Value – A Resource Pack for Managers and Trainers*, University of York, Social Policy Research Unit, York.

Qureshi, H. (1999) 'Outcomes of Social Care for Adults: Attitudes Towards Collecting Outcome Information in Practice', *Health and Social Care in the Community*, 7 (4): 257-265.

Qureshi, H. (2003) 'A Response to Dempster and Donnelly 'Outcome Measurement and Service Evaluation – A Note on Research Design': The Importance of Understanding Social Care Outcomes', *British Journal of Social Work*, 33 (1): 117-120.

Qureshi, H. and Nicholas, E. (2001) 'A New Conception of Social Care Outcomes and its Practical Use in Assessment with Older People', *Research, Policy and Planning*, 19 (2): 11-26.

This approach to practice, service and policy evaluation departs from a standard evidence-based model in four ways. First, it entails a criticism of any tendency to push for a hierarchy of evidence. '(T)here is no "hierarchy of research methods" that is independent of the question being asked' (Qureshi, 2004: 9). This is not a rejection or even criticism of randomized control trials as such, but rather a concern with 'the tendency to slip imperceptibly from the existence of a hierarchy of designs suitable for research on clinical effectiveness, to the existence of a "hierarchy of research methods" per se' (p. 9). 'Evidence is helpful, but rarely determines precisely what should be done to reach goals' (p. 20).

This language echoes House' early conclusion,

> Everyone agrees that information somehow informs decisions, but the relationship is not direct, not simple. Often the more important the decision, the more obscure the relationship seems to be. (House, 1980: 68)

House went as far as to say that, 'subjected to serious scrutiny, evaluations always appear equivocal' (p. 72). He argued that evaluations can be no more than acts of persuasion. 'Evaluation persuades rather than convinces, argues rather than demonstrates, is credible rather than certain, is variably accepted rather than compelling' (p. 73). Human services and social work evaluation researchers have generally plied their trade outside the evaluation community. While this has not always been to their disadvantage, the debate regarding service evaluation would have been enriched and pushed forward earlier, is there had been some mutual conversation on issues of evaluative judgement.

Second, there has been a push to accept a wider evidential base. Nicholas, for example in her work on carers, illustrates a growing recognition of the need to contextualize outcomes based policies. To assess outcomes for caregivers, Nicholas stresses the need to understand 'the complex, dynamic nature of care-giving which is interactive, contextual, temporal, based in relationships and on experience which changes over time' (Nicholas, 2003: 33). This leads to a wider acceptance of ways in which research findings may be useful for practice, without necessarily determining the form of intervention.

Sinclair and Wilson, in their discussions about effective fostering, make a central distinction between skilled performance in a particular situation [in this case 'responsive parenting'] and the prior conditions that make this likely – either conditions to do with the child, carer and their compatibility, or to do with the wider context (wider family; social worker, etc). They wanted to know why some cases were 'successful' or not and what processes underlie changes as some cases worsen and other improve.

They adopted an analytic induction approach with echoes of research and development tactics. Case interviews were followed by a review of the model. Further case interviews were succeeded by further modifications to the model. The case study they draw on confirms but also goes beyond the statistically derived model 'in identifying the processes involved in a way that is more precise and theoretically relevant' (Sinclair and Wilson, 2003: 1003, cf Wilson, Petrie, and Sinclair, 2003). This is an example of thoughtful, mixed-method development of good practice that develops the model from a large data set and utilizes a case study to check and deepen the conclusions (Wilson, Petrie, and Sinclair, 2003: 993). It can be placed as part of a strand of research on effective fostering that goes back to Parker (1966). As with much of British evaluative research, it does not make any attempt to make links to the evaluation community.

Third, the gradual development of government standards for evaluation and research evidence begins to illuminate the different kinds of evidence that can be cited. This may be to:

- Demonstrate the necessity of action to support *values*.
- Support the promotion of certain *preventative* interventions.
- Demonstrate the *existence and nature of a problem* to be solved. (Qureshi, 2004: 19)

Fourth and finally, service-focused evaluation in the UK and other countries gives greater emphasis to recognizing power dimensions of evaluation and developing some degree of inclusivity with service users. Qureshi argues that 'One can simultaneously have a concern for democracy, or inclusiveness, and an attachment to a hierarchy of evidence for effectiveness' albeit they will each provoke different evaluative questions (Qureshi, 2004: 13). This illustrates ways in which values and knowledge are brought together in the post paradigm war era. Paradigm language unhelpfully polarized positions on the place of theory, values and worldviews in evaluation. The debate was too often cast as being between the advocacy of incommensurability of worldviews and thus of choices of methodology, over against a position that, at its least, argued that differences of value, theory and worldview will never have conflictual implications for choice of method. Either position, so it seems to me, has only to be stated to be seen to be implausible. And if the latter position cannot be sustained, I wonder if the confidence of service outcome evaluators that service user inclusivity can be respected alongside a hierarchy of evidence for effectiveness may prove unduly sanguine. Adherence to ethical principles – eg through the democratization of research – *may* prove detrimental to service effectiveness. As Lewis some time ago expressed the general point, 'It is entirely possible that a manager who acts in an ethically commendable fashion may contribute to a less effective service for some and a more effective service for others' (Lewis, 1988: 282).

Intervention Research and Development

The broad stance on service evaluation remarked on in the previous paragraphs includes a thread of research and development. This R and D strand, however, has been especially marked in American social work intervention research. Intervention research has been fundamentally shaped by Rothman and Thomas' (1994) engineering perspective for intervention development. There are a limited number of intervention studies – 'about a dozen research reports a year (describe) an evaluated intervention in such detail that a practitioner might be able to replicate it' (Fraser, 2004: 212). A range of skills is needed:

> At once, intervention researchers must be clinical, substantive and methodological experts. They have to have good street sense. They have to be skilled in building partnerships with clinicians and agencies. Similar to good practitioners, they must be able to encode social cues, interpret social information, and regulate their own behavior to be effective in a variety of settings. (Fraser, 2004: 212)

A key bridging figure here is Bill Reid who died during the preparation of this handbook. Reid first became widely known through Anne Shyne and his book, *Brief and Extended Casework*, which reported an experimental study comparing short and long term social work intervention (Reid and Shyne, 1969). Planned short-term service provision yielded results at least as good as and possible better than open-ended intervention. In the context of the time, when long term casework was regarded as the ideal, 'in this particular race (Planned Short Term Intervention) needed only a tie to win' (p. 175).

Reid took the lead in developing and testing Task-Centred Practice – a short term, problem-solving approach to social work where the focus is on the problems that clients acknowledge as being of concern. Reid and Fortune describe the intervention as a 'short-term problem solving approach to social work practice' that 'fits well with current definitions of evidence-based practice' (Reid and Fortune, 2004: 226). With the cautious expansion of tested applications of task-centred intervention, it has latterly been presented as an 'open pluralistic practice system' with 'a core of values, theory and methods that could be augmented by compatible approaches' (p. 226-7). It is especially congenial to cognitive-behavioural, cognitive, and family structural therapies – ie an empirically backed approach that focuses on client action as a means of change.[5]

The model has been research-informed throughout, and has a strong empirical orientation (eg Reid, 1997). This connecting strand running though Reid's career provides the context for a range of concerns. *First*, his outcome research and review work on other studies was one plank in the gradual renewal of confidence in evaluative research (Reid, 1988, 1997; Reid and Hanrahan, 1982). His work noted the increasing 'dominance of structured forms of practice', in particular those influenced by 'the behaviour modification movement' (Reid and Hanrahan, 1982: 329). While he was convinced the helping professions can demonstrate they are effective, he warned that the practical significance of identified effects was often slight, and their durability ambiguous. He sometimes appeared doubtful about the methodological criteria of such studies. In his chastening and memorable metaphor, 'It is like trying to decide which horse won a race viewed at a bad angle from the grandstand during a cloudburst' (Reid, 1988: 48)!

In his observations on the direction of outcome research he commented favourably that 'The researcher as evaluator is giving way to the researcher as developer of models' (Reid and Hanrahan, 1982: 338). This reflects his *second* cluster of concerns. He regards his task-centred practice research as a step-by-step

5 There is a Task Centered web site at www.task-centered.com.

process of development, testing and further development. He sought to develop unobtrusive and practitioner-friendly methods for field testing the early trial versions of specific practice interventions (Reid, 1994b).

Reid's *third* contribution recommended ways in which considerations of epistemology and methodology should be applied to social work. For example, he explored the potential of 'change process research' (Reid, 1990). Practical and ethical constraints on experiments necessitate, in his view, the naturalistic study of process-outcome relations. A key notion about the process of change is that of understanding intermediate 'micro-outcomes' depicted through intensive study of smaller elements of practice. This gives central importance to the immediate context of practice. This avenue of research has the potential to be pulled towards either a stronger naturalistic, interpretive methodology, or towards more traditional notions of rigour. Reid opposed the latter and probably the former, and preferred to see the knowledge gained as 'one kind of provisionally valid knowledge' (1990: 144). Behind this careful steering was Reid's concern to reframe debate

> away from arguments about epistemological worldviews, and devote our energies instead to clarifying and resolving the specific issues embedded in these arguments. (Reid, 1994a: 465)

Reid is not the only significant figure in the intervention research field. Rothman and Thomas have made the most cited contribution (Rothman and Thomas, 1994). One insufficiently recognized failing of British social work evaluation lies in the absence of a research and development model in the development of social work intervention.

Single system evaluation

Human services evaluation has also proved a lively testing ground for the development of single system approaches to practice evaluation. Reports of single system evaluation have appeared in the social work literature, particularly in America, since the late 1960s. The strategy involves the intensive study of a one-client system, typically with before and after measures, as opposed to a more wide-ranging investigation of larger groups of service users. Single system designs have clear attractions over more traditional group experimental designs. Apart from the obvious resource reasons for not undertaking large group experiments, grouped data hide the very information that individual practitioners and service users need if they are to act directly on it. Group measures reveal *net* change, not *gross*, individual change. Single system designs avoid this problem. Unlike experimental, control group designs, that compare groups, single system designs make comparison between time periods for the same system, so that the individuals act as their own 'control' over time. Advocates of quasi-experimental, single system designs believe that such methods have advantages of practical feasibility, encouraging a systematic approach, improving assessment and planning decisions, continuous feedback on performance outcomes, and, for more rigorous varieties of design, the capacity to identify cause and effect.

There has been an interest in the extension of single system designs to non-behavioural interventions, which will continue to be a central point of growth and discussion. If greater flexibility can be demonstrated for the application of empirical designs, then their attraction will spread, and the argument that such designs can be applied to everyday realities of practice will be more persuasive than it has been so far.

Additional Developments in Outcomes Evaluation

Before moving away from outcome-oriented evaluative research, there are two contrasting areas of development that we have hinted at without comment. First, social work outcomes evaluation has played a part in the steady growth of research synthesis and meta-analysis. Second, the acceptance of the need for a wider evidential base, an interest in critical realism and sustained arguments from qualitative evaluators, have led to acceptance of the case for qualitative methods within outcomes research.

Synthesis and meta-analysis

The launch of the Campbell Collaboration has brought together people from Europe, the USA and elsewhere in a collaborative effort that is unusual within the human services. The demand for knowledge synthesis and practice prescriptions has also been strengthened in Britain through the establishment of the Social Care Institute for Excellence (SCIE).[6] The mode of operation of SCIE in its early years has included a multi-project programme designed to establish ground rules for knowledge utilization (e.g. Pawson, et al., 2003; Walter, et al., 2004) and to develop the basis for standards of good practice (e.g. Crisp, 2003).

We synthesize in order to generalize. For those who claim a hierarchy of evidence, meta-analysis stands at the head of pyramid. But meta-analysis has an ambiguous relationship to the use of randomized control trials. Its advocates regard meta-analysis not as an adjunct to randomized control trials but as a more credible basis of evidence. Randomized control trials (or the component studies in meta-analysis) then become a means to an end. This is a paradox. We must have randomized control trials, and the more the better, otherwise no meta-analysis, so the argument goes. But we must treat the results of any given randomized control trial with at best caution. 'We must be very cautious in interpreting a single set of results, even from a well-designed evaluation study' (Lipsey, 2003: 207).

Lipsey suggests five general conclusions from the application of meta-analysis to studies of programmes of intervention.

6 http://www.scie.org.uk.

1. Many programs are more effective than we thought.
2. Individual outcomes can easily produce erroneous results.
3. Method variations are related to outcome variations.
4. Program effectiveness is a function of identifiable program characteristics.
5. There is room for program improvement.

His second point poses the problem of how do we reconcile 'fact' that meta-analysis produces positive effect size but we cannot conclude from any given study that X works? Lipsey's response is that Type II errors, from small sample sizes, are part of the answer. The relevance of this point is accentuated because human services evaluations often depend on small samples. He also says that the lack of statistically significant results only says that we have failed to reject null hypothesis, not that we have confirmed the absence of effects. But he admits that this subtle distinction is lost on policy makers! He acknowledges that the sample size argument also counts against studies showing positive gains over against the control group. Treatment may be *worse* than we think.

His third point about the effect of method variations is also important for mixed method human services evaluations. Meta-analysis has demonstrated that the neutrality of the typical range of methods for outcome evaluation cannot be taken for granted. 'What we observe as program effects may reflect as much influence from the methods with which the program was studied, as the actual effects the program has on its intended beneficiaries' (Lipsey, 2002: 203). Fraser makes a similar point in his assessment of advances and challenges in intervention research. If outcome variance is due to in significant part to method, this may produce different results *between* methods, and, if unstable in its operation, may produce differences *within* the same method at different times. 'The plurality of our methods leads to complicated findings and fuzzy plausibility' (Fraser, 2004: 218). This shows that human services practitioners will need to exercise continued caution about synthesized judgements of effect.

Qualitative methods and outcomes

Scepticism and even antagonism still surface from time to time when qualitative evaluation methods are under consideration. Thyer, for example, has not found reason to retreat from his comment some years ago that

> Social work practitioner-researchers look in vain for qualitative research studies which have clearly demonstrated the effectiveness of social work intervention in solving problems of social importance (Thyer, 1989: 312)

There is a range of positions among those who take a more accepting line towards qualitative evaluation. These extend from a pragmatic 'horses for courses' position that sees method choice as epistemologically neutral and shaped simply by the practicalities of research planning and delivery (eg Cheetham, et al., 1992) to the reversal of this in which qualitative strategies are seen in some cases to be the method of choice where previously they would have been considered inappropriate (Patton, 2002; Shaw, 1999). In between lies a mixed method approach that is ready to accept that no single design can provide complete evidence. The language of triangulation is often drawn on as a metaphor for this approach and is well represented by Qureshi's work reviewed above. Fraser is among those with an essentially quantitative orientation to human services evaluation who urges qualitative researchers to address outcomes issues. 'If you are more oriented to qualitative research I ask you to study more than phenomena as they exist. Instead, devise a change strategy, implement it, and describe the processes leading to outcomes' (Fraser, 2004: 220). He accepts that it is impossible to develop culturally free methods. Culturally rooted concepts and categories 'are the core elements of constructs' (p. 219). Thus, for example, the use of scales raises the problem of 'scale equivalence' – alternate meanings may be given to items and response categories across people with different cultural backgrounds. This will be true both linguistically (meanings and nuances of words) and culturally (values attached to categories). The solution is *not* just greater sample size or sample diversity, but how we conceptualize. Conceptual differences (eg around race and ethnicity) may warrant separate activities within an intervention or even a separate culturally specific intervention.

This should not be read as a plea to replace one uniformitarian orthodoxy with another. On the one hand, a notion that *only* qualitative methods can examine unique, complex cases is clearly not accurate, as there is an interesting history of idiographic and ipsative quantitative methods for individual case analysis in psychology in the work of people such as Rogers, Allport, Cattell and Kelly. Likewise, I am not convinced that all forms and traditions of qualitative methodology lend themselves equally or even directly to evaluative purposes in the human services. Stake probably had this in mind when he remarked that 'to the qualitative scholar, the understanding of human experience is a matter of chronologies more than of cause and effect', and that 'the function of research is not…to map and conquer the world but to sophisticate the beholding of it' (Stake, 1995: 39, 43).

Understanding and Evaluating in Practice

This brief glance at ways in which qualitative methods contribute to understanding outcomes in human services has taken us some way from the strong versions of evidence based practice and meta-analysis that have been nearer the core of the chapter. The final part of this chapter takes us further still from evidence-based practice and policy. We will consider the connections between professional practice and evaluation research practice. We will also review the ways in which practitioners engage in disciplined inquiry. Finally, we will highlight the strong contribution that human services in general and social work in particular have made to the development of justice-based approaches to evaluation and research.

Qualitative Evaluation

Practitioners and evaluators may mutually benefit from considering how far the perspectives and methods of one provide a template for the other. The argument that qualitative research has a natural synergy with the processes of practice first strongly emerged in the writings of Jane Gilgun (1989, 1994) who proposed and elaborated the metaphor that practice fits qualitative research 'like a hand fits a glove'. Essentially, Gilgun's case is that practice and qualitative research share a number of common features: the focus on how informants construe their world is congruent with the social work injunction to start where the client is; the contextualization of data fits with the social work emphasis on understanding the person within their environment; 'thick' description of individual case studies is parallel to the social work individualization of social work processes of assessment and intervention; and so on. Martin Bloom exemplifies those who have been equally forceful opponents of the view that the perspectives and methods of qualitatively oriented inquiry find their reflection in good social work practice Bloom, 1999).

There is, of course, no unanimity in this. Padgett, a protagonist of qualitative research in social work, suggested that under closer scrutiny the glove really did not fit (1998a, 1999). Padgett reasserts the value of the contribution of qualitative research to the knowledge base of social work, but draws out a number of criteria by which she asserts that practice and research are very different undertakings, and that there are both scientific and ethical reasons for ensuring that the two are not conflated. Primarily she argues that both are located in different paradigms (practice is irredeemably theory and model driven, located within normative views of social or individual functioning whereas qualitative research is concerned with theory generation and is non-normative), goals and practice/research relationships. Practice has a series of mandates established between legal duties, the agency and service user which may be contested or in conflict but are presumed to be contributing to a notion of 'helping'; the goals of research are the development of knowledge and scholarship. Padgett's sting that provoked the strongest reaction was her argument that the conflation of research and practice was inherently unethical with compromises around standards of confidentiality, informed consent and withdrawal from research/ treatment (Padgett, 1998: 376).

My own position is that there is congruence at the level of logic between EBP and quasi-experimental evaluation. I am also persuaded that there is 'a sympathetic connection' between certain kinds of social work and qualitative kinds of data – 'talk, therapeutic conversation, agency records, narratives about experiences with organizations and macro systems' (Riessman, 1994: ix). The tie is proximate but neither universal, homogenous nor capable of straightforward transfer from one to the other. It requires methodological work, which I think can helpfully be described as involving 'counter-colonising' and 'translating' (Shaw, 1996). Counter-colonizing requires practitioners to challenge the conventional donor-client relationship between practice and social science, and act upon evaluation research methods rather than simply apply them. Translation raises issues of language and culture, and underscores the interpretative character of the process. Social workers need to develop a dialogic practice, both within social work and with methodologists. For example, Janesick's 'stretching' exercises for qualitative researchers are an example of work based on a learning rationale that provides a fertile basis for professional 'counter-colonising' and 'translating' (Janesick, 1998). The quality of 'methodological practice' will have an emergent, opportunistic and particularistic character. Whitmore's use of visual methods exemplifies this opportunist quality (Whitmore, 2001). To maximize the gains from this process social workers need to avoid remaining too much insiders. 'The familiar not only breeds contempt, it breeds darkness as well' (Eisner, 1988: xii). Above all, such 'methodological practice' will have a participatory and collaborative character.

Viewed through these lenses, we can observe how differences between evidence-based practice and more hermeneutically inclined evaluation are not superficial. They are present-day manifestations of differences extending back more than three hundred years, between evaluation undergirded by empirical philosophy, in which the mind is viewed as essentially passive in perception, and idealist philosophy, which emphasizes the active powers of the mind to create and transform reality. The postmodern turn in social work has yielded a mistrust of evaluation, in the sense of a search for foundational truth. Derrida and Foucault's critical appraisals of knowledge have led to uncertainty and an emphasis on 'the instability of meaning, the impossibility of arriving at foundational truths about the world, the myth of linearity and thus the impossibility of prediction, and the role of knowledge and technologies of cultural production in oppressive exercises of power and minority subjugation' (Penna, 2000: 262).

Practitioner evaluation Practitioner involvement in evaluation – research, development, or more general inquiry that is small-scale, local, grounded, and carried out by professionals who directly deliver those self-same services – is embraced across a wide range of professions as an essential ingredient of good practice.

McLeod has defined practitioner research as 'research carried out by practitioners for the purpose of advancing their own practice' (McLeod, 1999: 8). This definition has much going for it, although it is incomplete. First, it includes a statement of purpose, and hence incorporates an implicit criterion for assessing the quality of practitioner research. It is not adequate to define practitioner research simply as research carried out by practitioners, without grounding it on a basis of purpose. The boundaries between practitioner research and practitioners being trained as researchers will remain blurred, as will the relationship between practitioner research and, for example, Intervention Research of the kind discussed earlier in this chapter. Second, it makes explicit a practice rationale, rather than broader policy or academic rationales for research. Finally, it includes an implicit model of how practitioner research can be useful. McLeod seems to assume a fairly direct relationship between research and practice – or, as we may describe it, an 'instrumental' model of information use.

There have been several arguments in support of practitioner research in social work, two of the most frequently heard being the professional obligation to be self-evaluating, and the belief that research and practice draw on similar skills. McIvor aptly expressed these twin views when she says,

> The starting point…is the twofold belief that practitioners should be encouraged to engage in the evaluation of their own practice and that they possess many of the skills which are necessary to undertake the evaluative task. (McIvor, 1995: 210)

It is probably not helpful to search for the historical roots of practitioner research, although practitioners-as-researchers is no new idea. What is new is the range of arguments and exemplars offered for practitioner research, its independent emergence in British and American education in the 1970s, in American social work in the 1970s, and in a different form in 1980s British social work, and in the gradual deepening and diversification of the influence of qualitative methodologies on social work.

Practitioner research in social work is different between Britain and America. In the USA there is a vigorous 'scientific practitioner' movement based in general on outcome-oriented and quantitative methodology. We have already noted the importance of single-system designs in this context. The American social work journals have been the scene of continuing debate about the contribution of the empirical practice movement. Epstein has argued that both mainstream evaluation and social work practice have come to take 'psychic determinism' positions,

> that locate the source of human trouble inside the individual person, in some non-empirical site such as the soul, the spirit, the psyche, the mind, personality structures and similar venues. (Epstein, 1996: 115)

In doing so, evaluators and practitioners are 'concentrating on reading and changing the minds of poor people and those who are otherwise distressed and deviant' (p. 115). 'The problem in both cases is that the context is missing' (p. 116). The implicit answer to her appeal appears to include a more sociologically informed and qualitative practitioner research strategy. One approach to constructing such a strategy has been to analyse the differences and similarities in the data processing strategies of social work and qualitative research in order to assess ways in which they might be implemented (eg Lang, 1994; Ruckdeschel et al., 1994).

The limited empirical work on practitioner evaluation and research suggests it may be fruitful to consider its present character and future development in terms of the scheme shown in Figure 6.1 (Keane, Shaw and Faulkner, 2003):

A Project Ownership

Individual >>>>>>>>>>>>>>>>>>>>>>>>>>>>>>>>>	**Multiple**
No formal ethical approval	External formal ethical approval
Own practice as sole data source	*Cross-agency/cross-sector*
partnership	
No use plans beyond personal practice	Multiple planned uses
No funding	External funding from grant
giving body	
	Agency level agreement and
management	
	Service user involvement in project planning/fieldwork/utilisation
	Data from more than one agency
	Links with other practitioner research projects

B Research Methodology

Simple >>>>>>>>>>>>>>>>>>>>>>>>>>>>>>>>>>	**Complex**
Single data type	Multiple data sources and data
collection methods	
Lone researcher	*Collaboration with other PR*
researchers	
Low technology	*Computer assisted analysis*
Researcher has no methods training	*Utilisation takes place*
	Refereed published output
	Expert consultation resources

Figure 6.1 Dimensions of practitioner research in human services

I have not presented this typology as a normative framework – for example, it is *not* my view that the more complex the project the better it will be. But I am convinced that there is already great diversity in practitioner evaluation and this diversity will be linked to variation in the relevance, value and impact of practitioner evaluation in human services. The typology does raise questions as to the possibilities for kinds of practitioner evaluation that are rarely on show at the moment. I have *italicized* some features of practitioner evaluation at the right hand end of the two dimensions that – as far as I can judge – are rarely evident at present.

Visiting some of the origins and more recent directions in practitioner evaluation in social work prompts us to see it as a phenomenon that – rather than being special or narrowly associated with the place of social work in contemporary society – manifests a pervasive professional cluster of concerns about good professional practice. What evidence we possess suggests that the wider systems of which it is a part frequently hamstring the potential of such research to operate as more than a fringe operation – a 'street market' version of mainstream research. The probable volume of such research simply serves to underscore the irony and significance of this situation. Human service stakeholders need to foster ways in which social workers, service users, agency managers, academics, government departments, and universities can work to a transformative agenda for practitioner research – transformative for both practice and research. This will involve refashioning the interface between the methodology and methods of practice and research; generating practitioner research capacity; recognizing the subtlety and critical potential of a genuinely 'practical' agenda in practitioner research, and rescuing practitioner research from a simply technical information-providing function, that by-passes the challenge to promoting diverse forms of social justice.

Justice and Human Services Evaluation

Evidence, understanding – and justice. This final section of the chapter focuses on the third of the evaluative purposes in human services identified in the opening paragraphs. Different strands can be identified in the development of the idea of empowerment in social work. These include self-help, liberational, professional, managerialist and market models.

> Empowerment has become the site of key struggles over the nature and purpose of politics, policy, services and professional intervention. That is why its meanings are heavily contested and it is important to recognize its *regulatory* as well as its *liberatory* potential. (Croft and Beresford, 2000: 117).

In social work practice and policy in western nations professional and liberatory approaches have been most prominent, although considerable caution is necessary in generalizing, even across western countries and cultures.

> While professional approaches have focused on *personal* empowerment (bringing about change in the individual), the liberational approaches adopted by the disabled people's and service users' movements placer equal emphasis on personal and *political* empowerment. (Croft and Beresford, 2000: 117).

Croft and Beresford are talking about practice and policy, but their distinctions and cautions apply in a very similar way to how concern about the oppressive potential of human services in relation to eg race, gender and disability has emphasized the centrality of political, moral and human rights frameworks in shaping evaluative work. Evaluation is conventionally viewed as a relatively sophisticated means to a larger end. The problem focus, research design, fieldwork, analysis, reporting and dissemination of results are all seen as the work of experts seeking understanding that will be for the good of some present or future beneficiaries. One of the most far-reaching developments of recent years has been that practitioners within the human services increasingly have been challenged by forms of evaluation that are seen not as means to some external end but also (and for some advocates, solely) as ends in themselves. To borrow an apt phrase from Robert Stake, social workers have become 'reluctant to separate epistemology from ideology, findings from yearnings' (Stake, 1997: 471).

The forms taken by this radical challenge are varied and include feminist research, research within the disability movement, critical theory, justice-based commitments within research, participatory and reflective inquiry and qualitative evaluation as a dimension of direct practice. Advocacy positions cover a span of political stances. At one end is located *multi-partisan* and multi-vocal research. This is well established in some American evaluation research, for example in Lee Cronbach and Robert Stake, and also in much interpretive research. More explicit advocacy positions are associated with much British *reformist* policy evaluation, and with some participatory evaluation. Radical positions of critical inquiry include the majority of feminist inquiry, research from the disability movement and among mental health 'survivors', and the greater part of research that takes its primary impetus from neo-Marxist critical theory. These diverse positions stem largely from the different rationales that have been advanced for advocacy evaluation. There are three main rationales that parallel in some regards Croft and Beresford's ordering of empowerment positions.

Table 6.1 Foundations of advocacy evaluation

Foundation	Key words
Political	Power; empowerment; standpoint; structures
Postmodernism	Interpretation; meaning; local relevance
Interpersonal learning	Understanding; reciprocity

The foundation positions in Figure 6.2 are, of course, abstractions. There *are* those who take one main position, perhaps particularly when associated with relatively radical political rationales. But it is equally common to encounter those who bridge more than one position – either on practical and opportunistic grounds or on the basis of more general arguments. For example, Reason has been strongly associated with the development of reflective inquiry approaches, but belongs to no single 'camp'. He firmly rejects postmodernism as nihilistic and does not major on any political rationale. However, he distances himself from conventional science. Fetterman – probably the best known advocate of empowerment evaluation in the USA – sits closest to the third of these positions but has elements of the first. He regards empowerment evaluation as 'designed to help people help themselves and improve their program using a form of self-evaluation and reflection' (Fetterman, 2004: 585). Two examples where social work has made a distinctive impact on critical, empowerment evaluation are participatory empowerment evaluation, and user-led evaluation.

Participatory empowerment evaluation

Whitmore's account of an evaluation of a pre-natal programme for single, pregnant mothers illustrates how positive outcomes may on balance be achieved. The evaluation was carried out over several months by four women who had themselves been through the programme, with Whitmore as consultant to the project. There were tensions in the group, and communication failures. One member left and another protested to Whitmore that

> Our world is different from yours. The fear is that people always want to humiliate you, put you down (for being on welfare)...We have a different lifestyle from you. We just don't trust people the way you do. (Whitmore, 1994: 92)

Whitmore concluded that she could never entirely share the worlds of the women with whom she worked. 'My small words were often their big words. What I assumed was "normal talk", they saw as "professor words"' (p. 95). Martin arrived at similar conclusions from her own feminist participative research, concluding that such research 'places unrealistic expectations on the extent to which the researched can become involved in the research process', and that 'even when problems are a major concern to people (the researched) they have work and private lives which usually take priority, whereas research IS work for the researcher' (Martin, 1994: 142). But the strength of their final achievements is evidence that participatory evaluation with oppressed groups is not only political rhetoric.

User-led evaluation

Whitmore concludes from a subsequent participatory project with young people that

> We assumed that street-involved youth were in the best position to evaluate their own services and we were right. They could not have done this alone, however. As much as we want to believe in "community control", this has to be seen in context, and the reality is that marginalized populations will need our professional support and commitment in working with them. (Whitmore, 2001: 98)

This captures the edges between participatory evaluation and user-led and controlled evaluation. Social work has to some extent led the way on exploring the possibilities for a full-blown user-led evaluation. In Britain, for instance, there are examples in the fields of mental health, older people, and learning disabilities. My own involvement in projects of this kind suggests there are at least three ways this makes for better practice in the human services.

First, it shifts the focus of what professionals and evaluators think are key questions to those that sufferers and survivors think are central. The likely priorities that mental health sufferers and survivors place at the centre will probably include coping, identity, information needs, support needs, self-help, carers, women's issues, rights and opportunities.

Second, it challenges a reappraisal of what human services practitioners think is good intervention. For example, user-led evaluation prioritizes:

- An emphasis on telling stories (hence narratives).
- Ground level concerns. A comment from the floor in a national consultation of user researchers mentioned a Ghana proverb – 'A person who rides a donkey does not know the ground is hot'.
- Experience. In the same consultation, someone cited Paulo Freire as saying, 'Reading the world always precedes reading the word'.

Third, user-led evaluation yields a powerful sense of what is stigmatizing. What does it mean to live on a locked ward? How do users experience language? The 'service user' may be rejected because it implies a one-way consumption. 'Victim' carries similar passive connotations – as in Victim Support schemes. User evaluators may also avoid terms that define the whole person in terms of the role, as in 'carer'. 'Sufferer' – 'because I have suffered' as one woman said – and 'survivor' may seem stronger words.

Fisher (2002) has claimed that user controlled evaluation may lead to methodologically stronger evidence. It may:

1. Ensure a problem focus is less reliant on perspectives on social issues held by the dominant group.
2. Lead to more representative samples because of lower refusal rates.
3. Guarantee better data quality because participants will be less defensive, eg in interviews.
4. Lead to the development of outcome measures that:
    - Pay attention to the *processes* of service delivery.
    - Understand people within their *social context*.
    - Reflect the *diversity* of users' views on the quality of life.
5. Enable greater theoretical relevance and sensitivity to emerge during data analysis.

Possibly so, although the jury is still out. For the present, the benefits of user-led evaluation should not be treated as axiomatically better than other forms of evaluation. Nor should we slip into the solipsism of assuming only those who experience problems and services can understand them. It is not inevitable that evaluation that is justifiable on moral grounds will also be methodologically sounder. Also, there are ethical questions as to whether research principles around informed consent, and confidentiality/privacy are especially at risk in user-controlled research. Finally, even when an alliance of service users and research professionals is accepted as good practice, the role of independent academic judgement is not easily agreed. There are numerous methodological questions posed by empowerment evaluation. Are large dataset studies susceptible to empowerment evaluation (Truman, 1999)? More generally, does empowerment evaluation entail any prior methodological commitments, positively or negatively (cf Shaw and Gould, 2001: 169-172)? If human services *are* to be advocates, what implications does this have for debates about catalytic validity (Lather, 1986)?

Conclusion

We have reviewed three arenas of social work and human services evaluation, namely, evaluation designed to establish plausible *evidence* regarding best practice and then outcomes of policies, services and intervention; evaluation that aims to *understand* and learn about social problems, organizational responses, and direct practice; and evaluation seeking to promote *just* forms and outcomes of human services.

> Historically, the influence of science on direct social work practice has taken two forms. One is the use of the scientific method to shape practice activities, for example, gathering evidence and forming hypotheses about a client's problem. The other form is the provision of scientific knowledge about human beings, their problems and ways of resolving them. (Reid, 1998: 3)

Reid's distinction is fundamental and too little appreciated. The parts of this chapter reviewing evidence-based practice and evaluation of service outcomes emphasize the second form of influence. The final section on matters of justice and understanding accentuate the first form of influence. Both fields of work are the scenes of lively and mobile inquiry, thinking and practice.

References

Bloom, M. (1999) 'Single-system Evaluation' in Shaw, I. and Lishman, J. (eds) *Evaluation and Social Work Practice*. London: Sage.

Bogdan, R. and Taylor, S. (1994) 'A Positive Approach to Qualitative Evaluation and Policy Research in Social Work', in Sherman, E. and Reid, W. (eds) *Qualitative Research in Social Work.* New York: Columbia University Press.

Cheetham, J., Fuller, R., McIvor, G. and Petch, A. (1992) *Evaluating Social Work Effectiveness*. Buckingham: Open University Press.

Chelimsky, E. (1997) 'Thoughts for a New Evaluation Society', *Evaluation*, 3 (1): 97-118.

Conrad, K. (1985) 'Promoting Quality of Care: The Role of the Compliance Director', *Child Welfare*, 64 (6).

Corcoran, K. and Vandiver, V.L. (2004) 'Implementing Best Practice and Expert Consensus Procedures' in Roberts, A.R. and Yeager, K.R. (eds) *Evidence-Based Practice Manual: Research and Outcome Measures in Health and Human Services*. New York: Oxford UP.

Crisp, B., Anderson, M., Orme, J. and Lister, P. (2003) *Learning and Teaching in Social Work Education: Assessment*. London: Social Care Institute for Excellence.

Croft, S. and Beresford, P. (2000) 'Empowerment' in Davies, M. (ed.) *The Blackwell Encyclopaedia of Social Work*. Oxford: Blackwell.

Cronbach, L., Ambron, S., Dornbusch, S., Hess, R., Hornik, R., Phillips, D., Walker, D., and Weiner, S. (1980) *Toward Reform of Program Evaluation*. San Francisco: Jossey-Bass.

Davies, M. (2000) 'Nothing Works' in Davies, M. (ed.) *The Blackwell Encyclopaedia of Social Work*. Oxford: Blackwell.

Eisner, E. (1988) 'Educational Connoisseurship and Criticism: Their Form and Functions in Educational Evaluation', in Fetterman, D.M. (ed.) *Qualitative Approaches to Evaluation in Education*. New York: Praeger.

Fetterman, D. (2004) 'Empowerment Evaluation' in A.R. Roberts and K.R. Yeager (eds.) *Evidence-based Practice Manual: Research and Outcome Measures in Health and Human Services*. New York: Oxford UP.

Fisher, M. (2002) 'The Role of Service Users in Problem Formulation and Technical Aspects of Social Research', *Social Work Education*, 21 (3): 305-312.

Fraser, M.W. (2004) 'Intervention Research in Social Work: Recent Advances and Continuing Challenges', *Research on Social Work Practice*, 14 (3): 210-222.

Gardner, F. (2003) 'Critical Reflection in Community Based Evaluation', *Qualitative Social Work*, 2 (2): 197-212.

Gibbs, L. and Gambrill, E. (2002) 'Evidence Based Practice – Counterarguments to Objections', *Research on Social Work Practice*, 12 (3): 452-476.

Gibbs, L. and Gambrill, E. (2004) 'Measuring Skills and Reasoning Scientifically and Critically about Practice' in Roberts, A.R. and Yeager, K.R. (eds) *Evidence-Based Practice Manual: Research and Outcome Measures in Health and Human Services*. New York: Oxford UP.

Gilgun, J. (1994) 'Hand in Glove: The Grounded Theory Approach and Social Work Practice Research' in Sherman, E. and Reid, W.J. (eds.) *Qualitative Research in Social Work*. New York: Columbia University Press.

House, E. (1980) *Evaluating with Validity*. Beverley Hills: Sage Publications.

Howard, M.O., McMillen, C.J. and Pollio, D.E. (2003) 'Teaching Evidence Based Practice: Towards a New Paradigm for Social Work Education', *Research on Social Work Practice*, 13 (2): 234-259.

Janesick, V.J. (1998) *'Stretching' Exercises for Qualitative Researchers*. Thousand Oaks: Sage.

Kazi, M. (2003) 'Realist Evaluation for Practice', *British Journal of Social Work*, 33 (6): 803-818.

Keane, S., Shaw, I. and Faulkner, A. (2003) *Practitioner Research in Social Work and Social Care*. Cardiff: Wales Office for Research and Development.

Kirk, S. and Reid, W.J. (2002) *Science and Social Work*. New York: Columbia University Press.

Laird, S.E. (2003) 'Evaluating Social Work Outcomes in Sub Saharan Africa', *Qualitative Social Work*, 2 (3): 251-270.

Lang, N. (1994) 'Integrating the Data Processing of Qualitative Research and Social Work Practice to Advance the Practitioner as Knowledge Builder: Tools for Knowing and Doing' in Sherman, E. and Reid, W. (eds.) *Qualitative Research in Social Work*. New York: Columbia University Press.

Lather, P. (1986) 'Issues of Validity in Openly Ideological Research', *Interchange*, 17 (4): 63-84.

Lipsey, M.W. (2002) 'Meta-analysis and Program Outcome Evaluation', *Socialvetenskaplig Tidskrift*, 9 (2-3): 194-208.

Macdonald, G. (1999) 'Social Work and it Evaluation' in F. Williams, J. Popay and A. Oakley *Welfare Research: A Critical Review*. London: UCL Press.

Macdonald, G. (2000a) 'Critical Thinking' in Davies, M. (ed) *The Blackwell Encyclopaedia of Social Work*. Oxford: Blackwell.

Macdonald, G. (2000b) 'Evidence-based Practice' in Davies, M. (ed) *The Blackwell Encyclopaedia of Social Work*. Oxford: Blackwell.

Martin, M. (1994) 'Developing a Feminist Participative Research Framework' in Humphries, and Truman (eds) *Rethinking Social Research: Anti-Discriminatory Approaches in Research Methodology*. Aldershot: Avebury.

McIvor, G. (2000) 'The Evaluation of Effectiveness' in M. Davies (ed) *The Blackwell Encyclopaedia of Social Work*. Oxford: Blackwell.

McLeod, J. (1999) *Practitioner Research in Counselling*. London: Sage Publications.

Mullen, E. (2004) Facilitating Practitioner Use of EBP, in Roberts, A.R. and Yeager, K.R. (eds) *Evidence-Based Practice Manual: Research and Outcome Measures in Health and Human Services*. New York: Oxford UP.

Mullen, E. and Bacon, W. (2004) 'Implementation of Practice Guidelines and Evidence-Based Treatment', in Roberts, A.R. and Yeager, K.R. (eds) *Evidence-Based Practice Manual: Research and Outcome Measures in Health and Human Services*. New York: Oxford UP.

Munson, C.E. (2004) 'Evidence-based Treatment for Traumatized and Abused Children', in Roberts, A.R. and Yeager, K.R. (eds) *Evidence-Based Practice Manual: Research and Outcome Measures in Health and Human Services*. New York: Oxford UP.

Nicholas, E. (2003) 'An Outcomes Focus in Carer Assessment and Review: Value and Challenge', *British Journal of Social Work*, 33 (1): 31-47.

Okamato, S.K. and LeCroy, C.W. (2004) 'Evidence-Based Practice and Manualized Treatment with Children', in Roberts, A.R. and Yeager, K.R. (eds) *Evidence-Based Practice Manual: Research and Outcome Measures in Health and Human Services*. New York: Oxford UP.

Padgett, D. (1998) 'Does the Glove Really Fit? Qualitative Research and Clinical Social Work Practice', *Social Work*, 43 (4): 373-381.

Padgett, D.K. (1999) 'The Research-Practice Debate in a Qualitative Research Context', *Social Work*, 44 (3): 280-282.

Patton, M.Q. (2002) *Qualitative Research and Evaluation Methods*. Thousand Oaks: Sage Publications.

Pawson, R. and Tilley, N. (1997) *Realistic Evaluation*. London: Sage Publications.

Pawson, R., Boaz, A., Grayson, L., Long, A. and Barnes, C. (2003). *Types and Quality of Knowledge in Social Care*. London: Social Care Institute for Excellence.

Penna, S. (2000) 'Post-structuralism', in Davies, M. (ed) *The Blackwell Encyclopaedia of Social Work*. Oxford: Blackwell.

Proctor, E.K. and A. Rosen (2004) 'Concise Standards for developing Evidence-Based Practice Guidelines' in Roberts, A.R. and Yeager, K.R. (eds) *Evidence-Based Practice Manual: Research and Outcome Measures in Health and Human Services*. New York: Oxford UP.

Qureshi, H. (2004) 'Evidence in Policy and Practice: What Kind of Research Designs?', *Journal of Social Work*, 4 (1): 7-23.

Reason, P. (ed.) (1994) *Participation in Human Inquiry*. London: Sage Publications.

Reid, W.J. (1988) 'Service Effectiveness and the Social Agency', in Patti, R., Poertner, J. and Rapp, C. (eds) *Managing for Effectiveness in Social Welfare Organisations*. New York: Haworth.

Reid, W.J. (1990) 'Change-Process Research: A New Paradigm?', in Videka-Sherman, L. and Reid, W. (eds) *Advances in Clinical Social Work Research*. Silver Spring, MD: NASW Press.

Reid, W.J. (1994a) 'Reframing the Epistemological Debate', in Sherman, E. and Reid, W. (eds) *Qualitative Research in Social Work*. New York: Columbia University Press.

Reid, W.J. (1994b) 'Field Testing and Data Gathering on Innovative Practice Interventions in Early Development', in Rothman, J. and Thomas, E. (eds) *Intervention Research: Design and Development of Human Service*. New York: Haworth Press.

Reid, W.J. (1994c) 'The Empirical Practice Movement', *Social Service Review*, 68 (2): 165-184.

Reid, W.J. (1997) 'Research on Task-Centred Practice', *Social Work Research*, 21 (3): 132-137.

Reid, W.J. and Hanrahan, P. (1982) 'Recent Evaluations of Social Work: Grounds for Optimism', *Social Work*, 27: 328-340.

Reid, W.J. and Shyne, A. (1969) *Brief and Extended Casework*. New York: Columbia University Press.

Reid, W.J. and Zettergren, P. (1999) 'A Perspective on Empirical Practice' in Shaw, I. and Lishman, J. (eds) *Evaluation and Social Work Practice*. London: Sage.

Reid, W.J. and Fortune, A. (2004) 'Task-centred Practice: An Exemplar of Evidence-based Practice' in Roberts, A.R. and Yeager, K.R. (eds) *Evidence-*

Based Practice Manual: Research and Outcome Measures in Health and Human Services. New York: Oxford UP.

Riessman, C.K. (1994), 'Preface: Making Room for Diversity in Social Work Research' in Riessman, C.K. ed. *Qualitative Studies in Social Work Research*. Thousand Oaks: Sage Publications.

Roberts, A.R. and Yeager, K.R. (eds) (2004) *Evidence-Based Practice Manual: Research and Outcome Measures in Health and Human Services*. New York: Oxford UP.

Robinson, G. (2000) 'Prediction' in M. Davies (ed) *The Blackwell Encyclopaedia of Social Work*. Oxford: Blackwell.

Rothman, J. and Thomas, E. (1994) (eds) *Intervention Research: Design and Development of Human Service*. New York: Haworth Press.

Ruckdeschel, R., Earnshaw, P. and Firrek, A. (1994) 'The Qualitative Case Study and Evaluation: Issues, Methods and Examples' in Sherman, E. and Reid, W. (eds.) *Qualitative Research in Social Work*. New York: Columbia University Press.

Sackett, D., Rosenberg, W., Gray, J., Haynes, R. and Richardson, W. (1996) 'Evidence-Based Medicine: What it is and What it isn't', *British Medical Journal*, 312 (7023): 71-72.

Shaw, I. (1996) *Evaluating in Practice*. Aldershot: Ashgate.

Shaw, I. (1999) *Qualitative Evaluation*. London: Sage Publications.

Shaw, I. (2003) 'Qualitative Research and Outcomes in Health, Social Work and Education', *Qualitative Research*, 3 (1): 57-77.

Shaw, I. (2004a) 'William J Reid: An Appreciation', *Qualitative Social Work*, 3 (2): 109-115.

Shaw, I. (2004b) 'Qualitative Evaluation: Application of Reflective Practice in Direct Care Settings' in Roberts, A.R. and Yeager, K.R. (eds) *Evidence-Based Practice Manual: Research and Outcome Measures in Health and Human Services*. New York: Oxford UP.

Shaw, I. (2005) 'Practitioner Research: Evidence or Critique?', *British Journal of Social Work*, 35 (8): 1231-1248.

Sinclair, I. and Wilson, K. (2003) 'Matches and Mismatches: The Contribution of Carers and Children to the Success of Foster Placements', *British Journal of Social Work*, 33 (7): 871-884.

Springer, D., Abell, N. and Hudson, W. (2002a) 'Creating and Validating Rapid Assessment Instruments for Practice and Research: Part 1', *Research on Social Work Practice*, 12 (3): 408-439.

Springer, D., Abell, N. and Hudson, W. (2002b) 'Creating and Validating Rapid Assessment Instruments for Practice and Research: Part 2', *Research on Social Work Practice*, 12 (4): 768-795.

Stake, R. (1995) *The Art of Case Study Research*. Thousand Oaks: Sage Publications.

Stake, R. (1997) 'Advocacy in Evaluation: A Necessary Evil?' in Chelimsky, E. and Shadish, W. (eds.), *Evaluation for the 21st Century*. Thousand Oaks: Sage.

Thyer, B. (1989) 'First Principles of Practice Research' in *British Journal of Social Work*, 19 (4).

Thyer, B. (1998) 'Promoting Evaluation Research on Social Work Practice' in Cheetham, J. and Kazi. M. (eds) *The Working of Social Work*. London: Jessica Kingsley.

Truman, C. (1999) 'User Involvement in Large-scale Research: Bridging the Gap Between Service Users and Service Providers' in Broad, B. (ed) *The Politics of Social Work Research and Evaluation*. Birmingham: Venture Press.

Usher, C.L. (2004) 'Measuring and Evaluating Effectiveness of Services to Families and Children' in Roberts, A.R. and Yeager, K.R. (eds) *Evidence-Based Practice Manual: Research and Outcome Measures in Health and Human Services*. New York: Oxford UP.

Vanstone, M. (1999) 'Behavioural and Cognitive Interventions' in Shaw, I. and Lishman, J. (eds.) *Evaluation and Social Work Practice*. London: Sage Publications.

Walter, I., Nutley, S., Percy-Smith, J., McNeish, D. and Frost, S. (2004) *Improving the Use of Research in Social Care*. London: Social Care Institute for Excellence.

Whitmore, E. (1994) 'To Tell the Truth: Working with Oppressed groups in Participatory Approaches to Inquiry' in Reason, P. (ed.) *Participation in Human Inquiry*. London: Sage.

Whitmore, E. (2001) 'People Listened to What We Had to Say' in Shaw, I. and Gould, N. *Qualitative Research in Social Work*. London: Sage Publications.

Wilson, K., Petrie, S. and Sinclair, I. (2003) 'A kind of loving: a model of effective foster care', *British Journal of Social Work*, 33 (8): 991-1003.

Chapter 7
Evidence from Qualitative Evaluation*

Professional practitioners act or decline to act, feel confident or uncertain they have a sound basis for their actions and decisions, draw prescriptions or confess agnosticism, and all in the light (or gloom!) of the best evidence they can reasonably assemble. But what is the status of such evidence? Can professionals safely act on the assumption that it provides a good enough approximation to reality, which will transfer to similar new situations? Or should they remain deeply sceptical of all similar information on the grounds that it is the contingent, relative product of a unique local context, and may also represent the interests and constructions of the powerful?

There is a welcome vigour in current advocacy of the need to make evidence 'work' for professional practice. The very phrase, 'evidence-based practice' captures a confident belligerence, a tone of 'prove-it-or-else'. The language of goals, objectives, outcomes and effectiveness challenges reliance on sentimentality, opinion-based practice, intuition or lay knowledge. The phrase, along with its companion question, What Works?, has gradually crept into official formulations. The term was being used in academic literature on evaluation research from at least 1980 (Weiss, 1980: 387), and was common currency in official reports in the USA by the mid 1980s (US Department of Education, 1986). Although medicine is often seen as the model for aspirants to emulate (Sackett and Rosenberg, 1995), teaching, nursing, social work, youth policy, policing, prisons, pharmacy, librarians and probation work all have their performance measured against evidence-based criteria (Kirkpatrick and Lucio, 1995).

We pointed briefly in Chapter 1[1] to reasons why evidenced based practice should not be the first resort of professionals or evaluators eager to establish secure grounds for effective practice. However, the idea of evidence based practice helpfully problematizes the notion of evidence in two ways. *First*, evidence based practice helps support the important assumption that some central issues of evidence are not special to any given occupation but are shared across superficially very different professions. Evidence based practice promotes this assumption by insistently asking the same core questions of all and sundry. Qualitatively grounded forms of inquiry also promote the same assumption through a more

* Originally published as I. Shaw, 1999. 'Evidence from qualitative evaluation', Chapter 3 of *Qualitative Evaluation*. London: Sage. Reprinted with permission of Sage Publications Ltd.

1 This, and all other cross references in this chapter, refer to chapters in the original publication (Shaw, 1999).

inductive, bottom-up approach to understanding practice, shorn in part of prior assumptions that we already know what a given profession is really about. *Second*, evidence based practice forces attention towards direct practice rather than broader programme evaluation strategies and agendas, which have dominated the theorizing of evaluation.

This chapter explores the background issues that shape debate and practice regarding evidence. They are posed, perhaps too simply, as a series of alternatives.

- Should evaluation be based on a particular paradigm of evaluation practice, or on pragmatic, even opportunistic, initiatives?
- Can we discover an objective, real picture of the world, or are all evaluative accounts contingent relativities?
- Should evaluation be planned according to the demands of scientific rigour or practice relevance?

In Chapter 4 we move our footholds to consider how the answers to these questions need also to take into account a series of more 'use-oriented' questions.

- How do we know if we are doing evaluation right?
- Are the results of evaluation research used through direct application to problems or through a more general process of enlightenment?
- What ethical principles and decision rules should guide qualitative evaluation?
- How should our answers to these questions shape the methodology we use?

Paradigms and pragmatism

'Paradigm' is a thorny word. Indeed, it has become a 'bucket word' (Popper) to hold diverse meanings. If we take it in a general sense of 'a basic set of beliefs that guides action' (Guba, 1990: 17) we are only a little further forward. It would give even a mildly tendentious philosopher a heyday with each of the five key words in this definition! How many such 'basic sets of beliefs' are there? Convinced social science paradigmists do not always agree. Perhaps there are two – qualitative and quantitative, or positivist and postpositivist, or realist and idealist? Maybe there are three – realist, hermeneutic and critical theory? But possibly there are four – positivist, postpositivist, constructivist, and critical theory?

Before you despair and decide to skip this section altogether, the particular question at issue is fortunately slightly more straightforward. Is it the case that in order to be consistent, evaluators must choose one or another? Is there an inherent inconsistency in subscribing to the worldview of one approach but employing the methods of the other?

Filstead, for example, advocated a strong paradigm position, as a means of promoting qualitative evaluation (Filstead, 1979). He viewed the classic arguments between realism and idealism as lying at the root of the debate. Faith in reason became expressed through faith in science, and was exemplified in logical positivism. To those influenced by European idealist philosophies, the mind is the source of knowledge and the social world is created by individuals who live in it. Quantitative evaluation represents the first paradigmatic approach and qualitative evaluation the second. Jacob adopts a paradigmatic position in her frequently cited review of qualitative research traditions in American education research (Jacob, 1987). However, she criticizes the treatment of qualitative research as a single approach, and draws on Kuhn's notion of 'traditions' to identify five different schools of thought. Her plea is that applied researchers should align themselves with a tradition. 'Studies outside traditions are likely to be poorly focused, conceptually unclear, and weakly implemented' (Jacob, 1987: 38).

Take for a moment the distinction between quantitative and qualitative approaches to practice evaluation. Hammersley does not subscribe to a paradigm stance. However, he helpfully summarizes ways in which others have distinguished the elements of each pole. These can be represented as in Table 7.1 (Hammersley, 1992: Ch 10):

Table 7.1 Quantitative and qualitative paradigms

	Quantitative	**Qualitative**
Data is:	Quantitative	Qualitative
Fieldwork in:	Artificial settings	Natural settings
Empirical focus is on:	Behaviour	Meaning
Natural science model is:	Accepted	Rejected
Analysis proceeds by:	Deduction	Induction
Theorising seeks:	Laws	Patterns
Philosophy of:	Realism	Idealism

Guba argues that all such paradigms respond to three basic questions (Guba, 1990: 18):

- What is the nature of reality? A question of ontology.
- What is the nature of the relationship between the knower (inquirer) and the known (or knowable)? A question of epistemology.
- How should the inquirer go about finding out knowledge? A question of methodology.

In the following discussion we will pursue Guba's basic questions to discern three possible paradigm positions, realist postpositivism, critical evaluation, and constructivist evaluation. Each position includes major diversity over issues such as objectivity (realist postpositivism), the advocacy role of the evaluator (critical evaluation), and relativism (constructivism). But the three positions have general coherence and correspond closely to major developments in the philosophy of science (Bernstein, 1976; Outhwaite, 1987; Phillips, 1987a). We should be warned that the prefix 'post' is used in different and potentially confusing ways in the literature. For example, in the term *postpositivism*, 'post' is used to convey that this is a position that keeps some of the key ontological/epistemological premises of positivism, with some more or less radical changes to doctrines of realism and subjectivity. Thus, 'post' serves to signal a greater or lesser element of *continuity* with the position it conditions. However, in the term *postmodernism*, 'post' is used to convey that the key motives and *motifs* of the modernist enterprise are challenged. What unites adherents to this position is what is challenged. 'Post' in this context serves to signal the element of *discontinuity* with the position it conditions.

Realist postpositivism

Positivist is a convenient term of abuse that has been much over-used. Yet it is rarely a term which attracts public adherents. It is, as Raymond Williams long ago remarked, 'a swearword by which no-one is swearing' (Williams, 1976). Despite claims to the contrary, positivism has been in decline for at least 50 years. Attacks on practitioners or academics as 'positivists' are generally ill-informed and damaging (Shaw, 1999). Miles and Huberman do admit to being 'soft-nosed positivists' (1994), but this merely indicates their commitment to a thoroughgoing version of realism. Positivism is no longer a serious choice within qualitative evaluation research.

For the *positivist*, 'the business of science is to discover the true nature of "reality" and how it "truly" works'. It also has an objectivist epistemology, and the idea of an Archimedean point. Archimedes is said to have remarked that given a long enough lever and a place whereon he could stand, he could move the earth. 'Objectivity is the Archimedean point…that permits the inquirer to wrest nature's secrets without altering them in any way' (Guba, 1990: 19).

Phillips provides a plausible account of the reasons for the demise of positivism (Phillips, 1990a). Three developments have been crucial in creating near unanimity among social scientists that there are no absolute justifications of scientific assertions. *First*, the role of observation as the final arbiter has been revalued. For example, the acceptance that some mechanisms are unobservable led to the rejection of the belief that concepts can be reduced to a set of operational, observational statements. Equally influential has been the rejection of the assumption that observation can be theoretically neutral. The recognition that all observation is 'theory-laden' is shared by all three positions described here. In the words of Hanson, whose *Patterns of Discovery* fired people's imaginations on this issue, 'there is more to seeing than meets the eyeball'. 'Justificationism' – the view that knowledge equals proven knowledge – is almost universally rejected.

But realist postpositivists are united in arguing that theory laden observation does not entail relativism, and that it is possible to sustain a version of a correspondence view of truth – that research can represent social phenomena that are independent of it (Hammersley, 1995: Chapter 4; Phillips, 1990b).

Second, the relationship between theory and observation was shown to be more complex than previously thought. It became clear that theories are 'underdetermined' by nature, such that we are never able to say that we have the best theory, and a variety of theories can be constructed that are equally compatible with the available evidence. This has led to the unanimous rejection of 'foundationalism' – the view that research findings of indisputable validity can be a foundation for policy. We should note, however, that this should not lead to a belief that theories are always fallible whereas the empirical base for them is not fallible. Lakatos labels this position 'dogmatic falsificationism' (Lakatos, 1970). He rightly rejects the caricature that 'science grows by repeated overthrow of theories with the help of hard facts' (p. 97). This scepticism regarding the value of theory simply reinstates a new version of theory-free observation. Observations are so in the light of a given theory, and 'there are and can be no sensations unimpregnated by expectations' (p. 99). Therefore, although there are no *absolute* justifications, this does not mean there are *no* justifications. Yet while we may be warranted in holding particular views, we cannot assert that something is true, that our warrant is unchallengeable, or that it will for ever be warranted – '*nothing* can guarantee that we have reached the truth' (Phillips, 1990a: 43). There are ironic, invisible inverted commas whenever Popper speaks of 'experiment', 'empirical base', 'observation' 'applying theories' and so on. 'If a theory is falsified, it is proven false; if it is "falsified" it may still be true' (Lakatos, 1970: 108; Shaw, 1996a: Chapter 6). Popper's falsifying arguments have been criticized. Nonetheless, the thesis that science (and hence evaluation research) should be both critical and fallible is central – both as commitment and tension – in all realist postpositivism.

Third, the view that there is a steady accumulation of findings and theories, and that science grows thus, has been effectively challenged by Kuhn, Popper, Lakatos and others.

The continuity between positivism and postpositivism should not be overemphasized. Guba is surely engaging in tongue-in-cheek mischief when he says that the only alternative to relativism is absolutism (Guba, 1990). Phillips rightly insists, 'In no sense is (this) new philosophy of science…closely akin to positivism' (1990a: 39). Postpositivist evaluators and those influenced by them, actively engage in partial trade-offs, of rigour to gain relevance, precision to gain richness, theoretical elegance to gain local applicability, and measures of outcomes to promote inquiry into process, meaning and local context.

Critical evaluation

Critical theory – or more specifically *critical evaluation* – is a catch-all term to include neo-Marxist evaluation (Anderson, 1989; Lather, 1991; Popkewitz, 1990), some feminist positions (Dullea and Mullender, 1999; Swigonski, 1993), the work of Paolo Freire, and some forms of participatory inquiry (Reason and Rowan, 1981). These approaches are 'critical' in the sense that problems are conceptualized as part of the social, political and cultural patterns in which the evaluand is formed. The form of critical inquiry focuses on the contradictions of practice. Hence the basic logic is not preoccupied solely with the formal organization of argument, 'but also particular forms of reasoning that give focus to scepticism towards social institutions' (Popkewitz, 1990: 49). For example, critical evaluation of schooling is not merely about learning but has implications which continually relate the evaluation to larger issues of social production and reproduction (Carr and Kemmis, 1986). This typically involves an 'inversion' which entails 'making history fragile…thus poking holes in the causality that confronts us is daily life and that limits our possibilities' (Popkewitz, 1990: 49).

Hence, critical knowledge from evaluation is never neutral. 'It is always for some particular subject' (Comstock, 1982: 374). The production of knowledge is the production of values. This has major implications for the role of the evaluator.

> Social scientists are participants in the socio-historical development of human action and understanding. As such they must decide the interests they will serve. The only legitimate activity of a critical social scientists is to engage in the collective enterprise of progressive enlightenment. (Comstock, 1982: 377)

There are internal differences within critical evaluation at this point. For perhaps a majority of representatives of this position, the partisan role of science makes it an obligation to pursue political commitments through active participation in political movements. This 'entails a direct and explicit involvement in efforts to transform current social relations' (Popkewitz, 1990: 49). To quote Popkewitz' own position again, 'social scientists are partisans in the forming of social agendas through the practices of science' (p. 50). Thus activism is implicit, whereby inquiry discloses ways in which people are to challenge the world and locate themselves in its ongoing relations.

There are lively debates within critical research and evaluation. Neo-Marxists have strongly criticized the *a priori* theorizing tendency of critical theorists, and have called for 'critical inquirers to practice in their empirical endeavours what they preach in their theoretical formulations' (Lather, 1986b: 258). Others have insisted that both traditional and emancipatory research need to be interrogated, 'and *both* may be found wanting' (Humphries, 1997: 4.6). Critical evaluators need to acknowledge 'the permanent partiality of the point of view of those of us seeking to construct emancipatory research' (4.8). There are differences in the extent to which critical evaluators place emphasis on the classic Marxist concept of false consciousness. Those who place heavy emphasis on false consciousness are likely to place equally heavy weight on structural conditions, whereas those who place little or no emphasis on false consciousness will give central significance to inter-subjective meanings. Indeed, it may not be too much of an exaggeration to say that where people stand on this is the single most important determinant of the critical theorist's stance on epistemology and methodology. We return to some of these themes in the next chapter.

Constructivism

The third paradigm, *constructivism*, is perhaps best known through Guba and Lincoln's book on *Fourth Generation Evaluation* (Guba and Lincoln, 1989). The outline of their work in the previous chapter will stand for a sketch of the constructivist/interpretivist position. Their work has attracted inevitable discussion, both for its epistemological stance, and for its methodological strategy. Constructivism is also associated with the names of Smith and Schwandt. Schwandt seeks to recast evaluation in terms of practical acts of interpretation, often described for this reason as an interpretive or hermeneutic approach. He criticizes postpositivism on grounds of its alleged modernism.

> (We) resist three modernist tendencies: (1) ... to conceive of knowledge only as the acquisition of power to control self, society and nature; (2) .. to assume that method holds the key to knowledge; (3) ... to define the individual knower as in complete control of self, nature and social arrangements. (Schwandt, 1997: 78)

The approach he advocates involves the positions

> (1) that the social world..can only be studied from a position of involvement "within" it, instead of as an "outsider"; (2) that knowledge of that world is practical-moral knowledge and does not depend upon justification or proof for its practical efficacy; (3) That we are not in an "ownership" relation to such knowledge but we embody it as part of who and what we are. (p. 75)

Adherents of all three paradigms accept the position that observation is theory-laden. However, constructivism enthusiastically embraces the theory-ladenness of facts, the value-ladenness of facts, and the interactive nature of inquiry whereby the knower and the known are 'fused into a coherent whole' (Guba, 1990: 26). Hence the concern of the constructivist working out of a strictly relativist position is not so much with understanding more accurately but with understanding more deeply, more truly. Inquiry is not therefore an epistemological task but a moral and practical activity. No meaning has epistemic privilege. 'The kind of understanding one has of understanding makes a great deal of difference to the understanding one has of qualitative inquiry' (Smith, 1993: 199).

While a challenging variety of constructivist positions exist, these extracts helpfully catch the recurrent *motifs* of paradigm-based constructivism. The position is gaining increasing voice in the evaluation journals, stimulated by the 1989 'Alternative Paradigms Conference' (Guba, 1990), although these sources may perhaps be less vocal in Britain than in the USA.

The basic constructivist evaluative commitment is to story-telling. 'Stories are the closest we can come to experience as we and others tell our experience… Experience in this view, is the stories people live. People live stories, and in the telling of them reaffirm them, modify them, and create new ones' (Clandinin and Connelly, 1994: 415).

Much of the debate surrounding constructivism is focused on the relativist framework, and the feasibility and consistency with which that relativism is espoused (Heap, 1995; McLennan, 1995). There has also been concern regarding the even-handedness with which constructivists frame the debate. McLennan, for example, suggests extended criticism of some feminist postmodernism on the grounds that opposing views are persistently cast as 'absolutist'. He complains that this is 'a near scandalous truncation of the highly varied philosophical labours which have gone into this issue...(and) over-polemicizing to the point where scholarship simply does not come into the picture' (McLennan, 1995: 401). We have more to say on this issue in the second part of this chapter.

To return to our initial questions, is it the case that to be consistent, evaluators and practitioners must choose one paradigm? Is there an inherent inconsistency in subscribing to the worldview of one approach but employing the methods of the other? Lincoln answers eloquently in the affirmative.

> The adoption of a paradigm literally permeates every act even tangentially associated with inquiry, such that any consideration even remotely attached to inquiry processes demands rethinking to bring decisions into line with the worldview embodied in the paradigm itself. (Lincoln, 1990: 81)

Smith and Heshusias similarly conclude with a qualified 'no' in answer to the question whether quantitative and qualitative inquirers can even talk to each other. 'In the end, the two sides may be close to speaking different languages – a neutral scientific or value-free language versus a value-laden language of everyday discourse' (Smith and Heshusias, 1986: 11). Constructivists are not the only advocates of paradigm stances. Popkewitz acknowledges that accommodation occurs at the practical levels of hiring practices in universities and academic debate, but of the theoretical level, he says, 'Here, I guess, I leave the pluralism'.

> To include a disciplined sense of history into methodology...rejects "seeing" the discrete events, whether bound to "qualitative" or "quantitative" techniques, in isolation from the relation of events to historical formulations. (Popkewitz, 1990: 65)

Pragmatism

However, loud replies in the negative can be heard from different quarters. The mainstream position of evaluation theorists takes a mixture of postpositivist and pragmatic positions (Cook, 1985; Patton, 1990; Reichardt and Cook, 1979;

Scriven, 1997; Shadish, 1995). Chelimsky represents this mainstream position when she says,

> What should count is not the favoured method of a particular group, but rather how well we answer the question or achieve the purpose..it matters little which perspective or purpose has been adopted: honesty is critical and advocacy is not really an option. (Chelimsky, 1997: 109)

Some ethnographers have also argued for pragmatism. Hammersley, for instance, is strongly opposed to pragmatic arguments for the validity of research (1995). However, he is equally resistant to paradigm stances, and argues that for each of the seven elements of the divide between qualitative and quantitative methods (Figure 7.1), characteristics of each paradigm element can always be identified in examples of research conducted under the alternative paradigm. Miles and Huberman have also warned against the temptation in epistemological debates to 'operate at the poles'. 'In the actual world of empirical research, we believe that all of us – realists, interpretivists, critical theorists – are closer to the centre, with multiple overlaps' (Miles and Huberman, 1994: 4-5). Perhaps the most well-known ethnographic voice on this issue is that of Howard Becker. Writing of epistemological issues, he says, 'I think it is fruitless to try to settle them…These are simply the commonplaces, in the rhetorical sense, of scientific talk in the social sciences, the framework in which the debate goes on. So be it…There's nothing tragic about it' (Becker, 1993: 219). We should take an empirical perspective on such matters, treating them as 'a topic rather than an aggravation' (p. 222). But we should beware the paralysing effect of too much methodological discussion. 'We still have to do theoretical work, but we needn't think we are being especially virtuous when we do' (p. 221). Rather than regard such theoretical work as the responsibility of all qualitative researchers, he is content to view it as a specialism – the profession of 'philosophical and methodological worry' (p. 226)!

Support for some kind of pragmatism can be found also in Eisner and Stake. Eisner asks 'what can be more enslaving' than to have 'one framework, one language…one drummer to whom scholars and teachers…can listen', and suggests 'it is more a matter of seeing what works, what appears right for particular settings' (Eisner, 1991a: 211). We have already seen in Chapter 2 that Stake rejects the use of the term 'model' as raising false hopes.

Pragmatism is attractive for a variety of reasons, and makes for some unexpected bedfellows. We should distinguish between *methodological* pragmatism and *philosophical* pragmatism. Methodological pragmatism rests on an impatience with philosophy and an emphasis on real world evaluation and practice, and it is claimed that methods can be separated from the epistemology out of which they have emerged. The emphasis is thus on practical utility and the credibility of the methods used. Most of the pleas for pragmatism referred to above are of this kind. For example Patton puts forward a case for what he describes as a 'paradigm of choices'.

> A paradigm of choices rejects methodological orthodoxy in favour of *methodological appropriateness* as the primary criterion for judging methodological quality. (Patton, 1990: 38-9)

Gage envisages the time when there will be a triumph of pragmatic resolutions of paradigm differences, based on a realization that paradigm differences are based on researchers simply studying different topics, often from a different discipline perspective (Gage, 1989). The guidelines and regulations for professional education in perhaps all the English speaking countries typically take broadly pragmatic stances, despite lobbying from evaluation constituencies. For all those who hold this position, 'the specific methodology employed is less important than the overall approach to action and research' (Kelly, 1985: 144).

Methodological pragmatism typically leads to a rejection of both epistemological and methodological 'purism', a contentment with a 'good enough' methodology, and a pluralist approach to specific methods. Thus, in complaining about the 'philosophically besotted', Scriven says

> it is better to build on what might conceivably be sand…than not to build at all… It is a waste of time to try to solve the problems of epistemology without getting on with the job. (Scriven, 1997: 478, 479)

Reid argues to similar effect if more temperately for social work.

> Irreconcilable conflicts may indeed exist in the discourse of philosophers, but their perspectives are not essential to the task of resolving differences and building consensus in the practical worlds of social work. (Reid 1994b: 478)

Reid wants to 'redefine the nature of the mainstream so that qualitative methodology is part of it, not apart from it…Neither method is inherently superior to the other, but rather each provides the researcher with different tools of inquiry' (p. 477).

There are overlapping concerns between methodological pragmatism and *philosophical pragmatism*. However, there are important differences. Philosophical pragmatism draws especially on the work of American philosophers, and has been invigorated by recent work by Richard Rorty, whose arguments have exercised a growing influence (Rorty 1979, 1991).

> When confronted with a knowledge claim the pragmatist is less concerned with whether it is right and asks instead, "What would it be like to believe that?" "What would happen if I did?" "What would I be committing myself to?"…This shifts the focus of inquiry from verification and the appeal to method, to practice and an appeal to deliberation and conversation. (Schwandt, 1993: 18)

Reid applies a less relativist version of some of these ideas to social work. He believes such a stance 'will take us further than grand epistemologies that trade in abstract assertions about Truth, Reality and so on', and locates himself 'within the tradition of American pragmatism, especially as it has been set forth in the writings of Pierce, James, Dewey and Rorty' (Reid, 1994b: 472). He and Zettergren (1999) develop the interesting idea of empirical practice as a *perspective* which allows an interchange with humanist and advocacy approaches.

Pragmatic arguments have also been used within some work on feminist postmodernism – one of the unexpected bedfellows referred to earlier. The element of surprise stems from the radical's fear that pragmatism tends to political complacency.

> Characteristic of these methodologies are their orientation to decision making and hence to management, their primary emphasis on producing useful information, their practical and pragmatic value base, and their eclectic methodological stance. (Greene, 1994: 532-3),

Example 7.1 Can pragmatism be radical?

Rorty believes that pragmatist philosophy may be useful to feminist politics. He hopes that feminists will consider the possibility of dropping realism, and the notion that the subordination of women is intrinsically abominable. He also urges them to drop the claim that there is something called 'right' or 'justice' or 'humanity' which has always been on their side.

He is modest about the nature of the enterprise. 'Yoking feminism with pragmatism is like yoking Christianity with Platonism...something big and important, a vast social hope, is being yoked with something comparatively small and unimportant' (Rorty, 1991: 6).

Applying pragmatism in this way is utopian rather than radical. Radicals think there is a basic mistake deep down at the roots.

Pragmatists cannot be radicals in this sense, but they can be utopians. They do not see philosophy as providing instruments for radical surgery..Philosophy's function is rather to clear the road for the prophets and poets, to make intellectual life a bit simpler for those who have visions of new communities (p. 6).

It thus allows for an appeal to courage and imagination. 'On my view philosophy bites other philosophies, but not social problems as such' (p. 12).

The application of such more careful ideas of pragmatism to evaluation is still in its infancy. But it has the potential to critically integrate aspects of postpositivist, constructivist and empowerment approaches to evaluation. My own position lies with a strong version of the *fallible* realism of postpositivism, the *constructed* character of reality, and the central role of political and personal *interests*. On paradigms, my premise is that 'the relationship between paradigms and methods is an empirical question' (Pitman and Maxwell, 1992: 732). Yet I think that Hammersley overstates the weakness of the relationship between epistemology, values and methods. People's actions, in evaluation as much as in any other activity, *are* shaped by values and worldviews, and paradigm positions do *not* inevitably tend to the intolerance suspected by Atkinson and colleagues (Atkinson, Delamont and Hammersley, 1988). Professional practitioners and evaluators have sometimes been guilty of naïve pragmatism of the variety that says, 'if it works, it's true'. I agree with Greene when she dissents from the methodological pragmatism that avers epistemological purity does not get research done. Rather, 'epistemological integrity does get meaningful research done right' (Greene, 1990: 229).

As early an advocate of paradigms as Filstead conceded that 'the middle ground of blending the assets of both approaches throughout an evaluation is optimal', and as enthusiastic a proponent as Guba allows there is now a 'more ecumenical stance' in the shared acknowledgement that both verification and discovery methods can go on in all paradigms (Filstead, 1979: 43; Guba, 1990: 23). Guba and Lincoln's case is that disagreement is at the level of basic axioms, rather than methodological postures. Writing out of a postpositivist position, Reichardt and Cook are probably safe to stop at the point that 'paradigms are not the sole determinant of choice of methods', and to conclude there is a 'real but imperfect linkage between paradigm and method' (Reichardt and Cook, 1979: 16).

This essential tension between philosophical paradigms and practice is likely to remain contested. 'It matters to evaluators because it has important effects on how we envision and do our work' (Greene, 1996: 537). In discussing paradigmatic approaches we have touched on issues of realism and relativism, trade-offs between relevance and rigour, and the uses of evaluation. This fairly extended discussion of paradigms and pragmatism has signalled the kind of solutions I am likely to suggest for each of these issues.

Realism and Relativism

We opened the chapter with the dilemma of realism and relativism as it faces professionals in their day to day practice. Are practitioners working with fairly direct evidence of reality, with relativist constructs, or the standpoints of the powerful? 'Realism', as with paradigm, is a word that has attracted increasingly varied and differentiated meanings. Speaking of one variety of realism, Leplin wryly remarks that, 'Like the Equal Rights Movement, scientific realism is a majority position whose advocates are so divided as to appear a minority' (Leplin, 1984: 1).

Realism as applied to evaluation is usually assumed to demand an absolutist view of the role of evaluative inquiry, referred to as foundationalism. This is thought to involve a strict correspondence view of truth, that evaluation can fully represent realities independent of the inquiry process. We have noted already that this naive form of realism is a straw man, which retains the positivist adherence to the role of observation as discloser of the true nature of reality, and a confidence in the objectivity of the evaluator. However, this does not preclude the presence of strong versions of realism in some varieties of qualitative evaluation. Blumer and Harré are perhaps the best known representatives. For instance, Blumer argued that a constructivist view

> does not shift "reality", as so many conclude, from the empirical world to the realm of imagery and conception...(The) empirical world can "talk back" to our picture of it or assertions about it – talk back in the sense of challenging and resisting, or not bending to, our images or conceptions of it. This resistance gives the empirical world an obdurate character that is the mark of reality. (Blumer, 1969: 22)

Constructivism is not incompatible with realism. Indeed, this is simply to repeat the point we made about realist postpositivism in the context of paradigms. On this view of things we can maintain belief in the existence of phenomena independent of our claims about them, and in their knowability, 'without assuming that we can know with certainty whether our knowledge of them is valid or invalid' (Hammersley, 1992: 50).

A critical or fallible realism is the stance of most of those identified with postpositivism as well as Blumer and Harré. It is also the position of the majority of evaluation theorists such as Scriven, Campbell, House, Cook, Shadish, and, with some ambiguity, Stake.

> The essence of this position is that, although a real world, driven by real natural causes, exists, it is impossible for humans truly to perceive it with their imperfect sensory and intellective mechanism. (Cook and Campbell, 1979: 29)

A range of views co-exists within fallible realist evaluation. For example, the term 'objectivity' means different things to different realists, as does the idea of 'cause'. Some would not be very far from a strict positivist position in respect of their apparent belief that evaluation can provide an account closely approximate to reality. Others, such as the writer, take the position that, while some version of objectivity remains as a 'regulatory ideal' (Phillips, 1990a: 43), evaluative processes and results are always significantly jeopardized by interests, the social location of the evaluator and powerful stakeholders, and, in Guba's surprisingly realist phrase, 'nature's propensity to confound' (Guba, 1990: 19).

Such epistemological modesty does not necessarily lead to modest aspirations for social change. For example, Campbell's strong fallibilism is harnessed to a bold vision of an experimenting society, and from within social work Reid has asked, 'Is it better to make limited but well documented progress or to work toward more important goals with less certainty of what we have attained?' (Reid, 1988: 45). Yet fallible realist evaluators are less likely to pronounce confidently that they have got it right. They are likely to concur with Phillips when he admits that 'the objectivity of an inquiry does not guarantee its truth…*nothing* can guarantee that we have reached the truth' (Phillips, 1990a: 43).

The most influential developments in the last two decades have stemmed from the field of scientific realism. The most prominent advocates within evaluation are House in America and Pawson and Tilley in Britain (House, 1991; Pawson and Tilley, 1997a). Scientific realism is a complex field with more than its share of internal contradictions. Leplin, for example, lists ten claims that are characteristic of realism, but no majority of which is likely to be endorsed by any one realist. Yet

> What realists do share in common are the convictions that scientific change is, on balance, progressive, and that science makes possible knowledge of the world beyond its accessible, empirical manifestations. (Leplin, 1984: 2)

The counterpoint to this continuing commitment to a realist basis of evaluation is a radically relativist epistemology of evaluation, fashioned around assumptions that truth is a matter of consensus, facts do not have meaning except within some value framework, and causes and effects exist only in that they are imputed. Relativist evaluators unequivocally reject the whole idea of a correspondence view of truth. It requires 'independent access to both domains of mind and an independently existing reality', say Smith and Heshusias, 'which we cannot have' (1986: 10). Relativists believe that problems, findings and solutions from one context cannot be generalized to another. Evaluators are subjective partners with stakeholders in the literal creation of data, and act as orchestrators of a negotiation process. Hence, evaluation data have neither special status, but represent simply another construction to be taken into account in the move to consensus. There are consequently multiple shapers of accountability, no single one of which can be singled out for accountability.

The main criticisms of relativist evaluation are similar to those against social science relativism in general. It suffers from the well-known problem of being self-refuting, in that if it is true then it applies to itself. 'If it is true then it applies to itself; and therefore it is true relative to a particular culture or framework, and may be false from the perspective of other cultures or frameworks' (Hammersley, 1992: 49). Hammersley has also argued that one of the effects of relativism is that its adherents 'tend to oscillate between undiscriminating tolerance and ideological dogmatism'. The latter is a contsant risk, he and Gomm suggest, because there are no grounds within a specific community to oppose enforcement of the paradigm (Hammersley and Gomm, 1997: 3.3). This can lead to stalemate, sometimes encountered in evaluation, where each side is able to claim that their views are 'true'.

A further particular problem connected with relativist evaluation is that constructions become divorced from any anchor point to structures and interests. They appear little more than personal, mental constructs, as when Guba concludes that 'realities exist in the form of multiple mental constructions…It is the mind that is to be transformed, not the real world' (1990: 27). But reality is not simply and solely a mental product. It comprises social, collective acts, and these collective acts are material transactions with the world.

The confessedly relativist position of writers such as Guba, Lincoln, Smith and Schwandt also poses special difficulties for practising evaluators, deriving from the pressure on them to seek guidelines and support for their work which will give it credibility and trustworthiness.

> Evaluators sense particular pressure to invoke such procedures because the contexts of program evaluation continue to demand assurances of methodological quality and data integrity in evaluative work. This work can make no contributions to social policy and program decision making unless it is perceived as credible and trustworthy. (Greene, 1994: 537)

Relativism has as a consequence been troubled by practitioner struggles. Writing of qualitative evaluation Greene remarks that

> Many qualitative practitioners struggle with the dissonance invoked by the assumed mind-dependence of all social knowledge claims in the face of the contextual (as well as personal, ego-related) demands to "get it right", to "find out what's really going on in this setting". (Greene, 1996: 280)

The final argument that has been developed against some forms of constructivist and relativist evaluation and social problems research is that they are guilty of what has been called 'ontological gerrymandering' (Woolgar and Pawluch, 1985). The point requires a few sentences to explain the precise argument involved. Constructivist (or as Woolgar and Pawluch prefer, 'definitionist') arguments regarding social problems analyse changing definitions of behaviour and conditions, in terms of claims-making activities of the individuals concerned. A given deviant behaviour or condition – for example, child abuse, prostitution, drug abuse – becomes defined in society as gaining new or increased problem status. The most common definitionist argument is that since the basic background condition has not changed, variations in the definition of the condition must result from the social circumstances of the definers rather than from the condition itself. 'The lynch pin is the assumption that the condition itself does not vary' (Woolgar and Pawluch, 1985: 215). The problem arising from this explanatory strategy is, 'how do authors manage to portray statements about conditions and behaviours as objective while relativizing the definitions and claims made about them?' (p. 216).

> The successful social problems explanation depends on making problematic the truth status of certain states of affairs selected for analysis and explanation, while backgrounding or minimizing the possibility that the same problems apply to assumptions upon which the analysis depends. (p. 216)

It is this strategy of creating and managing boundaries between assumptions understood to be problematic and those understood not to be problematic, that Woolgar and Pawluch describe as 'ontological gerrymandering'. Constructivists proceding in this way fail to acknowledge that their assertions regarding the constancy of the background condition must itself be construed as a definitional claim.

Heap describes this problem in terms of monism and dualism. The meaning of monism taken by Heap is the metaphysical position that only one kind of thing exists, whereas dualism is the metaphysical position that two kinds of thing exist (mind/matter, body/soul, reality/representation, and so on). For example, the realist evaluation position described earlier in this section is clearly dualist – there is knowledge and there is 'knowledge' (representation). A strict relativist position is, on the other hand, monist. Evaluators are concerned with both the *domain* of inquiry (the evaluand) and the *inquiry* itself. For the consistent relativist 'the domain of inquiry is considered to consist of constructions, and the inquiry itself is seen to consist of constructions' (Heap, 1995: 55). There is no objective reality against which the inquirer's claim can be judged.

Heap's contention, persuasively illustrated from Guba and Lincoln's writings, is that there are deep inconsistences between the rhetoric and practice of fourth generation evaluation. While they argue constantly that the domain of inquiry is constructed, their methodology is assumed always in dualist terms. We have seen an example of this already, in Guba's phrase regarding 'nature's propensity to confound' (Guba, 1990: 19), where he presumes a world that is not simply a mental (or social) construction. Heap gives several other illustrations of Lincoln and Guba's presumption of the existence of independent, intersubjectively accessible evaluands in the domain of inquiry.

Woolgar and Pawluch, and Heap each conclude that the inconsistency apparent here cannot be eradicated. 'Perhaps all attempts at accounting (explaining) depend upon presenting at least some state of affairs as objective' (Woolgar and Pawluch, 1985: 224). Selective relativism of the kind Heap identifies in Guba and Lincoln may not be 'mere technical difficulties in social problems arguments, but pervasive features of all attempts to explain social phenomena' (p. 224). Heap skips Woolgar and Pawluch's 'perhaps'.

> Evaluation, and policy studies, can be taken up consistently and cogently only from a dualist social constructionist position...*Evaluation inquiries necessarily are dualist*. A monist position that there are no real evaluands, only constructions of them, entails the claim that there is nothing to evaluate, unless one wants to evaluate constructions of evaluands. (Heap, 1995: 58)

The arguments against relativist evaluation are generally persuasive. However, there are also serious difficulties attached to realist evaluation involving its assumptions regarding the overall progressive character of scientific knowledge.

Rigour or relevance?

Reid's choice between limited and well-documented goals or working to more important goals with less certainty, illustrates one of the central 'trade-offs' that appears to face evaluators. Some have argued for objectivity and validity as the highest imperatives of the evaluator. For the outside evaluator 'both distancing and objectivity remain correct and frequently achievable ideals' (Scriven, 1997: 483). Scriven's arguments for remaining distant, undertaking goal-free evaluation, the priority of summative evaluation over formative evaluation, and for dismissing 'so-called participatory design' as 'about as sloppy as one can get, short of participatory authoring of the final report' (p. 486), are unlikely to find favour with qualitative evaluators. I find them either wrong-headed or other-worldly. But they remain important strands in the argument for evaluative rigour.

However, the wind has been blowing strongly in the direction of addressing issues of relevance as well as, and in some cases instead of, traditional ideas of rigour. Ironically it was the honest doubting of writers such as Campbell that opened the way for such changes. For example, writing in 1974 when 'many of our ablest and most dedicated graduate students are increasingly opting for the qualitative, humanistic mode', he expounded his insistence that qualitative, commonsense knowing is the building block and test of quantitative knowing.

The mainstream among social work evaluators has for some time abandoned the claim that experimental and quasi-experimental designs, and single system designs, can yield confident information about cause and effect. It is widely conceded that we are involved in 'social inquiry for and by earthlings' (Cronbach, 1986).

The possibility for rigorous evaluation has also been conditioned by loss of faith in the rationality of organizational decision making, and by the extensive work done first in the mid 1970s on the nature of policy making, and the ways in which information is used in such processes. This fed through to changed views about how evaluation is and can be used to change programmes, projects and practices. The problem of relevance arises in a sharp form in qualitative evaluation because of its idiographic approach. The findings have to be made relevant by appeal to appropriate arguments about generalization, or to inference from the design and process by which the evaluation was carried out.

Where should we stand then on issues of relevance? The question involves six different aspects. We discuss the first four aspects in the final pages of this chapter, and the fifth and sixth aspects in Chapter 4.

1. How do evaluation problems emerge and gain agreement?
2. Should evaluators be concerned to develop theory?
3. How does scientific knowledge relate to common sense and professional knowledge?
4. Can evaluation results be generalized to other similar or even somewhat different settings or practices?

5. What are the criteria for a good evaluation?
6. How are – or ought – the results of evaluation to be used?

First, relevance involves issues of how evaluation problems emerge and are agreed. Arguments for practitioner evaluation and action research are often based on claims of increased relevance, and that 'any losses in research rigour are more than compensated for by gains in the acceptability of the research' (Kelly, 1985: 148). The development of 'responsive evaluation' by Stake and others has also widened the involvement of stakeholders in practical agendas of problem setting.

Second, the rigour *versus* relevance issue has been pulled in different directions by the unresolved question of whether evaluators should be concerned to develop theory. By theory, we mean substantive theory. Greene has previously complained that

> Contemporary discussions of qualitative approaches to evaluation are filled with clamorous dialogue about methodological theory and practice, but only whispers of concern about the nature and role of substantive or programme theory. (Greene, 1993: 26)

'Theory' is, of course, difficult to define. Indeed, in one important sense we have already argued from the theory-laden character of observation that there is no distinction between theory and fact. Even bracketing that consideration, difficulties may still exist because theory may refer to formal propositions, a worldview, or a working hypothesis. 'You can't pick up rocks in a field without a theory', as William James apparently said.

My own answer to the question whether qualitative evaluators should engage in substantive theory development is 'in some cases'. I do not accept the position of several theorists and writers on evaluation that theory development is the task of research, not of evaluation. But the question of theory development poses special questions for evaluation. It will not do for ethnographers to simply rap the knuckles of qualitative evaluators for not being good theorizing ethnographers (Atkinson and Delamont, 1993). Greene invites us to explicate our own theoretical predispositions, describe local programme theories ('locally meaningful theoretical perspectives on data interpretation': Greene, 1993: 38), attend to emergent theoretical issues, and integrate theory into evaluation conclusions and recommendations. The unanswered problem (acknowledged by Greene), is how such theorizing should reflect contested evaluative purposes.

Those who claim to do atheoretical evaluation are actually doing one or some combination of three other things:

1. They hold their theories tacitly, without reflecting upon them or stating them explicitly.
2. They hold them explicitly but deliberately withhold them from public view.

3. They pack structural concepts that properly belong to theory into their methodology where they are hidden from their view as well as ours. (Garrison, 1988: 24)

Greene has more recently detected 'an opening up of qualitative evaluation to the potential contributions offered by theoretical ways of looking and seeing' (Greene, 1996: 282). Such developments are none too early.

Third, developments in how we think regarding the logic of evaluation have also helped to draw on practical criteria of relevance. There has been a welcome influence of ideas regarding practical reasoning, informal and working logic, and the stimulating impact of neo-Aristotelian ideas of practical reasoning. These developments all help push a distinction between mainstream research rigour and more practical, everyday reasoning and logic, which also include ethical reasoning. We should note four questions.

- How should qualitative evaluators regard common sense knowledge – their own and others?
- How do practitioners think regarding evaluation?
- What is meant by arguing the practical character of a task?
- Does practitioner evaluation rely on similar or different forms of inquiry from those of the evaluative researcher?

Common sense knowledge, especially that possessed by those on the receiving end of evaluation, has for some time been given weight (Campbell, 1978; Mayer and Timms, 1970). Smith is pushing at an open door when he proclaims interpretivists think

> it is time to dispense with the long-standing claim that the knowledge of researchers is inevitably superior to, and thus can stand automatically in judgement of, the knowledge of others, such as parents and teachers. (Smith, 1992: 100)

Anthropologists, such as Geertz, have suggested several reasons why we should treat common sense as a cultural system – 'a relatively organized body of thought, rather than just what anyone clothed and in his right mind knows' (Geertz, 1983: 75). If it *is* a cultural system and not mere matter-of-fact apprehension of reality, then 'there is an ingenerate order to it, capable of being empirically uncovered and conceptually formulated' (p. 92). It is here, of course, that the argument 'bites' on qualitative evaluation. Pleas to treat common sense seriously must in part include pleas to treat it empirically. The common sense picture of the odd, the deviant, the tediously mundane, and the difficult, provide us with out-of-way cases. They are hence of use to us anthropologically, by setting nearby cases in an altered context.

Geertz undertakes this 'disaggregation of a half examined concept' (p. 93). He contends that the uses we gain from common sense are by understanding its 'stylistic features, the marks of attitude that give it its peculiar stamp' (p. 85), rather than its varied content. He identifies properties of 'naturalness', 'practicalness', 'thinness', 'immethodicalness', and 'accessibleness' as those general attributes of common sense found everywhere as a cultural form.

Common sense is much more than the explanation of the untutored citizen offered by the professional or academic expert. Recent reflections on the place of professional practice wisdom owe an indirect debt to this realization. If evaluation is to be relevant it cannot ignore the untutored (or tutored) ways in which practitioners endeavour to make evaluative sense of their practical activities (Shaw and Shaw, 1997a, 1997b). But this raises a further question. What do we mean when we describe such activities as 'practical'? In considerations of this question the renewed influence of Aristotelian views of theory and practice surfaces in various quarters, including ethnography (Hammersley, 1992), constructivism (Schwandt, 1993) and critical evaluation (Carr and Kemmis, 1986). The main effects of this have been twofold. First, it has led to a welcome reinstatement of the ethical dimension of reasoning and practice. Second, it has rescued notions of the practical from its status as second tier, derivative, and derived prescriptively from formal theory. Hence Schwab insists that by practical 'I do *not* mean...the easily achieved, familiar goals which can be reached by familiar means', but to 'a complex discipline...concerned with choice and action' (Schwab, 1969: 1, 2).

Reflection on common sense understandings also leads eventually to the question whether practitioner forms of evaluation rely on similar or different forms of inquiry from those carried out by the evaluative researcher. We will see in Chapter 6 that practitioner evaluation raises a range of interesting questions that differ from the arguments and solutions of some earlier programme evaluation theory.

Fourth, can evaluation results be generalized to other similar or even somewhat different settings or practices? For the moment we simply note the significance of the question posed. Generalization raises special problems in qualitative research. The greater the emphasis on the local and the contingent, the more wary one will inevitably be about extrapolating conclusions to other places and times. There are, no doubt, ways and means of addressing the task, some of which lend themselves with particular appropriateness to evaluative practice. Erikson, for instance, invites stimulating comparisons between inference in research and in the clinical setting (Erikson, 1959). Geertz has similarly suggested that the task of generalizing within rather than across cases is exactly like the clinical inference process (Geertz, 1973: 26).

The connection to questions of relevance *versus* rigour is apparent in terms of the familiar distinction between Type 1 and Type II errors – false positives, and false negatives. Cronbach has complained somewhere that evaluation researchers have been too prone to accept Type II errors (false negatives), out of a misreading of the risk of Type 1 errors. We have already noted in Chapter 2 that he is ready to trade off precision (fidelity') against relevance ('bandwidth'). There are more things in heaven and earth than are dreamt of in our hypotheses, he would doubtless say. Once we major on gaining control through enhancing the internal validity of evaluations, relevance is likely to suffer. '"External validity" – validity of inferences that go beyond the data – is the crux of social action, not "internal validity"' (Cronbach et al., 1980: 231).

Quantitative evaluation researchers are fond of accusing qualitative researchers of lack of precision, in their failure to turn their assertions of the typical into quantities. But qualitative evaluation should hold its position. The accusation fails to distinguish precision and wider accuracy. It is the latter that is important. Answers may be precise – but wrong.

We have considered three questions at the heart of understanding the evidence gained from qualitative evaluation. Should evaluation be based on a particular paradigm of evaluation practice, or on pragmatic, even opportunistic, initiatives? Can we discover an objective, real picture of the world, or are all evaluative accounts contingent relativities? Should evaluation be planned according to the demands of scientific rigour or practice relevance?

References

Anderson, G. (1989) 'Critical ethnography in education: origins, current status, and new directions' in *Review of Educational Research*, 59 (3): 249-270.

Atkinson, P. and Delamont, S. (1993) 'Bread and dreams or bread and circuses? A critique of case study research in evaluation', in Hammersley, M. (ed), *Controversies in the Classroom*. Buckingham: Open University Press.

Atkinson, P. Delamont, S. and Hammersley, M. (1988) 'Qualitative research traditions: a British response to Jacob', in *Review of Educational Research*, 58 (2): 231-250.

Becker, H. (1993) 'Theory: the necessary evil', in Flinders, D. and Mills, G. (eds), *Theory and Concepts in Qualitative Research: Perspectives from the Field.* New York: Teachers College, Columbia University Press.

Bernstein, R. (1976) *The Restructuring of Social and Political Theory*. Oxford: Blackwell.

Blumer, H. (1969) *Symbolic Interactionism: Perspective and Method.* Englewood Cliffs, NJ: Prentice-Hall.

Campbell, D. (1978) 'Qualitative knowing in action research', in Brenner, M. and Marsh, P. (eds) *The Social Context of Methods*. London: Croom Helm.

Campbell, D. (1979) 'Degrees of freedom and the case study', in Cook, T. and Reichardt, C. (eds), *Qualitative and Quantitative Methods in Evaluation Research.* Beverly Hills: Sage.

Carr, W. and Kemmis, S. (1986) *Becoming Critical: Education, Knowledge and Action Research.* London: Falmer Press.

Chelimsky, E. (1997) 'Thoughts for a new Evaluation Society', in *Evaluation*, 3 (1): 97-118.

Clandinin, J. and Connelly, F.M. (1994) 'Personal experience methods', in Denzin, N. and Lincoln, Y. (eds), *Handbook of Qualitative Methods*. Thousand Oaks: Sage.
Comstock, D. (1982) 'A method for critical research', in Bredo, F. and Feinburg, W. (eds), *Knowledge and Values in Educational Research*. Philadelphia: Temple University Press.
Cook, T. (1985) 'Postpositivist critical multiplism', in Shotland, R. and Mark, M. (eds), *Social Science and Social Policy*. Beverly Hills: Sage.
Cronbach, L. (1986) 'Social inquiry by and for earthlings', in Fiske, D and Shweder, R. (eds), *Metatheory in Social Science: Pluralisms and Subjectivities*. Chicago: University of Chicago Press.
Cronbach, L., Ambron, S., Dornbusch, S., Hess, R., Hornik, R., Phillips, D., Walker, D., and Weiner, S. (1980) *Toward Reform of Program Evaluation*. San Francisco: Jossey-Bass.
Dullea, K and Mullender, A (1999) 'Evaluation and empowerment' in Shaw, I. and Lishman, J. (eds), *Evaluation and Social Work Practice*. London: Sage Publications.
Eisner, E. (1991) *The Enlightened Eye: Qualitative Inquiry and the Enhancement of Educational Practice*. New York: Macmillan.
Filstead, W. (1979) 'Qualitative methods – a needed perspective in evaluation research', in Cook, T. and Reichardt, C. (eds), *Qualitative and Quantitative Methods in Evaluation Research*. Beverley Hills: Sage.
Gage, N. (1989) 'The Paradigm wars and their aftermath' in *Educational Researcher*, 18 (7): 4-10.
Garrison, J. (1988) 'The Impossibility of atheoretical research' in *Journal of Educational Thought*, 22 (1): 21-25.
Geertz, C. (1983) *Local Knowledge*. New York: Basic Books.
Greene, J. (1990) 'Three views on the nature and role of knowledge in social science', in Guba, E. (ed), *The Paradigm Dialog*. Newbury Park: Sage.
Greene, J. (1993) 'The Role of theory in qualitative program evaluation', in Flinders, J. and Mills, G., *Theory and Concepts in Qualitative Research*. New York: Teachers College Press.
Greene, J. (1994) 'Qualitative program evaluation: practice and promise', in Denzin, N. and Lincoln, Y. (eds), *Handbook of Qualitative Research*. Thousand Oaks: Sage.
Greene, J. (1996) 'Qualitative evaluation and scientific citizenship', in *Evaluation*, 2 (3): 277-289.
Guba, E. (1990) 'The Alternative paradigm dialog', in Guba, E. (ed), *The Paradigm Dialog*. Newbury Park: Sage.
Guba, E. and Lincoln, Y. (1989) *Fourth Generation Evaluation*. Newbury Park: Sage.
Hammersley, M. (1992) *What's Wrong With Ethnography?* London: Routledge.
Hammersley, M. (1995) *The Politics of Social Research*. London: Sage.

Hammersley, M. and Gomm, R. (1997) 'Bias in social research', in *Sociological Research Online*, 2, 1. <http://www.socresonline.org.uk/socresonline/2/1/2.html>

Heap, J. (1995) 'Constructionism in the rhetoric and practice of fourth generation evaluation', in *Evaluation and Program Planning*, 18 (1): 51-61.

Humphries, B. (1997) 'From Critical thought to emancipatory action: contradictory research goals?' *Sociological Research Online*. <http://www.socresonline.org.uk/socresonline/2/1/3.html>.

Jacob, E. (1987) 'Qualitative research traditions: a review' in *Review of Educational Research*, 57 (1): 1-50.

Kelly, A. (1985) 'Action research: what it is and what can it do?', in Burgess, R. (ed), *Issues in Educational Research*. London: Falmer Press.

Kirkpatrick, I. and Lucio, M. (1995) (eds) *The Politics of Quality*. London: Routledge.

Lakatos, I. (1970) 'Falsification and the methodology of scientific research programmes', in Lakatos, I. and Musgrave, A. *Criticism and the Growth of Knowledge*. Cambridge: Cambridge University Press.

Lather, P. (1986) 'Research as praxis' in *Harvard Educational Review*, 56 (3): 257-277.

Lather, P. (1991) *Getting Smart: Feminist Research and Pedagogy with/in the Postmodern*. New York: Routledge.

Leplin, J. (1984) (ed) *Scientific Realism*. Berkeley: University of California Press.

Lincoln, Y. (1990) 'The Making of a constructivist: a remembrance of transformations past', in Guba, E. (ed), *The Paradigm Dialog*. Newbury Park: Sage.

Mayer, J. and Timms, N. (1970) *The Client Speaks*. London: Routledge and Kegan Paul.

McLennan, G. (1995) 'Feminism, epistemology and postmodernism: reflections on current ambivalence', in *Sociology*, 29 (2): 391-409.

Miles, M. and Huberman, A. (1994) *Qualitative Data Analysis: an Expanded Sourcebook*. Thousand Oaks: Sage.

Outhwaite, W. (1987) *New Philosophies of Social Science*. London: Macmillan.

Patton, M. (1990) *Qualitative Evaluation*. Newbury Park: Sage.

Phillips, D. (1987) *Philosophy, Science and Social Inquiry*. New York: Pergamon.

Phillips, D. (1990) 'Postpositivistic science: myths and realities', in Guba, E. (ed), *The Paradigm Dialog*. Newbury Park: Sage.

Pitman, M. and Maxwell, J. (1992) 'Qualitative approaches to evaluation: models and methods', in LeCompte, M. and Preissle, J. (eds), *The Handbook of Qualitative Research in Education*. San Diego: Academic Press.

Popkewitz, T. (1990) 'Whose future? Whose past?' in Guba, E. (ed), *The Paradigm Dialog*. Newbury Park: Sage.

Popper, K. (1966) *The Open Society and Its Enemies* (II). London: Routledge and Kegan Paul.

Popper, K. (1989) *Conjectures and Refutations: The Growth of Scientific Knowledge*. London: Routledge.

Reason, P. and Rowan, J. (eds) (1981) *Human Inquiry; a Sourcebook of New Paradigm Research.* Chichester: John Wiley.

Reichardt, C. and Cook, T. (1979) 'Beyond qualitative *versus* quantitative methods', in Cook, T. and Reichardt, C. (eds), *Qualitative and Quantitative Methods in Evaluation Research.* Beverly Hills: Sage.

Reid, W. (1988) 'Service effectiveness and the social agency', in Patti, R., Poertner, J. and Rapp, C. (eds), *Managing for Effectiveness in Social Welfare Organisations*. New York: Haworth.

Reid, W. (1994) 'Field testing and data gathering on innovative practice interventions in early development', in Rothman, J. and Thomas, E. (eds), *Intervention Research: Design and Development of Human Service*. New York: Haworth Press.

Reid, W. and Zettergren, P. (1999) 'A Perspective on empirical practice', in Shaw, I. and Lishman, J. (eds) *Evaluation and Social Work Practice*. London: Sage.

Rorty, R. (1979) *Philosophy and the Mirror of Nature.* Princeton, N.J.: Princeton University Press.

Rorty, R. (1991) 'Feminism and pragmatism', in *Radical Philosophy*, 59: 3-14.

Sackett, D. and Rosenberg, T. (1995) 'On the need for evidenced based medicine', *Health Economist*, 4 (2): 249-254.

Schwab, J. (1969) 'The Practical: a language for curriculum' in *School Review,* November, pp. 1-23.

Schwandt, T. (1993) 'Theory for the social sciences: crisis of identity and purpose', in Flinders, D. and Mills, G. (eds), *Theory and Concepts in Qualitative Research: Perspectives from the Field.* New York: Teachers College Press.

Schwandt, T. (1997) 'Evaluation as practical hermeneutics', in *Evaluation*, 3 (1): 69-83.

Scriven, M. (1997) 'Truth and objectivity in evaluation', in Chelimsky, E. and Shadish, W. (eds), *Evaluation for the 21st Century.* Thousand Oaks: Sage.

Shadish, W. (1995) 'Philosophy of science and quantitative-qualitative debates: thirteen common errors', in *Evaluation and Program Planning*, 18 (1): 63-75.

Shaw, I. (1996) *Evaluating in Practice*. Aldershot: Ashgate.

Shaw, I. (1999) 'Seeing the trees for the wood: the politics of evaluating in practice', in Broad, B. (ed), *The Politics of Research and Evaluation.* Birmingham: Venture Press.

Shaw, I. and Shaw, A. (1997a) 'Keeping social work honest: evaluating as profession and practice', in *British Journal of Social Work*, 27 (6): 847-869.

Shaw, I. and Shaw, A. (1997b) 'Game plans, buzzes and sheer luck: doing well in social work', in *Social Work Research*, 21 (2): 69-79.

Smith, J. (1992) 'Interpretive inquiry: a practical and moral activity', in *Theory into Practice*, 31 (2): 100-106.

Smith, J. (1993) 'Hermeneutics and qualitative inquiry', in Flinders, D. and Mills, G. (eds), *Theory and Concepts in Qualitative Research: Perspectives from the Field.* New York: Teachers College Press.

Smith, J. and Heshusius, L. (1986) 'Closing down the conversation: the end of the quantitative-qualitative debate among educational inquirers', in *Educational Researcher*, 15 (1): 4-12.

Swigonski, M. (1993) 'Feminist standpoint theory and questions of social work research', in *Affilia*, 8 (2): 171-183.

U.S. Department of Education, (1986) *What Works: Research about Teaching and Learning.* Washington D.C.: U.S. Department of Education.

Weiss, C. (1980) 'Knowledge creep and decision accretion', in *Knowledge, Creation, Diffusion, Utilisation*, 1 (3): 381-404.

Williams, R. (1976) *Keywords: a Vocabulary of Culture and Society*. London: Fontana.

Woolgar, S. and Pawluch, D. (1985) 'Ontological gerrymandering: the anatomy of social problems explanations', in *Social Problems*, 32 (3): 214-227.

Chapter 8

Seeing the Trees For the Wood: The Politics of Evaluating in Practice*

Sentimentality, superstition and myth

When it comes to matters of research and evaluation social workers are vulnerable to sentimentality, marked by a nurturing of myths and a tendency to superstitious practices.

We are guilty of sentimentality, says Howard Becker,

> when we refuse, for whatever reason, to investigate some matter that should properly be regarded as problematic. We are sentimental especially, when our reason is that we would prefer not to know what is going on, if to know would be to violate some sympathy whose existence we may not even be aware of (Becker, 1970, pp. 132-3).

The sentimentalities and superstitious practices that specially concern me are those most closely associated with commitments that I myself share. The criticisms that make up the bulk of this chapter are drawn from a context in which I am committed to developing evaluation as a dimension of direct social work practice (Shaw, 1996, 1997). My conviction is that *qualitative* evaluation offers a promising way forward to achieve evaluating-in-practice. Participatory and collaborative methods, the cultivation of a reflexive practice, egalitarian engagements between researchers and academics in higher education and social workers, and the potential of work-based assessment methods in postqualifying social work programmes, are pointers to ways qualitative evaluating in practice can be developed.

I am also committed to listening to and learning from the case made for *emancipatory*, praxis-oriented evaluation, and to evaluating for and with service users. I have been very strongly influenced by feminists' arguments that women, as outsiders on the inside, 'occupy a special status – they become different people, and their difference sensitises them to patterns that may be more difficult for established insiders to see' (Collins, 1986, p S29). I do not wish to neglect this debt.

---

* Originally published as I. Shaw, 1999. 'Seeing the Trees for the Wood: the Politics of Practice Evaluation', in B. Broad (ed.) *The Politics of Research and Evaluation in Social Work*. Birmingham: Venture Press. Reprinted with permission of The British Association of Social Workers and Venture Press.

I am convinced that we need to develop a richer and more rigorous *empirical base* for such evaluation. For example, we need to give practitioners voice in talking about ways in which they evaluate in their day to day practice (Shaw and Shaw, 1997a, 1997b). I do not regard this as simply a preliminary ground clearing exercise, filling in the gaps of research knowledge that have hitherto been neglected in the social work research and evaluation enterprise, but as a continuing normative obligation. We also have reason to listen carefully when leaders of the empirical practice movement challenge social workers and social scientists committed to humanist, qualitative and participatory methodologies to begin detailing how they can be applied in practice.

And yet those who share these broad commitments are not immune from sentimentality, superstitious practices, and myth-making. Which myths – stories we live by – worry me? There are three that I will briefly touch on in this chapter.

- Quantitative methodology is politically manipulative, while qualitative methodology is not.
- Mainstream ('malestream') research and evaluation methods are politically manipulative while feminist methods are not.
- Expert, mainstream research and evaluation methods are politically manipulative, while emancipatory evaluation is not.

There are risks in embarking on such a course. I may perhaps be seen as a well-meaning but naive washer of only slightly soiled linen, who undermines hard-won positions by inadvertently attacking core beliefs, or possibly responsible for covert, quasi-positivist infiltration. I could have much more comfortably written a chapter to the majority position occupied by most social work audiences, in which I ventriloquised the voice of such hearers by worrying out loud about evidenced-based practice, the American empirical practice movement, or the possible resurgence of a confessional logical positivism.[1] I watch, from a distance, the staying power of the American debate on the scientific practitioner model with some dismay as (mainly) men exchange coded insults; plead their positions with moral fervour; talk past one another about practice wisdom, intuition, emancipatory evaluation, causal impacts of single-system designs, or the theoretical content of empirically based intervention; focus their endeavours on an unduly narrow vision of evaluation; snipe at practitioners for their alleged irrationality or ignorance; treat issues of gender as technical matters which can be softened if not eliminated by stronger adherence to rigorous evaluative designs; and dismiss or, on a good day, patronise, the advocates of qualitative methods for their alleged flight from

1 Positivism, in social work at least, is no longer 'a swear word by which no-one is swearing' (Williams, 1976, p. 239). It is still a swear word, as we go on the illustrate, but there is a small but vocal number of advocates willing to swear by the merits of positivism for social work (see, for example, Thyer, 1989, 1993; Rotheray, 1993).

reason or tendency to intellectual Ludditism. I have tried elsewhere to substantiate some of this worrying out loud (Shaw, 1996; 1998; Shaw and Shaw, 1997b).

The picture is not as bleak as I perhaps convey. There are, in Martin Bloom's phrase, occasional 'peace offerings' (Klein and Bloom, 1995), acknowledgements that the scientific-practitioner model may not hold all the answers (e.g. Robinson, Benson and Blythe, 1988; cf Penka and Kirk, 1991), and efforts to provide empirical support for the claim that the scientific-practitioner model is theory-free and transferable to very different practice models. From time to time there are also judicious, temperate hands steering through the smoke of the crossfire (E.g. Grasso and Epstein, 1988; Meyer, 1992, 1996; Thomas, 1978; and notably Reid, 1988; 1994 and 1999).

Such distant watching is increasingly a luxury. Evaluation developments in the United Kingdom are different from those in the United States, and should not be seen as simply American positions of a few years ago. Yet strong traces of all the negative characteristics of the American debate can be found in Britain, without, as yet, the 'peace offerings'.

This chapter is in part a peace offering in return, drawn from a commitment to qualitative, emancipatory evaluation, and addressed, among others, to evidence-based practitioners who share a commitment to keeping social work honest. However, it is not a plea for naïve pragmatism – that we should just get on with eclectic evaluation on the grounds that practitioners and, more importantly, service users could not care why and what we do, just whether people are helped by it. Rather, it is offered in a spirit of guarded reciprocal dialogue. Such exercises in guarded reciprocity should aspire to an outcome not too dissimilar from that described by Popper when he concluded that,

> Ironically enough, objectivity is closely bound up with the *social aspect of scientific method*, with the fact that science and scientific objectivity do not (and cannot) result from the attempts of an individual scientist to be 'objective', but from the *friendly-hostile co-operation of many scientists.* Scientific objectivity can be described as the inter-subjectivity of scientific method (emphasis original). (Popper, 1966, Vol. II, p. 217)

This inter-subjectivity consists, in Popper's view, of free criticism, marked by scientists refusing to take anyone's findings as unassailable, and also by scientific efforts to avoid talking at cross-purposes, which is demonstrated by trying to state their theories in a form which can be refuted (cf Hammersley, 1995, pp. 75-78). This chapter is intended as a provocation to conversation and practice marked by these qualities.

Quantitative *v* qualitative

Anecdotal impressions suggest that rejection of quantitative methods among many student social workers and practitioners is rather akin to popular images of the debate regarding evolution *versus* creation as an explanation of the origins of life. It is known that there are still some folk who practice quantitative methodology, but they are regarded as 'off the wall' and quirky survivors of a bygone age. News of the nascent revival of positivist epistemology, and enthusiasm regarding the pay-offs from experimental research designs has yet to spread. The late 1990s have witnessed an enthusiasm for evidence based practice, coming on the back of the more influential moves towards evidence based medicine. Evidence based practice has been given regional and national infrastructures through the 'What Works' conferences in the Probation Service, the formation of the Centre for Evidence Based Social Services Research at Exeter University, and Research in Practice (an initiative of the Association of Directors of Social Services aimed at the improvement and dissemination of child care research).[2] Nonetheless, the majority of social workers are incorrigible 'lovers of small numbers',[3] and will remain ready to embrace any of the several rationales for concluding that quantitative methodology is politically manipulative.

The choice is a serious one that extends far beyond a merely technical judgement about which research methodology produces the best results. In social work the model of research that dominated until the mid-1960s was a Fabian and democratic socialist policy research model, in which research was addressed – typically through survey methods – to the resolution of particular policy problems. The role of the researcher was seen as that of a social critic who would enlighten policy makers, agency managers, and practitioners (cf Bulmer, 1982; Shaw, 1996, chapter 2).

Social work research was increasingly influenced by two developments from the mid 1960s. First, there was the growth of Marxism. While Marxist practice had a weak empirical agenda, influence out of proportion to its scale was exercised through exemplar research such as Paul Willis' *Learning to*

2 'Evidence-based practice' has, in fact, both a narrow and a wider usage. The two usages have a large area of overlap. The broader meaning is marked by emphases on the obligation of social workers to ground their practice judgements in explicit evidence, a more explicit drawing on research findings, and a determination to disseminate research findings and make them accessible. It also includes an emphasis on outcome research rather than research about process, and a generally positive belief in the potential to apply research to practice and policy in an incremental fashion. The narrower sense of the term includes all of these features, but also typically includes a negativity towards qualitative research and evaluation, and an advocacy of particular methods of practice intervention (usually cognitive or behaviourally based). I have criticised the narrower concept in Shaw, 1996 (chapters 5 and 9) and Shaw and Shaw, 1997b.

3 The phrase is W.H. Auden's from his poem, 'Numbers and Faces'. 'Lovers of small numbers go benignly potty...Lovers of big numbers go horridly mad...'

Labour (Willis, 1977), and the dominant model of action research which emerged in the Home Office-funded Community Development Projects (cf Specht, 1976). Second, qualitative research, especially symbolic interactionism, began to emerge from the shadows of mainstream research. The precise reasons for this development have still to be documented in relation to social work, but the rapid expansion of university sociology degrees, and the perceived failure of randomised control group experiments first in America (e.g. Meyer, Borgatta and Jones, 1965) and subsequently in Britain (e.g. Goldberg, 1970) both played a part. Qualitative research was enriched by symbolic interactionist methodology books such as Denzin's *Research Act* (1970), which exercised a formative influence on several researchers who were later to become key figures in the social work research 'establishment'. It is only a slight oversimplification to observe also that the discipline of anthropology became transmuted in these years from a study of exotic societies into ethnography for urban society. The stronger emergence of qualitative sociologies in the field of education also exercised an indirect and seriously underemphasised influence on social work developments (and do so now). It is probable also that Labour governments in the 1960s and early 1970s facilitated a growing role for evaluation research.

Following this period, qualitative research and evaluation developed into three different strands. First, *critical ethnographies* of social work represented a radicalisation of the earlier model of social research in which the researcher's role was that of social critic. Much of this work was done on the fringes of mainstream social work in fields such as youth work and community work. Harvey has reviewed some of this work (Harvey, 1990). From the late 1980s this strand has developed into broader liberatory and *activist qualitative models* of research, influenced from within social work by the shift in critical attention from social class to issues of race, gender and disability. The influence of theorising about feminist standpoint, sketched in the next part of the chapter, has been one important driving force behind such developments.

The second strand is that of *interactionist ethnographies*. There have been few such ethnographies in social work, compared with medicine and education. Juvenile justice research was one strand in this work (e.g. Cicourel, 1968). A central focus of such studies (e.g. Pithouse, 1988), has been on discipline development, although a critical perspective on practice was never absent (e.g. Rees, 1978). From the mid-1980s this strand was subject to the growing influence of relativism and scepticism about epistemology. Guba and Lincoln's *Fourth Generation Evaluation* (1989) has been a central text in this development, along with subsequent developments in feminist postmodernism (e.g. Hekman, 1990), thus bridging trends in both ethnography and evaluation.

Third, there has been the gradual emergence of *qualitative evaluation* in social work. Until very recently social workers have elided different forms of evaluation, and qualitative forms have had no clear separate identity. Thus practitioner research in Britain and the scientific practitioner movement in the USA have been governed by a strongly utilitarian view of research and evaluation, in which matters of epistemology and methodology have been treated as important but essentially subordinate to pragmatic concerns about process and outcome of services (cf Fuller and Petch, 1995; Cheetham, 1998). However, there have been several attempts at synthesising developments in qualitative social work evaluation (e.g. Sherman and Reid, 1994; Shaw, 1996; White, 1998), and the writing and research generated by these, together with the current interest in emancipatory evaluation, are likely to make this area volatile for the next few years.

The risk of superstition and sentimentality arises when social workers committed to a qualitative stance generalise in undifferentiated ways about the role of research and evaluation. In doing so they are liable to misrepresent its impact and benefits. For example, I am very uncomfortable with social work attacks on positivism and quantitative methodology. Take the following not untypical comments selected from a student text:

> Positivists not only see their work as uncontaminated: they see themselves as pure and safe in their objectivity, an elite who have managed to transcend the constraints of subjectivity.

A problem of 'the positivist paradigm' is that

> the research endeavour is mystified; esoteric skills and techniques serve the interests of the powerful.

> the essential values of positivism, objectivity, neutrality and determinism are..at variance with the value base, and the purposeful and humble activities of social work practice.

Those whose research is framed by positivism are said to be guilty of

> spurious and dangerously simplistic solutions (Everitt, Hardiker, Littlewood and Mullender, 1992, pp. 6, 35, 55, 61; Mullender, Everitt, Hardiker and Littlewood, 1993/4, p 13).

Generalisations of this kind simply do not do justice to the problem. They caricature by omission the highly varied philosophical work that has been done in this field, betraying apparent unawareness of the far from straightforward arguments regarding objectivity, subjectivity, neutrality and determinism that are part and parcel of the position they target. Being 'dangerously simplistic' follows from superstitious myth-making wherever it occurs. These writers echo that 'weary critique of positivism' in the early 1980s, which in Silverman's view more or less lacked coherence outside the pages of undergraduate examination books (Silverman, 1997, p. 241). The omission of any discussion of critical realism, and failure to glimpse the radical discontinuities between positivism and most postpositivist positions, illustrate both the wearying character and lack of incoherence of which Silverman complains.

Take, for example, the use in this context of the word 'paradigm'. It is unhelpful in that it implies that all the characteristics of positivism come as a package, and also that there are no internal differences. 'It obscures both potential and actual diversity in orientation, and can lead us into making simplistic methodological decisions' (Hammersley, 1995, p. 3). When 'quantitative' and 'qualitative' are characterised as paradigms they are usually set against one another as polar opposites, with the diversity within both equally hidden. For example, emancipatory evaluations and interactionist ethnographies both fall within qualitative methodology, yet they take very different positions on a wide range of paradigm-like issues such as relations to practitioners, theorising, the potential for policy applications, and political involvement.

An associated problem is that committed advocates of qualitative evaluation research are prone to assume a too close association between epistemology and methodology. The tacit assumption is that evaluators can and do choose methodologies consistent with their epistemology. There has been an extensive debate especially in American literature regarding paradigms, with the debate ranging from the pragmatism of Patton and Firestone to the paradigm commitment of Guba and Lincoln, and Smith (Firestone, 1990; Guba, 1990; Smith and Hershuis, 1986; Patton, 1990). While there is no easy solution (see Greene, 1994, for a helpful assessment), the implicit and unquestioned strong paradigm position in some British advocacy of qualitative methods smacks of sentimentality. Furthermore, it unhelpfully shifts the focus of attention too far away from methodological concerns towards broader interpretive issues.

Feminist *v* malestream

It would provide 'aid and comfort to the barbarians' (Weiss, 1987) if the arguments of the previous paragraphs were hijacked, either to protect some advocates of quantitative methodologies from criticism on the grounds of their own sentimental and superstitious thinking and practices, or to reject the central thrust of feminist argument. The influence of feminism in many spheres of social work practice, research, and teaching has been almost breathtaking. For example 'feminism has literally revolutionised our sense of what today must count as "adequate" approximations to knowledge' (McLennan, 1995, p. 397).

There are two main positions within feminist social work, feminist standpoint theory, and postmodern feminism.[4] *Feminist standpoint theory*:

4 Until recently it was customary also to include feminist empiricism as a third position. Feminist empiricism seeks to criticise male ways of knowing from within a traditional position of science as a potentially objective knowledge form, and thus provide an empirical corrective to male bias. However, there has been forceful and generally

> disputes the traditional picture of science by proposing that the mainstream notion of scientific rationality is itself intrinsically masculinist, and thus not amenable to piecemeal correction by feminist scientists. On the contrary, feminists must openly abandon the quest for better "neutral" knowledge, replacing it with a clear emancipatory commitment to knowledge from the standpoint of women's experience and feminist theory (McLennan, 1995, p 392).

It draws its rationale from the arguments of Hartsock, Harding and others, and starts from Marx' position that a correct vision of society is available only from one of the two major class positions in capitalist society.

Hartsock, in a classic paper, reworks Marxist arguments about the division of labour to apply to the sexual division of labour, in which girls define themselves *relationally*, while boys do not. She develops her position to claim that these different experiences are replicated in later life as epistemological and ontological differences. This male experience replicates itself in the institutions of class society.

Hartsock notes that, given the power of the controlling group to define the terms for the community as a whole, a feminist standpoint is *achieved* rather than obvious. 'The standpoint of the oppressed represents an achievement both of science (analysis) and of political struggle on the basis of which this analysis can be conducted' (Hartsock, 1983, p. 288). It is a potentially hopeful position in that

> because it provides the basis for revealing the perversion of life and thought, the inhumanity of human relations, a standpoint can be the basis for moving beyond these relations..(A) standpoint by definition carries a liberatory potential (Hartsock, 1983, p. 289).

Put simply, in response to the patriarchal assumption that women are *less* able to understand, standpoint theory argues that they are *more* able to do so. It does so through two linked assertions, the double vision of the oppressed and the partial vision of the powerful – 'privilege and its invisibility to those who hold it' (Swigonski, 1993, p. 174).

Feminist standpoint theory when applied to social work evaluation espouses – if such a politically shaky verb may be used – a number of defining positions:

- Women's experience is seen as a more complete and less distorting kind of social experience.
- Objectivity is rejected for its inherent masculinist biases and distortions.
- Hierarchy within the research relationship is rejected as not simply bad method, but more importantly as both bad ethics and bad politics.

---

persuasive criticism to the effect that, at least in epistemological terms, feminist empiricism as a category 'does not really exist at all: either you have women empiricists or feminist standpoint epistemologists' (McLennan, 1995, p. 396).

- An activist and empowerment conception of evaluation is implied, as undertaken for explicitly political purposes. 'The research process itself can become a process of "conscientisation" for both the researcher and the subjects of the research' (Cook and Fonow, 1990, p 75). In a much quoted comment Cook and Fonow say, 'The purpose of knowledge is to change or transform patriarchy…Description without an eye for transformation is inherently conservative' (p. 79).

The risk of superstition arises once unresolved aspects of feminist standpoint theory are treated by social workers as unproblematic and therefore are prone to being sentimentalised. There are three problems regarding feminist standpoint theory which have received growing attention in the literature, but which social work standpoint theorists such as Swigonski fail to problematise.

First, there is an unresolved ambivalence within feminist standpoint theory, especially in regard to criticisms of objectivity (McLennan, 1995).

Second, as is by now well known, the argument for a privileged feminist perspective has been criticised from within feminist scholarship. For example, to Hawkesworth the idea 'appears to be highly implausible'. 'Given the diversity and fallibility of all human knowers, there is no good reason to believe that women are any less prone to error, deception or distortion than men' (Hawkesworth, 1989, p. 544).

Third, standpoint theory has been criticised for essentialising the concept of 'woman'. Third world, black and lesbian feminisms have together served to 'dissolve the conceptualisation of "woman"' (Olesen, 1994, p. 160). This creates problems for those who wish to argue that women's experience should have privileged status.

Standpoint theory is pulled one way by the realisation that, while affirming a radically different agenda for *what counts* as objective, it yet retains a search for universalising validation, and a different way by the emphasis on the diversity of women's experiences. Thus, while Gelsthorpe wises to retain the terminology of standpoint theory, there is little remaining of its substance when she concludes,

> We cannot assume that black/white, young/old, and so on, experience life in the same way...(We) choose standpoints and standpoints may change over time; they are transitional, not fixed points...This leads me to argue that women do have uniquely valid insights from their vantage points as women, but women are never *just* women…The same goes for men, of course… (Gelsthorpe, 1992, p. 215).

This kind of argument reflects the important influence of the *second* main position within feminist social work, *feminist postmodernism*. There is an important feminist postmodern strand in British social work, in which the work of Susan Hekman has been especially influential (Hekman, 1990). While it is difficult to be conclusive, it is likely that there has been a move away from standpoint feminism in social work, and that the position of Hekman and others captures the main *motif* of feminist social work in Britain at the turn of the century, at least within higher education. Millen expresses it thus:

> Instead of privileging female or feminine standpoint, feminist postmodernism suggests that there is a variety of contradictory and conflicting standpoints, of social discourses, none of which should be privileged: there is no point in trying to construct a standpoint theory which will give us a better, fuller…knowledge because such knowledge does not exist (Millen, 1997, 7.7).

While there are important variations within feminist postmodernism, stemming in part from ambiguity about what being postmodern entails, there are several recurring themes.[5]

- a movement away from essentialising concepts of women.
- A rejection of objectivism in favour of relativism.
- An engagement with pluralist and humanist research methodologies.
- A determination to politicise postmodernism and rescue it from any risk of political complacency.
- A strong claim that all knowledge is contextual and historically specific, and hence a hostility to cross-cultural explanations.
- A rejection of epistemology in exchange for discourse and rhetoric.

Our concern here is not primarily with the arguments of feminist postmodernism as such, any more than with the arguments of feminist standpoint theory, but with the constant risk that the advocacy of a methodology that expresses core beliefs will be prone to a failure to problematise, and thus a risk of superstitious sentimentality. We referred earlier to the hazards of using 'paradigm' language to attack perceived enemies. In addition, there is the danger that broad brush arguments will be used to bury rather than praise contrary positions, in the way we illustrated earlier in this chapter. For example, there is tendency in too much feminist work to caricature the position of modernist researchers, through allegations that they aspire to absolute truth through research, and that they claim it is possible to hold 'God's eye view' (cf Hekman, 1990, pp. 152-3; Nicholson, 1990, pp. 2, 3).

Relativist positions have also been troubled by practitioner struggles. Jennifer Greene is one of a number of people working from an educational context who have sharpened our understanding of qualitative approaches to evaluation.

> Many qualitative practitioners struggle with the dissonance invoked by the assumed mind-dependence of all social knowledge claims in the face of the

5 I am indebted to McLennan's influential essay at this point (McLennan, 1995). In addition to Hekman (1990), Flax (1990), Nicholson (1990) and Rorty (1991) represent important work.

> contextual (as well as personal, ego-related) demands to *"get it right"*, to *"find out what's really going on in this setting"* (Greene, 1996, p. 280. Emphasis in original).

A distinction needs drawing between 'strong' and 'partial' postmodernist positions. A strong position probably would adopt unequivocally all six of the above themes. In practice, it is likely that a range of more partial positions is being advocated, without always acknowledging the unresolved tensions that exist between them. If this is a fair reading, then it would help explain why postmodern statements sometimes seem to hedge their bets. For example, Millen asks 'How can we propose a political philosophy without some sort of epistemic unity?' (1997, 7.8). She clings to the aspiration that

> A dual role, where we use postmodern insights to continually critique the role of feminist research and the gendered aspects of mainstream research, but utilise modernist ideas to advance feminism's political agenda, may be possible (1997, 7.10).

She adds an immediate postscript that 'consensus is not, after all, a primary aim of feminism'. Millen makes a valuable point. We should beware of the chronic scepticism that marks epistemological purists. It is quite appropriate to be caught between different paradigms if this reflects the constituency of which we are a part. Indeed, it is likely to be a creative, if anxious, experience. To ask for a cut and dried position risks provoking accusations of the very masculinist thinking referred to earlier! But accepting unresolved diversity is still a problematic position for feminist evaluators, researchers and social workers. McLennan asks, in this context, if a hesitation in abandoning epistemic grounding may be due to 'the premonition that feminism as a distinctive theory and practice might dissolve with its absorption into postmodernism' (1995, p. 393).

Emancipatory *v* mainstream

There is a problem common to both feminist and emancipatory research. We noted that hierarchy within the research relationship is rejected by feminist analysis and practice as not simply bad method, but more importantly as both bad ethics and bad politics. However, there has been widening acknowledgement that activist research is not immune from the paradox and irony that 'our efforts to liberate perpetuate the relations of dominance' (Humphries, 1997, 3.5). For example, in a reflexive account of her own research in which she asks whether there can be a feminist ethnography, Stacey wonders 'whether the appearance of greater respect for and equality with research subjects in the ethnographic approach masks a deeper, more dangerous form of exploitation'. She concludes that 'conflicts of interest between the ethnographer as authentic, related person (ie participant), and as exploiting researcher (ie observer)' are 'an inescapable feature of the ethnographic method' (Stacey, 1988, p. 22). She exemplifies the plea that in making women's lives problematic feminists 'should not turn away from rendering their own practices problematic' (Olesen, 1994, p. 169) in her suggestion that feminists tend to suffer the 'delusion of alliance' (1988, p. 23). Martin (1994 and 1996) and Whitmore (1994) have portrayed this problem in participative research in areas of relevance to social work.

There is a welcome recent willingness, in Lather's apposite phrase, to 'protect our work from our own passions' (Lather, 1986a, p. 77). Humphries goes as far as to say that both traditional and emancipatory research need to be interrogated 'and *both* may be found wanting' (1997, 4.6). She asks 'surely it is possible to recognise the particularities of struggle without abandoning the metanarratives of emancipation and justice' (4.8). In doing so we need to acknowledge 'the permanent partiality of the point of view of those of us seeking to construct emancipatory research', and that 'an emancipatory intent is no guarantee of an emancipatory outcome' (4.8, 4.10).

> In sum, the development of emancipatory social theory requires an empirical stance which is open-minded, dialogically reciprocal, grounded in respect for human capacity, and yet profoundly sceptical of appearances and "common sense" (Lather, 1986b, p. 269).

Lather's transparent commitment displays both welcome aspiration yet the recurrent risk once more of sentimentality on the part of liberatory researchers. Lather's vigorous warnings against the theoretical imperialism within neo-Marxism – the 'circle where theory is reinforced by experience conditioned by theory' (Lather, 1986b, p. 261) – are salutary. 'Theory is too often used to protect us from the awesome complexity of the world' and

> Neo-Marxist praxis-oriented work too often falls prey to...the irony of domination and repression inherent in most of our efforts to free one another... In the name of emancipation, researchers impose meanings on situations rather than constructing meaning through negotiation with research participants (1986b, pp. 267, 265).

'Open-minded' research and evaluation present an unresolved tension within a tradition where too often 'one is left with the impression that the research conducted provides empirical specificities for more general, *a priori* theories' (Lather, 1986a, p. 76). Her desire for 'dialogically reciprocal' research is open to similar ambiguities. She openly admits to

> a lack of self-reflexivity in the empirical work that exists within critical inquiry... Too often, critical self-awareness comes to mean a negative attitude to competing approaches instead of its own self-critical perspective (1986a, p. 65).

Conclusion

Our concern throughout this chapter has been with the risks that attach to a commitment to qualitative and emancipatory evaluation. The tensions will not go away. Lather is arguing for a re-worked neo-Marxist position yet she catches pointedly the tensions that face all social work evaluation if it is to escape the risks of sentimentality, superstition and myth-making that are its constant temptation. We cannot retreat to the older traditions of research and evaluation where the applications of uses of research were only the vaguest responsibility of the researcher. The demands of social justice and citizenship challenge all our political sentimentalities. There is no 'Blue Peter' template for applying these demands. Yet unless we have

> an engaged, accountable…scientific citizenship, I fear that qualitative evaluation will be relegated to the sidelines of important debates about public issues..No longer can we shroud our citizen-selves behind our scientific subjectivities. We must become scientific citizens (Greene, 1996, pp. 286-7).

References

Becker, H. (1970) *Sociological Work*. New York, Aldine.

Bulmer, M. (1982) *The Uses of Social Research*. London, Allen and Unwin.

Cheetham, J. (1998) 'The evaluation of social work: priorities, problems and possibilities', in Cheetham, J. and Kazi, M. (eds), *The Working of Social Work*. London, Jessica Kingsley.

Cicourel, A. (1968) *The Social Organisation of Juvenile Justice*. New York, John Wiley.

Collins, P. (1986) 'Learning from the Outside Within: the Sociological Significance of Black Feminist Thought' *Social Problems*, 33 (6), pp. S14-S32.

Cook, J. and Fonow, M. (1990) 'Knowledge and Women's Interests: Issues of Epistemology and Methodology in Feminist Sociological Research', in Neilsen, J. (ed.) *Feminist Research Methods*. New York, Westview Press, pp. 69-93.

Denzin, N. (1970) *The Research Act in Sociology*. Chicago, Aldine.

Everitt, A., Hardiker, P., Littlewood, J. and Mullender, A. (1992) *Applied Research for Better Practice*. London, Macmillan.

Firestone, W. (1990) 'Accommodation: Towards a paradigm-praxis dialectic', in Guba, E (ed) *The Paradigm Dialog*. Newbury Park, Sage, pp. 105-124.

Flax, J. (1990) *Thinking Fragments*. Berkeley, University of California Press.

Fuller, R. and Petch, A. (1995) *Practitioner Research*. Buckingham, Open University Press.

Gelsthorpe, L. (1992) 'Response to Martin Hammersley's paper on feminist methodology' *Sociology*, 26 (2), pp. 213-218.

Goldberg, E. (1970) *Helping the Aged.* London, Allen and Unwin.

Grasso, A. and Epstein, I. (1988) 'Management by Measurement: Organisational Dilemmas and Opportunities', in Patti, R., Poertner, R., and Rapp, C. (eds) *Managing for Effectiveness in Social Welfare Organisations*. New York, Haworth.

Greene, J. (1994) 'Qualitative Program Evaluation: Practice and Promise', in Denzin, N and Lincoln, Y. (eds), *Handbook of Qualitative Methodology*. Thousand Oaks, Sage, pp. 530-544.

Greene, J. (1996) 'Qualitative Evaluation and Scientific Citizenship' *Evaluation*, 2 (3), pp. 277-289.

Guba, E. (1990) (ed) *The Paradigm Dialog*. Newbury Park, Sage.

Guba, E. and Lincoln, Y. (1989) *Fourth Generation Evaluation*. Newbury Park, Sage.

Hammersley, M. (1995) *The Politics of Social Research*. London, Sage.

Hammersley, M. (1997) 'A reply to Humphries' *Sociological Research Online* 2 (4), <http://www.socresonline.org.uk/socresonline/2/4/6.html>.

Harding, S. (1987) (ed) *Feminism and Methodology*. Buckingham, Open University Press.

Hartsock, N. (1983) 'The feminist standpoint: developing the ground for a specifically feminist historical materialism, in Harding, S. and Hintikka, M. (eds) *Discovering Reality*. Dordrecht, Reidl Publishing.

Harvey, L. (1990), *Critical Social Research*. London, Unwin Hyman.

Hawkesworth, M. (1989) 'Knowers, knowing, known: Feminist theory and claims of truth' *Signs: Journal of Women in Culture and Society*, 14 (3), pp. 533-555.

Hekman, S. (1990) *Gender and Knowledge: Elements of a Postmodern Feminism*. Cambridge, Policy Press.

Humphries, B. (1997) 'From critical thought to emancipatory action: Contradictory research goals?' *Sociological Research Online*, 2 (1) <http:www.socresonline.org.uk/socresonline/2/1/3.html>.

Kirk, S. (1990) 'Research utilisation: the substructure of belief', in Videka-Sherman, L. and Reid, W. (eds) *Advances in Clinical Social Work Research*. Washington, NASW, pp. 233-250.

Klein, W. and Bloom, M. (1995) 'Practice wisdom' *Social Work*, 40 (6), pp. 799-807.

Lather, P. (1986a) 'Issues of validity in openly ideological research' *Interchange*, 17 (4), pp. 63-84.

Lather, P. (1986b) 'Research as praxis' *Harvard Educational Review*, 56 (3), pp. 257-277.

Martin, M. (1994) 'Developing a feminist participative research framework' in Humphries, B. and Truman, C. (eds) *Rethinking Social Research: Anti-Discriminatory Approaches in Research Methodology*. Aldershot, Avebury.

Martin, M. (1996) 'Issues of power in the participatory research process' in de Koning, K. and Martin, M. (eds) *Participatory Research in Health*. London, Zed Books, pp. 82-93.

McLennan, G. (1995) 'Feminism, epistemology and postmodernism: Reflections on current ambivalence' *Sociology*, 29 (2), pp. 391-409.

Meyer, C. (1992) 'Social work assessment: Is there an empirical base?' *Research on Social Work Practice*, 2 (3), pp. 297-305.

Meyer, C. (1996) 'My son the scientist' *Social Work* Research, 20 (2), pp. 101-104.

Meyer, H., Borgatta, E. and Jones W. (1965) *Girls at Vocational High*. New York, Russell Sage Foundation.

Miller, J. (1992) 'Exploring power and authority issues in a collaborative research project' *Theory and Practice*, 21 (2), pp. 165-172.

Miller, J. and Martens, M. (1990) 'Hierarchy and imposition in collaborative inquiry: Teacher-researchers' reflections on recurrent dilemmas' *Educational Foundations*, 4 (4), pp. 41-59.

Millen, D. (1997) 'Some methodological and epistemological issues raised by doing feminist research on non-feminist women' *Sociological Research Online*, 2 (3), <http:www.socresonline.org.uk/socresonline/2/3/3.html>.

Mullender, A., Everitt, A., Hardiker, P. and Littlewood, J. (1993-4) 'Value issues in research' *Social Action*, 1 (4), pp. 11-18.

Nicholson, L. (1990) (ed) *Feminism/Postmodernism*. London, Routledge.

Olesen, V. (1994) 'Feminisms and models of qualitative research', in Denzin, N. and Lincoln, Y. (eds) *Handbook of Qualitative Methodology*. Thousand Oaks, Sage, pp. 158-174.

Patton, M. (1990) *Qualitative Evaluation and Research Methods*. Newbury Park, Sage.

Penka, C. and Kirk, S. (1991) 'Practitioner involvement in clinical evaluation' *Social Work*, 36 (3), pp. 513-518.

Pithouse, A. (1988) *Social Work: the Social Organisation of an Invisible Trade*. Aldershot, Hants, Avebury.

Popper, K. (1966) *The Open Society and Its Enemies*, Volume II. London, Routledge.

Rees, S. (1978) *Social Work Face to Face*. London, Edward Arnold.

Reid, W. (1988) 'Service effectiveness and the social agency', in Patti, R., Poertner, R., and Rapp, C. (eds) *Managing for Effectiveness in Social Welfare Organisations*. New York, Haworth.

Reid, W. (1994) 'The empirical practice movement' *Social Service Review*, 68 (2), pp. 165-184.

Reid, W. (1999) 'Empirical practice' in Shaw, I. and Lishman, J. (eds) *Evaluation and Social Work Practice*. London, Sage.

Robinson, E., Benson, D. and Blythe, B. (1988) 'An analysis of the implementation of single-case evaluation by practitioners' *Social Service Review*, 62 (2), pp. 285-301.

Rorty, R. (1991) 'Feminism and postmodernism' *Radical Philosophy*, 59, pp. 3-14.

Rotheray, M. (1993) 'The positivistic research approach', in Grinnell, R. (ed) *Social Work Research and Evaluation*. New York, F.E. Peacock.

Shadish, W., Cook, T.. and Leviton, L. (1990) *Foundations of Program Evaluation: Theories of Practice*. Newbury Park, Sage.

Shaw, I. (1996) *Evaluating in Practice*. Aldershot, Ashgate.

Shaw, I. (1997) *Be Your Own Evaluator: A Guide to Reflective and Enabling Evaluating in Practice*. Wrexham, Prospects Publishing.

Shaw, I. (1998) 'Practising evaluating', in Cheetham, J. and Kazi, M. (eds) *The Working of Social Work*. London, Jessica Kingsley, pp. 201-223.

Shaw, I. and Shaw, A. (1997a) 'Game plans, buzzes and sheer luck: doing well in social work' *Social Work Research*, 21 (2), pp. 69-79.

Shaw, I. and Shaw A. (1997b) 'Keeping social work honest: Evaluation as profession and practice' *British Journal of Social Work*, 27 (6), 847-869.

Sherman, E. and Reid, W. (1994) *Qualitative Research in Social Work*. New York, Columbia University Press.

Silverman, D. (1997) 'Towards an aesthetics of research', in Silverman, D. (ed) *Qualitative Research*. London, Sage, pp. 234-253.

Smith, J. (1992) 'Interpretive inquiry: a practical and moral activity' *Theory into Practice*, 31 (2), pp. 100-106.

Smith J. and Heshusius L. (1986) 'Closing down the conversation: the end of the quantitative-qualitative debate among educational inquirers' *Educational Researcher*, 15 (1), pp. 4-12.

Specht, H. (1976) *Community Development Projects*. London, National Institute for Social Work Training.

Stacey, J. (1988) 'Can there be a feminist ethnography?' *Women's Studies International Forum*, 11 (1), pp. 21-27.

Swigonski, M. (1993) 'Feminist standpoint theory and questions of social work research' *Affilia*, 8 (2), pp. 171-183.

Thomas, E. (1978) 'Research and service in single-case experimentation: Conflicts and choices' *Social Work Research and Abstracts*, 14 (4), pp. 20-32.

Thyer, B. (1989) 'First principles of practice research' *British Journal of Social Work*, 19 (4), pp. 309-323.

Thyer, B. (1993) 'Social Work Theory and Practice Research: the Approach of Logical Positivism' *Social Work and Social Sciences Review*, 4 (1), pp. 5-26.

Weiss, C. (1987) 'Where politics and evaluation meet', in Palumbo, D.J. (ed) *The Politics of Program Evaluation*. Newbury Park, Sage, pp. 12-46.

White, S. (1998) 'Analysing the content of social work: Applying the lessons of qualitative research', in Cheetham, J. and Kazi, M. (eds) *The Working of Social Work*. London, Jessica Kingsley, pp. 153-169.

Whitmore, E. (1994) 'To tell the truth: Working with oppressed groups in participatory approaches to inquiry', in Reason, P. (ed) *Participation in Human Inquiry*. London, Sage, pp. 82-98.

Williams, R. (1976) *Keywords: a Vocabulary of Culture and Society*. London, Fontana.

Willis, P. (1977) *Learning to Labour: How Working Class Kids Get Working Class Jobs*. Aldershot, Gower.

Chapter 9
Evaluation for a Learning Organization?*

At first glance evaluation and the idea of a learning organization do not seem to fit comfortably. Evaluation, so it may be said, is about outcomes, effectiveness, bottom lines and evidence-based practice – in sum, accountability. Learning organizations, on the other hand, are about systems, interaction, process, feedback and improvement.

The doubts are not easily dismissed. 'In essence, accountability is evaluation, and evaluation is accountability', remarked one senior manager in the National Science Foundation (House et al, 1996: 142).[1] The push-pull tension between evaluation purposes of accountability and learning are real. 'Although administrators and funders may state that they believe in organizational learning, the way evaluations sometimes are used is as a win-lose, "gotcha" game' (Stockdill, Baizerman and Compton, 2002: 19). 'Accountability-hungry funders and legislators who continue to demand outcomes within short periods of time' present one of the several challenges to evaluators and organizations interested in an organizational learning approach (Torres and Preskill, 2001: 389). Indeed, a plausible case can be made out for arguing that evaluation capacity building – 'the intentional work to continuously create and sustain overall organizational processes that make quality evaluations and their uses routine' – requires art, craft and skill that are very distinct from programme or project evaluation (Compton, Baizerman and Stockdill, 2002: 1).

I don't wish to overstate the tensions. On the one hand, proponents of learning organizations might bear in mind that lessons learned must be evidentially based, albeit in a variety of ways, and not simply unfalsifiable insights. In addition, in practice, if not in rhetoric, most evaluation is about incremental change and improvement.

> It is a distinctly Washington idea that those in the center of government can discover mechanisms to effect change in the periphery of the country. The search for discrete mechanisms of change has rarely been successful, probably because change is more complex, the result of many interacting factors in the local setting rather than the presence or absence of a few common elements. (House et al, 1996: 144)

---

* Shaw, I. (2004) 'Evaluation for a learning organization', in N. Gould and M. Baldwin *Social Work, Critical Reflection and the Learning Organization*. Aldershot: Ashgate.

1 The National Science Foundation (NSF) represents the American scientific community. It 'is one of the most prestigious agencies in Washington, and its director reports directly to the President' (House, 1996: 137).

Further grounds for not over-playing the tensions between accountability and learning models emerges from a recent discussion in which Kirk and Reid, in their critical appraisal of social work and science, have favoured arguments that implicitly narrow the gap between accountability evaluation and organizational learning. Accountability, they suggest, 'is not just a question of determining the effectiveness of whatever methods have been tested… It involves showing that the practitioner has used the best possible methods for the case at hand in the most suitable way – that he or she has engaged in "appropriate practice"'. This larger and fuzzier concept should, they believe, 'replace the one track idea of accountability as measurement of change' (Kirk and Reid, 2002: 91). They also back the approach that accountability be seen as an organizational responsibility, rather than that of individual practitioners.

This line of response to our initial doubts will, however, only take us so far. We should not only loosen the concept of accountability, but recognize that evaluation is not *only* about accountability, but is a fairly loose coalition of purposes and practices.[2] In particular, evaluation is often about learning and perhaps always about persuasion. Several writers have made this point. Owen and Lambert, in an early discussion, regard enlightenment as a 'first order use' of evaluation, and sometimes the prime motivation for commissioning an evaluation (Owen and Lambert, 1995).[3] Greene has more recently concluded that 'We must not just proclaim goodness or badness, but we must also offer conceptual, programmatic and theoretical insights relevant to that particular context *and* to others' (Greene, 2001: 398).

Michael Patton engaged in some fairly unflinching exchanges with Carol Weiss a quarter of a century ago, defending an instrumental, pragmatic position on evaluation purposes and uses, against her argument for enlightenment as the political reality of evaluation use. Yet he now acknowledges the use of evaluations to offer illumination and 'influence thinking and deepen understanding by increased knowledge' (Patton, 2001: 332).[4]

Preskill and Torres present all this as a principle and 'see evaluative inquiry as a kind of public philosophy whereby organization members engage in dialogue with clients and other stakeholders about the meaning of what they do and how they do it' (Preskill and Torres, 1999: 44). Ernest House long ago argued that evaluations never yield certain knowledge. 'Subjected to serious scrutiny, evaluations

2 For a useful and frequently cited discussion of the purposes of evaluation, see Chelimsky, 1997. I would add to her list, 'Evaluation for justice' (cf Shaw, 1999, chapter 1).

3 We have already noted, however, Stockdill et al's concern about the discrepancy between what funders say they want and the criteria they subsequently use to assess evaluation reports. I have been on the receiving end, for example, of criticism by the funders of an evaluation project funded to assess agency learning and justice issues, on the grounds of failing to test outcome hypotheses.

4 For a fuller outline of the development and significance of the enlightenment argument about evaluation use see Shaw, 1999: 28-30, 73-4, 92-5, 119.

always appear equivocal'. The aspiration after certain knowledge 'results from confusing rationality with logic. They are not identical…Evaluations can be no more than acts of persuasion' (House, 1980: 72). They are acts of argumentation, not demonstration. The requirement is for, as van der Knaap (1995) suggests, feedback and enlightenment, but also for argumentation. In summary, 'Evaluation persuades rather than convinces, argues rather than demonstrates, is credible rather than certain, is variably accepted rather than compelling' (p.73; cf House and Howe, 1999).

I risk digressing before even beginning. There *is* tension between evaluation and the development of learning organizations, which cannot neatly be resolved. We should not exaggerate the differences, but nor should we see them as simply negative factors.

By way of final preamble, it is worth emphasizing that the current interest in evaluation and learning organizations in social work in not some stand-alone development. The fields of health and education have both seen corresponding developments.[5] In all three fields there is a cluster of associated developments. Ideas about '*best practice*' can be read as an argument for practice that is less tied to a trust in the possibility of linear applications of research findings. *Reflective learning*, despite its more individualized approach, is a direct predecessor of the learning organization literature and still has something of value to contribute to organizational learning, as for example through the emphasis on cycles of action and learning. One reaction to arguments for evidence based practice has been to make a case for *knowledge based practice* – a process that suggests professional interaction, exchange and judgement, closely akin to the brief discussion of learning based practice below. I have already mentioned in passing the emerging literature on *evaluation capacity building*. This in turn owes a debt to the development literature and arguments for *sustainable development*. It is also linked to efforts to *mainstream evaluation*, which is argued to have occurred when evaluation is institutionalized as the ordinary way we do things in an organization. Finally, there are frequent references in the learning organization literature to the importance of *systems thinking*. The potential for reactivating links with the social work literature from the 1970s onwards, on intervention guided by systems approaches, is an obvious association of ideas, despite the characteristically thin treatment of evaluation issues in the majority of that literature. These links imply that we will gain far more from the interest in learning organizations if we avoid treating it as a *de novo* phenomenon, and hold it in dialogue with this family of cognate ideas, principles and practices.

In the following paragraphs I briefly outline the core requirements for the evaluative dimension of a learning organization. I then raise two potentially

5 Community based health programmes are one example in the health field (eg Shediac-Rizkallah and Bone (1998). In Britain, the Economic and Social Research Council has invested heavily in the Research Capacity Building Network for teachers. (See http://www.tlrp.org/ and http://www.cf.ac.uk/socsi/capacity/).

difficult questions, first about insider/outsider relations in a learning organization, and second regarding the underlying political thrust of pleas for a learning organization. I partly acknowledge these criticisms, but also respond to them through an outline of evaluating as a direct practice competence, and through a re-visioned practitioner research with a potential for organizational critique. I illustrate these points from recent projects in which I have been involved. I conclude with some cautionary comments about what we might hope for from embedding evaluation and evaluation capacity in a learning organization.

Evaluative requirements for a learning organization

There are four basic characteristics required if evaluation is to be embedded in a learning organization, *viz* an evaluation culture, an organizational focus for evaluation, a conscious attention to evaluation capacity building, and learning-based practice.

Evaluation culture

There has been little empirical work on the production of evaluation, and this hampers efforts to assess the characteristics of an evaluation culture in an agency. We can accept House's definition of an evaluation culture as 'those social arrangements and practices that sustain honest evaluative inquiry and utilization of findings' (House et al, 1996: 139). The work of House and his colleagues provides as good an indicator as we can find on the makings of an evaluative culture. Much hard, unseen work went into developing a culture in the National Science Foundation (NSF) whereby evaluation was accepted. This work was often described as 'building trust', and some staff seemed more adept and spent more time doing it than others. On the contrary, bad evaluations create a 'hang-over' effect. 'If you want to talk about one word – it's trust. And they felt that their trust had been damaged. Our trust, their trust in us had been damaged' (Research, Evaluation and Dissemination staff in NSF, House et al, 1996: 141).

Evaluation cultures cannot exist in isolation from organizational structures. Birleson describes the application of a learning organization to child and adolescent mental health services in Victoria (Au), and emphasizes the need to align structure and culture for learning. Existing structures tend to emphasize the roles of individual professional groups, and thus 'both structural and cultural change is usually required, although culture is less tangible and more poorly understood than structure' (Birleson, 1999: 268).

Organizational focus

Birleson's point about structures links to the need for an organizational focus. The point has been little developed, but it would seem that a focus on either project or programme evaluation, separate from an organization level, will overlook key factors in shaping the project environment.

Patton illustrates this point from a synthesizing evaluation of a large number of Aid to Families in Poverty (FIP) programmes in Minneapolis. 'An important breakthrough in our synthesis came when we understood that project and agency-wide cultures were systematically interrelated... We found that staff tended to treat participants the way they were treated as professionals within their organizations' (Patton, 1999: 96, 97). The systems connections between projects, programmes and organizations operated in both directions, however. 'Programs developed cultures that affected entire agencies and systems of which they were a part' (p. 97). This was particularly the case when projects gained the power and confidence that came from being unusually well resourced. Ordinary projects lacked the power or confidence to challenge system barriers to effectiveness. It was also true where projects and organizations shared a strong sense of mission. However, one important caveat that Patton emphasizes is that a project can be effective in terms of goal attainment measures, and yet make a low contribution to organizational mission (and *vice versa*). This reinforces our earlier point that accountability evaluation covers different territory from evaluation in a learning organization.

Evaluation capacity building

The issue of how organizations, programmes, governments and communities take on and sustain evaluation and its uses as ordinary, everyday practice is a central concern of this chapter. I cited the brief working definition given by Compton and colleagues earlier. More fully, they define evaluation capacity building as:

> A context-dependent, intentional action system of guided processes and practices for bringing about and sustaining a state of affairs in which quality program evaluation and its appropriate uses are ordinary and ongoing practices within and/or between one or more organizations/programs/sites. (Compton et al, 2002: 8)

This definition is limited somewhat because of its restriction of evaluation to programme evaluation. I return to this issue in the following part of the chapter. But that apart, it is a helpful summary of the process and concepts of capacity building.

I have mentioned already the claim that evaluation capacity building should helpfully be viewed as having different characteristics and requiring skills that are distinct from evaluation. It is a guided process that is ongoing and never complete. It is done collaboratively in teams, and in coalitions and other formal and informal partnerships. It supports the need for evaluation to be useful and conducted in an ethically responsible way. The key concepts include emergence, development, site learning, intention, sustaining and collaboration. A number of these ideas owe a considerable amount to the writing and experience in the field of third world development policy – an area that social work, to its loss, has generally bypassed. Patton remarks that 'Developmentally-oriented leaders in organizations and programs…don't aim for a steady state of effectiveness modelling because they're constantly tinkering as participants, conditions, learnings, and context change' (Patton, 1999: 110). The process demands skills of reflection, working in groups, both collaboratively and politically, together with a process orientation and a concern for rigour and relevance.

Learning based practice

Pleas for practice that is evidence-based, and 'best' frequently underplay what is entailed in learning a lesson, and the role of evaluation in this. While it is acknowledged that information is not the same as knowledge, there is nonetheless a simplistic emphasis in social work on the dissemination of research-based knowledge to practitioners. The notion of 'best practice' seems to enshrine the suspect assumption that there must be a single best way of doing something. On the contrary, 'Identifying specific intended uses with specific intended users can only be undertaken in a specific context and situation' (Patton, 2001: 331). This will require close attention to lesson learning, and heeding Patton's sharp interjection that 'all kinds of drivel passes for lessons learned' (Patton, 1999: 106). My own view is that a strong case can be made out for establishing what may be called a 'learning office' in a number of social work agencies, to facilitate appropriate practice in lesson learning.

Preskill and Torres (1999) have developed a Likert scale to measure organizational readiness for learning and evaluation (ROLE), consisting of 78 items grouped into six dimensions:

- Culture
- Leadership
- Systems and structures
- Communication
- Teams
- Evaluation

The aptness and usefulness of the scale needs field-testing. While it teases out different dimensions, the reliance of the authors on mean scores for interpreting the results risks overlooking the localized, context-specific nature of readiness for lesson-learning.

Organizational critique

I have argued that evaluation in learning organizations requires development of an evaluation culture, an organizational focus for evaluation, a conscious attention to evaluation capacity building, and facilitating learning-based practice. But if it is left without further comment, the suspicion may rightly lurk that there are conservatizing tendencies in the learning organization 'movement'. The suspicions are not without foundation. There are two reservations that I want to reflect on. First, a common sense inference might suggest that the processes I have described are best reserved for organizational insiders. This is worrisome, particularly if it is also linked to keeping a strong management hold on the process and direction of organizational learning. Second, does embedding evaluation in a learning culture result in a consensual, pluralist and incremental approach to organizational change, and militate against radical critique?

Insiders and outsiders

An 'insider' stance adopts the view that insiders are best positioned – or even solely positioned – to understand their daily world. Social work has been beset by various strong insider positions, not all of which are conservative in tendency.[6] It has a superficial plausibility. Applied to the previous discussion, it would encourage the view that outsiders – from other agency, government or higher education contexts – are largely or even wholly disqualified from participating in the process. But the insider/outsider split is not that simple. As Sue White concludes in her reflexive account of her own research,

> As anthropologists have debated the in/out, stranger/native, familiar/unfamiliar dichotomies, it has become clear that either/or distinctions of this kind are difficult to measure or sustain in ethnographic fieldwork. (White, 2001: 103)

In the same book, Hall (2001) and White record how they held both insider and outsider roles in relation to their research participants. Hall 'arrived' as an outsider but became in different ways a partial insider. White started as an insider, yet found herself undergoing a fruitful, if potentially hazardous, process of de-familiarization through which she became in some degree a marginal 'inside "out" member'. This suggests that, if only on learning grounds, an assumption that outsiders can and should be neatly identified and excluded is naïve and risky.

There are additional considerations. Outside facilitators have value-added benefits. For example, more obviously external facilitators, such as higher education colleagues, can paradoxically provide a key dimension of continuity. Embedding evaluation in the culture of an organization is an extended process that is never complete. If dependent only on insiders it risks being reliant on the enthusiasm of a limited number of good practitioners and managers, who in the nature of things are likely to move on. I have had some involvement with a strong practitioner research interest group in a social services department. The

6 See Shaw and Gould (2001), pp. 172-3 for an appraisal of strong insider positions in social work.

group attracted large numbers of practitioners to its varied meetings, and enjoyed a supportive but helpfully loose link to senior management in the agency. Yet when a key facilitator moved to another post, the group struggle to maintain its energy and activity levels. Furthermore, the experience of insider evaluation in large organizations and smaller agencies suggests that, for internal evaluations to be useful and credible, they must have high status in the organization and real power to make evaluation meaningful (Patton, 1999).

Outsiders-in have an important role to play in fostering the culture and structures of a learning organization. But the justification is not in terms of the supposed objectivity that distant outsiders bring to an organization.

Practitioners and organizational critique

The strength of the practitioner research interest group mentioned above stemmed to a significant degree from its relationship to agency management – given space to work, with membership open to managers, but run as a peer learning group. The thrust of this is rather different from the emphases of most literature on evaluation in a learning organization. I entered an earlier caveat about the definition of evaluation capacity building that Compton and colleagues provide, on the grounds that it envisages the evaluation link as being to programme evaluation. Patton, despite his acknowledgement that process evaluation is a key ingredient of organizational learning, tends to locate organizational leaders' relationship to evaluators as the key axis. Owen and Lambert also focus on the evaluator/organizational leader relationship (Owen and Lambert, 1995). Preskill and Torres make clear that their approach to evaluative inquiry for organizational learning is not a form of participatory evaluation.

I associate these emphases in my own mind with the downside to pleas for 'mainstreaming' evaluation such that it becomes a routine part of what happens. What is routine is taken for granted, and what is taken for granted is typically uninspected and part of an organizational equivalent of Thomas Kuhn's notion of 'normal science'. A comparison of American and British texts on evaluation and social work practice helps make the point. The American publishing market has a significant number of synthesizing textbooks on evaluation for social work students. The British market, to my knowledge, has not a single synthesizing social work textbook on this theme. By contrast, the British texts are all aiming, at least in part, to develop a position, and make an argument. It would be grossly unfair to imply that British writing is in some way 'better' than American, and the huge difference in market size doubtless contributes to the difference. But the more that any literature becomes dominated by 'mainstream' texts the less likely it is that practitioner critique will develop and be supported.

This risk of conservatizing tendencies has been noted. 'A concern is that in the ECB literature so far, other stakeholders' voices, in particular the individuals affected by the development programs, are not taken into consideration' (Stockdill et al, 2002: 17). They quote Hauge's report on the United Nations Development

Programme that 'It is better to have an imperfect answer from someone who has a legitimate claim to concern than a perfect answer from an expert whose mind is elsewhere' (p. 18). Some organizational learning writers are also open to engaging with action research models, and it is noticeable that the action research literature is beginning to offer a possible *rapprochement* between action research and learning approaches (eg Reason and Bradbury, 2000).

How can the possibility of organizational critique in the interests of good practice for service users be sustained? Two avenues look promising. First, through a re-visioning of the role of practitioner research, and second, through embedding evaluation processes as part and parcel of practice, rather than as something that is done to practice.

Practitioner research Practitioner research – evaluation, research, development, or more general inquiry into services that is small-scale, local, grounded, and carried out by professionals who directly deliver those self-same services – is embraced across the professions as good practice. Whether the practice be teaching, nursing, primary health care, pharmacy, counselling, psychotherapy, the various branches of applied psychology, the penal services, medicine or the human services, the desirability of practitioner research is for the most part unquestioned. Much of this activity trundles along with a low profile, rarely unsettling the status quo. It is almost stereotypically Kuhnian – minor puzzle-solving and ordinary. There are the exceptions, such as the classic, even heroic early developments in self-administered vaccine research, and the fashioning of the major depth psychologies in the consulting rooms of Vienna.

Practitioner research in social work is no exception. Fellow professionals, agencies and government welcome it as a contribution to the evidence base of social work that is modest in aspiration, small-scale, and for the most part non-contentious.

Yet there are characteristics of practitioner research that leave it in a weak position – entangled in, yet paradoxically insulated from, larger issues, and unlikely to influence social work services and practice. What are those characteristics? There are six that spring to mind.

Practitioner research often stands in a *client-donor relationship to social work agencies*. It is characteristically performed by direct service people in line posts, or by middle managers. It is often dependent for its completion on the consent of senior managers. In such cases it is employer led and agency owned.

Practitioner research in social work is also typically a *solitary* activity. The paradox of an activity that is both agency owned and solitary is more apparent than real. I estimate that over a half of all practitioner research in social work and social care in the UK is linked to the fulfilment of dissertation requirements for a master's degree.[7] Most practitioner research is solitary because it is non-collaborative

---

7 This estimate is taken from a preliminary screening audit of practitioner research in South-East Wales, undertaken in 2002.

and not part of a collective enterprise. Its *non-collaborative* nature springs from economic factors such as the agency costs of simultaneously releasing multiple members of staff to spend time doing research, and from the pressures towards lone research that stem from the assessment criteria that are part of post-qualifying activities and higher degrees in universities. Its *non-collective* character springs from rather different causes, associated with the absence of a critical agenda.

Practitioner research is almost always *insider research*. By 'insider' research, I refer to more than the organizational location and membership of the practitioner. Where I *work* and where I *stand* are two different matters. The point about practitioner research is that it has typically been insider research both in location and standpoint. This becomes transparent when we reflect on the relationship between practitioner research and user-led research. Fisher has argued that

> Genuine involvement of service users (cannot) be taken forward if the focus remains on the researcher-practitioner relationship. In a sense, the idea that problem formulation is/should be resolved through improving the relationship between practitioner and researcher is part of the problem… Indeed, there is a clear danger that in focusing on the modes of researcher-practitioner collaboration the voice of the service user is less prominent or simply outnumbered. (Fisher, unpublished)

Practitioner research stands in a donor-client relationship not only to social work agencies but also to the methodology of *social science research*. The subordinate stance of practitioner research is also not helped by an occasional insistence from its supporters that practitioner research is a special *genre* of research (eg Cochran-Smith and Lytle, 1990). I am not convinced by such territorial claims. Distinctions between 'academic' and practitioner inquiry, based on methodology or epistemology, are 'tenuous if not untenable' (Smith and Kleine, 1986: 55).

Finally, practitioner research tends to be bounded in both *professional and discipline* terms. Despite the well nigh universal professional interest in practitioner research, it is almost never the topic of inter-professional conversation and exchange.

This is a one-sided assessment ignoring the positive gains that come from local relevance, critical assessment of research findings, and so on. But the diagnosis suggests directions for a different prognosis. Practitioner research needs to be increasingly collaborative, collective, articulated to user concerns, the subject of active cross-professional conversation, and alert to the possibility of critique of both agencies and social science 'donors'. Knud Ramian has directed the development and testing of a collaborative practitioner research network strategy for social workers in mental health field in Denmark.[8] The central ingredients in the strategy are:

8 I am indebted to Knud Ramian's paper at the 2002 'Evaluation for Practice' conference in Tampere (Finland) and for our workshop collaboration.

1. A procedure for the selection of a small number of research teams.
2. No participants are allowed to work alone.
3. All teams in a network are committed to the same research question.
4. All teams adopt a case study strategy.
5. The network is organized around written contracts between the workplace and the network manager.
6. The network meets for a seminar every second month.

At the time of writing, the strategy has been tested in seven collaborative research networks including a total of 45 projects. The existing results show that the network strategy is a method that gives social workers the opportunity to learn, plan, carry out and report case studies. It is conceived in a form that promises well for the delivery of collaborative and collective effort.

While her analysis is not concerned explicitly with organizational learning, White illustrates two ways in which social workers can develop a critical, or analytic orientation to their practices. It is worth citing at some length.

> First, it was in part a product of particular personal and professional experiences. For example, I remember that, on one or two occasions when my second child was very small, I took him into work with me for a short while. He would sometimes be clingy and sometimes very independent, preoccupied with play, or other people, and hence almost indifferent to my presence. In the company of a group of my social work colleagues, I became acutely conscious that his behaviour could easily be read on any of these occasions as one of the many varieties of 'attachment disorder'. Had this been a clinical assessment, I thought about how vulnerable I would have been to such a diagnosis, and how resistance to it could easily have been written off as defensiveness or denial. Having used the theory routinely in my work for many years, this experience made me much more aware of its incredible malleability and virtual incorrigibility. There are few permutations of infant behaviour which escape its prolific explanatory potential. I came to see attachment theory (indeed all theory) less as a convenient tool, or template, and more as a powerful coloured lens, with the capacity to clarify (by eliminating the 'glare' which we experience when we try to make sense of complex relationships), but which may also cast the world in an over-simplifying monochrome.
>
> The second way in which a more meta-analytic orientation to day to day practices may develop … is related to 'techniques of organizing knowledge' (Strathern). If practitioners are exposed to different analytic and meta-analytic frameworks from outside their primary discipline, this increases the likelihood of them understanding their practices in new ways. In my own case, this influence came from my academic studies in sociology and social theory. (White, 2001: 105-6)

Evaluating-in-practice A second route to enabling a reformist organizational critique is through embedding evaluation processes as part and parcel of practice, rather than as something that is done to practice. As with practitioner research, the focus is on the world of direct practice rather than organizational leaders.

Patton hints at aspects of this when he supports helping people in organizations to think evaluatively so as to build evaluation into the organizational culture and engage in evaluation as part of ongoing organizational development. 'Using the processes of evaluation for organizational development and learning can be useful quite apart from the findings that may merge from these processes. Reasoning like an evaluator and operating according to evaluation's values have impacts' (Patton, 1999: 107).

We should not exaggerate the likeness of practice and evaluation, but there is what Riessman has called 'a sympathetic connection' between certain kinds of social work and qualitative kinds of data – 'talk, therapeutic conversation, agency records, narratives about experiences with organizations and macro systems' (Riessman, 1994: ix). The tie is proximate but neither universal, homogenous nor capable of straightforward transfer from one to the other. It requires methodological work, which I have described as involving 'colonizing' and 'translating' (Shaw, 1996, 1997). Colonizing requires practitioners to challenge the conventional donor-client relationship, and act upon research methods rather than simply apply them. Translation raises issues of language and culture, and underscores the interpretative character of the process. Social workers need to develop a dialogic practice, both within social work and with methodologists. For example, Janesick's 'stretching' exercises for qualitative researchers are an example of work based on a learning rationale that provides a fertile basis for professional 'colonising' and 'translating' (Janesick, 1998). The quality of 'methodological practice' will have an emergent, opportunistic and particularistic character. To maximise the gains from this process social workers need, once again, to avoid remaining too much insiders. 'The familiar not only breeds contempt, it breeds darkness as well' (Eisner, 1988: xii). Above all, 'methodological practice' will have a participatory and collaborative character.

I recently spent six months working on these ideas with senior practitioners and project managers in a large and geographically widely dispersed voluntary children's agency in Britain. Full days spent as a group were inter-laced with work-based learning projects. I conveyed to them my belief that evaluating in practice requires commitments to evidence, learning and justice, and illustrated the possibilities for methodological practice deriving primarily from qualitative methods.[9] This 'tripod', as the group aptly called it, was critically integrated into their day to day practice, and formerly routine events such as annual review days, case closures, and so on, became the subject of a new or renewed critical orientation.

---

9 Kirk and Reid develop a corresponding logic in their critique of science and social work practice in the USA (Kirk and Reid, 2002).

Conclusion in a minor key

I introduced this chapter with reflection on the tensions between some evaluation models and advocacy of a learning organization. I outlined the core requirements for the evaluative dimension of a learning organization. I then raised two potentially difficult questions, first about insider/outsider relations in a learning organization, and second regarding the underlying political thrust of pleas for a learning organization. I partly acknowledged these criticisms, but also responded to them through an outline of evaluating as a direct practice competence, and through a re-visioned practitioner research with a potential for organizational critique. I illustrated these points from recent projects in which I have been involved.

I am not, however, sentimental regarding the feasibility of introducing a critical transformation. Social change tied to barely visible increments remains a serious risk in learning organizations. The arguments remain weak on issues of gender and race (although see Rossiter's chapter in this book). In addition, there is a risk of insularity linked to an undue reliance on intra-organizational learning (there is scope here to draw from work on agency coalitions, eg Stevenson et al, 1996). Rejection of sentimentality, however, does not require abandonment of the project.

Acknowledgement

John Stevenson, University of Rhode Island, for first making me aware of important parts of this literature.

References

Birleson, P. (1999) 'Turning child and adolescent mental-health services into learning organizations' in *Clinical Child Psychology and Psychiatry* 4 (2): 265-274.

Chelimsky, E. (1997) 'Thoughts for a new evaluation society' in *Evaluation* 3 (1): 97-118.

Cochran-Smith, M. and Lytle, S. (1990) 'Research on teaching and teacher research: the issues that divide', in *Educational Researcher* 19 (2): 2-22.

Compton, D.W., Baizerman, M. and Stockdill, S.H. (2002) (eds) *The Art, Craft and Science of Evaluation Capacity Building*, New Directions For Evaluation, No 93. San Francisco: Jossey-Bass.

Eisner, E. (1988) 'Educational connoisseurship and criticism: their form and functions in educational evaluation', in D.M. Fetterman (ed) *Qualitative Approaches to Evaluation in Education.* New York: Praeger.

Fisher, M. (unpublished) 'The role of service users in problem formulation and technical aspects of social research'.

Greene, J. (2001) 'Evaluation extrapolations' in *American Journal of Evaluation* 22 (3): 397-402.

Hall, T. (2001) 'Caught not taught: ethnographic research at a young peoples' accommodation project' in I. Shaw and N. Gould *Qualitative Research in Social Work*. London: Sage Publications.

House, E.R. (1980) *Evaluating with Validity*. Beverley Hills: Sage Publications.

House, E.R., Haug, C. and Norris, N. (1996) 'Producing evaluations in a large bureaucracy' in *Evaluation* 2 (2): 135-150.

House, E. and Howe, K. (1999) *Values and Evaluation*. Thousand Oaks: Sage Publications.

Janesick, V.J. (1998) *"Stretching" Exercises for Qualitative Researchers*. Thousand Oaks: Sage.

Kirk, S. and Reid, W.J. (2002) *Science and Social Work*. New York: Columbia University Press.

Patton, M.Q. (1999) 'Organizational development and evaluation' in *The Canadian Journal of Program Evaluation* Special Issue, 93-113.

Patton, M.Q. (2001) 'Evaluation, knowledge management, best practices, and high quality lessons learned' in *American Journal of Evaluation* 22 (3): 329-336.

Preskill, H. and Torres, R.T. (1999) 'Building capacity for organizational learning through evaluative inquiry' in *Evaluation* 5 (1): 42-60.

Preskill, H. and Torres, R.T. (1999) *Evaluative Inquiry for Learning in Organizations*. Thousand Oaks: Sage Publications.

Reason, P. and Bradbury, H. (2000) *Handbook of Action Research*. London: Sage Publications.

Riessman, C.K. (1994) 'Preface: Making Room for Diversity in Social Work Research' in C.K. Riessman (ed) *Qualitative Studies in Social Work Research*. Thousand Oaks: Sage Publications.

Shaw, I. (1996) *Evaluating in Practice*. Aldershot: Ashgate.

Shaw, I. (1999) *Qualitative Evaluation*. London: Sage Publications.

Shaw, I. (1997) *Be Your Own Evaluator: a Guide to Reflective and Enabling Evaluating*. Wrexham (Wales): Prospects Publishing.

Shaw, I. and Gould, N. (2001) *Qualitative Research in Social Work*. London: Sage Publications.

Shediac-Pizkallah, M.C. and Bone, L.R. (1998) 'Planning for the sustainability of community based health programs: conceptual frameworks and future directions for research, practice and policy' in *Health Education and Research Theory and Practice* 13 (1): 87-108.

Smith, L. and Kleine, P. (1986) 'Qualitative research and evaluation: triangulation and multi-methods reconsidered', in D.D. Williams (ed) *Naturalistic Evaluation*. New Directions in Program Evaluation, No. 30, San Francisco: Jossey-Bass.

Stevenson, J.F., Mitchell R.E. and Florin, P. (1996) 'Evaluation and self-direction in community prevention coalitions' in D.M. Fetterman, S.J. Kaftarian and A.

Wandersman (eds) *Empowerment Evaluation: Knowledge and Tools for Self-assessment and Accountability*. Newbury Park CA: Sage Publications.

Stockdill, S.H., Baizerman, M. and Compton, D.W. (2002) 'Towards a definition of the ECB process: a conversation with the ECB literature' in D.W. Compton, M. Baizerman, and S.H. Stockdill (eds) *The Art, Craft and Science of Evaluation Capacity Building* New Directions For Evaluation, No 93. San Francisco: Jossey-Bass, pp 7-25.

Torres, R.T. and Preskill, H. (2001) 'Evaluation and Organizational Learning: Past, Present and Future' in *The American Journal of Evaluation* 22 (3): 387-395.

van der Knaap, P. (1995) 'Policy evaluation and learning: feedback, enlightenment or argumentation?' in *Evaluation* 1 (2): 189-216.

White, S. (2001) 'Auto-ethnography as reflexive inquiry: the research act as self-surveillance' in I. Shaw and N. Gould (eds) *Qualitative Research in Social Work*. London: Sage Publications.

PART III
Qualitative Research

I sketched something of the career of my ideas in the opening essay, including the fluctuating contribution made by quantitative methods. Over a fairly long period I have engaged in a number of quantitative studies – surveys (e.g. Shaw, 1977, 1985), mark-recapture methods (Shaw et al, 1996) and program evaluation (e.g. Shaw et al, 2009).

And yet, and yet. However strong my selective endorsements of quantitative research may be (Shaw, 2012a), qualitative inquiry loosens the tight predilections of surveys and randomized control trials, and enlarges perspective. Roy Ruckdeschel's and my launch essay for the journal *Qualitative Social Work* aimed to mark out that vision for social work research and practice (Shaw and Ruckdeschel, 2002), and that article opens this section of the book.

To take the difficult case, qualitative methodology enables a rewarding entry into those very fields where quantitative scholars believe themselves to be strong. I endeavour to set out this claim through an older essay on conceptualizing causal thinking in social work practice (Bull and Shaw, 1992), and through a more recent effort to show how qualitative strategies enable us to address a range of design and inferential problems associated with detecting the outcomes of social work intervention (Shaw, 2003b). The *Qualitative Social Work* journal has a special issue on qualitative intervention research in 2012.

I would not want to overclaim the merits of qualitative social work research. For example, unlike some commentators, I do not think qualitative methods have a special affinity with social work values that is not possessed by quantitative research. However, I have included a former book chapter that illustrates ways in which I believe qualitative inquiry affords us a sharpened hearing (Shaw, 1996b). I have tried once or twice to apply the same assumptions to thinking about research ethics in qualitative research, and the following article is my most recent effort to say something plausible about this field (Shaw, 2008b).

The final inclusion in this part of the book returns to the broad canvas, through a discussion of the consequences of qualitative research (Shaw and Gould, 2001, Ch. 11), and I hope to say more about this in a pending work with Sally Holland. This chapter has an earlier version of aspects of the chapter, also in this part, on qualitative contributions to outcomes research, but covers more extensive territory in viewing 'consequences' as a way of deliberately avoiding mere 'dissemination' or even active utilization, but the broad aftermath of the research act. I returned to that theme through empirical fieldwork carried out some years later (Shaw and Norton, 2007).

References

Bull, R. and Shaw, I. (1992) 'Constructing Causal Accounts in Social Work', *Sociology* 26 (4): 635-649.

Shaw, I. (1996b) 'Unbroken Voices: Children, Young People and Qualitative Methods', in Butler, I. and Shaw, I. (eds), *A Case of Neglect?* Aldershot: Avebury.

Shaw, I. (1977) 'Selecting for Social Work', *British Journal of Social Work* 7 (1): 55-72.

Shaw, I. (1985) 'A Closed Profession? – Recruitment to Social Work', *British Journal of Social Work* 15 (3): 261-280.

Shaw, I. (2003b) 'Qualitative Research and Outcomes in Health, Social Work and Education', *Qualitative Research* 3 (1): 57-77.

Shaw, I. (2008b) 'Ethics and the practice of qualitative research' *Qualitative Social Work* 7 (4): 400-414.

Shaw, I. (2012a) 'The Positive contributions of quantitative methodology to social work research: a view from the sidelines' *Research on Social Work Practice.*

Shaw, I., Bell, M., Sinclair, I., Sloper, P., Mitchell, W., Dyson, P., Clayden, J. and Rafferty, J (2009) 'An Exemplary Scheme? An Evaluation of the Integrated Children's System', *British Journal of Social Work* 39 (4): 613-626.

Shaw, I., Bloor, M., Cormack, R. and Williamson, H. (1996) 'Estimating the Prevalence of Hard to Reach Populations: Illustration of Mark-Recapture Methods in the Study of Homelessness', *Social Policy and Administration* 30 (1): 69-85.

Shaw, I. and Gould, N. (2001) *Qualitative Research in Social Work*. London: Sage Publications.

Shaw, I. and Norton, M. (2007) *Kinds and Quality of Social Work Research in Higher Education*. London: Social Care Institute for Excellence.

Shaw, I. and Ruckdeschel, R. (2002) 'Qualitative social work: a room with a view', *Qualitative Social Work: Research and Practice* 1 (1): 5-23.

Chapter 10
Qualitative Social Work: A Room with a View*

This journal comes to you with what might appear to be an out of the ordinary title: *Qualitative Social Work*. In this essay, we will attempt to explain what we mean by that term, and in addition introduce readers to the aims and purposes of the journal as well as to the contents of the first issue. The subtitle, a room with a view, perhaps suggests the notion of a room with a number of windows and corresponding multiple views of varying scenery. While not wanting to belabor the analogy, this journal is a kind of room with a view – or indeed, rooms with views. Further, the title suggests something about the journal's editorial position on the landscape of qualitative research and of social work. While there has been a tendency to see these as two separate landscapes, we in fact see these as one landscape, if a rather cluttered one. By way of a final note of introduction, this article was written in the days immediately following the events of September 11, 2001 in New York and Washington D.C. The world, whether one views it as postmodern of not, now seems a very different place. In a just world order, we need to keep open all channels of communication, all possibilities for dialogue. We hope this journal provides a forum, even if only in a small way, for facilitating some of that dialogue.

Qualitative Social Work: Research and Practice will provide a forum for those interested in qualitative research and evaluation and in qualitative approaches to practice. The journal provides a two-way bridge, between those engaged in qualitative research and those involved in the world of practice. It reflects the increasingly international and interdisciplinary nature of these worlds. The journal will not merely provide a platform for applying qualitative methodology and evidence from research to social work, but will be a forum for rigorous dialogue that promotes qualitatively embedded professional practice and inquiry. Hence, a central aim of the journal will be to promote and exemplify a qualitative informed professional practice, that is both challenged by, and in turn challenges, qualitative inquiry in its broadest conceptions.

This broad canvas includes, for example, exchange and conversation on:

- The role of critical perspectives within social work.
- The nature of reflective inquiry and practice.

---

* Originally published in the first number of *Qualitative Social Work*. I. Shaw and R. Ruckdeschel, 2002. 'Qualitative social work: a room with a view', *Qualitative Social Work: Research and Practice* 1(1): 5-23. Reprinted with permission of Sage Publications Ltd.

- The development of practitioner research that avoids naïve pragmatism on the one hand and an overly narrow commitment to evidence-based, empirical or scientific practice on the other.
- Developments in parts of the world in realist evaluation and inquiry, and attempts to develop principled integrations of qualitative and quantitative methodology in social work.
- The potential of interpretive and narrative approaches to research and practice.
- The possibilities of linking various disciplines through the evolving interest in cultural studies and its social critique of contemporary society.

We invite journal contributors to engage that to challenge the basic assumptions of social research and of practice and to do so with primary, though not exclusive, reference to the contexts of social work and the understanding and evaluation of practice. Social work research and practice will only be the weaker insofar as it develops solely within a social work context. Research and practice benefit enormously from the multiple perspectives that come from inter-disciplinary, multi-cultural approaches.

Moments and themes

'A study of social work research literature for information about qualitative methods would turn out to be a brief venture' (Goldstein, 1991: 101). The late Howard Goldstein's decade-old comment is, as Gould has observed, both true and untrue.[1] Somewhat paradoxically, while there is a very large qualitative literature in social work journals, and evidence of a strong upward trend in the use of qualitative methods on social work doctoral research, the impression remains in the majority of student texts on social work research, that qualitative research is an exotic minority pastime.

The periodization of qualitative research has come to be dominated by Denzin and Lincoln's historical overview of broad 'moments' (see also Denzin's paper in this issue).[2] While we do not think that research and practice are advanced by tight adherence to reconstructed historical periods, Denzin and Lincoln's work offers a sensitizing framework for thinking about the evolution of qualitative research in social work. As Gould puts it, '"moments" are not like geological seams which are

1 Gould has completed a helpful review of qualitative research in social work that cautiously maps 'moments', traces emergent themes, and considers the relationship between qualitative research and practice (Chapter 2 of Shaw and Gould, 2001). We acknowledge our debt to Gould's analysis in these following paragraphs.

2 There are several references such as this to articles that appeared in the first issue of *Qualitative Social Work.*

mined to extinction, but overlap and are often worked simultaneously' (Shaw and Gould, 2001: 34).

The substantive themes and preoccupations of qualitative social work research partially cut across historical 'moments', and appear to cluster around six nodes.

1. Analyzing taken for granted practices in social work, by submitting routine or mundane processes to scrutiny and analysis, in order to learn more about their function and how participants construct their roles within their working context.
2. Probing and exploring the behavior of social workers as an occupational group, and of service users, and opening up the interactions between them to scrutiny
3. The use of qualitative research to articulate the voice of the service user.
4. Organizational and professional adaptation to organizational life.
5. Understanding and evaluating complex policy initiatives.
6. Qualitative research on problems with which social workers are concerned.

There are obvious gaps in all this. For example, qualitative social work research has left itself too open to Thyer's implicit criticism, that the 'two purposes of evaluation research, process versus outcome studies, may be best respectively addressed by qualitative versus quantitative methodologies' (Thyer, 2000: 401). Also, practitioner research, and scientific or empirical practice, is only now beginning to take on board the rich potential of qualitative inquiry to generate understanding, collaborative initiatives, and critical perspective.

The literature on qualitative social work yields more than empirical themes, or the development of that research within the wider sphere of social science research. Indeed, the borders of research and practice perhaps inter-twine most closely when the question is posed if qualitative research methodology has a natural synergy with the processes of practice. The debate on this is still in its infancy. Gilgun argued from a grounded theory perspective some years ago that practice fits qualitative research 'like a hand fits a glove' (Gilgun, 1994). She suggested that the two share a number of common features, including a focus on construing the world, contextualizing data, 'thick description' of individual cases, deductive and inductive reasoning, processes of constant comparison and analytic induction, and an embeddedness in naturalistic settings. In contrast to this, Padgett has claimed that both are located in different paradigms. Practice is theory and model driven, while research is concerned with theory generation and is non-normative (eg Padgett, 1998). While this is not a distinction that we ourselves find very helpful, we do hope that responses and counter responses to these positions will find a home in this journal. The main point for the moment is that the debate is helpful, in that it widens the scope of relevance, and asks questions about the interlacing of research and practice in new ways.

Qualitative Social Work will provide a forum to explore and promote these themes and developments, through the challenge and enhancement of human services research, social work practice, and the social work commitment to critique, reform and change. The journal will be characterized by a broad-based engagement with research and practice, and a strong practice development aim. We intend that the journal will provide an opportunity to explore ways in which research utilization and dissemination issues can be explored creatively. The journal is committed to high standards of methodological writing (cf Seale's paper in this issue) but is also open to accounts written in alternative forms of discourse. It is the editorial policy of the journal to not only encourage established writers, but also to provide an outlet for emerging scholars, for the best material from qualitative dissertation work and for the perspectives of those whose voice is often not heard. We intend that the journal will promote excellence in whatever form it publishes.

It goes without saying that the journal is committed to qualitative research and practice. This is partly as a counter-balance to the asymmetry of existing social work journals, but primarily because social work will be enhanced thereby. However, writers for the journal will be encouraged to explore and challenge boundaries, rather than simply reinforce them. These boundaries include those of research and practice, qualitative and quantitative inquiry, discipline and profession, nation and community, and race, age and gender.

Human services research

Social work can have no place for sloppy research, a 'sentimental' refusal to question dearly held positions, naïve pragmatism in methodology, or stringent relativism. Social work research, and journals thereon, should be judged by the extent to which they promote social work inquiry marked by rigor, range, variety, depth, progression and concern with ethics. This is more likely to be achieved if we

1. Avoid ethnocentrism, by drawing on the best available knowledge within and beyond the boundaries of social work. Social work and its research enterprise are not hermetically sealed from cognate enterprises in the fields of education, health, criminal justice, and evaluation. Social work research has distinct characteristics[3] but social work research, though difficult, is not uniquely difficult or complex. We have no reason to be precious regarding the distinctiveness of our professional enterprise.

---

3 Just what those distinctive characteristics *are* is open to agreement. As a way into this question, one of us has argued that qualitative social work research should be more strongly grounded in an understanding of and puzzling about issues of context (Shaw and Gould, 2001, chapter 1). In that way, social work can *set* as well as *respond to* the research agenda.

2. Remember – but are not stifled by the realization - that regimes of truth are regimes of power.
3. Are critical, and eschew overly sentimental or Romantic positions of the kind that refuse to question dearly held positions. Naïve constructionism and relativism, attacks on so-called positivism, and uncritical adoption of the latest research vogue, whether it be of methods (eg focus groups) or methodology (eg critical realism), are among the less than helpful trends that leave us feeling intellectually and occasionally morally queasy.

Can qualitative social work research and practice deliver on these goals? Qualitative research, particularly when it has a strong applied agenda, has been criticized for being atheoretical or lacking rigor, for promoting a diluted, token form of ethnography,[4] and for being generally methodologically weak (eg Atkinson and Delamont, 1993). We think social work should resist knee-jerk 'not guilty' pleas to these charges. It does neither social work nor qualitative research a service to either caricature or unquestioningly dismiss criticisms from conventional or qualitative methodologists. Social work research too often lacks methodological imagination. Decisions about methods seem to be treated as technical matters, informed by a naïve sense of pragmatism. This unnecessarily strengthens the arms of critics, insofar as pragmatists 'exist in splendid isolation from developments and debates in research methodology outside of social work' (Trinder, 2000: 43).

In part response, we wish to see the emergence of a genuinely inter-disciplinary forum for the development of research and practice. Inter-disciplinarity may be demonstrated at three levels:

- Qualitative work undertaken from the perspective of different social science and humanities disciplines, and by inter-disciplinary collaboration. For example, the editors believe that social work has been weakened by the general absence of exchanges and links with the evaluation research community in the United States, Europe and more widely. We hope this journal will facilitate a creative exchange from within such communities.
- Work that explores the occupational boundaries between social work and other professions, for example, education, health, criminal justice and housing.
- Articles that enable theoretical, practice and methodological exchange between social work and other professions.

---

4 There are variations in usage that need to be accommodated in this discussion. For example, qualitative research traditions developed somewhat differently in the USA and Britain (Atkinson, Delamont and Hammersley, 1988; Jacob, 1987). It is usual to hear the term 'ethnography' used with relative precision in the USA, and in distinction from other qualitative research traditions, whereas in Britain it is also often used a catch-all category to convey a more thorough-going commitment to qualitative inquiry, as In Hammersley's 1992 book cited at this point in the article. It is sometimes used with that wider sense in this article.

But do we need to maintain the qualitative/quantitative divide in order to achieve such goals and counter indifferent research and practice? For example, is part of what's wrong with ethnography its existence in direct counterpoint to conventional methodologies (Hammersley, 1992)? Yes and no. Yes, insofar as it has contributed to the generation and maintenance of the positions criticized in the previous paragraphs. But no, if it is assumed that the choice is a distinction without a difference. For example, the division of the land offered by Thyer earlier in this article simply does not work. Sinclair, a leading British mainstream researcher on social work outcomes concludes that qualitative methods are in many ways more adapted to the complexity of the practitioner's world than the 'blockbuster' randomized control trial.

> Qualitative research draws attention to features of a situation that others may have missed but which once seen have major implications for practice. It counteracts a tendency to treat the powerless as creatures with something less than normal human feelings. It contributes to an ethically defensible selection of outcome measures. And, in combination with simple statistical description, it can lead to an informed and incisive evaluation of programs in social services. (Sinclair, 2000: 8)

Turning common assumptions on their head, he concludes that,

> Quantitative social work research does face peculiarly acute difficulties arising from the intangible nature of its variables, the fluid, probabilistic way in which these variables are connected, and the degree to which outcome criteria are subject to dispute. (pp. 9-10)

Does this mean that we should take a mix and match approach, in the confidence that greater diversity of method will produce findings that comfortably 'triangulate' with one another? Unfortunately using multiple methods does not inevitably lead to sounder consensual conclusions in an additive fashion. 'Simply using different perspectives, with the expectation that they will validate each other, does not tell us what to do if the pieces do not fit' (Trend, 1979: 83). Trend's advice is:

> That we give the different viewpoints the chance to arise, and postpone the immediate rejection of information or hypotheses that seem out of joint with the majority viewpoint. (p. 84)

He quotes approvingly Paul Feyerabend as saying 'It seems that it is not the puzzle solving activity that is responsible for the growth of knowledge, but the active interplay of various tenaciously held views' (p. 84).

Prematurely collapsing the boundaries of inquiry and method may be the wrong prescription to achieve this goal. It is our view that we should work for a principled synthesis where feasible, but should not assume that a synthesis will be possible in any given instance. In a discussion of mixed methods that helpfully sets the discussion in the context of paradigms rather than discrete methods, Greene and Caracelli argue for a synthesis that represents,

> a balanced, reciprocal relationship between the philosophy and methodology, between paradigms and practice. This...honors both the integrity of the paradigm construct and the legitimacy of contextual demands, and seeks a respectful, dialogical interaction between the two in guiding and shaping evaluation decisions in the field. (Greene and Caracelli, 1997: 12)

There are, of course, questions other than those of methodological strategy. For instance, the journal provides a forum for the development of qualitative practitioner research – an issue for which Fook's paper has considerable relevance. Most practitioner research is employer-led, 'applied', and based on an expectation that it should lead to results that are directly useful. Yet ironically practitioner research tends to be weak at the very point where it seems most strong – its practical usefulness. Its limitations include:

1. Insufficient reflection on what it means for social workers to be 'practical'.
2. A tendency to search for confirmatory rather than falsifying instances.
3. Unduly narrow views about how practitioner research can be useful for practice.
4. A weak connection with user-led research.

To correct these shortcomings, there needs to be as much emphasis on qualitative inquiry methods as presently is placed on more conventional, structured inquiry methods. Qualitative practitioner research is too often invisible in social work. McLeod describes what is missing as 'knowledge-in-context practitioner research' as against the scientific practitioner model (McLeod, 1999: 13). He identifies the key characteristics of such practitioner research as being 'Born out of personal experience and a "need to know"'. Its aim is to produce knowledge that makes a difference to practice, in which the investigator uses reflexive self-awareness throughout to gain access to implicit meanings. It 'addresses the moral and ethical issues associated with the combination of researcher and practitioner roles, and with a process of inquiry into the experience of perhaps vulnerable or fragile informants' (McLeod, 1999: 8). And, as he notes elsewhere, this need not be at the expense of concern with practice outcomes (McLeod, 2001, Chapter 10).

Social work practice

If this journal aims to challenge and enhance human services research then, in reciprocal fashion, it ought to question and enrich social work practice. It will do so in at least three ways. First, by demonstrating the value of qualitative research for social work practice; second, by promoting authentic evidence-based practice; and third, by fostering the development of evaluation and inquiry as a direct dimension of social work practice.

The first of these is deceptively straightforward. The journal will not merely be a stamping ground for epistemological debates – for those engaged in what Becker engagingly calls 'philosophical and methodological worry as a profession' (Becker, 1993: 226) – but will look for qualitative research that is practice-relevant. The journal includes within its panel of assessors/reviewers several who come from mainstream qualitative research. The papers by Denzin and Seale in this issue illustrate this commitment, and there will be further examples in forthcoming issues. Yet there is only a tiny proportion of qualitative research that reflects on its practitioner usefulness. This probably has little to do with any intrinsic difficulties in doing so. Indeed, one ethnographer argues that 'the real opportunities for sociological influence lie closer to the coalface than they do to head office, that the real opportunities for sociological influence lie in relations with practitioners, not with the managers of practice' (Bloor, 1997: 234).

In reviews of a street ethnography of HIV-related risk behavior among Glasgow male prostitutes, and comparative ethnographies of eight therapeutic communities, he suggests there are two ways in which ethnography might speak to the practitioner. *First*, in an argument akin to Gilgun's linking of grounded theory and social work practice, he suggests that ethnography may 'model' a service delivery that can be transferred to service providers. For example, 'ethnographic fieldwork, in its protracted and regular contacts with research subjects, has much in common with services outreach work' (p. 227). From his therapeutic community studies, Bloor suggests the very act of comparative judgment can model helpful service practice. 'Rich description of particular kinds of therapeutic practice can assist practitioners in making evaluative judgments about their own practices' (p. 229). *Second*, ethnographers may, where appropriate, draw practitioners' attention to practices they think worth dissemination and further consideration. Bloor and McKeganey list seven practices which seemed to them to promote therapy in their original settings (Bloor and McKeganey, 1989), and which they discussed with the practitioners in the therapeutic communities.

However, we do not think that applying qualitative research to social work is an unproblematic process. Some writers rightly dismiss 'cookbook' approaches to both research and its application (in fact cooking is a more apt metaphor that may be thought). Hence the journal will aim to promote authentic evidence-based practice without presupposing the meaning of that concept. There are three key points here. First, the journal will treat the obtaining of 'evidence' as something that needs careful work. Second, *Qualitative Social Work* will encourage the exploration of how practice is 'based' on and in evidence. For example, the journal welcomes the application of critical realist positions to social work, with their emphasis on the way causal mechanisms operate, and the consequent need to incorporate understanding of process in studies of outcomes, and so on. Also, the journal invites articles that promote a grounded understanding of research usefulness. Third, evidence based practice leads directly to questions of outcomes research. The journal will provide a forum for innovative qualitative research that explores social work outcomes.

The necessity for this last point has been hard learned. Silverman, in his study of HIV counseling, still found grounds to complain of the ways in which what he calls the Explanatory Orthodoxy of counseling research leads to a focus on either the causes or consequences of counseling. This approach 'is so concerned to rush to an explanation that it fails to ask serious questions about what it is explaining' (Silverman, 1997: 24), such that the phenomenon of counseling 'escapes'. Traditional formulations of causal inputs and outcomes need at the very least to be delayed until we have understood something of the 'how'. For sound evaluative reasons we will want to ask the explanatory 'why' questions. 'There is no reason not to, provided that we have first closely described how the phenomenon at hand is locally produced' (p. 35). A qualitative approach to evaluation analysis will start from the premise that 'the ends of the goals should emerge from the process, not the other way round' (Sherman and Reid, 1994: 152).

There are four hallmarks and trends in qualitative research that offer ways forward on this. First, some qualitative research designs can offer a limited degree of control in ways akin to quasi-experimental designs, and hence strengthen the possibility of outcome inferences (eg Yin, 1994). Second, qualitative research allows a greater sensitivity to the micro-processes of practice and programs, and hence to the understanding of the inter-weaving of formative and summative outcomes (eg Reid, 1990). Third, developments in symbolic interactionism and ethnomethodology have been applied to outcome questions (eg Miller, 1997, Mohr, 1997). Fourth, the impact of scientific realism has led to recognition of the fuzzy relationship between causes and consequences, and hence a more grounded and persuasive understanding of outcomes (House, 1991, Pawson and Tilley, 1997).

A different approach to questioning and enriching social work is through the development of evaluation and inquiry as a direct dimension of social work practice, as part and parcel of service delivery in much the same way as assessing, planning, communicating, enabling and so on. It is here that the reflective learning and practice strand may find a congenial domicile in the journal, and some of the theorizing work drawing on Foucault, Bourdieu, Habermas, Ricoeur, Latour and others.

There is a wide range of topics available to qualitative social work researchers to explore through reflective methods, including:

- The changing nature of practice
- The relationship between professional education and practice
- How practitioners develop practical knowledge
- The development of expertise
- The development and characteristics of tacit knowledge
- The development of professional identity
- The relationship between practice and continuing professional development (Shaw and Gould, 2001, adapted from Jarvis, 1999).

A current illustration of this issue is the debate over the application of qualitative methods to assessment of clinical practice. The evaluation of clinical practice, particularly in the U.S. has primarily focused on the application of quasi-experimental methods to the evaluation of one's own practice. The form this has taken has been that of the single system design or single subject design. The appeal of this design is pragmatic or perhaps even naively pragmatic in that it assumes an instrumental (as discussed previously) solution to evaluation of clinical practice and that the single subject design can at long last provide the link between research and practice. This logic is open to both insider and outsider critique and has been the subject of extensive debate at both levels. However, to critique single subject design from the vantage point of a qualitative perspective, as indeed one of the editors has done (Ruckdeschel and Farris, 1982) is to leave open what alternatives would be posed by a qualitative social work approach. Among other things, a qualitative approach to evaluation puts instrumental issues into context, a context that includes moral and political dimensions. On an instrumental level, it increasingly poses questions about the utility of emerging qualitative computer software. Such software has potential utility in solving the burden of audiotape transcription that confronts qualitatively inclined practitioners. Similarly, there are questions about the utility of qualitative analysis software such as Atlas, NUD*IST and Ethnograph. Thus the more instrumental aspects of the application of qualitative methods, while secondary to conceptual and moral issues, are fair game for dialogue in *Qualitative Social Work.* It is our view that a concern with the epistemological aspects of qualitative clinical evaluation (what is the nature of social work practice, how can we include the voice of those we serve in that evaluation, etc.) does not preclude an appreciation of instrumental issues (e.g. what data analysis packages are best; what is the utility of voice recognition software).

Reform and change

Once qualitative research and practice becomes limited to methodology and practice it runs the risk of political and policy complacency. Hence, *Qualitative Social Work* will debate social work's moral and political purpose, while holding it central.

Social work values

There are three immediate aspects to this role. First, *Qualitative Social Work* will address social work values. The appropriateness of this implied link between methodology and values sometimes has been questioned. For example, there is a debate in the empowerment research literature as to whether qualitative methodology – or any methodology – has distinctive value commitments. A diminished concern with methodological cogency has often been associated with an advocacy position on research, where instrumental procedures take second place to wider political issues. Lorenz summarizes this questioning stance as follows.

> It is not the choice of a particular research method that determines social work's position socially and politically. Rather it is the ability to engage critically in the political agenda of defining the terms on which knowledge and truth can be established which should form the basis for the search of appropriate research approaches in social work. (Lorenz, 2000: 8)

In a thoughtful analysis, Stanfield concludes that 'even in the most critical qualitative research methods literature there is a tendency to treat "human subjects" as the passive prisoners of the research process' (Stanfield, 1994: 168).

Others have been more optimistic regarding the affinity of qualitative methodology with moral or political agenda. Riessman, for example, has written about narrative methods through which 'an individual links disruptive events in a biography to heal discontinuities – what should have been and what was' (1994: 114). She makes a more general link between qualitative methodology and liberatory positions. 'Because qualitative approaches offer the potential for representing human agency – initiative, language, emotion – they provide support for the liberatory project of social work' (1994: xv).

Dingwall arrives at a similar conclusion, albeit from a different approach. In his consideration of the moral discourse of interactionism, he is impatient with the postmodern repudiation of moral concerns and is concerned with how the moral and empirical plug together. He reaches back to the philosophy of Adam Smith, for viewing sociology as studying the very preconditions for mutual society. 'If we have a mission for our discipline, it may be to show the timeless virtues of compromise and civility, of patient change and human decency, of a community bound by obligations rather than rights' (Dingwall, 1997: 204). This quotation deliberately contrasts with emancipatory models of research, and shows that qualitative analysis 'of what it might take to live a moral life' (p. 204) is neither novel nor the exclusive province of any single political position.

We hope that contributions to this journal will sharpen awareness of ways that qualitative research informed by critical concerns 'must neither ignore instrumental issues nor privilege them' (Vanderplaat, 1995: 94). We acknowledge that, while qualitative inquiry does not necessarily promote particular values, and is certainly not more 'ethical' than conventional research, it does, however, focus the attention helpfully on a range of key value questions for social work. The ethics of qualitative research design pose distinctive demands on principles of informed consent, confidentiality and privacy, social justice, and practitioner research (cf Murphy and Dingwall, 2001). Fieldwork ethics raise special considerations regarding power, reciprocity and contextual relevance. The analysis and dissemination of qualitative inquiry emphasize questions regarding the ethics of narrative research, outcomes and justice, and the utilization of research. The paper in this issue by Denzin and Gilgun and Abrams illustrate the kind of argument that might be made.

Welfare reform

Second, the journal intends to enhance and give critical 'bite' to the social work commitment to political change and reform. A hotly contested issue in American social welfare policy is that of the consequences of the massive change in the nature of the social welfare system wrought by the so-called welfare reform legislation of the 1990s – reforms closely paralleled elsewhere in the world. Investigations have focused on the organization of welfare departments, the change in welfare caseload dynamics over time, the patterns of work and welfare use of former welfare recipients, the barriers to employment, especially among poor, single mothers, and the functioning of children, especially school-age children. These investigations have relied on experimental and quasi-experimental designs and quantitative measures. Very few have employed qualitative strategies or methods. Those that have tend to rely on qualitative methods of data collection such as the use of questions with open-ended response formats or the use of focus-group interviews. These have yielded some useful descriptive information. What is lacking is the application of theoretical frameworks to help understand the significance of the data that have been obtained. For example, we need:

- Sophisticated analyses of the culture of welfare departments drawing on appropriate theoretical frameworks and ethnographic models.
- Substantive theory to account for variability in how welfare recipients respond to welfare workers or to employers, which draws on grounded theory methods.
- Longitudinal investigations of how work, welfare, and other survival strategies are learned and evolve over the life course, drawing on biographical approaches.

Indeed the very meaning of 'reform' is at issue. For example, the evaluation of consequences clearly seems to involve studying the quantifiable results of this legislation but also strongly suggests a need to better understand its impact on the poor and the disempowered from their vantage point. It follows that they may well conclude that it is not 'reform'. As in other instances of policy research, the voice of those impacted by policy change has neither been heard nor for that matter sought. Qualitative strategies and methods have a prominent role to play in the development of knowledge in this area of social policy. It is our intention to engage this concern in future issues of the journal.

Empowerment research

Third, *Qualitative Social Work* will provide a forum for empowerment research, including user-led and other forms of collaborative research. One of the most far-reaching developments of recent years has been that practitioners within the human services increasingly have been challenged by forms of inquiry that are seen not as means to some external end but also (and for some advocates, solely) as ends in themselves. To borrow an apt phrase from Robert Stake, social workers have become 'reluctant to separate epistemology from ideology, findings from yearnings' (Stake, 1997: 471). The idea that research ought not to be neutral but partisan turns conventional ideas of science and research on their head. Why has it happened?

1. Doubts have emerged as to whether science is progressive - the idea that research leads to knowledge, which in turn leads to improved practice. This enlightenment philosophy has been widely questioned – the assumption that 'increased knowledge will make people happy or better satisfied in some way' (House, 1980: 64).
2. The linked idea that science should simply describe without taking a value position has also been widely rejected. It is almost 30 years since Robert Merton criticized 'social sadism' and 'sociological euphemism' on these grounds (Merton, 1972).
3. The idea that scientific knowledge is fundamentally separate from citizen knowledge also has been widely questioned, stimulated by the work of sociologists of knowledge.
4. Power issues in research have thrown doubt on the justness of pluralist models of interests in research, and have led many to believe that power issues cannot be resolved simply by improving stakeholder representation.

These emerging positions may pose social work researchers and practitioners with an acute sense of dissonance that stems from arguing for rigorous methodology in one breath, and different forms of partisan advocacy based on the evidence, in the next. Yet we think it must be done.

> Absent an engaged, accountable position like scientific citizenship, I fear that qualitative evaluation will be relegated to the sidelines of important debates about pressing public issues.. No longer can we shroud our citizen-selves behind our scientific subjectivities. We must become scientific citizens. (Greene, 1996: 286-7)

Structure and format of the journal

The preceding discussion articulates the overall aims and purposes of *Qualitative Social Work: Research and Practice*. As noted at several points, our intent is that this journal serves as a forum for dialogue. The structure of the journal hopefully facilitates that dialogue. The following are the ongoing sections of the journal.

Main articles

These are intended to engage the central issues of qualitative social work. The article by Denzin and response by Gilgun and Abrams is representative of this dialogue. As noted, Denzin applies the historical model of seven moments in the history of qualitative research to social work. In essence, Denzin is asking the reader to consider or reconsider what social work can and should look like in the postmodern world. His view is informed by developments in the arena of cultural studies and is guided by his empowerment oriented feminist communitarian ethic. In their response, Gilgun and Abrams embrace the main elements of Denzin's perspective but attempt to introduce what they view as the unique elements of the contemporary social work context and thereby modify his position. As such, the exchange becomes a dialogue rather than a debate.

Seale, on the other hand, is interested in grounding the meaning of the term 'qualitative', the root word or term in qualitative methods and qualitative social work. In so doing he provides a reading of some of the issues reflected in Denzin's seven moments approach to the history of qualitative methods. Seale is asking us and indeed expecting us to go beyond a naïve or taken for granted understanding of the meaning of 'qualitative', and especially to make the case for methodological awareness as an essential component of the craft skill that qualitative researchers typically bring to their work.

Fook and Poindexter take us directly into the world of practice. Fook raises the question of how we can begin to develop theory in practice by utilizing a qualitative social work perspective. In so doing she gives us insights into the application of qualitative methodology into practice and implicitly challenges the view that qualitative methodology is atheoretical. By exemplifying a more inclusive approach to ways of theorizing, she illustrates qualitative social work as a room with a view. Similarly, Poindexter takes us into the world of the HIV-affected caregiver. She shows us how a narrative approach can provide an understanding of that world and how that understanding may shift depending on the type of narrative employed. Her article has implications on both the substantive and methodological level.

This introductory essay itself is illustrative of planned occasional editorial pieces by Shaw and Ruckdeschel. The intent is to provide a framing of the issues under consideration, even if at times that framing is provocative in nature. We would think that the likely readers of this journal would expect nothing less.

New Voices

These are articles by practitioners, dissertation and graduate students, academics at an early stage of their career, and others whose voices are often not heard. This will be more clearly reflected in future issues of the journal. The concept of 'voice' has been much discussed in the social work literature. Witkin has in his editorials in *Social Work* eloquently argued for active inclusion of the voices of those disempowered, oppressed, and unrepresented. As he has also noted, this is no doubt easier said than done (Witkin, 1999). Some voices, such as those of practitioners, have been underrepresented in the social work literature. In contrast, this journal hopes to reach out to the practitioner and to give her/him an opportunity to engage in the dialogue. While perhaps a problematic enterprise, it is a doable one. The make up of the Board of the journal, which includes practitioners, is one way to try to provide a structure that will encourage such voice. The voice of the 'client', a particularly disempowered and oppressed voice, presents a more difficult challenge. In this regard, the journal is open to alternative languages of discourse. The language of social science as represented in the United States by the APA style (American Psychological Association) is only one form of discourse, albeit a form highly privileged by many journals. The journal will be flexible on the details of referencing styles. APA style, for example, is less familiar to writers outside the US. We hope to go beyond this and, in concert with our contributors, seek out ways to address this imbalance. The alternating voices in Gilgun and Abrams' article illustrate one direction in which this commitment might take the journal.

Response and Commentary

This section includes responses to previous articles in the journal or contributions that initiate discussion of current research and practice issues. Here we intend to go beyond the typical reader response section of many journals. We seek a more pointed form of dialogue that will encourage the journal and its readers to engage particularly difficult issues. Dialogue and commentary that in a sense opens up spaces will be of highly valued.

Practice and Teaching of Qualitative Social Work

These are critical 'how-to' accounts and reflections on the methodology and practice of qualitative social work. The section title implies two separate but interrelated activities of considerable concern to the journal. In this essay, we have provisionally mapped the meaning of qualitative social work. We have suggested that the meaning will continue to evolve as the journal evolves. Given our intentions, that evolution will proceed and succeed only if our contributors are able to provide insight into how they go about the practice of qualitative social work. In this respect, we are not seeking to reproduce ourselves or to substantiate the title of the journal but rather to explore the possibilities of a qualitatively informed social work practice.

Teaching, in our view, is another form of social work practice. In the past two decades or so, there has been an international explosion in the teaching of qualitative methods in social work education. No longer can research and practice texts ignore the role of qualitative methods in social work education. The journal hopes to provide a venue for those engaged in the practice of teaching qualitative social work. The journal seeks to foster a profession that runs counter to the everyday wisdom that practical aptitude and teaching competence are rarely found at home together.

Technical Applications

These are reviews of developments that impact on qualitative research and practice such as qualitative analysis software and voice activated recording devices. Technology, as previously noted, is not separate from practice. There are in fact exciting new opportunities to use technology to facilitate practice. Technology will not solve the fundamental issues confronting the contemporary qualitative social worker, but it can facilitate data gathering and data analysis and who knows what else. The article by Schoech and Helton illustrates how one can use the Internet and the Web based chat room in a classroom context. It also suggests ways in which this type of approach and the attendant data can be analysed.

This introductory essay is both a statement of what this journal is about or hopes to be about and a call for you the reader to be a participant in the process. We hope that it is indeed a room with a view.

References

Atkinson, P. and Delamont, S. (1993) 'Bread and dreams or bread and circuses? A critique of case study research in evaluation', in Hammersley, M. (ed) *Controversies in the Classroom*. Buckingham: Open University Press.

Atkinson, P. Delamont, S. and Hammersley, M. (1988) 'Qualitative research traditions: a British response to Jacob', *Review of Educational Research*, 58 (2): 231-250.

Becker, H. (1993) 'Theory: the necessary evil', in Flinders, D. and Mills, G. (eds) *Theory and Concepts in Qualitative Research: Perspectives from the Field*. New York: Teachers College, Columbia University Press.

Bloor, M. (1997) 'Addressing social problems through qualitative research', in Silverman, D. (ed) *Qualitative Research: Theory, Method and Practice*. London: Sage.

Bloor, M. and McKeganey, N. (1989) 'Ethnography addressing the practitioner' in Gubrium, J. and Silverman, D. (eds) *The Politics of Field Research: Sociology Beyond Enlightenment*. Newbury Park: Sage.

Gilgun, J. (1994) 'Hand in glove: The grounded theory approach and social work practice research' in Sherman, E. and Reid, W.J. (eds) *Qualitative Research in Social Work*. New York: Columbia University Press.

Goldstein, H. (1991) 'Qualitative research and social work practice: Partners in discovery', *Journal of Sociology and Social Welfare*, XVIII (4): 101-119.

Greene, J. (1996) 'Qualitative evaluation and scientific citizenship', *Evaluation*, 2 (3): 277-289.

Greene, J. and Caracelli, V. (1997) *Advances in Mixed Method Evaluation: the Challenge and benefits of Integrating Diverse Paradigms.* New Directions For Evaluation, No 74, San Francisco: Jossey-Bass.

Hammersley, M. (1992) *What's Wrong With Ethnography?* London: Routledge.

House, E. (1980) *Evaluating With Validity.* Beverly Hills: Sage.

House, E. (1991) 'Realism in research', *Educational Researcher*, 20 (6): 2-9.

Jacob, E. (1987) 'Qualitative research traditions: a review', *Review of Educational Research*, 57 (1): 1-50.

Jarvis, P. (1999) *The Practitioner-Researcher.* San Francisco: Jossey-Bass Publishers.

Lorenz, W. (2000) 'Contentious identities – social work research and the search for professional and personal identities' paper from ESRC seminar series 'Theorizing social work research', National Institute for Social Work web site http://www.nisw.org.uk/tswr/lorenz.html.

McLeod, J. (2001) *Qualitative Research in Counseling and Psychotherapy.* London: Sage Publications.

McLeod, J. (1999) *Practitioner Research in Counseling.* London: Sage Publications.

Merton, R.K. (1972) 'Insiders and outsiders; a chapter in the sociology of knowledge', *American Journal of Sociology*, 78 (1): 9-47.

Miller, G. (1997) 'Contextualizing texts: studying organizational texts' in Miller, G. and Dingwall, R. (eds) *Context and Method in Qualitative Research.* London: Sage.

Mohr, W.K. (1997) 'Interpretive interactionism: Denzin's potential contribution to intervention and outcomes research', *Qualitative Health Research*, 7 (2): 270-286.

Murphy, E. and Dingwall, R. (2001) 'The ethics of ethnography' in Atkinson, P., Coffey, A., Delamont, S., Lofland, J. and Lofland, L. (eds) *Handbook of Ethnography*. London: Sage Publications.

Padgett, D. (1998) 'Does the glove really fit? Qualitative research and clinical social work practice', *Social Work*, 43 (4): 373-381.

Pawson, R. and Tilley, N. (1997) *Realistic Evaluation*. London: Sage.

Reid, W. (1990) 'Change-process research: a new paradigm?', in Videka-Sherman, L. and Reid, W. (eds) *Advances in Clinical Social Work Research.* Silver Spring, MD: NASW Press.

Riessman, C.K. (1994), 'Preface: making room for diversity in social work research' in Riessman, C.K. ed. *Qualitative Studies in Social Work Research.* Thousand Oaks: Sage Publications.

Ruckdeschel, R. and Farris, B. (1982) 'Assessing practice, a critical look at the single case design', *Social Casework*, 63 (5): 272-275.

Shaw, I. and Gould, N. (2001) *Qualitative Research in Social Work*. London: Sage.

Sherman, E. and Reid, W. (1994) (eds.) *Qualitative Research in Social Work.* New York: Columbia University Press.

Silverman, D. (1997) *Discourses of Counseling: HIV Counseling as Social Interaction*. London: Sage.

Sinclair, I. (2000) 'Methods and measurement in evaluative social work' Theorizing social work research. Paper from ESRC seminar series http://www.nisw.org.uk /tswr/sinclair.html

Stake, R. (1997) 'Advocacy in evaluation: A necessary evil?' in Chelimsky, E. and Shadish, W. (eds), *Evaluation for the 21st Century*. Thousand Oaks: Sage.

Stanfield, J. (1994) 'Empowering the culturally diversified sociological voice' in Gitlin, A. (ed) *Power and Method: Political Activism and Educational Research*. New York: Routledge.

Thyer, B. (2000) Review of I. Shaw and J. Lishman (1999) (eds) 'Evaluation and Social Work Practice', *British Journal of Social Work*, 30 (3): 401-402.

Trend, M.G. (1979) 'On the reconciliation of qualitative and quantitative analyses', in Cook, T. and Reichardt, C. (eds) *Qualitative and Quantitative Methods in Evaluation Research*. Beverly Hills: Sage.

Trinder, L. (2000) 'Reading the texts: Postmodern feminism and the "doing" of research' in Fawcett, B., Featherstone, B., Fook, J. and Rossiter, A. (eds) *Practice and Research in Social Work: Postmodern Feminist Perspectives*. London: Routledge.

Vanderplaat, M. (1995) 'Beyond technique: issues in evaluating for empowerment', *Evaluation*, 1 (1): 81-96.

Witkin, S. (1999) 'Constructing our future', *Social Work*, 44 (1): 5-8.

Yin, R.K. (1994) *Case Study Research*. Thousand Oaks: Sage.

Chapter 11

Qualitative Research and Outcomes in Health, Social Work and Education*

> Probation officers tended to 'de-couple' the *process* of supervision from the *outcomes* of someone being on a probation order. One person said that clients 'frequently get into more trouble but I don't think that in any way is a reflection on whether or not I have been effective'. There was a widespread belief that an element of luck operated in being effective. One might do 'brilliant work but if the circumstances are against you they will still re-offend'.
>
> Two social workers, talking about their practice.
>
> 'The fact that I can successfully get her to begin to think about something which might in the end turn a few little cogs in her mind is gonna be for her a success. If there is only a little, teeny chink in the wall of justification for offending then, yeah, I would probably take a little bit of credit for that'.
>
> 'You can spend a lot of time on a particular case and you feel you've done really well, only to find out that somebody rings up and tells you they're in (hospital) on the poisons unit. So, it's very hard to evaluate or to recognise whether you're doing a good job or not'.[1]

The purpose of this chapter is to outline ways in which qualitative research may contribute to research on outcomes in health, social work and education. It is a methodology paper with a practical purpose. Large tracts of inquiry work are concerned with questions about the benefits of a given policy initiative, programme, service or intervention – benefits that are likely to be couched in terms of outcomes, merit and so on.

An appraisal of the possible contribution of qualitative research to such endeavours is important for two reasons. First, it is plausible to claim a deepened methodological strength in qualitative research in the policy field. Government departments are in some cases more open to commissioning qualitative research for evaluative purposes (eg National Institutes for Health, 2001). I believe it is a desirable aspiration for health, social work and education researchers to support qualitative social science research that seeks to integrate rigor (substantive and

* Originally published as I. Shaw, 2003. 'Qualitative research and outcomes in health, social work and education', *Qualitative Research* 3(1): 57-77. Reprinted with permission of Sage Publications Ltd.

1 These extracts are taken from Humphrey and Pease, 1993, and Shaw and Shaw, 1997.

methodological) and relevance. This point will have local importance, for example in Britain, where the future of mainstream Social Policy undergraduate and postgraduate degrees is under serious threat. New alliances are necessary between 'applied' researchers and sociologists who take an integrative position on rigor and relevance. If we are to avoid reinforcing conventional wisdom about a 'horses for courses' approach to methodological choice, then we need an intellectually principled position on the relationship between different methodologies.

Second, wider developments underline the timeliness of this discussion. Government departments and research funding bodies in the USA, Britain, Australia, and Canada talk routinely of 'evidence-based policy and practice'. There are widespread initiatives to facilitate the integration of research into professional practice, which are echoed in research and development initiatives that bring health and social care into working proximity. Developments in Britain such as the Economic and Social Research Council's initiative on Evidence Based Policy and Practice (see for example http://www.evidencenetwork.org) aim to be a catalyst in the development of evidence-based practice. While these are welcome developments, there is a risk that advocates of conventional outcomes research may too heavily influence debates about evidence.

A couple of cautions are in order. For one thing, this chapter should not, of course, be read as a claim that qualitative research is better equipped than more traditional approaches to generate foundationalist knowledge of policy and practice outcomes. This would be crass. '*Nothing* can guarantee that we have recalled the truth' (Phillips, 1990: 43). In the human sciences knowledge of outcomes – especially of future ones – is not so much informative as advisory. 'Like the cry of the backseat driver: "You'll be in the ditch in a minute", such communications function more like *advice*. "Consider how you would like it if things turned out this way"... To receive such communications about ourselves may in a sense be informative; but it does not confront us with the "take-it-or-leave it" claim to our assent which is the hallmark of objective knowledge. We can falsify it' (McKay, 1988: 140, 141).

In addition, I would have unwittingly provided 'aid and comfort to the barbarians'[2] if what follows was received as a plea to replace one uniformitarian orthodoxy with another. On the one hand, a notion that only qualitative methods can examine unique, complex cases is clearly not accurate, as there is an interesting history of idiographic and ipsative quantitative methods for individual case analysis in psychology in the work of people such as Rogers, Allport, Cattell and Kelly. Likewise, I am not convinced that all forms and traditions of qualitative methodology lend themselves equally or even directly to evaluative purposes. Stake no doubt had this in mind when he remarked that 'to the qualitative scholar, the understanding of human experience is a matter of chronologies more than of

2 The phrase is borrowed from Carol Weiss' reflections on how neo-conservatives latched on to liberal research critiques of education in the 1970s.

cause and effect', and that 'the function of research is not…to map and conquer the world but to sophisticate the beholding of it' (Stake, 1995: 39, 43).

Finally, the way I approach this chapter probably betrays my British social science background. I talk of research and evaluation almost inter-changeably for much of the chapter. I may be wrong – indeed, for most USA readers I am certainly wrong, and evaluation is best understood as a distinct discipline. But the basic arguments are probably little affected by this.

In the first part of the chapter, I consider the relationship between quantitative and qualitative methods especially in relation to evaluative research. I discuss this from the position that there is a *real* but very *imperfect* linkage between philosophy and method. I concur with Greene when she concludes that 'epistemological integrity does get meaningful research done right' (Greene, 1990: 229). In the main part, I draw some preliminary conclusions regarding the contribution that qualitative methodology can make to outcomes research.[3]

Numbers and qualities

> These two purposes of evaluation research, process versus outcome studies, may be best respectively addressed by qualitative versus quantitative methodologies (Thyer, 2000).

Thyer captures in this single sentence the most common image of the relationship between quantitative and qualitative research, and links it to the related question of how such research should address issues of process and outcomes. John Stevenson expresses the position more subtly as follows:

> Despite the fascination I have with the narrative complexities in the programs I have evaluated, I see this as the background for the evaluation, worthy of attention as it affects the foreground, the movement toward finding replicable means of accomplishing desired ends. Is the qualitative salience of the process, and especially the conflicts and inconsistencies, the best guide to where attention should be paid? I see the process as seductive, and relevant only up to a point.[4]

The two sets of relationships – quantitative/qualitative and outcome/process – have often been expressed either in terms of a functional division of labor – what may be described as a *horses for courses* approach (eg Chelimsky, 1997), or in terms of a relationship of hierarchy, where aspects of one methodology are alleged to be intrinsically superior to the other. Macdonald advocates the latter position in a contribution – ironically – to a book that claims to seek a rapprochement between

3 This paper develops arguments made in Shaw, I. and Gould, N. (2001) *Qualitative Research in Social Work*. London: Sage, Chapters 1 and 11.

4 Personal communication.

quantitative and qualitative approaches. In discussing the case for randomised control trials (RCTs), she concludes that it is 'essential that *all* research designs deployed in outcomes research pay heed to the sources of internal validity that RCTs are best able to control' (Macdonald, 1999: 101). This is a give-away remark, illustrating that too often the emergence of methodological pluralism has had little impact on outcomes research.

The roots of these debates go back at least to the work of Campbell and Cronbach from the 1960s onwards in America. Their work, and the debates between them on issues of internal and external validity, process and outcomes, and rationality, has not been sufficiently taken into account by the current generation of evidence-based evaluators and supporters of scientific practice. In some cases, their contribution has not even been acknowledged. Cronbach remarked that it is 'rationalist to the point of unreality' to proceed on the basis that evaluation starts from agreement on goals (Cronbach et al., 1980: 129). All social programmes, he argued, have broad and vague goals, even supposedly targeted programmes. This is not escapism, as the rationalists would argue, but reflects the nature of programmes as operating within a climate of political accommodation. 'The first rule of the successful political process is, "Don't force a specification of goals or ends"' (p. 130). House correctly concludes that the traditional formulation 'is not the world of social programmes and, in general, is not the social world at all' (House, 1993: 135). Rather, we are engaged in 'social inquiry for and by earthlings' (Cronbach, 1986).

The lesson has been hard learned. Silverman, in his study of HIV counselling, still found grounds to complain of the ways in which what he calls the Explanatory Orthodoxy of counselling research leads to a focus on either the causes or consequences of counselling. This approach 'is so concerned to rush to an explanation that it fails to ask serious questions about what it is explaining' (Silverman, 1997: 24), such that the phenomenon of counselling 'escapes'. Traditional formulations of causal inputs and outcomes need at the very least to be delayed until we have understood something of the 'how'. For sound evaluative reasons we will want to ask the explanatory 'why' questions. 'There is no reason not to, provided that we have first closely described how the phenomenon at hand is locally produced' (p. 35).

The inadequacy of conventional outcome designs arises in part from the extreme difficulty of isolating inputs. Abrams' paper on the problems of measuring informal care summarised the position as follows:

> The resistance of informal social care to experimental evaluation has entirely to do with the problem of breaking down the intractable informality of the treatment; of reducing informal caring relationships to the sort of units, factors, events, variables, items needed if specifiable inputs are to be systematically related to specifiable outcomes (Abrams, 1984: 2).

The 'sheer weight and diversity of the "quasi-inputs" which appear to intervene between effects and their presumed causes' means that 'the fine web of conditions within which social action occurs is discovered in the course of the research instead of having been provided for in the research design' (p. 4). The force of Abrams' remarks should not be missed. It is not simply that experimental evaluation has technical limitations. Experimental and other comparable evaluation strategies inevitably disaggregate informal care, and rob it of its inherent systemic and holistic character. The problems stem from the intrinsic incapacity of such designs, rather than their technical imperfections.

At the heart of the question lie different 'root metaphors' of what research is basically about (Kushner, 1996). For mainstream outcomes researchers, inquiry is basically about order; for process researchers it is about conversation. Kushner suggests the key test is what keeps evaluators awake at night. For outcomes researchers it is not managing to distil the evaluation into a single unified story; for process researchers it is having only one story to tell.

We should not jump from this to the counter-conclusion that qualitative methodology has no problems of its own. Qualitative research, especially that of an interpretive cast of mind, has been criticised, for example, by Giddens who complains that interpretive sociology sits too close to philosophical idealism. Hence it is marked by:

- 'A concern with "meaning" to the exclusion of the practical involvements of human life in material activity'.
- 'A tendency to seek to explain all human conduct in terms of motivating ideals at the expense of the causal conditions of action'.
- 'A failure to examine social norms in relation to asymmetries of power and divisions of interest in society' (Giddens, 1993: 163-64).

Naïve constructivism, as applied to evaluation, 'risks losing sight of culture'. Individuals daily struggle to 'reconcile their hopes with the institutional hand they have been dealt' (Kushner, 1996: 198-199), and qualitative evaluation research must address this individual/culture relationship.

Fortunately, there have been constructive, if cautious, dialogues regarding the relative merits and characteristics of quantitative and qualitative methodologies. For example, in social work research, Reid in the USA and Sinclair in Britain have developed mediating positions. Reid seeks to 'redefine the nature of the mainstream so that qualitative methodology is a part of it not apart from it'. He regards quantitative research as strong when dealing with linkages, control, precision, and larger data sets, while qualitative research is able to depict system workings, contextual factors, and elusive phenomena, and provide thorough description. 'Neither method is superior to the other, but each provides the researcher with different tools of inquiry' that can be set against a single set of standards (Reid, 1994: 477).

Sinclair goes somewhat further, when he says that qualitative methods are in many ways 'more adapted to the complexity of the practitioner's world than the blockbuster RCT'.

> Qualitative research draws attention to features of a situation that others may have missed but which once seen have major implications for practice. It counteracts a tendency to treat the powerless as creatures with something less than normal human feelings. It contributes to an ethically defensible selection of outcome measures. And, in combination with simple statistical description, it can lead to an informed and incisive evaluation of programmes in social services. (Sinclair, 2000: 8)

He turns common assumptions on their head when he concludes that,

> Quantitative social work research does face peculiarly acute difficulties arising from the intangible nature of its variables, the fluid, probabilistic way in which these variables are connected, and the degree to which outcome criteria are subject to dispute. (pp. 9-10)

Qualitative researchers have also addressed the relationship between different methodologies in ways that fruitfully extend the debate (eg Bryman, 1988; Greene and Caracelli, 1997), and have explored the relative contributions different methodologies make to evaluation studies of process and outcomes.

It would be highly premature, however, to conclude that the debates should now be closed, and we should simply get on with evaluation research without wasting time on the profession of 'philosophical and methodological worry' (Becker, 1993: 226). For example, it is sometimes wrongly assumed that using multiple methods will lead to sounder consensual conclusions in an additive fashion. Naïve versions of triangulation arguments are sometimes resorted to in support of this argument (cf Bloor, 1997 for a helpful discussion of triangulation as a means of judging validity). One of the most insightful discussions of the problems raised by this assumption is Trend's early classic account of an evaluation of a USA programme designed to test the effectiveness of direct payment of housing allowances to low income families (Trend, 1979). In one case study, the *quantitative* data suggested that the programme was producing major improvements in housing quality. Yet all the *qualitative* data indicated the programme would fail. The major part of Trend's paper records his assiduous sifting of the data in an attempt to discover a plausible explanation that did not simplistically cut the Gordian knot, either by prioritising one kind of data above the other through paradigm arguments, or by premature syntheses. His conclusion still stands as a warning against such easy solutions:

> The complementarity is not always apparent. Simply using different perspectives, with the expectation that they will validate each other, does not tell us what to do if the pieces do not fit. (1979: 83)

His advice is:

> That we give the different viewpoints the chance to arise, and postpone the immediate rejection of information or hypotheses that seem out of joint with the majority viewpoint. (p. 84)

He quotes approvingly Paul Feyerabend as saying 'It seems that it is not the puzzle solving activity that is responsible for the growth of knowledge, but the active interplay of various tenaciously held views' (p. 84).

The inter-relationship of qualitative and quantitative methods is not only, nor even primarily, about choice of methods. It is about single cases or comparison; cause and meaning; context as against distance; homogeneity and heterogeneity. It entails judgements about validity and the criteria of quality in social work research, the relationship of researcher and researched, and measurement. Methodological choice is also inextricably relevant to issues of the politics and purposes of social research, values, participatory forms of research, interdisciplinary inquiry, and the uses of research.

How we understand the relationship between different methodologies will, of course, be closely linked to the position taken on paradigms. Hence, we have already anticipated our likely direction in our preliminary comments on paradigms. There are three broad positions (the terminology is that used by Greene and Caracelli, 1997). The *purist* position argues that different frameworks of inquiry embody fundamentally different and incompatible assumptions about the nature of social reality, claims to knowledge, and what it is possible to know. Multi-methods at the paradigm level are not an option. The *pragmatic* position is best represented by what we have described as a functional division of research labor. The position that is likely to prove most creative for qualitative outcomes research is that described by Greene and Caracelli as *dialectical*. This position accepts that philosophical differences are real and cannot be ignored or easily reconciled. We should work for a principled synthesis where feasible, but should not assume that a synthesis will be possible in any given instance. This represents,

> a balanced, reciprocal relationship between the philosophy and methodology, between paradigms and practice. This…honours both the integrity of the paradigm construct and the legitimacy of contextual demands, and seeks a respectful, dialogical interaction between the two in guiding and shaping evaluation decisions in the field. (Greene and Caracelli, 1997: 12)

One possible undesirable consequence is that an emphasis on the value of multiple, integrated methods may lead to a dilution of one or the other – a lowest common denominator position. It may also lead to a tendency to treat qualitative methodology (or quantitative) in an unduly homogenous way. Stake's recent confession should not be ignored. 'I have not had much luck in using qualitative and quantitative studies to confirm each other. The criteria of the one get lost in the events of the other. Consistencies, enrichments in meaning, can be found but, I think, seldom confirmations'.[5]

Partly in recognition of this, there is a need to develop the case for a dialectical mix of methods *within* qualitative research. This will need to proceed through the development of a set of critical features of knowledge for different qualitative methodologies. A helpful starting point for this is the paper by McKeganey and colleagues, in which they discuss the benefits and limitations of interviewing and observation methods as part of a study of professional decision-making when people may be offered a place in a home for the elderly (McKeganey et al., 1988; cf Shaw, 1999: 145-146). This initial analysis needs to be extended to a full range of qualitative strategies, and tied to the critical features of the associated knowledge claims (Greene and Caracelli, 1997: 12-13).

Evaluative judgements

Qualitative applications to outcome research can be facilitated by rethinking assumptions about how evaluative reasoning proceeds.

> Everyone agrees that information somehow informs decisions, but the relationship is not direct, not simple. Often the more important the decision, the more obscure the relationship seems to be. (House, 1980: 68)

House goes as far as to say that, 'subjected to serious scrutiny, evaluations always appear equivocal' (p. 72). He argues that evaluations can be no more than acts of persuasion. 'Evaluation persuades rather than convinces, argues rather than demonstrates, is credible rather than certain, is variably accepted rather than compelling' (p. 73). Evaluators have too frequently underplayed the role of judgement and hence of argumentation. This has resulted in an unduly technical, methods-oriented analysis, an over-confidence in quantification, and a tendency to represent knowledge in an impersonal, objectified form. Those who fail to accept the 'compelling' conclusions drawn from the evaluation are dismissed as irrational. If results are unequivocal then those who fail to accept them are 'wrong'.

There have been several attempts to take a different approach to thinking through the reasoning process involved in constructing justified evaluative arguments. These typically emphasise the complex connection between evidence and conclusions, and commence from the differences between formal and informal reasoning. Whereas formal reasoning assumes a tight fit between the premises and conclusions within an argument, informal logic 'deals with ordinary, everyday language, where rules of inference are less precise and more contextual' (Fournier and Smith, 1993: 317). The key question is whether good but non-

5 Quoted from a posting on EVALTALK – the discussion list of the American Evaluation Association – June 26th, 2001.

deductive reasoning is possible – ie reasoning that is not logically valid in a formal inferential sense. 'The consensus among informal logicians is that there can be logically good, but nonvalid reasoning' (Blair, 1995: 73).

This philosophical argument has direct practice implications because much evaluative reasoning is non-deductive. For example, we may sometimes engage in good all-things-considered reasoning, where there are reasons for and against a point of view but where the pros outweigh the cons. The argument by House cited above falls in that category. Also, there has been growing acceptance of the circumstances in which it may be legitimate to reason from *factual* evidence to *evaluative* conclusions, where there can be no logical relation of implication for such an argument. Finally, informal logicians have concluded that much reasoning is dialectical. Reasons for a claim are seen as a move in an argument – an attempt to persuade offered as part of an actual or possible exchange between parties who differ.

Process and outcomes

Given these more general arguments, how can qualitative research and evaluation address outcome questions? In four ways.

1. Through design solutions partly analogous to designs which entail a degree of control.
2. A shift of emphasis from internal validity to questions of external validity and generalisation, can lead to a greater sensitivity to the micro-processes of practice and programmes.
3. Developments in symbolic interactionism and ethnomethodology are susceptible to application to outcome questions.
4. Several approaches to analysis of qualitative data facilitate an enriched development of outcome judgements.

Design solutions

The development of case study designs, and the use of simulation methodology provide two contrasting illustrations of the development of qualitative design solutions analogous to designs, which entail a degree of control.

Qualitative design solutions have been pursued actively by those who have worked on the borders of qualitative and quantitative methodology. For example, Donald Campbell's early position was that 'one-shot' case study designs are uninterpretable with regard to causal attribution. However, through exchanges with Becker and Erikson, he came to the position that the analogy of degrees of freedom provides a major source of discipline for interpreting intensive, cross-cultural case studies. The logic entails testing theories against the predictions or expectations it stimulates, through a general process he describes as pattern matching, based on the premise that 'experimental design can be separated from quantification' (Campbell, 1978: 197). He developed a perspective which entailed a mutual commitment to both ethnography and comparative studies.

Campbell's approach has been developed in Yin's account of case study research (Yin, 1994). Patton has also illustrated how 'well-crafted case studies can tell the stories behind the numbers, capture unintended impacts and ripple effects, and illuminate dimensions of desired outcomes that are difficult to quantify' (Patton, 2002: 152). He makes a familiar distinction between programme improvement and individual outcomes, and argues that qualitative case studies offer a method for capturing and reporting individualised outcomes. Insofar as it is necessary to understand individual outcomes – and in many classroom, school-level, health interventions, criminal justice programmes, and human services interventions understanding of such outcomes is often vital – then quantitative, standardised measures will be inappropriate. Take, for example, education or human services programmes that aim at some form of individual autonomy and independence. 'Independence has different meanings for different people under different conditions… What program staff want to document under such conditions is the unique meaning of the outcomes for each client'. 'Qualitative methods are particularly appropriate for capturing and evaluating such outcomes', through the use, in particular, of inductive description (Patton, 2002: 158, 476).

Simulations offer a rather different design solution for qualitative inquiry, and have the potential to provide 'a unique and innovative tool that has not yet been widely applied' (Turner and Zimmerman, 1994: 335). They have two main applications – first, as an evaluative test for service discrimination, and second, as a qualitative proxy for control within a natural setting. The first application is essentially an export from the social psychology laboratory, which offers some control over stimuli but also suffers from some of the laboratory risk of, for example, artificiality and demand characteristics. But it is the second application that is more relevant for present purposes. One particular example of simulation – the simulated client – represents an advance on the use of vignettes in policy research. Those who evaluate the process of professional practice come face to face with the invisibility of practice. How may we learn the ways in which lawyers, teachers, general medical practitioners, or social workers practice? How would different professionals deal with the same case? Wasoff and Dobash used a promising innovatory method in their study of how a specific piece of law reform was incorporated into the practice of solicitors (Wasoff and Dobash, 1992; Wasoff and Dobash, 1996). The use of simulated clients in 'natural' settings allowed them to identify practice variations that could be ascribed with some confidence to differences between lawyers rather than the artefacts of differences between cases.

Suppose, for example, that one wishes to carry out a qualitative evaluation of decisions made by housing managers, medical staff, and social workers regarding the allocation of care management packages. Evaluators using simulated clients would prepare a small number of detailed case histories designed to test the practice decisions under consideration. A researcher or evaluator takes on the role of the client in the case history. The housing manager, relevant medical staff, and social workers each interview the 'client' within the 'natural' setting of their work.

There are limitations to the application of simulation methods. The method needs additional resources to prepare the case material, perhaps to act the role of clients, and to reflect on the quite detailed material that results from transcriptions of the interviews. The cost is therefore likely to be relatively high, and it requires reasonably high levels of research skills. It will be clear from the brief description that the method could not be a tool for evaluating particular cases, but would focus on specific *kinds* of practice. However, the use of simulated clients has several things going for it. First, some researchers, especially insider researchers who have completed professional training programmes, are likely to be familiar with the 'family' of role-playing methods from which it is drawn. Second, other methods are not always feasible for practical or ethical reasons. Simulated clients overcome the ethical problems of seeking the co-operation of genuine clients. Above all, thirdly, it makes practice visible.

Micro-processes

Qualitative research also contributes to outcomes when attention is given to the micro-processes of practice and programmes. This is one plausible response to the criticism made by Abrams quoted earlier in this paper. William Reid has been attracted by the potential of 'change-process' research. He does not reject the role of controlled experiments but concludes that 'practical and ethical constraints on experiments necessitate a reliance on the naturalistic study of these relations' (Reid, 1990: 130). This entails a focus on the processes of change during the period of contact between the professional helper and the client system. Rather than relying on aggregated, averaged summary measures of outcomes, this approach returns to the content-analysis tradition in social research, through a greater focus on micro-outcomes.

Reid applies his ideas to social work, although the logic applies to other forms of change-oriented professional service. A systemic view of intervention is at its root, in which professionals and service users are viewed in a circular, mutually influencing interaction. In this model 'conventional distinctions between intervention and outcome lose their simplicity' (p. 135). 'It then becomes possible to depict change-process research as a study of strings of intermixed i's and o's' – interventions and outcomes' (p. 136). While Reid seeks to defend experiments, he suggests a more naturalistic stance when he says that 'averages of process variables that are devoid of their contexts at best provide weak measures' (p. 137).

A different and interesting argument for using qualitative methods as a means of understanding micro-processes has been suggested by McLeod in a thoughtful assessment of the potential of qualitative methods for understanding outcomes of counselling. He suggests that qualitative interviews are more likely to elicit critical perspectives than questionnaires, arising from the 'demand characteristics' of extended interviews. 'In terms of producing new knowledge that contributes to debates over evidence-based therapy, it would appear that qualitative evaluation is better able to explore the limits of therapeutic *ineffectiveness*' (McLeod, 2001: 178). Combined with their potential for eliciting positive relations between intervention and outcome, he concludes, not unlike Patton, that 'Qualitative interviews appear to be, at present, the most sensitive method for evaluating the harmful effects of therapy and also for recording its greatest individual successes' (p. 179).

Ethnomethodology and symbolic interactionism

Ethnomethodology and symbolic interactionism suggest more general avenues of influence on outcomes inquiry. Two examples will serve to illustrate our point. First, Miller's work enriches our understanding of the importance of context in qualitative outcomes research. He discusses ways that institutional texts constructed to explain past decisions inevitably gloss over the openness and complexity of the decision-making process (Miller, 1997). He gives the mundane example of evaluation research on a bowel-training programme in a nursing home. The evaluation consisted of counting when and how patients had bowel movements. The programme was judged to have a successful outcome if patients used a toilet or bedpan and ineffective for those who continued soiling beds. One patient had soiled her bed. However, ethnographic methods enabled the researcher to observe a nursing aide contesting the definition of this incident as 'failure', on the grounds that the patient knew what she was doing and had soiled her bed as a protest act against staff favouring another patient. This illustrates how mundane, everyday life is illuminated by observing the context of text construction. This would not have found a way into the formal outcome record. Text production in institutions is 'micro-politically organised', and this includes textual outcome records.

Second, Denzin's interpretive interactionism has also had an impact on thinking about service outcomes (Denzin, 1989). Mohr, for example, extends Denzin's argument to the evaluation of clinical outcomes in health research. She argues that the method strives to inspect the relationships between personal difficulties, experiences, policies, interventions, and institutions. 'Interpretive interactionism permits intensive scrutiny of the ramifications and outcomes of various interventions' (Mohr, 1997: 284). It can:

1. Sort out different ways problems are defined.
2. Show how patients experience care. What it is about interventions they find helpful or not, and in what circumstances.
3. Identify 'secondary causes' eg contexts, culture, and the meanings patients bring.

'Strategic points for intervention can be identified by contrasting and comparing patients' thick descriptions, and these can be used to change, to improve, or to negotiate and renegotiate interventions' (p. 284). It is valuable when 'an outcome may not be readily apparent, and…the intervention is something that only the patient and not the professionals can define' (p. 285).

Qualitative analysis and outcomes

The fourth qualitative line of approach to methodological problems posed by conventional outcome research is rather different. Encouraged to some extent by recent developments in the realist school of the philosophy of science, fresh energy has been given to strategies for the analysis of outcomes and to cautious inferences about cause and effect (eg Henry, Julnes and Mark, 1998). As John and Lyn Lofland express it,

> Qualitative studies are not designed to provide definitive answers to causal questions...(but) it can still be an appropriately qualified pursuit. (Lofland and Lofland, 1995: 136, 138)

Miles and Huberman are even less reserved. 'The conventional view is that qualitative studies are only good for exploratory forays, for developing hypotheses – and that strong explanations, including causal attributions, can be derived only through quantitative studies'. They describe this view as 'mistaken' (Miles and Huberman, 1994: 147), and insist that qualitative evaluation research can,

1. Identify causal mechanisms.
2. Deal with complex local networks.
3. Sort out the temporal dimension of events.

They also argue that it is well equipped to cycle back and forth between different levels of variables and processes, and that a selective adoption of analytic induction provides a way of testing and deepening single case explanations.

Causal accounts will be local and 'now-oriented' (Lofland and Lofland, 1995: 141). Miles and Huberman develop analytic methods that address causal attribution in both single and multiple case explanations. For example, they advocate the use of field research to map the 'local causal networks' which informants carry in their heads and to make connections with the evaluator's own emerging causal map of the setting. Such maps start from 'causal fragments', which lead on to linked building of logical chains of evidence. Such causal networks

> are not probabilistic, but specific and determinate, grounded in understanding of events over time in the concrete local context – <u>and</u> tied to a good conceptualisation of each variable. (Miles and Huberman, 1994: 159)

Patton gives an example of how the creation of qualitative matrices is especially useful for exploring linkages between process and outcome. The analytic sequence entails the development of categorisations of types and levels of outcomes and of program processes. The categories are developed through orthodox qualitative analysis. The relationships between processes and outcomes may come either from participants or through subsequent analysis.

> In either case, the process/outcomes matrix becomes a way of organizing, thinking about and presenting the qualitative connections between program implementation dimensions and program impacts. (Patton, 2002: 472)

The following extract gives an illustration of how this approach can operate.

> Suppose we have been evaluating a juvenile justice program that places delinquent youth in foster homes ... A *regularly recurring process theme* concerns the importance of "letting kids learn to make their own decisions". A *regularly recurring outcome theme* involves "keeping the kids straight" … By crossing the program process ("kids making their own decisions") with the program outcome ("keeping the kids straight"), we create a data analysis question: What actual decisions do juveniles make that are supposed to lead to reduced recidivism? We then carefully review our field notes and interview quotations looking for data that help us understand how people in the program have answered this question based on their actual behaviors and practices. By describing what decisions juveniles actually make in the program, the decision makers to whom our findings are reported can make their own judgements about the strength or weakness of the linkage… (pp. 472-3)

Hence, while qualitative evaluation cannot resolve the problems of causal conclusions any more than quantitative evaluation, it can assess causality 'as it actually plays out in a particular setting' (Miles and Huberman, 1994: 10).

Part of this reasoning was anticipated by Cronbach's arguments regarding causal models. Rejecting the idea of causation as events that can be predicted with a high degree of probability, Cronbach developed twin arguments. First, he argued that causes are contingent on local interactions of clusters of events. More than one cluster may be sufficient, but no one cluster is necessary. Second, he accepted that there are usually missing events or conditions that affect the outcome of a given programme, but about which we know little. He was the first theorist to produce a plausible explanation of contextual factors in evaluation. Hence, he concludes that 'after the experimenter with his artificial constraint leaves the scene, the operating programme is sure to be adapted to local conditions' (Cronbach et al., 1980: 217). Furthermore, somewhat pessimistically, he concluded that 'a programme evaluation is so dependent on its context that replication is only a figure of speech' (p. 222).

Qualitative research and evaluation share a recognition of the irony of social causes and consequences. Much of the sociology of deviance was based on just this sense of irony, with its exploration of deviant roles as doing necessary 'dirty work'. It leads to the question of what functions are served by a particular practice that would not be served by its absence. What are the typical results of this phenomenon in this setting, and what ends are served thereby? Lofland and Lofland make the important observation that causal answers are by and large based on *passivist* conceptions of human nature. Qualitative inquiry has often steered away from causal accounts, not because the methodology is weak in that area but because of a commitment to an *activist* conception of human nature. The Loflands argue that an activist conception will lead to a focus on questions that address both structures and strategies. This will involve 'deciphering and depicting exactly what sort of situation the participants are facing' (Lofland and Lofland, 1995: 146), and understanding the 'incessantly fabricated' strategies people construct to deal with the situation.

Take for example, Silverman's work on HIV counselling. He is right to conclude that 'it is usually unnecessary to allow our research topics to be defined in terms of…the "causes" of "bad" counselling or the "consequences" of "bad" counselling' (Silverman, 1997a: 34), insofar as such topics reflect the conceptions of social problems as recognised by professional or community groups. Nonetheless, this does not require the abandonment of causal inquiry in qualitative evaluation. Inquiry into the ways in which professionals incessantly fabricate service forms and structures does promise a better way to understand causes. The voices of human services professionals that head this article illustrate the visibility yet elusiveness of outcomes in the search for meaning in narrative accounts.

Causal networks exist at the level of the individual case. Miles and Huberman also develop ways in which ordering and explaining can be tackled through cross-case displays of data. They are confident of the ability of qualitative inquiry to go beyond the problems of inferring from association ('the weasel word of quantitative researchers', p. 222). They summarise the process as follows.

> *Cross-case causal networking* is a comparative analysis of all cases in a sample, using variables estimated to be the most influential in accounting for the outcome criterion. You look at each outcome measure and examine, for each case, the stream of variables leading to or "determining" that outcome. Streams that are similar to or identical across cases, and that differ in some consistent way from other streams are extracted and interpreted. (p. 228)

They spell out the steps to accomplishing this analysis, but suggest that it may not be feasible for either larger or very small samples.

An example may make this process more visible. Shaw and colleagues describe a qualitative, case study evaluation of a rural activity centre for people with learning disabilities (Shaw, Williamson and Parry-Langdon, 1992). They observed and interviewed project participants, parents, carers, management group members, key workers and other professionals. Project records were analysed.

When describing and explaining the workings of the centre, the people who were interviewed appeared to draw on one or more of three different models of the scheme. These were a 'training for work' model, a 'personal and social growth' model, and an 'education for life' model. These operated in part as causal maps which entailed an array of model-specific positions on the aims of the project, optimal target groups, desirable programme patterns, staffing requirements, future development strategies, and likely or desirable project outcomes.

Table 11.1 Causal maps: participant models for a rural activity centre

	Training for Work	Personal/social growth	Education for life
Aims	Credible work skills for independent/ sheltered work	Personal and social growth	Alternative occupation to enhance the quality of life
Target group	Demonstrable ability to benefit; younger	Wide range of age and ability	Wide ability range; younger
Programme	Time limited stay; skill learning; assessment and review; contracts; move-one facility; integration into work	Open stay period; small project; small-group activities; counselling; liaison with carers and social work agencies	Loosely held time limits; the best learning context; interest-led contracts; community based activities and outside links; craft work and home making skills
Staffing	Education and special needs employment skills; plus volunteers	Social and group work qualifications; plus expert consultants	Education and social work qualifications; plus volunteers
Outcome	Regular throughput; work placements; normalisation of work patterns; skill learning	No clear distinction between programme and outcome	Wide range of social skills; integration into community networks; change of attitudes on the part of outside community members

Finally, to return to a general point made earlier, qualitative research facilitates the *valuation of outcomes*, and is opposed to the technicalisation of outcome research. While this is not exclusively the province of qualitative research, more conventional, and strictly evidence-based varieties of outcome research tend to treat such issues as technical matters. This links to the broader question of value and political issues.

> Evidence on effectiveness and outcomes and an emphasis on health gain and health outcome provide an apparently value-neutral, rational approach and means for rationing health and social care. Beneath the range of technical issues in assessing outcomes are political and social values that need to be explicit. (Long, 1994: 175)

Concluding issues

I have argued for ways in which qualitative research offers a distinctive and indispensable element in outcomes research in the fields of education, social work and health. Starting from the position that there is a *real* but very *imperfect* linkage between philosophy and method, the chapter reviewed the continuing grounds to doubt the adequacy of conventional controlled designs for understanding outcomes of projects, policies, practice and programmes. I then illustrated how qualitative research can contribute indispensably to outcomes research in four ways.

- Design solutions
- Sensitivity to the micro-processes of practice and programmes.
- Applications of symbolic interactionism and ethnomethodology.
- Qualitative analysis.

There are a number of problems and opportunities for continuing work that come into focus through this discussion. In the first instance, the focus on examining claims made in argument rather than starting from theoretical arguments, directs our attention to how researchers (and practitioners) actually do reason. This presents a forcible case for an empirical agenda.

Second, conventional controlled designs for outcomes research tend to be linked to an instrumental model of research as having direct utility for subsequent application. The problem with this – long since recognised by writers from Carol Weiss onwards (eg Weiss, 1988) – is that it does not square with evidence on how research is actually used, and it misunderstands the nature of the policy making process. It is based on a rationalistic model.

> The rationalist model of policy making sees it as a series of discrete events, where each issue to be decided is clearly defined, and decisions are taken by

> a specific set of actors who choose between well-defined alternatives, after weighing the evidence about the likely outcome of each. (Finch, 1986: 149-150)

Over against this, there has been development of an enlightenment model of research use. 'It offers far more space for qualitative research, through its emphasis on understanding and conceptualisation, rather than on providing objective facts' (p. 154). The enlightenment model, while valuable for its realistic depiction of research use, is not a universal description of how research information use operates. For example, practitioner research is likely to proceed on a more immediate instrumental view. Empirical work on information use is equally important as work on evaluative judgements.

Thirdly, the strategies discussed earlier tend to favour an incremental approach to social change. This is also the case of the enlightenment model of research use, which often assumes a piecemeal, social engineering position. This raises in turn the general question whether qualitative methods are especially congenial to advocacy methods in research. My view is that there is no necessary relation between the two, but in practice they have proved mutually reinforcing.

Finally, qualitative approaches to outcomes research tend to give greater prominence to theorising, but not in the caricature of research represented by the discredited belief that 'science grows by repeated overthrow of theories with the help of hard facts' (Lakatos, 1970: 97). Finch argues,

> First, that a concern with theory is quite compatible with qualitative research; second that a blend of theory and data is the hallmark of good qualitative work; and third, that this particular blend produces precisely the kind of work which is likely to make an impact upon policy because it offers theoretical insights grounded in evidence. (p. 174)

Greene (1993) specifies what this might entail. We should,

1. Explicate our own theoretical predispositions.
2. Describe locally held theories ('locally meaningful theoretical perspectives in data interpretation' (Greene, 1993: 38).
3. Attend to emergent theoretical issues.
4. Integrate substantive theory into research conclusions and recommendations.

Empirical work on evaluative judgements, developing plausible models of research information use, exploring the possibilities for interlinks between qualitative methodology, advocacy research and evaluation, and the diverse and complex relations between the theoretical and the practical, leave more than enough to be getting along with in the development of benchmark standards for qualitative outcomes research.

Acknowledgements

I am especially grateful to John Stevenson, for his detailed comments on an earlier draft of this chapter. Nick Gould shared work on the larger argument of which this chapter is a part.

References

Abrams, P. (1984) 'Evaluating soft findings: some problems of measuring informal care' in *Research, Policy and Planning* 2 (2): 1-8.

Becker, H. (1993) 'Theory: the necessary evil', in Flinders, D. and Mills, G. (eds) *Theory and Concepts in Qualitative Research: Perspectives from the Field.* New York: Teachers College, Columbia University Press.

Blair, J. (1995) 'Informal logic and reasoning in evaluation' in New Directions For Evaluation, No 68 *Reasoning in Evaluation: Inferential Links and Leaps*, ed D.M. Fournier. San Francisco: Jossey-Bass.

Bloor, M. (1997) 'Techniques of validation in qualitative research', in Miller, G. and Dingwall, R. (eds), *Context and Method in Qualitative Research.* London: Sage.

Bryman, A. (1988) *Quality and Quantity in Social Research.* London: Allen and Unwin.

Campbell, D. (1978) 'Qualitative knowing in action research', in Brenner, M and Marsh, P. (eds) *The Social Context of Methods*. London: Croom Helm.

Chelimsky, E. (1997) 'Thoughts for a new Evaluation Society', in *Evaluation* 3 (1): 97-118.

Cronbach, L. (1986) 'Social inquiry by and for earthlings', in Fiske, D. and Shweder, R. (eds), *Metatheory in Social Science: Pluralisms and Subjectivities*. Chicago: University of Chicago Press.

Cronbach, L., Ambron, S., Dornbusch, S., Hess, R., Hornik, R., Phillips, D., Walker, D., and Weiner, S. (1980) *Toward Reform of Program Evaluation.* San Francisco: Jossey-Bass.

Denzin, N.K. (1989). *Interpretative Interactionism*. Newbury Park, CA: Sage.

Finch, J. (1986) *Research and Policy: the Uses of Qualitative Methods in Social and Educational Research.* London: Falmer Press.

Fournier, D. and Smith, N. (1993) 'Clarifying the merits of argument in evaluation practice', in *Evaluation and Program Planning* 16 (4): 315-323.

Giddens, A. (1993) *New Rules of Sociological Method.* Stanford: Stanford University Press.

Greene, J. (1990) 'Three views on the nature and role of knowledge in social science', in Guba, E. (ed) *The Paradigm Dialog*. Newbury Park: Sage.

Greene, J. (1993) 'The role of theory in qualitative program evaluation', in Flinders, J and Mills, G., *Theory and Concepts in Qualitative Research.* New York: Teachers College Press.

Greene, J. and Caracelli, V. (1997) *Advances in Mixed Method Evaluation: the Challenge and Benefits of Integrating Diverse Paradigms*. New Directions For Evaluation, No 74, San Francisco: Jossey-Bass.

Henry, G.T., Julnes, G. and Mark, M.M. (1998) (eds) *Realist Evaluation: an Emerging Theory in Support of Practice.* New Directions For Evaluation, No 78, San Francisco: Jossey-Bass.

House, E. (1980) *Evaluating With Validity.* Beverly Hills: Sage.

House, E. (1993) *Professional Evaluation*. Newbury Park: Sage.

Humphrey, C. and Pease, K. (1992) 'Effectiveness measurement in the Probation Service: a view from the troops' in *Howard Journal* 31 (2): 31-52.

Kushner, S. (1996) 'The limits of constructivism' in *Evaluation* 2 (2): 189-200.

Lakatos, I. (1970) 'Falsification and the methodology of scientific research programmes', in Lakatos, I. and Musgrave, A. *Criticism and the Growth of Knowledge*. Cambridge: Cambridge University Press.

Lofland, J. and Lofland, L. (1995) *Analysing Social Settings*. Belmont: Wadsworth.

Long, A. (1994) 'Assessing Health and Social Outcomes' in Popay, J. and Williams, G. eds. *Researching the People's Health*. London: Routledge.

Macdonald, G. (1999) 'Social work and it evaluation' in Williams, F., Popay, J. and Oakley, A. *Welfare Research: A Critical Review*. London: UCL Press.

McKay, D.M. (1988) 'Value-free knowledge: myth or norm?' in McKay, D.M. *The Open Mind.* Leicester: Inter-Varsity Press.

McKeganey, N., MacPherson, I. and Hunter, D. (1988) 'How "they" decide: exploring professional decision making' in *Research, Policy and Planning* 6 (1): 15-19.

McLeod, J. (2001) *Qualitative Research in Counselling and Psychotherapy*. London: Sage.

Miles, M. and Huberman, A. (1994) *Qualitative Data Analysis: an Expanded Sourcebook*. Thousand Oaks: Sage.

Miller, G. (1997) 'Contextualizing texts: studying organisational texts' in Miller, G. and Dingwall, R. (eds) *Context and Method in Qualitative Research*. London: Sage.

Mohr, W.K. (1997) 'Interpretive interactionism: denzin's potential contribution to intervention and outcomes research' in *Qualitative Health Research* 7 (2): 270-286.

National Institutes of Health (2001) *Qualitative Methods in Health Research* http://obssr.od.nih.gov/publications/qualitative.pdf.

Patton, M.Q. (2002) *Qualitative Research and Evaluation Methods*. Thousand Oaks: Sage Publications.

Phillips, D. (1990) 'Postpositivistic science: myths and realities', in Guba, E. (ed), *The Paradigm Dialog*. Newbury Park: Sage.

Reid, W. (1990) 'Change-process research: a new paradigm?', in Videka-Sherman, L. and Reid, W. (eds) *Advances in Clinical Social Work Research*. Silver Spring, MD: NASW Press.

Reid, W. (1994) 'Reframing the epistemological debate', in Sherman, E. and Reid, W. (eds), *Qualitative Research in Social Work.* New York: Columbia University Press.

Shaw, I. (1999) *Qualitative Evaluation*. London: Sage.

Shaw, I. and Gould, N. (2001) (eds) *Qualitative Social Work Research*. London: Sage.

Shaw, I. and Shaw, A. (1997) 'Game plans, buzzes and sheer luck: doing well in social work' in *Social Work Research* 21 (2): 69-79.

Shaw, I. Williamson, H. and Parry-Langdon, N. (1992) 'Developing models for day care services' in *Social Policy and Administration* 26 (1): 73-86.

Silverman, D. (1997) *Discourses of Counselling: HIV Counselling as Social Interaction*. London: Sage.

Sinclair, I. (2000) 'Methods and measurement in evaluative social work' Theorising Social Work Research seminar. http://www.nisw.org.uk/tswr/sinclair.

Stake, R. (1995) *The Art of Case Study Research*. Thousand Oaks: Sage Publications.

Thyer, B. (2000) Review of Shaw and J. Lishman (1999) (eds) 'Evaluation and Social Work Practice' in *British Journal of Social Work* 30 (3): 401-402.

Trend, M.G. (1979) 'On the reconciliation of qualitative and quantitative analyses', in Cook, T. and Reichardt, C. *Qualitative and Quantitative Methods in Evaluation Research*. Beverly Hills: Sage.

Turner, M. and Zimmerman, W. (1994) 'Acting for the sake of research' in Wholey, J., Hatry, H. and Newcomer, K. (eds) *Handbook of Practical Program Evaluation*. San Francisco: Jossey-Bass.

Wasoff, F. and Dobash, R. (1992) 'Simulated clients in "natural" settings: constructing a client to study professional practice' in *Sociology* 26 (2): 333-349.

Wasoff, F. and Dobash, R. (1996) *The Simulated Client: a Method for Studying Professionals Working with Clients*. Aldershot: Avebury.

Weiss, C. (1988) 'If programme decisions hinged only on information' in *Evaluation Practice* 9 (1): 15-28.

Yin, R.K. (1994) *Case Study Research*. Thousand Oaks: Sage.

Chapter 12
Ethics and the Practice of Qualitative Research*

Commitments to developing disciplines and professions often lead protagonists to overstate the extent to which a special case should and can be made for the distinctives of that field. Research practice and ethics are no exception. In falling foul of this trap, the gains from shared common ground may be lost.[1] However, valuable work *has* been accomplished on developing an understanding of research ethics in social work (eg Butler, 2002) – valuable in part because it provides a community reference point. One drawback of such texts is that they leave the twin impressions that applying ethics to social work research works in a fairly standard way from one project to another, and that such applications are largely initial business, sorted and settled in the early phases of the research.

As a counterweight to these tendencies I will explore ways in which the practice of research ethics is presented afresh – and contextualized in distinct forms – at every stage of research. Elliot Eisner sharpens our sense of unease when he concludes:

> We might like to secure consent that is informed, but we know we can't always inform because we don't always know. We would like to protect personal privacy and guarantee confidentiality, but we know we cannot always fulfil such guarantees. We would like to be candid but sometimes candour is inappropriate. We do not like to think of ourselves as using others as a means to our own professional ends, but if we embark upon a research study that we conceptualize, direct, and write, we virtually assure that we will use others for our purpose. (Eisner, 1991: 225-6)

---

* Originally published as I. Shaw, 2008. 'Ethics and the practice of qualitative research', *Qualitative Social Work* 7(4): 400-14. Reprinted with permission of Sage Publications Ltd.

1 For example, in the UK the Social Research Association (http://www.the-sra.org.uk/documents/pdfs/ethics03.pdf), the more recent *Research Ethics Framework* from the Economic and Social Research Council (ESRC, 2005), and the British Sociological Association (http://www.sociology.org.uk/as4bsoce.pdf). For ethics statements in applied fields see The American Evaluation Association (http://www.eval.org/Publications/GuidingPrinciplesPrintable.asp) and the British Educational Research Association (http://www.bera.ac.uk/publications/pdfs/ethica1.pdf).

Codes, concerns and the social research community

A spate of concerns has run through social and medical research in the West over consent for storage of body organs, developments in genetics, and linked innovations in technology, and new problems in privacy issues have destabilized confidence in the ethical regulation of medical research. Concerns range from the use of chemicals in international sport to university science that could be exploited by terrorist networks. Mark Walport (Director of Wellcome Trust, a major UK medical research charity) reflected the growing recognition within the research community that these developments have led, perhaps ineluctably, to a growth of regulation when he remarked that 'Scientists have responsibilities. If the scientific community is resistant to self regulation it can't complain if governments with legitimate concerns decide to intervene' (*Times Higher Education Supplement* 14/11/03). Within the health research fields this has led to a growth of national and state level governance frameworks.

Within this climate of wide concern and weather of growing regulation a cluster of concerns has crystallized, often initiated by qualitative researchers. Has the discourse of research ethics gone beyond its appropriate reach and scope? As Hammersley (2000) claims, has methodology become inappropriately 'ethicized' such that broader methodological questions to get absorbed in a reductionist way into ethics? Does an over-reaching, wide-ranging governance become part of the embodied disposition – in Bourdieu's term, *habitus* – of social research? Linked to the perceived medical hegemony, does 'the template of medical research and the stirring of moral panic seem to work against the benefits of qualitative methods' (Van den Hoonaard, 2002: 176)?[2] More broadly, Adler and Adler – in an essay that is perhaps too obviously cross in tone – ask whether the American Sociological Association has 'totally capitulated' to demands of institutional review boards, and sociologists have become 'the "stoolies" of law enforcement' (2002: 39). They fear a danger as a consequence that some areas of qualitative research will become off limits, for example, studies of illegal activity or powerless groups, studying publicly accountable individuals or elites, and investigative/covert research.

The governance of ethics may on the one hand have proceeded too far, yet once misdirected may not go far enough. In efforts to elucidate this problem various writers have drawn distinctions as direction finders. Helen Simons (2006), in an excellent discussion of research ethics codes, draws on distinctions between rules, codes, standards, principles and theories.

---

2 I acknowledge my debt to Will van den Hoonaard (2002) for his carefully edited volume that gives us something on which to grip our ethical and moral climbing boots. The essays debate and illustrate the social organization of ethical review bodies, the appropriateness of medical and natural science models, the ethical dilemmas special to qualitative research, the concern that issues of risk and harm from research may have been exaggerated, and the ethical and methodological problems posed by signed consent in ethnography.

Florence Kellner borrows a distinction between the letter (codes) and the spirit (morality).[3] She uses this to argue that research issues are about morality not ethics – about an orientation to the other, the uniquely human. 'It is our morality, our diffuse, unlimited obligation to the welfare of the other, that must inform these more important aspects of our conduct in the field…Where ethical requirements and moral requirements conflict, the latter must take priority' (Kellner, 2002: 32).

Finally, John Johnson and David Altheide develop the widely expressed view that 'the contemporary focus on "research ethics" is really about issues other than research ethics' and that '"Ethics" has…collapsed into discourses of institutional control' (2002: 61). In contesting this they suggest there are in fact five spheres of ethics:

- Personal ethics. A broad sphere that may subsume other spheres.
- Research ethics. Their view is that strictly research ethics are the least problematic of all the areas.
- Intellectual ethics. How to select problems for investigation; how to sponsor and pursue such inquiries and discern and report the truth.
- Professional ethics.
- Corporate ethics. Eg legal obligations.

Johnson and Altheide are against codes. 'Try not to hurt anyone and when you hurt someone try your best to make amends' (2000: 67) is their suggested 'rule' though they admit the key terms – 'try', 'best', 'hurt' and 'amends' – are all problematic and so this could not be enforced. For myself, I am not arguing that codes of ethics are out of place. For example, part of Johnson and Altheide's fire is aimed at what they believe is the harmful encroachment of professional ethics. They are concerned that 'The ethical domain of professional ethics inexorably grows like a bamboo shoot in a rain forest' (2002: 65). My own view is that there are merits, though problems, in trying to link professional and research ethics (cf Butler, 2002 and Ungar and Nicholl, 2002). But I *am* concerned that reliance on codes alone risks compartmentalizing ethical aspects of research, and, as noted above, shutting them off into a preamble to research. Neither would I repeat the claim sometimes made, that qualitative research is somehow more ethical than quantitative research. No research strategies are especially privileged. To adapt a phrase from Ernest House, qualitative researchers do not live in a state of methodological grace (House, 1991: 245). But the ethical challenges of qualitative inquiry are easily neglected if the agenda posed by the methodological concerns of control, technology, and large datasets remains normative. Kellner interestingly concludes that there is a trust problem – researchers do not trust adjudication judgements and adjudicators mistrust researchers as cavalier, and suggests 'the most useful stance is to communicate good intentions to comply with the code' (2002: 33).

3 To recognize the undertones of this distinction we should see its source in Paul, II Corinthians 3v6 'The letter kills but the spirit gives life.'

Rather differently from this literature, the focus of this paper is on the *process* of research, and instead of taking the conventional ethical problems of randomized control trials as a benchmark I will focus on ethical questions raised by *qualitative* research. This risks too much simplicity. There are differences *within* both quantitative and qualitative approaches. Anne Ryen helpfully summarizes differences in the ethical 'tilt' of different qualitative research paradigms (Ryen, 2004). Although the primary reference is human services research, I have deliberately looked for precedent and stimulation to the work of writers outside the usual boundaries of social work, especially sociologists, education researchers and those working in the evaluation field.

I will develop three linked arguments. First, the ethics of qualitative research *design* pose distinctive demands on principles of informed consent, confidentiality and privacy, social justice, and practitioner research. I will focus only on consent – for its topicality, not because it is more important or difficult. Second, *fieldwork* ethics raise special considerations regarding power, reciprocity and contextual relevance. Third, ethical issues raised by the *analysis and uses* of qualitative inquiry emphasize questions regarding the ethics of narrative research, anonymization, and the utilization of research.

In all, we may end up 'chastened by the interpersonal and ethical complexities of even the simplest piece of research' (Weinberg, 2002: 94).

The ethics of consent and agreeing qualitative research strategies

There are at least five ways in which the ethics of consent take on a distinctive form and character in qualitative research. Jennifer Stacey, in an oft quoted phrase, referred to the problem of 'the delusion of alliance' in qualitative and feminist research, as a consequence of which participants may reveal more than they intend (Stacey, 1988). In 'traditional' research – experiments, surveys, structured interviews – it is probably relatively clear to the participant when the researcher is 'working' and when she is having 'time out'. The participants are likely to assume that when they are in informal settings, or their words and actions are not being overtly recorded, the researcher is having time out. But this is not likely to be the case in much qualitative research,[4] where the participants face the consequent risk of involuntary disclosure, and unwittingly the researcher becomes a covert investigator.

Second, there is an issue as to whether there are particular ethical issues in *evaluative* qualitative research. Simons (2006) suggests there *are* special considerations. Janet Finch, speaking out of a UK policy research tradition and reflecting on participant observation methods, suggests that covert *evaluation* is 'a particularly dangerous example of covert social research, because the findings

4 This does not apply to all qualitative research. For example, the boundaries of focus groups are generally clearly demarcated for participants.

are not being used merely to illuminate our knowledge of the social world, but potentially to change it' (Finch, 1986: 203).

Third, informed consent in qualitative research is often hazardous because it 'implies that the researcher knows *before* the event...what the event will be and its possible effects' (Eisner, 1991: 214). This is often not the case in qualitative research, where responsiveness and adaptability are seen as *strengths* of the method.

Fourth, issues of informed consent often appear sharpest in test cases. The development of qualitative research invests consent with personal dimensions. It involves engaged and therefore complex relationships. Strategies, as we have just noted, change during a project. It has a 'friendly façade', and thus risks pseudo-intimacy. The potential hazards of these issues may become especially acute in research and evaluation with people with learning disabilities. Thompson (2002) illustrates how engaging and disengaging become major issues and the risk of sharing too much, eg memories of abuse, is greater. In turn this raises the problem of the genuine voluntariness of the consent.

This is especially likely when people live in situations of external control (not just residential/housing projects), where consent becomes fragile. I was invited some years ago to be part of an advisory group for a project in the four home countries of the UK, funded by the Mental Health Foundation (MHF)[5] in which over twenty mental health service users were funded following a process of competitive tendering to undertake a small research project of their own devising. One user-researcher undertook study of home leave from a psychiatric hospital. He had been an in-patient, in part on a locked ward. For this project, which entailed interviewing people living in the community, a hospital nurse accompanied him throughout. He lived in an environment where decision-making opportunities were lacking and consent was heavily conditioned. Further, in circumstances where folk with learning disabilities live in the community they may, in Goffman's term, seek to 'pass' and more readily appear to acquiesce. This poses ethical challenges to the researcher.

> Do researchers have an ethical responsibility to serve in a dual role: first, as researchers with a project aimed at satisfying their research purposes, and second, as advocates … raising questions that the researchers know should be raised in order for (people) to make a competent assessment of the risks? (Eisner, 1991: 217).

Finally, there are special difficulties surrounding the ethics of consent and qualitative Internet research. There are three key questions. Can we treat all information taken from the Internet as public information? I think probably not, though this is far from agreed. Waruszynski (2002) and Kitchen (2002) give

---

5 For a downloadable summary of the project go to http://www.mentalhealth.org.uk/publications/?EntryId5=43591&char=S.

contrary answers. Second, are we free to exploit fully the results to which we have unfettered access? How does informed consent relate eg to material taken from chat rooms, or from listservs? Are there special issues of group consent? How can these be dealt with, assuming it is a real problem? Third, when it comes to interpretation and dissemination, who owns the story? I am not convinced that the same standards ought to apply to eg the material on a moderated discussion list or newsgroups and, say, a breast cancer survivors list.

Fieldwork ethics

Lofland and Lofland ask is it ethical to:

- See a severe need for help and not respond to it directly?
- Take a calculated stance towards other human beings?
- Take sides or avoid taking sides in a factionalized situation?
- 'Pay' people with trade-offs for access to their lives and minds?

(Lofland and Lofland, 1995)

They leave the questions on the table. All but the third of these questions can be approached through an example, which helps to make the central point of this paper that ethics decisions, even when we may believe there are shared normative principles, cannot be allocated in a decontextualized manner.

Example: qualitative research with homeless people.

This lengthy extract is drawn from contemporary notes of a round table discussion of ethics which took place at a symposium on homelessness and social exclusion organized in 1996 by the Paris-based Conseil National de L'Information Statistique (http://www.cnis.fr/). I have retained the round-table format in the following example, without disclosing the identity of the participants.

Chair She offered a preliminary map of the ethical issues in this field as linked to:

1. The purpose of any inquiry.
2. The balance of the value of the inquiry against the degree of intrusion.
3. Who are the beneficiaries? Is the respondent a beneficiary?
4. How is the information obtained?
5. How will it be used? Issues of privacy, and potential misinterpretation of the findings.

Discussant 1 argued that ethical issues are not *greater* in homelessness research but they do need *more careful formulation*. He believed that they include:

1. The right of refusal at the point of contact. But this right cannot be exercised on someone's behalf. The discussant was against the right of any group to make a collective decision on behalf of others not to participate.
2. The interview. There is a need for privacy of space. This may be a special difficulty in homelessness research.
3. The content of the interview. Ethical consequences arise from the fact that the emphasis of such interviews is frequently on negatives – on the deficiencies of the responder.
4. Ending the interview. Offering some trade-off is difficult due to the lack of an address, but it is a central issue.

Discussant 2 referred to possible payment of interviewees in a French homelessness research project. Within French research culture, payment is very rare. One the one hand it poses the problem of paternalism. Yet consent to be interviewed can result in people losing their turn at a soup kitchen or 'begging' time. Their solution was to give a telephone card at the end of the interview, but not to say in advance that this would happen. The card allowed contact with family and friends, and could not be used directly to harm themselves.

Discussant 3 was concerned with the ethics of longitudinal research carried out in America. He reported research in which 1,500 interviews were undertaken, from which 500 were followed through at two monthly intervals over about sixteen months. The ethics issues he identified were:

- *Paying*. It is the American standard practice in research to pay for long interviews. He acknowledged there might be risks attached to giving money, but argued for a non-paternalist stance on payment.[6]
- *Privacy*. There is a problem of knowing how the information will be used. For example, it could be damaging to a homeless person to ask a third party (perhaps an official) for information related to the individual's homelessness. It may jeopardize the likelihood that the agency supplying information will continue to offer 'service'. As a partial solution they gave a non-damaging title to the research. Instead of naming it 'The Course of Homelessness Study' they called it 'The Course of Housing Study'.
- Implications of obligations arising from long-term relationships with people.

Discussant 4, a Paris street level social worker, distinguished those who are 'sentenced to give' (social workers), and those who are 'sentenced to receive'.

6 Payment questions provide an example of research ethics decisions that have been insufficiently empirically grounded. For example, a user-researcher in the Mental Health Foundation project mentioned earlier, who had experienced sexual abuse as a child, commented 'I'd feel dirty if I was paid for talking about my experiences'.

After remarking that 'people who are homeless have been made cuckolds by life', he made his main point that it is what happens *after* the research that matters. 'How can we give back to them the knowledge they gave us?' Learning to receive is the key ethical issue. He acknowledged he had no complete answer to this problem of giving back. He had been involved in the organization of an art exhibition for homeless people, where the money gained was kept for collective use. He remarked that we also give back by keeping the information in ourselves. Listening as well as answering is part of giving back. Sometimes the person cannot be contacted or may die – but we are to become 'watchful' in our own behaviour.

Discussant 1 argued that the interview is not solely instrumental but does also have potential benefit for the interview-giver. It can enable people not to see life as fate (for example, by learning to read behind the figures). This should be part of our ethical concerns. Finally, we should not forget the collective benefits of research. Judgements of benefit do not have to be limited to the immediate beneficiary.[7]

Qualitative ethics, making sense and thereafter

As with the previous sections of this chapter, I offer little more than small parts of a jigsaw. Narrative, anonymization and research utilization are loosely connected, if at all, by a focus on the later stages of research and its consequences.

Narrative and life stories

Experience 'is the stories people live. People live stories, and in the telling of them reaffirm them, modify them and create new ones' (Clandinin and Connelly, 1994: 415). Ethical issues are raised by the fact that as we encourage people to tell their stories, we become characters in those stories, and thus change those stories. In presenting a life story there develops a 'complex relationship between the biography of the research subject and the autobiography of the researcher' (Mills, 2002: 109), with consequent ethical dilemmas. Mills, in her story of Hazel, the dental assistant, develops her main point that feminists have become unhappy with 'false consciousness' as an explanation of (eg) the non-political interpretations women often give in narratives of 'exploitation'. She is concerned that this can allow us to miss what we are being told, by concentrating on our own agenda and lived experience. She concludes there are always at least two voices in a narrative – when we research and write a life history/narrative we also write our own autobiography and, as Clandinin and Connelly observed, we become characters in their stories.

---

7 This example points to the importance of culture and qualitative ethics. This is a large and complex issue that I have left untouched in this paper. Ryen (2004) offers a useful introduction.

This can be positive but it also carries risks. Research and evaluating must be done with care and not as 'a raid on mislaid identities' (Dannie Abse's phrase, from his poem *Return to Cardiff*).[8] I recall the poignancy of listening as part of a research project early in my career to a woman in a South Wales valleys mining town talking at length about the experience of bringing up at home her son with serious learning difficulties, then in his early twenties. She reflected that this was the first time she had ever talked to someone about this experience.

Anonymization and confidentiality

Simons makes the familiar point that is it more difficult in qualitative research and participatory methods to protect privacy and confidentiality. Even if it is possible to anonymize this does not mean that privacy and confidentiality are respected. She argues that anonymization is a technical procedure which may offer some protection for an individual from public gaze, but the ethical promise in confidentiality is met in how one negotiates the use of the data. Hence anonymization needs to be decoupled from concerns with confidentiality and privacy (Simons, 2006).

Utilization and betrayal

A risk of betrayal arises partly from the greater closeness and consequent trust that may develop between researcher and participant. In quantitative research the greater distancing may make these issues less agonizing.

The risk of betrayal is increased because of the characteristic use of smaller samples, and the emphasis on the details of how people live their lives. Finch described from her playgroups research her 'sense that I could potentially betray my informants as a group, not as individuals' (Finch, 1986: 207). 'Where qualitative research is targeted upon social policy issues, there is the special dilemma that findings could be used to *worsen* the situation of the target population in some way' (Finch, 1985: 117).

Finch's particular interest was in what self-help playgroup provision would mean for working class women living in economically deprived areas. Over a three-year period, through observation and semi-structured interviewing, she was able to document the character of self-help playgroups in such areas.

> I uncovered situations where practice diverged wildly from bourgeois standards of child care and education which most policy makers and academics would take as the norm, and at times were downright dangerous. (1985: 117)

She was worried that the publication of her work would further reinforce 'those assumptions deeply embedded in our culture and political life that working class

8 The complete line is 'The journey to Cardiff seemed less a return than a raid on mislaid identities'.

women (especially the urban poor) are inadequate mothers' (p. 117). Those who had welcomed her for three years would thus be betrayed.

She had to work through these problems. Had she been guilty of taking a middle class norm and imposing it on these groups? Yet that norm *was* the one to which the women who ran the groups aspired. It was the participants' model and not simply hers. She eventually developed reasoning that avoided the 'deficit' model of explanation, and argued that to view working class mothers as incompetent is improper and naïve. She acknowledges she is not certain she has fully resolved the issues, and accepts that,

To argue like this is to take a frankly moral stance, far removed from the model of the objective social scientist… It seems to me that qualitative research on social policy issues will lead inevitably to explicit moral stances of that sort, and that it can never simply provide the 'facts' (Finch, 1985: 119-20).

Reflections

An embedded, contextualized stance in regard to the practice of ethics in qualitative research will foreground three wider issues that have been implicit in the paper. First, the democratization of social work research is one direction from which the politics of the research act have moved centre-stage. Participatory, emancipatory forms of research make conventional views of research ethics hard to sustain. Likewise, stakeholder models of evaluation raise new issues. It is plausible to suggest from a reading of the literature that a strong advocacy stance in research, e.g. within user led research from postmodernist or standpoint positions, has not as yet been associated with reflective work on the ethics of emancipatory research. The general approach to research ethics in user-led research has been to capture ethics in more holistic and possibly over-generalized responses.

Second, the gradual if belated increase in the awareness of research funders that qualitative research makes an important and distinctive contribution to policy and practice as well as to strategic research, poses fresh challenges to qualitative researchers to address ethics issues in a persuasive and original way when bidding for funding. The Office of Behavioral and Social Sciences Research in the National Institutes of Health (NIH) in the USA set up a working party a few years back on qualitative methods in health research. The NIH report has some interesting observations. Their experience of research bids was that applicants did not always address the ethics issues of qualitative inquiry.

> Qualitative research evokes consideration about confidentiality and the protection of participant identity. Ethical questions arise due to the special closeness that may develop between qualitative researchers and study participants. Since participant observation is a key methodology, the researcher will need to explain how they plan to address the issue of nonconsenting members of a group. It is not unusual for qualitative researchers to investigate "hidden" populations who

> engage in behaviour defined as deviant. Applicants studying individuals who may be subject to legal sanctions if their identities are revealed will need to specify procedures to ensure confidentiality (NIH, 2001)

I quote this not because they are original points or because I go along with the particular ways in which qualitative ethics are formulated, but because the NIH – known for its commitment to quantitative methods – is now recognizing them.[9]

Third, I mentioned when talking about Johnson and Altheide that I am not wholly averse to carefully linking professional and research ethics. Ungar and Nicholl argue there are similar goals for qualitative research and human services, ie 'to enhance the discursive power of silenced voices' (Ungar and Nicholl, 2002: 137). In ethics terms they argue we need supportive environments in which to nurture this discourse, while 'respecting the diversity of knowledge claims from marginalized groups' (p. 137). Describing themselves as 'affirmative postmodernists' (p. 148), they believe that the qualitative researcher and the social work practitioner both seek reflexivity (the researcher through choice of methods and the practitioner through choice of practice) and that 'qualitative research is an integral part of an anti-oppressive practice' (p. 151).

This returns us to the interweaving of ethics and morality – that 'welfare professionals have to be personal exponents of the values they presume to trade in professionally' (Clark, 2006a: 76, cf Clark, 2006b). Clark may be talking about social work practice, but his conclusion will stand for research. Good research practice 'is not sufficiently described either by technical competence or by grand ethical principle; it also subsists essentially in the moral character of the practitioner' (2006a: 88), whereby generic principles are context sensitive. Stand alone liberal ethics will not resolve conflicts.

References

Adler, P.A. and Adler, P. (2002) 'Do university lawyers and the police define research values?' in van den Hoonaard, Will C. (2002) (ed.), *Walking the Tightrope: Ethical Issues for Qualitative Researcher*. Toronto: University of Toronto Press.

Butler, I. (2002) 'A code of ethics for social work and social care research' *British Journal of Social Work* 32 (2): 239-248.

Clandinin, J. and Connelly, F.M. (1994) 'Personal experience methods' in Denzin, N. and Lincoln, Y. (eds) *Handbook of Qualitative Methods*. Thousand Oaks: Sage.

9 For a critique of the original report and a response from the Chair of the Working Group see the articles by Gilgun (2002) and Heurtin-Roberts (2002) in an earlier issue of *Qualitative Social Work*.

Clark, C. (2006a) 'The moral character of social work' *British Journal of Social Work* 36 (1): 75-89.

Clark, C. (2006b) 'Against confidentiality?' *Journal of Social Work* 6 (2): 117-136.

Eisner, E. (1991) *The Enlightened Eye: Qualitative Inquiry and the Enhancement of Educational Practice.* New York: Macmillan.

Finch, J. (1985) 'Social policy and education: problems and possibilities of using qualitative research', in Burgess, R. (ed) *Issues in Educational Research: Qualitative Methods*. London: Falmer Press.

Finch, J. (1986) *Research and Policy: the Uses of Qualitative Methods in Social and Educational Research.* London: Falmer Press.

Gilgun, J. (2002) 'Conjectures and refutations: governmental funding and qualitative research' *Qualitative Social Work* 1 (3): 359-375.

Hammersley, M. (2000) *Taking Sides in Social Research*. London: Routledge.

Heurtin-Roberts, S. (2002) 'Thoughts on qualitative research methods at the NIH' *Qualitative Social Work* 1 (3): 376-379.

House, E. (1991) 'Evaluation and social justice: where are we now?' in McLaughlin, M. and Phillips, D. (eds) *Evaluation and Education: at Quarter Century*. Chicago: Chicago University Press.

Johnson, J. and Altheide, D.L. (2002) 'Reflections on professional ethics' in van den Hoonaard, W.C. (2002) (ed.), *Walking the Tightrope: Ethical Issues for Qualitative Researchers*. Toronto: University of Toronto Press.

Kellner, F. (2002) 'Yet another crisis coming? Coping with guidelines from the Tri-Council' in van den Hoonaard, W.C. (2002) (ed.), *Walking the Tightrope: Ethical Issues for Qualitative Researchers*. Toronto: University of Toronto Press.

Kitchen, H.A. (2002) 'The Tri Council on cyberspace: insights, oversights and extrapolations' in van den Hoonaard, W.C. (2002) (ed.), *Walking the Tightrope: Ethical Issues for Qualitative Researchers*. Toronto: University of Toronto Press.

Lofland, J. and Lofland, L. (1995), *Analysing Social Settings*. Belmont: Wadsworth.

Mills, E. (2002) 'Hazel the Dental Assistant and the research dilemma of (re) presenting a life story' in van den Hoonaard, W.C. (2002) (ed.), *Walking the Tightrope: Ethical Issues for Qualitative Researchers*. Toronto: University of Toronto Press.

Office of Behavioral and Social Sciences Research, (2001) *Qualitative Methods in Health Research* National Institutes for Health, Washington DC http://obssr.od.nih.gov/publications/qualitative.pdf.

Oguz, N.Y. (2003) 'Research ethics committees in developing countries and informed consent' *Journal of Laboratory and Clinical Medicine* 141 (5): 292-296.

Ryen, A. (2004) 'Ethical Issues' in Seale, C. et al (eds) *Qualitative Research Practice*. London: Sage.

Shaw, I. (2003) 'Ethics in qualitative research and evaluation' *Journal of Social Work* 3 (1): 7-27.

Simons, H. (2006) 'Ethics in evaluation', in Shaw, I., Greene, J. and Mark, M. *Sage Handbook of Evaluation*. London: Sage.

Stacey, J. (1988) 'Can there be a feminist ethnography?' *Women's Studies International Forum* 11 (1): 21-27.

Thompson, S.A. (2002) 'My research friend? My friend the researcher? My friend, my researcher? Mis/Informed consent and people with developmental disabilities' in van den Hoonaard, W.C. (2002) (ed.), *Walking the Tightrope: Ethical Issues for Qualitative Researchers*. Toronto: University of Toronto Press.

Ungar, M. and Nicholl, G. (2002) 'The harmony of resistance: qualitative research and ethical practice in social work' in van den Hoonaard, Will C. (2002) (ed.), *Walking the Tightrope: Ethical Issues for Qualitative Researchers*. Toronto: University of Toronto Press.

Waruszynski, B.T. (2002) 'Pace of technological change: battling ethical issues in qualitative research' in van den Hoonaard, W.C. (2002) (ed.), *Walking the Tightrope: Ethical Issues for Qualitative Researchers*. Toronto: University of Toronto Press.

Weinberg, M. (2002) 'Biting the hand that feeds you, and other feminist dilemmas in fieldwork' in van den Hoonaard, W.C. (2002) (ed.), *Walking the Tightrope: Ethical Issues for Qualitative Researchers*. Toronto: University of Toronto Press.

Chapter 13
Constructing Causal Accounts in Social Work*

Professional Language and Causal Thinking

Sociologists have conducted work on the discourse of occupations such as medicine and education (e.g. Mishler 1984; Jackson 1968; Lortie 1975), and have shown some interest in the talk of social workers (Philp 1979; Dean 1989; Rojek, Peacock and Collins 1988; Pithouse 1987; Pithouse and Atkinson 1988; Whan 1979; Jones 1990). Shaped especially by the frameworks of Wittgenstein and Foucault, this writing is part of a wider auxiliary literature on rhetoric and theorizing in the human sciences, lay theorizing, analyses of the significance of narrative and text in the construction of personal identity, conversations between women and men, and feminist constructions of a sociology for women (Furnham 1988; Pollner 1987; Shotter and Gergen 1989; Simons 1989; Stanley 1990). However, analyses of causal accounts have not been central to this work. Causal attributions and accounts are one facet of the prism of occupational discourse. Our concern in this paper is with the social construction of causal accounts within the occupational community of social work, and with developing an orientation towards producing an ethnography of social workers' use of causal understandings in making their work accountable to a range of audiences. Our interest is in the possible significance of different kinds of causal accounts resorted to by social workers, the occupational 'triggers' for different kinds of causal accounting, and the purposes of such attributions and accounts.

Causal Accounts

Following Lyman and Scott's early distinction between an explanation and an account, an explanation does not include untoward action and does not have critical implications for relationships. An account, on the other hand, is 'a linguistic device employed whenever an action is subject to evaluative enquiry' (1970: 112).

The giving of accounts is central to social work. We do not wish to argue that social work is unique in the 'invisibility' of its trade (Pithouse 1987), but elucidating the significance of social work accounts for practice and management

* Originally published as Bull, R. and Shaw, I. (1992) 'Constructing Causal Accounts in Social Work', *Sociology* 26(4): 635-49. Reprinted with permission of Sage Publications Ltd.

demands careful, flexible scrutiny of the empirical instances where such accounts take place. 'Motives' and 'rules' of behaviour are, in part at least, prior to and independent of behaviour, but what is done is not entirely separate from the motives for doing it. People cannot know what they do without invoking a motive, so action itself *involves* motive. Hence, although description of any action is always defeasible (i.e. it is always possible in principle to argue against it), it still makes sense to investigate reasons and accounts (Hughes 1980).

> Rule following, convention obeying, meaning giving or any other form of self monitoring by the individual concerned is fatal to the idea that the heart of an explanation lies in the causal story (Harré and Secord 1972: 168).

Following Wittgenstein, more recent work on explanations and naive, un negotiated accounts, while taking issue with some aspects of Harré's theories, has continued to emphasize vocabularies, grammars and narrative conventions, and the implications of rule-governed behaviour which are 'not to do with the inevitability of causal necessity but with the inexorability of moral necessity' (Harré 1989: 35; Harré, Margolis, Deese and Lamiell 1989).

In one of the few significant pieces of work on social work talk done so far, Pithouse and Atkinson explored the character of 'case talk' as one example of talk between social workers in a childcare team in an area office of a local authority social services department. They conclude that such talk takes on a dramatic narrative character in which causal accounts are relatively marginal. Case presentations take the form of a moral tale, in which the cause of any failure is typically ascribed to the client rather than the social worker, where there is little explicit theorizing, and in which behaviour is not related to specific causes but is part of the narrative drama.

> The experienced worker, through soundings, brief forays and insightful observations of family relations, can construct a mosaic of suspicion that confirms the presence of 'problems' without specifying the precise cause or cure.. The construction of a 'case' is thus a *rhetorical accomplishment* (Pithouse and Atkinson 1988: 197).

We share this emphasis on the centrality of language in constituting social reality. The recounting of an event not only describes the event but produces conclusions about it by the particular selection of incidents which make up the recounting (Smith 1978). However, in seeking to assert more forcefully the significance of causal accounts and attributions in the professional discourse of social workers, we argue the importance of developing an analysis in two directions.

First, case talk between social workers in the same team is only one of several forms of spoken narrative and recital, which take place in a wide range of quite different contexts. Social work talk may be with other social workers in the same *team,* as in Pithouse and Atkinson's analysis of case talk. Such exchange will also involve *other social workers* in the same organization or agency, and *other staff* in the same organization who are not social workers. In addition, social workers are typically engaged in occupational discourse with *social workers in other organizations,* or with *other professionals,* in the same organization (for example, medical social workers based in hospitals and medical or paramedical staff), and in other organizations (for example, probation officers' talk with police officers, lawyers or magistrates), and with non-professional auxiliary staff such as volunteers and foster parents. Thus, there is a range of intra- and inter-organizational micro-settings within which there might be competing, conflicting or otherwise variant modes of causal thinking, and this considerably widens the scope for an ethnographic agenda.

Second, we also believe that the utilization of the *metaphor* of narrative drama may itself lead to a framework in which inspection of the causal texture is not central to the analytic task. In the text presented by Pithouse and Atkinson, causal attributions *are* present and are part of the fabric of the narrative. They report a social work team meeting in which a social worker and team leader discuss a 'case' of a girl on a supervision order who had been shoplifting again. In trying to explain this behaviour the social worker says,

> But her criminality is in *(pause)* er, strange really, it's almost a mania. It has a quality about it that's almost psychologically driven. I don't know if that's the proper use of the term 'psychology' but – you know – the drive is there, er, because of an abnormal psychology, there's something there all right (Pithouse and Atkinson 1988: 189).

A moment later this is echoed by the team leader confirming, 'yes, there's something *there* in the family'.

The theory is part of the shared assumptions about aetiology between social worker, team leader and watching members of the team, and is nonetheless formative and central to the narrative for being implicit. The social worker suggests a determinist view of the family's behaviour as 'psychologically driven'. Moreover, this kind of causal explanation appears to carry with it a message about the diminished performance expectations that can reasonably be anticipated from the social worker.

A similar and very explicit example of a causal case account being used as a professional safety net occurs later in the same text. In drawing the threads together into the final denouement of the narrative, the social worker asserts an argument about culture:

> this is quite a delinquent family, we're not going to change that fact of their life-style – it's cultural – I'm not going to change this you know – I don't intend to (Pithouse and Atkinson 1988: 192).

Whether in any precise sense, *cultural* or psychological factors are at work is largely immaterial to whether or not the account is accepted and 'honoured' by the audience. In either case a causal account is presented to justify and gain colleague and management agreement for an expectation of *limited* and *imprecise* effects from the social worker's intervention, and for a style of work described earlier by the social worker as 'continually chipping away at the family' (p. 191).

This meta-analysis raises a number of possible issues about causal talk and explanation in occupational discourse. The implicitness of theory is just one feature of this account that suggests that social workers' theories of cause are more akin to 'lay' theorizing than to formal scientific theories.

Furnham (1988: 1-121) has concluded that lay theories are often implicit rather than explicit, with tacit, non-specified assumptions. They are frequently ambiguous, allowing people to hold two mutually incompatible or contradictory ideas or beliefs at the same time, and not be particularly troubled by that inconsistency. Thus we observed that the social worker could comfortably appeal to both 'psychology' and 'culture' as explaining the relative resistance to change of the family under discussion. Lay theories also tend to proceed by seeking for verification rather than falsification, confirmatory rather than disconfirmatory evidence. They also often confuse correlation and cause by interpreting a relationship between two variables in a unidirectional manner based on an implicit theory.

Interesting as this conjunction of lay and scientific theories may be, it is culturally highly specific. There is evidence, for example, that some tribal cosmologies fix the search for causal explanations in everyday life centre stage. Thus, Shona cosmology emphasizes the continuity between the physical and the spiritual, and places the search for causal understandings of illness within a complex network of natural, social and spiritual environments. Medical diagnosis, treatments, programmes of prevention and responses to sexually transmitted diseases all fall within a framework of lay theorizing quite different from that envisaged by Furnham (Reynolds 1986; Mugadza 1991).[1]

In this very selective comparison of lay and scientific theories we are not of course saying that scientific theories are 'better', and neither are we arguing that there will always be a qualitative difference between scientific and lay theories. Indeed, there are significant similarities as well as differences. However, we do argue that professional causal accounts may be usefully viewed in the context of everyday explanation.

The re-inspection of Pithouse and Atkinson's work also suggests the relevance of recent work on accounts within service exchanges. For example, Iacobucci (1990) has illustrated that in certain contexts service talk, while it is ostensibly 'relational', may also have a use for accomplishing a task goal. Whether such talk is relational or task oriented depends not on the actual content of the talk but on the way participants orient to the talk as it emerges in the interaction. Thus, while social workers may not appeal to causes in a formal sense, they may yet be centrally concerned with giving explanations and reasons (Draper 1988: 15-27), and a variety of causal accounts may form a central part of the structuring of their occupation.

---

1 Norma Hall drew this evidence to our attention from her work and that of her students among Shona women in Harare.

A Methodology of Account-Giving in Social Work

Thus far we have argued that sociological analyses of occupational discourse have given scant attention to the probable existence and significance of causal accounts. Analyses of social workers' case talk call for an investigation of causal attributions as part of their professional 'survival kits', and need to be extended to include a wider range of professional discourse within and across organizational boundaries. A far more elaborated account of the significance of 'explanations' is necessary. In what follows we argue that exploration of such issues about social work talk and causality calls for an ethnographic approach.

Ethnographic field research has oscillated between suspicion and celebration of members' representations of social reality. Our stance on the status of such accounts seeks to take seriously the theoretical value of our commonsense notions of causal explanation, yet also accepts the limitations and fallibility of these folk theories as guides to an explanation of actions or beliefs held by social workers (Yearley 1988). In the knowledge that 'people do have strong intuitions...concerning the presence or absence of causes in particular instances', we need to look for the 'systematic rules and strategies for assessing cause in .. everyday inference' (Einhorn and Hogarth 1986: 3).

Lakoff and Johnson (1980) argue that while causation is a basic human concept, it is not unanalysable and 'undecomposable', but is made up of a cluster of other components which together make up the *gestalt* we experience as causation. This prototypical concept of causation operates as a yardstick against which we measure 'other kinds of causation which are less prototypical…actions or events that bear sufficient family resemblance to the prototype' (1980: 71). Their work is part of a wider literature on the significance of metaphor in the human sciences which illustrates ways in which causation is elaborated through use of metaphorical extensions (e.g. Black 1979; Boyd 1979; Kuhn 1979; Martin and Harré 1982).

The implications of this discussion for the beginnings of an ethnographic study of social work accounts of cause lie in the realization that causation inevitably has fuzzy boundaries, though it is not entirely fluid. 'The concept is viable because we continue to function successfully in terms of it' (Lakoff and Johnson 1980: 72). Yet judgements of cause are always likely to involve uncertainty. Hence an initial task for such a study is the exploration of ways in which social workers use ideas of cause in everyday language in the place of work, which will include an inspection of the contexts in which causal accounts are used, and the purposes they appear to have.

This basic task entails addressing a range of distinct questions which facilitates a more textured understanding. For example, do social workers engage in kinds of 'mundane reasoning' which, in the face of what may appear as contradictory testimony, holds fast to its suppositions and regards the objectivity of the world and a shared intersubjective experience as 'incorrigible propositions' (Pollner 1974; Pollner 1987)? Do social workers hold to a prototypical causal *gestalt?* What are assumed to be the essential components for a causal account? What other kinds of non-prototypical causation are seen as existing? Do social workers distinguish a range of related but distinct kinds of cause? When does an explanation cross the boundary between being 'causal' and 'not-causal'? How do social workers manage the inevitable uncertainty in their probabilistic causal judgements? What metaphors do social workers draw on in talking about causes?

For example, Lakoff and Johnson discuss the use of the 'emergence' metaphor in such statements as 'the mother nearly went crazy *from* loneliness', or 'she hit her child *out of* desperation', where the state (loneliness, desperation) is viewed as a 'container', and the act or event as an object that emerges from the container.

However, this approach is insufficient by itself. As part of a more incisive research strategy we also include 'Garfinkeling' – 'the technique of disrupting the social fabric to discover in the consequent reaction its generating rules' (Harré and Secord 1972: 150). For our purposes we take the social workers' social fabric to consist of the taken-for-granted assumptions and socially constructed realities of everyday professional life.

We need a 'grid' to approach this. One key question is 'What are the characteristics of events that trigger causal reasoning?' Einhorn and Hogarth marshall the evidence from cognitive psychology that people engage in causal reasoning in order to make sense of the world, and therefore it is likely to be unusual, abnormal or unlikely events that arouse causal interest (1986: 5). Schön's discussion of metaphor as central to the task of accounting for our perspectives on the world is also integral to this context. In one of the few applications of this debate to social policy, he argues that,

> 'metaphor' refers both to a certain kind of product – a perspective or frame, a way of looking at things-and to a certain kind of process – a process by which new perspectives on the world come into existence (Schön 1979: 254).

In exploring tentative hypotheses for 'trigger' events of causal accounts, we suggest that it may prove of central importance to understand how social workers explain and account for things 'going wrong'. While the very idea of 'making a mistake' assumes rule-governed, rather than determined, behaviour, it is arguable that we often refer to *causes* when something has gone wrong (Hughes 1980: 83, 89).

To clarify, within the category of 'going wrong' we include 'mistakes', 'crises', a worsening of the client's 'problem' notwithstanding the social worker's efforts, and also when positive or even negative predictions or explanations appear to be contradicted by events. Thus, negative predictions may come unstuck, and, while this may be good for the client, it is to us still an example of 'going wrong'.

Lyman and Scott's analysis is helpful at this point. They distinguish two kinds of account, *viz:* 'excuses' and 'justifications'. An excuse is offered when someone accepts that the action is bad, wrong or inappropriate, but responsibility is denied. Justifications take the form of accepting responsibility, but denying the pejorative quality of the action. Taking this as the essence of the distinction, accounts can thus be more fully categorized within the following paradigm (Figure 13.1).

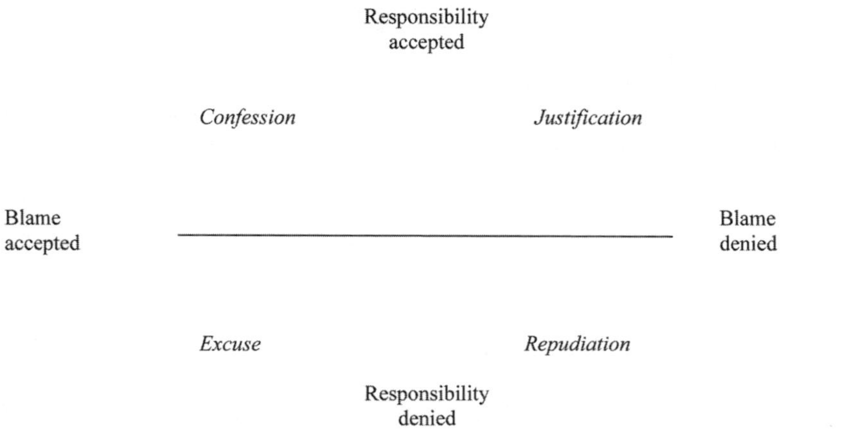

Figure 13.1 Social work 'accounts'

A critical area of work in this respect is that by Pomerantz, in her cluster of studies of blamings as one example of attributions of responsibility. She identifies various uses of what she calls 'extreme case formulations' in conversations designed to convince others through complaining, accusing, justifying or demanding (Pomerantz 1978; Pomerantz 1986).

We believe that work of this kind offers a rich programme for research into the strategies social workers adopt in accounting for things that 'go wrong'. For example, do social workers engage in exercises of 'retrospective rationality' (Bettman and Weitz 1983)? Do social work teams define peaks and troughs, good times and bad times, in their occupational activities? If so, how are these explained both within the group and to wider audiences? In addition, from our re-analysis of the text presented by Pithouse and Atkinson we can observe the way in which causal attributions perhaps operate as a kind of 'anticipatory justification' for limited achievements in the future – to adapt Bettman and Weitz's (1983) expression, a 'prospective rationality'.

Such accounts cannot be seen in the free-floating vacuum, but are shaped, if only with partial consistency, by the background expectancies held by the social worker. Thus a key question for an ethnography of social work accounts is whether such accounts are 'honoured' by peers, clients and managers (Blumstein 1974; Selwyn 1991). Early and more recent work has emphasized ways in which choices among causal explanations are dependent on cultural contexts, and that cultural and cognitive processes mutually inform and constrain each other (Lee 1950; Mulkay and Gilbert 1983; Nuckolls 1991).

We have highlighted just one possible 'trigger' of causal accounting by social workers. Other areas of inquiry include exploration of social work talk about prevention and risk taking (Brearley 1982). Notions of prediction, probability and 'if then' judgements are at the heart of 'risk' talk and thus appear to entail some kind of causal account.

Social workers' record keeping and report writing may also be particularly illuminating as triggers for causal accounts. Reports have a high status in social work, and are often regarded as expressing 'social work at its most detached and objective' (England 1986). Yet, as England goes on to point out,

> Formal reports in social work are necessarily incomplete . . . they are in essence 'extracts' from more comprehensive critical accounts. Their weakness is that, in social work practice, these more comprehensive accounts are rarely written (1986: 128).

In their reports prepared for courts, social workers and probation officers often resort to deterministic explanations of the behaviour of defendants (Hardiker 1977). For instance, a report might argue the cumulative and inescapable effect of childhood or economic disadvantage as a reason for not imposing a custodial sentence. Probation officers often appear to resort to strategies intended to keep offenders 'down tariff'. These strategies are apparently based on causal assumptions about the damaging effects of social work intervention, and an appeal to some kind of labelling theory. These are examples, in Lyman and Scott's terms, of an 'excuse'.

Records raise slightly different questions, in that, while reports have an essential prospective rationality, records are largely an exercise in retrospective constructions and accounts. Records are accounts also from the rather different standpoint of decisions about what counts as a 'case' unit. Smith and Harris drew attention to the significance of the taken-for-granted way in which case records usually cover one individual. Ideologies of need and judgements about causes of need are both inherent in these decisions about record keeping (Smith and Harris 1972).

Other examples of aspects of occupational work which may repay inspection include practices surrounding the admission of young people to local authority assessment units, and decisions reached by such units about the 'causes' of problems and future actions. Report writing and inter-disciplinary case conferences form the audience for such practices. Also, decisions in social work team meetings about work allocation, and related judgments about whether to close a particular case seem, *prima facie,* to be practices which involve appeal to reasons, explanations and causes.

In developing an ethnography of account making we need throughout to make the commonsense theories of social workers and managers integral to the investigation, without abandoning our 'empirical fishing lines'.[2]

2 The phrase is Graham Swift's in his novel, *Waterland.* The full sentence reads, 'There are times, (they come round really quite often) when good, dry, textbook history

Explanations as 'Survival Kits'

What sociological insights can we anticipate from such a study? Our discussion of accounting for things 'going wrong' points to possible ways in which explanations may serve in part as 'survival kits'. There are several dimensions to this.

Social work explanations as justificatory or excusing accounts may vary in the extent to which they refer to factors which are amenable or unamenable to change. Strongly 'causal' explanations, referring to factors which are unamenable to change, may, as we have seen, carry the political/professional sub-text 'I cannot be expected to do anything about this problem'.

Several aspects of this call for investigation. For example, do court reports operate in some kind of negotiated manner as 'excuses' for defendants? What kinds of accounts of poor 'corporate' performance are resorted to by social work agencies (Bettman and Weitz 1983)? Do causal accounts function as a cloak of understanding? For example, in a different context Begelman has discussed the way in which we may 'define' something by categorizing it as a member of a larger class (Begelman 1970). So 'delusions' may be defined as a symptom of mental illness. But categorization may be confused with causal explanation, and understanding is made less likely when it is assumed that categorized labels have somehow explained the acts of those to whom such labels are applied.

Social Work Practice

We have contended that social work literature has given little attention to grounded inter- and intra-professional accounts of reasons and causes in occupational activity. In these end paragraphs we reflect on the reorienting perspective that this critique offers for some of the debates about social work practice and management that provide part of everyday fare within social work writing.

Sheldon has observed that in social work practice 'no treatment ever seems to be abandoned ', and has commented on the corresponding 'supermarket principle' of social work education, whereby 'students are encouraged to believe anything they like from the vast literature available to them' (1978: 12).

This criticism of social work's lack of rationality is also reflected in the professionally influential arguments of Goldberg and others, in developing their work on 'case' accountability, that social workers apparently found it difficult to envisage the circumstances in which they would close their cases. Working without an operational sense of means and ends, causes and outcomes, they had difficulty in formulating a plan for the future rather than a description of the present situation, and as a result expected their cases to remain open more or Jess indefinitely (Goldberg 1976: 6, 10).

---

takes a plunge into the old swamp of myth and has to be retrieved with empirical fishing lines' (1983: 74).

Sheldon's solution is to see the problem as an immature primitivism out of which social workers must grow. But this positivist ethnocentrism will not suffice. A perspective which recognizes social workers as engaged in giving and making accounts will allow us to pause and ask *why* this happens. Alan Paton's metaphor in his novel, *Too Late the Phalarope,* about our struggle to understand our fellow human beings, is apt. The character Kappie, in seeking to understand his friend,

> Sat there like a man with a puzzle with a hundred pieces, with a picture all but complete, with six or seven pieces that would not fit at all, whatever way you turned them; so that you knew this could not be the picture at all, but that the real picture must be something strange and different, and that the parts that looked complete must be something quite other, if these six or seven pieces were to be made to fit (Paton 1971: 141).

We need the intellectual grace to recognize the significance of the pieces that do not fit – the 'obdurate character of the real world', as Blumer long-ago remarked (Blumer 1969: 21-47). 'Theory is good' remarked Charcot, 'but it does not prevent things from existing' (Freud 1962: 3.13).

Evidence of the role of causal accounts as part of the lay theories of social workers and other professionals would also provide a different lens through which to appraise arguments for the significance of systems theory for social work practice. Systems theory has been regarded as having wide implications for how social workers think about cause and effect and prediction, by throwing doubt on the linear model of cause and effect. Emery and Trist (1962) have argued that systems theory creates new possibilities for behaving, feeling and believing, and identifies determinants that cannot be traced back to the individual actor in isolation but must be referred to the system *per se.* Systems theory 'replaces a linear approach to causation and emphasizes an understanding of cause by the observation and interpretation of functional consequences both manifest and latent' (Whittaker 1974: 93).

Social work writers sometimes espouse systems theory as a crusade, which enables practitioners to increase both the breadth of assessment *and* the possibilities for intervention, thus enabling social workers to 'think about the unthinkable' (Hartmann 1970).

Whittaker hints at the underlying problem in this argument when he acknowledges that systems theory leaves 'unsettled the choice of strategy or technique of helping' (1974: 94). But he does not go far enough. Rather, in our view it magnifies uncertainty for the social worker, in that while it increases almost to infinity the possibilities for intervention, it does not help the social worker choose *which* intervention, but leaves her entangled in conceptual cobwebs. Fischer makes this very point in allowing for the way in which systems theory suggests a different causal model, but observing that

> such knowledge does not necessarily or automatically prescribe what to do in those situations . . . the extent to which utilization of such knowledge actually benefits caseworkers' intervention practices is unclear (1978: 58).

This importation of a particular model of causality into talk about social work is some distance away from the world of reasons, explanations, causes and accounts inhabited by social workers, and presents practitioners with the problem of living in good faith and avoiding a philosophy of despair. Systems theory may loosen the 'bundles of causal threads' (Bunge 1979: 123), but the social worker may in the end be left threadbare.

Sainsbury (1975) some time ago made the point that social workers distinguish 'good' and 'successful' work. Ask a social worker if she has had a 'good' day or a 'successful' day, and she is likely to make a clear distinction. 'Successful' work follows a clear linear pattern, and social workers rarely claimed that they had had a successful day. 'Good' work accounts for work which finds its end in itself. This illustrates the way in which some social workers may draw on what for them is an occupationally necessary distinction, and respond to a particular *gestalt* of causal thinking.

Client Accounts

We have restricted our attention to accounts given by and between occupational members. Yet there has been a significant vein of studies of client accounts. The initial development of these studies was due to a number of factors including the decline in social work of the treatment ideology which, through its preoccupation with the relatively *hidden* causes of behaviour, rather than behaviour *per se,* produced among other things an aversion from clients' own assessments of the meaning of problematic situations. Consumer studies, with their emphasis on client rationality and common senses explanations, were thus part of this reaction against the medical model, and evidence of a greater interest in what people *do,* rather than what they *are.* Pessimism about the productiveness of experimental research designs in social work, allied to a concern about the dehumanizing effects of bureaucracy, led to user studies in the United Kingdom focusing on standards of service delivery, rather than on its outcome. The general influence of interpretive sociologies within social work also made practitioners cautious of scorning the natural attitude. Social workers increasingly questioned the idea that there is only one standard of rationality to apply to the interpretation of human behaviour (Shaw 1984).

Judgements about outcomes are, of course, relative to both context and culture. No-one who has read Primo Levi's account of 'A Good Day' in Auschwitz (Levi 1987: 77-82) can fail to appreciate this relativity as it applies, for example, to institutional life.

Yet paradoxically these studies were carried forward on the tacit – and as we have tried to show, mistaken – assumption that we already knew the *social worker's* voice. Furthermore there has been limited attention to consumer's own causal constructions since the formative work of Mayer and Timms (1970). And while their research made a fundamental contribution to social workers' understanding, it was sometimes marred by a recurring tendency to place social workers' accounts within a formal professional framework, and compare what they describe as clients' 'unicausal-moralistic-suppressive' ascriptions of cause with this formal framework, as if it was the event itself.

Accounts of Management Practice

Bettman and Weitz (1983) have identified strategies engaged in by organizations in accounting for 'good' and 'bad' years, in terms of such factors as the balance sheet and market share. Causal explanations tend to be constructed which locate causes of bad years in external and unstable factors outside the organization, and therefore beyond its control. Farr's work on motivation in industrial contexts showed similarly that favourable outcomes tended to be attributed to the self and unfavourable ones to the environment. The self was seen as causing job satisfaction and the environment as causing job dissatisfaction (Farr 1977). Social work management judgements about performance 'balance sheets' invite analogous exploration in terms of strategies adopted by senior management to decide and account for whether they are in the 'red' or the 'black'.

The general point here is the extent to which causal factors are judged to be within the control of the participants. We have made this point in our discussion of explanations as justificatory accounts, and parallels can be drawn with thinking about social work management and organizations. Bettman and Weitz utilize a potentially fruitful framework in adding the ideas of the *locus* of cause (whether it is perceived as internal or external to the organization) and its *stability* (short-run or long-term in its influence) to the question of whether the event is seen as modifiable or controllable.

Comparable ideas have been developed by Emery and Trist (1962), in their work on the ways in which organizations' understanding of their environments influence corporate strategies. Davies has applied these ideas to social work practice with individuals (1977: 95-100), and Peter Leonard has argued that social workers typically intervene after the points at which causal factors operate (1971). We have tried to advance the case that ethnographic work would illuminate ways in which causal accounts shape strategies adopted by social work organizations in dealing with changing environments (Chaffee 1985).

Conclusion

We have argued that, while causal accounts lie at the heart of social work, sociological research and theorizing have very largely ignored their occupational centrality. We have proposed an orientation towards the production of an ethnography of how social workers give accounts of their work, which would focus particularly on an inspection of the management of events that 'go wrong' as triggers for causal accounting.

Acknowledgments

Various people have exercised a positive influence on our work in this paper. Those we are most aware of because most recent are Paul Atkinson, Tia DeNora and Norma Hall.

References

Begelman, D.A. 1970. 'Behavioural Classification' in M. Hersen and A.S. Bellack. *Behavioural Assessment: A Practical Handbook.* Oxford: Pergamon Press.

Bettmann, J.R. and Weitz, B.A. 1983. 'Attributions in the Board Room: Causal Reasoning in Corporate Annual Reports'. *Administrative Science Quarterly* 28: 165-183.

Black, M. 1979. 'More About Metaphor' in A. Ortony (ed.) *Metaphor and Thought.* Cambridge: Cambridge University Press.

Blumer, H. 1969. *Symbolic lnteractionism: Perspective and Method.* New Jersey: Prentice-Hall.

Blumstein, P.W. 1974. 'The Honouring of Accounts'. *American Sociological Review* 39: 551-561.

Boyd, R. 1979. 'Metaphor and Theory Change: What is 'Metaphor' a Metaphor for?' in A. Ortony (ed.) *Metaphor and Thought.* Cambridge: Cambridge University Press.

Brearley, P. 1982. *Risk and Social Work.* London: Routledge.

Bunge, M. 1979. *Causality and Modern Science.* New York: Dover Publications.

Chaffee, E.E. 1985. 'Three Models of Strategy'. *Academy of Management Review* 10: 89-98.

Davies, M. 1977. *Support Systems in Social Work.* London: Routledge.

Dean, R.G. 1989. 'Ways of Knowing in Clinical Practice'. *Clinical Social Work* 17: 116-127.

Draper, S.W. 1988. 'What's Going on in Everyday Explanation?' in C. Antaki (ed.) *Analysing Everyday Explanation: A Casebook of Methods.* London: Sage.

Einhorn, H.J. and Hogarth, R.M. 1986. 'Judging Probable Cause'. *Psychological Bulletin* 99: 3-19.

Emery, F.E. and Trist, E.L. 1969. 'The Causal Texture of Organisational Environments' in F.E. Emery (ed.) *Systems Thinking.* Harmondsworth: Penguin.

England, H. 1986. *Social Work as Art.* London: Allen and Unwin.

Farr, R.M. 1977. 'On the Nature of Attributional Artifacts in Qualitative Research'. *Journal of Occupational Psychology* 50: 3-14.

Fischer, J. 1978. *Effective Casework Practice: An Eclectic Approach.* New York: McGraw-Hill.

Freud, S. 1962. 'Charcot' in *Standard Edition of the Complete Psychological Works of Sigmund Freud* 3. London: Hogarth Press.

Furnham, A.F. 1988. *Lay Theories: Everyday Understanding of Problems* in *the Social Sciences.* Oxford: Pergamon Press.

Goldberg, E.M. 1976. 'Towards Accountability for Social Workers: A Case Review System for Social Workers'. *British Journal of Social Work* 6: 3-22.

Hardiker, P. 1977. 'Social Work Ideologies in the Probation Service'. *British Journal of Social Work* 7: 131-154.

Harré, R.J., Margolis, J., Deese, J. and Lamiell, J.T. 1989. 'Language and the Science of Psychology'. *Journal of Social Behaviour and Personality* 4: 165-188.

Harré, R.J. 1989. 'Language Games and Texts of Identity' in J. Shotter and K.J. Gergen (eds.) *Texts of Identity.* London: Sage.

Harré, R.J. and Secord, P.F. 1972. *The Explanation of Social Behaviour.* Oxford: Basil Blackwell.

Hartmann, A. 1970. 'To Think About the Unthinkable'. *Social Casework* 51: 467-474.

Howe, D. 1987. *An Introduction to Social Work Theory.* Aldershot: Wildwood House.

Hughes, J. 1980. *The Philosophy of Social Research.* London: Longman.

Iacobucci, C. 1990. 'Accounts, Formulations and Goal Attainment Strategies in Service Encounters'. *Journal of Language and Social Psychology* 9: 85-99.

Jackson, C. 1968. *Life in the Classroom.* New York: Holt, Rinehart and Winston.

Jones, M. 1990. 'Understanding Social Work: A Matter of Interpretation?' *British Journal of Social Work* 20: 181-196.

Kuhn, T.S. 1979. 'Metaphor in Science' in A. Ortony (ed.) *Metaphor and Thought.* Cambridge: Cambridge University Press.

Lakoff, G. and Johnson, M. 1980. *Metaphors We Live By.* Chicago: University of Chicago Press.

Lee, D. 1950. 'Lineal and Non-Lineal Codifications of Reality'. *Psychosomatic Medicine* 12: 89-97.

Leonard, P. 1971. 'The Challenge of Primary Prevention'. *Social Work Today* 2.5: 2-4.

Levi, P. 1987. *If This is a Man.* London: Sphere Books.

Lortie, D.C. 1975. *School Teacher.* Chicago: University of Chicago Press.

Lyman, S.M. and Scott, M.B. 1970. *A Sociology of the Absurd.* New York: Appleton Century-Crofts.
Martin, J. and Harré, R. 1982. 'Metaphor in Science' in D. Miall (ed.) *Metaphor: Problems and Perspectives.* Brighton: Harvester Press.
Mayer, J. and Timms, N. 1970. *The Client Speaks.* London: Routledge.
Mishler, E.G. 1984. *The Discourse of Medicine: Dialectics of Medical Interviews.* Norwood: Ablex Publishing.
Mugadza, W. 1991. 'Shona Culture and Its Influence on Solving Family Problems' unpublished.
Mulkay, M.J. and Gilbert, G.N. 1983. 'Scientists' Theory Talk'. *Canadian Journal of Sociology* 8: 179-197.
Nuckolls, C.W. 1991. 'Culture and Causal Thinking: Diagnosis and Prediction in a South Indian Fishing Village'. *Ethos* 19: 3-51.
Paton, A. 1971. *Too Late the Phalarope.* Harmondsworth: Penguin.
Philp, M. 1979. 'Notes on the Form of Knowledge in Social Work'. *Sociological Review* 27: 83-111.
Pithouse, A. 1987. *Social Work: The Social Organisation of an Invisible Trade.* Aldershot: Gower.
Pithouse, A. and Atkinson, P. 1988. 'Telling the Case: Occupational Narrative in a Social Work Office' in N. Coupland (ed.) *Styles of Discourse.* London: Croom Helm.
Pollner, M. 1974. 'Mundane Reasoning'. *Philosophy of the Social Sciences* 4: 35-54.
Pollner, M. 1987. *Mundane Reason.* Cambridge: Cambridge University Press.
Pomerantz, A. 1978. 'Attributions of Responsibility: Blamings'. *Sociology* 12: 115-121.
Pomerantz, A. 1986. 'Extreme Case Formulations: A Way of Legitimizing Claims'. *Human Studies* 9: 219-229.
Reynolds, P. 1986. 'Concepts of Childhood Drawn from the Ideas and Practice of Traditional Healers in Musami'. *Zambezia* 13: 1-10.
Rojek, C., Peacock, G. and Collins, S. 1988. *Social Work and Received Ideas.* London: Routledge.
Sainsbury, E. 1975. *Social Work with Families.* London: Routledge.
Schön, D.A. 1979. 'Generative Metaphor: A Perspective on Problem Setting in Social Policy' in A. Ortony (ed.) *Metaphor and Thought.* Cambridge: Cambridge University Press.
Selwyn, J. 1991. 'Applying to Adopt: the Experience of Rejection'. *Adoption and Fostering* 15: 26-29.
Shaw, I. 1984. 'Consumer Evaluations of the Personal Social Services'. *British Journal of Social Work* 14: 277-284.
Sheldon, B. 1978. 'Theory and Practice in Social Work: A Re-examination of a Tenuous Relationship'. *British Journal of Social Work* 8: 1-22.
Simons, H.W. 1989. *Rhetoric in the Human Sciences.* London: Sage.
Smith, D.E. 1978. 'K is Mentally Ill'. *Sociology* 12: 23-53.

Smith, G. and Harris, R. 1972. 'Ideologies of Need and the Organisation of Social Work Departments'. *British Journal Social Work* 2: 27-45.

Stanley, L. (ed.) 1990. *Feminist Praxis.* London: Routledge.

Swift, G. 1983. *Waterland.* London: Heinemann.

Whan, M. 1979. 'Accounts, Narrative and Case History'. *British Journal of Social Work* 9: 489-499.

Whittaker, J. 1974. *Social Treatment: An Approach To Interpersonal Helping.* Chicago: Aldine.

Yearley, S. 1988. 'Settling Accounts: Action, Accounts and Sociological Explanation'. *The British Journal of Sociology* 39: 578-599.

Chapter 14

The Consequences of Qualitative Social Work Research*

Throughout this book [Shaw, I. and Gould, N. (2001)] the writers and contributors have trodden the contested borderlands between research and practice. In so doing, they have persistently questioned and challenged commonly held understandings about both. They have said less about the technical requirements and methods of good qualitative research, and more about the mind-set, values and logics that are essential if qualitative social work research is to prove rigorous and relevant. We have not quite exhausted our agenda. In this final chapter we will confront some conventional positions regarding the contribution of qualitative inquiry to practice.

The following statements probably sound non-contentious. We need:

1. Clear evidence regarding the outcomes of social work.
2. Instrumental, practical uses from research if social work and human services more generally are to benefit.
3. Research that has clear implications that can be applied to social work practice.

We do not disagree. Outcomes evidence, useful research, and theory that entails a practice agenda, are certainly core requirements. But we have qualms about the too-easy tacit connection that is frequently made between these assertions and the role of qualitative research. Proponents of the functional 'horses for courses' approach to research methodology frequently assume that qualitative inquiry is somehow less well equipped to meet these requirements than surveys, longitudinal designs, single system designs or randomised control trials. We noted in the opening chapter that representatives from within quantitative outcome research have accepted that such an approach is narrowing and blinkered. However, we have found no grounds for advocates of qualitative research to be complacent about the merits of their methodologies. We conclude this book with an exploration of the three questions of social work outcomes, the uses of research, and the relations of practice and theory.

---

* Originally published as Shaw, I. and Gould, N. (2001) 'The consequences of qualitative social work research' in *Qualitative Research in Social Work*. London: Sage. Reprinted with permission of Sage Publications Ltd.

Process and outcomes

By way of preamble we should first clarify what we mean by 'outcomes'. Second, we need to rethink the assumptions we make about how evaluative reasoning proceeds.

Outcomes

We need to distinguish between general outcomes, social work outcomes and social work service outcomes (cf Long, 1994). Research findings, or policy implementation, are examples of outcomes in general. 'Social welfare outcomes' includes the effect on social welfare of any type of process, including not only social work services but also informal care, health care, housing, education and so on. 'Social work service outcomes' refers to the effects of social work services. These will be mainly social welfare outcomes, but by no means exclusively so. We should also distinguish between final and intermediate outcomes, and what can be called process-based outcome measures.

There is no implicit valuation of good or bad in the concept of 'outcome' and valuation of outcomes thus becomes a major issue. An outcome is more than a technically measured end point. It involves a valuation of that end point. These points become relevant when we make decisions about the methodology for researching outcomes.

Evaluative judgements

Second, there has been insufficient attention to philosophical contributions to the field of evaluation logic.

> Everyone agrees that information somehow informs decisions, but the relationship is not direct, not simple. Often the more important the decision, the more obscure the relationship seems to be. (House, 1980: 68)

House goes as far as to say that, 'subjected to serious scrutiny, evaluations always appear equivocal' (p. 72). He argues that evaluations can be no more than acts of persuasion. 'Evaluation persuades rather than convinces, argues rather than demonstrates, is credible rather than certain, is variably accepted rather than compelling' (p. 73). Evaluators have too frequently underplayed the role of judgement and hence of argumentation. This has resulted in an unduly technical, methods-oriented analysis, an over-confidence in quantification, and a tendency to represent knowledge in an impersonal, objectified form. Those who fail to accept the 'compelling' conclusions drawn from evaluation are dismissed as irrational. If results are unequivocal then those who fail to accept them are 'wrong'.

There have been several attempts to take a different approach to thinking through the reasoning process involved in constructing justified evaluative arguments. These typically emphasize the complex connection between evidence and conclusions, and commence from the differences between formal and informal reasoning. Whereas formal reasoning assumes a tight fit between the premises and conclusions within an argument, informal logic 'deals with ordinary, everyday language, where rules of inference are less precise and more contextual' (Fournier and Smith, 1993: 317). The key question is whether good but non-deductive reasoning is possible – i.e. reasoning that is not logically valid. 'The consensus among informal logicians is that there can be logically good, but nonvalid reasoning' (Blair, 1995: 73).

This philosophical argument has direct practice implications because much evaluative reasoning is non-deductive. For example, we may sometimes engage in good all-things-considered reasoning, where there are reasons for and against a point of view but where the pros outweigh the cons. The paper by House cited above falls in that category. Also, there has been growing acceptance of the circumstances in which it may be legitimate to reason from factual evidence to evaluative conclusions, where there can be no logical relation of implication for such an argument. Finally, informal logicians have concluded that much reasoning is dialectical. Reasons for a claim are seen as a move in an argument – an attempt to persuade offered as part of an actual or possible exchange between parties who differ.

Qualitative research and outcomes

Following that preliminary ground clearing, we now sketch our views regarding the ways in which qualitative research and evaluation can address outcome questions.

First, there are design solutions analogous to those conventional outcome designs that entail a degree of control.

Second, the shift of emphasis from internal validity to questions of external validity and generalization, has led to a greater sensitivity to the micro-processes of practice and programmes.

Third, developments in symbolic interactionism and ethnomethodology have been applied to outcome questions.

Fourth, the impact of scientific realism has led to a radical rethinking of notions of causality.

Campbell and 'theory-infirming' case studies

Qualitative design solutions have been pursued actively by those who have worked on the borders of qualitative and quantitative methodology. For example, Donald Campbell's early position was that 'one-shot' case study designs are uninterpretable with regard to causal attribution. However, through exchanges with

Becker and Erikson, he came to the position that the analogy of degrees of freedom provides a major source of discipline for interpreting intensive, cross-cultural case studies. The logic entails testing theories against the predictions or expectations it stimulates, through a general process he describes as pattern matching, based on the premise that 'experimental design can be separated from quantification' (Campbell, 1978: 197). He suggested a paradigm which entails a whole-hearted commitment to both ethnography and comparative studies. Campbell's approach has been developed in Yin's account of case study research (Yin, 1994; cf Shaw, 1999, Ch 7).

Micro-processes

William Reid has been attracted by the potential of 'change-process' research. He does not reject the role of controlled experiments but concludes that 'practical and ethical constraints on experiments necessitate a reliance on the naturalistic study of these relations' (Reid, 1990: 130). This entails a focus on the processes of change during the period of contact between the professional helper and the client system. Rather than relying on aggregated, averaged summary measures of outcomes, this approach returns to the content-analysis tradition in social research, through a greater focus on micro-outcomes.

Reid applies his ideas to social work, although the logic would presumably apply to other forms of change-oriented professional service. A systemic view of intervention is at its root, in which professionals and service users are viewed in a circular, mutually influencing interaction. In this model, 'conventional distinctions between intervention and outcome lose their simplicity' (p. 135). 'It then becomes possible to depict change-process research as a study of strings of intermixed i's and o's' – interventions and outcomes (p. 136). While Reid seeks to defend experiments, he suggests a more naturalistic stance when he says that 'averages of process variables that are devoid of their contexts at best provide weak measures' (p. 137).

Ethnomethodology and symbolic interactionism

Developments in symbolic interactionism and ethnomethodology have enabled qualitative researchers to add a rich, transformative leavening to otherwise flat, two-dimensional depictions of outcomes. Two examples will serve to illustrate this point. First, we saw in Chapter 1 how Miller's work enriches our understanding of the importance of context in qualitative research. He discusses ways that institutional texts constructed to explain past decisions inevitably gloss over the openness and complexity of the decision-making process (Miller, 1997). He gives the apparently mundane example of evaluation research on a bowel-training programme in a nursing home. The evaluation consisted of counting when and how patients had bowel movements. The programme was judged to have a successful outcome if patients used a toilet or bedpan and ineffective for those who continued soiling beds. One patient had soiled her bed. However, observation methods enabled the researcher to view a nursing aide contesting the definition of this as 'failure' on the grounds that the patient knew what she was doing and had soiled her bed as a protest act against staff favouring another patient. This illustrates how observing the context of text construction illuminates mundane, everyday life. This would not have found a way into the formal outcome record. Text production in institutions is 'micro-politically organized', and this includes textual outcome records.

Second, Denzin's interpretive interactionism has had a surprising impact on thinking about service outcomes (Denzin, 1989; Mohr, 1997). Mohr, for example, extends Denzin's argument to the evaluation of clinical outcomes in health research. She argues that the method leads us to inspect the relationships between personal difficulties, experiences, policies, interventions, and institutions. 'Interpretive interactionism permits intensive scrutiny of the ramifications and outcomes of various interventions' (1997: 284). It can:

1. Sort out different ways problems are defined.
2. Show how patients experience care. What it is about interventions they find helpful or not, and in what circumstances.
3. Identify 'secondary causes' eg contexts, culture, and the meanings patients bring.

'Strategic points for intervention can be identified by contrasting and comparing patients' thick descriptions, and these can be used to change, to improve, or to negotiate and renegotiate interventions' (p. 284). It is valuable when 'an outcome may not be readily apparent, and…the intervention is something that only the patient and not the professionals can define' (p. 285).

Cause and causal models

The fourth qualitative line of approach to the methodological problems posed by outcome evaluation is rather different. It stems from the stimulus provided by changed thinking regarding the nature of cause, and the corresponding models of causal hypotheses which flow from that thinking. The central idea is of underlying causal mechanisms that cannot be understood by surface workings and measurement. Hence, 'events themselves are not the ultimate focus of scientific analysis...Reality consists not only of what we can see but also of the underlying causal entities that are not always discernible' (House, 1991: 4). The underlying reality produces actual events, of which we have empirical experiences and sense impressions.

This is often described as a generative concept of causality.

> When we explain an outcome generatively, we are not coming up with variables or correlates that associate with one another; rather we are trying to explain how

> the association itself comes about. The generative mechanisms thus actually *constitute* the outcome. (Pawson and Tilley, 1997: 408)

The conventional concept of causation as regularities and associations is dismissed in favour of causal entities which have 'tendencies interacting with other tendencies in such a way that an observable event may or may not be produced' (House, 1991: 5). House quotes Manicas and Secord saying that, 'For the standard view of science, the world is a determined concatenation of contingent events; for the realist, it is a contingent concatenation of real structures. And this difference is monumental'. Hence, instead of merely documenting the sequence and association of events, the realist seeks to *explain* events.

While this view of cause does not necessarily require a qualitative methodology, it does clearly lend itself to such methods.

> Qualitative studies are not designed to provide definitive answers to causal questions..(but) it can still be an appropriately qualified pursuit. (Lofland and Lofland, 1995: 136, 138)

Miles and Huberman are even less reserved. 'The conventional view is that qualitative studies are only good for exploratory forays, for developing hypotheses – and that strong explanations, including causal attributions, can be derived only through quantitative studies'. They describe this view as 'mistaken' (Miles and Huberman, 1994: 147), and insist that qualitative evaluation research can,

1. Identify causal mechanisms.
2. Deal with complex local networks.
3. Sort out the temporal dimension of events.
4. Is well equipped to cycle back and forth between different levels of variables and processes.
5. Analytic induction provides a way of testing and deepening single case explanations.

Causal accounts will be local and 'now-oriented' (Lofland and Lofland, 1995: 141). Miles and Huberman develop analytic methods which address causal attribution in both single and multiple case explanations. For example, they advocate the use of field research to map the 'local causal networks' which informants carry in their heads and to make connections with the evaluator's own emerging causal map of the setting. Such maps start from 'causal fragments' which lead on to linked building of logical chains of evidence. Such causal networks

> are not probabilistic, but specific and determinate, grounded in understanding of events over time in the concrete local context – *and* tied to a good conceptualization of each variable. (Miles and Huberman, 1994: 159)

Much of this reasoning was anticipated by Cronbach's arguments regarding causal models. Rejecting the idea of causation as events that can be predicted with a high degree of probability, Cronbach developed twin arguments. First, he argued that causes are contingent on local interactions of clusters of events. More than one cluster may be sufficient, but no one cluster is necessary. Second, he accepted that there are usually missing events or conditions that affect the outcome of a given programme, but about which we know little. He was the first theorist to produce a plausible explanation of contextual factors in evaluation. Hence, he concludes that 'after the experimenter with his artificial constraint leaves the scene, the operating programme is sure to be adapted to local conditions' (Cronbach et al, 1980: 217). Furthermore, 'a programme evaluation is so dependent on its context that replication is only a figure of speech' (p. 222).

Qualitative evaluation cannot resolve the problems of causal conclusions any more than quantitative evaluation, but it can assess causality 'as it actually plays out in a particular setting' (Miles and Huberman, 1994: 10). For example, qualitative evaluation and research share a recognition of the irony of social causes and consequences. Much of the sociology of deviance was based on just this sense of irony, with its exploration of deviant roles as doing necessary 'dirty work'. In evaluative terms, we may ask the question what functions are served by a particular practice that would not be served by its absence. In less functional terms we may ask what are the typical results of this phenomenon in this setting, and what ends are served thereby? Lofland and Lofland make the important observation that causal answers are by and large based on passivist conceptions of human nature. Qualitative inquiry has often steered away from causal accounts, not because the methodology is weak in that area but because of a commitment to an activist conception of human nature. The Loflands argue that an activist conception will lead to a focus on questions that address both structures and strategies. This will involve 'deciphering and depicting exactly what sort of situation the participants are facing' (Lofland and Lofland, 1995: 146), and understanding the 'incessantly fabricated' strategies people construct to deal with the situation.

Take for example, Silverman's work on HIV counselling. He is right to conclude that 'it is usually unnecessary to allow our research topics to be defined in terms of…the "causes" of "bad" counselling or the "consequences" of "bad" counselling' (Silverman, 1997: 34), insofar as such topics reflect the conceptions of social problems as recognized by professional or community groups. Nonetheless, this does not require the abandonment of causal arguments. Inquiry into the ways in which professionals incessantly fabricate service forms and structures does promise a better way to understand causes.

Miles and Huberman also develop ways in which ordering and explaining can transcend the level of the individual case through cross-case displays of data. They are confident of the ability of qualitative inquiry to go beyond the problems of inferring from association ('the weasel word of quantitative researchers', p. 222). They summarise the process as follows.

> *Cross-case causal networking* is a comparative analysis of all cases in a sample, using variables estimated to be the most influential in accounting for the outcome criterion. You look at each outcome measure and examine, for each case, the stream of variables leading to or 'determining' that outcome. Streams that are similar to or identical across cases, and that differ in some consistent way from other streams are extracted and interpreted. (p. 228)

They spell out the steps to accomplishing this analysis, but suggest that it may not be feasible for either larger or very small samples.

Qualitative research also facilitates the task of valuation of outcomes, and is opposed to the technicalization of outcome research. This is not exclusively the province of qualitative research, but more conventional, and strictly evidence-based varieties of outcome research tend to treat such issues as technical matters. This links to the broader area of value and political issues.

> Evidence on effectiveness and outcomes and an emphasis on health gain and health outcome provide an apparently value-neutral, rational approach and means for rationing health and social care. Beneath the range of technical issues in assessing outcomes are political and social values that need to be explicit. (Long, 1994: 175)

Making use of qualitative research

A focus on outcomes leads fairly directly to the wider question of how qualitative research might be useful for social work policies, programmes, projects and practice. At the broadest level, research would be judged useful if it demonstrably contributed to one or more of the following.

- Better policies, services and practice.
- Strengthened the moral purpose of social work.
- Promoted methodological rigour, scope, depth and innovation.
- Strengthened the sense of social work's intellectual nature and location.

We tend to make simple distinctions between research that has a direct, applied purpose and research that is basic, and hence where direct use questions are less relevant. This does not work (just as the related sharp distinction between 'research' and 'evaluation' does not work either).

Conventional quantitative research on outcomes is linked to a confidence in the instrumental utility of research. The problem with this is that it does not square with evidence on how research is actually used, and it misunderstands the nature of the policy making process. It is based on a rationalistic model.

> The rationalist model of policy making sees it as a series of discrete events, where each issue to be decided is clearly defined, and decisions are taken by a specific set of actors who choose between well-defined alternatives, after weighing the evidence about the likely outcome of each. (Finch, 1986: 149-150)

The important figure for this question is Carol Weiss, whose work in the 1970s explored how political considerations intrude on evaluation. She addressed three related issues.

First, she delineated the political context in which evaluation is located. Although she has been primarily concerned with evaluation and policy research at the federal level, her empirical work with policy and programme staff resonates throughout evaluation theory and practice. This underlines importance of being clear about the audiences for any inquiry.

Second, she exposed the limitations of conventional instrumental views of the political use of information, through her conceptualization of use as enlightenment. With her colleagues she interviewed 155 senior officials in federal, state and local mental health agencies. Officials and staff used research to provide information about service needs, evidence about what works, and to keep up with the field. However, it was also used as a ritualistic overlay, to legitimize positions, and to provide personal assurance that the position held was the correct one. At a broader conceptual level, it helped officials to make sense of the world. For all these purposes, 'It was one source among many, and not usually powerful enough to drive the decision process' (Weiss, 1980: 390). As for direct utilization of research, 'Instrumental use seems in fact to be rare, particularly when the issues are complex, the consequences are uncertain, and a multitude of actors are engaged in the decision-making process' (p. 397).

Research use was also reflected in officials' views of the decision-making process. Decisions were perceived to be fragmented both vertically and horizontally within organizations, and to be the result of a series of gradual and amorphous steps. Therefore, 'a salient reason why they do not report the use of research for specific decisions is that many of them do not believe that they make decisions' (p. 398). Hence the title of her paper – 'Knowledge creep and decision accretion'. This provided the basis for her conclusion that enlightenment rather than instrumental action represents the characteristic route for research use.

The enlightenment model 'offers far more space to qualitative research, through its emphasis on understanding and conceptualization, rather than upon providing objective facts' (Finch, 1986: 154).

Third, Weiss imbued models of use with a realistic view of the public interest. More than anything she has struggled towards a realistic theory of use. Others subsequently have developed such realistic views. For example, Chelimsky suggests that evaluation may have a deterrence function. 'In other words, the mere presence of the function, and the likelihood of a persuasive evaluation, can prevent or stop a host of undesirable government practices' (Chelimsky, 1997: 105).

Several cautious remarks are in order. First, we should not become over-pre-occupied with models of research use. Chelimsky believes ‘it is often the case that…evaluations are undertaken without any hope of use’. Expected non-use is characteristic of some of the best evaluations, including ‘those that question widespread popular beliefs in a time of ideology, or threaten powerful, entrenched interests at any time’ (p. 105). Thus, ‘there are some very good reasons why evaluations may be expert, and also unused’ (p. 105). Chelimsky’s comments are both sane and plausible.

> To justify all evaluations by any single kind of use is a constraining rather than an enabling idea because it pushes evaluators towards excessive preoccupation with the acceptability of their findings to users, and risks turning evaluations into banal reiterations of the status quo. (Chelimsky, 1997: 106)

Second, the enlightenment model should not be adopted as universally appropriate. For example, practitioner research is likely to proceed on a more immediate instrumental view.

Third, the adoption of enlightenment assumptions about research use can easily translate into a defensive posture, arising from the fact that they can readily be used to support an incrementalist approach to social change. The step from an empirical recognition that policy and practice change often proceeds through incremental enlightenment to a tacit assumption that this is how social change ought to proceed may be logically insupportable, but it is deceptively easy.

Fourth, in counterpoint to the previous point, we should avoid being unduly sanguine about the ability of research to change social work. Hammersley has criticized some professionally-driven research approaches on the grounds that they are based on too narrow a concept of research relevance and an overly optimistic faith in the ability of research to influence policy and practice. While he is writing about education, his remarks are relevant to social work. He suggests two grounds for concluding ‘there are good reasons to believe that research cannot routinely solve teachers’ problems’ (Hammersley, 1993: 430). ‘There is no scientific method that guarantees results’ (p. 430) and teacher circumstances are diverse and unlikely to be amenable to action in any routine sense. Rather, ‘sound practice cannot amount to the straightforward application of theoretical knowledge, but is an activity that necessarily involves judgement and draws on experience as much as on…scientific knowledge’ (p. 430).

Fifth, there is often an important connection between research use and ethics. Consider the ethical and political dilemmas about how research material is used. These issues are sometimes sharper in qualitative research. This arises partly from the greater closeness and consequent trust that may develop between evaluator and participant. In quantitative research the greater distancing may make these issues less agonizing. The risk of betrayal is also increased because of the typical use of smaller samples, the consequent difficulties of protecting the confidentiality of individuals, and the emphasis on the details of how people live their lives. Finch describes from her playgroups research her 'sense that I could potentially betray my informants as a group, not as individuals' (Finch, 1986: 207). 'Where qualitative research is targeted upon social policy issues, there is the special dilemma that findings could be used to worsen the situation of the target population in some way' (Finch, 1985: 117).

But none of these caveats reduces the overall value of careful elaboration of what we mean when we speak of research being useful. For instance, everyday social work discussions of evidence-based practice frequently proceed on a misconception at this point. Practice is not and cannot be 'based' on evidence in the straightforward and unproblematic way envisaged by many of its advocates. The discussion of theory and practice in the final pages of this chapter yield further reasons for this conclusion.[1]

Theorizing research and practice

In Chapter 10 we discussed the three practice-related problems of research and professional practice, reflective inquiry and identity, and whether qualitative inquiry can prove enabling and emancipatory. These all have implications for how we think about the relationship between *practice and theory*. Fook's chapter raises a cluster of such issues, both explicitly and implicitly. For example, is it possible to retain the language of 'bias' in qualitative research? Does it make sense to talk about the relationship between theory and fact? Is it possible to generalize from qualitative research? Whitmore is also concerned about generalization. Hall and Scourfield both draw on the logic of grounded, inductive theorizing, which is familiar in much qualitative and ethnographic work. In this part of the final chapter, we will consider ways in which qualitative research contributes to developments in theory, practice and method in social work.

Readers of a book on qualitative social work research will need no convincing that research ought to enhance practice. They may need greater persuasion that it ought to enhance theorizing, either by researchers or practitioners. If they consider theory at all, then practitioners are likely to regard it as something developed by social scientists, advocated during training, and available as a rather abstract framework that may be applied to practice. We opened this book by declaring our understanding of practitioners who flinch at the thought of swallowing the latest dose of expert knowledge. Their misgivings about theories and theorizing are sometimes reinforced by their realization that 'interpretive and social constructionist approaches are … ambivalent in regard to the ability of researchers to generate explanations' (Brodie, 2000: 2). This stems from a variety of factors. Qualitative researchers sometimes appear to take a hands-off approach to explaining and making judgements. They favour a descriptive rather than prescriptive approach

---

1 For a more extended consideration of the uses of qualitative research see Shaw, 1999.

to values, and prefer that research should be 'oriented to understanding the case more or less as a whole, not for patching its pieces and fixing its problems' (Stake, 1991: 77). This stance goes back to the roots of qualitative research, which provide researchers with 'powerful disincentives to assert responsibility for more than their story. The applicability of the story to other contexts is a judgement left to others' (Greene, 1993: 40-41). Local relevance and the human story are regarded as the primary goals of qualitative research, and not generalizability.

This open-minded stance can give qualitative research in social work 'a prima donna image' (Simon, 1986: 52). 'In insisting that ethnographers have the freedom to define problems after they get into the field, ethnography's representatives inadvertently may do more to keep ethnography out of policy research than to keep pretenders out of doing ethnography' (p. 55).

Theory and theorizing

Qualitative researchers have not adopted a unanimous stance of theoretical indifference. Finch, for example, has argued that a concern with theoretically informed empirical research is quite compatible with qualitative research, that a blend of theory and data is the hallmark of good qualitative work, and that 'this particular blend produces precisely the kind of work that is likely to make an impact upon policy because it offers theoretical insights grounded in evidence' (Finch, 1986: 174). Greene (1993) specifies what this might entail. We should,

- Explicate our own theoretical predispositions.
- Describe locally held theories ('locally meaningful theoretical perspectives in data interpretation' (Greene, 1993: 38)).
- Attend to emergent theoretical issues.
- Integrate substantive theory into research conclusions and recommendations.

'Theory' is, of course, elusive. Once we acknowledge the theory-laden character of all observations, then the distinction between theories and data acquires an inevitable haziness. Even if we accept the need to use the language of theorizing, difficulties continue to occur because 'theory' may refer to formal propositions, worldviews, or working hypotheses. Social work practitioners often use the term in a colloquial sense to refer to models of intervention.

More recently, attention has helpfully moved to recognize the similarities and differences between lay and expert knowledge. The assumption that researchers possess expert knowledge that is different from and inherently superior to 'citizen science' has been widely questioned. The conclusion has been widely reached that 'the products of systematic inquiry will not necessarily be better than the presuppositions built into traditional ways of doing things. It is a modernist fallacy to assume otherwise' (Hammersley, 1993: 438).

Reflection on the cultural significance of common-sense knowledge, practical knowledge, praxis, tacit knowledge and lay theorizing has substantially reconfigured conventional ideas of the relationship between theory and practice, and served to question the assumptions behind some forms of quantitative inquiry.

Common sense

Campbell gave early expression to some of these ideas. Writing in 1974 when 'many of our ablest and most dedicated graduate students are increasingly opting for the qualitative, humanistic mode' (1979: 49), he expounded his insistence that qualitative, common sense knowing is the building block and test of quantitative knowing.

Anthropologists, such as Geertz, have suggested several reasons why we should treat common sense as a cultural system – 'a relatively organized body of thought, rather than just what anyone clothed and in his right mind knows' (Geertz, 1983: 75). If it is a cultural system and not mere matter-of-fact apprehension of reality, then 'there is an ingenerate order to it, capable of being empirically uncovered and conceptually formulated' (p. 92). It is here, of course, that the argument 'bites' on qualitative research. Pleas to treat common sense seriously must in part include pleas to treat it empirically. Common sense pictures of the odd, the deviant, the tediously mundane, and the difficult, provide us with out-of-way cases, and are hence of use to us anthropologically, by setting nearby cases in an altered context.

Geertz undertakes this 'disaggregation of a half examined concept' (p. 93). He contends that the uses we gain from common sense are by understanding its 'stylistic features, the marks of attitude that give it its peculiar stamp' (p. 85), rather than its varied content. He identifies properties of 'naturalness', 'practicalness', 'thinness', 'immethodicalness', and 'accessibleness' as those general attributes of common sense found everywhere as a cultural form.

Common sense is, however, not to be seen as a way of sense-making characteristic only of untutored citizens, and explained by the professional or academic expert. Recent reflections on the place of professional practice wisdom owe an indirect debt to this realization. If evaluation is to be relevant, it cannot ignore the common sense ways in which practitioners endeavour to make evaluative sense of their practical activities (Shaw and Shaw, 1997a, 1997b). In a similar way, recognizing the role of informal logic means that we also need to discover how researchers draw conclusions about evidence.

Tacit knowledge

Common sense knowledge will often be tacit knowledge. The notion that experts have tacit knowledge was first introduced by Polanyi (1958). The idea has been refined and applied to fields as diverse as medical practice and laser building, social work and the development of nuclear weapons. Tacit knowledge can be defined as knowledge or abilities that can be passed between experts by personal contact but cannot be, or has not been, set out or passed on in formal statements, diagrams, verbal descriptions or instructions for action (Collins, 2000).

The question arises whether tacit, implicit understanding is in tension with more explicit, planned, qualitative research. Stake may seem to suggest as much when he and Trumbull argue that

> For practitioners..formal knowledge is not necessarily a stepping stone to improved practice..We maintain that practice is guided far more by personal knowings. (Stake and Trumbull, 1982: 5)

Although they do not dismiss formal knowledge, 'the leverage point for change too often neglected is the disciplined collection of experiential knowledge' (pp. 8-9). On this view, good qualitative inquiry will reveal tacit knowledge – 'the largely unarticulated, contextual understanding that is often manifested in nods, silences, humour and naughty nuances' (Altheide and Johnson, 1994: 492). There are actions, judgements and recognitions which we accomplish spontaneously. We do not have to think about them prior to performance. We are often unaware of having learned to do them. While we may remember once being aware of the understanding necessary for action, we typically are now unable to describe the knowings that our actions reveal. It has become 'thinking as usual' knowledge.

> Tacit knowledge exists in that time when action is taken that is not understood, when understanding is offered without articulation, and when conclusions are apprehended without an argument. (Altheide and Johnson, 1994: 492)

The research problem posed by this largely non-discursive knowledge is 'how to talk about what is seldom spoken about' (p. 493). Qualitative researchers in social work often seem ambivalent regarding such knowledge, tending to oscillate between seeing it as potentially liberating or constraining (cf Scott, 1990). However, there is nothing intrinsically wrong about an implicit, unarticulated theory. 'Reality is what we choose not to question at the moment', and 'the better shape science is in, the more the positions are implicit' (Becker, 1993: 220). A consequence of prioritizing qualitative work in social work ought to be that different kinds of tacit knowledge are recognized. The significance of personal contact and practical knowledge sharing between social work practitioners will be brought out, and sources of trust and mistrust between social workers made clear (Collins, 2000). This is a big agenda, and one that social work has only begun to tackle.

Practical knowledge

But this raises a further question. What do we mean when we refer to 'practical' knowledge? There has been a renewed influence of Aristotelian views of theory and practice on writers in diverse fields such as ethnography (Hammersley, 1992), constructivism (Schwandt, 1993) and critical evaluation (Carr and Kemmis, 1986). The main effects of this have been twofold. First, it has led to a welcome reinstatement of the ethical dimension of reasoning and practice. Second, it has rescued notions of the practical from its status as second tier, derivative, and derived prescriptively from formal theory. For example, Schwab's influential paper on understanding curriculum argued for a language of the practical rather than the theoretical. By practical 'I do *not* mean...the easily achieved, familiar goals which can be reached by familiar means' (Schwab, 1969: 1), but rather 'a complex discipline...concerned with choice and action' (pp. 1-2).

Schwandt distinguishes theoretical knowledge ('knowing that'), craft or skill knowledge ('knowing how'), and practical-moral knowledge ('knowing from'). Ethical reasoning takes place through practical wisdom. Schwandt wishes to recast evaluative research within this kind of practical hermeneutics. When we talk about 'application', something more is intended than the instrumental sense of practicality, but the more fundamental sense of making something relevant to oneself. This involves a particular kind of knowledge – 'knowing from within or practical-moral knowledge', which 'requires not cleverness in application but understanding' (Schwandt, 1997: 76). 'Practical-moral knowledge aims to actually move people, not simply give them good ideas' (p. 81).

The contributors to this book have no interest in downplaying analytical knowledge. Reid may be correct when he concludes that 'flawed research may be better evidence than "low grade" practice wisdom' (Reid, 1994: 476). But we do hope to persuade social workers to abandon the polarized tensions between 'theory' and 'practice'. To this end, an appreciation of 'practical hermeneutics' will help deliver social workers from seeing good practice and good qualitative research as the inculcation of hierarchical knowledge-from-above.

Local relevance and general knowledge

We reminded ourselves at the start of this discussion of theory and practice that qualitative researchers have emphasized the importance of the locally relevant story, and the applicability of the story to other contexts has tended to be a judgement left to others. Miller and Crabtree put is as follows: 'Local context and the human story…are the primary goals of qualitative research and not "generalizability"' (1994: 348). There is no way that qualitative researchers should have cold feet about the main thrust of this position, under pressure from advocates of tight evaluation designs, and research funders who talk darkly about 'anecdotalism'. Schwab had in mind the application of curriculum initiatives to schools, but his remarks hold good for analogous applications of intervention initiatives in social work agencies.

> The curriculum will be brought to bear not in some archetypal classroom but in a particular locus in time and space with smells, shadows, seats and conditions

> outside its walls which may have much to do with what is achieved inside. (Schwab, 1969: 12)

Does this mean, then, that advocates of qualitative work in social work should give up any thought of claiming wider relevance and generality for their work? Indeed, should we go still further and – in the name of political and philosophical opposition to modernism – reject any act of generalization across social contexts as an act of despotism (Lyotard, in Seale, 1999: 13)? We do not think so. Questions of generalization are closely similar to those regarding outcomes that we discussed earlier in this chapter. They take us immediately back to the basic mind-set that we bring to qualitative inquiry, and to the inadequacies of the functional division of labour approach – the horses for courses line of argument – that we have reasoned against during this book. That line of argument could be put in the following way. Qualitative and quantitative methodologies have their particular strengths. Qualitative research is strong on elucidating process and meaning – quantitative research is the prime vehicle if we need to make inferences regarding causes and outcomes, and if we need to draw conclusions that can be applied more generally. In much social work research, so the reasoning goes, we need to draw exactly the kinds of inferences that quantitative research facilitates.

Before we can directly answer the questions, if and how qualitative research can provide a grounding for inferences to other local contexts, we need to heed the implications of our previous consideration of the relationship between scientific and citizen theorizing. If the two are in closer proximity to one another than conventional ideas of science might lead us to assume, then we should also avoid treating ideas of generalization as technical matters constrained within an expert field of discourse.

Processes of drawing judgements about wider application and relevance are not limited to scientists. The process of generalization is present in all learning, and a grasp of generalization in qualitative research will be stronger for an awareness of how we generalize lessons in everyday life. Eisner distinguishes 'generalizing' in the sense of the exact application of what was learned in situation A to situation B, from 'transfer', in which we recognize that all situations are different to some extent. The expression 'transfer of learning' captures exactly his implicit distinction.

> Since no generalization can fit an individual context perfectly, modification is always necessary. This modification requires judgement on the part of intelligent practitioners. (Eisner, 1991: 212)

Pugh has demonstrated the value of reflecting on ideas of categorization, particularization, prototypes and stereotyping for social work practice (Pugh, 1998, 2000). Starting from a discussion of generalizing and particularizing in cognitive processing, he develops a critique of unduly simplistic ideas of stereotyping as they have been applied to anti-discriminatory practice. Discussions of this kind are immediately helpful for social work practice, and they are also valuable for the links they point to between everyday, professional and research thinking about those processes. For example, practitioners' understanding of processes of clinical inference will be enriched from a comparison with inferential processes in qualitative research (Erikson, 1959; Geertz, 1973).

Qualitative research contributes to conclusions about wider generality in several ways. First, by questioning an over-optimistic reliance on inferences from internal validity in controlled intervention studies, and by cautioning against the naïve transfer of logics of representativeness and probability from conventional research designs. Second, and more positively, by a productive emphasis on theoretically defensible strategies of generalization, such as naturalistic generalization, analytical generalization and thick description.

Internal and external validity

The expression 'internal validity' was coined by Donald Campbell, to describe the confidence with which inferences could be drawn about the relationship between independent and dependent variables within programmes. Of what use, he would argue, is generalizing a relationship if one doubts the relationship itself. His elaboration of threats to internal validity is likely to remain the standard statement.

Lee Cronbach argued in response to the work of Campbell on internal validity and Scriven on the centrality of summative evaluation, that '"external validity" – the validity of inferences that go beyond the data – is the crux of social action, not "internal validity"' (Cronbach et al, 1980: 231). For Campbell, internal validity is about the relations between interventions and outcomes in a given random sample. For Cronbach, experimental designs that rely on rigorous inferences are weak at the very point they claim to be strong – i.e. as context free statements that will safely generalize. 'Campbell's writings make internal validity a property of trivial, past tense, and local statements' (Cronbach, 1982: 137). Cronbach prioritizes the understanding and explanation of mechanisms operating in a local context, in order that plausible inferences can be drawn regarding other settings, people and interventions that are of interest to policy-makers. It is extrapolation that matters, and validity that goes beyond the data – 'a prediction about what will be observed in a study where the subjects or operations depart in some respect from the original study' (Cronbach, 1986: 94).

Cronbach's arguments are largely unfamiliar within social work, but they have methodologically radical implications, that bear on both qualitative and quantitative research. The issue for him is how we can establish research that will enable us to generalize to people, interventions and settings that were not sampled and are different. In order to achieve this local, contextualized understanding he rejects the notion of research in which 'the program is to play statue while the evaluator's slow film records its picture' (Cronbach et al, 1980: 56), in favour of case studies that draw primarily though not exclusively on qualitative methods. It is not 'before and after', but 'during-during-during' as he somewhere says, and 'planning inquiry…is the art of recognizing tradeoffs and placing bets' (Cronbach, 1986: 103).

We have given space to these arguments partly because they are absent from much routine debate within social work research. We are convinced that this 'tough-minded master of conceptual distinctions' (Scriven, 1986: 15) provides qualitative social work research with a rigorous framework that creates 'truly unique alternatives sensitive to the scholarly need for general knowledge and the practitioner need for local application' (Shadish et al, 1990: 375).[2] There are some problematic aspects and limitations to Cronbach's theory (Shaw, 1999: pp 25-35, Chapter 5), yet these are outweighed by the relevance of his work for debates within qualitative evaluation research about generalization, causal explanations, multi-site case studies, and the policy relevance of research.

Statistical generalization

Qualitative researchers have rightly been wary of the conventional logic of generalization based on probability sampling. However, models of statistical generalization have occasionally been used effectively, for example with multiple case studies. Sinclair reported a large-scale study of hostels for young male offenders that utilized an impressive range of data to draw conclusions regarding the effect of hostel environments on offending (Sinclair, 1971). He went on to argue with others that

> The comparison of a large number of institutions within a single study enables a serious weakness of descriptive case studies to be overcome. This is the difficulty of linking the precise features of the care provided with its immediate and long term effects. (Tizard et al, 1975: 3)

Yet the problems usually outweigh the gains. Conclusions based on probabilities are of limited utility in specific cases. While we might know that 'on average' a particular project, social work intervention, or correctional programme has a given chance of being successful, this does not help us to weigh the particular contingencies for a specific choice. We lose 'case identity', and are left with faceless generalizations. Also, the typical situation facing practitioners, carers or agency managers is not one of exact generalization, but, to repeat Eisner's term, transfer to settings or interventions which are different to some degree.

2 Shaw has described and drawn extensively on aspects of Cronbach's work as applied to qualitative evaluation methodology in the fields of education and human services (Shaw, 1999).

Analytical generalization

Beginning social work researchers often find it hard to envisage an alternative to statistical approaches to generalization. They may tend to revert to analogies with samples and populations, along with assumptions of minimum viable sample sizes. However, using case study designs as an example, when selecting more than one case the logic is not that of sampling but of replication. 'Each case must be selected so that it either (a) predicts similar results (a *literal replication*) or (b) produces contrasting results but for predictable reasons (a *theoretical replication*)' (Yin, 1994: 46).

By way of parenthesis, we should note that Yin's argument should not be confused with the idea that we can extrapolate from particular agencies, families, and other complex unities, on the grounds that the smaller case is a microcosm (literally, a 'little world') of the larger world. This doctrine of a constant analogy between universal nature (the macrocosm) and human nature (the microcosm) is a seductive argument, because it may seem to solve our problems in one move. There certainly are instances where samples of one have intrinsic interest, and we do not need to take the extreme position that cases simply share a common difference. But faith that individual 'cases' are microcosms is a chimera – in Geertz' terms, 'palpable nonsense', and 'an idea which only someone too long in the bush could possibly entertain'! (Geertz, 1973: 22).

A common theoretically guided approach to generalization is analytic induction. The method proceeds by employing the notion of a 'generic problem', which is applied through explicit and implicit comparisons of instances (Atkinson and Delamont, 1993). The use of this constant comparative method, including the identification of critical and deviant cases, enables the identification of common features between cases. This brief description of analytic approaches illustrates that inferences about generalization are logical ones rather than statistical. Qualitative methods lend themselves more readily to logic of this kind, because 'the place of generalization in social work is closer to the constructivist, naturalistic orientation…than to the position of logical positivists' (Reid, 1994: 470).

Vicarious generalization

A different approach to generalization is associated with logic that seeks to bridge the experience yielded by the research and the experience of the research participants and audience. Stake and Trumbull have evaluative research in mind when they say:

> We believe that program evaluation studies should be planned and carried out in such a way as to provide a maximum of vicarious experience to the readers who may then intuitively combine this with their previous experience. (Stake and Trumbull, 1982: 2)

These are 'self-generated knowings, naturalistic generalizations, that come when, individually, for each reader, each practitioner, new experience is added to old' (p. 5). It is the evocation of personal experience that leads, in their view, to the improvement of practice.

Eisner's ideas of connoisseurship and criticism are based on the same broad approach to generalization. Eisner poses the interesting question of the different points of focus for generalization. He wants to include in this the superficially paradoxical idea of 'retrospective generalization', which occurs when we see our past in a new light, naming something so that we can find a new significance in an array of past experience. We 'find a fit between a general statement and our personal histories. New ideas can reconstruct our past' (Eisner, 1991: 206).

Approaches based on personal experience are difficult to assess, and are open to the criticism that they diminish the possibility of generalizing inferences that challenge the wider, structural status quo. They tend to assume a consensual moral framework, and fit well with Stake's emphasis on stakeholder case studies. The basic ideas are challenging, but they need development.

Thick description

What defines anthropology is the kind of intellectual effort it is – an elaborate venture in 'thick description'. So reasoned Geertz, in what has become a point of reference for subsequent discussion. It is difficult to read a text on qualitative research without running into the expression. It is his vision of the relationship between the obscure and the public, the small and the broadscale, which carries appeal. His argument is inspirational rather than didactic, and is constructed around a fieldwork account of Jews, Berbers and French in Morocco in 1912, and an elaborate story of sheep stealing. He stresses the microscopic character of ethnographic descriptions. 'The anthropologist characteristically approaches… broader interpretations…from the direction of exceedingly extended acquaintances with extremely small matters' (Geertz, 1973: 21). He confronts grand realities of Power, Faith, Oppression, Prestige, Status and Love, 'but he (*sic*) confronts them in contexts small enough to take the capital letters off' (p. 21). Anthropology involves 'looking at the ordinary in places where it takes unaccustomed forms', so that 'understanding a people's culture exposes their normalness without reducing their particularity' (p. 14). 'What generality it contrives to achieve grows out of the delicacy of its distinctions, not the sweep of its abstractions' (p. 25).

In his eminently quotable phrase, 'small facts speak to large issues, winks to epistemology, or sheep raids to revolution' (p. 23). Hence, 'The essential task of theory building…is not to codify abstract regularities but to make thick description possible, not to generalize across cases, but to generalize within them' (p. 26). The vocation of interpretive anthropology 'is not to answer our deepest questions, but to make available to us answers that others, guarding other sheep in other valleys, have given, and thus to include them in the consultable record of what man has said' (p. 30).

The argument for qualitative research has never been that its claims for generalizability are outstandingly strong. Yet this brief overview demonstrates that qualitative methods should not be avoided because of the fear that their claims for wider relevance are especially weak. This is not the case. Kushner concludes,

> I try always to stay confused by this issue. I believe viscerally in the uniqueness of cases – and this leads me to believe in the necessity to measure quality of…processes anew in each context…On the other hand my commitment to social justice demands a distributive principle which insists upon comparative measures…The tension is irresolvable, I think. But..this tension is a rich one. (It) lies at the heart of case study approaches. (Saville Kushner)[3]

Theory and practice

We have engaged in an act of attempted persuasion about the centrality and relevance of concerns about theory and its relationship with practice in qualitative research. First, theory must be reconnected to everyday reasoning by practitioners and service users. Second, qualitative research should not be sidelined on the specious grounds that it is weak at the particular points social work most needs a research input. In countering this we opened the chapter with a discussion of the ways qualitative social work research challenges and deepens understanding of human service outcomes, and closed it by exploring ways that we can make plausible claims to wider generalities while sustaining the local and particular.

What conclusions can we draw?

In the first place, we should not be precious about our theories. Too much time spent discussing theory is paralysing. We need to defend social work against attacks, and hence need those people who pursue 'philosophical and methodological worry as a Profession' (Becker, 1993: 226). But while we still have to do theoretical work, 'we needn't think we are being especially virtuous when we do it' (p. 221). There are some circumstances where theory has been overemphasized. For example, emancipatory researchers, especially some of those whose work is underpinned by neo-Marxism, should not feel too aggrieved by Lather's vigorous insider warnings against theoretical imperialism – the 'circle where theory is reinforced by experience conditioned by theory' (Lather, 1986b: 261). 'Theory is too often used to protect us from the awesome complexity of the world' and

> In the name of emancipation, researchers impose meanings on situations rather than constructing meaning through negotiation with research participants. (1986b: 267, 265)

---

3 This is extracted with permission from an exchange about case studies of schools, on the American Evaluation Association Discussion List in November 1998.

Too often, 'one is left with the impression that the research conducted provides empirical specificities for more general, *a priori* theories' (Lather, 1986a: 76).

Lather's remarks point to our second conclusion – that at their worst 'scientific concepts can reinforce a vast array of dangerous or hateful political and moral agendas' (Jacob, 1992: 495).

Third, we should not retreat behind the bunker of the threat of abuse by theory to protect ourselves against the demand that theory and critique must go hand in hand. When theory/practice relationships are viewed as the failure of practitioners to apply the theories developed by those who are engaged in empirical and theoretical pursuits, this distorts reality. To regard theory and practice problems as breakdowns in communication that afflict practitioners is to fail to recognize that practical problems of this kind occur in the course of any theoretical undertaking. To assume that they can somehow be identified and tackled in theory and then 'applied' in practice tends to conceal how they are generated out of practice. As Parton reminds us, practice informs the development of theory as much as, if not more than, vice versa (Parton, 2000). To put it more specifically, theoretical problems in social work have in part a social work character. We made this point in our reflections on the limitations of practitioner research in the previous chapter. Fahl and Markand's point about psychology will stand for social science in general when they conclude that 'if existing academic psychology and existing professional psychological practice can only be brought together with difficulty, then this "only" says that this type of psychology needs to be criticizes and developed' (Fahl and Markand, 1999: 75).

Fourth, we should concur with Hall when he questions in his chapter the idea that research is either 'academic' or 'applied'. He remarks that 'one can see what is meant by this distinction…but all social research, inasmuch as it is about and results from an engagement with the social world, is "applied"'.

Finally, our vision of the relationship between social work and research must never be utopian – but it must always be radical. It was possibly Einstein who said that 'Things should be as simple as possible, but not any simpler'. Qualitative theory and research should persistently entice us with glimpses of the possibility of seeing the world differently. 'The impact of theory will perhaps be greatest where the ideas have sufficient "fit" with the issues professionals encounter on an everyday basis, while at the same time providing an alternative framework within which to understand these issues' (Brodie, 2000).

In our consideration of generalization in qualitative research we implicitly questioned strong versions of relativism in social research. It is true that 'in effect you have to be a relativist if you are going to study any historical moment in science' (Jacob, 1992: 500). White has drawn on Hacking's work in her contribution to this book, and he expands this stance to argue that relativism can helpfully be adopted as an interesting way of thinking if one is trying to understand a person or another culture (Hacking, 1999). But this willing suspension of belief as an attitude of mind should not be confused with relativism – that combination of 'intuitionism and alchemy' (Geertz, 1973: 30).

> Science can be socially framed, possess political meaning, and also occasionally be sufficiently true, or less false, in such a way that we cherish its findings. The challenge comes in trying to understand how knowledge worth preserving occurs in time, possesses deep social relations, and can also be progressive…and seen to be worthy of preservation. (Jacob, 1992: 501)

References

Altheide, D. and Johnson, J. (1994) 'Criteria for assessing interpretive validity in qualitative research', in Denzin, N. and Lincoln, Y. (eds) *Handbook of Qualitative Research*. Thousand Oaks: Sage.

Atkinson, P. and Delamont, S. (1993) 'Bread and dreams or bread and circuses? A critique of case study research in evaluation', in Hammersley, M. (ed) *Controversies in the Classroom*. Buckingham: Open University Press.

Becker, H. (1993) 'Theory: the necessary evil', in Flinders, D. and Mills, G. (eds) *Theory and Concepts in Qualitative Research: Perspectives from the Field.* New York: Teachers College, Columbia University Press.

Blair, J.A. (1995) 'Informal logic and reasoning in evaluation', in D.M. Fournier (ed) *Reasoning in Evaluation: Inferential Links and Leaps*, New Directions For Evaluation, No. 68. San Francisco: Jossey-Bass.

Brodie, I. (2000) 'Theory generation and qualitative research: School exclusion and children looked after', paper from ESRC seminar series 'Theorising social work research', National Institute for Social Work web site http://www.nisw.org.uk/tswr/brodie.html.

Campbell, D. (1978) 'Qualitative knowing in action research', in Brenner, M. and Marsh, P. (eds) *The Social Context of Methods*. London: Croom Helm.

Campbell, D. (1979) 'Degrees of freedom and the case study', in Cook, T. and Reichardt, C. (eds), *Qualitative and Quantitative Methods in Evaluation Research.* Beverly Hills: Sage.

Carr, W. and Kemmis, S. (1986) *Becoming Critical: Education, Knowledge and Action Research.* London: Falmer Press.

Chelimsky, E. (1997) 'Thoughts for a New Evaluation Society', in *Evaluation*, 3 (1): 97-118.

Collins, H. (2000) 'Tacit Knowledge, Trust and the Q of Sapphire' Cardiff University School of Social Sciences. Working Paper. <http://www.cf.ac.uk/socsi/>

Cronbach, L. (1982) *Designing Evaluations of Educational and Social Programs.* San Francisco: Jossey-Bass.

Cronbach, L. (1986) 'Social Inquiry by and for Earthlings', in Fiske, D. and Shweder, R. (eds), *Metatheory in Social Science: Pluralisms and Subjectivities.* Chicago: University of Chicago Press.

Cronbach, L., Ambron, S., Dornbusch, S., Hess, R., Hornik, R., Phillips, D., Walker, D., and Weiner, S. (1980) *Toward Reform of Program Evaluation.* San Francisco: Jossey-Bass.

Denzin, N. (1989) *Interpretive Interactionism.* Englewood Cliffs, NJ: Prentice Hall.

Eisner, E. (1991) *The Enlightened Eye: Qualitative Inquiry and the Enhancement of Educational Practice.* New York: Macmillan.

Erikson, E. (1959) 'The Nature of Clinical Inference', in Lerner, D. (ed) *Evidence and Inference.* Illinois: Free Press.

Fahl R. and Markand, M. (1999) 'The Project "Analysis of Psychological Practice" or: An Attempt at Connecting Psychology Critique and Practice Research', in *Outlines*, 1: 73-98.

Finch, J. (1985) 'Social Policy and Education: Problems and Possibilities of Using Qualitative Research', in Burgess, R. (ed) *Issues in Educational Research: Qualitative Methods.* London: Falmer Press.

Finch, J. (1986) *Research and Policy: the Uses of Qualitative Methods in Social and Educational Research.* London: Falmer Press.

Fournier, D. and Smith, N. (1993) 'Clarifying the Merits of Argument in Evaluation Practice', in *Evaluation and Program Planning*, 16 (4): 315-323.

Geertz, C. (1973) *The Interpretation of Cultures: Selected Essays.* New York: Basic Books.

Geertz, C. (1983) *Local Knowledge.* New York: Basic Books.

Greene, J. (1993) 'The Role of Theory in Qualitative Program Evaluation', in Flinders, J. and Mills, G., *Theory and Concepts in Qualitative Research.* New York: Teachers College Press.

Hacking, I. (1999) *The Social Construction of What?* London: Harvard University Press.

Hammersley, M. (1992) *What's Wrong With Ethnography?* London: Routledge.

Hammersley, M. (1993) 'On the Teacher as Researcher', in *Educational Action Research*, 1 (3): 425-445.

House, E. (1980) *Evaluating With Validity.* Beverly Hills: Sage.

House, E. (1991) 'Realism in Research' in *Educational Researcher*, 20 (6): 2-9.

Jacob, M.C. (1992) 'Science and Politics in the Late Twentieth Century', in *Social Research*, 59 (3): 487-503.

Lather, P. (1986) 'Research as Praxis' in *Harvard Educational Review*, 56 (3): 257-277.

Lofland, J. and Lofland, L. (1995) *Analysing Social Settings.* Belmont: Wadsworth.

Long, A. (1994) 'Assessing Health and Social Outcomes', in Popay, J. and Williams, G. (eds) *Researching the People's Health.* London: Routledge.

Miles, M. and Huberman, A, (1994) *Qualitative Data Analysis: an Expanded Sourcebook.* Thousand Oaks: Sage.

Miller, G. (1997) 'Contextualizing Texts: Studying Organisational Texts', in Miller, G. and Dingwall, R. (eds) *Context and Method in Qualitative Research.* London: Sage.

Miller, W. and Crabtree, B. (1994) 'Clinical Research', in Denzin, N. and Lincoln, Y. (eds) *Handbook of Qualitative Methods*. Thousand Oaks: Sage.

Mohr, W.K. (1997) 'Interpretive Interactionism: Denzin's Potential Contribution to Intervention and Outcomes Research' in *Qualitative Health Research*, 7 (2): 270-286.

Parton, N. (2000) 'Some Thoughts on the Relationship between Theory and Practice in Social Work' in *British Journal of Social Work*, 30 (4): 449-463.

Pawson, R. and Tilley, N. (1997) 'An Introduction to Scientific Realist Evaluation', in Chelimsky, E. and Shadish, W. (eds) *Evaluation for the 21st Century*. Thousand Oaks: Sage.

Polanyi, M. (1958) *Personal Knowledge*. London: Routledge and Kegan Paul.

Pugh, R. (1998) 'Attitudes, Stereotypes and Anti-discriminatory Education' in *British Journal of Social Work*, 28 (6): 939-959.

Reid, W. (1990) 'Change-process Research: A New Paradigm?', in Videka-Sherman, L. and Reid, W. (eds) *Advances in Clinical Social Work Research*. Silver Spring, MD: NASW Press.

Reid, W. (1994) 'Reframing the Epistemological Debate', in Sherman, E. and Reid, W. (eds), *Qualitative Research in Social Work*. New York: Columbia University Press.

Schwab, J. (1969) 'The Practical: A Language for Curriculum' in *School Review,* November, pp. 1-23.

Scott, D. (1990) 'Practice Wisdom: The Neglected Source of Practice Research' in *Social Work*, 35 (6): 564-568.

Scriven, M. (1986) 'New Frontiers of Evaluation' in *Evaluation Practice*, 7 (1): 7-44.

Seale, C. (1999) *The Quality of Qualitative Research*. London: Sage Publications.

Shaw, I. (1999) *Qualitative Evaluation*. London: Sage Publications.

Shaw, I. and Shaw, A. (1997a) 'Keeping Social Work Honest: Evaluating as Profession and Practice' in *British Journal of Social Work*, 27 (6): 847-869.

Shaw, I. and Shaw, A. (1997b) 'Game Plans, Buzzes and Sheer Luck: Doing Well in Social Work' in *Social Work Research*, 21 (2): 69-79.

Silverman, D. (1997) *Discourses of Counselling: HIV Counselling as Social Interaction*. London: Sage.

Simon, E.L. (1986) 'Theory in Education Evaluation, Or, What's Wrong with Generic-Brand Anthropology?' in D. Fetterman and M. Pitman (eds) *Educational Evaluation – Ethnography in Theory, Practice and Politics*. Newbury Park: Sage.

Sinclair, I. (1970) *Hostels for Probationers*. London: HMSO.

Stake, R. (1991) 'Retrospective on "The Countenance of Educational Evaluation"', in McLaughlin, M. and Phillips, D. (eds) *Evaluation and Education at Quarter Century*. Chicago: University of Chicago Press.

Stake, R. and Trumbull, D. (1982) 'Naturalistic Generalizations' in *Review Journal of Philosophy and Social Science*, 7: 1-12.

Tizard, J., Sinclair, I. and Clarke, R. (1975) (eds) *Varieties of Residential Experience*. London: Routledge and Kegan Paul.

Weiss, C. (1980) 'Knowledge Creep and Decision Accretion' in *Knowledge, Creation, Diffusion, Utilisation*, 1 (3): 381-404.

Yin, R.K. (1994) *Case Study Research*. Thousand Oaks: Sage.

Chapter 15
Unbroken Voices: Children, Young People and Qualitative Methods*

The hallmark of this book[1] is a sociology of childhood expressed through a series of illustrations of the ways in which a *qualitative* sociology enriches our understanding of childhood. Furthermore, this book is not only a qualitatively grounded sociology *about* children but one in which the voices of children and young people are directly heard pulled taut against the voices of adults. It is both a sociology *of* children and childhood, and a sociology *for* children and childhood. 'Children and childhood' is no accident. There is no homogeneous 'childhood', just as there is no undifferentiated qualitative method waiting to be applied to childhood. To assume so would be to run the risk of the sociological sadism against which Robert Merton warned, when the interests of the person are swallowed in the abstractions of the sociologist. There is a plurality of childhoods. But having said this we are equally opposed to disaggregating our understanding of childhood, such that the unique 'child' erases the common characteristics and rights of children.

There is no tradition within sociology for studying childhood. Work in this field only began in the 1980s, although major initiatives such as the Childhood as a Social Phenomenon project at the European Centre in Vienna (Qvortrup, Bardy, Sgritta and Wintersberger, 1994), and benchmark collections of readings (James and Prout, 1990; Waksler, 1991) demonstrate the considerable distance that has been travelled over a short time. Qualitative sociologists are not alone in their concern for children's voices and rights to be heard. Saporitti and Qvortrup have made effective cases regarding the 'conceptual and numerical marginalisation of children' (Qvortrup, 1990: 80) and against the bias of social statistics (Saporitti, 1994) – bias both in the ways social statistics are assembled and the uses to which they are put. Saporitti demonstrates the ways in which our social accounting systems make childhood invisible. In many governmental statistics children do not count either as units of observation or as units for analysis.

Saporitti illustrates the potential for exploiting statistics to present a very different picture in which the child becomes central. We lack 'a systematic and coherent set of demographic, social and economic indicators appropriate for

* Originally published as Shaw, I. (1996) 'Unbroken Voices: Children, Young People and Qualitative Methods', in Butler, I. and Shaw, I. (eds), *A Case of Neglect?* Aldershot: Avebury. Reprinted with permission of Ashgate Publishing Ltd.

1 Butler, I. and Shaw, I. (1996) *A Case of Neglect*. Aldershot: Avebury.

assessing the social status of childhood in contemporary industrial societies' (p. 190). He is committed wholeheartedly to a theoretically driven attempt to provide empirical support for a new sociology of childhood, and not just to the collection of new statistics. He applies this strategy to statistics dealing with population structure, dependency ratios, family statistics, poverty and fertility. For example, he charts the ratio between children and elderly people. Instead of seeing these statistics as an indicator of the problem of ageing populations he sees it as a 'co-existence ratio' – a measure of the shifting balance and relationship between the elderly and children. On fertility statistics he observes that 'all theories advanced to explain the decline in fertility consider children a "dependent variable" in a world of adults: in other words, all these theories focus on adults' (p. 209). He invites us to consider whether there may be a relationship between the decline in fertility and images of childhood, and whether the decline in fertility will mean lower status for children or children being treated as a precious social good.

Saporitti provides a radical and persuasive example of an argument for a *quantitative* approach in which a sociography of childhood is central. Yet it does not and cannot go far enough. At the purely pragmatic level, official statistics are very rarely child based (ie the unit of collection is not the child, and the analysis is not about children), and this limits the extent to which a creative re-reading of this kind can be carried out. Statistics on children vary greatly in availability, quality, scope and comparability across time. Comparative analysis across time and space is difficult. Saporitti admits that

> Thus we are often compelled to resort to methodological and technical devices that frequently leave us with 'artefacts' rather than well grounded and valid indicators of childhood status (Saporiti, 1994: 195).

There are more significant limitations. The method inevitably yields an adult perspective, which does not require any direct understanding of the child's own view. In addition, at its best it poses interesting questions which can be tabled but not resolved. Butler has already made the point that changing ratios of children to older people may or may not indicate changing *relationships* between people across the generations (cf Pilcher, 1995). Social demography will not give us sufficient answers.

A growing interest in qualitative studies of children has led to a shift away from traditional methods such as experiments and hypothesis testing strategies. Qualitative studies fall into two broad clusters. The identification of consistent trends and stages in children's development within social, family and educational contexts has provided the thrust for many studies, and has influenced the work reported here by Pugsley, Coffey and Delamont. More typically associated with qualitative work has been the second cluster of studies 'involving naturalistic observation and micro-ethnography where the focus is on discovering and describing stable features of children's life-worlds' (Corsaro and Streeck, 1986: 29). One area of growth has been ethnographies of pre-school years (eg Corsaro,

1985; Mandell, 1988), which served to bring to the fore the way in which previous studies had overemphasised development processes at the expense of direct consideration of what the events of everyday life look like in childhood. These studies also served to show, by way of contrast, how researchers, with occasional exceptions (eg Denzin, 1977), had tended to remove themselves from the social context of children's peer activities.

Studies of children fall into three kinds (Fine and Sandstrom, 1988). There are those that find children to be more mature or capable than we have expected. Fine and Sandstrom conclude that they 'know of no study that has found that children are more "childish" than we have given them credit for' (p. 72), though they admit this could be the product of social science ideologies, in which researchers want to make their work important by showing their informants are talented. The work described by Crowley, and also the analysis of children's involvement in prostitution, by Crowley and Patel, illustrate this tradition of social research. Second, there are studies that find children and young people to be more tendentious and rebellious – studies that act in effect to de-romanticise childhood. In contrast with American research, British research has often been about working class youth. The work of people such as Paul Willis (1978) has addressed the problem of how the class system is produced, and is more broadly theoretical than American work. Williamson describes research with young people in the British youth services in a later chapter of this book which is influenced by this tradition. Finally, there are those studies that have shed light on how socialisation by peers occurs among children and young people. Much of this work has been done in the context of schooling, setting a secret process of education alongside formal schooling (e.g. Bowles and Gintis, 1976). Parry's account in this volume of participant observation in naturist clubs considers socialisation processes in a different setting.

The work of Piaget and Kohlberg has been foremost in casting an image of childhood marked by a series of developmental stages. From the perspective of mainline, functional socialisation theories, qualitative work with children is viewed as finding age-appropriate ways for the 'knowing' adult to learn about children. The special nature of research methods with children is regarded as stemming from the limited extents to which children are able to comprehend language, articulate subjective experience and sustain affective relationships (eg Parker, 1984). This deficit model surfaces in the ways researchers worry to their readers about doing research. For example, Bierman and Schwartz's account of clinical interviews warns that pre-school children

> *have trouble* holding more than one concept at a time in mind. Additionally, their conceptions are *limited* to ideas that can take concrete, observable forms. They are *unable* to consider alternative perspectives..They are *just learning* how to interpret others' emotions (Bierman and Schwartz, 1986: 268, emphasis added).

There are disturbing consequences of a deficit model of this kind for the understanding of the cultures of children. Indeed, children are unlikely to be seen as having their own culture, or at most that culture will be seen according to its approximation to the culture and world of adults. Criticism of this position has steadily grown. Jenks rejects the influence of Piaget and also that of Talcott Parsons as a form of ethnocentrism in which

> the continuous lived social practice of being a child..is ignored. This unilateral manipulation of the child within socialisation theories condemns him to be an absent presence, a nominal cipher without an active dimension (Jenks, 1992: 13).

One of the major forces initiating a welcome corrective to this research was the work of Cicourel on children's language (1974), which presented a view of children as capable of having their own culture, generationally transmitted by children. Pugsley's chapter illustrates the kind of understanding that emerges from studies of this kind. On this very different view of children they are seen to possess interpretive competence equal to or even greater than adults, and as being potentially 'more creative, more honest, in short, in some ways more human than adults' (Goode, 1986: 84). This challenges the mainstream assumption that adult intervention is essential in order to gain competence. Goode regards the model of children as *tabula rasa*, growing in developmental stages, as an ethnocentric 'adultism' in which researchers reveal themselves as parents writing slightly abstract versions of their own or other peoples' children – a concern reflected in Butler and Williamson's chapter.

It does not need saying that there are diverse cultures of childhood just as there are of adulthood. Age, social class, ethnic identity and, beyond a certain age, gender all pattern the cultures of childhood. Indeed, we would not wish to pose a stark choice of culture *versus* developmental stages. It is not either/or. We must accept children's world views as a legitimate, lived reality, and yet also accept the significance of the constant change and growing that occurs in childhood. Parry's work described in this book how ideas of culture and development may mutually enrich our understanding of children.

Unfortunately participation in 'Kid Society' (the term is Glassner's) is not guaranteed to all who are young. Not all children attain to being a kid. 'It is possible to undergo the physical processes of growth and maturation which we associate with childhood without ever becoming a kid' (Goode, 1986: 88). Goode's work and relationship with Christina, a profoundly deaf-blind child, in which he used 'mimicking, remaining passively obedient during interaction, prolonged observation, video-taping interaction and simulated deaf-blind experiences' (p. 94), demonstrate how 'adultcentric' research can be transformed, and how he 'had become her student in order to become her tutor' (p. 100).

Understanding Children

Understanding the world of understanding children pulls with both fascination and mystification. How many of us have delved into Iona and Peter Opie's books both to learn and to recall (eg Opie and Opie, 1959; 1969; cf Opie and Opie, 1991)? Our 'problem' with children's society is their closeness and social distance. 'Our proximity to children may lead us to believe that we are closer to them than we really are – only differing in that...children are still growing up...and they are often wrong' (Fine and Sandstrom, 1988: 34). This is the problem of ethnocentrism to which Goode refers, though it is made worse by the fact that we do not recognise it as problematic.

Can we understand children? My own answer to this question is 'Yes, but our understandings, though real, will always be approximate and provisional'. 'The participation of our youth leaves a permanent door to kids' culture. There is a Peter Pan in each of us' (Goode, 1986: 101). Siegert takes a similar position in his valuable reflections on the paradox of adults interviewing children. While he thinks the possibility of adults understanding children cannot sensibly be denied, he acknowledges the possibility that

> children reveal in contexts of peer activity social competences which differ from the interviewer's "model of the competent speaker" and, therefore, remain uninterpreted or are, at worst, not even admitted as displays of social competence (Siegert, 1986: 367).

This links to a problem evident throughout qualitative sociology, which is how we account for thinking-as-usual, taken for granted knowledge. Good ethnographies display tacit knowledge, described by Altheide and Johnson as 'the largely unarticulated, contextual understanding that is often manifested in nods, silences, humour and naughty nuances'. Tacit knowledge exists 'in that time when action is taken that is not understood, when understanding is offered without articulation, and when conclusions are apprehended without an argument' (Altheide and Johnson, 1994: 492). This is a special issue in research with young children, where the evidence suggests that children rely less on precise verbal explications and concentrate more on non-verbal cues. Thus, while adults may often describe children's talk as 'babbling',

> Unintelligible noise is both part of children's involvement with each other and a device to exclude adults from their play. Children often do not understand others' precise meanings. They require less detail and specification to create acts (Mandell, 1988: 449).

In circumstances where 'shared meanings, perhaps only roughly understood' are sufficient, and where children have the ability to filter out irrelevant sound and monitor and anticipate adult intrusions, tacit knowing takes on a particular form which may be all the more difficult for adults, and children themselves, to elicit. The social age of children is relevant to this point. With pre-school children, for example, the problem of knowing their culture is especially difficult. For children approaching adolescence with its associated transitions, the worlds of meaning of adults and childhood overlap, and that overlap will be a central task of interpretation. By adolescence, 'the game of life is being played for keeps even when the players find the rules somewhat obscure' (Fine and Sandstrom, 1988: 60). Age begins to be less important in differentiating oneself, and class and gender become still more important.

Because of these changing worlds it is relevant to ask if young people understand children, and to be aware of the implications of asking older children and young people to reflect back on their recollections of their own childhoods. At this point there is common ground between children, young people and adults. Qualitative work with children should be regarded as a process of narrative inquiry. Children are both living their stories in an experiential text, but also telling their stories as they talk to their own selves and explain themselves to others. We may describe this as a simultaneous process of 'storying' and 'restorying' (Connelly and Clandinin, 1990). The thrust of a qualitative strategy is to make these neighbours into strangers and thence into peers, if we are to obtain a sense of what it means to be a child, and be able to view the world 'through their hearts and minds'. In doing so we struggle to mine our own experience, and be challenged to breach our well constructed defences. It is not without its rewards. 'While children are constructing their own worlds, they sometimes permit us to stand with them to enjoy the monuments they have made' (Fine and Sandstrom, 1988: 76-77).

Our claim that we can understand children in ways which are real if approximate and provisional needs further defence. Are we not living in a world of socially constructed actions? On what grounds do we assert this degree of realism in our accounts of childhood? One of the recurring themes of this book is about how people understand and respond to social problems. There are two broad options on offer in deciding what is intended by a 'social problem'. We may describe these as the *objectivist* option and the *constructivist* one. For the objectivist, a social problem is a social condition that is widely regarded as undesirable, has been caused by the actions or inactions of people, and is thought to affect a relatively large number of people. This view fits commonsense definitions of social problems, but raises two difficulties. First, it minimises or even denies the subjective dimension. It fails to take into account that a social problem is such because enough people *believe* it to be so. Child prostitution, the experiences of children in their families, schooling, and so on, may come to be regarded as social problems without there being any necessary alteration in the social condition. Second, objectivist definitions leave us with no way of seeing what different social problems have in common (Best, 1989).

Constructivist perspectives focus on the processes by which some people designate some social condition as a problem. In other words, social problems are understood in terms of a series of claims-making activities. Hence, social problems refer to two very different things from each perspective. For the objectivist social problems are social conditions. For the constructivist, social problems are claims making activities, and the social conditions may be of little interest in their own right. A given social condition may be construed as several different social problems. Child prostitution, for instance, may be seen as a problem about policing, male oppression, the breakdown of family life or welfare state provision for homeless people. The stances of contributors to this book are by and large unsympathetic to objectivist perspectives, but neither can they be labelled simply as constructivist. A common sense reading of most of these chapters probably will lead the reader to conclude that the writers believe the views and perspectives of the children and young people to whom they spoke are more true to reality in some ways than adult accounts. This of course poses a tricky point for constructivists. Do they see the world as entirely constructed – and therefore without any knowable connection to 'real' social conditions – or are qualitative accounts in some significant sense stories about how the world really is? Is a social problem a process whereby meanings come to be shared, accepted or disputed, or is it also some kind of plausible statement about actual social conditions?

Best helpfully distinguishes between *strict* constructivists and *contextual* constructivists (Best, 1989: 243-253). Strict constructivists accept entirely the distinction between knowable claims and unknowable social conditions, and in consequence refuse to make any assumptions about the real world. The difficulty with this position is that it does not sit comfortably with most qualitative research, including the research described in this volume. Constructivists often appear to be making a case along the lines that *new* and *unwarranted* claims are being made – unwarranted because insufficient grounds, warrants and conclusions (Best, 1987) have been evidenced to make a persuasive case. Best believes that such a case can be justified in terms of contextual constructivism. Qualitative sociologists of this ilk accept that they are making some assumptions about social conditions. 'Contextual constructionists argue that any claim can be evaluated...(they) assume that they can know – with reasonable confidence – about social conditions' (Best, 1989: 247). It is possible, albeit imperfectly, to know the social context in which claims are made.

Contextual constructionist approaches obviously cover a wide span, from those who appear to assume that, say, official statistics are pretty reasonable estimates of social conditions, to those who believe they are occasionally rough approximators, but not often. This range of positions is reflected in the chapters that make up the substantive core of this volume.

So, what makes a child or young person's account a good one? First, it will bear some relation to our approximate understanding of real social conditions – it will display what Hammersley calls 'subtle realism' (Hammersley, 1992). The position of most contributors in the following chapters is that children and young people's accounts are, in Williamson's words, 'special but not uniquely privileged'. 'Experience' is not its own justification.

> Merely taking experience into account does not reflect on how that experience came to be. In short, oppressive systems are replicated rather than criticized in the unquestioning reliance on "experience" (Olesen, 1994: 167).

Second, it will be a plausible account. It will be coherent, and make sense of all the available information. While accounts will not always resolve every puzzle, they will make better sense than other possible narratives, and will do so in ways that are not fraught with obvious contradictions, stupidity and so forth. There are sometimes special difficulties when applying this criterion to children's accounts. Corsaro's observational study of pre-school children aged between two and four years included the use of video evidence to check out whether the children gave comparable interpretations of events on film. He gives examples of extracts from taped interviews with two boys talking about a given episode on film, in which Corsaro tried to use a form of member validation described by Cicourel as 'indefinite triangulation'. His conclusion is that,

> use of indefinite triangulation with children of this age is a difficult process. Young children seldom reflect on past activities in this fashion, and when asked to do so they often find the task tedious and uninteresting (Corsaro, 1985: 141).

Ethics

Sociologists' codes of ethics have often failed to give special thought to ethical issues in research involving children. Ethnographers can lay no claim to be exempted from this neglect. Indeed, proponents of qualitative research have on occasion raised their voices in defence of the argument that qualitative research is in some senses more ethical than experimental or survey traditions, on the grounds, for example, that it is less likely to objectify those on whom researchers rely for evidence.

This argument cannot be sustained. The ethical issues created by ethnographic inquiry may find distinctive expression, but they are no less acute. Indeed, it has more recently been acknowledged that ethnography raises especially acute considerations arising from the extent to which it is intrusive in peoples' lives (eg Stacey, 1988). This intrusiveness demands particular sensitivity when children are the subjects of inquiry. The risk of betrayal of trust – to which social workers and teachers are acutely exposed – is of equal importance to researchers. Butler and Williamson, in their portrayal of a child-centred picture of children's worst experiences and deepest anxieties, illustrated also in their chapter in this book, observe the different dimensions of trust. The readiness of some children to say to these relatively passing researchers that they could trust 'someone like you' (Butler and Williamson, 1994: 33) illustrates the problems of easy trust and the potential for ethical abuse that such trust presents. Methods that call on personal experience inevitably raise these questions. 'When we become characters in their stories we change their stories' (Clandinin and Connelly, 1994: 422), which, while it can be positive, carries risk and underlines the need to care for those who share their stories with us.

Fine and Sandstrom offer one of the clearest discussions of ethical issues, and suggest that there are three main areas where such issues arise. These are in the fields of informed consent, the possibility of harm and risk to children, and decisions about how to respond to unpleasant or unacceptable behaviour on the part of children and young people.

We have already pin-pointed one aspect of the problem of *informed consent* in talking about the dangers of easy trust. Indeed, *adult* consent to undertake work with children is often more time consuming and difficult to negotiate. The understandable warnings from schools about 'stranger danger' add to this difficulty. Also, despite the best efforts of researchers, it is likely that younger children in particular will fit the researcher into their world however clear the explanation given (cf Corsaro, 1985). A further complication may arise from considerations of confidentiality. Children and young people may have different views from adults and *want* to be named! In their discussion of children's rights in AIDS research, Rotheram and Koopman point out that ethnographic research raises ethical tension between confidentiality and clinical concerns very acutely, because ethnographers are more likely to witness unacceptable or risky behaviour. In these circumstances 'the researcher needs both morality and strategy; the first without the second is ineffectual; the second without the first is cruel' (1992: 160). When it comes to occasions where the young person refuses to participate, it is our view that there are no special circumstances. The right to refuse is as strong for the child as for the adult and should be given similar weight.

What is the responsibility of adult researchers in potentially harmful situations? Aggression, mischief and cruelty are examples from everyday experience. Ethical concerns arise more frequently in participant observation research. Adults in the vicinity of the research will act as if the researcher is caring for their interests even when the researcher does not believe that is part of the research bargain. Mandell (1988) reports one incident when she found herself watching and not intervening when a risk of moderate harm was evident. More commonly, participant observers are likely to find themselves involved in some level of 'reactive policing' when called on to intervene by one child against another.

The balance is difficult to strike. Disclosure of physical, emotional or sexual harm needs anticipatory planning, so that researchers do not respond without thought when it happens. Special issues arise in some of the participant research carried out in youth gangs or networks, though they fall largely outside the span of research reported in this volume. The usual approach of adopting a gang role that allows non-involvement in overtly unethical or criminal behaviour is not without its moral tensions (Polsky, 1971; Parker, 1974; Williamson, 1981: 516-520).

Harm to the child shades over into more general instances of unpleasant or unacceptable behaviour. Fine and Sandstrom believe that

> Children must be permitted to engage in certain actions and speak certain words that the adult researcher finds distressing. Further, in some instances, the researcher must act in ways that are at least tacitly supportive of these distressing behaviours (Fine and Sandstrom, 1988: 55).

Take as examples the occurrence of racist or sexist talk, or minor theft. The natural tendency of sensitive and aware researchers, along with social workers or teachers, may be to *challenge* the former and seek to *understand* the latter. But they also need to observe and try to understand the former, though they also need to avoid responding in ways that make sexist or racist talk more salient than it otherwise would be. The wider issue of the possible sexual dimension of relations between researchers and informants has been neglected and requires discussion (cf Bloor and McKeganey, 1989).

In general, it is important that the researcher first listen to the story, and that it is the informant who tells the story. This requires the 'mutual construction of the research relationship in which both (informants) and researchers feel cared for and a voice with which to tell their stories' (Connelly and Clandinin, 1990: 4). Researchers are not there to conduct 'a raid on mislaid identities' (the phrase is Dannie Abse's from his poem, *Return to Cardiff*).

Methods of Inquiry

We observed earlier that strongly held beliefs about childhood as an unfolding of developmental stages has constrained the methods of many researchers, and led to a model of child interviewing which it is believed 'can help the clinician assess the developmental sophistication of the child's interpersonal style and social-emotional reasoning' (Bierman and Schwartz, 1986: 276). However, interviewing strategies in research with children and young people have developed from this position in two directions. *First*, there has been a welcome and quite widespread acceptance of children as persons who have similar rights to those of adults in regard to giving informed consent to research access.

Most of the chapters in this book start from this very premise. For example, Butler and Williamson, in work reported here and elsewhere, gave children the choice as to how they wished to be interviewed – whether singly, in pairs or in groups. They had warm-up sessions with children and young people to convey this ethos and freedom to pursue a particular line of thought. They put them in control of both the tape recorder and the length of interview. When conducting an individual interview they accepted that it 'does not lend itself to tight structures and defined sequences. Children jump around and researchers have to jump with them' (Butler and Williamson, 1994: 30). This often included responding to children's humour and recognising the importance children seemed to attach to researchers conveying 'serious listening inside a funny shell' (p. 46).

The *second* development in interviewing with children and young people is, if anything, more far reaching. At its heart it involves a major reversal of how we view the interview, so that it is seen not as a source of information from young informants, but as data in and of itself. For instance, talking to adolescents is not a means of gaining information about socialisation processes but, from this perspective, is itself an instance of socialisation. Baker's 'second look' at interviews with adolescents exemplifies this approach. She argues that 'the key to turning the interview into a resource is to view it as a real event in the real world – not only as a means of access to data but as data' (Baker, 1983: 501, 508). This allows her to see the way the interviews display their character as adult-young person social encounters in which adults are questioning adolescents. The questions contain an implicit adult theory of adolescence and answers contain an implicit adolescent theory of adulthood. Interviews are an occasion for the management of identity.

Much of this analysis has come to depend on the proliferation of technology in analysing text. Corsaro and Streeck warned some time ago of the implications of the researcher's greatly expanded information processing capacity, which becomes much greater than that of the individual who is talking. 'The problem is especially acute when studying young children because researchers naturally tend to interpret the data from an adult rather than a child perspective' (1986: 28). But this does not lessen the persuasiveness of Baker's analysis. 'Interviews are socialisation sites. In these interviews adolescents are invited to show membership in the adult language community by making sense of the questions and developing the discourse with the interviewer' (pp. 516-517).

Siegert has drawn similar conclusions from his analysis of the paradox of seeking to measure children's competences through interviews. Data from such interviews give insight into competences displayed by children when they interact with adults. Interviews with young children are often conducted in educational settings, where children assume that adult questions have an adult right answer. The paradox of such research is that children are asked to give information about behaviour that occurred in an *egalitarian* context, in a setting which itself is highly *asymmetrical*. He concludes that 'data from interviews which are conducted by an adult interviewer give us more insight into competences displayed by children in interaction with adults...It is questionable, however, if these findings can be generalised to other contexts, especially to contexts of peer interaction' (Siegert, 1986: 373). Conclusions of this kind clearly have implications beyond the research encounter, and also are relevant to problem solving talk between adults and children in health, social work and educational settings.

Siegert suggests that peer relations may be better investigated through participant observation and group discussions. The extent to which participant observation is possible for adults researching children is an important area of continuing debate, and one where the central problem concerns the membership role adopted by the researcher. This may range from the detached observer, not unlike the use of observation facilities in clinical and therapeutic practice, through the reactive, 'special friend' adopted by Corsaro in his excellent study of children in a nursery school (1985), to the 'responsive, interactive, fully involved participant observer role with the children, in as least an adult role as possible', practised and advocated by Mandell (1988). She presses the advantages of taking a role which minimises social distance, suspends judgements on children's immaturities, engages in joint action with children, and risks being taken for a fool. Her position has been criticised (e.g. Fine and Sandstrom) on the grounds that it is not possible to 'bracket' adult/child differences during research. The underlying issue is whether qualitative research with children is in essence different from similar research with adults. Mandell is ready to 'apply adult-adult research strategies to adult-child studies' (p. 436). In either case the researcher engages in a reflective activity which distinguishes participant observation with children from that with adults, in that they may mine their own experience. This 'differentiates this type of participant observation from most others in which we have never experienced the emotions, social position, or even some of the culture of the group being studied' (Fine and Sandstrom, 1988: 76).

Focus groups offer an alternative method of qualitative inquiry which can and should be further developed with children (Morgan, 1988; Morgan, 1993; Kreuger, 1994). A variant of focus group is illustrated by Bond's account of a day's programme for three ten year old short term foster girls, in which their views were being sought about a family centre. A group discussion format was set up. Dressing up, food, paint, cooking, poster preparation, photography and a presentation were used in an innovative attempt to learn service user views from children (Bond, 1990-1991). However, the application of focus groups methods to social work and research on children has thus far been very limited (Shaw, 1996). The work reported by Katz in this volume offers an important extension of this research.

Personal texts also offer special opportunities for understanding with children and young people. For example, journals provide a way of giving accounts of experience. Children and adolescents often keep journals of their thoughts, activities and stories. Most of these remain private, and it is usually only the accident of history that brings to public view the childhood writings of an Anne Frank or the Bronte children. Childhood memories of those who come within the sphere of influence of social workers are more often emotions recollected in the relative tranquility of older years (e.g. Courtney, 1989). But it is likely that some children and young people with whom practitioners work keep journals as attempts to make sense of their experiences – 'capturing fragments of experience in attempts to sort themselves out' (Clandinin and Connelly, 1994: 421). Adults speaking of their experiences as a child do, of course, raise special difficulties for the hearer. Who is speaking?

> Is it the adult interpreting the childhood experience, in which case it is the adult speaking. Or is it the adult expressing the child's story as the child would have told the experience, in which case it is the child speaking (p. 424).

Recent developments in the field of life histories and life course sociology also prompt researchers to innovative methods of qualitative inquiry with children and young people, as in Burchardt's account of step-children's memories (1990), and Bowen's (1993) application of life history methods to understanding and working with school non-attenders.

The 'practical' implications of engaging in qualitative inquiry cannot be sidestepped (Shaw, 1996). The value of an empirical grasp of kids' culture, the transformation of traditional methods of professional investigation, and the radical implications of understanding for and with children, extend far beyond discipline boundaries. The clearest evidence for this can be found in the subsequent chapters.

Do we need a special qualitative sociology of childhood? This is not, perhaps, the best way to present the question. Rather, just as for John Milton 'New presbyter is but old priest writ large', so for the qualitative inquirer for and with children, the demands, challenges and opportunities of research are those of general qualitative sociology spotlighted, accentuated and 'writ large'.

References

Altheide, D. and Johnson, J. (1994) 'Criteria for Assessing Interpretive Validity in Qualitative Research' in Denzin, N. and Lincoln, Y. (eds) *Handbook of Qualitative Research*, Sage, Newbury Park.

Baker, C. (1983) 'A Second Look at Interviews with Adolescents' in *Journal of Youth and Adolescence*, Vol. 12, No. 6.

Best, J. (1987) 'Rhetoric in Claims Making' in *Social Problems*, Vol. 34, No. 2.

Best, J. (ed) (1989) *Images of Issues: Typifying Contemporary Social Problems*, Aldine de Gruyter, New York.

Bierman, K. and Schwartz, L. (1986) 'Clinical Child Interviews: Approaches and development Considerations' in *Child and Adolescent Psychotherapy*, Vol. 3, No. 4.

Bloor, M. and McKeganey, N. (1989) 'Ethnography Addressing the Practitioner' in Gubrium, J. and Silverman, D. (eds) *The Politics of Field Research: Sociology Beyond Enlightenment*, Sage, Newbury Park.

Bond, M. (1990-1991) '"The Centre, It's for Children": Seeking Children's Views as Users of a Family Centre' in *Practice*, Vol. 7, No. 1.

Bowen, D. (1993) 'The Delights of Learning To Apply The Life History Method To School Non-attenders' in Broad, B. and Fletcher, C. (eds) *Practitioner Research.* Whiting and Birch, London.

Bowles, S. and Gintis, H. (1976) *Schooling in Capitalist America*, Routledge, London.

Burchardt, N. (1990) 'Stepchildren's Memories: Myth, Understanding and Forgiveness' in Samuel, R. and Thompson, P. *The Myths we Live By*, Routledge, London.

Butler, I. and Williamson, H. (1994) *Children Speak: Children, Trauma and Social Work*, Longman, London.

Cicourel, A., Jennings, K., Leiter, K., MacKay, E., Mehan, H. and Roth, D. (1974) *Language Use and Schools Performance*, Academic Press, New York.

Clandinin, D. and Connelly, F. (1994) 'Personal Experience Methods' in Denzin, N and Lincoln, Y. (eds) *Handbook of Qualitative Research*, Sage, Newbury Park.

Connelly, F. and Clandinin, D. (1990) 'Stories of Experience and Narrative Inquiry' in *Educational Researcher*, Vol. 19, No. 5.

Corsaro, W. (1985) *Friendship and Peer Culture in the Early Years*, Ablex, Norwood, New Jersey.

Corsaro, W. and Streeck, J. (1986) 'Studying Children's Worlds: Methodological Issues' in Cook-Gumperz, J., Corsaro, W. and Streeck, J. (eds) *Children's Worlds and Children's Language*, Mouton de Gruyter, Berlin.

Courtney, C. (1989) *Morphine and Dolly Mixtures*, Honno, Cardiff.

Denzin, N. (1977) *Childhood Socialisation*, Jossey Bass, San Francisco.

Fine, G. and Sandstrom, K. (1988) *Knowing Children: Participant Observation with Minors*, Sage, Newbury Park.

Goode, D. (1986) 'Kids, Culture and Innocents' in *Human Studies*, Vol. 9, No. 1.

Hammersley, P. (1992) *What's Wrong With Ethnography?*, Routledge, London.

Jenks, C. (ed) (1992) *The Sociology of Childhood*, Gregg Revivals, Aldershot.

Kreuger, R. (ed) (1994) *Focus Groups: a Practical Guide for Applied Research*, Sage, Newbury Park.

Mandell, N. (1988) 'The Least Adult Role in Studying Children' in *Journal of Contemporary Ethnography*, Vol. 16, No. 4.

Morgan, D.L. (1988) *Focus groups as Qualitative Research*, Sage, Newbury Park.

Morgan, D.L. (ed) (1993) *Successful Focus Groups: Advancing the State of the Art*, Sage, Newbury Park.

Olesen, V. (1994) 'Feminisms and Models of Qualitative Research' in Denzin, N. and Lincoln, Y. (eds) *Handbook of Qualitative Research*, Sage, Newbury Park.

Opie, I. and Opie, P. (1959) *The Lore and Language of Schoolchildren*, Oxford University Press, Oxford.

Opie, I. and Opie, P. (1969) *Children's Games of Street and Playground*, Oxford University Press, Oxford.

Opie, I. and Opie, P. (1991) 'The Culture of Children', in Waksler, F. (ed), *Studying the Social Worlds of Children: Sociological Readings*, Saxon House, Farnborough.

Parker, H. (1974) *View From the Boys*, David and Charles, Newton Abbott.

Parker, W. (1984) 'Interviewing Children: Problems and Promise' in *Journal of Negro Education*, Vol. 53, No. 1.

Pilcher, J. (1995) *Age and Generation*, Oxford University Press, Oxford.

Polsky, N. (1971) *Hustlers, Beats and Others*, Penguin, Harmondsworth.

Qvortrup, J. (1990) 'A Voice for Children in Statistical and Social Accounting: A Plea for Children's Right to be Heard', in James, A. and Prout, A. (eds)

Constructing and Reconstructing Childhood: Contemporary Issues in the Sociological Study of Childhood, Falmer, Basingstoke.

Qvortrup, J., Bardy, M., Sgritta, G. and Wintersberger, H. (eds) (1994) *Childhood Matters: Social Theory, Practice and Politics*, Avebury, Aldershot.

Rotheram, M. and Koopman, C. (1992) 'Protecting Children's Rights in AIDS Research', in Stanley, B. and Sieber, J. (eds) *Social Research on Children and Adolescents: Ethical Issues*, Sage, Newbury Park.

Saporitti, A. (1994), 'A Methodology for Making Children Count', in Qvortrup, J., Bardy, M., Sgritta, G. and Wintersberger, H. (eds), *Childhood Matters: Social Theory, Practice and Politics*, Avebury, Aldershot.

Shaw, I. (1996) *Evaluating in Practice*, Ashgate, Aldershot.

Siegert, M. (1986) 'Adult Elicited Child Behaviour: The Paradox of Measuring Social Competence Through Interviewing' in Cook-Gumperz, J., Corsaro, W. and Streeck, J. (eds) *Children's Worlds and Children's Language*, Mouton de Gruyter, Berlin.

Stacey, J. (1988) 'Can There be a Feminist Ethnography?' in *Women's Studies International*, Vol. 11, No. 1.

Waksler, F.C.W. (1991) (ed), *Studying the Social Worlds of Children: Sociological Readings*, Saxon House, Farnborough.

Williamson, H. (1981) *Juvenile Justice and Working Class Community*, Unpublished PhD Thesis, University of Wales.

Willis, P. (1978) *Learning to Labour*, Saxon House, Farnborough.

PART IV
Research, Theory and Practice

A connecting strand in this part of the book is to illustrate how research around social work practice and its contexts supports theorizing about social work. This does not exhaust the themes in these five pieces. An alternative description of my preoccupations would be to say that an understanding of the practice, organizational and wider cultural contexts of social work and research steers us away from facile and culturally myopic understandings of the social work project.

The opening essay harks back to the preoccupation – largely unhelpful in my view – with various target and measurement oriented management models that were prominently to the fore across the whole of the public sector in the 1990s, and linger to this day. While I drew on contemporary sources, I would not wish to demur from the broad conclusions I reached at that time.

The next three inclusions all focus more directly on social work practice. Together they capture a line of research and argument that continues to interest me. First, I do not have confidence in arguments about social workers' evaluation practices that start from and are largely determined by prior assumptions about good practice. To borrow words from my appreciation of Reid earlier in the book, he 'seemed to take a position that, for me, has much going for it – to regard the relationship between paradigms and methods as an *empirical* question. Thus, with Kirk, he lamented that "we know comparatively little about notions of bias, error, mistakes and truth – the actual epistemologies used – in the ordinary practice of social work" (Kirk and Reid, 2002: 17). He took a similarly inductive stance when remarking that "the bottom line for research utilization is what happens in the field among practitioners"' (Kirk and Reid, 2002: 194). By way of illustration of this stance, I include an article that gives an account of part of a study of social worker's judgements of successful and unsuccessful social work (Shaw and Shaw, 1997). This essay is also here as witness to the joy of writing with one's daughter.

Second, I have found increasingly that the apparently mundane activity represented by small scale, practitioner research poses a range of profoundly challenging issues about the nature of research, the relationship between academic disciplines and professional practice, and the scope of scientific knowledge. The article with Alex Faulkner, included here, is from an earlier project, and has been followed up with subsequent work with Neil Lunt and others (Lunt et al, forthcoming; Shaw and Lunt, 2011, Shaw and Lunt, forthcoming) that deepens the analysis of the work included here.

Third, claims to originality in research – social work or otherwise – are easily made and less readily grounded. So I may be mistaken if I say that one area – perhaps *the* one area – where I have possibly been able to say something original is in writing about evaluating in practice. I said a little about this area in the opening essay. Because the argument is primarily about practice – of a form I sometimes refer to as sociological practice – the 2010 brief essay appears in this part of the book. It is not as developed an exposition and exemplification of the argument as I would wish (cf Shaw, 2011a) but serves to introduce the general case.

This part of the book is bookended with another more general article, which in this case picks up the question of culture and research. Jointly written with a former doctoral student Khalid Al-Awwad, we reflect on how judgements about the nature and quality of social work research are shaped by the political, faith-based, and social systems of the country in which it takes place. I want at this point to pay tribute to the many research students with whom I have worked during my career, and to the extent to which I have learned from those who engage with a research enterprise developed in primarily Western nations, but in countries where the various contexts depart at many points from the university world they have joined. This article is included in part to make that tribute. The linking theme of practice, agency and research contexts is something that continues to entice me (e.g. Shaw, 2010a).

References

Kirk, S.A. and Reid, W.J. (2002) *Social Science Work: A Critical Appraisal*. New York: Columbia University Press.

Lunt, N., Ramian, K., Shaw, I., Mitchell, F. and Fouché C. (in press) 'Networking practitioner research: the state of the art' *European Journal of Social Work*.

Shaw, I. (1995) 'The Quality of Mercy: the Management of Quality in the Personal Social Services' in Kirkpatrick, I. and Lucio M. (eds), *The Politics of Quality in the Public Sector*. London: Routledge, pp. 128-150.

Shaw, I. (2010a) 'Places in time: contextualizing social work research' in Shaw, I., Briar-Lawson, K., Orme, J., and Ruckdeschel, R. (eds), *Sage Handbook of Social Work Research*. London: Sage Publications.

Shaw, I. (2010d) 'Evaluating in Practice' in Evans, T. and Hardy, M. with Shaw, I. *Evidence and Knowledge for Social Work*. Cambridge: Polity Press, pp. 152-164.

Shaw, I and Al-Awwad, K (1994) 'Culture and the Indigenization of Quality in Third World Social Research' *Journal of Social Development in Africa* 9, 1: 59-71.

Shaw, I. and Faulkner, A. (2006) 'Practitioner Evaluation at Work' *American Journal of Evaluation* 27, 1: 44-63.

Shaw, I. and Lunt, N. (2011) 'Navigating Practitioner Research' *British Journal of Social Work* 2011; doi: 10.1093/bjsw/bcr025.

Shaw, I. and Lunt, N. (forthcoming) 'Constructing practitioner research' *Social Work Research.*

Shaw, I. and Shaw, A. (1997) 'Game Plans, Buzzes and Sheer Luck: Doing Well in Social Work' *Social Work Research* 21, 2: 69-79.

Chapter 16

The Quality of Mercy: The Management of Quality in the Personal Social Services*

Introduction

The idea of a 'mixed economy of welfare' in which the statutory agencies are no longer the sole or even primary service providers received its first sharpened statement in Britain in the mid-1980s. Norman Fowler, then Secretary of State, reasoned that the state has not, cannot and should not monopolize the personal social services. He argued for a strategic view of all the sources of care in any area, and for the recognition that the direct provision of services is only one aspect of local provision and that other forms of care are also available. He pressed for a new 'enabling role' for local authority social services which promoted the fullest possible participation of other sources of care. This initiative was a relatively late flowering of the Conservative government's commitment to rolling back the frontiers of the state, and part of central government's programme to control local authority spending and promote cost effectiveness. With this flagging of government intentions, the lead vehicle for the introduction of quality management in the personal social services in the United Kingdom was on the road.

The government's initial targets were services providing care in the community for the elderly, people with physical or learning disabilities and those with mental health problems. Since then, the objectives of a mixed economy of welfare and cost-effective services have been extended to all personal social services in the United Kingdom. Care in the community reforms, the Children Act 1989, a beefed up Social Services Inspectorate within the Department of Health, new local authority inspection units for social services departments, national standards and performance measures for the Probation Service, strategic plans and successive versions of performance expectations for supported housing projects, and a government-led scrutiny, succeeded by new departmental policies and guidance for relations between government departments and voluntary organizations, have followed hard upon one another's heels. Education and training for the personal social services has also been reformatted by these service changes and by the rapid introduction of quality management into higher education.

* Originally published as Shaw, I. (1995) 'The Quality of Mercy: the Management of Quality in the Personal Social Services' in I. Kirkpatrick, and M. Lucio (eds), *The Politics of Quality in the Public Sector*. London: Routledge, 128-50. Reprinted with permission of Taylor and Francis.

The languages of cost-effectiveness, service user satisfaction, empowerment, commercial models of quality management, monitoring and evaluation, service contracts, partnerships, staff supervision, financial decentralization and outcome assessments have permeated the planning, management and delivery of British social services.

In this chapter we pursue the central theme of this book, by seeking to deconstruct the concept of quality, showing how it is actually used in the personal social services. The core of the following argument is that the rhetoric of quality in the personal social services is politically and managerially driven. It entails an argument about partnership which is pursued as a way of managing a shift in state/voluntary sector relations, a rational managerialism which may threaten the professional role in social welfare, and a rhetoric about choice and satisfaction which paradoxically hinders the effective voice of the service user. We will show how quality arguments are used in the personal social services by different people for different purposes, and that the rhetoric of quality is justified on grounds as varied as risk protection, staff control, customer satisfaction or user empowerment, managerial control of the voluntary sector, cost-effectiveness, the need for decentralization, and various forms of partnership.

However, while the politics of policy agenda setting are important, we also need to appreciate the difficulties which arise when policy agendas are implemented. In the course of this chapter we question whether quality does indeed act as a 'relay device', linking government 'mentalities' and policies with everyday organizational realities as a way of introducing organizational change. We will illustrate that quality policies in the personal social services are implemented imperfectly for a variety of reasons. Agreement about appropriate service outcomes is often more apparent than real, and employees responsible for service delivery will bring their own lay explanations of policy to bear when evaluating or planning services. As a result, agreement about quality and standards becomes the subject of social negotiation, thus making standards partly contingent on their immediate service contexts.

The growth of supervision and surveillance of street-level staff has been a hallmark of these recent changes. This leads to one of the unresolved questions about the effects of quality management Will it lead to a change in the nature of the professional task in welfare services? However this question is answered, we will argue that those who implement quality management usually have not recognized the extent to which risk management and discretionary behaviour constrain the extent to which new management practices can take root.

Finally, the case for a new customer/provider/purchaser relationship in which 'everything we do is driven by you' has not prevented service users from remaining marginalized. This is because a quality culture may not increase user choice, measures of customer satisfaction within the personal social services are problematic, customer satisfaction initiatives are paradoxically usually management-led, and the extent of user involvement is likely to remain variable, ambiguous and, on occasion, minimal.

Quality initiatives in the personal social services

Pfeffer and Coote identify four broad approaches to quality, according to whether the purpose is to convey prestige (the 'traditional' approach), meet standards set by experts (the scientific approach), measure customer satisfaction (the managerial or 'excellence' approach) or make the customer more powerful (the consumerist approach) (Pfeffer and Coote 1991).

Accounts of quality developments in the personal social services have often been limited to specific segments. However, the following map of quality initiatives throughout the personal services demonstrates the broadly comparable trends and arguments which characterize and buttress quality management in this field. To summarize, somewhat pessimistically and oversimply, politicians are primarily interested in quality as cost-effectiveness, managers aim for organizational and staff performance controls, and welfare professionals welcome quality as a mechanism that will guarantee professional survival in an uncertain world.

In consequence, the meaning of quality remains elusive, because it is made to service different purposes both by different people and by the same people at different times. Quality becomes fought over in both the macro- and micro-political battles of welfare provision. The definition of quality is also difficult because quality is often used to refer to a process of quality assurance, whether it be through user involvement, inspection, joint objective setting, new forms of service management or compulsory competitive tendering. The final benchmark of quality must be the outcome of services and not only the process by which quality of service is assured.

Local authority social services

In 1986, the Audit Commission, which is charged with monitoring the effectiveness of local government financial arrangements and value for money, produced an influential critique of care in the community. The commission identified key financial problems around a mismatch of resources and services, and a lack of bridging finance to fund the transition to community care, together with organizational fragmentation and inadequate staffing arrangements. It also gave emphasis to the existence of 'perverse incentives' within the benefit system: 'Social Security policies appear to be working in a way directly opposing community care policies' so that 'the more residential the care the easier it is to obtain benefits and the greater the size of the payment' (Audit Commission 1986: 44). The commission argued that this tempted providers to go for residential rather than community care. The report provided a benchmark for later reforms and an actuarial, value for money orientation to the direction of those reforms.

Government proposals for reform of community care gained momentum during the late 1980s. The Griffiths Report (1988) introduced the proposal that local authorities should design and purchase community care services rather than be the major providers. The government moved with speed. A White Paper *Caring for People* (HMSO 1989) was followed by legislation (Community Care and National Health Service Act 1990). This act required social services departments to prepare Community Care Plans covering a three year period. Plans were to include arrangements for quality assurance and systems for safe guarding service standards, including complaints procedures. Contracts between purchasers and providers were required to include monitoring systems and break-out clauses-a theme which continues to be reiterated by government departments.

In the White Paper, quality control systems were clearly viewed as a necessary adjunct of the proposed 'move away from the role of exclusive service provider to that of service arranger and procurer' (HMSO 1989: 5.6). To this end, the Social Services Inspectorate (SSI), based in the Department of Health (DH), was given a substantially strengthened role. Local independent inspection units accountable to each director of social services were set up to inspect local authority, voluntary and private residential homes, although the independence of these local inspectorates from local providers is not entirely clear. The Chief Inspector now reports annually to the Secretary of State on the effectiveness of these arrangements. Driven by the Citizen's Charter, the 1993 SSI report, through its new Chief Inspector, adopted a bullish, up-beat tone, advocating 'more explicit standards, openness, full and accurate information, choice, accountability and non-discrimination' (Social Services Inspectorate 1993a: 3.1).

The range and influence of the inspectorate's work is growing noticeably. Employing more than 100 inspectors and still growing, global reviews of whole departments are now being undertaken jointly with the Audit Commission. The SSI is also augmenting its output through buying in work from major charities such as the Nuffield Foundation. There are several themes and aspirations in the work of the national inspectorate. Emphasis has been placed on 'the involvement of users and carers in planning and conducting inspections, defining the criteria to be applied, and reporting the findings' (SSI 1992c: 5.4), and satisfaction has been expressed at the extent to which this is taking place (SSI 1993a: 2.7). Recurrent anxieties have also been voiced over the need to improve managerial supervision of staff in personal social services. Thus, 'the variable quality of professional supervision is worrying ... deficiencies in supervision appeared in inspections of all services' (1992c: 13). The Chief Inspector has also supported a shift to managerialism, in which 'no individual fieldworker should be regarded as self sufficient' (SSI 1992c: 13). This managerialism is mirrored in the recurrent pleas and plans for a partnership of 'jointly agreed policies and practices, and fully agreed and understood interdisciplinary working arrangements' (SSI 1993a: 3.4), which will lead to a shared position among all interest groups.

In contrast, the commercially led route to quality accreditation ('kite marking') of services that satisfy the British Standards Institution (BSI) has as yet had a slight and patchy influence on the personal social services. Some privatized residential units have been accredited, and also a number of privatized services within the welfare sector. Discussions between the BSI and representatives of social work services have yet to produce much in the way of specific guidance, although a major voluntary organization, the Pre-School Playgroups Association, has recently promoted a process that leads to an accreditation of individual pre-school playgroups (British Standards Institution 1993). At least one local authority social work Inspection Unit – the Highland region in Scotland – has received the BSI mark of accreditation. Quality concerns have also been demonstrated in the plethora of guidance and good practice documents flowing from the Children Act and the Care in the Community legislation. Standards in residential care and day care have been disseminated through the SSI's Caring for Quality series, now Inspecting for Quality (e.g. SSI 1989, I990a, 1990b, 1992a, 1992b, 1993b). Guidance for social workers carrying out the recently designated care management and assessment role has been produced both for managers and for practitioners (SSI 1991a, 199lb). The corresponding Guidance and Regulations for the Children Act runs to ten volumes, to which must be added an influential review of residential child care by the retiring Chief Inspector of the SSI and guidelines for working with child sexual abuse (Utting 1991; Department of Health 1991). The SSI also commissioned a more reflective assessment of the meaning of quality and its assessment (James *et al.* 1992).

The voluntary sector

The plans to introduce purchaser/provider relationships into the organization of community care through a mixed economy of statutory, voluntary and private care was paralleled by a Home Office scrutiny of funding and departmental links with agencies and projects in the voluntary sector. The consequent report, published in 1990, was liberally sprinkled with complaints that 'Departments were not agreeing objectives and targets with core funded bodies by which the success of the grant could be measured', that there were 'rarely any plans against which performance could be compared' and that, while monitoring of projects was often more intensive, there was 'very little rigorous evaluation of core funding' (Home Office 1990: 3.5.8, 3.7.6, G21, G28).

Familiar themes of quality management permeated the report's recommendations. Value for money and cost-effectiveness were seen as central to the role of government funding. 'We think that Departments should look for added value whenever they decide to give a core or project grant' (Home Office 1990: 3.4.6), by which it is meant that grants should carry commitments to additional fund-raised monies, service charging and volunteer input. The perceived need to strengthen partnership between voluntary agencies or projects, and government departments also figured largely in the scrutiny. The most important aspects of partnership were regarded as joint objective setting between the department and the voluntary body, monitoring requirements, user feed back and three-yearly evaluations of all larger long term grants. 'Strategies expressed through objectives' encapsulates the aim (3.3.15).

These recommendations were complementary in purpose to the wider restructuring of personal social services outlined above. The report paralleled the purchaser/provider split in community care with its proposal that 'Departments should look actively at the scope for using voluntary bodies as agents to deliver services which are currently by statutory authorities' (3.5.24). This efficiency scrutiny led immediately to a government action plan and subsequent departmental strategies, and was also followed by the establishment of Charities Evaluation Services, intended as a nationwide resource for charity evaluation.

However, departmental strategies seemed on occasion to be significantly more tentative than the original proposals. For example, the Welsh Office version of joint objective setting was that 'these objectives are set wherever possible (sic) in consultation with the appropriate voluntary organizations' (Welsh Office n.d: 8). Anecdotal evidence suggests some government departments may be highly selective in engaging in systematic joint formulation of objectives. Charities Evaluation Services has had a rather patchy impact, with large areas of the country still without a regional base.

Supported housing and housing associations

We have illustrated that the introduction of quality management into the care in the community field cannot be viewed in isolation, but must be seen in the context of parallel government thinking for the voluntary sector. Likewise, thinking regarding the voluntary sector ties in closely at several points with Department of the Environment guidance and regulations for supported housing funded through housing associations via the London-based Housing Corporation, and with recent developments in Home Office policies for the Probation Service. The government provides an estimate of approximately £2 billion in annual grant to the voluntary sector. Of this, more than 50 per cent goes to housing associations, although the majority of this funding is spent on the development and management of general needs housing, rather than supported housing for people with special needs. The costs of employing staff to provide care and support in supported housing projects are provided from outside this budget.

The 1980s witnessed a sustained reaction against traditional large-scale hostel provision, with its shared eating, sleeping and catering facilities. Capital and revenue funding systems for housing associations changed radically, and housing associations have been part of the wider shifts towards a planned rather than an incremental approach and the stress on consumer involvement in service provision. Performance monitoring and quality assurance policies have increasingly taken root as the preferred tools of funding agencies for developing and appraising supported housing.

The Housing Corporation continues to feel its way in this area. It replaced its Performance Expectations guidance with a Performance Criteria handbook which concentrates on the basic minimum requirements rather than covering good practice recommendations as well (Housing Corporation 1989, 1992a).

Changes in the revenue funding system have also served to sharpen the preoccupation of housing associations and agencies with financial performance indicators for management Guidance from the federal bodies representing housing associations has also encouraged the development of explicit housing management performance indicators (National Federation of Housing Associations 1987). User satisfaction and tenant participation are increasingly pursued as a key criterion for appraising special needs housing association performance, and agreed guidance is appearing in this field (e.g. Housing for Wales 1993a, 1993b).

Probation service

Following the establishment of national standards for the supervision of offenders in the community (Home Office 1992c) and the introduction of internal monitoring and inspection, the Home Office embarked on an annually revised Three Year Plan which sets quality targets for the Probation Service deriving from the Citizen's Charter. The 1994-7 plan introduced for the first time a series of key performance indicators against which the work of probation officers were to be measured. Intended to 'help assess the performance of the Probation Service, both nationally and at area level', 'the indicators are designed ... to be of use at local level and to support good practice and the effective and efficient use of resources' (Home Office 1994: 14, 15). For example, the performance of each service will be measured against 'predicted and actual reconviction rates for persons subject to community orders by type of order' (1994: 14). The first quality objective for 1994-5 was 'to monitor and evaluate the introduction of performance indicators'. The consequences of this initiative will unfold through the mid years of the decade. However, it is worth emphasizing that quality measures here, and throughout the personal social services, have tended to be limited to those most easily obtained and those easily measured. Only one of the ten Home Office key performance indicators requires a qualitative measure.

Part of this Home Office strategy involves the establishment of partnership arrangements on the basis of either competitive tendering or joint planning with both the voluntary and the commercial sectors. This is to be funded by a top slicing of 'around 5 per cent' of each probation area's revenue budget (Home Office 1992b: 28). However, given the tentative nature of local accommodation strategy planning, the continued, uncertain Home Office uncertain murmurs about the role of the independent sector and the talk of parceling out areas of work that are not within the 'core' of probation practice, the balance of power between the Probation Service and the voluntary sector remains weighted to the managerial interests of purchasers.

Social work education

We indicated at the beginning of this chapter that social work education and training has been reformatted to service the quality concerns of government departments. The Central Council for Education and Training in Social Work (CCETSW) developed the rules and regulations required of all accredited social work courses, and set learning outcomes of knowledge, skills, values and competences (Central Council for Education and Training in Social Work 1991). These detailed regulations require structures for student assessment, internal and external monitoring systems, review and inspection arrangements, and new powers for providers.

The CCETSW received much negative public attention during 1993, which led the government to appoint a new chair committed to reviewing and changing CCETSW structures and policy. The interested departments also conducted a wide-ranging policy and financial management review of the organization, which charged CCETSW with the requirement to discover and respond to customer and user views, strengthen its arrangements for enforcing standards and ensure quality in training programmes. Heavy warnings were also made about the implications of public spending deficits for the funding of CCETSW in the next five years, and the subsequent demand that it develop improved systems for demonstrating that it is making cost-effective use of its annual revenue budget of £32 million (DH 1993b). It remains to be seen how far the newly revised social work training regulations (CCETSW 1995) weaken or change the elaborate apparatus of quality management in social work education.

The recurrent themes in this brief survey are cost-effectiveness, joint objective setting between interested providers, strengthened account ability of welfare professionals, explicit standards and performance monitoring, and customer satisfaction. This suggests that quality initiatives in the personal social services are, in Pfeffer and Coote's terms (1991), a mixture of expert approaches intended to meet agreed standards, and a managerial or excellence approach designed to measure customer satisfaction.

It is our view that relations between the state, statutory welfare and the voluntary sector, the accomplishment of managerial control, and a determination to incorporate the customer's voice comprise the basic agenda of these quality initiatives. The extent to which a satisfactory resolution of these themes has been accomplished will be the focus of the second part of this chapter.

The rhetoric of quality

The question of whether this rhetoric of quality reflects what happens on the ground is to miss a central point. Indeed, we would argue that there is no way that the rhetoric could 'work' in some unambiguous, instrumental manner, if only because different interest groups arguing for quality have different and possibly incompatible objectives. This dilemma is occasionally recognized in official documents. For example, in the Department of Health guidance on the training implications of the NHS and Community Care Act 1990, the countervailing tendencies behind political drives for quality were neatly recognized in the warning that pressures for training 'are likely to be internal (the desire to raise throughput and quality while holding or reducing costs) and external as a result of user empowerment and possible resource constraints/competition' (DH I993a: 17).

Not that debates about quality should be rejected as irrelevant or misleading. There are several instances of public good arising from quality concerns within the personal social services. Citizens' concerns about standards of service are drawn into the public arena, and channels are provided for earlier disclosure of unacceptable practices. Quality management has stimulated some instances of good practice involving practitioners, managers and service users (James *et al.*1992: 2.4, 2.7). The ENQUIRE System of quality assurance developed by the King's Fund is a further example of quality management which offers a more positive experience. It includes the establishment of Quality Action Groups, where professionals, users, carers, volunteers and others work together to evaluate the impact of different types of service, and in which information is presented in a way that is more likely to facilitate participation by users (Richards and Heginbotham 1992). These positive developments demonstrate that good service standards are not only a matter of obtaining good resourcing.

Yet quality management has not been accepted wholesale in the personal social services. For example, market forces and quality control mechanisms do not always sit side by side comfortably. This is because sustaining quality management often entails a costly quasi-governmental apparatus. Thus, the government has been caught back-pedaling sharply on some aspects of quality control. Tim Yeo, a minister at the Department of Health, wrote in 1993 to directors of Social Services urging them to be less assiduous in registering day care services under the 1989 Children Act – a circular that caused acute anxiety and opposition from groups such as the Pre-School Playgroups Associations in England and in Wales (DH 1993c). This was followed later in the same year by a letter from the same government department indicating that the government was considering softening the requirements which they introduced in 1984 for the regulation of residential homes for the elderly.

Since April 1993, the implementation of the new community care requirements has been marked by a significant number of bulk purchase agreements between Social Services departments and existing providers whereby, for instance, all housing association contracts to provide places in residential care for elderly persons are renewed en bloc without competitive tendering and sometimes at existing prices. This seems to be a euphemism for the abandonment (temporarily at least) of significant features of the 'excellence' culture.

However, despite the positive benefits of quality mechanisms, and the limited degree to which quality management has permeated the personal social services, reflection on the developments discussed in the first part of this chapter suggests that, on balance, the public good has not been demonstrably served. First, the promotion of partnership marks a major and worrying shift in relations between the state and the voluntary sector. Second, quality management in the personal social services is marked by a rational managerialism which may threaten the traditional professional role in welfare activity and lead to a marginalization of the service user. Finally, talk of customer satisfaction and choice often hinders rather than promotes real attention to the voice of the service user. We develop each of these themes in the remainder of this chapter.

Partnership, the state and the voluntary sector

Partnership language has been used to describe collaborative arrangements between purchasers and providers, statutory and voluntary or private agencies, central government departments and local departments, agencies or projects, and between service providers and users. Our case in the following paragraphs is that partnership arrangements threaten to establish a disturbing shift in relationships between the state and the voluntary sector.

The split between local authorities as service purchasers and a wider spread of agencies as service providers opens the way for a disaggregation of services and creates for the state a newly sharpened problem of how diverse voluntary, statutory and private providers can be integrated within a common government strategy. In response to this it appears clear that quality control measures have been viewed by the government as a mechanism for managing these fissile tendencies. The review of quality measures sponsored by the SSI partly recognized this in its conclusion that the community care reforms placed the tensions between central and local, diversity and uniformity under strain. 'Quality assurance can be seen as one mechanism to manage the tension between uniformity and diversity' (James *et al.* 1992: 2.7.2). The mechanism is not straightforward. For example, the Home Office is encouraging the development of partnerships between Probation Services and the independent sector. Yet, as Smith has pointed out: 'The paradox is that the more probation work is "hived off" or contracted out to the independent sector the harder it is to achieve the levels of accountability the Home Office now expects' (Smith *et al.*1993: 34).

This tension is managed, in part, by government emphasis on a culture of working together through jointly negotiated and shared objectives – a strategy that we noted in our examination of the Home Office scrutiny of the voluntary sector. This is one of the main mechanisms used by the government to achieve an attempted depoliticization of quality. Partnership talk provides the rhetoric of depoliticization. The managerialism that we illustrate below provides the vehicle through which this depoliticization takes place.

Studies of informal and voluntary care in the 1970s provided a point of rejuvenation for sociological work (Offer 1990). Philip Abrams – the most influential contributor to what Offer has aptly termed 'the sociology of morals' – warned about the dangers that could occur when government or local authority departments colonized the voluntary sector (Abrams 1984).

Partnership policies pose precisely this risk. There are two associated dangers. First, the values of the state sector may penetrate the voluntary sector – the phenomenon of colonization. As a result, the major voluntary organizations – for example, the Children's Society, National Children's Home, Barnados and the major special needs housing associations – may come to dominate the sector, lose their independence and critical edge, and unwittingly elbow out the smaller voluntary organizations. The diversity of the voluntary sector could be lost. Second, with this radical shift in relations between the central state and the local state, the new commercially oriented private sector will prove best equipped to take advantage of the welfare economy, to the disadvantage of smaller voluntary groups.

A rather different solution to this development is proffered in a research report which received widespread attention for its authors' proposal that voluntary organizations should have their charitable status withdrawn and split into either non-profit service providers or traditional campaigning and innovatory bodies (Knight 1993). In the first category would be the big voluntary agencies already bidding for contracts in the health, education and social services markets.

A similar risk exists in the sphere of influence of the Probation Service- the 'risk of a loss of genuine independence in the independent sector as it becomes colonized by a probation service concerned to demonstrate efficiency, effectiveness and economy in the achievement of its core tasks' (Smith *et al.* 1993: 34).

Valuable grassroots work accomplished on developing partnership between service providers and service users (Marsh and Fisher 1992) will be vulnerable to the neutralizing tendencies of these macro-political developments.

The new managerialism

The work carried out through the SSI and the enormous growth of guidance documentation from government departments assume that a new and strong management style – both at senior and middle management levels – will provide the vehicle through which quality management will be made part of the warp and woof of services. This managerialism drives the aspirations for partnership and functions to increase super vision of professional staff. Managers in social work have traditionally been in a powerful position relative to the professionals who deliver social work services (Howe 1991), unlike medicine, where managers have until recently been relatively weak in relation to doctors. Social work managers almost always come up through the professional ranks and are not usually introduced from outside the profession as management specialists. This, paradoxically, may strengthen their position by giving them dual claims to both managerial and professional authority.

The introduction of quality measures into this equation creates an additional complication. The risk exists that social work management will be moulded into a rational straitjacket, which sets an impossible agenda for welfare agencies by requiring that the organizational core should control the periphery and that all staff should know what to do in all circumstances.

What consequences are likely to follow for the role of professionals in the personal social services? Those who received a social science education during the 1960s and 1970s probably accepted without too much question a critique of professional power – a critique of excessive claims and limited achievements, failures of professional responsibility, absence of professional neutrality, trampling on citizens' rights, lack of accountability and so on (Wilding 1982: 85-128). In the policy climate of the 1980s and 1990s when the government has said 'precisely so' to this battery of criticisms, there have been few commentators willing to ask whether a damaging transformation of professional roles may be occurring.

There are three important related questions. First, has the wide-scale introduction of quality management weakened the professional role in social work, or is professional power in the process of remaking the role and retaining power? Second, are operational professional values – the actual values inherent in day-to-day practice – being transformed? Third, is there a shift towards either increased indeterminacy or greater rationality in the carrying out of the professional task?

It is too early to make firm generalizations regarding the impact of recent changes in public sector management on professional power, and rather contrary interim conclusions have been reached by different contributors to this book. There are, however, several straws in the wind that suggest social work professionals may be in a weaker position, and Pfeffer and Coote are in no doubt that 'one of the main effects of the changes has been to begin to limit the power of the "caring" professionals' (Pfeffer and Coote 1991: 12).

It seems plausible to suggest that a significant minority will become quasi managers through taking on a care management role, whereas the introduction of quasi-professional tasks will weaken professional influence. If the welfare task comprises market commodities, local authority social workers may become 'welfare traders' where, for example, debt collecting skills rival the importance of counselling.

The shift should not be overstated. The grassroots reality of social work management and practice is probably rather different from the rhetoric of planning, analysis, standards, evaluation and so on. For example, in research currently being undertaken by the writer, a Principal Social Services Officer (PSSO) in a Social Services department child care team described her role in supervising social workers' assessment tasks in a way which underscores the ambiguity of assessment, discretionary judgements, and risk taking:

> Assessment is very broad ... we use it to cover a lot of things. Everything is seen as needing assessment Assessing risk and assessing service requirements are needed throughout. A senior practitioner may be involved. The concerns that

> decide this are maintaining independence, the protection of the social worker, and my judgements about people's expertise....
>
> The senior practitioner acts as a filtering system. The PSSO will use discretion, and the PSSO/senior practitioner relationship is very crucial. Senior practitioners are not meant to be line managers ... a contentious issue but that's the structure.
>
> Each social worker and social work assistant has two-weekly diaried sessions with a senior practitioner ... but they often have to be cancelled. Planned supervision sessions are constantly at risk because of the over-riding claims of having to respond to crises.

This extract illustrates the way in which quality assurance can operate as a managerial device to ensure safety and risk protection (cf. Bull and Shaw 1992), and in reality departs from the managerial model officially advocated for work in child protection cases where social work is regularly appraised against objectives, standards and operational criteria (SSI l993b; Pithouse 1987).

Managerialism is also growing rapidly in voluntary organizations. Line management structures are being adopted throughout the voluntary sector. While this may give voluntary organizations greater credibility with funders, it is likely to lead to a loss of volunteer involvement. The language of governance is in the air. Commercial models, strengthened by the publication of the Cadbury Report on the financial aspects of corporate governance (Cadbury 1992), are being transferred to voluntary organizations. Additional incentive has followed from the Charities Act 1992, which has heightened preoccupations with accountability among trustees of voluntary organizations (Charities Commissioner 1993).

Yet again, experience at the street level of service delivery is likely to be somewhat different, and be marked by management practices leading to indeterminate outcomes. Recent work in the supported housing field has shown how the negotiation of definitions of need at the point of referral, the brokerage of rulemaking and breaking during people's stay in projects, and the chronic ambiguity surrounding move-on as a goal of supported housing all underline the extent to which goals are, to a significant degree, socially constructed from the point of entry, through daily Jiving in the scheme, to leaving such projects (Shaw and Williamson 1992).

Evidence for the 'distortion' of quality indicators at the level of day-to-day implementation can also be illustrated from the social work education field. A study of methods, skills and knowledge used by social work practice teachers to evaluate the competence of social work students demonstrated that practice teachers tended to rely on intuitive 'gut feelings' in assessing students. The extent to which underlying models of competency outcomes were shared by the interested parties was thrown into doubt by this research (Williamson and Jefferson 1989).

The User at the Margins

The new managerialism is not only rational and inimical to professional autonomy, but may also lead to the marginalization of the consumer. In one of the most thorough reviews of quality assurance practices in social services departments, the pessimistic conclusion was reached that:

> Again and again we found definitions of Quality Assurance in use and evidence of standard setting which overwhelmingly represented the view of managers and professionals rather than those of service users. We found these systems had in general at least as much to do with achieving bureaucratic efficiency and good professional practice as improving outcomes for users. (James *et al.* 1992: 2.1.3)

Unless a heavily cynical view is adopted, this potential marginalization of the user is not what was intended by the framers of the Children Act and the community care reforms. 'Both aim to replace systems dominated by professionals with approaches based on partnership with service users ... The focus ... has been on ways to make it easier for children, parents, users and carers to participate and be heard' (SSI 1992c: 5.2, 5.3).

There are several reasons why, at the very least, the jury must remain out on the impact of this alleged culture change on the personal social services. The central issues are the extent to which service users have real choice, the question of whether it will prove possible to reach a partnership of views with service users on appropriate and desirable outcomes, and the ambiguity and even conservatising effects of drawing on user assessments of satisfaction as a basis for managing service developments.

Policies of choice for service users are not a guarantee of quality for many customers of the personal social services. There are three reasons for this. First, the sovereign consumer is a far *cry* from 'most dependent people whose needs come within the remit of the personal social services ... (and who) are tied because of frailty, illness, fear, handicap, low income or habit to their local area' (Barclay 1982: 220). Second, welfare clients who believe they are in receipt of an unsatisfactory service often cannot choose an alternative because they are involuntary users. The emphasis on providing exit options for welfare clients frequently chooses to ignore this obvious reality. Third, this inability to shop around often may be compounded by the fact that the need for given services may be confined to a small number of people in the population and alternatives, therefore, will not be available in any given area. For example, specialist drugs and alcohol units or day care facilities for people with certain disabilities are likely to hold a monopoly in any one area. This may be exaggerated following the introduction of local government reform, leading to smaller unitary authorities.

There is already some evidence that the introduction of contracting may serve to increase the likelihood of this problem occurring. For example, early evidence from a study of the development of relationships between purchasers and providers through the process of contracting suggested that, in the majority of contracts the authors had studied, 'the existence of the contract did nothing to increase user choice of services'. A common reason for this was that 'services provided through the contract became the only service meeting a particular need for a particular client group in a particular locality' (Common and Flynn 1992: 35). Choice becomes a reality for purchasers, not for service users.

> Restructuring may have been advanced as a way of enhancing choice – and thereby quality – but in practice, in health and personal social services, the right to choose falls not to individual patients and clients, but to those who hold the purse strings. (Pfeffer and Coote 1991:22)

Pfeffer and Coote make the point that users are both citizens – interested in services as a member of the community – and customers who are interested as individual users. They are also frequently providers of care. 'We are interested as citizens in planning and as customers in delivery' (1991: 26). If users are to exercise influence and choice then they must be empowered in both their customer and citizen roles.

The problematic nature of user choice has to be viewed in the light of difficulties in interpreting user judgements of services they receive. For example, it is well documented that user statements of satisfaction with a given service may have a conservatizing effect on policy developments. There is ample evidence that high satisfaction levels can co-exist with high problems or poor service (Shaw and Walton 1979; Shaw 1984; Ste Croix 1992).

There are several reasons why this may be so. For instance, service users may have low expectations of service quality arising from previous experience of these services or wider life experience. Also, when asked to suggest how existing services can be improved, they may find it difficult to grasp a wider framework of services than that with which they are already familiar. More generally, responses to service users' evaluations must take into account the impact of the power differential between users and providers. Satisfaction thus has a rather tenuous relationship to meeting needs. 'Meeting needs is not the same as satisfying tastes or wants' (Pfeffer and Coote 1991: 13).

It may appear trite to observe that a person's satisfaction with the outcomes of a service will depend on their prior assumptions regarding the aims of a service. Yet we still have limited evidence regarding the kinds of criteria which citizens will adopt in appraising a service. In a recent evaluation of supported housing schemes debate about move-on, integration into the community and policies of normalization underlay many of the attempts by participants to make sense of their daily and working lives (Shaw and Williamson 1992). For example, in one housing scheme for people with learning difficulties, a woman had recently left and was now living in a nearby local authority housing development, newly married to a partner who also had learning difficulties. When scheme staff and others were asked what they would regard as a measure of success or failure, this event was often raised: 'I don't know whether they've settled where they are now

... We may have made a mistake, we altered her life completely, we relieved her of too much'. This committee member's doubt was expressed still more strongly by a staff member who cited the incident as an example of where the home had failed. Both of these respondents interpreted this particular outcome in negative light because they believed the project's goal was the provision of a permanent home. However, another staff member who was emphatic that the project should aim to provide rehabilitation to permanent housing quoted the same example as evidence of where they were succeeding.

The implications are clear. Instances of people moving out of the project were interpreted as quite contrary evidence for success or failure depending on the views that each person held regarding project aims.

A rational, actuarial approach to performance measures of outcomes, based on an assumption of shared service objectives, is also at risk from processes of lay theorizing and policy making. Such processes appear to be part of the way both service employees and users typically endeavour to make sense of guidance from above.

Normalization polices in supported housing schemes provide an illustration of this process of lay policy construction. A staff member in a scheme providing for people with learning disabilities was asked about the aims of her project:

> Normalization ... as far as you can go. For example, I say "Go and change your shirt", and John complains, 'Don't talk like that', and I say, 'It's normalisation, John'. He asks me to shave him and I tell him to shave himself ... he wanted me to insert pessaries for his haemorrhoids!

Government and academic statements of normalization policies are relatively elaborate, and based on general values and statements. In contrast, street-level staff fashion ways in which guidance from above can be made understandable and feasible in day to day work.

This brief discussion of service outcomes and day-to-day policy implementation illustrates that agreed practices of care, support and management over matters as central as major house rules or as apparently mundane as gardening are kept in place as the uncertain outcomes of negotiated realities between residents, paid employees, outside professionals in housing or welfare networks, and purse-holders from provider agencies and organizations.

Conclusion

We have argued that the implementation of a culture of quality within the personal social services is likely to remain at risk because it does not recognize the contingent, socially negotiated characteristics of much street-level management practice. A rational, quality control model of management demands major behavioural changes on the part of social workers. The difficulties of these changes tend to be underestimated and their desirability taken for granted. The service user can easily become marginalized. Quality culture may not increase customer choice, and the apparent liberal values behind advocacy of user satisfaction as a criterion of quality compete with several inbuilt tendencies to conservatism. Quality cultures typically fail to recognize the power differentials between providers and users.

Yet the rhetoric of quality management has some way to go before it bums out. It provides a convenient catch-all forum within which competitive political, managerial and professional interests are played out. It will continue to function as one of the central managerially led mechanisms in an attempt to unify social service provision under a disaggregated, purchaser/provider split, and it will continue to provide an impetus for the partially achieved shift in relations between the state and the voluntary sector.

Pfeffer and Coote (1991) advocate an alternative approach to defining and assuring quality, designed to achieve common goals and meet individual needs – a democratic approach, which acknowledges the differences between commerce and welfare. Such an approach, they believe, must pursue equitable opportunities for all, responsiveness to individual needs, and a commitment to making the public more powerful, both as citizens and as customers.

Tensions between these goals will remain, for reasons we have discussed in the later part of this chapter. It is our conviction that an undue preoccupation with quality process is not the way forward, but rather a determination to place quality outcomes centre stage. Gatehouse has suggested six tests of whether quality has been achieved. Does the service meet the needs of the individual client or carer? Are services available to people irrespective of location, race, gender, belief or ability to pay? Are consumers satisfied and is their distress or difficulty reduced? Are the expectations of consumers, providers and tax payers satisfied? Are no more resources than necessary used to achieve the stated aim? (Gatehouse 1992). Squaring the circle of these tests, of relevance, equity, effectiveness, social acceptability and efficiency will never prove easy. But it is the real quality agenda facing the personal social services.

References

Abrams, P. (1984) 'Realities of neighbourhood care', *Policy and Politics* 12: 413-29.

Audit Commission (1986) *Making a Reality of Community Care*, London: HMSO.

Barclay, P. (1982) *Social Workers: Their Roles and Tasks*, London: Bedford Square Press.

British Standards Institution (1993) Correspondence.

Bull, R. and Shaw, I. (1992) 'Constructing causal accounts in social work', *Sociology* 26: 635-49.

Cadbury, A. (1992) *Report of the Committee on the Financial Aspects of Corporate Governance*, London: CCETSW.

Central Council for Education and Training in Social Work (1991) *Rules and Requirements for the Diploma in Social Work*, London: CCETSW.

Central Council for Education and Training in Social Work (1992) *Setting Quality Standards for Residential Child Care*, London: CCETSW.

Central Council for Education and Training in Social Work (1995) *Requirements for Qualification in Social Work*, London: CCETSW.

Charities Commissioners (1993) *Charities: The New Law*, London: Charity Commissioners for England and Wales.

Common, R. and Flynn, N. (1992) *Contracting for Care*, York: Joseph Rowntree.

Department of Health (1991) *Working with Child Sexual Abuse*, London: Department of Health.

Department of Health (1993a) *Training for the Future*, London: HMSO.

Department of Health (1993b) *Policy and Financial Management Review of the Central Council for Education and Training in Social Work*, London: Department of Health.

Department of Health (1993c) *The Children Act and Day Care for Young Children: Registration*, LAC (93)1, London: Department of Health.

Gatehouse, G. (1992) 'Ensuring quality in the new culture', in Allen, I. (ed) *Purchasing And Providing Social Services in the 1990s*, London: PSSI.

HMSO (1989) *Caring For People: Community Care in the Next Decade and Beyond*, London: HMSO.

Home Office (1990) *Efficiency Scrutiny of Government Funding of the Voluntary Sector*, London: HMSO.

Home Office (1992a) *Partnership in Dealing With Offenders in the Community*, London: Home Office.

Home Office (1992b) *Three Year Plan: 1993-1996*, London: Home Office.

Home Office (1992c) *National Standards for the Supervision of Offenders in the Community*, London: Home Office.

Home Office (1994) *Three Year Plan for the Probation Service 1994-1997*, London: Home Office.

Housing Corporation (1989) *Performance Expectations*, London: Housing Corporation.

Housing Corporation (1992a) *Performance Criteria*, London: Housing Corporation.

Housing Corporation (1992b) *Tenant Participation Strategy*, London: Housing Corporation.

Housing Corporation (1993a) *Making it Work: A Guide to Tenant Participation for Housing Associations*, Cardiff: Housing for Wales.

Housing Corporation (1993b) *Measuring tenant Satisfaction*, Cardiff: Housing for Wales.

Howe, D. (1991) 'Knowledge, power and the shape of social work practice', in Davies, M. *The Sociology of Social Work*, London: Routledge.

James, A., Brooks. T. and Towell, D. (1992) *Committed to Quality: Quality Assurance in Social Services Departments*, London: HMSO.

Knight, B. (1993) *Voluntary Action*, London: CENTRIS.
Marsh, P. and Fisher, M. (1992) *Good Intentions: Developing Partnership in Social Services*, York: Joseph Rowntree.
National Audit Office (1989) *Control and Management of the Probation Service in England and Wales*, London: HMSO.
National Federation of Housing Associations (1987) *Standards for Housing Management*, London: NFHA.
Offer, J. (1990) 'The Sociology of Welfare', in Davies, M. (ed.) *The Sociology of Social Work*, London: Routledge.
Pfeffer, N. and Coote, A. (1991) *Is Quality Good for You?* A *Critical Review of Quality Assurance in Welfare Services*, London: Institute for Public Policy Research.
Pithouse, A. (1987) *Social Work: the Social Organisation of an Invisible Trade*, Aldershot: Avebury.
Richards, H. and Heginbotham, C. (1992) *ENQUIRE: Quality Assurance Through Observation of Service Delivery*, London: Kings Fund College.
Shaw, I. (1984) 'Consumer Evaluations of the Personal Social Services', *British Journal of Social Work* 14: 277-84.
Shaw, I. and Williamson, H. (1992) *Management and Welfare: Evaluation of Special Needs Housing in Wales*, Cardiff: Housing for Wales.
Shaw, I. and Walton, R. (1979) 'Transitions to residence in homes for the elderly', in Harris, D. and Hyland, J. (eds) *Rights in Residence*, London: Residential Care Association.
Smith, D., Paylor, I. and Mitchell, P. (1993) 'Partnerships between the independent sector and the probation service', *Howard Journal* 32: 25-39.
Social Services Inspectorate (1989) *Homes are for Living In*, London: HMSO.
Social Services Inspectorate (1990a) *Inspecting Home Care Services*, London: HMSO.
Social Services Inspectorate (1990b) *Guidance on Standards for Residential Homes for People with a Physical Disability*, London: HMSO.
Social Services Inspectorate (1991a) *Care Management and Assessment: Practitioner's Guide*, London: Department of Health.
Social Services Inspectorate (1991b) *Care Management and Assessment: Managers' Guide*, London: Department of Health.
Social Services Inspectorate (l992a) *Guidance on Standards for the Residential Care Needs of People with Specific Mental Health Needs*, London: HMSO.
Social Services Inspectorate (1992b) *Guidance on Standards for the Residential Care Needs of People with Learning Disabilities/Mental Handicap*, London: HMSO.
Social Services Inspectorate (1992c) *Concern for Quality: The First Annual report of the Chief Inspector, Social Services Inspectorate 1991-1992*, London: HMSO.
Social Services Inspectorate (1993a) *Raising the Standard: Second Annual report of the Chief Inspector*, London: HMSO.

Social Services Inspectorate (1993b) *Evaluating Performance in Child Protection*, London: HMSO.

Ste Croix, de, R. (1992) *Can Quality be Assured in an Uncertain World?*, Bristol: School of Advanced Urban Studies.

Utting, W. (1991) *Children in the Public Care*, London: HMSO.

Welsh Office (n.d) *Welsh Office Funding of the Voluntary Sector: A Strategic Statement*, Cardiff: Welsh Office.

Wilding, P. (1982) *Professional Power and Social Welfare*, London: Routledge.

Williamson, H. and Jefferson, R. (1989) *Assessment of Practice: A Perennial Concern?*, Cardiff: University of Wales.

Chapter 17
Game Plans, Buzzes and Sheer Luck: Doing Well in Social Work*

Introduction: Images of Evaluating

There has been an animated, even passionate, debate about the relative merits of 'positivist' and 'humanist' versions of social work. Yet, in our view, the way in which the debate has been conducted has been, in several respects, unhelpful. Not that there is nothing to debate. But social workers have tended to adopt entrenched positions which make it difficult to get fully inside or outside the argument. Advocates of qualitative research have been dismissed as 'intellectual Luddites' (Thyer, 1995: 97), while, from the opposing trenches, some protagonists of qualitative research dismiss those they label positivist as dangerously simplistic elitists, whose values are 'at variance with the value base, and the purposeful and humble activities of social work practice' (Everitt *et al.*, 1992: 61). Hence, positivism becomes 'a swear-word by which nobody is swearing' (Williams, 1976: 239), and we are sometimes left with the impression that if only we were courageous enough to 'deconstruct' a problem, we would be nine tenths of the way to its solution. While a commitment to evidencing practice lies at the heart of the best work of both positivist and humanist strategies, Augustine's comment is apposite for some representatives of both camps – 'total abstinence is easier than perfect moderation'.

To move forward in this debate we need to take several steps backwards, and reflect on the little we know about social workers' existing valuating practices. Elks and Kirkhart have called for a fresh approach to such research,

> One that is exploratory rather than confirmatory, building a model of evaluation from practitioners' own accounts rather than superimposing an ideal model and testing for conformity (Elks and Kirkhart, 1993: 555).

Research of this kind is necessary if we are to develop a plausible strategy for evaluating in practice. Our fundamental argument is that social workers' accounts of self evaluating indicate that an informed evaluating in practice strategy cannot afford to ignore the existing realities of social work. To build a

---

* Originally published as Shaw, I. and Shaw, A. (1997) 'Game Plans, Buzzes and Sheer Luck: Doing Well in Social Work', *Social Work Research* 21(2): 69-79. Reprinted with permission of the National Association of Social Workers, and Rights Link.

model of evaluating in practice, we need to start with the realities of day-to-day practice and with social workers' experiences and accounts of how they evaluate their work, rather than impose an abstract and decontextualised framework of evaluation. We need to work 'from the bottom up', grounding our model of evaluation on an appreciation of practitioners' own accounts, rather than superimposing an ideal model 'from the top down' which will necessarily lack meaning in the context of everyday social work practice.

A general conclusion from the small amount of work done in this field has been that practitioners have an implicit model of practice evaluation, a 'pragmatic-professional model', 'characterised by its down-to-earthness, immediacy and practical relevance' (Elks and Kirkhart, 1993: 557). Effectiveness tends to be seen in input rather than output terms, distinctions between means and ends are not fixed, and effectiveness remains complex and contingent (Humphrey and Pease, 1992). Social workers appear to have two contrasting 'models' of evaluation – 'evaluation proper' and self evaluation – which represent two distinctive sets of characteristics. These images of evaluation are essentially separate. On the one hand is formal evaluation – 'Evaluation with a Capital E' – which is experienced as largely alien to the realities of social work. On the other hand, this 'map' of formal evaluation is in complete contrast with social workers' 'maps' of their actual day to day evaluations of practice (Shaw, 1996; Shaw and Shaw, 1997).

Research evidence about these maps of evaluation has only provided a small part of the picture – the straight edges and corners of the jigsaw. The picture of evaluating in action needs filling in by considering certain key questions, such as how social workers account for practice that, in their view, goes 'well' or 'less well', and what evidence do they draw on in accomplishing such productions of their work? The evidence outlined in this paper pursues these questions, through an exploration of social workers' evaluating practices in specific cases.

Methodology

A series of in-depth, unstructured interviews was carried out with fifteen social workers practising in a wide cross-section of British public and voluntary agencies, including adult services in the community, child protection teams and in the Probation Service. Local agency practice teacher, and social work course lists provided the ingredients of a sampling grid from which potential respondents were randomly drawn. All practitioners invited to take part in interviews which would explore their views about evaluating within their everyday practice agreed to participate. Experienced practitioners, accredited practice teachers and newly qualified social workers made up the sample. 'Qualitative research', McCracken aptly remarks, 'does not survey the terrain, it mines it' (McCracken, 1988: 17). Consequently, potential research participants were selected from an intentionally wide compass of experience and presumed expertise, in order to allow a range of 'test cases' for analytic categories emerging during the research.

Each social worker talked in detail to one or other of the authors about different instances of their work. The heart of the interview involved the respondents talking about two recent examples of their work, one in which they thought they were doing the work well, and one in which they thought they were practising less well. They were asked to describe the work, and to say how they knew whether it was going well or not. They were encouraged to identify the evidence specific to each instance of their work. They were also invited to consider whether the service users would have reached a similar view and if they might have used similar or different criteria in evaluating the service received. Practitioners appeared to find little difficulty in identifying examples of work they believed had gone well or less well, although reflecting on their tacit strategies and evidence proved more demanding. One of the authors has argued elsewhere that close inspection and exploration of extreme, marginal, unusual or problematic social work practice is a fruitful trigger to render tacit understandings and accounts explicit (Bull and Shaw, 1992: 640-641). The uncertainty of practitioners' day to day hold on professional knowledge, and their means of coping with this uncertainty, are central to this inquiry.

In the analysis of the narrative accounts produced through these interviews we attempt to glimpse and systematically reconstruct aspects of practitioners' views of their world. Our interest is in what medical sociologists have called the 'clinical gaze' (Atkinson, 1995: 5). To accomplish this the analysis of the interview transcripts proceeded from an identification of social workers' cultural categories, based as far as we were able on a disingenuous resistance to supplying assumptions and understandings. For example, we took metaphors seriously, and have retained practitioner categories in organising much of what follows. To avoid foreclosing prematurely on analytic conclusions we pursued a cycle from inspection, to preliminary themes, and to clusters of themes. We alternated this cycle with attempts to falsify emergent analytic categories through review of deliberately 'different' interview transcripts. To assess the plausibility of our analyses, preliminary results were distributed to all participating practitioners, and their observations invited on the emerging themes and interpretations.

An emphasis on ways in which social workers construct a sense of of 'good' practice demands two cautiuons. First, it 'does not imply that social actors whimsically conjure reality out of thin air'. Reality is not simply and solely a mental product – it comprises social, collective acts. These collective acts are material transactions with the world. Therefore, '"reality" is not to be viewed as a construct in the sense that "there is nothing there" independently of social actors' (Atkinson, 1995: 43), and while we choose to bracket particular categories, (eg 'social work', 'evaluation'), we do not deny their material existence. Second, it commits us to holding an enduring tension between what is and what ought to be. 'Good' practice as enviasged by these social workers may overlap only partly with more generally held judgements of good practice. Yet, while existing practice cannot be taken as a recipe for what *ought* to be, it does provide one plank for constructing an evaluating in practice which is simultaneously true to social workers' accounts of what lies close to the core of their practice, while also offering a critical starting point for appraising and refashioning that practice.

Unstructured interviews are, of course, open to some methodological reservations. It is not always clear that they possess the ecological validity of responses captured 'on the wing' in a natural setting, and, unlike other qualitative methods such as participant observation, they are less likely to disclose the *processes* through which such occupational constructions are produced. Nonetheless, we are convinced of their value. The significance of the accounts offered by these practitioners hinges on whether they prove conceptually generalisable. They are likely to do so insofar as they display coherence, unity, explanatory power, and fertility.

The social workers we spoke to set a fundamental agenda of practice issues. The central questions raised by their accounts are *firstly*, what practice evaluating *strategies* do social workers employ? What essentials do social workers believe need to be in place if work is to have a chance of going well? *Secondly*, what *evidences* do social workers draw upon in deciding how well a piece of work has gone? Strategies and evidencing obviously dovetail and overlap, but for the sake of clarity they are presented separately in this paper. We will offer a concluding commentary on the data and point to ways we believe the research provides a stimulus for the development of evaluating in practice.

Strategies for 'Good' Practice

The practitioners' narratives suggest that their strategies for evaluating can be understood in the light of three implicit organising considerations. Did they have a '*game plan*'? Were they working with '*good*' *clients*? Were they enjoying *good luck*? These issues are summarised in Figure 17.1.

A 'game plan'

The possession of a *game plan* depends, using the terms of our respondents, on three issues – keeping *control* of the work, carrying out '*constructive practice*', and '*staying in the ball park*'. The issue of control was a constantly recurring theme, and having a 'game plan' made control possible, although not certain:

> I have a kind of game plan in my head which I just do…I think most social workers, or *good* social workers rather, know their capabilities, know their skills, know what they should be doing and they get on with it.

A key feature of remaining in control is being able to 'juggle' in relation to both clients and to other agencies and professionals:

- An implicit 'game plan' comprising:
  - The ability to exercise 'control' in work with clients and other key actors
  - A purposeful and 'constructive' practice strategy
  - Keeping practice within the rules of the 'ball game'
  - Constant watchfulness
  - Knowledge built on life and professional experience
  - A sense of 'timing'
- Having a 'good' client
- Recognising the significant part played by 'sheer luck', including:
  - The unpredictable nature of social work practice
  - Factors that mitigate against blame for poor practice

Figure 17.1 Strategies for good practice

> You do this sort of juggling act with all this information.
>
> I've got two strands here – I've got to think about the little girl's needs and her future well-being, and also her mother's needs and her future well-being, and ideally try to marry those two things.
>
> I think I've got all the issues at the forefront of my mind and I think I'm working well with all the other key people in this case.

Being in control keeps the practitioner one step ahead, and the social workers often attributed poor social work practice to a loss of or a failure to gain this kind of control.

> I'm finding it difficult to work with this couple..I felt a bit out of control and it made me very anxious.
>
> They're using their son's welfare as a bargaining tool and…I've not been able to have any impact into that change. I'm slightly in a heavy flow tide and you're being dragged along with it, having no control over what's actually happening to you...I'm just not happy that we've lost control of that situation.

Control and *constructive practice* were closely inter-linked. When the social workers felt they had failed to remain in control of a case or exert appropriate influence over the situation, their concern was frequently with the absence of 'constructive' or 'purposeful' practice. The absence of clear assessments, plans and objectives was a frequent self-criticism, and there was strong belief in the need for workable, 'evaluable' plans, without which intervention risked becoming aimless:

> I don't know where I'm going to. I haven't got a workable plan with that case, and for me that's quite important…If we haven't got anything to start with we're bound to get lost.

> I never got to grips with them about why I was going to be visiting again…I'm not even sure she knew why I was visiting or if she even wanted me there.

Failure in a case was often attributed to the failure to be proactive:

> She had no interest whatsoever in the probation order, and then I fell into that role with her, of not trying to confront.

Being proactive rather than reactive was a virtue frequently extolled by these social workers, where a successful case often involved the social worker adopting a proactive role:

> If they didn't hassle you, you were going to hassle them.

For this practitioner 'hassling' was a sign of attentive, active intervention. Being proactive involves a certain kind of relationship between practitioner and service user – a relationship of trust – which is not always easy to achieve:

> Maybe sort of conflicting more..if she saw me as a friend and someone to confront her offending.

Being in control and being constructive are two parts of a game plan. More difficult to identify but also important is '*staying in the ball park*'. A probation officer described a pre-sentence report in which a very low tariff sentence was recommended but where a custodial sentence was given. In attempting to reflect on the extent to which he felt he had misread the situation, the probation officer concluded,

> If the judge had said, 'No. Conditional discharge isn't serious enough, I'll *fine* her', then I'd say, 'Fair enough'. I was in the ball park, you know.

An important point is being made by this practitioner. He believed he had been outside the ball park in the sense that he had unwittingly but completely misjudged the rules of the game. The rules may be relatively encompassing, but practice is not possible unless the players are on the same turf.

Having a 'game plan' is a *general* strategy. However, this general strategy may not be effective without an approach *specific* to a particular individual, group or family. There were three core elements to how practitioners viewed this kind of understanding. These were constant *watchfulness and awareness*, '*the knowledge*', and the possession of *good timing.*

> It needs a trained eye, an experienced eye (to have) a confident view of what is taking place.

> You're really looking at the situation all the time..Evaluation is something which I do by thinking, by observing, the dialogue with the client, the dialogue with people I work alongside from other agencies and this agency..You have to be constantly aware.

Not only does the social worker have to be watchful and aware, but some practitioners also referred to possessing 'the knowledge', which for most of them was based on a blend of professional and personal experience.

> You do rely on your own life experience...I rely on my own personal experience but also my professional experience...I think I've got the knowledge.

Finally, applying a general 'game plan' to a specific situation is believed to require the possession of 'good timing' on the part of the practitioner:

> I felt the timing for the children was essential, that they were placed with the adopters when the baby was quite small...I felt a sense of satisfaction that I had managed to set the plans up, not made too quick a decision in either direction, and that the outcome was good for everybody.

> I chose the timing wrongly..and the outcome was to damage our relationship for a couple of months...It was that judgement, it was actually about timing, and I think your timing goes when you're under pressure.

Good clients

Having a general 'game plan' and a more specific understanding of indivudal service users may fail if the social worker is working with someone they do not regard as a 'good client'. Lack of informed consent, no motivation to change, a personal mistrust of the social worker, over-familiarity and an inability to change were among the characteristics to which social workers referred. When present to a significant degree they excluded an individual from being not only a *good* client, but even a client at all in any meaningful way. These characteristics of a 'bad' client were all evident in many of the examples given by practitioners of work that had not gone well.

The mirror image hallmarks of a 'good' client were referred to by several practitioners.

> She was coping with the bereavement, trying to contemplate being a single parent..she was able to talk about the kind of support she would have..she was beginning to plan...she was talking about her deceased husband in quite a healthy way. She was clearly projecting into the future..So really she was measuring herself in a way which I would have looked at as well.

'Just sheer luck'

Whatever personal game plans may be in place, and however experienced and wise a social worker may be, there remains an element of unpredictability near the heart of social work practice. According to the social workers to whom we spoke, whether work goes well or badly is not the product only of rational and intelligent planning. At its simplest, it is reflected in the assumption of one social worker that 'there's always an element of good fortune in these things'.

> Whether it was because the time was right for her and I was just lucky that I connected, I don't know. I think it was just sheer luck. It's a bit like gambling and roulette, and every now and then you score the right number and you make a good connection with somebody.

> I've been trying to help (the group) for three or four years. I don't know what happened. I was really dreading it, and I went in and I flew through it. I mean it was like flying, it was such a brilliant experience for me...It was a one-off.

The unpredictability of social work practice applies equally well to work that goes badly, although none of the practitioners used the term 'bad luck' to describe it:

> You can spend a lot of time on a particular case and you feel you've done really well, only to find out that somebody rings up and tells you they're in (hospital) on the poisons unit. So, it's very hard to evaluate or to recognise whether you're doing a good job or not.

The commonly expressed belief that cases are capable of 'blowing up into a total nightmare' assumes that there are aspects of work beyond the control of even the seasoned game planner. This has implications for the *accountability* of social workers. If outcomes are no easier to predict than a number on a roulette wheel, then social workers cannot be held accountable for work going wrong, or praised for work going well. Most of the social workers we spoke to were almost always able to identify substantial mitigating factors when work had not gone well:

> I suppose I feel there has been a failure – even if it wasn't necessarily mine.

Various reasons were suggested as mitigating factors, but the most commonly recurring ones were the recurrent issue of *control*, and the *circumstances and constraints of daily work*:

> I don't feel I did the piece of work as well as I might have done, but having said that, there were elements in it that were totally out of my control.

> I would count it as bad practice...(but) it wasn't my fault, there were a lot of other things involved, but I would say it was bad practice..The only grounds for that being the nature of work here gets you into that state sometimes.

The conclusion from listening to these social workers is that, although they usually identify substantial mitigating factors when a case does not go well, they also often demur when work turns out happily. However, practitioners rarely, if ever, choose to duck out of all responsibility. Indeed, they often set themselves very high standards. 'I think I sometimes beat myself with a stick' is probably true of many social workers.

We have looked at the social workers' *strategies* for good and bad practice. How do these strategies work in particular cases? What *evidence* do social workers draw upon in deciding whether their work has gone well or less well?

Evidence for Quality

Inviting social workers to evidence the quality of their work – to identify how they knew whether they were doing well or less well in specific instances – yielded a high degree of agreement among people, regardless of previous experience, expertise or agency settings. The perceived quality of their work depended, for them, on the responses they made to a range of emergent criteria which we may pose as a series of questions. These questions are outlined in Figure 17.2.

1. Does the work produce emotional rewards or penalties for the social worker?
2. Was the case or problem hitherto 'stuck' or moving?
3. Was there client 'movement'? Did the intervention win steady, incremental change?
4. Did the social worker achieve a moral balance in the case?
5. Did the social worker receive corroborating evidence from the client and especially from fellow professionals on the quality of their work?

Figure 17.2 Evidence for quality of work

Emotional rewards and penalties

It might be thought that social workers, weaned knowingly or unknowingly on the heritage of Biestek's principle of controlled emotional involvement, would at least be wary of admitting the emotional impact of the work they do, and even more so of giving it a central place in reaching decisions about how well their work was going. To the contrary. Barely any of the practitioners we spoke to failed to locate the evidence of the emotions as central to their direct practice evaluating. Even the rare sceptic admitted as much:

> There was a certain amount of gut feeling on my part to know how it was going, which I think is quite a problem when you come to evaluating. How can you separate your gut feeling from what's actually happening?

'Quite a comfort', 'excites', 'enjoy', 'flattering', 'reassuring', 'a brilliant experience for me', 'a sense of satisfaction', 'real pleasure' and 'a good feeling' are just a scattering of the phrases that came immediately to practitioners' minds when they were asked how they knew they were doing well in particular cases. The recognition that good feelings were not common only served to make them more appreciated:

> It makes a change. I mean we don't often get real pleasure in child protection work. Is it important? Yeah, a sense that something good has come out of the work that we've done, yeah I think that's important.

> Yes, on the whole it's been a very positive order for both of us. It's nice to have a client that responds because most of them don't. But this one is so keen. I think he's got a lot out of it.

> The buzz was there. People wanted to work. I was on form. The other thing it was a one-off...The buzz was there, people were involved, everybody was talking, everybody felt safe.

Work that had not gone well was equally liable to be demonstrated by reference to the evidence of the emotions.

> It's a gut reaction that I feel. My gut reaction is, 'Oh God, I'm dreading the next network meeting', and there's something wrong if I'm dreading the next network meeting.

> I'm getting absolutely nowhere with her, and so it makes me feel quite frustrated, and I think that frustration sometimes shows..I don't get any sense of satisfaction in any of the interactions I have with her. It effects me as a worker I think.

> I wasn't getting anything out of the relationship with (the client), and she wasn't getting anything out of the probation order.

The influence of the emotions on practice sometimes led to moral judgements, and to a concern that good practice could thus be put at risk:

> My frustrations show when I'm with her and that's not helpful – to her, to the kids, or to me.

Stuck or slowly moving?

Evidence of good practice was all the more persuasive if it was achieved in the context of problems which had hitherto been 'stuck', and had therefore been achieved against the odds.

> I felt it was quite important because she'd been on probation so many times and really had talked about anything and everything. Probation officers had pretty much done it all before. Weighed up against other clients…I thought of her as a success...because the task was always going to be massively more difficult to start with.

Being 'stuck', of course, was just as likely to be seen as evidence that practice was going badly:

> I've almost got stuck into that pattern of feeling exasperated with her, as she is with Social Services.

> She's ended up now having another baby and it feels like I'm on a treadmill for the second time around because similar things are happening.

Securing change matters, and client 'movement' was seen as a vital clue to the progress of a case.

> His confidence improved, he was dressing better, he'd make eye contact with you.

> I had the opportunity to return to this woman, and...I asked specifically to return...I felt that I could measure at that point that she'd taken in a lot of what I'd said the day before.

Social workers often are struggling to draw a line from what happens within the process of intervention to change in the service user's life outside of social work. In doing so, they rarely made any distinction between *outputs* – the products which may of may not have anything to do with the intervention – and direct *outcomes*.

> The relationship with the mother is much better, the bedwetting's improved, school situation's been sorted out, offending and truanting's stopped. So those were the practical things that indicated to me that things were successful, and also there's the boy and his mother's words and attitudes.

The evidence cited by the same social worker for work that had *not* gone well was virtually a mirror image of the positive outputs:

> The lad's behaviour isn't improving and the lad doesn't seem to be any happier. Things like the offending doesn't seem to have slowed. The school attendance hasn't improved

These comments by social workers indicate that signs of client 'movement', or indeed the absence of such movement, are relied on as an important source of evidence that work is going well or less well, albeit without being attributed to specific interventions on their part. However, client 'movement' must be placed in the context of these practitioners' assumptions about the nature of social work practice, which they frequently characterised as achieving progress through *small, incremental steps*. The social workers we spoke to placed great stress on the achievement of small, incremental goals and this was reflected in the evidence they cited for quality of practice. Grand goals tended to be eschewed and slow incrementalism favoured when evidencing both 'good' and 'bad' practice.

> The fact that I can successfully get her to begin to think about something which might in the end turn a few little cogs in her mind is gonna be for her a success. If there is only a little, teeny chink in the wall of justification for offending then, yeah, I would probably take a little bit of credit for that.

> I got sucked into the idea of thinking 'This is a situation that can be cured', which I think was the wrong thing to be looking at. It should have been more, 'This is a situation which can be stabilised' rather than hoping that if I could put in some sort of basic practical support it was all going to go away.

'At the end we'd reached all the goals that were set. They weren't big ones, but we'd reached all of them'. Most of these social workers were more than happy with steady, step by step change of this kind.

Doing a moral deal

A matter for concern that surfaced time and again in social workers' accounts of evidence for quality was whether their social work practice followed implicit moral rules. If a moral balance could be demonstrated, then this in itself was seen as evidence of good practice:

> He wrote to me to thank me for the report 'cos he said he knew he had to be punished but he wanted the court to see both sides of the story, and that is just what the report is for. There's two ways of looking at it.

A similar assumption lay behind the frequently expressed fear that work that did not go well had not given the client a fair deal. This fear rose to the surface several times in connection with a concern that social work services may in and of themselves make matters worse. Work that had gone well was often evidenced on the grounds that *no harm had been done* when there seemed to be initial reasons to fear a risk of harm.

> The most important thing at the end of the day is that two little boys could have been lost within a system that sometimes takes far too long. They're not lost, they are two very happy, confident, loved little boys.

Evidence that work had not gone well was often presented in terms of the damaging impact of the welfare system:

> I felt like a total mug, certainly in terms of effectiveness. Not only totally ineffective but also possibly worsened a bad situation by colluding with this man in the belief that everything was all right, and wasted a good deal of time in supposed counselling sessions.

> We weren't able as a centre to keep confidentiality. Everybody got involved so it was a real mess. When I look back there was no need to involve so many people..I can't imagine how that woman felt that everybody knew what was going on in her life. I think she felt intimidated.

Social workers were not so much concerned at this point with whether social work achieved any demonstrable impact, but with whether the process of service delivery had been achieved with integrity. In this respect, perhaps the most reflective account was given by a social worker who tellingly illustrated how personal evaluation methods can form a coherent strategy:

> I'd use an informal system of measurement to see whether I'm doing what I see as being a good job. I've thought about this quite a lot and personally I've worked back to very basic rules: whether I've made it a little bit easier to understand for people; whether I've made the pathway through to it a little bit easier and a little bit less stressful; whether I've given them sufficient information; whether I've made it a little bit less dramatic, a little bit easier to

> pick up the threads afterwards. Carrying out those responsibilities, I suppose I have to humanise it.

Thus, when describing work that had gone well, this same practitioner concluded, 'I haven't alienated this lady...I think she was able to grasp that she was an important part of this whole problem and she wasn't just someone being forgotten about'. Practising with integrity is, for these social workers, an important facet of good quality practice.

Confirmation from colleagues

Gaining corroboration that work had gone well was often mentioned. Direct feedback from clients was rarely given as evidence for the quality of work. When it did come, it was a rare red letter day. For example, a message to one social worker *via* her line manager that a member of the group she was working with 'was singing your praises all over the place.he just thinks you're wonderful' came as an unexpected 'buzz' to the practitioner. The relative absence of appeal to service user feedback, and the comparative indifference of most of the practitioners to the views of the people with whom they worked, raises issues about the probable difficulties of achieving partnership and an enabling practice which are beyond the scope of this paper. The two main reasons given by practitioners for their indifference were, first, that service users often worked to a different set of priorities when they assessed the value of the service they received, and second, that there were important instances of work when service user satisfaction was not relevant or would not make sense to agency users (Shaw, 1996).

The corroboration of fellow professionals was, however, mentioned far more frequently:

> If you get the same ideas and evaluations reflected back from other people, that tends to reassure you that your view is reasonably accurate.

> From the dialogue I have with the other professionals in the case, we all tend to agree on the same issues. We don't necessarily agree on how to resolve them but we all agree what those issues are.

There is an important caveat hidden in the second of these quotations. Corroboration may be possible on assessment of the issues, but it is seen as significantly less likely on plans and interventions – 'how to resolve issues'. This is perhaps why outside evidence from fellow professionals often seemed to be held more lightly than evidence from immediate social work colleagues, and why it could be the source of difficulties.

When work had gone less well, failures often were attributed to a breakdown of professional corroboration.

> I was asking people around me who one would think they'd know, and they didn't, or they agreed with me it wasn't so serious. It's almost like you're colluding with everyone else's ignorance, so you all agree on what probably works and you find out it's completely wrong.

Instead of appealing to the confirmation of fellow social workers, one practitioner looked more widely to the affirmative, collective experience of being a black woman:

> Black women in Britain share something in common which is an oppressive system and family pressures and community pressures. I think Black women have to get together and learn from each other. Different black women's refuges are talking to each other and saying, "Right, how would you deal with this?"

The research reported in this paper sheds light on two aspects of the micro-sociology of social workers' knowledge. *First*, what practice evaluating *strategies* do practitioners employ? These social workers' evaluating strategies were generally constructed from the possession of a 'game plan'. This consisted of an overall strategy of keeping or achieving control, accomplishing purposeful practice, and following rules of collectively acceptable practice, and was linked to a watchfulness, understanding and sense of 'timing', specific to work with each individual, family or group. This 'game plan' was contingent on two volatile and hard-to-predict factors. First, whether the service user was viewed by the practitioner as a 'good' client, and second, the untoward operation of 'sheer luck'.

Second, the data enables us to draw provisional conclusions about the *evidences* social workers draw on in deciding whether or not they are practising well. In their efforts to elicit evidence for work that went well, social workers judged their practice according to whether they could give positive responses to a range of emergent criteria. Did their work produce emotional rewards? Was the case 'moving'? Did intervention win steady, incremental change? Was practice accomplished without inflicting harm through the operations of the welfare system? Was corroborating evidence available from fellow professionals regarding the quality of their work?

Commentary: Implications for a 'Grounded' Model of Evaluation

If we are correct in believing that research of this kind is one essential ingredient of a plausible strategy for evaluating in practice, the evidence points to four considerations which must shape the development of such a strategy. They relate to practice accountability, explaining causes, the nature of social work evidence, and the interplay of knowing and feeling in social work. The development of evaluating in practice will prove fundamentally flawed if it fails to recognise these themes.

Accounts and Accountability

The research elicited recurring instances of ways in which practice regarded by social workers as having gone less than well is likely to trigger deep uncertainties in the mind of the reflective practitioner. Am I responsible? Should I take the blame? Could it have been avoided? The dilemma is unforgivingly sharp. There are two realities that need to be brought into conjunction.

First, we have illustrated a widespread sense that outcomes, both good and bad, are beyond prediction and will never cease to jump out and surprise the practitioner. Social workers – at least the ones we spoke to – are characterised by this uncertainty. Second, social workers display a hesitation about claiming credit for 'good' work or blame for 'bad' work. The two realities – predicting and accountability – are linked. In the words of one probation officer,

> I think, bearing in mind the fact that you can't predict what judges are going to do, you can't predict what magistrates are going to do, in a sense you can't take the blame for a failure. If you can't take the blame if it doesn't work, how can you take the credit if it does?

Causes and Accounts

We have seen that in their day to day work social workers do not give formal cause and effect explanations of events. They are more concerned with rules, conventions and the meaning of their work, on the one hand, and with uncertainty and approximations to knowledge on the other. A number of writers have reasoned that such

> Rule following, convention obeying, meaning giving or any other form of self monitoring is fatal to the idea that the heart of an explanation lies in the causal story (Harré and Secord, 1972: 168; cf Pithouse and Atkinson, 1988).

Rule governed behaviour is 'not to do with the inevitability of causal necessity but with the inexorability of moral necessity' (Harré, 1989: 35).

Yet although rhetoric and moral persuasion are crucial aspects of daily practice, social workers also regard themselves as working towards a knowledge of cases which will serve as a good enough grasp of identifiable personal or social problems. Their 'game plans' equip them with a sense of 'know-how'. Incomplete and maybe flawed causal understandings are an ingredient of this know-how. 'People do have strong intuitions concerning the presence or absence of causes in particular instances' and it is probable that 'systematic rules and strategies' exist 'for assessing cause in…everyday inference' (Einhorn and

Hogarth, 1986: 3). Although it inevitably has fuzzy boundaries, the concept of cause is a viable one if only because we continue to function well enough in terms of it. While social workers may not appeal to causes in a formal sense, they are centrally concerned with giving explanations and reasons.

Social worker accounts of work that is going well or not are simultaneously attempts to explain a problem, and a professional safety net. A causal account may secure colleague and management approval for limited achievement in the past and in the future (cf Bull and Shaw, 1992). Social workers offer both *retrospective* and *prospective* rationalities for limited and imprecise effects from social work intervention, and for an incremental style of work described by one of our respondents as 'chipping away' (cf Pithouse and Atkinson, 1988).

Complex and ambiguous evidence

We noted the conviction of social workers that the evidence facing them in day to day practice will always prove more or less ambiguous and complex, and open to competing interpretations.

> I personally don't feel a hundred per cent certain about anything I do. I think it's so difficult when you're working with individuals.

One practitioner employed an apt simile to suggest

> It's like snap photographs – one individual photograph isn't going to tell you very much. Over a period of time, that's how we see things, but that's not easy.

Evidence believed to be complex or ambiguous is less likely to fit comfortably with the quasi-experimental logic underlying evaluation models advocated by mainstream proponents of empirical practice.

Knowing and feeling

The endemic uncertainties of these social workers are not unreasonable. Luck, cloudy accountability, complex evidence and inherently uncertain outcomes all combine to suggest that practitioners are unlikely to feel assured about the value and impact of their work. Yet paradoxically these social workers often appeared confident they knew what they were doing. They worked from an assumed knowledge, a tacit understanding based on having a 'game plan', knowing your targets, and a reliance on proven 'gut feeling'. It is echoed in the remarks of a prison psychiatrist in a study of social workers dealing with child sexual abusers. 'It's a sort of intangible thing. It's a feeling you get that somebody's being genuine; sometimes it rings true and sometimes it doesn't' (Waterhouse, Dobash and Carnie, 1995: 161). A social worker in that same study said of sexual abuse perpetrators, 'You begin to get an instinct for them, when he's being honest and when he isn't' (p. 171).

The social workers we spoke to called heavily on their own emotional reactions to practice, alongside their 'gut feeling'. Social work is an occupation that entails emotional labour. Social workers run with a tension between a training and agency culture which cultivates a 'managed heart' (the phrase is Hochschild's (1983)), and an enriching utilisation of the evidence of their emotions as they evaluate their day to day work. They would probably agree with Erikson that the clinician's own feelings and opinions are an essential ingredient of clinical inference.

> The evidence is not 'all in' if he does not succeed in using his own emotional responses during a clinical encounter as an evidential source and as a guide to intervention (Erikson, 1959: 93)

Conclusion: Evaluating in Practice

Qualitative inquiry of the kind aspired to in this paper, marked by a sustained willingness to begin with respondent categories, and a fuller acceptance of the frequent proximity of scientific and 'lay' knowledge, poses questions for the empirical practice movement in social work. The empirical practice movement is buoyant on both sides of the Atlantic (eg Reid, 1994; Blythe, Tripodi and Briar, 1995; McGuire, 1995; Thyer, 1995). Its most enthusiastic protagonists are persuaded that a sea-change is afoot, leading to a fundamental shift in the practice, research basis and, in consequence, the status of social work (eg Fischer, 1993; Cook, Cooper and Cordray, 1992; Macdonald, 1994). It is believed that empirically-evaluated practice, based on largely behavioural and cognitive strategies, promises a social work that demonstrably works. Insofar as social work has yet to achieve this new stature, the responsibility is laid firmly at the door of practitioners, employers, social work educators, and 'intellectual Luddites' who advocate alternative evaluation strategies based on qualitative sociology (Sheldon and Macdonald, 1989-1990; Thyer, 1995).

There are straws in the wind, however, to suggest that such optimism is not delivering the goods. Some earlier proponents of empirical practice have backpeddled on the claim that the evaluation of empirical practice can identify effective interventions (Thomas, 1978; Kagle, 1982; Kazdin, 1982), with the consequence that the empirical practice movement has 'emerged as a complex combination of a practice model and a research agenda' (Reid, 1994: 169). Anxieties have been voiced about the possible costs of rigour at the expense of risk and enterprise (cf Reid, 1988). Practice and practitioners remain stubbornly resistant to the enticements of single-system designs (eg Robinson *et al*, 1988). A few researchers working in this tradition have acknowledged the possibility that the 'clinical mind sets' of practitioners need to be given greater centrality if we are to understand and develop practitioner involvement in evaluation (eg Penka and Kirk, 1991). Concerns have been expressed by senior figures within social work regarding quantitative formulations of effectiveness, narrow behavioural definitions of problems, and an overemphasis on client change outcomes as 'a new means test' within this tradition (eg Meyer, 1984: 323). Furthermore, the growth of a public sector performance culture in America and Europe during the 1980's led to fears that the empirical practice movement may be unduly influenced by 'management-by-effectiveness' approaches and the politics of quality (Lewis, 1988; Grasso and Epstein, 1988; Shaw, 1995 and 1996).

We have stressed that practitioners' existing evaluating practices as described in this paper are *not* offered as a blueprint for evaluating in practice. They do, however, provide the starting point from which social workers can 'think big and do small' (Meyer, 1992: 299), and develop an evaluating in practice that is neither decontextualised nor dominated by academics (Reid, 1994: 167, 181). Evaluating by practitioners cannot be dismissed as 'the confused impressions of the mob' (Durkheim), but must start from the tacit knowledge of social workers. Evaluating in practice is an activity in which the sources of understanding and action are not automatically picked off the surface, but in which they are tacit. Skilful action 'often reveals a knowing more than we can say' (Schon, 1983: 51). This 'thinking as usual' (the phrase is from Alfred Schutz) involves making innumerable judgements of quality for which we cannot state adequate criteria, and skills for which we cannot state the rules and procedures. It involves 'the largely unarticulated, contextual understanding that is often manifested in nods, silences, humour and naughty nuances' (Altheide and Johnson, 1994: 492). Practitioners carry out these actions spontaneously, so that one probation officer could say to us, 'It's making me think very hard, you know, about things that you just don't think about on a day-to-day basis'.

The choice of how we evaluate our own practice is more than a technical debate about different methods of gaining evidence. It is, in Karl Popper's term, a choice between metaphysical programmes (Popper, 1992: 148-151) which, while they are not falsifiable, can and should be rationally criticised and argued for. Our own position is that research evidence of the kind reported in this paper stimulates the emergence of an evaluating in practice shaped by a translation and creative colonising of the methodology and methods of qualitative sociology. We have not choosen to plead for a qualitative evaluation of social work, invaluable as that will prove, but for a qualitative social work, in which evaluation carried out for and with the service user is a dimension of direct practice (Shaw, 1996). Such evaluating offers at one and the same time both a fundamental part of practice and the possibility of its radical critique.

References

Altheide, D. and Johnson, J. (1994) 'Criteria for Assessing Interpretive Validity in Qualitative Research' in Denzin, N. and Lincoln, Y. (eds.) *Handbook of Qualitative Research*, Thousand Oaks: Sage.

Atkinson, P. (1995) *Medical Talk and Medical Work*, Thousand Oaks: Sage.

Blythe, B., Tripodi, T. and Briar, S. (1995) *Direct Practice Research in Human Service Agencies*, New York: Columbia University Press.

Bull, R. and Shaw, I. (1992) 'Constructing Causal Accounts in Social Work' in *Sociology*, Vol. 26, No. 4.

Cook, T., Cooper, H. and Cordray, D. (eds) (1992) *Meta-Analysis for Explanation*, New York: Russell Sage.

Elks, M. and Kirkhart, K. (1993) 'Evaluating Effectiveness from the Practitioner's Perspective' in *Social Work*, Vol. 38, No. 5.

Einhorn, H. and Hogarth, R. (1986) 'Judging Probable Cause' in *Psychological Bulletin*, Vol. 99, No. 1.

Erikson, E. (1959) 'The Nature of Clinical Inference' in Lerner, D. (ed) *Evidence and Inference*, New York: Free Press.

Everitt, A., Hardiker, P., Littlewood, J. and Mullender, A. (1992) *Applied Research for Better Practice*, London: Macmillan.

Fischer, J. (1993) 'Empirically Based Practice: The End of Ideology?' in Bloom, M., (ed) *Single-System designs in the Social Services: Issues and Options for the 1990s*, New York: Haworth.

Grasso, A. and Epstein, I. (1988) 'Management by Measurement: Organisational Dilemmas and Opportunities' in Patti, R., Poertner, J. and Rapp, C., (eds) *Managing for Effectiveness in Social Welfare Organisations*, New York: Haworth.

Harré, R. (1989) 'Language Games and Texts of Identity' in Shotter, J. and Gergen, K. (eds) *Texts of Identity*, Newbury Park, CA: Sage.

Harré, R. and Secord, P. (1972) *The Explanation of Social Behaviour*, Oxford: Blackwell.

Hochschild, A. (1983) *The Managed Heart – Commercialisation of Human Feeling*, Berkeley: University of California Press.

Humphrey, C. and Pease, K. (1992) 'Effectiveness Measurement in the Probation Service: a View from the Troops' in *Howard Journal*, Vol. 31, No. 2.

Kagle, J. (1982) 'Using Single-Subject Measures in Practice Decisions: Systematic Documentation of Distortion?' in *Arete*, Vol. 7, No. 1.

Kazdin, A. (1982) *Single Case Research Designs*, Oxford: Oxford University Press.

Lewis, H. (1988) 'Ethics and the Managing of Service Effectiveness in Social Welfare' in Patti, R, Poertner, J. and Rapp, C. (eds) *Managing for Service Effectiveness in Social Welfare Organisations*, New York: Haworth.

Macdonald, G. (1994) 'Developing Empirically-Based Practice in Probation' in *British Journal of Social Work*, Vol. 24, No. 4.

McCracken, G. (1988) *The Long Interview*, Newbury Park: Sage.

McGuire, J. (ed) (1995) *What Works? – Reducing Reoffending*, Chichester: Wiley.

Meyer, C. (1984) 'Integrating Research and Practice' in *Social Work*, Vol. 29, No. 4.

Meyer, C. (1992) 'Social Work Assessment: Is There an Empirical Base?' in *Research on Social Work Practice*, Vol. 2, No. 3.

Penka, C. and Kirk, S. (1991) 'Practitioner Involvement in Clinical Evaluation' in *Social Work*, Vol. 36, No. 6.

Pithouse, A. and Atkinson, P. (1988) 'Telling the Case: Occupational Narrative in a Social Work Office' in Coupland, N. (ed) *Styles of Discourse*, London: Croom Helm.

Popper, K. (1992) *Unended Quest*, London: Routledge.

Reid, W. (1988) 'Service Effectiveness and the Social Agency' in Patti, R., Poertner, J. and Rapp, C., (eds) *Managing for Effectiveness in Social Welfare Organisations*, New York: Haworth.

Reid, W. (1994) 'The Empirical Practice Movement' in *Social Service Review*, Vol. 68, No. 2.

Robinson, E., Benson, D. and Blythe, B. (1988) 'An Analysis of the Implementation of Single-Case Evaluation by Practitioners' in *Social Service Review*, Vol. 62, No. 2.

Schon, D. (1983) *The Reflective Practitioner*, New York: Basic Books.

Shaw, I. (1995) 'The Quality of Mercy: the Management of Quality in the Personal Social Services', in Kirkpatrick, I. and Lucio, M. *The Politics of Quality in the Public Sector*, London: Routledge.

Shaw, I. (1996) *Evaluating in Practice*, Aldershot: Ashgate.

Shaw, I. and Shaw, A. (1997) 'Keeping Social Work Honest: Evaluating as Profession and Practice' in *British Journal of Social Work*, Vol. 27, No. 6.

Sheldon, B. and Macdonald, G. (1989-90) 'Implications for Practice of Recent Social Work Effectiveness Research' in *Practice*, Vol. 6, No. 3.

Thomas, E. (1978) 'Research and Service in Single-Case Experimentation: Conflicts and Choices' in *Social Work Research and Abstracts*, Vol. 14, No. 4.

Thyer, B. (1995) 'Promoting an Empiricist Agenda within the Human Services: An Ethical and Humanistic Imperative' in *Journal of Behaviour Therapy and Experimental Psychiatry*, Vol. 26, No. 2.

Waterhouse, L., Dobash, R. and Carnie, J. (1995) *Child Sexual Abusers*, Edinburgh: Central Research Unit, Scottish Office.

Williams, R. (1976) *Keywords: a Vocabulary of Culture and Society*, London: Fontana.

Chapter 18

Practitioner Evaluation at Work*

Evaluations can contribute to democratic governance, to social betterment, to organizational learning, and more. But how do we know which types of evaluation are more likely to make what kinds of contributions? The idea that it would be helpful to increase the evidence base about evaluation practices and their consequences is not new (e.g. Shaw, Greene, and Mark, 2006). With such empirical data, the evaluation community could construct a "descriptive theory" of evaluation, or an empirically based assessment of what evaluations look like under different conditions and with what consequences. Viewed from this perspective, a growing evidence base about practitioner evaluation could help answer questions about which approaches to evaluation, implemented how, and under what conditions, lead to what kind of improvements in professional practice.

Practitioner involvement in evaluation, research, development, and other forms of disciplined inquiry that are small scale, local, grounded, and carried out by professionals who directly deliver those selfsame services is embraced across a wide range of professions as an essential ingredient of good professional practice. Whether the practice is teaching, nursing, primary health care, public and sustainable health, occupational therapy, pharmacy, counseling, psychotherapy, applied psychology, the penal services, medicine, or the social services, the desirability of practitioner evaluation is for the most part unquestioned. However, the degree of institutionalization of the activity in different public service occupations and organizational cultures appears to vary widely.

Despite this almost normalized acceptance of practitioner evaluation, scarcely anything is known about its character, homogeneity or diversity, outcomes, motives, and forms of practice. This article explores the character and practice of doing practitioner evaluation in one profession, social work, but is written with an eye toward plausible connections with other professions and occupations. Other professions can be treated as similar to the extent that they function in similar organizational contexts with similar constraints. Professionals delivering human services, typically with individual responsibility for managing a set of "cases" (but without the clearly defined technology of, for example, medicine), and supervised in bureaucratic hierarchies, represent

* Originally published as Shaw, I. and Faulkner, A. (2006) 'Practitioner Evaluation at Work' *American Journal of Evaluation* 27(1): 44-63. Reprinted with permission of Sage Publications Ltd.

the contexts to which these findings and arguments might apply. Social work in the United Kingdom has many differences of context and setting but here can be assumed to be similar in important respects to social work in the United States. Our participants were mainly employed in local government, public-sector social services departments rather than private, faith-based, or not-for-profit voluntary agencies.

We do not assume that we know the exact nature of practitioner evaluation. Our research treats this as emergent rather than precast. However, a preliminary set of operational criteria distinguishing practitioner evaluation suggests that it is marked by

- the direct collection and analysis of data;
- professionals setting its aims and outcomes;
- intended practical benefits for professionals, service organizations, and/or service users, usually expected to be immediate and "instrumental";
- practitioners conducting a substantial proportion of the inquiry ("insider" evaluation);
- a focus on the professionals' own practice and/or that of their immediate peers (it is self-evaluation, in which the "self" is the immediate community of colleagues);
- a small scale and a short term;
- a usually self-contained nature, in which the evaluation is not part of a larger evaluation program;
- not usually being part of externally required accountability or quality assurance activities;
- data collection and management that are typically carried out as lone activities; and
- a subject focus that is typically evaluative, though sometimes descriptive, developmental, or analytical.

We unpack and elaborate these characteristics as we present data from a research project, but they serve for our purpose. In a North American context, practitioner evaluation falls somewhere between the empowerment evaluation strand associated with David Fetterman and the literature on reflective practice associated with writers such as Schön, Reason, and Heron. This bridging of empowerment and reflection can be seen more widely in recent accounts of the territory occupied by action research (e.g., Reason and Bradbury, 2000).

Why is research on practitioner evaluation in social work of importance and interest to the evaluation community? It is so for a number of interconnected reasons. First, it represents an area of hidden and invisible evaluation and research practice. If, by analogy, we cannot understand the significance of education or caring unless we take into account informal learning, teaching, and caring, so we cannot understand the social mesh of more formal evaluation apart from its more informal, less visible counterparts. Second, social work as a profession has been relatively slightly engaged with the evaluation community, and a fuller exchange between the social work and evaluation communities is overdue. Third, there has been a tendency to treat the binary divides between formal and informal and insider and outsider evaluation as rather self- evident. It is our intention to problematize these relationships. Fourth, and connected to the previous, the kinds of knowledge drawn on by evaluators and professionals are typically treated as rather similar. Hence, when professionals are urged to apply evaluation-generated knowledge to their practice, any failure to do so tends to be treated as a failure of practice nerve rather than a failure of evaluation. By taking the process of doing practitioner evaluation more seriously and inspecting it closely, we may question how helpful it is to conceive of all forms of evaluation as representing science-based methods of generating knowledge and recognize the struggles for understanding, interpretation, application, and critique that mark practitioner evaluators' projects (cf. Fahl and Markand, 1999; Polkinghorne, 2000; Schwandt, 1999; Shaw, 2005). Fifth, there is an ongoing challenge to make evaluation useful to practitioners. We draw out in our conclusion the implications for the evaluation community as we see them. Sixth, to reiterate our opening paragraph, the evaluation community will be enriched through reflective research about evaluation as practiced. Research on evaluation will not replace all judgments about wise evaluation practice but instead can significantly aid judgment. Research on evaluation, like evaluation itself, will raise questions about generalizability, contextuality, and applicability to specific situations.

Society's modes of producing knowledge and interrogating itself are changing in the emerging "knowledge economy," and at the same time, public service communities look to research and evaluation knowledge for legitimation. The watchwords of the new knowledge-related practices include *evidence-based practice*, *best practice*, *science-based practice*, *knowledge diffusion and management*, *getting research into practice*, and *collaboration*. Research is becoming increasingly problem oriented and more socially open (Nowotny, Scott, and Gibbons, 2001). A consequence of this is an increasing diversification of "research-active" actors and agencies. Thus, Callon (n.d.) distinguished between the "confined research" of professional, dedicated research institutions and "research in the wild" that emerges as concerned social groups, such as patient advocacy groups, begin to engage in knowledge practices that reach the public arena. Indeed, Callon suggested that the major distinction is not between those who do and do not have access to research practice but between different modes of organizing and practicing research. This article considers a third mode of the social organization of research: that conducted by public service practitioners about public services. Such reflexive inquiry has been termed practitioner evaluation. It is interesting to compare our opening list of criteria with Callon's characterization of research in the wild: direct concern with the outcomes of research, researchers as both its subjects and objects, overlap between the production and appropriation of knowledge, personal stakes and incentives, and a research process that is one of identity formation.

Criticisms have been leveled (e.g., Shaw and Gould, 2001, pp. 158-164), however, on the grounds that practitioner evaluation

- has tended to treat the nature of evidence too naively;
- is characterized by an absence of cross-professional development and hence is isolated;
- has a passive "beneficiary" relationship with social service agencies and hence a restricted notion of usefulness, a too unquestioning insider standpoint;
- has a similar beneficiary relationship with the evaluation profession;
- manifests a severely limited engagement with service users that in turn encourages the unspoken assumption that practitioner expertise need not be challenged by the understandings of service users;
- has typically ignored ways in which styles of inquiry can perform as models for how practice itself should take place; and
- has a too conventional writing "voice."

The agenda of evaluation in public services has been castigated on the grounds that "researchers have had scant interest in studying the intertwining, personalistic, and crisis-like problems of daily practice" (Stake and Trumbull, 1982, p. 4). They prefer to "fiddle with models" and focus on change efforts, and in consequence, their evaluations have "not presented practitioners with the vicarious experiencings which could alter conviction and practice" (p. 11). The growth of interest in, for example, clinical expertise (Taylor and White, 2000; White and Stancombe, 2003) and the sociology of practical knowledge (e.g., Collins, 2000, 2001; Schwab, 1969) has softened the basis for the criticisms that Stake and Turnbull (1982) put forward over two decades ago, but their allegation still sticks to much practitioner evaluation. Pressures for accountability and an emphasis on outcomes do support evaluation in this environment but not a form of evaluation perhaps best suited to inform daily practice.

Inquiry Methods

This article presents an empirically based characterization of key dimensions of social work practitioner evaluation. The first stage involved a survey to map and analyze practitioner evaluation in social work in a defined geographical area of southeastern Wales that took place over

3 years beginning January 1, 1999. The aim was to identify as wide a range as possible of different models of practitioner evaluation across a range of types of social work practice, such as family work, child protection, disability assessment, and substance abuse, including administrative, service delivery, and client issues.

Table 18.1 Classification of studies (N = 42)

	Practitioner Owned		Agency Owned	
	Formal Approval	**No Formal Approval**	**Formal Approval**	**No Formal Approval**
University degree link				
Single data type	7	9	0	0
Multiple data types	3	4	2	0
No University degree link				
No Single data type	0	1	0	7
Multiple data types	0	0	6	3

We did not aim for a complete census of activity. We obtained information on practitioners and projects from a variety of sources, including directors of social service departments,[1] social work research centers, public lists of publications and reports, and university student project lists. We identified 42 projects and the associated (lead) practitioners and are satisfied that this represented a substantial proportion and broad cross-section of the relevant practitioner projects. A short, telephone-administered screening questionnaire was then used to conduct a preliminary audit of project characteristics, including their design, methods, ownership, accountability, and purposes.

From this data set, we developed a classificatory instrument that would differentiate the projects and provide a basis to initiate theorizing. The four classification criteria were whether participants regarded a project as practitioner owned or agency owned, whether the data collection relied on a single data type or multiple data types, whether the work was associated with a university qualification, and whether a formal approval process had been undertaken. The analytic categories stemmed initially from our shared sense of the possible problematics of practitioner evaluation. We developed a provisional typology of cases. The classification of the different types of practitioner involvement was used as the basis for the second stage of the project, a theoretical sample of eight case studies designed to provide more detailed examples of the main patterns of variation in evaluation project characteristics.

The questions we explored through the case studies included the following: Why do professionals become involved in evaluation? To what extent is it solitary or collaborative? What kinds of questions and problems are addressed? What inquiry methods are used? Does practitioner evaluation have close or more distant links to wider research priorities? Does practitioner evaluation foster or

1 Social service departments have been the main public-sector employers of social workers.

hinder professional identity? What relationship do active evaluating professionals have to their employing organizations, and do they see it as career development? What assumptions do professionals hold about the kinds of uses of evaluation? What conditions have to be met if the results of practitioner evaluation are to be generalized to other professionals, practices, and settings? How does practitioner evaluation relate to research that aims to promote citizen involvement? How does it relate to "academic" research projects and university researchers? What ethical questions are raised in practitioner involvement in evaluation?

The classification suggests a considerable diversity and some revealing patterns among practitioner evaluation projects. Notably, all but 1 individual-owned project were being conducted as part of the requirements for university degrees, while only two of 18 agency-owned projects were so linked (Table 18.1). However, we are using Table 18.1 primarily to show how we arrived at our case studies. The results of the first phase of the study are discussed in their own right elsewhere (Shaw, 2005). The cases sampled on the basis of this framework are encapsulated in Table 18.2.

Almost all of the project topics had some kind of evaluative purpose, and all were oriented to reaching judgments of worth or merit. The characteristic project activity was clearly evaluation. However, practitioners typically referred to their work as "research." We have made no effort to "doctor" their language, originating, as it probably did, from the tendency in U.K. social work to use the term *research* in a wider sense to describe all forms of disciplined inquiry. This makes for some degree of unavoidable alternating between the terms *evaluation* and *research* throughout the article as the practitioners' voices are heard. Each case study involved a week's fieldwork and included a preliminary report. They were made up of interviews with project participants and other relevant local colleagues and access to some project documentation. Interviews were recorded and transcribed, and the thematic analysis of qualitative data was initiated from an inductive identification of themes and patterns, pursuing a general logic of the elaboration of fresh themes and the falsification of prima facie ideas. In a lightly deliberative (House and Howe, 1999) and self-consciously reflexive project of this kind—"research into research," as one person expressed it to us—the "coding" is as much indigenous (Holstein and Gubrium, 1995) as external and takes place and unfolds as an integral part of the interview process, not just beforehand or afterward.

The holistic character of the practitioner evaluation experience serves as a caution against undertaking heavy thematic analysis. Recognizing this, in the analysis below, our intentionally "wide-angle" managing of the themes commences by looking primarily toward the evaluator: the doing of practitioner evaluation in its most immediate sense. We then explore the contextualization of practitioner evaluation within its most immediate sense. We then explore the contextualization of practitioner evaluation within its practice, agency, and professional cultures. The third focus is again outward but this time through the lens of shifting practice and research borderlines. We conclude the article with

Table 18.2 Case study sample: Descriptive summary

(Lead) Practitioner	Project Field	Inquiry Topic as Expressed by Social Workers	Practitioner or Agency Owned	Single or Multiple Data Type	Linked or Not to a Univesity Qualification	Formal Approval or Not
Sarah	Challenging behavior	Evaluation of the effects of physically and verbally aggressive challenging behavior on care staff members working with people with learning difficulties	Practitioner	Single	Linked	No formal approval
Helen	Care management	How are social workers reacting to care management?	Practitioner	Single	Linked	Formal approval
Jane	Community reenablement	Community reenablement scheme comparing the service benefits of a traditional day hospital and a day center	Agency	Multiple	Not linked	No formal
Rhian	Community profile	Community and demographic study of two housing estates	Agency	Single	Not linked	No formal
Hazel	Neglect in child care	Looking at the common understanding of what is "neglect"	Agency	Multiple	Not linked	Formal approval
Bethan	Child protection	Evaluation of the extent and results of parental participation in child protection case conferences	Practitioner	Multiple	Linked	Formal approval
Deborah	Self-help	Looking at the two worlds of self-help and social work and how they interact	Practitioner	Multiple	Linked	No formal
Catherine	Family therapy	Evaluation of the usefulness of systemic family therapy	Practitioner	Multiple	Linked	Formal approval

some tentative weaving and stitching of the first and second-order concepts and inferences.

Doing Practitioner Evaluation

Our account of doing practitioner evaluation in social work in the United Kingdom addresses its solitary or collaborative character, insider and outsider ascriptions and achievements, reflective moments regarding competence and capacity, and glimmers of fascination with the work.

Networks, Support, and the "Solitary" Evaluator

> In our provisional criteria for characterizing practitioner evaluation, we described it as typically an activity in which data collection and management are carried out as lone activities. The case studies uniformly questioned this simplistic view. Sarah might have classified her evaluation as a solitary project. She was a lone evaluator whose project did not have stakeholder ownership from anyone else, and there were no external expectations about its impact, apart from the university context. Yet the issue felt far less straightforward to her:

It was solitary. But it had to be collaborative in terms of I had to get other people's co-operation with that, to interview support workers and to have their kind of agreement because it is quite a sensitive topic to a certain extent...So it was collaborative in that sense in that I explained to them how much they were part of it and how I would feed back information to them.

This suggests that the most simple of projects needs to be viewed systemically if its dynamics are to be grasped. The role of the support workers in this case was as evaluation collaborators, with more power than the conventional image of the evaluator-respondent relationship suggests.

Interested parties to the projects were often mentioned. Friends, fellow students, university tutors,[2] and other practitioners all cropped up in roles as varied as mentors, supporters, sounding boards, shapers, and advisors. The significance of the shaping roles of key advisers is difficult to be precise about. Although it may be assumed that networks and collaboration are more visible and planned in agency-owned projects, the distinctions are probably far more diffuse in practice. Rhian led a public housing agency-initiated community profile that was well regarded by the agency. Yet she viewed the project as a solitary activity: "The Housing Officer came out with me once or twice and a Tenant Participation Officer came out with me once. But no, it was pretty much single-handed."

2 Tutor is here and subsequently used in the sense of "academic research advisor" or "major professor."

Practitioners did not experience solitariness as a totally negative factor. Hazel, for example, who led a multiagency project, viewed the research as partly hers and partly the working agency's, but she was the driving force: "I drove it. Very clearly I drove it."

The role of support and networks is important, though it is not easy to draw simple conclusions or to identify the factors that are associated with supportive projects. It appears clear that projects that are deemed successful are often those that enjoy a variety of congruent roles that include both support and shaping influences. Yet for some, the individualism of the evaluation "project" (in its broader sense of "mission") is what drives the evaluator, and it is possible that the evaluation role attracts some practitioners who are by nature solitary workers. The descriptors solitary and collaborative are complex and may not even be alternatives.

Inside or Outside?

The changing role of a practitioner when carrying out evaluation emerged as an important theme. One of the difficulties associated with being an evaluator is the reliance on informants (insiders), and therefore, there is no definite boundary between inside and outside. Sue White (2001) referred in this sense to "the necessity for translation back and forth of 'experience-near' and 'experience-distant' concepts" (p. 104).

Some practitioners emphasized the positive benefits of being an insider. Bethan exploited her "insider role" to gain data from other agencies involved in case conferences, using her position as a chair of child protection conferences. Deborah experienced her position as less straightforward. She had dual roles in the early stages of the evaluation. As a social worker, she was an insider talking to senior social work practitioners about the approach to the research, but she was an "outsider" in Alcoholics Anonymous. Hazel regarded herself as on the margins of her team and antisocial. Her outsider status was enhanced by her temporary relocation out of the team to undertake the project. Yet paradoxically, she saw herself as an insider on the (possibly contestable) grounds that

> I think people said things to me during the interviews that they wouldn't have said to an outside researcher. At least I hope they wouldn't. Because I was horrified at some of the things that were said to me about practice.

This is a rather unusual, and perhaps not persuasive, claim that social workers would be more likely to say something like this to an insider than to an outsider. The senior manager in this project appeared to hint that to do a multiagency project outside of practice might be seen as almost disloyal. When she went back to the team, her mentor concluded that she may not have been welcomed back wholeheartedly.

One of the more reflective accounts of moving away from being solely an insider came in Catherine's relation of the way her evaluation work had altered her relationship with her professional peers. She had moved from inside to outside:

> Well you enter into a very different relationship with your peers when you start saying, "Well do you do drawing with children or not? So why is it that you don't do drawing with children?" Which carries the possible statement "Shouldn't you?" even if it is not meant to. Curiosity can become quite threatening I think in peers.

This raises fundamental questions. The unspoken threat in accountability-oriented evaluation can be all too real: "The very proposal to evaluate has political impact. To ask about the virtue of Caesars wife is to suggest that she is not above suspicion" (Cronbach et al., 1980, pp. 163-164).

Reflective Moments

A significant theme, which pervaded all the case studies, was the practitioners' self-assessments of their capabilities. The predominant emphasis was not on evaluation skills but on personal and interpersonal qualities. Sarah, in the challenging behavior study, listed determination, inquisitiveness, being articulate, and having a creative outlook among the skills required. Rhian highlighted confidentiality, the way of approaching service users, politeness, patience and "being clear about who I was and what we were doing." Catherine stressed "being doggedly determined," having "a good analytical mind," and taking account of other peoples' viewpoints. She added that "the research in many ways mirrored my professional training course and then when I came to do interviews broadly speaking people skills. And the most difficult research was researching peers. But I knew it would be."

Seen together, these comments raise several interesting questions. There has been serious discussion in the social work literature as to whether the skills required of an evaluator are similar to or different from those required of a practitioner. Hazel, in a passing aside that nobody else in her working agency had "the capacity or the ability to undertake practitioner research," would presumably have felt that the two kinds of work required rather different qualities and skills, whereas Catherine, in her observation that "the research in many ways mirrored my professional training course," seemed to find important resonance and echoes of inquiry skills in her learning of social work skills. Other practitioners may be identifying more generic values and skills that make up a good researcher, whereas others refer to qualities associated with a high level of general intelligence, such as having a good analytical mind. These varying constructions of "research" highlight our earlier emphasis on alternative forms of knowledge in evaluation and in professional practice.

The Glimmer of Methodological Excitement

A stereotypical image of practitioner evaluators' decisions and choices about their methodology would probably be one of a fairly conventional, pragmatic, "necessary evil" approach. Indeed, some accounts given to us support this and were fairly conventional. However, it would be misleading if we dismissed practitioner evaluation methodology as low-level, pragmatic muddling along. Practitioner evaluators may tend to take somewhat ambivalent positions in relation to evaluation methodology. Sarah illustrated this extensively. She laughed as she commented that

> There are all these different arguments for different methods and—you know—different types of like evaluation and all that kind of thing. I do find that quite challenging to my mind and I don't know whether it is because I don't find it as interesting as the actual sort of results of the piece of research. I must admit when I am reading a journal article the bit I am less interested is probably the research method and I am probably not alone in that.

This approach can lead to a dependence on the advice of others that may make the methodological coherence and strength of project methodology somewhat fragile. Methodological modesty and ambivalence were, however, sometimes linked to elements of growing awareness. This could be seen in Bethan's relatively sophisticated study of parental participation in child protection case conferences. The key decisions were made at the beginning, but she subsequently reflected, "I think I probably started too widely as perhaps a naïve practitioner and then took much data on board—all of which to me was very interesting and which I would have liked to pursue."

Learning on the job raises a range of important questions, even for those who undergo basic postgraduate training in evaluation methods. For instance, it makes it more likely that practitioners will be open, for good and ill, to the advice of other project stakeholders. An unusual but striking example came in Deborah's self-help study, which involved multiple types of data, including both participant observation and semi-structured interviews. She listened to advice from within Alcoholics Anonymous and was able to adapt by using a participant observational method:

> They were basically telling me they thought it would be far more useful to carry on coming to the groups and seeing how it happened. I don't know, I suppose it's probably just the way I viewed research or whatever, I thought that this was basically a good way to go. But talking to the people who I was observing if you like, they didn't, they thought a different method would be better so I went with that.

This is a strong, even remarkable, example of the potential for methodological adaptability in practitioner evaluation, one that was shaped entirely by the voluntary group beneficiaries. Although this project included no formal involvement of service users in the management of the project, it was probably the strongest example of the potential of such collaboration in our study.

An equally positive, if more conventional, example of methodological choices and development was afforded by the family therapy project. Catherine explained that

> I grew as I was doing it so, at first it was how do I get my head around this to meet these criteria of the course requirements. But as I did it, it made more and more sense and whilst I wouldn't have wanted to do a piece of research into research, which is what you are doing, I can see why people would get excited about that. I can see what the glimmer of excitement was.

The fragile potential of practitioner engagement with methodology raises the question of how key parties to practitioner evaluation "sort" evaluation problems that are doable and those that are not. How do they facilitate the elusive chemistry of feasible but imaginative and creative work that holds the mind and enthusiasm of the evaluator through the long months of keeping it alive and thriving? Most practitioner evaluation probably depends for its health and well-being on passion about the evaluation problem and its solution.

To summarize this part of our analysis, we have presented data that suggest that the practitioner's self-identification as an individual with an "evaluator" role with particular motivations is important to the performance of these forms of inquiry in social work practice, regardless of whether a project is actually "owned" individually or corporately. Like professional evaluators, the practitioners in our sample were sensitive to the professional and methodological issues around access to and rapport with evaluation "subjects," in this instance often their own colleagues, as manifest in their experience of the transformations and tensions in their insider and outsider roles. Interestingly, in some cases, their commitment to evaluation designs within a project is characterized by flexibility and ambivalence, which suggests a fragility of expertise on one hand but on the other hand suggests the openness to intra-project methodological innovation characteristic of participatory action research.

Colleagues, Contexts, and Professionals

The identity and individual aspects of social work practitioner evaluation, explored above, attains much of its immediacy through its adjacency to individuals and structures that share in the practitioner evaluator's occupational and practice world. We explore this contextualization of practice, agency, and professional cultures in this section. This includes handling the ethical dimensions of projects, the assumptions and claims regarding the "property rights" of the research, the extent to which conversations regarding practitioner evaluation cross professional or occupational domains, and the actual or hoped-for value of the evaluation in terms of its possible use.

Practitioner Evaluation Ethics

In our case studies, four had obtained formal organizational approval for the projects and four had not. Formal approval may be related more to the topic and client group involved rather than the type of ownership. Our data show a lack of standardization of approach to ethical approval for evaluation in U.K. social work practice, which would contrast strongly with procedures in, for example, health care research. We found a lack of certainty stemming in part from a lack of shared understanding as to what "ethics decisions" might entail. For example, in the challenging behavior project, Sarah had a strong sense of ethical obligation: "You don't have to ask for their consent but they are being spoken about. I guess ... myself if someone was talking about me in a piece of research I would be quite uneasy."

Jane, in the community reenablement project, did not have to apply to the ethics committee for ethical approval: "I took some advice in the Trust [i.e., hospital organization] with regard to whether it's research or evaluation. Because it's evaluation I didn't have to request the Ethics Committee. They weren't interested." Although it is very difficult to understand the process being described here, even within the U.K. context, it shares with a number of others how a practitioner evaluator recalls advice given, in which perceived expert advice is treated as constraining. This suggests the need to understand how practitioners construct and explicate the nature of ethical issues in research and the possibility that practitioner evaluation decisions take place in a subordinate power relationship.

Ongoing decisions about ethics and consent were also apparent in the self-help study. Deborah decided not to seek access to "closed" meetings: "You know I suppose in a sense it would have been totally unethical to go to a closed meeting because that is not for anybody other than members of the group." The example illustrates a possible risk that practitioners may be too easily discouraged from seeking ethical approval because of a lack of experience in weighing the seriousness of ethical obstacles. Ethical concerns may then inappropriately override reasonable evaluation strategies, thus posing a question raised more widely since the turn of the century (e.g., Adler and Adler, 2003; Hammersley, 2000). "The contemporary focus on 'research ethics' is really about issues other than evaluation ethics. Ethics has ... collapsed into discussions of institutional control" (Johnson and Altheide, 2003, p. 61).

In the child neglect project, there was a strong awareness about research ethics issues. The senior social work manager recalled a detailed discussion: "But we did kick around all sorts of perspectives, from deontological perspectives, consequentialism—We actually ran the gamut of approaches to try and test out where there would be real ethical dilemmas the research would throw up." The practitioner evaluator did not mention this occasion, but it was nonetheless exceptional in that the account was told as an evaluation expert story, rather than as a practitioner or agency story, the only such instance in the study.

Of course, the ethics of access and approval, evaluation roles, and social work issues are very complex, whether one approaches them as a practitioner or as a professional evaluator. Our data raise particular issues about difficulties associated with the practitioner's location within organizational power structures and about tensions between practitioners' own experiences of ethical dilemmas and the confidence that existing ethical approval procedures may or may not engender.

Whose Practitioner Evaluation?

Ownership has wide ranging implications for agency resources, evaluation capacity, evaluation training, and the best possible value of project outcomes. Ownership of a project was used as a dichotomous variable in our preliminary classification of these social work projects. The case studies reinforced the significance of ownership but suggested a greater complexity and subtlety of interest, stakes, and accountabilities.

The community profile, for example, was a solitary inquiry, but Rhian received strong support from a network within the housing area office, from the area and assistant area manager, and from the housing officers. Consequently, the ownership of the project did not remain static and became a joint partnership between housing and community development agencies. This is unlikely to occur when there is a university qualification involved for the (lead) evaluation practitioner. Sarah was definite that she owned the challenging behavior project:

> I suppose you could say it was affected by my tutor in terms of she helped me to shape … how I thought about a problem and about the question I was trying to answer. But still that ownership is mine because I think at the end of the day she is just prompting me to think around things and I came up with the answers from her prompting.

More commonly, practitioners saw it as less clear cut. Deborah considered a different aspect of ownership, bringing service user involvement to the fore: "If I'd had more time to take the project back and get people to comment on it, I think they would have owned it a little bit more and I think that would have been better."

In this analysis, it is useful to distinguish between (a) services that promote user or consumer involvement; (b) evaluation that obtains data directly from service users; and (c) evaluation that involves service users in the development, management, and ownership of a project. A clear conclusion from the case studies is that social work practitioners actively back service user involvement in decisions about services, but none of the projects engaged service users in any direct way in the evaluation. A partial explanation may lie in the tension between being both a practitioner and a researcher. For example, Deborah expressed the following view:

> That has huge ethical implications ... doesn't it, because the practitioner has a working relationship with service-users and how difficult is that to get research? How easy is it to say 'no I don't want to be involved or whatever' if someone is doing direct research. All of it is a minefield really.

So Deborah could point to the potential role conflicts in the practitioner-researcher relationship with service users and research participants. At a time when professional confined research and formal evaluation is itself striving to move toward an increasing engagement with "users" at every stage, from agenda setting to the assessment of evaluation results, there may be an opportunity here for a productive dialogue between the grassroots experience of practitioner evaluators and professional evaluation communities.

Cross-Sector Practitioner Evaluation?

Our starting point was that practitioner involvement in evaluation is embraced across a wide range of professions. Yet we found that the making of a common cause between social work and education, housing, health, and the like—joined-up practitioner evaluation—was almost completely absent. Part of the reason for this may well be the partial invisibility of practitioner evaluation within the professions. Our preliminary exploration of cross-sector exchange did little more than confirm this. The practitioner evaluators were aware of the potential relevance of their work for other professionals, but often, this seemed more in hope than expectation.

The stakeholders in the community profile project had been more proactive in setting up cross-sector dissemination. The housing officer pinpointed future cross-professional plans. The drawback of such initiatives is that they are likely to be seen as professionals from one sector seeking to "educate" those from another, and the dissemination is less likely to be owned by the receiving agency. The community reenablement scheme was set up as a multiagency project, and it gained focus from a favorable political wind. Jane, the project manager pointed out that

> All sorts of things have been happening to be honest with you. This project has happened in the right political climate basically. It's been looked on very favourably by the Audit Commission [a national U.K. body that reviews public services' performance].

Overall, there was some modest and significant evidence of cross-sector exchange in the case studies. The general picture shows some positive hints, but some of this seemed more aspirational that actual, and there was no evidence at all of links between practitioner evaluators working in different sectors.

Uses of Practitioner Evaluation

Although the use agenda was fairly prominent, actual uses presented a more limited picture. The challenging behavior project yielded a not untypical account. The written output from Sarah's project was a master's dissertation, and she produced an additional written summary for support workers within her own agency. There was no expectation from the host agency that the evaluation should be made available across sectors. Her response was not untypical, revealing an almost poignant disappointment that a project involving extended commitment should, in effect, become invisible:

> I'd just like it that somebody read it, I would just hope that they would find it interesting, really. I suppose you've got that feeling ... although it was a social work dissertation, a lot of the literature was psychology based because it is behavioral psychology that has been interested in this topic.

There was also a strong aspirational quality to practitioners' accounts of evaluation use. It may be reasonable to conclude that evaluation results are more likely to have an impact when they resonate with planned or serendipitous priorities within the host agencies. This interpretation gains support from Helen's project, in which a strong mentor role existed. He cited her findings and conclusions as being crucial, with other research, for strategic discussions about the future nature of mental health services. He emphasized that "we want to base those developments upon research that ... not only [the] practitioner researcher has undertaken, but research and evidence-based practice from elsewhere within the U.K. So it fits into that scenario."

Wider opportunities for an evaluation to have an impact were unusual and were not easily accomplished. For example, the evaluator in the child protection project envisaged publishing a paper but added,

> Well, my tutor is talking about publishing it although I presume because it was such a wide research project that he will pick on some certain aspect of it to publish. So I don't know whether anything will come from that. What he is also saying is that there is sufficient information in there should I wish to continue or me to carry on with the research based on the data that I've got or to do some more Action Research on particular aspects of what I've studied so far.

This comment is interesting. First, it affords yet a further example of the implicit power relations in practitioner evaluation. Although the unnamed tutor would doubtless demur from the idea that it was his decision, the assumptions behind the remark "I presume ... that he will pick on some certain aspect of it to publish" assumes that the expertise on decisions to publish lies fully with universities. Second, the remarks also hint at possible ways in which a project may lead on to a research-active career, through the shaping and steering role of the tutor.

Although this example has positive aspects, the power relations in the practitioner evaluation culture can have less positive outcomes. Catherine, who had only just completed the research, outlined her dissemination plans:

> I've written a paper based upon it and I'm seeking publication for that. It's for a journal, the *Peer Review*, but that's still in progress. I've presented my research data and my reflections upon it at a Family Therapist conference earlier this year and I am going to present it to my colleagues here in a couple of months. … So it has had

> those kind of things which are quite exciting and encouraging for me but the main impact it's had is upon my practice.

Her hopes were generally untarnished, but the apparent invisibility to her of the journal world and the peer review process (her apparent assumption that "peer review" was the name of a journal) and the implicit reliance on the mentoring of someone in higher education both underline the fragility of dissemination plans for good project results.

Use questions are important in the context of current concerns regarding knowledge use in social work (e.g., Walter, Nutley, Percy-Smith, McNeish, and Frost, 2004). Practitioner evaluation helpfully focuses attention on use as reflected in the work of frontline social work professionals. "The bottom line for research utilization is what happens in the field among practitioners" (Kirk and Reid, 2002, p. 194). As things stand, use and general impact have a serendipitous quality, and we draw more general conclusions about this issue in the closing discussion.

In summary, in this second section, we have considered data on the "social" and organizational aspects of social work practitioner evaluation in our case studies in Wales, including ethical approval, ownership, and use. Our interpretation of the data has emphasized the tentativeness of these practitioners in approaching ethical issues and the world of dissemination. This reflects, perhaps, tensions in the insider-outsider role but also the lack of a strong institutionalization of the practitioner evaluator role in social work provider organizations. Even those projects that were agency owned appeared to be conducted almost exclusively single-handedly rather than as team projects.

Practice and Evaluation

The angle of vision in this third cluster of evidence from the research is outward once more but this time through what we earlier described as the lens of shifting practice and research borderlines. The themes here share a concern with the underlying question of the relationship between practice and evaluation in social work. We ask, how does practitioner evaluation relate to academic evaluation and research? How strong is the link between evaluation and practice?

Practitioner and Academic Evaluation

We have referred to the push and pull of insider and outsider identities. We mentioned the case for regarding practitioner evaluation as a distinctive genre of evaluation, fundamentally different from mainstream academic evaluation (cf. Cochran-Smith and Lytle, 1990, for this case made in relation to teacher-researchers or Callon's [n.d.] research in the wild).

The comments of the practitioners on academic research and practitioner evaluation reveal a depth of perceived contrast (Table 18.3). *Evidence based* was the only term common to both, perhaps illustrating the degree to which this term

Table 18.3 Practitioner terms for academic and practitioner evaluation

Academic	Practitioner
Evidence based	Evidence based
Detached	Interactive
Structured	Experience
Larger scale	Understanding
Rigorous	Valid
	Real world
	In depth

has become embedded in everyday accounts of practice. Several more negative characteristics were also mentioned about academic research, including limitations of understanding, experience, and "grasp."

Helen viewed practitioner evaluation as more "interactive" and more "valid": "I am doing the job that I am researching. That's the difference—you are actually in the workplace doing the same thing." Sarah also expressed reservations about academic research: "But then I would say perhaps mainly somebody who does it as a job who has not been in the social work field for a while might forget how things work in the real world as well." Jane took this emphasis further and portrayed academic research as more removed from the grass roots: "With practitioner research you live and breathe it. You live and breathe it and you know it so much in depth." The only exceptions to this favorable comparison of small-scale practitioner evaluation at the expense of academic research came, perhaps not surprisingly, from the non-practitioners—academics and managers—linked to the projects.

We must confess some anxiety. If this were to represent the general picture as seen by practitioners, then efforts to develop conversations between social work evaluators in the universities and even interested practitioners would have made little headway. These contrasts tend to assume a conventional insider stance and to tacitly treat all academic evaluation in a manner that is too insufficiently differentiated. It is possible, though we have to draw on other evidence to support this reflection, that practitioners associate academic evaluation ("Evaluation with a capital E" as someone labelled it) with larger scale projects by outsiders that are commissioned by senior agency managers and hence as dissociated from practice (Shaw and Shaw, 1997). We also have misgivings about this polarization on the grounds that it seems to undermine the potential for practitioner evaluation as a basis for critique of practice (Shaw, 2005).

Linking Practice and Evaluation?

Despite these concerns, we do not think that the previous passage fully represents the practitioners' positions. Indeed, in their general accounts of the relationship between practice and research, the general emphasis was positive, suggesting a congruence and mutual payoff. Hazel claimed,

> I think that possibly my background made it easier for me to do the study, than it might have done for somebody who didn't have that background, because I was able to hit the ground running more quickly, I think, than other people might have been able to do.

The direction is treated as straightforward: How helpful is research for practice? Although practitioners' criticisms of academic research could have provided a basis for them to challenge it, this was never stated, still less spelled out in the case studies. There was, by contrast, the seed of a less common but creative approach to schematizing the relationship of research and practice. Catherine concluded, "The methodology fitted the framework of my professional practice and in that sense I think it was bang on." The evaluation project had a strong effect on the way she subsequently conducted her working practice:

> I think that's made a huge, huge difference of how I sit with families and I learnt through doing the research that people love to pass their views. So that's made really a big difference. It has also made a very big difference doing the research to my understanding of when one can appropriately ask children to speak of you in the presence of their parent or even when not in presence of their parent.

We think that this is an important question. Whereas most discussions of the relationship of research and practice are based on the relevance of findings for practice, these comments are about the relevance of evaluation methodology for practice. In a comparable way, Deborah seemed to suggest ways in which practitioner evaluation promoted what may be called, without importing too much baggage, reflective practice:

> It made me look at research methods again and it did mean looking at evaluating information and how to get information and what were the best ways and what sort of information you would get from different research methods. More generally it has helped me to look at things and since then as well you know things like setting up groups.

Research and practice share a complex relationship, and the comments of the practitioners helpfully serve to disabuse us of the merits of simplistic dichotomies between the real world and the ideas world, research and practice, and theory and practice. This is partly because evaluation is not as simple as we often wish to think, and neither is practice.

Practitioner Evaluation: Reflection, Rethinking, and Resonance

The case studies in this article have offered an exploratory inquiry into a type of evaluation activity and an area of social work where relatively little is known. The study reveals some of the reasons this may be the case: low-key, small-scale projects, in which the power relations often work to reinforce the subordinate role of the evaluators and the evaluation possesses an inherent low visibility. And yet time and again, we have been prompted to the realization that practitioner evaluation in social work poses questions and issues that act as gateways to several of the major debates within social work and other professions in which such evaluation is a major if partly invisible dimension: the quality of practice and research, evidence-based interventions, career development, power, expertise, the kinds and quality of professional knowledge, ethical decision making, and the like.

Our initial attempt at a pragmatic set of characteristics of practitioner evaluation still seems not wholly unhelpful. But we do, however, want to emphasize three limitations of this preliminary approach. First, several of the key defining terms have proved to be far more complex and even ambiguous than anticipated. Terms such as *use*, *insider*, and *own account* are useful as much for the complexities they raise as for the directions in which they point. Second, we must come clean and admit that we realized that we were covering up key distinctions, as for example when we said that practitioner evaluation focuses on professionals' own practices and/or those of their immediate peers. The extensive evidence about the varying ownership and degrees of "privacy" within practitioner evaluation shows the limitations of this. Indeed, our efforts to classify practitioner evaluation only illuminate its striking degree of diversity. Third, this is a pragmatic definition, seeking to encapsulate what is and not what might conceivably be. For that reason, we would not advise adopting a definition of this kind as the basis for a policy or funding framework to enrich and develop practitioner evaluation in social work or any cognate field of work.

The same broad point about the limitations of a pragmatic approach to definitions applies to the classification scheme we developed from the telephone survey (Table 18.1). Yet we believe, with that caveat, that it has proved productive. It challenges future simplistic assumptions that practitioner evaluation can be treated as a homogeneous aspect of social work. The four distinct groupings of practitioner evaluation that can be detected in Table 18.1 have areas of overlap but clear differences.

We suspect that one conclusion, tempting to some, is that what we might call "private" versions of practitioner evaluation, typically practitioner owned, should be discouraged. We do not believe that this is the right response, for two reasons. First, we do not think that the evidence supports an association of low quality with private practitioner evaluation, and it is on the quality that we believe the stress should initially be laid. Nevertheless, we think that ownership and investment by colleagues, service users, and cross-sector agency interests are evident all too infrequently. Second, we think that an easy discouragement of private practitioner evaluation simply on the grounds it is private probably hides an unduly narrow set of assumptions about how it is or ought to be useful. Restricting knowledge use (evidence-based practice) to a direct and immediate relationship between inquiry and action fails to recognize the less direct but potentially just as potent kinds of relationship that may exist. For example, the usefulness of a high-quality private practitioner evaluation project that leads to the practitioner seeking to be- come a career social work evaluator cannot be judged only or even mainly by its short-term instrumental impact on agency practice.

We are not, however, complacent regarding the limitations of existing evaluation of this kind. A fuller development of multiple ownership would lead, helpfully in our view, to

- cross-agency and cross-sector practitioner evaluation partnerships,
- the use of practitioner evaluation data from more than one agency in the same project, and
- programmatic possibilities through, for example, links between projects.

The development of somewhat more sophisticated evaluation methodologies would lead, equally helpfully, to

- collaboration between practitioner evaluators,
- computer-assisted data analysis,
- the actual use of practitioner evaluation beyond the practitioner's own personal sphere of work, and
- published output from practitioner evaluation.

But again, we resist a practitioner-blame stance that supports a general shift to either multiple ownership or more complex methodology. The choice of methods made by the practitioners was diverse and did not support a conclusion that practitioners are methodologically naive or lacking in imagination. There was, perhaps, some degree of conventionality about the choice, and there were some obvious gaps. Quantitative skills were probably lacking throughout the practitioner group, and there were few more thoroughgoing qualitative designs. We were not able to elicit firm evidence about the quality of evaluation for any given method, and in particular, we were too distant from the projects to gain a strong sense of the standards of data analysis. We suspect, however, that this approach to assessing evaluation skills may reflect a more university-driven criterion compared with the apparently artless emphasis on a wide range of personal skills that we noted coming from the practitioners themselves. The question is not merely abstract. If practitioners understand evaluation skills in terms of qualities such as determination, inquisitiveness, being articulate, and having a creative outlook, this raises important questions about evaluation and practice training, the implementation of evidence-based practice, reflective learning, and so on. Our own conclusions are that polarized arguments to the effect that evaluation and practice are, or are not, akin to one another are probably unhelpful. Even when there are valuable ways of linking the two, there will need to be processes of active "translation" to make the one "work" for the other (cf. Shaw, 1996). We do not intend to imply a one-way process but one in which evaluation and practice are each challenged by the knowledge of the other.

Our evidence suggests other factors that shape methodological choice, including an apparent reliance on the advice of either those in positions of authority in the agency, or academic "experts." The narrative voice of the case studies tacitly reinforces this conclusion, in that project stories, with just one solitary and striking exception, were told in a practitioner voice and not in the voice of the (confident) evaluation insider. We wonder whether such apparent dependency may make the methodological coherence and strength of project methodology somewhat fragile. Nonetheless, this methodological modesty and even ambivalence was often linked to interesting elements of growing awareness and learning on the job. We believed at the outset that practitioner evaluation may be marked by undue methodological simplicity. We now think that this is an unwarranted overgeneralization. But this does not mean that all is well. The tendency for evaluation practitioners to be marginalized renders their survival capacity at constant risk.

Part of the reason for this might be a strong view that practitioner evaluation is and ought to be insider research, defined as including a privileged access to knowledge. This claim to privileged understanding was certainly made forcefully by the majority of our participants, in ways that make for uncomfortable reading by academic social scientists. We observed it especially strongly in the distinctions practitioners made between practitioner and academic research (Table 18.3). The claim should not be treated as incidental, because it is a claim to how we discover truth about social work. We can consider this point in terms of what Robert Merton (1972) years ago described as the insider doctrine, which claims in its strong form that particular groups have monopolistic access to particular kinds of knowledge. But Merton concluded that it is important to consider claims to knowledge as privileged rather than monopolistic: "We no longer ask whether it is the Insider or the Outsider who has monopolistic or privileged access to the truth; instead we begin to consider their distinctive and interactive roles in the process of truth seeking" (p. 36). This conclusion has much to recommend it as a starting point for assessing the role of the practitioner evaluator and truth claims in practitioner evaluation. We think three provisional conclusions follow from our evidence about the practitioner evaluation role.

1. The role of practitioner evaluator as both inside and outside, and as moving between the two, is sensitive and frequently difficult or even on occasion hazardous.

2. There is an ever present risk of marginalization for practitioner evaluators. This stems mainly from the frequent points at which relationships of authority and power shape the decisions, for good and ill, about access, methods, and the use of evaluation results.
3. Despite the tendency that we have just noted to polarize practitioner and academic evaluation, there were hints that the two roles are both exposed to elements of risk of marginalization.

This does not mean that we are pessimistic about the future of practitioner evaluation. For example, the creative mirroring of evaluation and research and practice that we observed in several of the case study projects raised valuable questions about the possibilities of a positive exchange between the two. Whereas most discussions of the relationship of research and practice are based on the relevance of research findings for practice, these practitioner comments were about the relevance of research methodology for practice. Similarly, Kirk and Reid (2002) followed a number of previous writers and distinguished between science as a source of knowledge and evidence and science as a model of how practice should take place. For example, evidence-based practice is either (or maybe both) of these: applying both evidence and critical thinking. Practitioner evaluation also has elements of both of these, and discussion is confused when we do not recognize this. Practice and practitioner evaluation may also mutually benefit from considering how far the perspectives and methods of one provide a template for the other. For example, is social work akin to evaluation in the sense that it is marked by "the systematic collection of data, the cautious use of inference and the consideration of alternative explanations, the application where possible of research based knowledge, and the discriminating evaluation of the outcomes of one's efforts" (Reid, 1995, p. 2040)?

This takes us back to the question of the uses of practitioner evaluation. We found several instances of an aspirational-but-not-quite-there quality in the ways practitioners talked about the impact of their work. Practitioners were strongly committed to contributing to improving social work. Yet factors seemed to conspire against them. The hopes of a wider audience, seen for example when practitioners hoped for the publication of their results, appeared less sanguine. The implicit power relations in practitioner evaluation play out here once more. Practitioners seem dependent on others, even to name a journal. This is not always completely negative. Committed mentors and tutors who recognize what they see as scholarly potential may go to some lengths to encourage and facilitate emerging researchers. But even when further evaluation work was seen as desirable, practitioners did not want to separate the practice-research tie-up. As Jane put it, her possible doctoral research would not entail a "move on to anything that's not related to intermediate care and to inter-agency working."

The implications for change that may be pursued in the light of this study need considerable care. But implications do exist, and not only for practitioners and agencies. Evaluation capacity building, the kinds and quality of knowledge in professional work, relations between universities and professional practice agencies, intellectual property rights, and the regulatory conventions governing postgraduate evaluation in universities all appear to be challenged by the prevalence, form, and identity of practitioner evaluation.

References

Adler, P.A. and Adler, P. (2003). Do university lawyers and the police define research values? In W.C. van den Hoonaard (ed.), *Walking the Tightrope: Ethical Issues for Qualitative Researchers* (pp. 34-42). Toronto, Canada: University of Toronto Press.

Callon, M. (n.d.). *Economy of Qualities, Researchers in the Wild and the Rise of Technical Democracy*. Retrieved October 16, 2005, from http://www.cts.cuni.cz/seminar/callon.htm.

Cochran-Smith, M. and Lytle, S. (1990). Research on teaching and teacher research: The issues that divide. *Educational Researcher*, 19, 2-22.

Collins, H. (2000). *Tacit knowledge, trust and the Q of sapphire* (Cardiff University School of Social Sciences Working Paper #1). Retrieved October 16, 2005, from http://www.cf.ac.uk/socsi/publications/workingpapers/abstracts/wrkgpaper1-ab.html.

Collins, H. (2001). What is tacit knowledge? In T. Schatzki, K. Cetina, and E. von Savigny (Eds.), *The Practice Turn in Contemporary Theory* (pp. 107-119). London: Routledge.

Cronbach, L., Ambron, S., Dornbusch, S., Hess, R., Hornik, R., Phillips, D., et al. (1980). *Toward Reform of Program Evaluation*. San Francisco, CA: Jossey-Bass.

Fahl, R. and Markand, M. (1999). The project "analysis of psychological practice" or: An attempt at connecting psychology critique and practice research. *Outlines*, 1, 73-98.

Hammersley, M. (2000). *Taking Sides in Social Research*. London: Routledge.

Holstein, J. and Gubrium, J. (1995). *The Active Interview*. Thousand Oaks, CA: Sage.

House, E. and Howe, K., (1999). *Values and Evaluation*. Thousand Oaks, CA: Sage.

Johnson, J.M. and Altheide, D.L. (2003). Reflections on professional ethics. In W.C. van den Hoonaard (Ed.), *Walking the Tightrope: Ethical Issues for Qualitative Researchers* (pp. 59-69). Toronto: University of Toronto Press.

Kirk, S., and Reid, W.J. (2002). *Science and Social Work*. New York: Columbia University Press.

Merton, R.K. (1972). Insiders and outsiders: A chapter in the sociology of knowledge. *American Journal of Sociology*, 78, 9-47.

Nowotny, H., Scott, P. and Gibbons, M. (2001). *Re-thinking Science: Knowledge and the Public in an Age of Uncertainty*. Cambridge: Polity.

Polkinghorne, D. (2000). Psychological inquiry and the pragmatic and hermeneutic traditions. *Theory and Psychology*, 10, 453-479.

Reason, P. and Bradbury, H. (2000). *Handbook of Action Research*. London: Sage Ltd.

Reid, W.J. (1995). Research overview. In R.L. Edwards and J.G. Hopps (Eds.), *Encyclopedia of Social Work* (19th ed., Vol. III). Washington, DC: NASW Press.

Schwab, J. (1969, November). The practical: A language for curriculum. *School Review*, 1-23. Schwandt, T. (1999). On understanding understanding. *Qualitative Inquiry*, 5, 451-464.

Shaw, I. (1996). *Evaluating in Practice*. Aldershot: Ashgate.

Shaw, I. (2005). Practitioner research: Evidence or critique? *British Journal of Social Work*, 35, 1231-1248.

Shaw, I. and Gould, N. (2001). *Qualitative Research in Social Work*. London: Sage.

Shaw, I., Greene, J., and Mark, M. (2006). Editorial essay. In I. Shaw, J. Greene, and M. Mark (Eds.), *Handbook of Evaluation: Policies, Programs and Practice*. London: Sage.

Shaw, I. and Shaw, A. (1997). Keeping social work honest. *British Journal of Social Work*, 27, 847-869.

Stake, R. and Trumbull, D. (1982). Naturalistic generalizations. *Review Journal of Philosophy and Social Science*, 7, 1-12.

Taylor, C. and White, S. (2000). *Practising Reflexivity in Health and Welfare: Making Knowledge*. Buckingham: Open University Press.

Walter, I., Nutley, S., Percy-Smith, J., McNeish, D., and Frost, S. (2004). *Improving the Use of Research in Social Care Practice*. London: Social Care Institute for Excellence.

White, S. (2001). Autoethnography as reflexive inquiry. In I. Shaw and N. Gould (Eds.), *Qualitative Research in Social Work* (pp. 100-115). London: Sage Ltd.

White, S., and Stancombe, J. (2003). *Clinical Judgement in the Health and Welfare Professions: Extending the Evidence Base*. Maidenhead: Open University Press.

Chapter 19
Evaluating in Practice*

A subterranean distinction has rumbled along beneath the chapters of this book.[1] Sometimes the argument has been organized with the general aim of showing how substantive knowledge from different kinds of research and inquiry can make for good social work practice. The previous chapter is a good example of this approach, as is Chapter 2. On other occasions the authors have focussed more of how different ways of disciplined thinking and inquiry constitute indispensable elements of practice. Chapter 4 is an example of this approach.

The distinction is neither accidental nor lacking consequence. Bill Reid, the inventor of task-centred intervention, expressed it as follows:

> Historically, the influence of science on direct social work practice has taken two forms. One is the use of the scientific method to shape practice activities, for example, gathering evidence and forming hypotheses about a client's problem. The other form is the provision of scientific knowledge about human beings, their problems and ways of resolving them. (Reid, 1998: 3)

The example Reid gives of how ways of disciplined thinking and inquiry constitute indispensable elements of practice is 'gathering evidence and forming hypotheses about a client's problem'. The authors have referred to this approach in Chapter 2. It is one of the hallmarks of evidence-based practice, and has been strongly influenced by research that aims to test effectiveness through experiments. In this chapter we take a different approach. Some influential social work writers believe that experimental studies of intervention, using quantitative methods, are the best, perhaps only trustworthy way of identifying the outcomes of social work. Thyer and Fischer in the USA and Macdonald and Sheldon in the UK have been associated with this position. Some writers take a further step and argue that a corresponding logic and approach is needed by social workers in their direct practice – i.e. they believe that social work ought to be like scientific research in its logic and aims. This is sometimes represented through using what are usually called single system designs (e.g. Kazi, 1998; Bloom, 1993, 1999).

---

* Originally published as Shaw, I. (2010) 'Evaluating in Practice' in T. Evans and M. Hardy with I. Shaw *Evidence and Knowledge for Social Work*. Cambridge: Polity Press, 152-164. Reprinted with permission of Policy Press.

1 This and subsequent references to chapters refer to Evans, T. and Hardy, M. (2010). *Evidence and Knowledge for Social Work*. Cambridge: Polity Press.

We take a broader view. In this chapter we outline an approach to an evidenced, understanding and just practice that embeds qualitative methods 'translated' and 'inhabited' for the purposes of practice rather than research. You can hear echoes of and consistencies with this approach in Chapters 3, 4 and 6.

Three aspects of the approach need emphasizing. First, evaluating in practice is not about the application of research findings to practice but about the *method* of inquiry and evaluation. We may label this the difference between research as a 'source' for practice and research as a 'model' for practice. Second, evaluating in practice is a cluster of practice skills and not research skills as such. Third, our orientation draws primarily on the rich literature and practice of *qualitative* inquiry and evaluation.

Translating and inhabiting

A demanding set of skills is necessary to achieve this shaping of practice – skills that we convey through the use of metaphors such as 'translation' and 'inhabit' and through ideas of transfer of learning. To inhabit some place does not happen simply by being there. It involves actively making it our home over a period of time. This process can be described as one of 'counter-colonizing' (e.g. Shaw, 2009). Implicit in this metaphor is a recognition that social workers often face the dominance of social science and research 'experts' over practice 'beneficiaries', and suggests in a contrary fashion the potential for practice to challenge social science, and thus contest conventional ways of seeing expert/beneficiary relationships. To translate and communicate are equally demanding. Film often illustrates this, in ways comedic (e.g. *Lost in Translation*) or dramatic (e.g. *Babel*). The tasks of translating and inhabiting exemplify that the relationship between doing social work and doing research is one of conjunction but difference.

Practitioners'-eye view

In the opening chapter the authors emphasized the importance of distinguishing different sources of knowledge in social work, and summarized the argument of Pawson and colleagues that there are five sources of knowledge:

- Organizational knowledge, gained from the management of social work and social care.
- Practitioner knowledge gained from the conduct of social work and social care.
- Policy community knowledge present in and gained from the wider policy environment.
- Research knowledge gathered relatively systematically and with a pre-planned design for how the knowledge will be gathered and generated.
- User and carer knowledge, gained from the experience of service use and reflection thereon. (Pawson *et al.*, 2003)

Evaluating in practice does not fit exclusively into any one of these, although it is aimed primarily at strengthening practitioner knowledge (cf White and Riemann, in press). Practitioner knowledge is likely to be partly tacit, and passed on by word of mouth and observation and expertise. Because this is so we need to understand the realities of day-to-day practice, and to hear accounts of how work is evaluated, rather than impose an abstract framework of evaluation. We can see something of this by attending to some replies given by practitioners when asked to describe their work, and to say how they knew whether it was going well or not.

All the social workers in this research (Shaw and Shaw, 1997a, 1997b) distinguished two types of evaluation – 'evaluation proper' on the one hand, and self evaluation of work with service users on the other hand. Evaluation proper, or 'Evaluation with a capital E' as someone labelled it, was the term practitioners used when they wished to refer to evaluation originating in legal or administrative requirements, planned and implemented by senior agency staff, and filtered through line managers. This model was widely regarded as being part of a change in culture in which evaluation has become 'a big buzz word':

> Historically I think that Social Services have tended to be 'woolly' and maybe 'airy-fairy'...there was a view of social workers who responded without having any clear strategy...that we were bumbling and not to say incompetent...I think social workers began to wake up to that really, that we have to be more methodical and more exact in our approach. I think that change began to happen about ten years ago.

This model was not rejected by social workers, but it did not relate in an easy fashion to their own practice.

> I think there's a lot of people that, when they say "evaluation" are asking you to evaluate things that are almost unimportant, things that are essentially quantifiable... Nobody ever asks you to evaluate whether what you did was worth doing.

This apparent distinction between evaluation as a species of counting and evaluating as a measure of worth was made by the majority of the people in the research. The latter was typically seen as lacking priority due to the 'tidal wave' of work.

> You haven't got the day-to-day emphasis on it...so it's something you have to want to do yourself. In terms of doing your own evaluation, that is something which is purely down to the individual.

Yet social workers did not wish to be complicit in this. For some, at least, evaluation was not simply a matter of evidence, but 'caught up' issues of belief and values.

> For me my evaluating skills are caught up with what I believe, and the reason I believe I am doing this. And why I'm doing this ultimately is because I want to protect and help children and families, and I want them to get a good service.

If this is so, then evaluating in practice is not and should not remain a peripheral aspect of social work. It is partly a matter of how to do evaluating, but it is also about the purpose and value of social work. Evaluating in practice involves a set of commitments that draw partly on reflective practice (Chapter 4) and partly on respect for the voice and experience of the service user (Chapter 3). These entail a commitment to reflexivity, to 'thinking big and doing small', to appreciating the significance of those who are 'outsiders on the inside', and to rendering explicit what we know and do not know.

An example of how aspects of these commitments can be demonstrated may be borrowed from a helpful recommendation about preparing questions for a research interview. McCracken (1988) recommends that long qualitative interviews are preceded by the investigator reviewing his/her personal experience of the topic of interest. This nicely illustrates an example of how qualitative research methods can be translated for practice, and is especially useful when we draw in some way on our personal experience in trying to understand the circumstances and problems facing the person we are about to interview. Eliciting such prior experience has two paradoxically 'opposite' effects. First, 'deep and long-lived familiarity with the culture under study has, potentially, the grave effect of dulling the investigator's powers of observation and analysis, but 'it also has the advantage' of giving the investigator an extraordinarily intimate acquaintance with the object of study' (McCracken, 1988: 32). For 'investigator' we can substitute 'practitioner'. Such a cultural review (McCracken's term),

> Calls for minute examination of [our] experience. The investigator must inventory and examine the associations, incidents and assumptions that surround the topic is his or her mind...the object is to draw out of one's own experience the systematic properties of the topic. (p. 32)

In so doing we demonstrate reflexivity and render explicit what we know and do not know. Our experience of applying this exercise is that the hard work of 'inhabiting' this cultural review in a way that provokes strange and challenging perspectives on social work problems is sometimes ducked in exchange for a quick and hence less helpful listing of obvious items.

Evidence, understanding and justice

We opened the chapter by describing evaluating in practice as an evidenced, understanding and just practice. The three principles can be spelt out as follows:

1. In the light of the best evidence about what works well for service users
2. So that service users and carers receive service that is fair, just and enabling
3. So that they, service users, carers and the organisations in which they work gain the capacity to learn about and understand both problems and ways in which they can be solved. It should lead to new learning capacity.

A case example will help make the point.[2]

> A social work student, working in a Social Services Department team, describes the work he undertook with a man and his partner. Gwynn Davies was in hospital at the time the work was referred.
>
> Mr Davies is a 52 year old man who is registered disabled. He has chronic mobility problems arising from bronchial problems, and needs annual hospitalisation to clear his chest of infection. His first marriage ended in divorce and he has been living with Mrs Watkins and her 14 year old daughter, Stephanie, in her house for the past three and a half years. They live in a South Wales valley town.
>
> Mrs Watkins visited the office in a distressed state, to tell the duty social worker that she was unable to accept Mr Davies back into her home because he repeatedly exposed himself to Stephanie. Mr Davies was interviewed on the ward. The first interview was difficult. He appeared to deny or evade the issues raised by his partner, and found it difficult to accept that Mrs Watkins would not let him return. He made it clear he had no intention of searching for alternative accommodation. He seemed more interested in his weight lifting prowess, and at one stage removed his shirt to show his body and asked the social worker what age he thought he was.
>
> Subsequent progress over the following days was slow, and goal setting was difficult. Mrs Watkins continued to visit him on the ward and appeared to act as if relations between them were free from problems. The student discussed with Mrs Watkins the mixed messages she was giving to Mr Davies. He and the practice teacher spoke to the child protection team, conveying their serious concern about Stephanie's welfare.
>
> Hospital staff regarded the student's concerns as misplaced and wanted Mr Davies home as soon as possible. This eventually led to communication difficulties between the hospital and the student.
>
> Reluctantly accepting that the relationship had broken down, at least temporarily, Mr Davies was provided with a list of private landlords, and the local authority was notified of his threatened homelessness. A local housing association visited him in hospital. At this period Mr Davies required constant encouragement to undertake tasks for himself, e.g. using the telephone.
>
> The local council offered him a flat, which he refused on the grounds that he could not manage the steps. Medical evidence was obtained, but the Council was not willing to accept that this provided sufficient grounds to make an alternative offer. He then accepted a bedsit letting, and said he intended to keep in touch with the housing association, but was not happy with the outcome of the social work that had been provided.

2 This anonymised case history is used with the consent of the practitioner.

In asking whether this was good practice, the general question is, did the practitioner embed the three practice principles in his work? But we should be more specific. If the concern is about evidence, examples of questions we may have in mind include:

1. Did the student have a clear hypothesis regarding the problem and its solution, which could be tested by the eventual outcome?
2. Was any intervention clearly specified and capable of being measured?
3. Do we know if the outcomes were the result of the student's practice?
4. What would count as evidence of success or otherwise for each of the professionals interested in this case?

If justice issues are in view, questions would include:

1. Did the social worker take seriously the risk of sexual or physical harm to the women involved?
2. Did the intervention give proper recognition to the power differentials, e.g. between those involved in professional relationships, or on the basis of gender?
3. Were the participants able to give feedback on whether their experience of social work had been helpful?
4. Was the service use enabled to collaborate with the social worker in judging whether the intervention had been helpful?

Understanding and learning raise different questions:

1. Did the student explore his own personal knowledge of the problem gained through his own background and life experience?
2. Were there opportunities for those involved to reflect on the process of intervention as well as on the problems?
3. Were 'lay' explanations of the problem (i.e. those explanations put forward by Stephanie, Mrs Watkins and Gwynn Davies) treated with equal seriousness as the explanations put forward by professionals?
4. Was evaluation participatory?

How these questions are answered is of course a matter of judgement. But to suggest possible answers to just the third principle, we might conclude that Mr Davies appears to have reached a gradual, unspoken conclusion that it would not be possible for him to resume his relationship with Mrs Watkins and Stephanie where it was left off. This suggests that the work done by the student had an impact on what initially seemed an intractable position. Other aspects were not dealt with clearly. For example, there is not apparent reflection on the student's personal, taken-for-granted knowledge. Neither was there any participatory evaluation. The recognition of lay explanations was difficult, and recognized to be so by the student. There were sharply divergent views between the partners. Also, the student was concerned that the views conveyed by Mrs Watkins may not represent the whole truth about her relationship with Mr Davies. A related issue was the socio-legal context of practice and its influence on practitioners' ability to hear and give weight to lay explanations

In noting that the student working with Gwynn Davies did not use any participatory evaluation, we are indicating that the work with this case does not illustrate the direct application of qualitative methods. We have outlined one example of such methods, through McCracken's cultural review. In a single chapter we can do little more than provide pointers to the rich opportunities for developing evaluating in practice. It will require a readiness to explore literature that rarely appears on the reading lists of social work programmes. In the table below we have suggested starter reading for each practice method. This is perhaps the core resource in this chapter. But of course, the references are offered as resource materials where the work of inhabiting and translating usually remains to be done by the reader.

Table 19.1 Methods and resources for evaluating in practice

Qualitative Methods	Resources
Ethnography	Riemann, 2005
Autoethnography	White, 2001
Life history; [auto] biography	Bowen, 1993; Clandinin and Connelly, 1994; Thompson and Holland, 2005
Documents	Prior, 2003; Shaw, 1996: 151-157
Focus Groups	Bond, 1990-91; Shaw, 1996: 158-161; Zeller, 1993
Narrative	McLeod, 1997; Neander and Stott, 2006; Riessman and Quinney, 2005; Wahlström, 2006
Qualitative interviews	Butler, 1996; Holstein and Gubrium, 1995; McCracken, 1988; McPherson, Hunter and McKeganey, 1986; Scourfield, 2001
Participant observation	Corsaro, 1985; Fine and Sandström, 1988; Mandell, 1988; Shaw, 1996: 135-141
Participatory inquiry	Forbat and Atkinson, 205; Kearney and Hyle, 2004; Traylen, 1994; Whitmore, 1994 and 2001
Self-observation	Rodriguez and Ryave, 2002
Simulations	Wasoff and Dobash, 1992 and 1996.
Visual methods	Mitchell, forthcoming

Self observation

The idea of systematic self observation yields one example where the writers themselves sense that some degree of transfer may be feasible. Rodriguez and Ryave (2002), explore the use of 'systematic self-observation' (SSO) as a research strategy. As a qualitative research tool they see SSO as training informants 'to observe and record a selected feature of their everyday experience' (p. 2). The focus is on understanding the ordinary, in particular the covert, the elusive and the personal. In an effort to overcome the 'numbness to the details of everyday life' (p. 4) respondents are asked to observe 'a single, focused phenomenon that is natural to the culture, is readily noticeable, is intermittent...is bounded...and is of short duration' (p. 5) and also to focus on the subjective.

The recording involves writing a narrative about the situation, the participants, what occurred, the words spoken and thoughts/feelings experienced at the time (i.e. not retrospectively), and doing it as soon as possible after the event. In observing they are instructed in no way to act differently than usual, to never produce instances nor to judge the propriety of the action – 'do not judge it, do not slow down, do not speed up, do not change it, do not question it – just observe it' (p. 17). They refer to a key skill as gaining a 'new mindfulness' about everyday life. In their own studies they have used the method to research telling lies, telling secrets in everyday life, withholding compliments and the role of envy in making social comparisons in everyday life.

Rodriguez and Ryave suggest that their approach might have an application within therapy in that:

1. Naming something can help
2. The task of observing without judging 'accesses the roots of the trouble in the tacit dimension' (p. 57) e.g. by identifying triggers/antecedents to problem behaviour etc
3. The write-up can act as therapeutic 'time-out'
4. Submitting data to others is a public 'owning up'
5. Sharing with others who are doing the same activity gives a sense of not being alone with a problem.

They are being speculative, not having tried it in this way – and so am I. But we would suggest a wider potential use, and one that adopts a social systems perspective and does not assume the 'client' is simply a target for change. Compared with the single system designs for evaluating intervention that we alluded to at the beginning of this chapter, systematic self observation may well be a preferred component of evaluating-in-practice in two respects:

1. It would allow a more contextualized and richer understanding of the nature of a problem in a service user's life, as part of an assessment and planning process.

2. Single system approaches are committed to behavioural approaches that typically proceed by counting and measuring incidence and prevalence of problems. SSO is, as we have noted 'more appropriate for the study of hidden or elusive domains, like the motives, memories, thought processes, withheld actions, thoughts and/or emotions that accompany overt behaviours' (p. 11).

We have expanded two examples of evaluating in practice – a cultural review and systematic self observation. The application of the cultural review was to the practitioner, whereas the illustration of SSO was primarily focused on the service user. Evaluating in practice applies equally to both. This kind of practice evaluation and inquiry is not a solitary activity, but one that readily involves communities of practice. Peter Reason's cycles of action and inquiry can be seen in this context (e.g. Reason, 1994). Hilary Traylen, for example, drew on Reason's work and offers a model of practice that has clear applications to evaluation and team work in social work (Traylen, 1994). She undertook a co-operative inquiry project with health visitors, in which five health visitors met with her monthly over approximately nine months, to address issues of hidden agenda in their practice, which were not revealed when they visited families. They decided to work on how they might appropriately confront families. Over the cycles of participatory work they heard each others' methods, agreeing and refining inquiry methods to be adopted in their own visits, and then applied them in the action phases of the cycle. The method owes something to models of action research. The approach – like any evaluating in practice – is not easy. The practitioners were heavily preoccupied in the early months with action rather than the inquiry process, and found it took some time to achieve the best balance between the two. However, reflection revealed the centrality of story-telling methods and the empowering impact of each cycle of inquiry.

Developing good practice

We have suggested several ways through which good evaluating in practice can be developed. They can be summarized as six working rules that draw to varying degrees on the principles regarding evidence, justice and understanding. First, concentrated critical reflection on our own practice is essential. This will include close attention to how we describe practice and people, and the relationship of that description to planned and actual outcomes.

Second, to repeat an earlier point, practitioners must come to know what they know. They must work to elicit, where possible,[3] their tacit, taken-for-

3 Some forms of tacit knowledge can probably be made explicit, but others are by their nature tacit. This is not a psychodynamic model of unconscious knowledge, but a sociological way of thinking about knowledge.

granted knowledge, and assess its relevance, for good or ill, for their practice. This will include the reviewing of personal and cultural knowledge that we have described. But it will also include acting on the wider applications of the insistence of, e.g. black feminist writers, that black women must 'learn to trust their own personal and cultural biographies as significant sources of knowledge' (Collins, 1986: 29). This is a difficult balancing act. On the one hand we should aim constantly to falsify our hunches and hypotheses, by watching for evidence that will help question conclusions arrived at too conveniently. On the other hand, there is a danger we may become paralysed into inaction by the uncertainty of our understanding. Reid has suggested that, if practitioners focus their energies on the achievement of effective but probably modest results from intervention research, this can 'discourage more radical but possibly less testable innovations'. He goes on to ask, 'Is it better to make limited but well documented progress or to work towards more important goals with less certainty of that we have attained?' (Reid, 1988: 45).

Third, practitioners must begin with the knowledge that service users and carers bring to them. This means more than listening to service user views, important and inescapably unsettling as that must always prove. It also includes openness to a view of the world that may be entirely at odds with our preconceptions.

Fourth, practitioners should exploit the implications of the analogy between some research methods and direct practice methods. We have sketched examples in this chapter of how this can be done through a process of translating and inhabiting qualitative research and evaluation methods. We have assumed, though not said, that qualitative methods offer a rich seam of work that will challenge social work to a much wider vision of practice-relevance. Social work is perhaps best seen as a field of study and a profession that draws on ideas and knowledge from a range of other disciplines – psychology, social policy, sociology, law, and medicine to instance an incomplete list.

Fifth, evaluating in practice requires a model of team and colleague work. We noted Hilary Traylen's use of Reason's model of participatory inquiry that involves successive cycles of inquiry and action.

The sixth working rule is that practitioners must engage in participatory evaluation with service users. As first steps to achieving this, social workers must insert themselves in the other's story as a way of coming to know that story. Whitmore's compelling accounts of participatory inquiry with oppressed black women and with young people, and Martin's reviews of feminist participatory research demonstrate both the rewards and difficulties of doing so (Martin, 1994; Whitmore, 1994, 2001).

Whitmore's account of an evaluation of a pre-natal programme for single expectant mothers was carried out over several months by four women who had themselves been through the programme, with Whitmore as consultant to the project. There were tensions in the group. One member left, and there were communication problems. One participant protested to Whitmore that

> Our world is different from yours. The fear is that people always want to humiliate you, put you down... We have a different lifestyle from you. We just don't trust people the way you do. (Whitmore, 1994: 92)

But the strength of their final achievement, leading also to presentations to the project advisory group, a conference, and a university class, was evidence that participatory evaluation with oppressed groups goes beyond rhetoric. A consideration arising from this kind of work arises from the recognition of feminist analysis that there is no single women's experience which transcends boundaries of class, race, education and language. Whitmore concluded that she could never entirely share the worlds of the women with whom she worked. 'My small words were often their big words. What I assumed was "normal talk" they saw as "professor words"' (p. 92).

These working rules clearly owe debts to the 'tripod' of evidence, understanding and justice. Tacit knowledge with its links to understanding; the service user's voice, and participatory inquiry take us back to justice; falsifying our prior assumptions borrows the ideas of the philosopher Karl Popper, and demands evidential standards. Developing evaluating in practice is part of a wider agenda. During this book we have found it impossible to avoid mention of important controversies about the nature and purpose of social work. 'Is social work primarily a technology-driven methodology, or is it a set of ideas, values and beliefs, about individuals and society?' (Witkin, 1992: 267). Our answer is the one that Witkin gives. Evaluating in practice is not limited to determining whether practice is effective, but must also be a means of empowerment and social change. 'By oversubscribing to the empirical model, we risk valuing effectiveness questions over moral ones, goal achievement over goal worthiness, and empirical data over personal lived experience' (p. 267). Evaluating in practice challenges social work students and practitioners to new understandings and new methodology. It recognizes throughout the significance of workers' present evaluating-as-it-is practices. Most importantly, it holds the promise of keeping social work honest.

References

Bloom, M. (1993) ed. *Single System Designs in the Social Services*. New York: Haworth.

Bloom, M. (1999) 'Single system evaluation' in Shaw, I. and Lishman, J. (eds) *Evaluation and Social Work Practice*. London: Sage Publications.

Bond, M (1990-91) '"The centre, it's for children": seeking children's views as users of a family centre' in *Practice* 7 (2).

Bowen, D. (1993) 'The delights of learning to apply the life history method to school non-attenders' in Broad, B. and Fletcher, C. (eds) *Practitioner Social Work Research in Action*. London: Whiting and Birch.

Butler, I. and Williamson, H. (1996) '"Safe?" Involving children in child protection' in Butler, I. and Shaw, I. (eds) *A Case of Neglect? Children's Experience and the Sociology of Childhood*. Aldershot: Avebury.

Clandinin, J. and Connelly, M. (1994) 'Personal experience methods' in Denzin, N. and Lincoln, Y. (eds) *Handbook of Qualitative Research*. Thousand Oaks: Sage Publications.

Collins, P. (1986) 'Learning from the outsider within: the sociological significance of black feminist thought' in *Social Problems* 33 (6).

Corsaro, W. (1985) *Friendship and Peer Culture in Early Years*. Norwood, NJ: Ablex.

Fine, G. and Sandström, K. (1988) *Knowing Children: Participant Observation with Minors*. Newbury Park: Sage Publications.

Forbat, E. and Atkinson, D. (2005) 'Research as social work: participatory research in learning disability' in *British Journal of Social Work* 35 (4): 425-434.

Holstein, J. and Gubrium, J. (1995) *The Active Interview*. Thousand Oaks: Sage Publications.

Kazi, M.A.F. (1998) *Single-Case Evaluation by Social Workers*. Aldershot: Ashgate.

Kearney, K.S. and Hyle, A.E. (2004) 'Drawing out emotions: the use of participant-produced drawings in qualitative inquiry' in *Qualitative Research* 4 (3): 361-382.

Mandell, N (1988) 'The least adult role in studying children' in *Journal of Contemporary Ethnography* 16 (4).

Martin, M. (1994) 'Developing a feminist participative research framework' in Humphries, B. and Truman, C. (eds) *Rethinking Social Research: Anti-Discriminatory Approaches in Research Methods*. Aldershot Avebury.

McCracken, G. (1988) *The Long Interview*. Newbury Park: Sage Publications.

McLeod, J. (1997) *Narrative and Psychotherapy*. London: Sage Publications.

McPherson, I., Hunter, D. and McKeganey, N. (1986) 'Interviewing elderly people: some problems and challenges' in *Research, Policy and Planning* 5 (2).

Mitchell, W. (2009) '"I know how I feel": listening to young people with life-limiting conditions who have learning and communication impairments' *Qualitative Social Work*. OnlineFirst. first published on October 1, 2009 as doi:10.1177/1473325009346460.

Neander, K. and Stott, C. (2006) 'Important meetings with important persons: narratives from families facing adversity and their key figures' in *Qualitative Social Work* 5 (3): 295-311.

Pawson, R., Boaz, A., Grayson, L., Long, A. and Barnes, C. (2003) *Types and Quality of Knowledge in Social Care*. London: Social Care Institute for Excellence.

Prior, L. (2003) *Using Documents in Social Research*. London: Sage Publications.

Reason, P. (1994) 'Three approaches to participative inquiry' in Denzin, N. and Lincoln, Y. (eds) *Handbook of Qualitative Research*. Thousand Oaks: Sage Publications.

Reid, W. (1988) 'Service effectiveness and the social agency' in Patti, R., Poertner, J. and Rapp, C. (eds) *Managing for Effectiveness in Social Welfare Organizations*. New York: Haworth.

Reid, William J. (1998) 'Empirically-supported practice: Perennial myth or emerging reality?' *Distinguished Professorship Lecture*. New York: State University at Albany.

Riemann, G. (2005) 'Ethnographies of practice – practicing ethnography' in *Journal of Social Work Practice* 19 (1): 87-101.

Riessman, C. and Quinney, L. (2005) 'Narrative in social work: a critical review' in *Qualitative Social Work* 4 (4): 391-412.

Rodriguez, N. and Ryave, A. (2002) *Systematic Self Observation*. Thousand Oaks: Sage.

Scourfield, J. (2001) 'Interviewing interviewers and knowing about knowledge' in Shaw, I. and Gould, N. *Qualitative Research in Social Work*. London: Sage Publications.

Shaw, I. (1996) *Evaluating in Practice*. Aldershot: Ashgate.

Shaw, I. (2009) 'Qualitative social work practice research', in Briar-Lawson, K., Fortune, A. and McCallion, P. *Advancing Practice Research in Social Work*. New York: Columbia University Press.

Shaw, I. and Shaw, A. (1997a) 'Keeping social work honest: evaluating as profession and practice', in *British Journal of Social Work* 27 (6): 847-869.

Shaw, I. and Shaw, A. (1997b) 'Game plans, buzzes and sheer luck: doing well in social work', in *Social Work Research* 21 (2): 69-79.

Thompson, R. and Holland, J. (2005) '"Thanks for the memory": memory books as a methodological resource in biographical research' in *Qualitative Research* 5 (2): 201-219.

Traylen, H. (1994) 'Confronting hidden agendas: co-operative inquiry with health visitors' in Reason, P. (ed) *Participation in Human Inquiry*. London: Sage Publications.

Wahlström, J. (2006) 'Narrative transformations and externalizing talk in a reflecting team consultation' in *Qualitative Social Work* 5 (3): 313-332.

Wasoff, F. and Dobash, R. (1996) *The Simulated Client: a Method for Studying Professionals Working with Clients*. Aldershot: Avebury.

White, S. 'Auto-ethnography as reflexive inquiry: the research act as self surveillance' in Shaw, I. and Gould, N. *Qualitative Research in Social Work*. London: Sage Publications.

White, S. and Riemann, G. (in press) 'Researching our Own Domains: Research as Practice in "Learning Organizations"' in Shaw, I., K. Briar-Lawson, J. Orme and R. Ruckdeschel (eds) *Sage Handbook of Social Work Research*. London: Sage Publications.

Whitmore, E. (1994) 'To tell the truth: working with oppressed groups in participatory approaches to inquiry' in Reason, P. (ed.) *Participation in Human Inquiry*. London: Sage Publications.

Whitmore, E. (2001) 'People listened to what we had to say: reflections on an emancipatory qualitative evaluation' in Shaw, I. and Gould, N. *Qualitative Research in Social Work*. London: Sage Publications.

Witkin, S. (1992) 'Should empirically-based practice be taught in BSW and MSW programs? No!' in *Journal of Social Work Education* 28 (3).

Zeller, R. (1993) 'Focus group research in sensitive topics' in Morgan, D.L. (ed.) *Successful Focus Groups: Advancing the State of the Art*. Thousand Oaks: Sage Publications.

Chapter 20

Culture and the Indigenisation of Quality in Third World Social Research*

Western Export Models of Social Research

Impressionistic, *ad hoc* evidence strongly suggests that Arab research – not to mention social research elsewhere in the developing world – is marked by a heavy reliance on quantitative methods, and in particular, survey models.

We find the implications of this both unsettling and paradoxical. Unsettling, because in terms of the potential for significant sociological analysis and understanding of analytic and policy issues, surveys offer at best a partial and limited tool. Paradoxical, because, on the one hand, survey research demands resources relating to population information, language and data analysis that are frequently in short supply, and on the other hand, because survey methodology reflects in a quiet subtle manner a paradigm of western pluralism that sits uncomfortably with societies holding distinctive values of social solidarity and homogeneity, authority and the proper transmission of knowledge.

For example, survey research, with its stress on criteria of external validity, demands adequate sampling frames which are rarely available even in urban areas within the Arab world. Informal anecdotes of how to access to respondents was negotiated, retold among Arab research students, suggest that a tell-it-how-it-really-is account of how researchers obtain their sampling frames would be very illuminating.

Not that perfect sampling frames are just lying around in western countries, waiting for the researcher to ask for them. Indeed, one of the ironic consequences of the high status of the western survey export model is that Arab researchers may be tempted into an overly sanguine belief about the ease and quality of survey research in the West, and a reluctance to consider the possibility that the problems of research in Arab cultures may simply be the problems of the West writ large – albeit sometimes horrendously large (Bulmer and Warwick, 1993).

We have implied already that survey models must also be viewed through the prism of western pluralism. It is certainly true that beliefs about society held by

* Originally published as Shaw, I. and Al-Awwad, K. (1994) 'Culture and the Indigenization of Quality in Third World Social Research', *Journal of Social Development in Africa* 9(1): 59-71. Reprinted with permission Professor Rodreck Mupedziswa and the *Journal of Social Development in Africa.*

English-speaking heirs of a broadly Judeo-Christian civilisation may not be shared by others. Harré (1989: 23) suggests that members of such societies believe that:

1. They are autonomous individuals.
2. Despite being trapped in a web of conventions and an apparently inexorable natural order, they are agents.
3. They have both individually and collectively, a past and a future, and so have histories.

It is against this cultural backdrop that we must place the argument of Hakim that survey research offers one of the most democratic forms of research method. Methods and procedures can be made visible and accessible to non-specialists and specialists working in other disciplines, which makes for a research method mode transparent and accountable than many other methods used by researchers (Hakim, 1987: 48-49).

Regardless of whether such assumptions are actually true for all, some or any members of western societies, the egalitarian premises of survey research are sometimes rejected at all levels of society in developing countries. For instance, simple random sampling carries the implicit assumption that the views of an Arab sheik and a Moslem village woman will be of potentially equal significance in reaching persuasive sociological understandings. This assumption will often be challenged in Arab society both by those in positions of power and those of lower status and influence. Further, respondents may not share with Western individualism the assumptions about the circumstances in which 'truth-telling' ought to be expected.

Related to this, 'conventional' (i.e. western eyes) methods of data analysis are assumed by European and American social scientists to be relatively neutral and value-free. Survey researchers, it is presupposed, will almost routinely uncover evidence of variance, and will produce tables, typically in the form of cross-tabulations, which will differentiate replies according to this or that category of respondent. Yet it is not too distant from the truth to suggest that, far from being neutral, such methods of data analysis assume a pluralist society, where, within certain normative boundaries, differences of opinion and behaviour are acceptable and a reflection of 'normal' society.

This was illustrated in a recent extensive questionnaire and interview survey of service standards in public sector organisations in a major Arab country, carried out by one of the authors (Al-Awwad, 1991), which yielded very little differentiation between respondents, allied to a strong tendency on the part of the organisation staff to offer conformist responses – conformist both to line managers' perceived views ('what did my line manager answer to that question?') and to the social norms of power holders within that society.

Survey methods in developing countries are sometimes caught in a apparent time-warp, where neither the criticisms (eg Cicourel, 1964), nor the measured defences (eg Marsh, 1982; Bryman, 1988) of surveys are part of the common currency of debate. For example, while individualism is not inherently endemic to survey strategies (Marsh, 1982: 60-62), it is too frequently reflected in decisions by survey planners in the Arab world to investigate the responses of *individuals* to a given programme, rather than *households* or other appropriate economic or social collectivities (Ibrahim, 1987: 32).

We argue later the strategic potential of qualitative research methodologies in developing countries. For the present we need to point out the way in which survey methods lead to a characteristic approach to substantive policy concerns which is marked more by an investigation and discussion of policies and system-wide features of services, than by an investigation of the realities of programme and service provision and outcomes. In a recent assessment of education research in developing countries the authors point out the implications of this emphasis, where:

> the kinds of evaluation methods that have typically been used most frequently in developing countries make it difficult to penetrate any marked divorce between policy and practice (Vulliamy *et al*, 1990: 17).

Urban Research

In Western countries social research is mainly an urban activity. The same is true in developing countries. It is estimated in Egypt, for example, that 75 per cent of research is done in urban areas in a country where about 50 per cent of people live in rural districts.

The buying of the western export model of research is sometimes linked to a corresponding importation of western research apparatus with a built-in urban bias, purchased by people working in urban organisations. In an eloquent and disturbing analysis of rural development, Robert Chambers argued some years ago that:

> Not only do urban-based professionals and officials often not know the rural reality; worse, they do not know what they do not know... For academics it is cheaper, safer and more cost-effective in terms of academic output to do urban rather than rural research... Rural research is mainly carried out by the young and inexperienced. For them rural research i s a rite of passage, an initiation which earns them the right to do no more, giving them a ticket to stay in town (Chambers, 1983: 6, 7).

The 1950s background of safari research – intrusive, white-run treks to collect and take away research specimens – has changed, but there is still the issue of the relation between indigenous and outside researchers, and the parallel relationship between research and development. Evaluation programmes run the risk of being seen by developing country customers more as a means of attracting resources for development than as impartial or critical reviews of the adequacy of such programmes.

Given the cultural and political context this is perhaps not surprising. Western social researchers sometimes appear to treasure the experience of an embargoed research report as a mark of street credibility during their career development. For researchers within much of the Arab world the political risks inherent in their work are much more real and up front. The development of research evaluations that can both work within, yet successfully challenge a socially homogenous parent culture makes a level of demand that us alien to the experience of most radical practitioners or researchers working in the West.

Knowledge and Research in Arab Culture

From their cultural and epistemological distance, Western academic social scientists, until very recently, have failed to appreciate the texture of Muslim culture with its implications for the role of the individual, ideas of social solidarity, patterns of reciprocal obligation, and so on. Harré's brief discussion of Islamic moral psychology in the context of psychological paradigms is a rare exception (Harré, 1989: 32). Hence western research and sociology texts transferred to Arab culture will inevitably be experienced as abstract and artificial.

Within Arab Muslim society religious knowledge is both the paradigmatic and the most highly valued form of knowledge. Within a traditional Arab culture the key issue is the culturally perceived relationship between a given field of study and the religious sciences (i.e. those bodies of knowledge which are thought to elucidate the *Quran*). Lines of continuity rather than discontinuity are sought from 'old' to 'new' knowledge, so that sociology may tend to be seen as old religious philosophy writ large.

This is not to say that there is no scope for 'secular knowledge' within Arab Muslim culture. Though some intellectual innovations are regarded as contrary to Islamic law, others are accepted so long as they do not explicitly contradict those principles. Hence, for sociology or social research methodologies, the question at issue becomes one of where they stand in relation to the religious sciences and secular knowledge. Thus there is an active debate within those parts of the Arab world where sociology is a distinct discipline as to whether there should be an 'Islamic Sociology', in which the concepts of sociology are 'Islamicised', and a corresponding debate about whether social workers ought to be accountable to religious leaders.

Learning is traditionally carried forward through memorising the *Quran*, based on mnemonic systems. Drawing on research carried out in parts of North Africa, Eickelman has argued that both religious and secular knowledge:

> throughout the Islamic world are thought to be transmitted through a quasi genealogical chain of authority which descends from master or teacher (shaykh)

> to student (talib) to ensure that the knowledge of earlier generations is passed on intact (Eickelman, 1978: 492).

In fieldwork carried out in Morocco, Eickelman found that:

> Former students emphasised that throughout the long process of memorising the Quran they asked no questions concerning the meaning of verse, even among themselves, nor did it occur to them to do so (Eickelman, 1978: 494).

Insofar as learning is influenced by such traditional patterns, 'understanding', unlike within western traditions, is measured not by any ability to 'explain' text, but by the ability to use particular *Quranic* verses in new and appropriate contexts.

An almost automatic Western conclusion from this account will be that such learning systems will lead inevitably to a deadening of any sense of inquiry. Given the wider features of Arab Muslim learning, which include some informal peer learning, this is a risky assumption. However, it does suggest possible reasons why there is a limited indigenous sociological voice in the Arab world, and why the debate about the development of sociology may become drawn into a polarisation of uncritical translated paraphrasing of western sociology and research texts under the guise of Arab authorship, versus an Islamicising of social science to a point where there appear few if any common *motifs* with western sociological enterprise.

Social science and social life end up inhabiting different worlds, and there is a tendency to uncritically adopt structural functionalist theories, backed by a superficial quoting of selected verses from the *Quran* as justification, thus sanctifying a particular brand of theorising. The model of a man *(sic)* of learning is also often allied to accepted popular notions of social inequality as a natural fact of the social order, and a restricted sense of social responsibility to criticise or change society.

Scholars are not in agreement on the extent to which the critical elements of this account should be attributed to either formal or lay versions of specifically *Islamic* culture. Indeed, it has also been argued that it is the *political* rather than *religious* environments of most if not all Arab regimes which are not conducive to either an open, interactive educational process or to a research-generated social critique of political systems (Massialas and Jarrar, 1983: 109-113).

An important contribution to this debate is presently being made by those who argue that the writing of the 14th C (Christian calendar) writer, Ibn Khaldun, provides the basis for a truly indigenous Arab-Muslim sociology, through his organising concept of *Al'Assabiyya*, through which he sought to explain how and why things are as they are (Dhaouadi, 1990).

It would be beyond the scope of this paper to attempt a dialogue with this line of argument. Ibn Khaldun's work appears to allow for a theory of social change within Arab-Muslim civilisation, and offers an explanation which goes some way to avoiding an either/or, political, economic, *versus* religious model of

Arab societies. His conceptual organising principle also provides the potential for a genuinely indigenous sociology.

Yet we are left with a number of unresolved problems in setting a direction for social research in the Arab world. Ibn Khaldun's level of explanation leads naturally to a concentration on a rather deterministic, evolutionary grand theorising. What is also needed is a research framework for analytic social policy that stimulates theoretical and empirical work at the levels of professional behaviour, service development and delivery, and policy implementation. We remain unconvinced that this tradition of sociological thinking will prove productive in these aspects of discipline and research development.

Within the cultural context of the Arab world it will prove no surprise that social research tends to be carried out largely by men. The memory of a male Kuwaiti government official, carrying out interview research with mothers about adoption and fostering, mediated through women social workers employed by the state, illustrates a particular challenge that Arab societies face in hearing the voice of women as family members and users of services.

In an interesting ethnographic study of craftswomen in part of Egypt, Lynch observes the neglect of efforts to conceptualise and document women's work, along with the assumption that the woman's contribution is mainly confined to 'housework' and therefore has only a marginal contribution to development. This, women's work is regarded as 'helping out' and not employment and does not show in census or employment figures:

> Western oriented in education and lifestyle, government bureaucrats attempt to deal with rural issues which they little understand because of class and cultural differences (Lynch, 1984: 3).

If some such analyses will hold water, how can an ethos of commitment to the indigenisation of quality social research be sustained within the Arab world? We want to suggest that there are five general ways in which this might occur, all of which target the underlying issue of a culturally pertinent social science scholarship. We would advocate first, the development of *scholarly association*, second, a sustained reflection on appropriate styles of *scholarly discourse*, third, the *institutionalisation of quality research*, fourth, the growth of a research methodology which entails a sustained commitment to the value of *qualitative research* styles, and finally, the fostering of a sensitive *reciprocity* with western social science. Each of these must take place within a wider debate about the role of the university and the social value of social science within the Arab world.

1. Scholarly Association

Professional and academic groups already exist in most Arab countries, and the gradual growth in parts of the Arab world of regular conferences is itself partial evidence of such association. Yet we are asking for something further than this.

To suggest just one example, we do not regard it as being in the long term interests of either sociology or social work for joint associations to act as the main bodies of association. Sociology and social work have long been uncomfortable, yet inseparable bedfellows, at their closest in uneasy coalition, and at their most distant locked in alienated, adversarial conflict. In the words of one commentator, social work and sociology have tried for more than a century to live down their common ancestry (Lee, 1976).

Today echoes of this debate can be heard in countries as varied as China, Taiwan, Canada, southern Africa, Nigeria, the former Yugoslavia, Britain, the United States, Switzerland, Sweden and other European countries as well as in the Arab world. We are not convinced by the substantial literature in the West that argues the essential common interests of sociology and social work – 'if only they realised it'. The sharp discontinuity of theory and practice apparently experienced by all social and community workers is for us the essence of a necessary mutual state of critical, creative tension.

However, in advocating scholarly association we are not restricting our thoughts to formal organisations. The fostering of *informal* collaboration and discussion is needed, so that shared *writing* and *collaborative research* can be developed. In a recent conference comment on research activity in Egypt, there was noted '*an observed variety of research subjects with the absence of a scientific coherence between them*' (Sawsan Osman, 1992). Without some such developments on the lines just suggested, Arab social science will continue to be marked by low-level duplication of effort, lack of cumulative, discipline development, and a limited scholarly impact.

The result is almost a caricature of western individualism, with very strong pressure to complete PhD work, which in turn can produce quantity at the expense of quality. Career progress is tied too closely to the chain of masters degree, doctoral degree, publishing at all costs, and thence promotion. This eventuates in pressure to look for the easiest research projects, and the suspicion that plagiarism and the overt misuse of student research may be widespread (Farah, 1976; Nuor, 1987; Khoder, 1992).

2. Styles of Academic Exchange

We suggested earlier that the ideals and realities of academic life and culture within the Arab world cannot be viewed in isolation from indigenous patterns of learning and education, with their characteristic stance of explaining and questioning, and the associated model of a man of learning. It is at least worth debate as to whether the didactic model of teaching in many Arab schools and universities, with its absence of discursive content, acts against the generation of individual scholarship, and in part leads to the re-cycling of accepted ideas in Arab social science literature.

A self-reinforcing schooling of this kind may in turn yield a reluctance either to give or receive intellectual criticism, and to a lack of appropriate styles of scholarly criticism. Thus conference papers often feel, at least to western ears, like a presentation of justificatory accounts, without any element of self-critical 'testability', and discussion tends to be at the level of generalities rather than of points which may have specific implications for thought or action.

Sociologists in the Arab world need to consider whether the development of sociology has been marked too heavily by an uncritical import of western, especially European, theorising; a widespread reliance on straight translations of western texts; a lack of culturally specific methodology; and a theoretical generalism which has often led to superficiality.

One way forward will involve the development of good Arabic journals. There are very few journals in the social science field that are indigenous to the Arab speaking world. The limited collaborative work that does go on seems to be western-led (eg Tessler *et al*, 1987). Young scholars completing doctoral work are usually obliged to write in *English* or sometimes *French*, for journals published *outside their own countries*. We are not naive about the difficulties surrounding the establishment of new journals which may be thought to have explicit social or political implications, but remain convinced that the emergence of cross-national sociology journals, perhaps with a sociology of social problems focus, and the nurturing of a younger generation of scholars – men and women – are major issues that must be addressed in the near future.

3. Institutionalising Quality Research

A common theme of the foregoing has been the need to find appropriate ways of institutionalising an indigenous social science research committed to work of critical quality.

The lack of a research infrastructure is one consequence of the weakness of social science within the Arab world. Physicists, engineers and doctors are understandably valued, whereas a recent, small-scale study of Egyptian researchers employed in a range of research settings identified inadequate central government policies for social research as the single most important hindrance to the fostering of effective social research (Abo El-Nasr, 1991). If issues of research sponsorship, collaborative activity and the achievement of a culturally specific independence of scholarly work are to be accomplished, then social research needs to develop an institutional base.

Here it is easier to identify problems than to be confident of ways forward. The establishment of independently funded research institutes, of research units within university departments with programme funding, the consolidation of the growing service, development and policy research work currently being undertaken through some of the major charities such as Oxfam (Pratt and Boyden, 1985; Marsden and Oaldey, 1990), the provision for funding of research studentships at post-doctoral level, and the establishment of financial partnerships across the divide between higher education and the private sector of industry and business, are all but pointers to a strategy that needs sustained cultivation *(cf* Vulliamy *et al*, 1990:

21-25, who make some of these points in the context of educational research). Such a strategy would involve the development of research outside as well as inside the higher education sector.

4. Research Methodologies

After a long history of being wedded to quantitative designs, some writers have detected the beginnings of a case study and ethnographic approach within research in developing countries, particularly in the field of education (Vulliamy *et al*, 1990).

With its associated emphasis on methodology as a context-related social process, qualitative research offers a strategy which is more likely to yield an indigenous research. It will open up a range of new substantive dimensions of familiar issues through a focus on the processes of service delivery and organisational life, identify unintended consequences through the ways in which policy implementations depart from scripts, uncover the phenomenology of how change is actually experienced, and foster the curiosity of distance and anthropological strangeness for urban Arab researchers working within their own societies, in rural and urban areas.

5. Reciprocity with the West

Aspects of the institutionalisation of quality research for which we have argued will entail working with Western organisations such as the Ford Foundation and the major charities. But this Arab/Western dialogue must be no one-way traffic. For example, the existence and recognition of Islamic/Arab cultures in France, Britain, Germany and elsewhere means that sociology and social research in these nations need to learn from their academic peers in Arab and other Muslim cultures in order to expand and develop their own academic research and practice.

The growing extent of institutional movement means that the transmission of expert knowledge needs to go in multiple directions. While practical considerations may mean that scholars will continue to look to USA/Britain/France for accreditation and expertise, increasingly academics and practitioners need to look to the recognition of indigenous intellectual traditions. The 'metropolitan' centres of learning also need to shed their colonial appropriation of expert knowledge and cultural capital.

In this way – and only in this way – appropriately planned study in the West not only has a continuing role, but paradoxically can prove one of the best ways of developing a culturally relevant social science. We want to witness the development of an international sociology, without accepting the full force of arguments for globalisation (Albrow and King, 1990) which, in our view, run counter to a number of the considerations raised in this paper. Learning in the Arab world will continue for the foreseeable future to depend heavily on the translation of English and French language texts (the appropriate *selection,* high quality *translation,* and educational *use* of such texts are issues in themselves), but the cultural contextualisation of Western scholarship cannot easily be achieved outside the academic communities that generate such material. There is a real sense in which Arab students who have been taught research methodology through straight translations of western texts may at some point arrive in the West not having understood that methodology.

Reciprocity should also entail the careful development of co-supervision schemes for Arab world students, such as the Egyptian Channel Scheme that operates between Egyptian and British universities, and enables assistant lecturers registered for doctoral work in their own university to experience collaborative supervision with a British university, and spend time studying in the United Kingdom.

Exchange must operate at the intellectual level as well as the institutional, and while it is beyond the scope of this article to cover this territory, the risk of neocolonialism might in part be avoided by arrangements for western scholars to spend limited but fairly substantial periods of time teaching and conducting research in developing countries.

Conclusion

We have tried to illustrate ways in which the cultural and epistemological contexts of societies shape the fundamental character and existence of social science and in particular social research. We have been conscious in doing so that we have been treading difficult territory, and may not have expressed our position with the evenhandedness it demands. Nonetheless, we are convinced that the ramifications of the Western export model of research together with the pervasive influence of Arab and perhaps Muslim traditions of learning and schooling, constitute the environment within which debate about the indigenisation of quality in Arab social research must be conducted.

We have identified a specific agenda of considerations, primarily around the institutionalisation of scholarship, but also in regard to reciprocity in Arab/ Western social science and the widening of the paradigms within which research methodology is framed in the Arab world.

While we have limited our illustrations to the Arab world – and in reality to the still more restricted parts of that world with which we are to a greater or lesser degree familiar – it is our view that corresponding tasks face social science elsewhere in the developing world. Social science will otherwise be fundamentally weakened, both in those countries and in the West.

References

Abo El-Nasr, M. (1991) 'Obstacles to Social Research and Social Work Research in Developing Countries with Special Reference to the Egyptian Experience', unpublished paper.

Al-Awwad, K. (1991) 'Service Provision in Saudi Public Sector Organisations: An Open System Approach', PhD Thesis, University of Wales, College of Cardiff.

Albrow, M. and King, E. (eds) (1990) *Globalisation, Knowledge and Society: Readings from International Sociology*, Sage, London.

Bryman, A. (1988) *Quantity and Quality in Social Research*, Unwin Hyman, London.

Bulmer, M. and Warwick, D.(eds) (1993) *Social Research in Developing Countries*, UCL Press, London.

Chambers, R. (1983) *Rural Development: Putting the Last First*, Longman, Harlow.

Cicourel, A. (1964) *Method and Measurement in Sociology*, Free Press, New York.

Dhaouadi, M. (1990) 'Ibn Khaldun: The Founding Father of Eastern Sociology', in *International Sociology*, 5, pp 319-335.

Eickelman, D.F. (1978) "The Art of Memory: Islamic Education and Its Social Reproduction", in *Comparative Studies in History and Society*, 20, pp 485516.

Farah, Muhamed S. (1976) *Deraset fel Mugtam'a Al Masry (Studies in Egyptian Society)* Dar al Ketab, Alexandria.

Khoder, A. (1992) *Azmat at Bahth at Elmi fi at Alam al Arabi (The Crisis of Research in the Arab World)*, Al-Hojeland Office, Riyadh.

Hakim, C. (1987) *Research Design*, Unwin Hyman, London.

Harré, R. (1989) 'Language Games and Texts of Identity', in J. Shotter and K.J. Gergen (eds) *Texts of Identity*, Sage, London.

Ibrahim S.E. (1987) 'Agony and Ecstasy of Social Research in the Arab World', in M. Tessler, M. Palmer, T.E. Farah and B.L. Ibrahim *The Evaluation and Application of Survey Research in the Arab World*, Westview Press, Boulder.

Lee, A.M. (1976) "What Kind of Sociology is Useful to Social Workers?", in *Journal of Sociology and Social Welfare*, 4, pp 4-13.

Lynch, P.D. (1984) *Craftswomen in Kerdassa, Egypt*, International Labour Office, Geneva.

Marsden, D. and Oakley, P. (1990) *Evaluating Social Development Projects*, Oxfam, Oxford.

Marsh, C. (1982) *The Survey Method*, Unwin Hyman, London.

Massialas, B.G. and Jarra, S.A. (1983) *Education in the Arab World*, Praeger, New York.

Nuor, O.A. (1987) "ElmAlsokan" in *Arab Journal for the Humanities*, 7, pp 176-179.

Pratt, B. and Boyden, J. (eds) (1985) *The Field Directors Handbook*, Part 3, OUP/OUP/Oxfam, Oxford.

Sawsan O. and Latif, A. (1992) "Identity of Social Work in Egypt An Analytical View and Future Outlook", paper presented at the International Conference on Social Work and the Future in Developing Countries, January, Cairo.

Tessler, M., Palmer, M., Farah, T.E. and Ibrahim, B.L. (1987) *The Evaluation and Application of Survey Research in the Arab World*, Westview Press, Boulder.

Vulliamy G., Lewin, K. and Stephens, D. (1990) *Doing Educational Research in Developing Countries*, Falmer, Basingstoke.

PART V
Service Users and Research

The field of user research is one of the least settled – and most unsettling – areas within social work research. Unsettling because it poses difficult questions – about structured and personal forms of discrimination; about the perceived dangers in several quarters of scientific hegemony; about the gendered male dominance of science and the majority position of women among service users; and about the scarcely veiled anger that many service users – and user researchers – feel towards those with whom they have to do in the state. The issues are complicated by the diversity of sometimes overlapping justice-based research positions – Postmodern, Feminist, Standpoint, Marxist, Fabian and the obligation-based position reaching back to Adam Smith.

I want to depart from the previous section introductions and expand slightly on the possible positions that have been taken on the power and regulatory force of service user knowledge in social work research. I want to cast this in the language of research quality, drawing as I do on my work with Norton and others that I have referred to several times. I see these positions as separate alternatives.

First, *some quality dimensions carry greater weight than others*. This may be argued from a belief that scientific knowledge always takes precedence over e.g. knowledge based on experience (hence rigour, accuracy and 'inner-science' criteria will always be more important than 'outer-science' criteria). It may also be argued from, for example, a strong 'standpoint' position that the knowledge of the oppressed will always carry greater validity than that of the oppressor. On the other hand, if a researcher believes that identifying outcomes of programmes is the most important way to progress social work services then randomized, controlled, clinical trials are likely to be seen as providing the 'gold standard, the Rolls Royce of evaluation approaches' (Chelimsky, 1997: 101). Yet, speaking about the field of evaluation, even Chelimsky concedes that the discipline needs standards of quality and practice that make sense for the entire field, not just one segment of it. 'It will be critical for the standards to be inclusive of all legitimate purposes of evaluation, and not merely serve to sanctify one perspective at the expense of another' (Chelimsky, 1997: 108). We can transfer the caution to social work when she warns of evaluation that it 'is not monolithic, but we have behaved as if it were' (Chelimsky, 1997: 104).

Second, it is possible to hold a viewpoint that *quality criteria will always be contingent on local context* and the perspectives of the stakeholders, and cannot be 'assigned' in advance. This position was one that Norton and I often found claimed by those to whom we spoke, but one we were less sure was consistently held.

A third position claims that *'inner' and 'outer' science criteria of quality are both indispensable*, and that they should be brought to bear on any given research project or output. However, they should not be applied through a framework of 'criteriology' (Stake, 2004), but at a level of generality that does not require us to 'weight' dimensions against one another. This is a highly condensed way of expressing a position that we expand in more detail elsewhere (Shaw and Norton, 2007). I found myself in sympathy with a position put to us by different people throughout the project – that 'outer-science' norms (eg being useful or emancipatory) are neither more nor less important than 'inner science' epistemic norms. Understood in this way, criteria developed for assessing the quality of social work research in particular contexts should still touch in one way or the other *all* of the general dimensions (Furlong and Oancea, 2005), but with a flexibility and level of specificity tailored to the particular project. Hence, it seems reasonable to suggest that quality should usually be assessed against a working rule that good research will usually be 'good' on more than one dimension. For example, it will not be 'good' *only* because it has been useful, *or* rigorous, *or* emancipatory.

I said in the opening chapter that I believe the criticism of early 'consumer opinion' studies by emancipatory researchers may have been misplaced. I have made several efforts to grasp the nature and significance of user knowledge. Two of those attempts are included in this collection (Shaw, 1976, 1984a). Both are from early in my career, and though I think they are far from complete, I am not sure I think the central conclusions are too far off the mark. I recall it as the first intellectual problem I gave a sustained effort to understand. Jennifer Platt's sociological analysis of the work of the Institute of Community Studies shaped my thinking in the first instance.

My preoccupations have shifted from hearing the voice of the 'consumer' (the term of the time) to embedding that within a weak standpoint position of the kind I explored in the piece on consequences of research included in Section 3. The next two pieces appeared a thirteen and sixteen year gap after the later of the first two articles. There are elements of continuity. The one on participation and the rhetoric of quality was written in the period when I was also working on the quality management discourse. The one from 2000 takes issues of justice as its *motif* – a category that was just finding its feet in the social work literature.

There is less differentiation between the first four pieces in this section than has been true of the choices in the previous sections. There is overlap and development between the pieces. The final inclusion is of a different kind, and acts as a tailpiece not only to the book as a whole but more specifically to the last two sections. It is an unpublished paper given to the Inter Centre Network for the Evaluation of Social Work Practice (INTSOCEVAL) in 2009. INTSOCEVAL is known in limited circles, but it is a significant network of a small number of representatives of research centres and departments, mainly but not exclusively in Europe. I have found membership of this network over the last decade provoking and challenging. I tried to place in conjunction the knowledge and values about social work research held by service users and practitioners, highlighting the significant differences. The presentation was based on four research projects – two regarding practitioner research and two linked to my good fortune in being involved in user research projects.

References

Chelimsky, E. (1997) 'Thoughts for a New Evaluation Society', *Evaluation* 3 (1): 97-118.

Furlong, J. and Oancea, A. (2005) *Assessing Quality in Applied Educational Research*. Swindon, ESRC.

Shaw, I. (1976) 'Consumer Opinion and Social Policy', *Journal of Social Policy* 5 (1): 19-32.

Shaw, I. (1984a) 'Consumer Evaluations of the Personal Social Services', *British Journal of Social Work* 14 (3): 277-284.

Shaw, I. (1997) 'Participation, Empowerment and the Rhetoric of Quality' (1997) in Pithouse, A and Williamson H. (eds) *Engaging the User in Welfare*. Birmingham, Venture Press.

Shaw, I. (2000) 'Just inquiry? Research and Evaluation for Service Users' in Kemshall, H. and Littlechild, R. (eds) *Participation in Social Care: Researching for Practice.* London, Jessica Kingsley.

Shaw, I. 'Postscripts on Users' and Practitioners' Research', Paper to 2009 Annual Meeting of the Inter-Centre Network for the Evaluation of Social Work Practice, Kristiansand, Norway. Unpublished.

Stake, R.E. (2004) *Standards-Based and Responsive Evaluation*. Thousand Oaks, Sage Publications.

Chapter 21

Consumer Opinion and Social Policy: A Research Review*

A significant proportion of research in social work shows a strong disposition to take into account the standpoint of the people receiving the social service in question. A focus on the opinion of the client, or, more fashionably, the 'consumer', marks part or the whole of a growing number of studies.[1]

This concern to understand the perspective of the consumer – the person directly involved in the situation of interest, but without any specialized training or role to play in relation to it – as distinct from the 'producer' or the general public, has been produced and moulded by a number of factors. The influence of politically left-wing opinion on social work stands for a favourable interpretation of the value of working-class culture. This has hit social work later than social administration, and has resulted in a distaste for the professionalization of social work practice, in so far as such professionalism implies an inability on the part of the client to diagnose his own needs, or discriminate among the range of possibilities for meeting them. Furthermore, the interest in 'client power',[2] the

---

* Originally published as Shaw, I. (1976) 'Consumer Opinion and Social Policy', *Journal of Social Policy* 5(1): 19-32. Reprinted with permission of Cambridge University Press.

1 The discovery of consumer opinion is the major concern of the following studies: P.M. Voelcker, 'Juvenile Courts: The Parents' Point of View', *Br. J. Criminology* 1 (2), 1960, pp. 154-66; J. Mayer and N. Timms, *The Client Speaks,* London: Routledge and Kegan Paul, 1970; A. McKay, E.M. Goldberg and D.J. Fruin, 'Consumers and a Social Services Department', *Social Work Today* 4 (16), 1973, pp. 486-91; J. Triseliotis, *In Search of Origins*, London: Routledge and Kegan Paul, 1973; D. Marsden, *Mothers Alone*, Harmondsworth: Penguin, 1973; P. Morris, J. Cooper and A. Byles, 'Public Attitudes to Problem Definition and Problem Solving', *Br. J. Social Work* 3 (3), 1973, pp. 301-20; O. Gill, *Whitegate: An Approved School in Transition*, Liverpool: Liverpool University Press, 1974; E. Sainsbury, *Social Work with Families*, London: Routledge and Kegan Paul, 1975. It is a partial concern in the following: Z. Butrym, *Medical Social Work in Action*, Occasional Papers on Social Administration, London: Bell, 1968; A. Cohen, 'Consumer View: Retarded Mothers and the Social Services', *Social Work Today* 1 (12), 1971, pp. 39-43; E.M. Goldberg, *Helping the Aged*, London: Allen and Unwin, 1970; M. Bayley, *Mental Handicap and Community Care*, London: Routledge and Kegan Paul, 1973; see also N. Timms, *The Receiving End*, London: Routledge and Kegan Paul, 1973; M. Shaw, *Social Work in Prison*, London: HMSO, 1974.

2 R. Holman, 'Client Power', *New Society* 31, Nov. 1968; A. Sinfield, *Which Way for Social Work?*, London: Fabian Society, 1969.

growth of consumer groups, and the disillusion with traditional forms of political representation have led to a partial breakdown of the structural isolation[3] of social work clients, and therefore an increased motivation to discover their evaluation of the services offered. This diversification of interest is consistent with the current preoccupation with finding more meaningful indices of social need.

Furthermore, in the realm of casework theorizing, the decline of analytic viewpoints and concepts, which encouraged practitioners to discount or explain away any views the client may have, has made it easier for social workers to be alert to rational meaning in the clients' account of his experience. Thus, Goffman points out that the psychiatrist is often under pressure to treat the outpourings of the patient not as directly usable statements of information, but rather as signs of the illness itself, to be discounted as direct information. 'But to treat the statements of the patients as signs, not valid symptom reporting, is of course to deny that the patient is a participant as well as an object in a service relation.'[4]

Finally, developments in research have provided both negative and positive reasons for grounding social work research more firmly on the client's own account of services received. The evaluative and experimental research of the 1960s led into a *cul de sac*. Results depressingly and predictably revealed marginal benefits either from social work in general, or from one variety of social work help as against another variety. One methodological approach that seemed to provide a way out of the *impasse* was that of close exploration and inspection of the meaning of social work to those who participate in it – an approach congenial with the resurgence of interest in qualitative research. British sociology appeared to provide a partial model for such research in the work of the Institute of Community Studies, which, in its programme of study into the relationship between the social services and working class family life, proceeds on the assumption that the policy makers and administrators are insufficiently aware of the needs or views of the working-class people who form the bulk of the users of the social services.[5]

Typical studies of this kind are based on fairly small samples of current or recent users of a particular social service. Respondents are interviewed with the aid of a loosely structured schedule, containing a large proportion of open-ended questions, and are asked to describe their experience of the service they received. The research approach is descriptive, with no formal hypotheses, and the account relies heavily on extracts from the interview to illustrate the opinions, attitudes and behaviour of the respondents. Professional and administrative conceptions of the service, as derived from the literature, are sometimes used as a basis for comparison. The study concludes with a number of policy recommendations. These recommendations are typically for improvements or rationalizations in

3 Mayer and Timms, *op. cit.,* pp. 15-16.

4 E. Goffman, *Asylums*, New York: Anchor Books, 1961, pp. 367-8.

5 J. Platt, *Social Research in Bethnal Green*, London: Macmillan, 1971, Introduction. Working-class people still form the bulk of social service clients, although the elderly and chronically sick and handicapped probably cut across class lines.

the delivery of existing services, rather than criticisms of an overall deficiency in the extent of the service or suggestions for the implementation of new kinds of services. The studies listed above[6] illustrate the wide range of issues within which recommendations have been made.

Value Commitments

The purpose of this review is to assess the commitment to the consumer and the efforts to formulate policy recommendations, as found in this loosely linked collection of research studies carried out in Britain, and particularly to evaluate the potentiality of social work consumer opinion in formulating social policy. Two main points will be made. First, that it is difficult to know when the opinion of the consumer has been understood properly. Second, that even when the views of consumers are known to us, the question of how these views are utilized in the formulation of policy is problematic.[7] 'A whole programme of research'[8] may be needed, but clarification of the precise purpose and utility of such research is an important prerequisite.

Two further points can be made as a preface to the discussion. It needs emphasizing that the derivation of prescriptions for action is a central concern in this literature. The studies by Butrym[9] and Goldberg[10] fail to work their data about consumer opinion into the main fabric of the work in ways that are more than incidental and peripheral to the main arguments, but these are exceptional, as a comparison with the work of Bayley, Mayer and Timms, Gill, Triseliotis and Marsden[11] makes clear. For example, Triseliotis starts off his book on adult adoptees in search of their natural parents by saying: 'It was hoped that answers to certain questions might not only give further understanding of the adoption situation but also point towards desirable areas for legal reform and for practice changes'.[12]

The second remark, by way of introduction, is that the commitment to take into account the standpoint of the consumer of social policy is a value judgement, the full consequences of which cannot be known until the investigation of viewpoints has taken place. A willingness to tolerate diversity and a belief that dignity and

6 See fn. 1 above.

7 This review is concerned with the sociological or methodological contributions made by the literature only in so far as these impinge on the way in which policy recommendations are formulated.

8 Mayer and Timms, *ibid.*, p. 1.

9 Butrym, *op. cit.*, pp. 69-82.

10 Goldberg, *op. cit.*, pp. 171-82, 189-90.

11 In the light of our earlier comments, it is worth recalling that Marsden has been associated with the work of the Institute of Community Studies for some years.

12 *Op. cit.*, p. 2.

respect are due to the individual as such are two values present in the literature. Also, the basic commitment tends to suggest at least an implicit conflict of interest between the consumer and the producer.

Discerning Consumer Opinion[13]

Our discussion so far might imply that the role of social work consumer is a clearly defined one, mutually agreed by all concerned. Recent evidence suggests that this is not so. In their study of people connected with Southampton Social Services Department, McKay and her colleagues found that the status of consumer is not a clear one for the client. Of the clients in their sample who thought they were still in contact with the social worker, 10 per cent were registered as 'closed' cases by the department. In contrast, two-thirds of those who thought they were 'closed', were registered as 'active'.[14] This helps to explain why, despite the work done so far, we have limited knowledge of the user's perspective in the social services, in that it is not easy for the researcher to maintain a clear and systematic distinction between the views of the social worker and those of the client. The views of 'producers' and consumers become confused, usually at the expense of the consumer.

This partly accounts for the stereotyped response frequently obtained to questions about levels of satisfaction experienced by clients, for example by Goldberg and McKay. The failure to distinguish the views of social worker and client is more obvious in Butrym's study of patients referred to medical social workers (MSWs), where the view of social work activity accepted by the researcher vitiates any use that might have been obtained from patients' views. For example, she analyses patients' descriptions of social work help in terms of whether it fitted the model of material or emotional help. On finding that only three out of 28 patients can be exclusively classified in one or the other category, she dubiously concludes that the figures 'reflect both the patients' recognition of the psycho-social nature of social work, and the medical social workers' adherence to this reality.[15]

The recent research by Cohen suggests that the difficulty experienced by users of a social service in finding a language with which to talk about and evaluate services is a further obstacle to discovering the clients' views. He illustrates their lack of vocabulary and familiarity with the services, and the feeling that the actions of social workers were either arbitrary or absurd.[16]

This problem may have been greater for Cohen's sample of mentally handicapped mothers than for other groups, but this can scarcely be said of other

---

13 This section is indebted to ideas outlined by Noel Timms in his Introduction to *The Receiving End, op. cit.*

14 McKay *et al., op. cit.*, p. 490.

15 *Op. cit.*, p. 74.

16 *Op. cit.*, pp. 39-40.

difficulties experienced by these same women in giving a clear evaluation of the services received. The very idea of evaluating was alien to them – a reluctance to criticize which stemmed in part from the feeling some women had that the service received was a favour rather than a benefit to which they had entitlement. This appears to reflect feelings about the individual presenting the service rather than the adequacy of provision. In Cohen's words, 'If the service is presented by someone regarded as likeable and well meaning the clients may feel disloyal or unfair to him if they criticise the service he represents.'

This particular problem pervades the literature. McKay records the difficulty she experienced in differentiating between consumers' attitudes towards the department, the services received and the individual worker.[17] Bayley found that the appraisal given by the families of mentally handicapped people of the service provided by mental welfare officers depended on the quality of the current relationship with a particular officer.[18] Again, Voelcker, in his study of how the parents of boys appearing in juvenile court understood the procedures, found that parents had a favourable picture of individual probation officers, but little sympathy for probation as a method of treatment.[19]

A further problem arises when the assumptions which lie behind apparently straightforward questions may not be shared by the interviewee. For instance, social work may be viewed by the client as a bartering relationship, entered into for the purpose of gaining specific material ends. The relationship itself may be regarded simply as a means to an end and not part of the end itself. Hence, 'If social work is seen as the "interference" one has to tolerate in order to receive the service, the consumer's evaluation may concern only a part of what the researcher defines as the service... [We] must know what the consumer sees as the boundaries of service.'[20]

Voelcker falls into the same trap of interpreting respondents' comments in the light of assumptions they do not share. He remarks that only two of the parents 'realized the impossibility [*sic*] of keeping to a close schedule' in court hearings. Again, when discussing their views about the methods of disposal used by the magistrates, he concludes that 'many parents have either a wrong or confused interpretation of all types of disposal'.[21] Voelcker apparently has failed to realize that views and activities which seem random to an outsider have order and pattern for a participant.

Finally, pressures of an organizational and professional nature may distort the voice of the client so that it simply echoes back whatever the professionals or the organizations wish to hear. When this happens, attempts to make sense

---

17 McKay, *ibid.,* pp. 488-9.

18 Bayley, *op. cit.*, p. 302.

19 Voelcker, *op. cit.*

20 Cohen, *ibid.,* pp. 42-3. The element of bargaining was found in the studies by Cohen and Mayer and Timms.

21 *Op cit.*

of the client's viewpoint are foredoomed. For example, Butrym tries more than once to explain away disagreements in the responses of patient and social worker. In dividing reasons for referral to the social worker into the two categories of environmental and emotional reasons, a disagreement level of 43 per cent between patients and MSWs is dismissed as not reflecting 'a basic disagreement, but rather a difference in emphasis which hardly seems surprising...'. Again, when asking patients 'what sort of training do you think an almoner ought to have?', Butrym is making the assumption, shared by her fellow professionals, that some sort of training is a good thing. This may have been self-evident to her, but it was an assumption clearly not shared by the patients, who had an ideal picture of an MSW which did not include systematic or prolonged training. Small wonder that only a handful of patients could give a clear answer to the question.[22]

Thus, there are a considerable number of reasons which make it difficult to discern the genuine voice of the client.

Utilizing Consumer Opinion

We have already remarked that some studies are concerned only superficially to work consumer opinion into their recommendations. Also, Gill's study is aimed only generally at evaluating consumer opinion of grass roots policy changes. However, the assumption is clearly present in all the literature under review that consumer opinion can be used in the formulation of social policy.

Despite this, the precise ways in which consumer opinion is to be utilized are rarely made explicit. Mayer and Timms recognize limitations on the extent to which client appraisals shape policy decisions without specifying these limitations in more than general terms,[23] but this is a step further than most studies.

Platt's analysis of the research done by the Institute of Community Studies makes fruitful suggestions about restrictions on the use of consumer opinion as a guide to policy.

Limitations on use of Consumer Opinion

First, there should be no other significant groups of consumers whose viewpoints differ from those in the sample. Other things being equal, if there are such groups an equally good case can be made out for acting on *their* opinions.[24] Unless this point is recognized, minority opinion among consumer groups is likely to exercise a disproportionate influence or be completely overlooked. This condition is more likely to be met when the consumers in question are members of an easily identifiable group. For this reason, Bayley's study convinces one that the particular

22 *Ibid.*, pp. 73, 76-7.
23 *Ibid.*, pp. 2-3.
24 Platt, *op. cit.*, p. 35.

group of consumers has been adequately sampled. The condition has not been met in the studies by Triseliotis and Mayer and Timms. Triseliotis samples adult adoptees who applied to the Registrar General in Edinburgh, asking to be supplied with information from their original birth entries. He is unable to say whether this group of people was similar in important respects to adoptees who did not make a search, and, in view of the fact that people applying to Register House are only a small proportion of adult adoptees, we have no grounds for thinking that the suggestions they make are typical. The same point applies to Mayer and Timms' sample of past clients of the Family Welfare Association.

In the study by McKay, the researchers obviously feel that the sample of clients ought to be comparable with a wider population. Hence she spends some time comparing the client group with the population of Southampton as a whole. However, the reasons for doing so are not clear – as one would expect, the two groups are different, but what implication this has for using client opinion for administrative changes in the social services department, we are not told.

A second condition that must be met is that consumer opinions should be relatively permanent. If their opinions are responsive to changes in their circumstances, opinions may change, even as a result of policy changes designed to satisfy their opinion. A number of the studies under review do not give satisfactory grounds for thinking that this condition has been met. Indeed, the only study that explicitly recognizes the problem is that by McKay, where a follow-up study is planned, to monitor changes in opinion. The difficulty of meeting this condition should not blind us to the fact that opinions collected in circumstances where appraisals of the situation are likely to be fluid[25] are poor indices of general and long-run commitments held by consumers.

Third, consumer opinion must rest upon informed consideration of the possible range of alternatives for dealing with the problem. In McKay's study, it was found that clarity of expectations about what help would be given was related in various ways to the amount of prior knowledge clients possessed about the department. People unclear about what kind of service is available are likely to be still less clear when asked to make suggestions about improvements in the service. This has consequences of considerable significance if the opinions of consumers are to be acted upon, in that resulting proposals are liable to take the existing pattern of life as given, thus producing an inbuilt conservatism. Causes become defined conventionally and the scope of the search for reform is limited.[26] The study by Butrym is particularly weak in this respect. The opinions of patients were ill-informed, and they had no conception of the range of alternative policy and administrative changes, or of the likely consequences of acting on the opinions they were asked to express. In Triseliotis' research radical proposals are ruled out,

25 For instance, the studies by Butrym, Gill, and Mayer and Timms.

26 This point is discussed in Platt, *op. cit.*, Ch. 2, and in P. Marris and M. Rein, *Dilemmas of Social Reform,* Harmondsworth: Penguin, 1972, Ch. 8.

by the fact that 70 per cent of adoptees wanted the existing system of access to the original birth entry to be continued.[27]

This set of conditions may appear unduly stringent and restrictive. Indeed, in some cases effective rejoinders can be made. For example, speculation by participants in a social setting, about the causes and consequences of aspects of that setting, can partake of the character of a self-fulfilling prophecy. In W.I. Thomas' words, 'if men define situations as real they are real in their consequences'. Policy-makers need to be aware of such effects. In addition, it might be replied that these conditions only apply when the researcher transmits the opinions of respondents without comment. Alternatively, the researcher may collect data on the *attitudes* and *behaviour* of consumers in policy-relevant areas, rather than their *opinion*, and make recommendations which he thinks likely to be acceptable to the respondent. This second rejoinder is often effective, in that it assumes consumers' wishes should be deferred to, but avoids the assumption that consumers know how these wishes can best be achieved. It is no longer necessary to ask that consumers know the range of alternatives in front of them.

The literature under review cannot be rigidly allocated to one of these categories or the other, in that most studies contain recommendations based on a mixture of consumer opinion and attitudes and behaviour. The work by Bayley and Cohen relies largely on attitudes and behaviour, and is stronger as a consequence. Bayley, for instance, delineates in telling detail the experience of mothers caring for their seriously handicapped children at home. He shows the crucial significance of the mother's attitude, and the way in which families manage the 'daily grind' of looking after their children by creating a 'structure for coping'. Occasional visits of emotional support from social workers are inappropriate, when 'structural' help is needed that is regular, reliable and punctual, and directly related to the family's structure for coping with the daily grind and mundane slog of caring for the handicapped. He develops the concept of interweaving the informal helping and caring processes already active in society, with the social services, and radically criticizes the inadequacy of seeing voluntary service as supplementary to the official services, rather than the basis upon which all other care is built. His recommendations for a scheme of residential care in locally based hostels differ from the government White Paper, *Better Services for the Mentally Handicapped*,[28] which advocates full hospital care for the profoundly handicapped. One of the reasons for this is that by examining the attitudes and behaviour of the families in his sample, Bayley – unlike the White Paper – has built the families' perceptions of what they need into his recommendations.[29]

However, there are two conditions which must still be met. First, there should be no other significant consumer groups whose attitudes and behaviour differ. Second, their attitudes and behaviour must be relatively permanent. This

27 *Ibid.*, p. 142.

28 Cmnd. 4683, London: HMSO, 1971.

29 Bayley, *op. cit.*, Ch. 19.

second desideratum may be difficult to achieve in that the researcher and policy-maker may wish to assume that behaviour and attitudes have been freely chosen by the consumer. Platt's comment is apposite. 'It is dangerous to infer that wishes, especially "real" (i.e. unverbalized) ones, are expressed in behaviour.'[30] While certain consequences may follow from the consumers' behaviour, these consequences may not represent their intentions. They may be latent functions of the consumers' behaviour, neither consciously intended or even perceived by them.

In our discussion of clients' opinions it has been assumed that the opinions elicited are about policies yet to be chosen. This is, in fact, the case in some studies, but often, as in the cases of Goldberg, Gill and McKay, opinions asked for refer to past or current policies, rather than to possible future ones. It is deceptive to think that recommendations based on such opinions are accurate representations of what the client would choose. Opinion about the future cannot automatically be assumed from opinions about the past or present. Dissatisfaction with the present does not necessarily indicate preference for future change and to assume otherwise is to run the risk of undue radicalism.[31]

Research Methods and Policy

The discussion has so far centred on the logical problems involved in deriving policy recommendations from consumer opinion. There is also a number of points about the research methods adopted in the literature under review which bear directly on the utility of subsequent prescriptions for change.

For instance, the studies are typically descriptive, and explanatory material, if it is present at all, is at a very general level. It is out of place here to discuss the development of theorizing in this research, beyond making the point that a clear purpose guiding the collection of data is necessary if useful policy decisions are to be forthcoming. The research is at its most interesting and provocative in discussing or speculating about explanations.

This point becomes significant when we examine the analysis of material, and the tendency in some cases to resort to 'ideal type' explanations. When summary statements are made about a whole sample, it tends to imply not merely that a majority, or all of them, share certain characteristics now, but that they are likely to do so in the future. 'To make more differentiated statements indicates the dependence of current characteristics on contingencies, and so is likely to imply superior predictions and explanations as well as more accurate description.'[32]

For example, Triseliotis reports that 70 per cent of his sample wanted the existing Scottish system of access to original birth entries to be retained and

30 *Ibid.*, p. 37.

31 J. Platt, 'Survey Data and Social Policy', *Br. J. Sociology* 23 (1), 1972, pp. 77-92.

32 Platt, *op. cit.*, 1971, p. 96.

improved. This becomes 'almost all of the adoptees' in his discussion, and recommendations are made on the basis of majority opinion in the sample. Again, 80 per cent of the adoptees found the search for their origins helpful in one sense or another, and the 20 per cent 'deviant cases' receive relatively little weight.[33] If individual preferences are used as a basis for social policy, then the possibility of conflicting preferences is raised. General policy will be unable to resolve such conflicts. Gill's study is a further example of explanations being presented as ideal types. Indeed, the only study to deal with this issue in a systematic fashion is that by Mayer and Timms, where the opinions of working-class clients are classified according to whether they were satisfied or dissatisfied with the help, and whether the problems they presented to the agency were predominantly material or interpersonal in character. The use of classificatory devices is clearly essential in this kind of research, although the criteria used by these authors for distinguishing clients on the grounds of satisfaction with service received did not prove highly discriminating, and furthermore, they found it more difficult to obtain good accounts from satisfied clients than from dissatisfied ones. In later discussion of their research, this has led to a concentration of attention on the findings from disenchanted clients.[34]

A second criticism of the research methods used in these studies is the over-reliance on intensive interviewing as a means of tapping the views of client participants. While this is one important way of delineating the distinctive perspectives of all participants in a particular setting, it provides a poor independent measure of what actually happens. If the researcher and policy-maker do not wish to assume that the participants' accounts are the only valid ones, the use of different data collection methods is indicated, which complement rather than replace interviewing methods. Participant observation methods, although subject to various kinds of bias, are a fruitful means of obtaining qualitative assessments of settings and actors in those settings, which are partially independent of the actors' own perspectives. The studies under review make no use of participant observation for this particular purpose.[35]

The third point on methodology refers to the sampling methods used. We made the point earlier that there should be no other significant group of clients whose opinions or attitudes and behaviour differ from the sample. Yet this is only a part of the problem, in that samples consisting only of consumers, however representative they may be, inevitably give a partial and at times misleading picture of the current state of affairs. Consequently, they beg the question of which set of values should be applied to policy change, by familiarizing the researcher with only one set of values apart from his own. The policy-maker needs to know the opinions of 'producers' and the general public if he is to avoid acting on a too narrow picture

33 *Op. cit.*, pp. 139, 142, 160.

34 *Op. cit.*, pp. 22-3, 136-48.

35 Gill uses participant observation, but attempts no independent assessment of the setting.

of the current situation.[36] And he needs to consider whose value judgements may be regarded as relevant. Present or future populations? Those directly affected or also those indirectly affected. In the case of Triseliotis' study, for example, the opinion of adopters, natural parents and adoptees who make no search for information about their origins would have been equally relevant to the policy-maker.

Unless an overall perspective is achieved, based on accounts of subjective opposites, research studies are bound to serve the interests of social criticism more than the interests of objective analysis.[37] The implication of this for research methodology is that sampling must be based on a population of *relationships* and not *individuals*. In virtually every case, the work under review is based on samples of individuals, and yet the researchers are generally interested in drawing conclusions about a research population of problems, each of which is perceived by social workers and clients. In such cases the conclusions cannot be upheld from the data. The study of patients referred to medical social workers is a partial exception to this criticism,[38] but the weaknesses in the author's overall research .strategy minimize the potential value of the sampling method. Again, McKay's study in Southampton is part of a wider survey of social workers and clients,[39] but social worker—client relationships as such were not sampled. Gill's study of `Whitegate' is also based solely on consumers, when the opportunity to sample relationships provided by the institutional setting could have resolved some of the problems this sampling technique involves in studies of fieldwork agencies. The weakness is particularly apparent when he comes to discuss staff-inmate relations in the school.[40] Mayer and Timms base their book almost entirely on a sample of consumers. At points in the book they appear to realize the defects of the method (e.g. p. 140), and, as they remark, much of the book is about insight-orientated casework procedures. A small sample of caseworkers was made, but this appears as something of an afterthought, and we have no definite knowledge how the information from this sample has been used by the authors. Marsden's work on fatherless families shows a careful regard for problems of interpretation and utilization of data, and the general failure to obtain information from DHSS officials, etc., complementary to that from the mothers, was not easily avoidable.[41]

---

36 Cf. Morris *et al.*, *op. cit.*; G. Smith and R. Harris, 'Ideologies of Need and the Organisation of Social Work Departments', *Br. J. Social Work* 2 (1), 1972, pp. 27-45.

37 As an example of this, using life histories, see A.J. Manocchio and J. Dunn, *The Time Game: Two views of a Prison*, Beverley Hills: Sage, 1970.

38 Butrym, *op. cit.*

39 Cf. J.E. Neill, D.J. Fruin, E.M. Goldberg and R.W. Warburton, 'Reactions to Integration', *Social Work Today* 4 (15), 1973, pp. 458-65.

40 Gill, *op. cit.*, Chs. 2 and 6.

41 Marsden, *op. cit.*, pp. 8-10, Ch. 12. Sainsbury's recent research with Family Service Unit families (*Social Work with Families*, *op. cit.*) is a significant advance on earlier studies in that he sampled agency-client relationships.

Conclusions

It has been argued that a loosely related body of research has been carried out in social work, in which the focus of attention is on the opinions, attitudes or behaviour of the people who receive particular services. One of the main purposes of this research is the formulation of recommendations for policy change. If such research is to make a useful contribution to the development of social policy, it must come to terms with two problems. First, it is problematic to know when the opinion of consumers has been meaningfully appreciated. Second, the utilization of consumer opinion entails careful research strategy if it is to be fruitfully achieved.

The danger of relying overmuch on consumer opinion is a new one for social work to face. Whereas in the past social workers have tended to regard case accounts given by professionals as records of what really happened, we need to avoid the opposite trap of regarding client accounts in a similar light. For the present, it is probably best for the researcher and policy-maker to bear in mind the four elements of the client's perception of what service is offered, the worker's perception of the service offered, the official description of the service, and the actuality of what service is given.[42]

The positive values of consumer research need little elaboration. They sensitize the public and the welfare professions to the human consequences of social planning, and draw social workers' attention to subcultural differences between them and those they try to help. This implies the need for a better climate of understanding, and therefore the need for better information flow from Social Service Departments about the whole range of services. Consumer surveys are only one of the possible devices for attaining this goal. Direct representation of consumers on local authority committees may serve to convey to the committees the feelings expressed in the studies reviewed here. However, although this possibility has been actively canvassed,[43] such individuals are unlikely to be representative of wider client groups, in the sense of being typical clients, and there remains a difficult link to be forged between the concepts of popular participation and traditional representative democracy.

Having recognized that client and professional opinion are unlikely to be completely consensual, it follows that policies should provide an element of choice, which can only be provided if alternative service patterns are available to individuals. All-or-none solutions, while cheaper to operate, ignore the real diversity of preference among service consumers.

Some difficulties are likely to remain, as, for example, the risk of treating opinion about the present as if it was prescription for the future, and the liability to inbuilt conservatism arising from the fact that clients are unlikely to be acquainted

42 O. Stevenson, Editorial, *Br. J. Social Work* 3 (3), 1973, p. 299.

43 R. Holman (ed.), *Socially Deprived Families in Britain*, London: Bedford Square Press, 1970, pp. 191-5; *Report of the Committee on Local Authority and Allied Personal Social Services,* Cmnd. 3703, London: HMSO, 1968, paras. 491-4, 628.

with the range of alternatives open to them.[44] Further, bias is always likely in consumer surveys carried out by consumer groups or social service departments. The research is at its best when it comes to terms with its research method and does not purport to give rigorous measures of the incidence of opinions in the population, and when client opinion is utilized in conjunction with other kinds of research evidence.[45]

---

44 The criticism of conservatism can be modified by distinguishing, as does Rein, between 'needs-resource' research, 'distributive' research and 'allocative' research. Much social work research in the past has been of the 'needs-resource' kind, aimed at identifying disparities between needs and services, and leading almost inevitably to a demand for more services of the kind already existing. The research reviewed here is mainly 'distributive' in character, aimed at the reallocation of existing resources within the social services. As such, it is less conservative, in that the existing form of services does not remain unquestioned. Its conservatism lies in leaving aside the possibility that alternative programmes are needed to reach the stated objective. (M. Rein, *Social Policy*, New York: Random House, 1970, Ch. 22)

45 A weakness of Bayley's careful study is that recommendations are drawn largely from the 53 intensive visits to the homes, and the extensive analysis carried out of records of all cases of mental handicap in Sheffield is largely overlooked.

Chapter 22
Consumer Evaluations of the Personal Social Services*

Client assessments of social work practice and the organizational context in which it is located have become in recent years part of the accepted wisdom of how to improve the initiation and delivery of the personal social services. Although there is room for doubt as to the policy impact of such assessment[1], woe betide the commentator, of whatever ideological hue, who fails to offer due deference to the value of consumer research. The arrival of these studies has been consolidated in the attempts of some writers to collate, synthesize and extract practice lessons from these studies (Rees and Wallace, 1982; Timms and Timms, 1977, pp. 68-75; Davies, 1981, Ch. 2).

It has been widely noted that both the 1959 Younghusband Report, and the Seebohm Report a decade later, bemoaned their failure to obtain the views of clients. Although their regrets were expressed in a noticeably half-hearted fashion, it would be harder for comparable committees to escape with such neglect in the coming years. Hence the attention given by the Barclay Committee to views of social work (Barclay, 1982, Ch. 11).

The purpose of this review is to explore some of the policy questions raised by user studies of this kind with particular reference to the problems of using 'client satisfaction' as an index of policy evaluation in the personal social services. From one point of view it does not matter what name is given to the users of the personal social services. Yet there is a strong normative element in the recent plethora of new designations, stimulated by a desire to emphasize individual rights, and a claim that the user of welfare services is in all important respects like other people. To borrow the title of a recent BASW publication, clients are fellow citizens (BASW, 1981).

There is an important interactive element in this naming process, in that the roles of the clients and social workers are denned in relation to each other. For

---

* Originally published as Shaw, I. (1984) 'Consumer Evaluations of the Personal Social Services', (1984), *British Journal of Social Work* 14(3): 277-284. Reprinted with permission of Oxford University Press.

1 Goldberg and Warburton's study (1979, p. 133) illustrates the lack of impact of consumer assessments. While one third of their consumer sample favoured some form of participation, and several made specific suggestions, 'despite extensive discussion of these findings little progress was made in initiating a dialogue between consumers and social services providers'.

example, if a client is a recipient, the social worker is the provider. This bland simplistic, static conception of the social worker role is amplified slightly when the client is described as an applicant. This implies an elective, allocative role for the social worker, and points up the elements of rationing and eligibility which frequently are present in social welfare. It also brings out the negotiable nature of social work interaction, and recognizes the significance of the organizational contexts in which social work takes place. These comments also apply to the notion of claimant, although there are important differences. Claimant implies a stronger emphasis on rights to welfare than the term applicant. As a corollary of this, there is less room for the exercise of discretion by the worker. A claimant carries more power than an applicant. Finally the use of the word claimant often implies a statement about the value and importance of corporate action, particularly through claimants unions.

Consumer and customer are in many respects comparable terms. A customer buys a product from a salesman. In the goods sector this implies among other things choice, price competition, brand comparison and demand stimulation. These features apply only slightly or not at all in the welfare sector (Gartner, 1977). The term consumer is slightly different. Customer implies some degree of regular and continuing relationship to a supplier, whereas consumer indicates a more abstract figure in an abstract market (Williams, 1976). This strong undercurrent of emphasis on client autonomy is misleading, and is part of a tendency to idealize the client role. Moreover, the overall influence of the consumer movement has tended toward political conservatism. One commentator has gone as far as to claim that 'the consumer movement has little guidance to offer beyond the need to seek more information about price and quality and more consumer representation. It has little to say about how information or representation will bring about change... (or) about what that change ought to be' (Creighton, 1977, p. 121). Nonetheless, the emphasis on consumer choice and rights has produced the strong research interest in the client's perspective, which is to be welcomed.

Following the seminal work of Mayer and Timms a number of user studies have been published. Two of the most recent studies in this field report a long overdue extension of consumer research to statutory work and community work (Sainsbury *el al.,* 1982; Bryant and Bryant, 1982).

The emergence of this research is due to a number of factors, which can only briefly be touched on here. Social workers have tended to adopt a more favourable interpretation of the value of work class culture since the 1960s. This development may be linked to the decline in social work of the treatment ideology which, through its preoccupation with the relatively hidden *causes* of behaviour, rather than behaviour *per se,* produced among other things aversion from the client's own assessment of the significance of problematic situations. Client studies, with their emphasis on rationality and common sense, are thus part of the reaction against the medical model, and evidence of a greater interest in what people *do,* rather than what they *are.* Pessimism about the productiveness of experimental research, allied to a concern about the dehumanizing effects of bureaucracy, has led to user studies in the UK studies focussing on standards of service delivery, rather than on its outcome. Finally, the general influence of interpretive sociologies has made social workers cautious of scorning the natural attitude. The social worker has increasingly questioned the idea that there is only one standard of rationality to apply to the interpretation of human conduct.

Client Satisfaction

A high proportion of studies during that last decade have reported high levels of consumer satisfaction. In the States, Beck found that 80 per cent of her sample reported the services to be helpful or very helpful (Beck, 1974). 64 per cent of Woodward's sample were satisfied or very satisfied (Woodward *et al.*,1978). The reported studies carried out by the National Institute for Social Work in this country yield satisfaction ratings of 71 and 73 per cent (McKay *et al.*,1973; Glampson and Goldberg, 1976). These findings were not very different from Goldberg's earlier study of elderly clients, in which 77 per cent of the experimental group and 48 per cent of the comparison group expressed satisfaction (Goldberg, 1970). More recently, a study of client perspectives in a general practice attachment indicated that 85 per cent of the sample were satisfied (Comey, 1981). In addition, it has frequently been found that clients report higher satisfaction levels than anticipated by the social workers (e.g. Beck and Jones, 1974; Glampson and Goldberg, 1976). In their review of client studies, the Barclay committee found that the average satisfaction level was around 66 per cent, and the average dissatisfaction ratings were about 20 per cent (Barclay, 1982, p. 167).

However, recent literature in this field has placed a number of question marks against the ready incorporation of these ratings into prescriptions for policy in the personal social services. The value of satisfaction ratings cannot be estimated without taking into amount the implication of three interconnected general propositions. First, satisfaction with service may often co-exist with criticism of that service. Second, satisfaction verdicts are influenced by the frame of reference within which they are reached. Third, judgements about satisfaction need to be clearly distinguished from judgements about the more favourable interpretation of the value of work class culture since the 1960s. To borrow Rees and Wallace's phrase 'helpful people and useful outcomes' are not the same thing (Rees and Wallace, 1982, p. 81). It is only when these considerations are taken on board that the difficult and neglected question of the usefulness of these studies can be tackled.

Satisfaction and Criticism

Personal satisfaction and criticism of services can often co-exist (Barclay, 1982, p. 160). A recent series of research initiatives in the field of public opinion and the welfare state, has emphasized the existence of 'a deep ambivalence in public opinion about welfare' (Judge, *et al.*, 1983; Beedle and Taylor-Gooby, 1983;Taylor-Gooby, 1983). Whereas previous work in this field has focussed on public opinion about welfare outputs, Taylor-Gooby and his colleagues explore public attitudes to welfare state financing. For example, in the most recent article, Judge concludes that strong support for the privatization of welfare 'can co-exist with, and need not contradict, an equal public enthusiasm for state welfare' (Judge *et al.*, 1983, p. 469). In exploring the meaning and implication of this ambivalence, the authors focus on the interplay between values and interests, to show how 'positive evaluations of the idea of a welfare state are not incompatible with distrust of the present set-up' (Beedle and Taylor-Gooby, 1983, p. 37). The interrelations of values and interests has not yet been explored in user studies of welfare services (though see Timms' recent comments on the significance of values in such studies, Timms, 1983, pp. 22-24).

Satisfaction in Context

'Client evaluations are not simply related to the receiving or not receiving of ... help ... They are relative to context, to knowledge of services available, to expectations, to help received in past encounters, to help received from other sources, to perceptions of the 'pleasantness' of the social worker' (Rees and Wallace, 1982, p. 72). Unless such factors are taken into account, 'we can never be sure whether the high rate of client satisfaction is related more to factors like lack of knowledge or limited expectations, than the actual helpfulness of social service contact' (Rees and Wallace, 1982. p. 77).

Recent studies provide numerous examples of positive evaluations of services apparently influenced by frames of reference. Children when asked if they wish to stay in their present foster home may answer in the affirmative, whereas when asked who they would like to live with, are likely to express a preference for family or friends. Again, more than 70 per cent of a sample of new residents in homes for the elderly said they had wanted to become residents, and thought it best to remain in the home. Yet only 30 per cent felt free from anxiety and distress during the admission process, and over half the sample admitted a sense of loss in their present situation, as compared with their former one (Bush *et al.*, 1977; Shaw and Walton, 1979).

These discrepancies appear to reflect the respondents' perceptions of what is possible and what is ideal. For such evaluations to provide an adequate basis for policy, opinion must rest on a relatively informed consideration of the range of possible alternatives (Platt, 1971, Ch. 2; Shaw, 1976). If this rubric is not observed it may result in inbuilt conservation. A clear example of this failing can be seen in Margaret Bone's comprehensive survey of the Youth Service. On the one hand, young people were critical of the range of activities offered by youth clubs. However, when they were asked to indicate the activities that, ideally, they would like the subsequent list bore an uncanny resemblance to the actual activities already available (Bone, 1972, pp. 91-96). Therefore, 'unless the service and options offered to clients cover the range of possible options, the client's responses are going to be circumscribed by the narrowed range of options they are offered' (Bush *et al.*, 1972, p. 499).

User studies need to pay greater attention to the social context of meaning. A tendency to take mutually shared knowledge for granted is apparent in the lame

Table 22.1 Consistency levels in responses to various 'satisfaction' questions

Items	**per cent agreement between judges**
Satisfied/very satisfied with service	66
No problem obtaining service	91
Services were comprehensive and adequate	89
Feel better/much better with regard to original problem	46
Attribute change at least in part to treatment	55
Would return if felt the need	97

Source: Woodward *et al.*, 1978.

suggestion of the LASS Research Liaison Group working party on Directions for Research in Social Work and the Social Services (LASS RLG, 1980), that clients should fill in the National Institute for Social Work case review form, as a way of incorporating a client perspective into case management! To take this suggestion seriously, we should note the unduly consensual assumption that, by collecting data on two sides of a question, we arrive at a balanced picture (Becker, 1970).

The literature on subjective social indicators has identified some of the moulding influences at work on satisfaction responses (Abrams, 1976; Gordon, 1977; Carley, 1981). Abrams borrows and develops a covering law model of the independent variables shaping satisfaction levels. To simplify somewhat, he suggests that objective conditions and personal history are mediated through perceived conditions, expectations and aspirations to produce satisfaction levels (Abrams, 1976, pp. 12-13). On this understanding we would expect a weak relation between objective conditions (e.g. service input) and satisfaction. Furthermore, similar perceived conditions (e.g. judgements about standards of service) may yield varying correlates with satisfaction because of varying expectations, aspirations or personal history – although perceived conditions will prove a better predictor of satisfaction than objective conditions.

Analysis of this kind, suggest Rees and Wallace, can help us understand factors which might otherwise appear puzzling. For example, the well known reluctance of some consumers to evaluate the service received (e.g. Bayley, 1973; McKay *et al.*, 1973; Cohen, 1971; Sainsbury *et al.*, 1982) may be understood in terms of personal norms, expectations, reference group theory or orientations to help-seeking. Again, the problem – too rarely researched or even recognized – of impermanence and fluidity in consumer verdicts, may be contingent on factors such as changing knowledge and expectations, or even emotional state. In a rare attempt to test the durability of satisfaction responses, Woodward and her colleagues carried out a follow-up survey, using independent judges, some two weeks after the various questions were first asked. Table 22.1 reports their findings (Woodward *et al.*, 1978).

One of the most highly volatile items was that which measured the extent to which change was attributed to treatment. This finding might help explain the poor correlation between satisfaction ratings and outcome measures. So far, the studies in this country, perhaps because of the qualitative, intensive, small sample size approach, have given little attention to this question, with the exception of Sainsbury and his colleagues, who provide trend data collected at three different points in time (Sainsbury *et al.*, 1982).

'Helpful People and Useful Outcomes'

We noted above the frequently occurring discrepancy between 'satisfaction' and 'help' ratings. The incongruity may occur in either direction. Clients may rate themselves, or be rated, as having been helped, and yet express disatisfaction with the service. Conversely absence of evidence regarding help may co-exist with expressions of satisfaction. In the first case, satisfaction ratings may be unduly radicalizing, whereas in the second case they exercise a conservatizing influence. The general drift of the evidence suggests that the latter problem is more likely to occur than the former.

Rees and Wallace cite the work of M.B. Jordan, who suggests that clients may explain this incongruity in terms of the burden of work or lack of resources faced by the social worker. 'Over time, the clients came to regard the social workers as being as much victims of the situation as themselves. The social workers were perceived as being relatively powerless to help given the limitations of their work situation' (Jordan, quoted in Rees and Wallace, 1982, p. 84). If clients are socialized to view social workers as powerless, this may act to cool out and pacify the client, by obscuring the fact that help is not forthcoming.

Using User Studies

Although it places a series of question marks against an unquestioning embrace of consumer studies in the personal social services, the literature shows an underlying commitment to clarify those factors which will enable us to hear the client's voice more clearly. In order for this voice to provide more than a superficial gloss on the professional and bureaucratic edicts of practitioners, managers and academics, we need to make haste more slowly, and cultivate a more serious sense of puzzlement.

The policy use of consumer studies remains problematic. Despite giving heed to criticism of earlier reports, the Barclay Committee's discussion of views of social work still seems rather 'in the air', and we are left with the impression that client views are marginal to the main proposals of the report. Part of the problem stems from the fact that inferences about proposals for *change* need to be drawn from client assessments of *existing* services. Platt's discussion of an analogous issue arising from the Institute of Community Studies research still provides one of the most cogent analyses of this and related issues (Platt, 1971, 1972).

Recent blurring of the client role, through emphasis on reciprocity and informal helping networks, serves to complicate the matter further. Furthermore, 'the question of which person's needs or wishes are to be given priority in a situation in which several people are involved .. remains to be studied, let alone answered' (Rees and Wallace, 1982, p. 115). Behind this is a more fundamental question. How much weight we attach to satisfaction rests on how much we think 'satisfaction' contributes to 'welfare'. Indeed, the goal of satisfaction may in some cases conflict with the goal of a just society.

References

Abrams, M. (1976) *A Review of Work on Subjective Social Indicators, 1971-1975*, London: SSRC.

Barclay, P. (ed.) (1982) *Social Workers. Their Role and Tasks*, London: Bedford Square Press.

Bayley, M. (1973) *Mental Handicap in the Community*, London: Routledge and Kegan Paul.

Beck, D.F. and Jones, M.A. (1974) 'A new look at clientele and services of family agencies', *Social Casework* 55, 589-599.

Becker, H. (1970) 'Whose side are we on?' in *Sociological Work*, Chicago: Aldine Press.

Beedle, P. and Taylor-Gooby, P. (1983) 'Ambivalence and public opinion about taxation and welfare', *Policy and Politics* 11, 15-39.

Bone, M. (1972) *The Youth Service in England and Wales*, London: HMSO.

British Association of Social Workers (1981) *Clients are Fellow Citizens*, Birmingham: BASW.

Bryant, B. and Bryant R. (1982) *Change and Conflict*, Aberdeen: Aberdeen University Press.

Bush, M., Gordon, A.C. and LeBailly, R. (1977) 'Evaluating child welfare services: a contribution from the clients', *Social Service Review* 51, 491-501.

Carley, M. (1981) *Social Measurement and Social Indicators*, London: Allen and Unwin.

Cohen, A. (1971) 'Consumer view: retarded mothers and the social service', *Social Work Today* 1, 39-43.

Comey, R.H. (1981) Client perspective in a general practice attachment', *British Journal of Social Work* 11, 159-170.

Creighton, L.B. (1977) The limits of consumerism', *Social Policy* 8, 121-125.

Davies, M. (1981) *The Essential Social Worker*, London: Heinemann.

Gartner, A. (1977) 'Consumers in the service society', *Social Policy* 8, 2-8.

Glampson A. and Goldberg, E.M. (1976) 'Post Seebohm social services: the consumers view', *Social Work Today* 8, 6.

Goldberg, E.M. (1970) *Helping the Aged*, London: Allen and Unwin.

Gordon, I. (1977) 'Subjective social indicators and urban policy analysis', *Policy and Politics* 5, 93-111.

Gutek, B.A. (1974) 'Strategies for studying client satisfaction', *Journal of Social Issues* 34, 44-56.

Judge, K., Smith, J. and Taylor-Gooby, P. (1983) 'Public opinion and the privatization of welfare', *Journal of Social Policy* 12, 469-490.

Local Authority Social Services Research Liaison Group (1980) 'Directions for research in social work and the social services', *British Journal of Social Work* 10, 203-217.

Mayer, J. and Timms, N. (1969) *The Client Speaks*, London: Routledge and Kegan Paul.

McKay, A., Goldberg, E.M. and Fruin, D. (1973) 'Consumers and a social services department'. *Social Work Today* 4, 486-491.

Platt, J. (1971) *Social Research in Bethnal Green*, London: Macmillan.

Platt, J. (1972) 'Survey data and social policy', *British Journal of Sociology* 23, 77-92.

Rees, S. and Wallace, A. (1982) *Verdicts on Social Work*, Aldershot: Arnold.

Sainsbury, E., Nixon S. and Phillips, D. (1982) *Social Work in Focus*, London: Routledge and Kegan-Paul.

Shaw, I. (1976) 'Consumer opinion and social policy', *Journal of Social Policy* 5, 19-32.

Shaw, I. and Walton, R. (1979) 'Transition to residence', in Harris, D. and Hyland J. (eds.) *Rights in Residence*, Bristol: Residential Care Association.

Taylor-Gooby, P. (1983) 'Moralism, self interest and attitudes to welfare', *Policy and Politics* 11, 145-160.

Timms, N. (1983) *Social Work Values*, London: Routledge and Kegan Paul.

Timms, N. and Timms, R. (1977) *Perspectives in Social Work,* London: Routledge and Kegan Paul.

Williams, R. (1976) *Keywords*, Glasgow: Collins Fontana.

Woodward, C.A., Santa-Barbara, J., Levin, S. and Epstein, N.B. (1978) Aspects of consumer satisfaction with brief family therapy, *Family Process* 17, 399-407.

Chapter 23
Engaging the User: Participation, Empowerment, and the Rhetoric of Quality*

The plea for user involvement has been a feature of good social work practice at least since the writers of the Seebohm Report pointed towards the restructuring of social work services which took place in 1970. The 'terms of engagement' altered over the following quarter-century, and the shifting realities of service users' and carers' experiences of social work are produced in the meeting of policy, guidance, rhetoric and statute from the state, and action, lobbying, and rhetoric, from citizen advocacy groups and user movements. This chapter opens with a brief sketch of the policy and service contexts within which debate about the potential for service users as participating and empowered citizens has been played out. These contexts sensitise us to the point and counterpoint of the various rhetorics of participation and quality. We outline the main *motifs* in the Conservative government's case for participation, and explore the reinforcing impact of the performance culture and management-by-effectiveness strategies, before turning to alternative rhetorics of participation and quality. There are various reasons for concluding that the advocacy of service user participation will always prove problematic when worked out in a context of state purchased services. But the thrust of this book is against a pessimistic resort to an outsider stance and for the advocacy of service users as critical outsiders-on-the-inside. This stance is an uncomfortable one, but one which enables participation through consumerist strategies, individual planning, service policy development, self-empowering and self-help groups, and advocacy evaluation.

The Rise of the Citizen

The languages of cost effectiveness, service user choice, satisfaction, empowerment, commercial models of quality management, monitoring and evaluation, service contracts and agreements, partnerships, staff supervision, financial decentralisation and assessments of outcomes permeate the present rhetoric of planning, management, and delivery of British social services. In this

---

* Originally published as Shaw, I. (1997) 'Participation, Empowerment and the Rhetoric of Quality' (1997) in Pithouse, A. and Williamson H. (eds) *Engaging the User in Welfare*, Birmingham: Venture Press. Reprinted with permission of The British Association of Social Workers and Venture Press.

chapter we will explore the importance for the practitioner of conceptualising the user in a relatively *wide* span of contexts which, in addition to those listed in the previous sentence, also include evaluation and advocacy.

The Conservative government agenda in the 1980s of cost-efficiency, control, and competition held the attraction of applying commercial models of quality to the public sector. The government sought a reform of the public sector through emphasis on improving outputs by stressing consumer interests and improving consumer satisfaction. This produced a 'want regarding' standpoint where, in place of experts deciding consumer needs, 'the needs and demands of consumers determine the content and organisation of services' (Kirkpatrick and Lucio 1995: 29). The philosophy of the enterprise culture and the sovereign consumer supported a pivotal stress on quality and an attack on professionals which was parallel in some respects to the government's earlier attack on restrictive practices in the trade unions.

The Audit Commission report on community care in 1986 provided the benchmark for later reforms and an actuarial, value for money orientation to the direction of those reforms (Audit Commission 1986). The National Health Service and Community Care Act (1990) required social services departments to produce Community Care Plans which include arrangements for quality assurance, local inspection units, complaints procedures and systems for safeguarding service standards. The Social Services Inspectorate (SSI) based in the Department of Health was given a beefed up role, and immediately began to advocate 'more explicit standards, openness, full and accurate information, choice, accountability and non-discrimination' (SSI 1993: 3.1). There have been several themes and aspirations in the work of this national inspectorate, including the perceived need to improve the supervision of staff ('The variable quality of professional supervision is worrying') and a shift to a managerial approach in which 'no individual field-worker should be regarded as self sufficient' (SSI 1992: 13).

Prominent emphasis has been placed on 'the involvement of users and carers in planning and conducting inspections, defining the criteria to be applied, and reporting the findings' (SSI 1992: 5.4; SSI 1995). Although satisfaction was at one point expressed by the Chief Inspector at the extent to which user involvement was taking place (SSI 1993: 2.7), the rate at which it has been implemented is still very patchy. Only a minority of inspections have directly involved users and carers (SSI 1994: 2.2; 3.1) and the degree to which such involvement goes beyond a consumer survey consultation, and achieves some degree of advocacy and empowering is as yet very limited (SSI 1994: 3.2).

The Home Office carried out a review of agencies and projects in the voluntary sector in 1990 which focused on performance against funding, and adopted a 'strategies expressed through objectives' approach (Home Office 1990: 3.3). This led to the establishment of Charities Evaluation Services, intended as a nationwide resource for charity evaluation, and also stimulated voluntary agencies' interest in self-evaluation and evaluation by outsiders. Similar trends were evident in the field of supported housing and housing associations, where performance monitoring and quality assurance policies increasingly took root as the preferred tools of government funding agencies for developing and appraising supported housing. User satisfaction and tenant participation have been earnestly sought as key criteria for appraising performance in these schemes.

Following the establishment of National Standards for the supervision of offenders in the community (Home Office 1992, 1995a), the Home Office publishes an annually revised Three Year Plan, which incorporates Key Performance Indicators against which the work of probation officers may be measured (Home Office 1994, 1995b). The application of these performance indicators to probation officers' pay, whereby remuneration is tied to the reconviction rates of supervised offenders, has been under active consideration within the Home Office *(The Guardian*, 10 April 1996).

Cost-effectiveness, joint objective setting, strengthened accountability of welfare professionals, managerial effectiveness, explicit standards, performance monitoring, and customer involvement, choice, and satisfaction are recurring themes in the pleas and provisions for quality in the personal social services. These different *standards* reflect distinct underlying *approaches* to quality. Pfeffer and Coote have identified four broad approaches to quality (Pfeffer and Coote 1991; Coote 1994). The 'traditional' approach is based on a 'no expenses spared' concept that assesses whether one product or service is better than another. This approach is not relevant to social service provision. The second, 'scientific' approach measures quality by expert standards against which a service is assessed according to its fitness for the task intended. The Social Services Inspectorate routinely uses a standards-based approach to evaluate services. The third, managerial or 'excellence' approach starts from a customer orientation as the key to service success. Rejecting mass production and mass consumption models, quality is based on demonstrating managerial effectiveness by giving the customers what they want. This approach to consumer satisfaction continues to shape the government policies for a mixed economy of welfare. Finally, the 'consumerist' approach to quality casts customers in an active role by focusing on their wishes rather than those of managers, and by claiming to seek consumer empowerment. This approach to excellence has influenced the margins of service provision in some voluntary agencies, a number of social services departments, and the work of some self-advocacy groups.

Rhetoric of Participation and Quality

The meaning of quality remains elusive because it is made to serve different purposes by different people and by the same people at different times. Quality becomes a potential battleground for both the micro and macro political battles of welfare provision. When the going gets tough, quality as cost effectiveness is likely to appeal to funders and politicians, quality as performance control will attract managers, and the resort to quality as a mechanism for professional survival in an uncertain world will tempt practitioners. Meanings are also ambiguous because quality is often used to refer to a *process* (quality assurance), and only sometimes to a service *outcome*. The government's use of the rhetoric of participation and quality has four recurring themes (Kirkpatrick and Lucio 1995). *First*, 'value for money' is central to any debate about service quality. It is conducted in constant tension with economic retrenchment. *Second*, the rhetoric of quality is used to legitimate organisational change, whether this be in social services, health, police, libraries, the fire service, British Rail or the Royal Mail. *Third*, it has been employed to establish a disturbing shift in relationships between the state and the voluntary sector. *Fourth*, it has been closely associated with a reassertion of the managerial prerogative (Kelly 1991) through greater managerial control and the flourishing of management-by-effectiveness strategies. The third and fourth points are inspected more closely in the following paragraphs.

Partnership language has been used to describe collaborative arrangements between purchasers and providers, statutory and voluntary or private agencies (the independent sector), central and local government, and between service providers and users. The split between local authorities as service purchasers and a wider spread of agencies as service providers opened the way for a disaggregation of services and created for the state a newly sharpened problem of how diverse voluntary, statutory and private providers could be integrated within a common government strategy. In response to this it appears clear that quality control measures have been viewed by the Government as a mechanism for managing these fissile tendencies. The review of quality measures sponsored by the Social Services Inspectorate partly recognised this in its conclusion that the community care reforms placed the tensions between central and local, and diversity and uniformity under strain. 'Quality assurance can be seen as one mechanism to manage the tension between uniformity and diversity' (James, Brooks and Towell 1992: 2.7.2). The mechanism is not straightforward. For example, the Home Office has spasmodically encouraged the development of partnerships between Probation Services and the independent sector. Yet, as Smith, Paylor and Mitchell (1993: 34) have pointed out:

> The paradox is that the more probation work is 'hived off' or contracted out to the independent sector the harder it is to achieve the levels of accountability the Home Office now expects.

This tension is managed in part by government emphasis on a culture of working together through jointly negotiated and shared objectives – a strategy that also appeared in the Home Office *Scrutiny* of the voluntary sector (Home Office 1990). This is one of the main mechanisms used by the Government to achieve an attempted depoliticisation of quality. Partnership talk provides the *rhetoric* of depoliticisation. The managerialism that we illustrate below provides the *vehicle* through which this depoliticisation takes place.

Philip Abrams – the most influential contributor to what Offer has aptly termed 'the sociology of morals' (Offer 1991) – warned about the dangers that could occur when government or local authority departments colonised the voluntary sector (e.g. Abrams 1984). Partnership policies pose precisely this risk. There are two associated dangers. First, the values of the state sector may penetrate and colonise the voluntary sector. As a result the major voluntary organisations – for example, the Children's Society, NCH Action for Children, Barnardo's, and the major supported housing associations – may come to dominate the sector, lose their independence and critical edge, and unwittingly (or not!) elbow out the smaller voluntary organisations. As a consequence, the diversity of the voluntary sector could eventually be lost. The second and parallel risk is that, with this radical shift in relations between central and local government, the commercially oriented private sector will prove best equipped to take advantage of the welfare economy, to the disadvantage of smaller voluntary groups. A similar risk exists in the sphere of influence of the Probation Service – the 'risk of a loss of genuine independence in the independent sector as it becomes colonised by a probation service concerned to demonstrate efficiency, effectiveness and economy in the achievement of its core tasks' (Smith, Paylor and Mitchell 1993: 34).

The fourth hallmark of the government's rhetoric of participation and the consumer is that changes justified on the basis of a sovereign consumer are often associated with greater managerial control and the flourishing of a management-by-effectiveness strategy. It is no accident that part of the confusion surrounding the language of empowerment stems from talk of management strategies such as Total Quality Management which claim the empowerment of *staff* through a delegation of responsibilities down the hierarchy (McArdle, Rowlinson, Proctor, Hassard and Forrester 1995; Kerfoot and Knights 1995). Managers who are concerned with outcomes, 'single-minded and obsessed with clients' (Rapp and Poertner 1988: 24) may be preferable to agency management systems dominated by input and process issues such as quantity of service provided, and numbers and types of clients served. However, the growth of the performance culture and its application to social work organisations risk creating a threat of undue managerialism which will defeat efforts at participation and empowerment. The concerns are threefold:

- managing by measurement risks producing a concentration on easily measurable aspects of practice
- organisational behaviour will change in order to score well on measurable criteria
- agency performance requirements will take precedence at the expense of the service user.

Etzioni (1964: 9) remarked long ago that 'Frequent measuring tends to encourage over-production of measurable items and neglect of less measurable items'. Conrad (1985), describing the extensive annual Programme Assessment System which New York's foster care agencies were required to operate, wryly noted how performance statistics resulted in precisely this negative, unintended consequence. Plans, contracts, placements, numbers of visits, and other more easily measured outputs gain higher profiles within social work agencies, and informal or less easily measured aspects of practice become invisible. A similar example can be seen ten years on from Conrad's study, in that only one of the Home Office Key Performance Indicators for probation officers requires a qualitative measure.

It is an easy but significant step from this to a position where the organisation changes its behaviour in order to score well on those criteria. Numbers become reified as true indicators of quality. The organisation will seek to control intakes and jettison 'weak' cases, and agency members will be tempted to distort how the work of the agency appears. Conrad's salutary vignette illustrates how accountability systems can serve to undermine the quality of care they were mandated and developed to protect and enhance – 'the very individuals the reforms aim to rescue can become the victims of its remedy' (Conrad 1985: 642). Her research revealed how decision makers were tempted to place the agency's performance requirements above the best interests of the child. For example, in order to achieve programme targets, children were sometimes reunited with families when professional judgement would suggest the contrary. Specialist agencies were known on occasion to refuse to accept deeply troubled children as a means of avoiding the risk of performing poorly. Thus, while accountability standards of the kind increasingly generated in British social work are doubtless partly intended to codify good practice, these requirements may 'encourage agency personnel to make decisions for which the agency will be rewarded, good casework practice or not, and to avoid those for which sanctions will result' (p. 646). It is hard, therefore, to dissent from Grasso and Epstein's (1988: 89) conclusion that 'emphasis on quantitative measures of effectiveness and efficiency has resulted in a number of different types of goal distortion and displacement' in which the service user becomes marginalised.

Alternative Rhetorics

Service users' and carers' experiences of social work are produced not only from the dominant rhetoric of the Citizens' Charter but also from the action and lobbying of advocacy and user groups. The Government has concentrated on increasing individual consumer influence rather than on the collective rights of citizens. The assumption has been that the consumer can exercise the freedom to choose and go elsewhere, or effectively complain and press for change. The first option – that of *exit* – is associated with the growth of market competition and privatisation, whereas the latter – that of *voice* – supports the promotion of needs-led services, consumer satisfaction and carer panels. The distinction between exit and voice is helpful in understanding the power relationships between people and organisations. Put simply,

> the market model, in theory at least, gives individuals the power of exit – dissatisfied customers can take their business elsewhere. The democratic process, again in theory at least, relies on individuals or groups having the power of voice – dissatisfied customers obtain a response by taking political action. (Burns, Hambleton and Hoggett 1994: 31)

While voice and exit options can co-exist in the same organisation they are fundamentally very different. Exit belongs to the realm of economics while voice belongs to the realm of politics. The versions of empowerment underlying recent government changes depend almost entirely on the exit mechanism. However, Burns et al's caveat 'in theory at least' is important. 'Concepts of user-oriented and user-led services are more strongly to be observed in rhetoric than practice' (Barnes and Wistow 1992: 8). The conclusion drawn from an early review of quality assurance practices in social services departments was:

> Again and again we found definitions of quality assurance in use and evidence of standard setting which overwhelmingly represented the views of managers and professionals rather than those of service users. (James, Brooks and Towell 1992: 2.1)

Policies of choice for service users based on the exit option are not a guarantee of partnership for many customers of the personal social services. There are three reasons for this. First the sovereign consumer is a far cry from 'most dependent people whose needs come within the remit of the personal social services ... [and who] are tied because of frailty, illness, fear, handicap, low income or habit to their local area' (Barclay 1982: 220). Second, welfare clients who believe they are in receipt of an unsatisfactory service often cannot choose an alternative because they are involuntary users. The emphasis on providing exit options for welfare clients frequently chooses to ignore this obvious reality. Third, this inability to shop around often may be compounded by the fact that the need for given services may be confined to a small number of people in the population and alternatives therefore will not be available in any given area. For example, specialist drugs and alcohol units, or day care facilities for people with certain disabilities, are likely to hold a monopoly in any one area. This may be exaggerated following the introduction of local government reform, leading to smaller unitary authorities. The exit option is frequently not about service user empowerment. It is the contracting authority rather than the service user that is the real consumer, so that the only real choice is in the hands of the contract manager or expert professionals. Unless a heavily cynical view is adopted, this potential marginalisation of the user is not what was intended by the framers of the Children Act 1989 and the community care reforms. 'Both aim to replace systems dominated by professionals with approaches based on partnership with service users...The focus...has been on ways of making it easier for children, parents, users and carers to participate and be heard' (SSI 1992: 5.2, 3). The White Paper *'Caring for People'* (1989), however embryonically, did provide an opportunity for working towards genuine user partnership, representation, and accountability.

There are alternative ways of thinking about participation and empowerment which stem from different political traditions. For example, there is a social democratic tradition which was strongly represented in the proposals for a decentralised service structure captured in the early 1980s Barclay Report. More recently there have been arguments for empowerment based on a right to quality of service plus the right to be involved in both the management and planning of services in ways which are not centrally imposed or manufactured. User involvement does, of course, cover a range of possible meanings, best viewed as occurring somewhere on a continuum from consultation through consumerist models to self-advocacy and to user control of services. Self-advocacy approaches have a clear commitment to promoting the empowerment of users, and extending their capacity to participate in decisions about the design, management, and review of services. Consumerist strategies tend to be more service provider led and are targeted at improving the quality of services by making them more responsive and sensitive.

User involvement strategies are also clarified by disaggregating the broad category of 'user'. Users should be distinguished from carers, and there are important distinctions between voluntary and involuntary users, long- and short-term users, and current and potential users (Barnes and Wistow 1992). Client groups may be in competition with each other, and users are also citizens. 'We are interested as citizens in planning and as customers in delivery' (Pfeffer and Coote 1991: 26). The distinction between voluntary and involuntary service users is given too little recognition in the language of consumerism. Fisher refers to two kinds of problem that occur, and which mean that 'allegiance to agreements is not matched by practice particularly when the user is involuntary or at risk' (Fisher 1992: 58). The problem of what Fisher calls the *'third mandate'* occurs where explicit legal sanction for action is missing, but intervention is imposed on the client, as when case conferences or reviews take place. The problem of escalation occurs when the original mandate gets extended to other areas. Agreements with involuntary clients tend to be coercive, conditional or constrained by resource problems. Passive consent is too often taken to mean agreement. Fisher (1992: 60, 61) wisely warns that 'we must avoid interpreting consent to an offer of a single resource or service as a positive choice' and 'resist the temptation to use "word-magic" to rewrite user compliance as positive choice'.

Achieving Participation and Empowerment

Distinctions need to be made between involvement and participation, and more-far-reaching empowerment strategies. In some instances it is misleading to use the language of empowerment to describe participation and involvement. Several writers have made the point that power is not something which can be given but only taken (e.g. Jack 1995; Braye and Preston-Shoot 1995). On the few occasions when statutory and official guidance mention empowerment, what is usually intended 'is enablement, in the sense of promoting participation and involvement, not empowerment, in the sense of professionals giving up their power and control' (Jack 1995: 18). Despite the inevitable problems arising from the interplay of different policy agendas of participation and empowerment, it would be unfortunate defeatism to withdraw from the field and remain critics from the outside. We are convinced that there remains a role for professionals. If service users and social workers are to be critical outsiders-on-the-inside then participatory and empowering practice needs to be pursued right across the continuum from consumerism to collective self-advocacy. We illustrate the potential for these initiatives in the final part of this chapter.

Consumerism

Critical feedback from service users is still of relatively recent origin within social work and is a long way from becoming part of the fabric of routine practice. Perhaps the most familiar kind of service user feedback is that associated with the tradition of research which endeavours to ascertain service user satisfaction. Best practice in this area will recognise that:

> Client feedback is not a panacea. It is one thing to be aware of a problem and another thing to do something about it... Nevertheless... it provides a counterforce to the one-sided provider perspective that is present in many social welfare agencies. (Weissman 1988: 219)

In order to avoid the simplistic assumption that a single question about satisfaction will provide a gauge of service quality, social work practice should be based on the following criteria. First, service users or their representatives should be consulted regarding how they wish their views to be canvassed. Second, mechanisms must be in place to take up any action arising from service users' appraisals. Practitioner and management acceptance of client feedback will depend on believing that beneficial change is possible as a consequence. These mechanisms must include ways in which serious allegations against social workers are to be handled. Third, routine satisfaction information needs to be enriched by more occasional, and more thorough, exercises. These should be carried out by someone who is not in a position to invoke sanctions, real or imaginary, against service users who criticise services. Fourth, satisfaction information is too often restricted to the collection of views regarding the delivery of services and perceived benefits. It should be widened to include efforts to learn people's views about a particular problem, and their opinions about the benefits and risks of introducing service changes. Fifth, social workers should not rely on global ratings of service user satisfaction. Satisfaction must always be understood in the light of service users' aspirations and expectations. It will be helpful to distinguish between preferred (or ideal) expectations and practical (or realistic) expectations. A general response saying 'satisfied' may mean:

> I've evaluated the service and I'm happy with it.
> I don't think I have the ability to evaluate but I do have confidence in the staff, *or*
> The service was appalling but I don't like to criticise; after all they're doing their best.

Finally, a word of caution. Consumer satisfaction should not normally be regarded as an indication of practice success. 'That is tempting and unfair. It is simply too easy to make people... happy about their experience' (Fike 1980: 46).

When these criteria are bypassed the consequence is that a strategy which appears at first glance to promise empowerment for service users can too easily prove a prop for conservatism and inaction. The risk is that 'through high levels of relatively meaningless expressions of satisfaction an illusion of consumerism is created which seldom does anything but endorse the *status quo*' (Williams 1994: 515). Power differentials between professionals and service users are too easily underestimated by consumerists. The more that people see themselves as powerless, the more likely they are to adjust their aspirations regarding what they can reasonably expect to gain from their exchange with social workers. Effective consumerism depends on a refusal to accept paternalism, and on the possibility of active consumers, not passive clients. Hence, user involvement that is to any degree committed to empowerment must include the development of quality and performance measures based on criteria owned by service users and carers. 'A more participatory agency practice begs a more participatory research' (Beresford 1992: 18). The public service orientation on which such an approach is premised cannot resolve all the remaining dilemmas. For example, social work participation must focus on people as both service user and citizen – the individual service user for whom the service is provided, and the collective citizen to whom the local authority is accountable. 'There will remain a dilemma between the collective view, even when grounded in actual views, and the view of particular individuals' (Stewart and Clarke 1987: 169).

Self-Help

During the last 15 years social workers have gradually come to accept that 'most community care is provided by people who are not professionals, for people who are not service users' (Jack 1995: 15). The important link between this and the argument for participation and empowerment has not always been pursued. Self-help requires self-empowerment (Adams 1996). Jack's helpful consideration of this issue concludes with the contention that 'true empowerment in community care is attainable only through self-help activity and user-led services' (1995: 38).

We should not conclude from this that the role of professionals is redundant. The work of Smale and his colleagues helpfully points to the model of assessment that lies behind social work practice, and distinguishes between *questioning, procedural* and *exchange* models of assessment (Smale and Tuson 1993). In the questioning model, 'It is assumed that the worker is an expert in people, or their problems, or both'. In the exchange model,

> It is assumed that all people are expert in their own problems and that there is no reason to assume that the worker will or should ever know more about people and their problems than they do themselves, and certainly not before they do. (Smale and Tuson 1993: 18)

This model of assessment may not readily generalise to settings where service users are involuntary participants, or have been 'sentenced to social work'. However, it gives proper recognition to the leading contribution of self-help within social care. It requires professional expertise in the process of problem solving, and the ability to work towards a mutual understanding of the 'problem' with all the major actors. But it also assumes that people are experts in themselves. The enabling professional thus contributes to the process of user self-empowerment.

Advocacy Evaluating

Consumerist strategies, described a moment ago, need to move hand in hand with a recognition of the inadequacy of the exit option for most service users and a determination to develop the voice option. The voice option is incorrigibly messy, and includes a range of responses graduating from grumbling to active protest. Carers groups of the kind developed in the Birmingham Community Care Special Action Project (CCSAP), self-advocacy groups exemplified by the work of *People First,* activist groups of service 'survivors' in the field of disability, and a gradual revival of confidence in the workings of local democracy all contribute to this 'rainbow coalition' (Wistow and Barnes 1993; Pitcairn 1994; Burns, Hambleton and Hoggett 1994). Advocacy evaluation for and with the service user poses an uncomfortable challenge for social workers. For example, feminist positions start from the proposition that when evaluating practice the practitioner must ask questions which make sense within women's experience, and must evaluate practice *for* women. Some feminists believe that this principle requires a strong participative commitment, and have worked with people as co-researcher participants in the interests of empowering rather than exploiting them. Evaluating is seen as being *'for* the subjects of research, to advance their causes' and therefore practitioners need to 'work towards the active participation of members of oppressed groups in every phase of their research activities' (Swigonski 1993: 178). Social workers engaged in anti-discriminatory evaluation are invited by Humphries and Truman (1994: 1, 3) to demonstrate a 'conscious partiality with those who are marginalised or invisible, or whose experiences have been distorted by traditional research', which exhibits a 'conceptual imperialism' based on male power, and is 'white, Eurocentric heterosexual and able-bodied'. Anti-discriminatory evaluation requires 'an active involvement in challenging assumptions based on unequal social relations, through reflexive, explicitly committed participation in the process of social change' (Humphries and Truman 1994: 14).

Perhaps the most important challenge raised by this argument is that it changes the *process* of evaluation and not simply the *outcomes.* In this respect it has much in common with *participatory research,* initiated largely through Third World development programmes. There has been a shift in social development evaluation towards a qualitative approach, caused by changing understandings of the meaning of social development which emphasise grassroots involvement (Marsden and Oakley 1990; Everitt and Hardiker 1996). Michael Edwards, who has worked within Non-Governmental Organisations (NGOs), presents the argument persuasively. He complains about the absence of strong links between understanding and action, and about

> ...the devaluation of popular knowledge; the values and attitudes of researchers and practitioners that prevent them from working as equals; the control of knowledge by elites; and a failure to unite understanding, action, relevance and participation. (Edwards 1989: 133)

He insists that 'participatory research is the vehicle for understanding and changing the world simultaneously' (p. 128). In the telling words of a Mexican proverb which he quotes, 'we make the path by walking it'. This explicitly liberationist strategy raises a series of inescapable questions which transfer with equal potency to evaluations by social workers. First, what do we mean by claiming that evaluation is 'relevant'? The meaning of relevance is one of the most controversial debates in social development. Second, what is the relationship between grassroots evaluating and 'higher level' evaluation? One of the dangers of recent post-Marxist shifts to enthusiastic adoptions of explanations based on culture, diversity, agency and actor constructions is that the relationship between the micro level of individual practice and the structural level is ignored. How can social workers be committed to evaluation at the micro level and still keep the macro issues firmly on the table? The questions raised by people such as Edwards – 'unashamedly polemical born out of years of frustration' (Edwards 1994: 279) – are in some ways more sharply uncomfortable for social workers than the more global statements that characterise feminist methodology. They are certainly more neglected.

We have mentioned self-help and advocacy movements. These have been active in the fields of learning disabilities and physical disabilities. We should add to these the work of groups representing children and young people in care. However, limited progress has been made in other fields. A potentially valuable precedent is that set by the National Coalition for the Homeless, based in Washington DC. On the basis that homeless people must lead their own movement and seek their own voice if homelessness is to end, the coalition is committed to promoting the leadership of homeless and formerly homeless people. In the 1996 presidential election year they conducted a survey and campaign by activists, service providers, and homeless or formerly homeless people to assess the state of empowerment within the anti-homelessness movement. The focus was on pressing local service providers to promote the participation, leadership and organisations of homeless people, and develop ways in which groups of such people could become part of the local service system. The variety of homeless-led empowerment groups which they explored included art/photography, peer tutoring and education, street newspapers, women's issues, substance abuse recovery, homeless people's conferences, political advocacy, and client councils. The campaign was effectively enhanced through use of discussion lists on the World Wide Web.

Conclusion

Consumerist strategies, advocacy evaluation, and self-advocacy groups illustrate the range of participatory and empowering strategies open to social workers and those for and with whom they practice. We have made no secret of the fact that such strategies will always entail ambiguities and problems. New practice will raise new problems – problems experienced by service users, by practitioners, and within the wider political and policy context. The work of the Birmingham Community Care Special Action Project suggests the risk that *users,* as against carers, may become marginalised. Wistow and Barnes (1993: 292) acknowledge that 'It is possible that carers' voices were heard in greater number and more directly than those of direct service users' (1993: 292). They also observe that:

> Empowerment as control by users over decision making and service delivery mechanisms implies time-consuming and energy-sapping demands in what are already frequently over-demanding lives. (Wistow and Barnes 1993: 296).

For example, they quote a woman who wrote when returning a questionnaire, 'because of the situation I am in, sometimes it is hard to find time or *mind* to sit and fill in forms or write letters. After caring for someone all you want to do is rest' (Barnes and Wistow 1992: 99). Problems in accomplishing an enabling role for professionals will also persist through the limited extent to which *practitioners* experience service user feedback as relevant to their own work. In research exploring how social workers endeavoured to evaluate their own work, practitioners gave reasons why they thought service user feedback was difficult to deal with (Shaw 1996: 63-71). One of the most common reasons was a belief that evaluation priorities were not shared between practitioners and service users. An example given was when inappropriately ambitious goals were believed to be held by clients and families.

> Oh, they wouldn't see my role as being effective at all. Not unless I can get her a new house tomorrow. The mum, where she sees effectiveness is, is quite different to where I see effectiveness is.

> They want some kind of pill that she can take and make it all better. As far as their daughter is concerned it was either cure or nothing.

More interesting, perhaps, were those cases where social worker and client both apparently thought that the work went well, but where practitioners were convinced that subtle but important divergence existed on priorities. Probation officers tended to think that, even if things had gone well, clients were less likely to rate the reduction of offending as the first priority. Speaking about the outcome of a group for offenders one officer said,

> She'd probably say, 'Yeah, it's all right' in a sense that I got a couple of things for her. I wrote a couple of letters so that she didn't have to come into town to get her dole cheque. She'd probably say I've been reasonably understanding, that I gave her the benefit of the doubt. I can't imagine her speaking highly of the fact that I pressed her on exactly why she shoplifted. I don't think she'd be terribly impressed by that.

Social workers tended to explain divergent priorities in terms of clients being more preoccupied with their personal well-being than the social worker would have preferred. A community worker, reflecting on the successful planning stages for a black women's information and self-help group, concluded,

> I think they would be quite happy, because it's something they've been asking for, the opportunity to be with other women, the children will be looked after in the creche, it will be like a day out for them, taking them out of the house. But I think they will see the information being not as important as I see it. 'We'll be out of the house, we'll have a nice lunch, the kids will be looked after, we'll be together' I think that would be the list of priorities for them.

In so far as social workers believe they are working to different agenda from service users, the potential for full partnership in assessment, planning and evaluation of services will be curtailed. Finally, uncertainties will continue to exist in a context of social and political change. For example, the continued growth of information technology in the human services field will raise increasing issues related to choice, access and empowerment. Social workers and service users will rightly become concerned about the positive and negative consequences of the spread of the information society. The implications for direct social work practice, and the applications of technology to independent living, are only two present areas where IT and empowerment questions overlap. Telematics, telework, virtual reality, data gloves, robotics, and satellite-based health education in Africa and elsewhere, are all on the near horizon, and pose distinctive questions for social work. Will such developments increase choice? Will cost factors lead to further inequitable resource distribution? Will information technology in social work become led by outcome oriented management interests, whereby presently uncharted regions of private life become opened to corporate colonisation? There is much to be said in favour of the case for a bill of rights for information technology in the human services (Glastonbury and LaMendola 1992).

Under a possible change of administration after a long period of Conservative government the rhetoric of participation and empowerment may change, and the language of social justice and the communitarianism associated with the American sociologist Amitai Etzioni may gain greater currency and acceptance. There has certainly been an embracing of Etzioni's ideas across the political spectrum, although they have been interpreted in different ways and remain contested and still essentially rhetorical (see Atkinson 1995). Rhetoric based on social justice and greater local autonomy is preferable to rhetoric stemming from narrow market economics. But, while there is no such thing as *empty* rhetoric, communitarianism implies a social harmony which, at its worst, may provide little change from the Conservative governments' attempts to depoliticise the debate about partnership, quality, and empowerment.

'Empowerment happens not just because powerful people give away power, but because oppressed people engage in wresting it from them' (Braye and Preston-Shoot 1995: 100). But a professional exchange model recognises that the expertise, experience and knowledge of both service users and professionals are essential elements of such empowerment.

References

Abrams, P. (1984) 'Realities of Neighbourhood Care', *Policy and Politics*, Vol. 12, pp. 413-29.

Adams, R. (1996) *Social Work and Empowerment*, London: Macmillan.

Atkinson, D. (ed.) (1995) *Cities of Pride: Rebuilding Community, Refocusing Government*, London: Cassell.

Audit Commission (1986) *Making a Reality of Community Care*, London: HMSO.

Barclay, P. (1982) *Social Workers: their Roles and Tasks*, London: Bedford Square Press.

Barnes, M. and Wistow, G. (eds.) (1992) *Researching User Involvement*, Leeds: University Nuffield Institute for Health Services Studies.

Beresford, P. (1992) 'Researching Citizen-Involvement: a Collaborative or Colonising Enterprise?' in Barnes, M. and Wistow, G. (eds.) *Researching User Involvement*, Leeds: University Nuffield Institute for Health Services Studies.

Braye, S. and Preston-Shoot, M. (1995) *Empowering Practice in Social Care*, Buckingham: Open University Press.

Burns, D., Hambleton, R. and Hoggett, P. (1994) *The Politics of Decentralisation*, London: Macmillan.

Conrad, K. (1985) 'Promoting Quality of Care: The Role of the Compliance Director', *Child Welfare*, Vol. 64:6, pp. 639-49.

Coote, A. (1994) 'Performance and Quality in Public Services' in Connor, A. and Black, S. (eds.) *Performance, Review and Quality in Social Care*, London: Jessica Kingsley.

Department of Health (1989) *Caring for People: Community Care in the Next Decade and Beyond*, London: HMSO.

Edwards, M. (1989) 'The Irrelevance of Development Studies', *Third World Quarterly*, Vol. 11:1, pp. 116-35.

Edwards, M. (1994) 'Rethinking Social Development: the Search for "Relevance"' in Booth, D. (ed.) *Rethinking Social Development: Theory, Practice and Research*, London: Longman.

Etzioni, A. (1964) *Modern Organisations*, Englewood Cliffs: Prentice Hall.

Everitt, A. and Hardiker, P. (1996) *Evaluating for Good Practice*, London: Macmillan.

Fike, D. (1980) 'Evaluating Group Intervention' in *Social Work with Groups*, Vol. 3:2 pp. 41-51.

Fisher, M. (1992) 'Users' Experiences of Agreements in Social Care' in Barnes, M. and Wistow, G. (eds.) *Researching User Involvement*, Leeds University Nuffield Institute for Health Service Studies.

Glastonbury, B. and LaMendola, M. (1992) *The Integrity of Intelligence: a Bill of Rights for the Information Age*, London: Macmillan.

Grasso, A. and Epstein, I. (1988) 'Management by Measurement: Organisational Dilemmas and Opportunities' in Patti, R., Poertner, J. and Rapp, C. (eds.) *Managing for Effectiveness in Social Welfare Organisations*, New York: Haworth.

Home Office (1990) *Efficiency Scrutiny of Government Funding of the Voluntary Sector*, London: HMSO.

Home Office (1992) *National Standards for the Supervision of Offenders in the Community*, London: Home Office.

Home Office (1994) *Three Year Plan for the Probation Service, 1994-1997*, London: Home Office.

Home Office (1995a) *National Standards for the Supervision of Offenders in the Community*, London: Home Office.

Home Office (1995b) *Three Year Plan for the Probation Service, 1995-1998*, London: Home Office.

Humphries, B. and Truman, C. (eds.) (1994) *Rethinking Social Research: Anti-Discriminatory Approaches in Research Methodology*, Aldershot: Avebury.

Jack, R. (1995) (ed.) *Empowerment in Community Care*, London: Chapman and Hall.

James, A., Brooks, T. and Towell, D. (1992) *Committed to Quality: Quality Assurance in Social Services Departments*, London: HMSO.

Kelly, A. (1991) 'The "New" Managerialism in the Social Services' in Carter, P., Jeffs, T. and Smith, M. (eds.) *Social Work and Social Welfare Yearbook 3*, Buckingham: Open University Press.

Kerfoot, D. and Knights, D. (1995) 'Empowering the "Quality" Worker?: The Seduction and Contradiction of the Total Quality Phenomenon', in Wilkinson, A. and Willmott, H. (eds.) *Making Quality Critical*, London: Routledge.

Kirkpatrick, I. and Lucio, M. (1995) (eds.) *The Politics of Quality*, London: Routledge.

Marsden, D. and Oakley, P. (1990) (eds.) *Evaluating Social Development Projects*, London, Oxfam.

McArdle, L., Rowlinson, M., Proctor, S., Hassard, J. and Forrester, P. (1995) 'Total Quality Management and Participation: Employee Empowerment or the Enhancement of Exploitation?' in Wilkinson, A. and Willmott, H. (eds.) *Making Quality Critical*, London: Routledge.

Offer, J. (1991) 'The Sociology of Welfare' in Davies, M. (ed.) *The Sociology of Social Work*, London: Routledge.

Pfeffer, N. and Coot, A. (1991) *Is Quality Good for You? A Critical Review of Quality Assurance in Welfare Services*, London: Institute for Public Policy Research.

Pitcairn, K. (1994) 'Exploring Ways of Giving a Voice to People with Learning Disabilities' in Humphries, B. and Truman, C. (eds.) *Rethinking Social Research: Anti-Discriminatory Approaches in Research Methodology*, Aldershot: Avebury.

Rapp, C. and Poertner, J. (1988) 'Moving Clients Centre Stage Through the Use of Client Outcomes' in Patti, R., Poertner, J. and Rapp, C. (eds.) *Managing for Service Effectiveness in Social Welfare Organisations*, New York: Haworth.

Shaw, I. (1996) *Evaluating in Practice*, Aldershot: Ashgate.

Smale, G. and Tuson, G. (1993) *Empowerment, Assessment and Care Management*, London: HMSO.

Smith, D., Paylor, I. and Mitchell, P. (1993) 'Partnerships Between the Independent Sector and the Probation Service', *Howard Journal*, Vol. 32, pp. 25-39.

Social Services Inspectorate (1992) *Concern for Quality: the First Annual Report of the Chief Inspector*, London: HMSO.

Social Services Inspectorate (1993) *Raising the Standard: the Second Annual Report of the Chief Inspector*, London: HMSO.

Social Services Inspectorate (1994) *Putting People First: the Third Annual Report of the Chief Inspector*, London: HMSO.

Social Services Inspectorate (1995) *Partners in Caring: the Fourth Annual Report of the Chief Inspector*, London: HMSO.

Stewart, J. and Clarke, M. (1987) 'The Public Service Orientation: Issues and Dilemmas', *Public Administration*, Vol. 65:2, pp. 161-77.

Swigonski, M. (1993) 'Feminist Standpoint Theory and Questions of Social Work Research', *Affilia*, Vol. 8:2, pp. 171-83.

Weissman, H. (1988) 'Planning for Client Feedback: Content and Context' in Patti, R., Poertner, J. and Rapp, C. (eds.) *Managing for Service Effectiveness in Social Welfare Organisations*, New York: Haworth.

Williams, B. (1994) 'Patient Satisfaction: a Valid Concept?', *Social Science Medicine*, Vol. 38:4, pp. 509-16.

Wistow, G. and Barnes, M. (1993) 'User Involvement in Community Care: Origins, Purposes and Applications', *Public Administration*, Vol. 71, pp. 279-99.

Chapter 24
Just Inquiry?: Research and Evaluation for Service Users*

Introduction

How can research and evaluation strategies be used to promote user participation and involvement? The question is still fairly novel, and there is by no means universal agreement that such purposes should be part and parcel of inquiry. Social work research is conventionally assumed to involve a rigorous application of methodology in order to provide answers to policy, practice or conceptual problems. Lincoln and Guba define research as a 'type of disciplined inquiry undertaken to resolve some problem in order to achieve understanding or to facilitate action' (Lincoln and Guba 1986, p.549). Research is viewed as a relatively sophisticated means to a larger end. The problem focus, research design, fieldwork, analysis, reporting and dissemination of results are all seen as the work of experts undertaken for the good of some present or future beneficiaries.

This book starts from a very different point. Social care practitioners have increasingly been challenged by the emergence of forms of inquiry which are seen not as means to some future end but as ends in themselves. This is captured in this book's editorial vision of a research enterprise that mirrors practitioners' goals of participation and involvement. To borrow Stake's apt phrase, social workers have become 'reluctant to separate epistemology from ideology, findings from yearnings' (Stake 1997, p.471). The forms taken by this radical challenge are varied and include:

- participatory reflective inquiry and practice
- participatory inquiry for empowerment
- evaluating as direct practice
- feminist research
- justice-based commitments within research.

There are various strands of *participatory reflective inquiry* which go under names such as co-operative inquiry, action science, action inquiry, and participatory

* Originally published as Shaw, I. (2000) 'Just inquiry? Research and evaluation for service users' in H. Kemshall and R. Littlechild (eds) *Participation in Social Care: Researching for Practice*. London: Jessica Kingsley. Reproduced with permission of Jessica Kingsley Publishers.

action research, and are associated with the writings of Heron, Reason, Whyte, Schön, Argyris and Eisner. In a familiar passage Schön says:

> both ordinary people and professional practitioners often think about what they are doing, sometimes even while doing it. Stimulated by surprise, they turn thought back on action and on the knowing which is implicit in the action.. As [the professional] tries to make sense of it, he [*sic*] also reflects on the understandings which have been implicit in his action, understandings which he surfaces, restructures and embodies in further action.
>
> It is this entire process of reflection-in-action which is central to the 'art' by which practitioners deal well with situations of uncertainty, instability, uniqueness and value conflict. (Schön 1983, p.50)

The strengths of Schön's argument are common to the majority of reflective inquirers:

1. Reflective evaluating is about *tacit knowledge*. It is a disciplined activity in which the sources of understanding and action are not automatically picked off the surface. Skilful action often reveals 'a knowing more than we can say' (Schön 1983, p.51).
2. Reflective evaluating involves *reflexivity* – a testing by reflection. Erikson's injunction is apt. We should constantly be trying to 'force our favourite assumptions to become probable inferences' (Erikson 1959, p.94). Practitioners are not simply users but generators of knowledge.
3. There is an inherent comparability between 'professional' and lay persons' capacities for displaying the elements of reflective inquiry.

Schön's analysis is original and provocative. He is, for example, the only theorist in the field of practitioner and reflective evaluation who has developed a model which is not specific to any one profession. Despite the gendered framework of his observation, the transformative implications of his position become clear when he reflects on the relationship envisaged between professionals and those with whom they work. The relationship

> takes the form of a literally reflective conversation.. He attributes to his client, as well as to himself, a capacity to mean, know and plan. He recognises that his meanings may have different meanings for his client than he intends.. He recognises an obligation to make his own understandings accessible to his client.. [He] tries to discover the limits of his expertise through reflective conversation with the client. (Schön 1983, pp.295-296)

However, in addition to the absence from his analysis of gender and broader power issues, Schön does not seem to envisage any directly participative dimension. His examples focus extensively on the practitioner in discussion with colleagues and supervisors, rather than involving students, children or other service users. Heron and Reason have developed a much more explicitly collaborationist vision of reflective inquiry. Reflective practice in social work has been developed in the work of England (1986), Gould and Taylor (1996) and Fook (1996). Participatory research approaches committed to *empowerment* have taken this a significant step further and have included some degree of emphasis on an explicitly liberationist strategy, an educative dimension through consciousness raising, and an integrated commitment to political action and social transformation. There are four main strands to this commitment. First, early appeals for participatory evaluation drew their strength from a redistributive welfare position. For example, Holman pleads for 'research from the underside' because 'the values I hold are such that I long for the end of poverty and the promotion of equality. My interest in research is just this, how can research help the poor?' (Holman 1987, p.669).

Second, there have been efforts to bring Third World development research closer to development practice. Edwards draws on his experience of working in non-governmental organisations when he laments the creation and perpetuation of a series of divorces, the most complete of which 'lies between research output and the subjects of this research – poor people themselves' (Edwards 1989, p.128). While he is insistent that method has not been the only problem, he nonetheless insists that 'participatory research is the vehicle for understanding and changing the world simultaneously' (p.128). In the telling words of a Mexican proverb which he quotes, 'we make the path by walking it'.

Participatory strategies have also followed from some versions of feminist research. For instance, feminist standpoint theory draws on an activist view of evaluation as undertaken for explicitly political purposes, as committed to empowerment, and entailing a model of evaluation that works towards the participation of members of oppressed groups in every phase of research activity. Once we concede that the purpose of research includes 'to enact rather than simply state' (Lather 1991, p.123), then the researcher will endeavour to 'maximise the research process as a change-enhancing, reciprocally educative encounter' (Lather 1986, p.72), in which the process is more important than the product. The work of Humphries (e.g. Humphries 1999; Truman, Humphries and Mertens 1999) and Mullender (e.g. Dullea and Mullender 1999) has been at the forefront of feminist approaches to social work inquiry in Britain.

Finally, empowerment approaches to social work research and evaluation have been driven by a training agenda of supporting the development of practitioners committed to combating discrimination and oppression in its various forms. Beresford, Fisher (e.g. Evans and Fisher 1999), Everitt and Hardiker (e.g. Everitt and Hardiker 1996) have each contributed significantly to working out the implications of this agenda for research.

The 1990s have witnessed the emergence of an approach to evaluation that blends aspects of both reflective practice and empowerment evaluation. The underlying premises of this approach are that all professionals should be reflective, enabling and rigorous evaluators-in-practice, and that qualitative methodology offers the basis of such a 'methodological practice' (Fook, Munford and Sanders 1999; Shaw 1996, 1997; Shaw and Lishman 1999; Tanner and Le Riche 1999). In summary, evaluating in practice is committed to a view of evaluative *purpose* which is *for* service users, and to an evaluative *process* which involves:

1. participatory evaluating with service users
2. reflecting on tacit knowing-in-practice
3. describing practice in ways that render access to its strengths and weaknesses feasible
4. mutual reflexivity of both practitioner and service user
5. legitimation through falsifying and establishing an empirically supported.

In essence this entails a view of evaluation as just as much a part of direct practice as assessing, planning, or delivering intervention.

There is a sense in which each of the approaches described so far can claim a commitment to social justice. Hence the implication of the chapter title that no research is merely inquiry, but raises problems and challenges for a just practice. Yet social work research and evaluation have failed to address the issues raised by literature and practice which specifically focus on ideas and ideals of justice. Such issues are almost entirely absent in the North American empirical practice movement, the British practitioner research literature, and the slowly growing literature from America, Britain and Australia on reflective inquiry. They are, of course, present in an axiomatic form in much of the literature on empowerment forms of evaluation, but remain largely uninspected.

We should not regard this as simply one more gap to fill. Whether we recognise it or not, issues of politics and associated questions of justice are present in our day-to-day practice. Weiss argued that political considerations intrude in three ways in evaluation. She is talking about broader policy and programme evaluation, but much of what she says probably applies to social work practice.

First, the programmes and policies being evaluated are themselves generated by political decisions. Second, evaluation entails political considerations because its reports enter the political arena. The nature and processes by which research is used cannot be understood outside a political framework. Third, there are politics implicit in the evaluation process itself. Research tends to accept the broad premises of the programme, and serious research 'gives an aura of legitimacy to the enterprise' (Weiss 1987, p.57). In consequence 'Most evaluations – by accepting a program emphasis on services – tend to ignore the social and institutional structures within which the problems of the target groups are generated and sustained' (p.57).

We cannot be neutral about justice issues. As the evaluation theorist Ernest House remarked some time ago, we 'do not live in a state of methodological grace' (House 1991, p.245).

The successful development of direct practice implications of these commitments is the litmus test of the authenticity of our claims to mutuality, respect and empowerment. Rather than attempt an overview of such developments,

I will use the central part of this chapter to give examples of ways in which these commitments may be worked out within social work practice.

Mutuality, Respect and Empowerment in Practice Inquiry

Reflective practice

Hugh England, in his valuable discussion of social work as art, analyses what constitutes a rounded description and appraisal of practice. He perhaps goes too far when he concludes that 'without adequate description there can be no possibility of evaluation' (England 1986, p.155), but his assertion is helpful for good practice because without such description we certainly will not force our favourite assumptions to become probable inferences. He rightly insists that social work practice 'must be subject to a description and analysis which can determine quality' (p.139). It has to be described in such a way that it renders access to and evaluation of its strengths and weaknesses feasible. By making clear the links between 'understanding, action and effect' (p.154), practitioners will be able to conclude whether they have plausibly and adequately helped.

England's concern is not with participatory practice, yet the implications are readily transferable. Whether or not they are able to reach agreement, social workers, service users, carers, and others who are part of the change agent system, need to make explicit the 'inventories of evidential signs they regularly but unwittingly scan' (Erikson 1959, p.82).

A useful application of reflective practice is peer interviewing, either between practitioners or between a service user and someone chosen by the service user. The core strategy involves enabling practitioner and service users to unpick the assumptions they have made regarding whether or not social work intervention went well. Questions that may trigger such reflection include asking one another to describe examples of work undertaken, and to be explicit about what aspects went well or less well. Participants may also ask one another to be clear about how one knows that something went well or not, and what evidence was drawn on in the particular instance under review. It may also be worth exploring whether the practitioner or service user believes that other key 'stakeholders' share their views about the quality and outcomes of the work, and if they would have used the same or different criteria in deciding whether the work had gone well.

Participatory inquiry for empowerment

Whitmore's account of an evaluation of a pre-natal programme for single, pregnant mothers illustrates how positive outcomes may on balance be achieved. The evaluation was carried out over several months by four women who had themselves been through the programme, with Whitmore as consultant to the project. There were tensions in the group, and communication failures. One member left and another protested to Whitmore that:

> Our world is different from yours. The fear is that people always want to humiliate you, put you down [for being on welfare].. We have a different lifestyle from you. We just don't trust people the way you do. (Whitmore 1994, p.92)

Whitmore concluded that she could never entirely share the worlds of the women with whom she worked. 'My small words were often their big words. What I assumed was "normal talk", they saw as "professor words"' (p.95). But the strength of the group's final achievements is evidence that participatory evaluation with oppressed groups is not only political rhetoric.

Social workers have sometimes been slow to reflect on models of empowering participatory practice in other occupations. A sensitive and arresting example of participatory research is provided by Miller's account of three years' collaborative research with teachers who had until that time been her postgraduate students. They aimed to 'extend the concept of teacher as researcher into reciprocal and interactive forms' with an emancipatory agenda (Miller 1990, p.ix). The accounts portray the sustained commitments of the group as they 'continue to struggle with ways in which the intentions and forms of emancipatory pedagogy and research both attract and confound us' (Miller and Martens 1990, p.45).

The group worked together for at least six years. They kept transcripts of their meetings, and each group member agreed to keep a journal. They had early misgivings about the term emancipatory research, as a kind of 'authoritative discourse' (Miller 1990, p.16) from someone else. There was a constant struggle 'not to impose the concept of empowerment upon others in the name of liberation' (p.18). The recurring issues they faced included:

- The worry that there might be 'nothing there'
- A constant re-surfacing of 'conceptualisations of knowledge determined by someone else's research' (p.71). The standard separation of research and practice 'confounded our efforts to conceive of research as praxis' (13.73)
- The uncertainty, in the words of one member, of 'are we doing this right?'
- No one to talk to outside the group who shared their assumptions about becoming creators rather than transmitters of objective knowledge. The typical school does not encourage or welcome inquiry and reflection on work. The irony of their inquiry was that they were part of an institution that perpetuated the technical rationality model of research and evaluation which they wished to challenge
- 'The halting and undulating nature of our quest to become challengers' (p.70).

The group was unwilling to regard their collaboration as practitioner research. 'We wonder if the label, teacher-as-researcher, in fact contributes in subtle ways to those theoretical and practical distinctions that continue to obscure the ways in which teaching itself is a "quiet form of research"' (p.150). They were also concerned that practitioner research provides little if any challenge to the often hierarchical nature of university-formulated research agendas and interpretations of classroom teachers' work (Miller and Martens 1990). Such questions offer a challenge to some forms of practitioner research in social work. Most British examples of practitioner research in social work are not participatory and tend to rest on unduly pragmatic approaches to decisions about methodology.

There are ethical risks in participatory inquiry and practice. Feminist work has provided some of the most sensitive accounts of such dilemmas, and of the need to 'protect us from our own passions' (Lather 1986, p.77). For example, Acker and her colleagues, in their study of the relation between women's attempts to move into the labour market and changes in their consciousness, tried three strategies to reduce unequal power and acknowledge the subjectivity of the participants, although they admit they did not solve this problem (Acker, Barry and Esseveld 1983):

1. They encouraged the interviewee to take the lead in deciding what to talk about. This did not always work. The women often wanted to be asked questions. However, the approach did work better for those women with whom they had more than one interview.
2. They established reciprocity, by offering to tell women something of themselves. This was accepted and often invited, and 'we formed friendships with many of the women' (p.428).
3. 'However, we recognized a usually unarticulated tension between friendship and the goal of research. The researcher's goal is always to gather information, thus.. attempting to create a more equal relationship can paradoxically become exploitation and use' (p.428).
4. They showed their written material to the women. However, they did not do so with all of them. They admit that they shared most with 'those who identified themselves as consciously trying to change.' They were therefore the women who 'most shared our worldview', and 'we have to admit some reluctance to share our interpretations with those who, we expected, would be upset by them' (p.428). This raises the issue of whether the evaluator should share interpretations with those whose explanations are radically different from their own. This is the 'tension between the goal of reducing the power differences between the researcher and the researched and the difficulties of carrying this out when there is a lack of agreement on the meaning of experiences' (p.429).

For example, when they asked the women to read their draft manuscript, the latter typically wanted 'more of our own sociological analysis. They wanted us, the researchers, to interpret their experience to them' (p.429). They concluded that 'If we were to fulfil the emancipatory aim for the people we were studying, we had

to go beyond the faithful representation of their experience, beyond "letting them talk for themselves"' (Acker *et al.* 1983, p.429).
There are five minimum requirements that must be met if participatory inquiry is to be more than a rhetorical flourish: first, clarify and mutually agree the *purpose of participation*. It is unlikely to work if some participants see it as democratising while others view it as directly challenging to existing power structures (Barnes and Wistow 1992).

Second, be clear with each other regarding the different *kinds of 'users'* who may have an interest. Fisher, for example, suggests that much participatory evaluation is naïve in underplaying the differences between voluntary and 'captive' clients. 'A problem in the new voluntarist language of welfare consumerism is that too little recognition is given to users who are "captive"' (Fisher 1992, p.55).

Third, establish genuine mechanisms for continued collaborative work. Verbal agreements are usually too non-specific, and are liable to chronic decay.

Fourth, seek agreement on the recurrent risks of intrusion and imposition. 'Whether intrusion into your life takes place in the name of "helping" or "researching" the experience, it seems, can feel all too similar if you are on the receiving end' (Davis 1992, p.37).

Finally, agree the harm to be avoided and the benefits to be gained by those who collaborate. In reflecting on an extensive project to involve carers in the processes of planning and review in an English local authority social services department, Barnes and Wistow caution that there are dangers in giving insufficient thought to whether meeting the needs of the service planning system, and meeting the needs of users and carers who become involved in that system, are incompatible.

> Providers should be sensitive to the demands they are placing on people whose lives are already complex and demanding. They should be ready to ensure that people derive some direct benefits from participation, as well as ensuring that...participation is justified by the outcomes it achieves. (Barnes and Wistow 1994, p.91)

Evaluating in practice

We noted earlier that the underlying premises of this approach are that all professionals should be reflective, enabling and rigorous evaluators-in-practice, and that qualitative methodology offers the basis of such a 'methodological practice'. Qualitative methodology provides a wide range of methods that can potentially be 'translated' and 'colonised' by professional practitioners (Table 24.1).

Table 24.1 Methods for qualitative evaluating in practice

Personal texts and narrative
Life histories
Interviewing
Focus groups
Participant observation
Participatory inquiry
Simulations
Member 'validation'
Cultural reviews

We should avoid naïve versions of this argument. It is *not* the case that social work and any particular forms of research involve the same logic and processes (Shaw 1999). The metaphors of translation and colonisation are inadequate descriptors of the extensive bridging work that 'methodological practice' calls for, but they do caution us against simplistic solutions. We should also note that it is *methodological* practice that is called for rather than any specific *methods*. In research, *method* usually refers to the techniques through which data is collected (e.g. sampling, participant observation, questionnaires). *Methodology* is a broader term, which takes into account the theoretical and value premises that lie behind research, and the social processes through which it is carried out.

Evaluating in practice applies both to direct practice for and with service users, and to indirect practice that seeks to improve services more generally. Focus groups provide one example of the former, and developments in simulations illustrate the latter.

Focus groups have three particular advantages for evaluating in practice. First, the group interaction is itself the data – 'the interaction is the method' (Jarrett 1993, p.198). Kitzinger says in summary that the method 'enables the researcher to examine people's different perspectives as they operate within a social network and to explore how accounts are constructed, expressed, censored, opposed and changed through social interaction' (1994, p.159). Second, focus groups are a form of participatory evaluation. They are valuable when there is a power differential between participants and decision makers, and hence have considerable potential for application within qualitative evaluation. Finally, they introduce a valuable approach to learning the extent of consensus on a particular issue. 'The co-participants act as co-researchers taking the research into new and often unexpected directions and engaging with each other in ways which are both complementary...and argumentative' (Kitzinger 1994, p.166).

The majority of writers in this field have opposed the application of focus groups to anything other than research or formal evaluation purposes. In my view this is an unhelpful generalisation. Focus groups also have a particular contribution to make to practitioner and participatory evaluating. Exercises in problem-setting, project development, anti-discriminatory practice, addressing projects that have become 'stuck', consumer feedback exercises, and evaluating sensitive topics are all ways in which focus groups have something to offer to qualitative evaluating. Gibbs summarises the case for focus groups:

> [They] are particularly useful when there are power differences between the participants and decision makers or professionals, when the everyday use of language and culture of particular groups is of interest, and when one wants to explore the degree of consensus on a given topic. (Gibbs 1997)

Despite the promise of this method, focus groups should be used within their limitations. The current, almost knee-jerk, adoption of group interviews labelled focus groups, regardless of their mode of operation, has been too undiscriminating. Focus groups, for example, always rely on interaction within the group based on topics that are supplied by the facilitator. There is little evidence on the relative benefits of focus groups and interview methods, and there are situations where focus groups should probably not be used. They should not be used if the practitioner's intention is to improve participants' communication or group skills. More generally, they should not be adopted for therapeutic purposes, or when the main purpose is to secure immediate action. If information, understanding or explanation is not central to the group's agenda, then other methods of intervention should be used. It may also be difficult to identify clearly individual messages within the group. There are other practical constraints on focus group work. If personal views cannot readily be expressed in such a context, or if breaches of confidentiality are likely to be a problem, then the method should not be used. When group members know each other particularly well, focus groups are also ill advised. Finally, bearing in mind the benefits of homogeneous group membership, it is not advisable to run focus groups comprising both service users or carers and practitioners.

Simulations have the potential to provide 'a unique and innovative tool that has not yet been widely applied' in evaluation (Turner and Zimmerman 1994, p.335). One application typically entails the use of paired role players (man/woman; white/black; able-bodied/with a disability). The pairs present themselves separately to a given service, as similar in terms of eligibility and need. 'To date, paired role playing has been used principally to test for racial and ethnic discrimination in housing and employment' (Turner and Zimmerman 1994, p.332); but the method will work equally well in evaluating the allocation of scarce resources in social work, where the element of judgement and discretion is present. For example, a variant of the method using just one researcher has been planned whereby a professionally qualified social work student with a sight disability will apply for advertised social work posts, and systematically vary whether the disability is disclosed; this provides a test of the operation of non-discriminatory employment policies.

A second application is more recent, and represents a development of the use of vignettes in policy research. Those who evaluate the process of professional practice come face to face with the invisibility of practice. How may we learn the ways in which social workers practise? How would different practitioners deal with the same case? The methods I have discussed hitherto do not directly address this problem. Wasoff and Dobash have, however, used a promising innovatory method in their study of how a specific piece of law reform was incorporated into the practice of solicitors (Wasoff and Dobash 1992, 1996). The use of simulated clients in 'natural' settings allowed them to identify practice variations that could be ascribed with some confidence to differences between lawyers rather than to differences between cases.

Suppose, for example, that one wishes to carry out a qualitative evaluation of decisions made by housing managers, medical staff and social workers regarding the allocation of community care packages. Evaluators using simulated clients would prepare a small number of detailed case histories designed to test the practice decisions under consideration. A researcher, practitioner or service-user representative would take on the scripted role of the client in the case history. The housing manager, relevant medical staff, and social workers would each interview the 'client' within the 'natural' setting of their work.

The use of simulated clients has several things going for it. First, social workers are familiar with the 'family' of methods from which it is drawn. Second, other methods are not always feasible for practical or ethical reasons. Simulated clients overcome the ethical problems of seeking the co-operation of genuine clients. Above all, the method makes practice visible. It will be clear from the brief description that this method could not be a tool for evaluating particular cases, but would focus on specific *kinds* of practice. There are limitations to the application of simulation methods. They require resources, time and skills, and they should avoid ethical problems of covert evaluation and entrapment.

Evaluating for social justice

Social workers will need a clear head and free time if they are to delve into the literature on theories of social justice. John Rawls's ideas of justice as fairness mingle with theories of justice based on participatory democracy, and more relativist views of justice operate in tension with neo-Marxist and feminist critical theories. Yet social workers do not need to resolve such intractable debates in order to recognise the daily demands for just practice and inquiry. Janet Finch's research on playgroups illustrates the point (Finch 1985).

Finch's particular interest was in what self-help playgroup provision would mean for working class women living in economically deprived areas. Over a three-year period, through observation and semi-structured interviewing, she was able to document the character of self-help playgroups in such areas.

> I uncovered situations where practice diverged wildly from bourgeois standards of child care and education which most policy makers and academics would take as the norm, and at times were downright dangerous. (Finch 1985, p.117)

She was worried that the publication of her work would further reinforce 'those assumptions deeply embedded in our culture and political life that working class women (especially the urban poor) are inadequate mothers' (p.117). Those who had welcomed her for three years would thus be betrayed. She had to work through these problems. Had she been guilty of taking a middle-class norm and imposing it on these groups? Yet that norm *was* the one to which the women who ran the groups aspired. It was the participants' model and not simply hers. She eventually developed reasoning which avoided the 'deficit' model of explanation, and argued that to view working-class mothers as incompetent is improper and naïve. Finch acknowledges that she is not certain she has fully resolved the issues, and accepts that:

> To argue like this is to take a frankly moral stance, far removed from the model of the objective social scientist.. It seems to me that qualitative research on social policy issues will lead inevitably to explicit moral stances of that sort, and that it can never simply provide the 'facts'. (Finch 1985, pp.119-120)

Social work practice and inquiry that promotes empowerment, mutuality and respect will be enriched by a more explicit adherence to standards of justice. Ernest House, the American evaluation theorist, develops the example of negotiating a fair and demanding evaluation agreement (House 1980, chapter 8), in which *all* participants should meet the conditions that they:

- should not be coerced
- are able to argue their position
- accept the terms under which the agreement is reached

- negotiate. This is not simply 'a coincidence among individual choices' (1980, p.165)
- do not pay excessive attention to one's own interests
- adopt an agreement that effects all equally
- select a policy for evaluation that is in the interests of the group to which it applies
- have equal and full information on relevant facts
- avoid undue risk to themselves arising from incompetent and arbitrary evaluations.

House adheres to a reformist view of social justice, which will not secure the agreement of everyone, yet his demanding standards regarding evaluation agreements go well beyond those which typically operate within the field of social work inquiry.

Questions – and Answers?

I have suggested that social workers face a wide-ranging challenge from forms of inquiry that are viewed as ends in themselves. These include participatory reflective inquiry and practice, participatory inquiry for empowerment, evaluating as direct practice, feminist research, and justice-based commitments within research. The examples sketched in the main part of this chapter pose as many questions as they answer. For example, there are *ethical* problems about threats to confidentiality, informed consent, covert inquiry, and the delusion of alliance that qualitative methods sometimes foster (Shaw 1999). The risks of imposition, which have been carefully documented by feminist writers and by some reflective practitioners, will not go away.

There is also a cluster of puzzling problems about who carries out these kinds of inquiry and just what claims are being made about its character. The relationship between participatory forms of inquiry and more traditional forms of research is a vexed issue, and attracts easy generalisations which often fail to do justice to the question.

Work also needs to be undertaken on how such forms of reflective, empowering and methodological practice can be developed. This work will include:

1. Empirical work on how practitioners make evaluative sense of their day-to-day work. Professionals' existing evaluating practices do not provide a blueprint for how such practice should be evaluated. They do, however, provide a starting point from which professionals can begin the development of an evaluating in practice that avoids a decontextualized imposition of ideal models (Shaw and Shaw 1997, 1999).
2. Collaborative practice of the kinds of work discussed in this chapter.
3. The development of opportunities for doctoral work in these fields.

4. Inter-professional learning. The tendency to regard professional competences as exclusive to a given profession is unhelpful.
5. Greater attention by mainstream ethnographers to the evaluative uses of ethnography (e.g. Bloor 1997).

My own sympathies are for a reformist evaluation, which would have the evaluator seek out the data most likely to support programmes that benefit the dispossessed. I recognise the acute sense of dissonance that can arise from arguing for a rigorous evaluative methodology in one breath, and a reformist, partisan advocacy based on the evidence, in the next. But I stay with it for the present.

References

Acker, J., Barry, K. and Esseveld, J. (1983) 'Objectivity and Truth: Problems in Doing Feminist Research'. *Women's Studies International Forum* 6, 4, 423-435.

Barnes, M. and Wistow, G. (1992) (eds) *Researching User Involvement*. Leeds: Nuffield Institute for Health Services Studies, University of Leeds.

Barnes, M. and Wistow, G. (1994) 'Involving Carers in Planning and Review' in A. Connor and S. Black (eds) *Performance, Review and Quality in Social Care*. London: Jessica Kingsley Publishers.

Bloor, M. (1997) 'Addressing Social Problems through Qualitative Research' in D. Silverman (ed) *Qualitative Research: Theory, Method and Practice*. London: Sage.

Davis, A. (1992) 'Who Needs User Research? Service Users as Research Subjects or Participants' in M. Barnes and G. Wistow (eds) *Researching User Involvement*. Leeds: Nuffield Institute for Health Services Studies, University of Leeds.

Dullea, K. and Mullender, A. (1999) 'Evaluation and Empowerment' in I. Shaw and J. Lishman (eds) *Evaluation and Social Work Practice*. London: Sage.

Edwards, M. (1989) 'The Irrelevance of Development Studies'. *Third World Quarterly* 11, 1, 116-135.

England, H. (1986) *Social Work as Art*. London: Allen and Unwin.

Erikson, E. (1959) 'The Nature of Clinical Inference' in D. Lerner (ed) *Evidence and Inference*. Illinois, IL: Free Press.

Evans, C. and Fisher, M. (1999) 'Collaborative Evaluation with Service Users' in I. Shaw and J. Lishman (eds) *Evaluation and Social Work Practice*. London: Sage.

Everitt, A. and Hardiker, P. (1996) *Evaluating for Good Practice*. London: Macmillan.

Finch, J. (1985) 'Social Policy and Education: Problems and Possibilities of Using Qualitative Research' in R. Burgess (ed) *Issues in Educational Research: Qualitative Methods*. London: Falmer Press.

Fisher, M. (1992) 'Users' Experiences of Agreements in Social Care' in M. Barnes and G. Wistow (eds) *Researching User Involvement*. Leeds: Nuffield Institute for Health Services Studies, University of Leeds.

Fook, J. (ed) (1996) *The Reflective Researcher: Social Workers' Theories of Practice Research*. St Leonards, NSW: Allen and Unwin.

Fook, J., Munford, R. and Sanders, J. (1999) 'Interviewing and Evaluating' in I. Shaw and J. Lishman (eds) *Evaluation and Social Work Practice*. London: Sage.

Gibbs, A. (1997) *Focus Groups*. Social Research Update, no. 19, Department of Sociology, University of Surrey.

Gould, N. and Taylor, I. (eds) (1996) *Reflective Learning for Social Work*. Aldershot: Ashgate.

Holman, B. (1987) 'Research from the Underside'. *British Journal of Social Work* 17, 6, 669-683.

House, E. (1980) *Evaluating with Validity*. Beverly Hills, CA: Sage.

House, E. (1991) 'Evaluation and Social Justice: Where Are We Now?' in M. McLaughlin and D. Phillips (eds) *Evaluation and Education: At Quarter Century*. Chicago: Chicago University Press.

Humphries, B. (1999) 'Feminist Evaluation' in I. Shaw and J. Lishman (eds) *Evaluation and Social Work Practice*. London: Sage.

Jarrett, R. (1993) 'Focus Group Interviewing with Low Income Minority Populations' in D. Morgan (ed) *Successful Focus Groups: Advancing the State of the Art*. Newbury Park, CA: Sage.

Kitzinger, J. (1994) 'Focus Groups: Method or Madness?' in M. Boulton (ed) *Challenge and Innovation: Methodological Advances in Social Research on HIV/AIDS*. London: Taylor and Francis.

Lather, P. (1986) 'Issues of Validity in Openly Ideological Research'. *Interchange* 17, 4, 63-84.

Lather, P. (1991) *Getting Smart: Feminist Research and Pedagogy with/in the Postmodern*. New York: Routledge.

Lincoln, Y. and Guba, E. (1986) 'Research, Evaluation and Policy Analysis: Heuristics and Disciplined Inquiry'. *Policy Studies Review* 5, 3, 546-565.

Miller, J. (1990) *Creating Spaces and Finding Voices: Teachers Collaborating for Empowerment*. New York: State University of New York Press.

Miller, J. and Martens, M. (1990) 'Hierarchy and Imposition in Collaborative Inquiry: Teacher-Researchers' Reflections on Recurrent Dilemmas'. *Educational Foundations* 4, 4, 41-59.

Schön, D. (1983) *The Reflective Practitioner: How Professionals Think in Action*. New York: Basic Books.

Shaw, I. (1996) *Evaluating in Practice*. Aldershot: Ashgate.

Shaw, I. (1997) *Be Your Own Evaluator*. Wrexham: Prospects Publishing.

Shaw, I. (1999) *Qualitative Evaluation*. London: Sage Publications.

Shaw, I. and Lishman, J. (eds) (1999) *Evaluation and Social Work Practice*. London: Sage Publications.

Shaw, I. and Shaw, A. (1997) 'Keeping Social Work Honest: Evaluating as Profession and Practice'. *British Journal of Social Work* 27, 6, 847-869.

Shaw, I. and Shaw, A. (1999) 'Game Plans, Buzzes and Sheer Luck: Doing Well in Social Work' in S. Kirk (ed) *Research Methods: Current Social Work Applications*. Washington, DC: NASW Press.

Stake, R. (1997) 'Advocacy in Evaluation: A Necessary Evil?' in E. Chelimsky and W. Shadish (eds) *Evaluation for the 21st Century*. Thousand Oaks, CA: Sage.

Tanner, K. and Le Riche, P. (1999) 'Work in Progress: The Contribution of Observation to the Development of Good Practice and Evaluation' in I. Shaw and J. Lishman (eds) *Evaluation and Social Work Practice*. London: Sage.

Truman, C., Humphries, B. and Mertens, D. (1999) *Research in an Unequal World*. Aldershot: Avebury.

Turner, M. and Zimmerman, W (1994) 'Acting for the Sake of Research' in J. Wholey, H. Hatry and K. Newcomer (eds) *Handbook of Practical Program Evaluation*. San Francisco, CA: Jossey-Bass.

Wasoff, F. and Dobash, R. (1992) 'Simulated Clients in "Natural" Settings: Constructing a Client to Study Professional Practice'. *Sociology* 26, 2, 333-349.

Wasoff, F. and Dobash, R. (1996) *The Simulated Client: A Method for Studying Professionals Working with Clients*. Aldershot: Avebury.

Weiss, C. (1987) 'Where Politics and Evaluation Met' in D. Palumbo (ed) *The Politics of Program Evaluation*. Newbury Park, CA: Sage.

Whitmore, E. (1994) 'To Tell the Truth: Working with Oppressed Groups in Participatory Approaches to Inquiry' in P. Reason (ed) *Participation in Human Inquiry*. London: Sage.

Chapter 25
Users' and Practitioners' Research

My aim in this closing chapter is to contribute in a small way to placing social work research as it bears on practitioners, service users, academic faculty, citizens, and the welfare policy community. 'Small' because citizens, the policy community and to some extent the academic community remain on the sidelines of the issues posed by this approach to research, and because I'll stick to empirical groundwork. I am drawing on five different projects over the present decade – hence the 'postscripts' of the title.

I participated in 2002-3 in a user-involved evaluation of a pilot advocacy service for people in residential care for older people. At the same period I was part of a Wales national advisory group for a network of user-led mental health research funded by the UK's Mental Health Foundation. I was simultaneously working on a study of practitioner research in social care. Fourth, with a team of colleagues I subsequently completed a study of the kinds and quality of social work research in UK universities (Shaw and Norton, 2007). Finally, over 2008-09 Neil Lunt, Fiona Mitchell and I completed a systematic review of practitioner research and an evaluation of innovative agency sponsored practitioner research networks (Lunt et al, forthcoming; Mitchell, Lunt and Shaw, 2010; Shaw and Lunt, 2011 and forthcoming; cf Shaw, 2005; Shaw and Faulkner, 2006).

I want to open the chapter with some reflections on aspects of the nature of the claim – made with increasing force, at least in parts of northern Europe and some UK Commonwealth countries – that the hidden voice of service users in social work research should be an equal partner or perhaps the primary voice in some – maybe all – social work research.

User-engaged research is perhaps a challenge that Norwegian colleagues will appreciate, with your commitment to egalitarianism as a national value, however much that value may be challenged and to some extent weakened by the forces of globalization, capitalism, liberalism and so on.

Academic orientations

What sort of a claim is it? The main intellectual tension associated with this development has been about the relationship between user research and mainstream university research. I think that is important and have tried to put some empirical flesh on the bones of the issue (cf Shaw and Norton, 2007). In a series of case studies of research practice in a number of UK universities, perhaps the least won of all positions related to differences regarding the response that social work should give to the various arguments for democratizing the research process. To put the issue candidly, are participatory, user-led, emancipatory and other responsive modes of research generally superior to and/or more in tune with social work values than more traditional modes of research relationship? Given the diversity of positions, it risks oversimplifying to suggest there was a predominant stance. But the majority view may be that:

1. User and carer involvement is in most instances preferable;
2. It is a necessary mark of good research in some cases;
3. It should not be viewed as necessary in all situations;
4. It may be counter-productive if not critically considered and justified during the research design process.

This argument could be expressed as saying that standards of quality in user-engaged research should not be different from those in mainstream social research, but that such research can be defended on the grounds that it yields good quality research highlighting issues that are less frequently addressed by academic-led research (cf Fisher, 2002).

Provisional inferences from this work would include:

1. The foundations for believing that user research agenda and academic research agenda are discontinuous are probably weak.
2. The assumption that academic social work research agenda are homogenous is probably mistaken.
3. The assumption that academic social work research routinely privileges science-knowledge over user-knowledge does not seem well founded.
4. Most university social work researchers are unlikely to accept a position that routinely accords epistemological privilege to user knowledge.

What would be helpful to know is the extent to which these points would be echoed in the user research community.

But I want to spend the main part of this paper trying to provide the basis for a discussion about a different, very rarely discussed, but equally important tension – that regarding the differences between the general orientations of *user* research and *practitioner* research. While there have been recurrent efforts to set out shared interests between service users and practitioners (eg Beresford and Croft, 2004, British Association of Social Workers, 1988) I keep finding myself drawn back to think and find out about this apparently mundane if widely prevalent form of research.

Orientations of user researchers

The term 'user' is widely used in the UK to refer to those on the receiving end of social work. There has been a variety of words used – client, consumer, patient, claimant. I suspect that the term 'client' may still be the one most commonly used in agencies. 'Service user' – and 'carer' – are the most common terms in social work education and in regulatory and policy documents in the UK.

Does it matter? It certainly matters to those to whom the terms are applied, as we will see. It may matter for additional reasons. There is, as we are well aware, a tendency over time for the moral 'pitch' of language to degenerate. Classically, 'Approved Schools' in Britain soon came to be regarded with '*dis*approval'. 'Borstal' – simply the name of a pleasant English village where the first such institution for offenders was located – came to be synonymous with places where *no-one* wishes to live. So with 'client'. Of itself it is a term with a variety of associations, most of which convey the idea of someone who enjoys the expertise of others, and who often actively chooses to be their client. It comes in time to be a term in social work for someone who has *no* choice and who, to use Pincus and Minahan's ever-useful distinction – is as much the target as the beneficiary of professional intervention.

The language 'pitch' is not only moral but also about power – the language shifts usually include a change from active agent to passive, acted-upon. There are already signs that the term 'user' will fall into disfavour among those so identified, for partly similar reasons and also perhaps, as a consequence of the very success of the movement, which leads to a mainstreaming of what was previously marginal, and a consequent wish to regain critical 'bite' by reaffirming non-member status.

What are the implications of engaging in user-led research for the focus and character of the research itself? The Mental Health Foundation (mhf.org.uk) sponsored a UK-wide 'Strategies for Living' Project at the turn of the century whereby service users could bid for small grants to carry out research of their own choosing and direction. About 22 projects were initially funded, and were supported by Advisory Committees at country level (ie Wales, England, Scotland and Northern Ireland). National facilitators were appointed for each of the home countries. In the case of Wales, with which I was particularly associated, the facilitator was also a mental health sufferer, and, as far as I know, all but one of the Advisory Group were also current mental health service users. A UK wide meeting of all projects strongly supported the following inferences.

First, user-led research and evaluation shifts the focus from what practitioners think are *key questions for research* to those that sufferers and survivors think are central. The key themes at a national meeting of the grant holders for this project were:

- Coping
- Identity
- Information needs
- Support needs
- Self-help
- Carers
- Women's issues
- Rights and opportunities.

This list carries a quite different emphasis from the focus on service delivery and direct practice in the practitioner research study.

Second, user-led research shifts the focus of what is regarded as *good intervention*. It prioritizes:

- An emphasis on telling stories (hence narrative).
- Ground level concerns. Someone quoted what she believed to be a Ghana proverb – 'A person who rides a donkey does not know the ground is hot'. This gives a different meaning to expressions like 'needs-led' and 'Best Value'.
- Experience. Someone cited Paulo Freire, 'Reading the world always precedes reading the word'.

Third, user-led research provides *a powerful sense of what is stigmatizing,* for example through users' experience of language. They may reject the liberal term 'service user' because it feels to them to imply the very passivity and powerlessness that its proponents seek to avoid (the service-user as engaging in one way consumption). The term 'victim', as in 'Victim Support Schemes', may be rejected for the same reason. People are also likely to be uncomfortable with terms that define the whole person in terms of the role – eg 'carer'. They may prefer 'sufferer' – 'because I *have* suffered' as one woman said to me – and 'survivor'.

Orientations of practitioner researchers

What do we know, by way of comparison, about the orientations of practitioner researchers? By 'practitioner research' I have in mind practitioner involvement in evaluation, research, development, or other forms of disciplined inquiry that are small-scale, local, grounded, and carried out by professionals who directly deliver those self-same services. By 'practitioner research' I have in mind practitioner involvement in evaluation, research, development, or other forms of disciplined inquiry that are small-scale, local, grounded, and carried out by professionals who directly deliver those self-same services.

Literature on practitioner research, especially as it is more likely to be understood in Europe and Australasia rather than in the USA, is of fairly recent origin. In its development it has understandably focused on three main themes. First, there was a modest but useful literature on how to set about doing small scale practitioner research (e.g. Cheetham, 1994, Cheetham, 2002, Edwards and Talbot, 1994, Fuller and Petch, 1995, Lang, 1994). Second, there were several efforts to develop a case for the special nature of practitioner research, as against university-based academic research (eg Elks and Kirkhart, 1993, Mullen and Hess, 1995), which sometimes engaged with ideas regarding reflexivity and critical reflection (eg Fook, 2001; Schön, 1983). Finally there was some literature that sought to bring together examples of good practice in practitioner research (eg Broad and Fletcher, 1993).

Practitioner research has sometimes been seen within wider categories that capture the distinctive character of *social work* research. In Finland, for example, the idea of 'practice research' (Satka et al, 2005) has been adopted with some success to convey a coherent identity in dialogue with funders and government.

> Practice research in social work knowledge production is practice-based and practice-oriented. The interest is on practice development, and more conscious use of social work methods and instruments. Practice research was seen neither as administrative inquiry nor as academic pursuit; it makes use of social theory and well-known and recognized research methods but its goal is to improve social work practice. The criterion of adequacy is its relevance for the field work. The ideas of pragmatism, action research and ethnography are near to the concept. (Saurama and Tukiala, n.d.)

The concept has been found useful elsewhere in the Nordic countries (eg by Lars Uggerhøj in Denmark) and efforts have been made to develop wider authority for the idea of practice research (eg *The Salisbury Statement*, 2009).

A gradual realization of the volume and potential significance of practitioner research has prompted a number of diversely sponsored and motivated networks of such initiatives in the first decade of the century. Knud Ramian in Denmark has probably done more than any other individual to promote active networks of projects, but little of his important work has been published in English. Significant networks have operated in New Zealand through the GRIP project (Lunt et al, 2008) and in the UK through the 'Strategies for Living' project imaginatively funded by the Mental Health Foundation.

From 2006 to 2010 the Children's Workforce Development Council sponsored a programme of funding for approximately sixty or seventy projects a year, contracting out the mentoring and co-ordination of the scheme since 2008 to Making Research Count. While this is a major collective initiative the projects are networked in a fairly limited fashion.

What do we know of the substantive focus of research that is carried out by practitioners? In a study of 42 such projects in South Wales, the central focus of all but one of the topics was classified as either 'service delivery' (29) or 'direct practice' (12). A very small number were linked in secondary or 'accidental' ways to service user concerns and one was related to training (Keane, Shaw and Faulkner, 2003a).

The problem foci seem starkly different from those of service users, though it would probably require more direct evidence before we could generalize more confidently. But I want to push on from this, to capture the experience and nature of practitioner research in social work. My developing understanding through work with social work practitioners is that the nature of practitioner research is something that emerges from the action, rather than something that prescribes the form of the experience in advance. It is only in the doing of practitioner research that the recurring questions take shape.

I have come to see practitioner research is a form of practice that sits creatively but uncomfortably between the established cultures of research and professional practice. The fieldwork data from the Lunt Mitchell and Shaw project has deepened my misgivings regarding ways in which the identity of practitioner research has been located, in particular when judgements are made regarding its relative proximity to practice or to research. I doubt whether it is helpful to envisage practitioner research as being either 'inside' or 'outside' practice or research. The understanding that seems best to depict the experience of practitioners is to see them, in their practitioner-as-researcher work, as possessing a sociality outside, or at least on the margins of, *both research and practice* – an uncomfortable but creative marginalization marked by an identity that is neither research nor practice.

To turn more explicitly to this study, the practitioner research initiative of the sponsoring agency and the partnered university school of social work aimed at supporting practitioners to develop and undertake their own small-scale research projects. The Project sought to have an impact at three levels – individual, team, and organization. Two cohorts of practitioners were recruited, to commence in 2006 and 2007. Our fieldwork took place in 2008 and 2009.

Practitioners were provided with training and support to undertake a small-scale research project. Training took the form of a series of structured, face-to-face training days with ongoing one-to-one support provided by an academic tutor via contact by telephone and email throughout the research process. Teaching content was aimed towards small-scale research and leaned towards qualitative rather than quantitative inquiry methods.

We found ourselves drawn to understand the data as shedding light on two orientations towards the practitioner research experience. First, the fieldwork shed light on a range of personal and relational questions of a broadly *linear* nature.

- What predisposed them to become engaged in practitioner research?
- What understanding did they bring with them to their involvement and how did this understanding shift and change during their projects?
- What were the push and pull factors that led down pathways to the diverse research topics?
- How did the interplay of agency managers, cohort colleagues, practice colleagues, university and tutors serve to support, encourage (or discourage), focus, shape, sustain and (re)direct the projects?
- What elements of the research experience figure most prominently in the accounts of the practitioners?
- What were the outcomes, impacts and consequences of projects and programme?
- What difference did it make that the projects and practitioners were part of a planned network of events?

If this list of roughly linear considerations formed the warp of the initiative – running vertically down through time – a weft of analytic ideas regarding language, memory, moral accountability, ownership, meaning, value, and social work practice ran horizontally across each of the themes. This suggests that the elements of practitioner research have to be understood as interwoven, and bringing together and containing different career/life concerns that otherwise may remain scattered. It is this second cross-woven set of ideas that I pursue here. I take a moderate symbolic interactionist position, in exploring how language, ascriptions of meaning, and interpretation provide a social environment through which the nature and meaning of practitioner research emerge.

The cross-weave of practitioner research

I have taken much of the claims about the data on trust, so that I can get through the points with brief illustrative data.

1) Practitioner researchers engage with a language and culture that is strange yet potentially rewarding for practice and research. They find themselves located in a culture that lies between 'practice' and 'research' but is fundamentally shaped by and challenges both.

> People speak in a different language, people use different words for different things. (Alison)

> It's something that I haven't ever done before, so to be able to talk about, undertaking a piece of research or a study in this way, I quite like that, I quite like to be learning new things and we talked before about the language, the process and that was all new to me, and then being able to see it through and I'm quite excited at this point in time about getting it written and completed and that's about a sense of achievement for me. (Shona)

Perhaps all of the participating practitioners came into the initiative with little or no conscious recall of previous knowledge, experience or expertise in research. These personal histories – albeit, as we will shortly see, susceptible to reconstruction – proved two-edged. The discovery of a new language community may entice or put off; entry may prove enduring or, more often, fragile. There were numerous instances of practitioners recalling or representing these cultural processes. Alison was explaining to the interviewer how she had worked through thinking of a question and objectives, her aims and how she was going to do it, and broke off to ask 'Does that sound the terminology?' Passing hesitations over terms and language typify the ease with which cultural membership is lost. These practitioners are reaching for and recalling an elusive language. Several practitioners understood this as entailing an acquired way of thinking, a particular kind of research 'gaze' which provided a position from which to look at practice in a new way, with new understandings that made old assumptions implausible, as for Lorna who thought 'that sounds stupid but I hadn't quite clocked just how much that was the case'.

> I suppose it was something like that that was the motivation.. having the opportunity to step back a bit and look at something in the way you don't have time to do and in a disciplined way (Focus Group 2)

Similarly for Alan, acquiring a research gaze

> Definitely helped me to get inside the mind of some of the…service users and fathers in particular – to see things from their perspective. It was a real insight. You know – their quotes…were very honest and to the point and some of it was very hard to hear.

At its most powerful practitioners saw this as placing them at the behest of the evidence, whatever it might be saying, in a way that almost frightened them. Lesley expressed this most strongly, when she picked up the word 'objective' to talk to other members of the focus group as a way of expressing what she had in mind . She defined objective as

Taking on board what people say and wanting them to say something else. I think that frightens me a little bit.. I just, to hear what people say, and to transcribe it and then use that information and not skew say with things that I want to hear.

This echoed a compelling remark she had made earlier regarding the fieldwork process:

> I was persuaded to have it much more open and I am anxious about that because.. I feel like I might lose control of what people say in that way.. You are asking open questions and gathering information from them, not really questions, just what they are saying.. I don't know, I just feel a bit...eh, the truth...

2) Practitioner researchers are typically engaged in negotiating an uncertain world, which is at its heart an effort to learn what it's about.

Something as potentially powerful as a new culture and language will perhaps inevitably entail uncertainty. When we listen to Alison's comment that 'I tried to put as much wording in of what people had actually said because I thought that's what it is about', we are hearing someone tentatively endeavouring to identify the essential nature of practitioner research. This will occasionally lead practitioners into new aspirations.

> It's opened up a whole range of things that I've never done before and so I would like to pursue maybe ways of combining the two, if that is possible, in a more proactive way, I don't know if that's about, I don't know how even to go about that. (Shona)

This runs counter to much of the literature about practitioner research, which presents it as a slimmed down, instrumental novice form of practice that is best tackled by learning simple rules for research. My view is that the uncertainty of practitioners is not down simply to ignorance or lack of skills, but is at least as much an endemic feature of a research practice that sits creatively but uncomfortably between the established cultures of research and professional practice.

3) The location of practitioner research as lying both within and outside of core professional work poses difficult challenges of moral accountability for their work within their practice cultures.

Practitioners' reflections regarding the significance of a network initiative, sometimes referred to the importance of group norms. In most instances this was raised in the context of practitioners' feelings of accountability for their project. The existence of group frames of reference also cropped up in discussing the relationship of practitioners to their practice colleagues outside the cohort. In all these a moral dimension was loud. We spoke to one person who had withdrawn from the initiative. The difficulties that were beyond her control left her saying 'It was hanging over me'. 'I had never failed to complete something'. She was 'giving myself a hard time' because 'it was something I wanted to do' – something that would have been 'good for me, good for the organization'. Even when at the instigation of the agency the project was closed, she said that a line had not been drawn under it. 'It relieved me' but 'from my point of view…I would still want to complete that work'.

Jean felt bad that she was at risk of 'squandering' her opportunity. Others were scrupulously sensitive to the use of time. The following comments were made in the first cohort focus group:

> I kind of felt when I was doing the actual interviews that that was set around time that was convenient for children and young people but at other times I could, I felt – you know people – "you're doing your research again". Well it kind of felt like skiving to take too much time off.

Social workers who, by their own standards, fell behind were unlikely to be forgiving of themselves.

> It's no excuse for me, he's as busy as I am. *Have there been advantages taking part?* It doesn't feel like it at the moment, it just feels like a millstone to be honest. (Lesley)

4) Involvement in practitioner research stirs reflection on the meaning and value of professional work. For some practitioners this may be overly demanding in the context of the perceived constraints of their core work.

Participants had much to say on the themes of the worth, meaning and value of the initiative, ranging from 'It's a fantastic opportunity, it's a great thing' to 'It lost meaning for what it was about'. In the main it should be said that occasions when a depth of disappointment was expressed were only possible because of the counterbalancing depth of appreciation. The initiative was something in which large hopes had been invested. The final appraisals were unanimously positive if diverse – 'interesting', 'difficult', 'stretching'.

One focus group of practitioners who had concluded their projects included the following exchange, which exactly reflects the way such appreciation was typically couched.

> C: I think we have been lucky that [agency] invested in doing it and gave us the opportunity to do it
> A: We have been lucky
> D: I also think, despite my moaning, the advantages far outweigh the disadvantages, it's not something I regret doing
> A: So glad I did it
> D: Yes absolutely. In the main, it's been positive
> B: We have focused on challenges and learning and things but I would agree that, you know, looking back I would do things differently but I'm still glad that I did it.

Yet for a number of participants it was the strength of feeling about a project unfinished that predominated, and the sense that the wider agency programme had been foregrounded at the expense of the individual projects.

> I really wanted something for the kids who took part in that, you know this wasn't really necessarily something for me but it was more about the kind of process that they took part in and that feels like that's kind of disappeared and that it has been something more *corporate*. (Focus Group 1)

> I ended up somehow presenting my research project three times to a public audience which I'm really, I am not really sure why. I kind of got into this situation where I did it at a staff conference and two other kinds of conferences and that felt like it.. it lost meaning for what it was about. (Focus Group 1)

One consequence of this was a feeling of having muted voices or becoming invisible. Two further pointed, almost poignant comments from that same focus group will serve.

> I just kind of feel that it's almost like as if I'm not sure if I did it. Does that make sense? I kind of feel as if I've gone in, I've done it, I've come back out and it's not really been noticed.
>
> It's just I feel as if I've kind of gone in and done it and I go away to Edinburgh and I disappear every so often to do things like this and I come back but you know nobody's really aware of what I've done. And I kind of think that's a shame because it feels like it's been a major piece of work for me – for *me*. I

> think, I look at and I think I can't believe I actually did that but it feels like it's disappeared into the air somehow.

What provides the ground for their disappointment? We believe it is a conviction of the profound dissonance between the central drivers of their projects and the perceived tendency to corporatism. Evidence not dealt with in this article emphasized how bettering practice was the way most practitioners in both cohorts expressed their motivation. Yet that perhaps does not quite do justice to the way in which, with hindsight, they saw their projects' *raison d'être* – that the voice of the service user should be heard. The most evocative statements of this kind are given in Box 25.1. They illustrate how the nature of practitioner research was something that emerged from the projects, and may not have been the way most people saw things at the outset.

Box 25.1 Practitioners hearing the voice of the service user

It actually reminded me of how hard that can be sometimes for kids - and I don't pretend to remember this every day - but sometimes actually it allowed me to think, to be free of all the other things, the letters and phone calls and just thinking just generally how hard it must be to buzz the buzzer, to come to this building. That really came through for me when I did the research programme. (FG1)

And I think what my research can be is, speaking from the perspective of the child or young person, (is) a kind of real challenge to some of the formal services that are set up for helping children. (FG1)

I think that was really important that kids could actually have a voice and say "well this is what I feel about this". I think that's good to know that potentially would be kept and even if they said things contrary to possibly where the organisation was at it would still be put in a document and not kind of be put aside. For all, that was really important. (FG1)

The fathers' own words were so powerful and evocative that I really wanted to capture their views. (Alan)

The people that I spoke to I was just, I felt privileged that I spoke to them to be honest because (they) told me things and I thought 'oh my god where am I going to put this or can I put this down' because it wasn't what I was asking them!. So a lot of the information that I got I didn't use which was I think just people telling me their story basically. (Alison)

If this is true, why might this change have taken place? I suspect the answer lies in the process of learning and discovery that took place in most of the projects. The doing of practitioner research was itself almost an epiphany, at least for a significant core. This is a large claim, and one that if true has significant implications for sponsoring agencies.

5) The nature of practitioner research is something that emerges from the experience, rather than something that prescribes it in advance. It is only in the doing of practitioner research that its critical identity takes shape.

If this is true, what does it suggest about some of the weightier aspects of the research-practice relationship? This can most easily be viewed by revisiting the outsider/insider debate. In setting out the practitioners' experience of research in their projects we sensed that they rarely held consistently to either 'pure' view. It is not original to say that 'Terms such as *use*, *insider*, and *own account* are useful as much for the complexities they raise as for the directions in which they point' (Shaw and Faulkner, 2006: 59). But we think the projects convey this with a richness and detail that *is* perhaps original.

Practitioners occasionally identified with the merits of an insider position, though it tended to be with circumspection. Alan, for example, argued that

> Although it makes it a compromise on objectivity slightly … one of the strengths of practitioner research is you've got people on hand that you already have a relationship with, who you can pick up the phone and say 'I am doing a piece of research – would you be willing to participate?' and that personal connection undoubtedly helps – there is no doubt about that.

This relatively neutral distinguishing comments should be placed alongside others that seem to assume recognition of the benefit that can be gained from incorporating aspects of mainstream academic research. The value of perspective and standing back were often mentioned. 'It is very easy in this line of work, you know, you are constantly busy, to not get a chance to take a step back from that and do some reading and some perhaps more formal research in your work' (Alan). He seemed to think he had not fully exploited this opportunity. 'That was a challenge, putting time aside and spending more time reading the kind of research, and I think if I had done that and incorporated more of that into my study it would have been a bit more authoritative'. I conclude with this example of the way practitioner research can, in Gillian's words, 'open up so many possibilities I had not thought of'.

> I think what I am and what I would like to be are different. I am a practitioner and that is my job, so that's what I have to do and I'm bound by the context of that because that is my income, that is my livelihood. I would like to be more of a researcher. It's opened up a whole range of things that I've never done before and so I would like to pursue maybe ways of combining the two

Practitioner research networked projects are in general valued by participants, and do make for important differences, although not always in ways planned for or anticipated.

Conclusion

We suggested when describing how practitioners were negotiating uncertainty that practitioner research is a research practice that sits creatively but uncomfortably between the established cultures of research and professional practice. The fieldwork data from this project deepened our misgivings regarding ways in which the identity of practitioner research has been located, in particular when judgements are made regarding its relative proximity to practice or to research. We doubt whether it is helpful to envisage practitioner research as being either 'inside' or 'outside' practice or research. The understanding that seems best to depict the experience of our practitioner participants is to see them, in their practitioner-as-researcher work, as outside, or at least on the margins of both research *and* practice – an uncomfortable but creative marginalization. It suggests in turn the kinds of questions that should be asked of user research.

This perspective has consequences for how practitioner research – and perhaps user research – can best be learned. If it is correct to reject a view of practitioner research as a bolt-on to everyday core practice this leads to a position in which support and facilitation for practitioner research are not simply about providing information on methods and techniques. A practice that has an intrinsic emergent quality to it cannot be reduced to a set of prior rules or textbook prescriptions. There is something of an Aristotelian craft in such research, where creativity, skill and identity are involved. But it is not a form of learning that can or ought to be reducible to the individual. The sociological links to the practical. In many settings the problems of development of practitioner research are often framed in a 'deficit' way – that researchers lack skills, time, support etc. These considerations may be true but must be counterbalanced by this wider 'becoming', and supported, where they emerge, by wider communities of practice.

References

Beresford, P. and Croft, S. (2004) 'Service users and practitioners reunited' in *British Journal of Social Work* 34 (1): 53-68.

British Association of Social Workers (1981) *Clients are Fellow Citizens*. BASW: Birmingham.

Broad, B. and Fletcher, C. (1993) (eds) *Practitioner Social Work Research in Action*. London: Whiting and Birch.

Cheetham, J. (1994) 'The social work research centre at the University of Stirling: A profile' in *Research on Social Work Practice* 4 (1): 89-100.

Cheetham, J. (2002) 'Practitioner research' in M Davies (ed) *Encyclopaedia of Social Work* Oxford: Blackwell.

Elks, M. and Kirkhart, K. (1993) 'Evaluating effectiveness from the practitioner's perspective' *Social Work* 38 (5): 554-563.

Fisher, M. (2002) 'The role of service users in problem formulation and technical aspects of social research' *Social Work Education* 21 (3): 305-312.

Fook, J. (2001) 'Identifying expert social work: qualitative practitioner research', in Shaw, I. and Gould, N. (eds) *Qualitative Research in Social Work*. London: Sage Publications.

Fuller, R. and Petch, A. (1995) *Practitioner Research: the Reflexive Social Worker*. Buckingham: Open University Press.

Keane, S., Shaw, I. and Faulkner, A. (2003) 'Practitioner Research in Social Care: an Audit and Case Study Analysis', Report to Wales Office of Research and Development in Health and Social Care.

Lang, N. (1994) 'Integrating the data processing of qualitative research and social work practice to advance the practitioner as knowledge builder: tools for knowing and doing' in Sherman, E. and Reid, W. (eds) *Qualitative Research in Social Work*. New York: Columbia University Press.

Lunt, N., Fouché, C. and Yates, D. (2008) *Growing Research in Practice: Report of an Innovative Partnership model*. Wellington: Families Commission.

Lunt, N., Ramian, K., Shaw, I., Mitchell, F. and Fouché, C. (in press) 'Networking practitioner research: the state of the art' *European Journal of Social Work*.

Lunt, N., Shaw, I. and Mitchell, F. (2009) Practitioner Research in CHILDREN 1st: Cohorts, Networks and Systems, Report prepared for The Institute for Research and Innovation in the Social Services: http://www.iriss.org.uk/resources/practitioner-research-social-services-literature-review-summary Accessed 26 July, 2011.

Mitchell, F., Lunt, N. and Shaw, I. (2010) 'Practitioner research in social work: a Knowledge Review' *Evidence and Policy* 6 (1): 7-31.

Mullen, E. and Hess, P. (1995) *Practitioner-Researcher Partnerships*. Washington, DC: NASW Press.

Practice Research: The Salisbury Statement, http://www.socsci.soton.ac.uk/spring/salisbury/The_Salisbury_Statement_on_practice_research_May_2009.pdf. Accessed 26 July, 2011.

Satka, M., Karvinen-Niinikoski, S., Nylund, M. and Hoikkala, S. (toim.) (2005) *Sosiaalityön käytäntötutkimus*. Palmenia Kustannus, Helsinki.

Saurama, E. and Tukiala, A-K (n.d.) The alternative story – the quest for practice research' Unpublished Report.

Schön, D. (1983) *The Reflective Practitioner: How Professionals Think in Action*. New York: Basic Books.

Scottish Executive (2006) *Changing Lives. The report of the 21st Century Social Work Review*. Edinburgh: The Scottish Government.

Shaw I. (2005) Practitioner Research: Evidence or Critique? *British Journal of Social Work* 35 (8): 1231-1248.

Shaw, I. and Faulkner, A. (2006) 'Practitioner evaluation at work' *American Journal of Evaluation* 27 (1): 44-63.

Shaw, I. and Gould, N. (2001) *Qualitative Research in Social Work.* London: Sage Publications.

Shaw, I. and Lunt, N. (forthcoming) 'Constructing practitioner research' *Social Work Research.*

Shaw, I. and Lunt, N. (2011) 'Navigating Practitioner Research' *British Journal of Social Work* 2011; doi: 10.1093/bjsw/bcr025.

Shaw, I. and Norton, M. (2007) *The kinds and quality of social work research in UK universities.* Using Knowledge in Social Care – Report 17. London: Social Care Institute for Excellence.

Uggerhøj, L. (nd) 'Practice research in Social Work – "hands on" knowledge production' http://vbn.aau.dk/fbspretrieve/16485228/Brasilien_opl_g.pdf. Accessed 26 July 2011.

Index of Names

Subject Index